THE CHALLENGE TO THE CROWN

THE CHALLENGE TO THE CROWN

Volume 1: The Struggle for Influence in the Reign of Mary Queen of Scots, 1542–1567

Robert Stedall

Book Guild Publishing

Sussex, England

First published in Great Britain in 2012 by
The Book Guild Ltd
Pavilion View
19 New Road
Brighton, BN1 1UF

Typesetting in Garamond by
YHT Ltd, London

Printed and bound in Great Britain by
CPI Group (UK) Ltd, Croydon, CR0 4YY

A catalogue record for this book is available from
The British Library.

ISBN 978 1 84624 646 3

'The Scottish nobles saw no point in pursuing any policy out of principle, once it no longer suited their purpose, even if they were being bribed to do so.'

Lady Antonia Fraser (*Mary Queen of Scots* p. 27)

Contents

CONTENTS

CONTENTS

Front jacket image: The Bath of Diana is an allegorical painting of Mary (depicted twice) by the French court artist, François Clouet. As a Huguenot, he strongly resented her ultra-Catholic Guise uncles (depicted as satyrs) gaining control of Government when Mary became Queen, following the death of Henry II in a jousting accident. *Musée des Beaux Arts, Tours/* ©*Réunion des Musées Nationaux.*

Preface

This book forms the first of two volumes of the history of the Scottish monarchy during the reigns of Mary Queen of Scots and her son, James VI. After Mary's enforced abdication during her imprisonment at Lochleven in 1567, the infant James replaced her as king, supported in his earlier years, as she had been, by successive regencies. This book deals with the period up to Mary's abdication, while the second volume covers the time from James's accession at the age of thirteen months until his invitation to take the English throne in 1603. Taken together, they show how close Scotland came to divesting itself of the Stuart dynasty, but how James's native cunning enabled him to reassert the Crown's authority, positioning him for an enthusiastic greeting as King of England on Elizabeth's death.

To appreciate the difficulties faced by Mary Queen of Scots, it is essential to have an understanding of the three great conflicts which caused such turmoil during her reign. Firstly, there were the competing efforts of France and England to maintain influence over the Scottish government. English belligerence had forced Scotland and France into a defensive alliance, in part to protect Scotland from English invasion and in part to protect France by allowing diversionary attacks to take place from the north. Secondly, there was religious conflict between Catholics and Reformers, during the spread of the Calvinist movement through Scotland. This had been incited by Henry VIII in his efforts to protect England, after its break with Rome, from the risk of a Catholic counter-Reformation being launched across its northern border. The Scottish Reformation also provided a platform for discontented members of the Scottish nobility to make a stand, with English support, against a Scottish government dominated by French and Catholic interests. Thirdly, there was the feudal conflict between central government and the traditional Scottish nobility, who ruled their remote personal fiefdoms while maintaining only a loose affiliation to the Scottish Crown. With the Crown financially weakened by successive debilitating regencies and the cost of fending off English aggression, it could no longer afford the cost of maintaining a standing army, and it relied on Scottish magnates for military support and the Catholic Church for funding.

There was a further difficulty, which was also faced by Elizabeth in England. The Tudor belief in the dynastic right of an anointed monarch to govern was being questioned by Reformers in Scotland and the Protestant government in England, both of whom believed that the monarchy should be accountable to the people. When Mary's right to rule was challenged, resulting in her imprisonment, those opposing her needed legal justification for the treasonable steps that they were taking. While James and Elizabeth developed the political acumen to survive this attack on their authority, Mary's naivety let her down, and it would become a problem for successive Stuart kings throughout the next century.

The history surrounding Mary is confused by hostile propaganda put about by her opponents in Scotland and by the English government. The English had no wish to encourage a charismatic and Catholic monarch, who would act as a catalyst for those seeking a counter-Reformation in Britain. Mary was not only the dynastic heir to the English Crown, but, through her mother, Marie of Guise, was a member of the fiercely imperialistic and Catholic Guise family. This called for desperate actions by those determined to maintain a Protestant government in England and one that was politically supportive in Scotland. It is a measure of their success that they completely undermined Mary's rule, giving her a place in history which her own abilities in government would never have justified.

Rumour and falsified evidence have resulted in conflicting assessments of key parts of Mary's story. There is a huge literature on the murders of Riccio and of her husband, Lord Darnley. Many recent scholarly studies of Mary, by Lady Antonia Fraser, John Guy and Alison Weir, for example, have painted her as an innocent in the midst of intrigue, let down by those who might have helped her, and debased by unjustified propaganda. They portray her as a Catholic martyr (as she wished her audience at Fotheringhay to believe), unfairly condemned both in her lifetime and by history. Their view is not shared by Dr Jenny Wormald, Roderick Graham or Susan Doran, who believe that she saw the murder of her husband as a political necessity. None of these assessments is totally convincing, and this book attempts to resolve the uncertainties. Yet to each of these eminent historians I owe a debt of gratitude for their scholarship and research. Leonie Frieda's study of Catherine de Medici and Rosalind Marshall's meticulous assessment of Queen Mary's women have been invaluable sources on Mary's childhood in France and, in the latter case, of her domestic arrangements in Scotland. The study of English politics draws significantly on J.E. Neale's *Elizabeth I*.

I have chosen to use the titles by which people were known in their day, referring to Darnley, for example, as King Henry after he married Mary. I have adopted the current spellings of names where practicable, although the Bethunes are also spelt Beaton, Beton and Betoun in various sources (and are pronounced 'Beaton' today, although it would appear that they were originally pronounced 'Betoon' as in the French/Flemish town that they came from in the thirteenth century). With the Ker or Kerr family, who all descend from one root, I have referred to the Cessfords as Ker and the Ferniehirsts and Lothians (including Cessford's brother, the Lothian ancestor Mark, Commendator of Newbottle) as Kerr, again to accord with current practice.

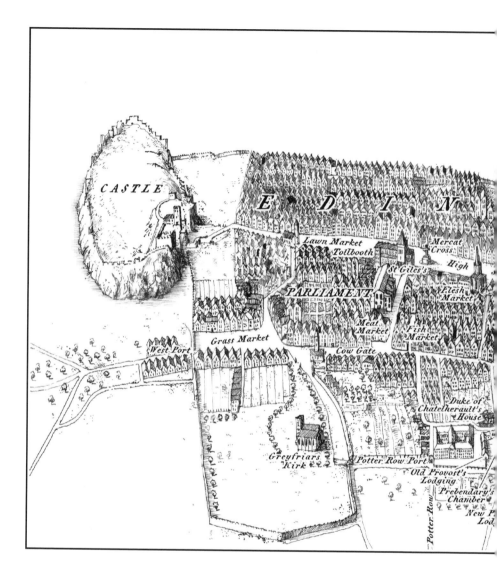

Edinburgh. Drawn by David Atkinson, Handmade Maps Limited. Adapted from a map of Edinburgh by James Gordon, 1647, National Library of Scotland.

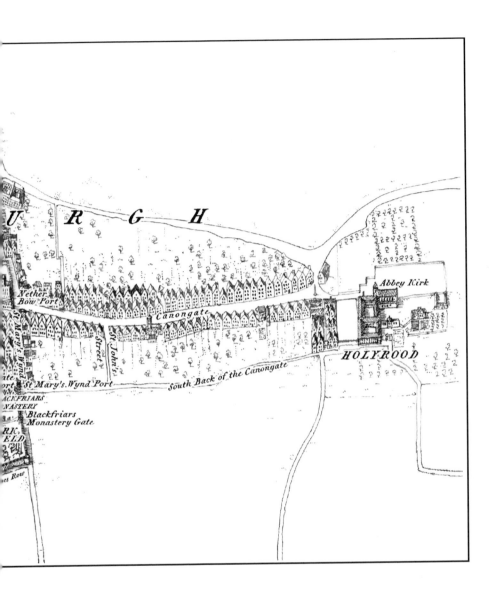

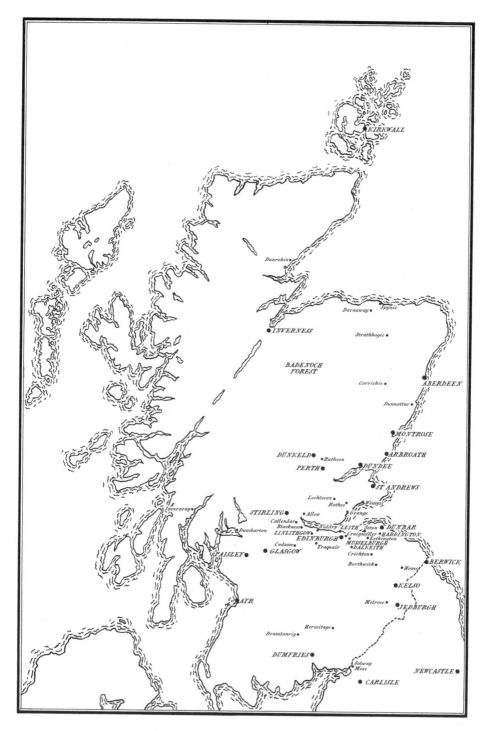

Scotland. Drawn by David Atkinson, Handmade Maps Limited.

Part 1 Beginnings

1

Introduction

In 1529, John Stewart, 3rd Earl of Atholl, aged twenty-two, entertained the Papal Nuncio with the young James V, aged seventeen, to a hunt on his estates. He had constructed a special woodland palace twenty miles from the nearest dwelling with its walls strewn with tapestries and the floor with flowers. He offered beer, red and white wine and *aqua vitae,* served with an array of fish, meats and fowl, including swan and peacock. Deer and wild boar for the hunt were brought in by cart from other areas and huge numbers were collected up to create a memorable occasion for Atholl's important guests with their hunting dogs. When the festivities were over, the temporary palace was destroyed. The extravaganza was thought to have cost him £1,000 Scots per day.* The Nuncio was incredulously impressed. He considered it 'a great marvel that such a thing could be in Scotland, considering that it was named the arse of the world in other countries'.[1] As he so inelegantly recognised, this demonstration of wealth was not the norm and ready money was in short supply. Scottish nobles could rarely demonstrate such trappings of opulence and refinement.

Even James V was hopelessly impoverished, a result of absurd military ambitions by his father, James IV, who had been killed surrounded by most of the Scottish nobility at the Battle of Flodden in 1513, after making a Scottish diversionary attack in support of the French, who faced an invasion across the Channel by the young Henry VIII. The infant James V was left to be King of Scotland, with his mother, Margaret Tudor, Henry VIII's sister, becoming Regent. She immediately remarried Archibald Douglas, 6th Earl of Angus, by whom she produced a daughter, Lady Margaret Douglas, but, despite his support, the Scots would not allow the sister of the English king to be their regent for long. She was forced to resign in favour of John Stewart, 2nd Duke of Albany, heir to the throne after James V. Albany was a

---

* There were 5.5 pounds Scots to a pound sterling, with a mark valued at two-thirds of a pound and a crown valued at a quarter.

naturalised Frenchman, who lived in France with his fabulously wealthy, but childless, wife, his first cousin, Anne, daughter of John de la Tour, Count of Auvergne. Her mother was Jeanne de Bourbon-Vendôme, a descendant of Louis IX, and the Bourbon dynasty was next in line to the French throne after the Valois kings. Anne's sister, Madeleine, had married Lorenzo de Medici, nephew of Pope Leo X, and by Lorenzo was the mother of Catherine de Medici. Anne's first cousin, Antoinette de Bourbon, was the wife of Claude, Duke of Guise. These connections provided Albany with unrivalled influence both at the French court and with the Papacy.

Albany arrived in Scotland and, despite speaking no Scots, showed his administrative ability in holding together rival factions of the nobility, but the French wanted him to invade northern England with a Franco-Scottish army. After the disaster of Flodden, the Scots were at best lukewarm about supporting him and refused to cross the border into England to assist his small French contingent, who led the way. On 24 May 1524, he went back to France, never to return, after decimating the Scottish Crown's remaining resources. Yet, before leaving, he cemented the 'Auld Alliance' by negotiating for James to marry a French princess, and chose for him his wife's first cousin, Marie de Bourbon, daughter of Charles, Count of Vendôme. He also set up the Court of Session to centralise the Scottish legal system under the Crown's control, after gaining papal consent to fund judges out of church revenue, although this was not put into effect until 1532. Feudal laws, which had been administered by local magnates in their own fiefdoms, had drawn scorn from French civil servants brought in to achieve order. Those responsible for administering justice often had a vested interest in the outcome, which caused feuding between rival interests. Little charity was shown; pregnant women were hanged and sacred ornaments in nearby churches or monasteries were ransacked.

After Albany's departure, there was a struggle for influence between the English party in Scotland, still led by Angus and Margaret Tudor, despite them becoming estranged, and the French party, which was now headed by Archbishop James Bethune of St Andrews providing it with the financial backing of the Scottish Catholic Church. James Hamilton, 1st Earl of Arran and his son James, who succeeded him as 2nd Earl in 1529, stood between these polarised interests, hoping to advance their position as heirs to the throne after the childless Albany. To be assured of the young King's loyalty, rival advisers, even members of the Church, provided attractive daughters of noble families to become his mistresses. As a result, he sired at least seven illegitimate children by different partners over a period of years, opening him to criticism from Protestant preachers. The eldest of these, born in 1531, was Lord James Stewart, the son of James, Lord Erskine's daughter Margaret,* who was already the wife of Sir Robert Douglas of Lochleven.

By now, Henry VIII in England was contemplating a break with Rome to enable him to divorce Catherine of Aragon and to marry Anne Boleyn. He was determined to avoid the Catholic-dominated French party from gaining control on his northern border. To undermine Catholic authority, he infiltrated a group of Protestant preachers into Scotland to target the Church's shortcomings. He also arranged the distribution of bibles in the vernacular, avidly welcomed by those who had no access to Catholic scriptures written in Latin.

The Scottish Catholic Church enjoyed an annual income of about £300,000 Scots, estimated at half of the gross national product of the nation. Its coffers had benefited from the more well-to-do buying a passport to heavenly glory with bequests in their wills. It took little for Reformist preachers to suggest that worldly munificence offered no assurance of redemption in the afterlife, causing impoverished Scots to flock to a less financially demanding religious regime.

It was inevitable that the Crown would look to the Scottish Catholic Church to provide it with resources. Successive Scottish kings had sought greater control over its wealth and were in practice responsible for the appointment of bishops after 1487. This had allowed them to appoint their kinsmen, legitimate and illegitimate, and those of powerful magnates to lucrative Church benefices often as laymen. When James V took control of church funds in 1535, the abbacies of Kelso, Melrose, Coldingham, St Andrews and Holyrood were granted to his illegitimate sons. In 1542, Regent Arran granted the abbacies of Arbroath and Paisley for his younger sons, with revenue surplus to their needs funding the building of his 'greit hous'. The Church's loss of revenue progressively reduced its charitable benefactions for schools or to assist the sick and the poor. Whereas the priesthood had previously been a stepping stone for educated men to become lawyers, civil servants and educators, the stipends remaining available failed to attract suitable candidates. The funding of schools in the towns now fell to wealthier burghers, who were encouraged by the Reformers to take civic pride in their munificence. Legal and government appointments started to be filled by a newly educated meritocracy brought up as Reformers, rather than by the protégés of the Catholic Church, and they belittled the declining education of the priesthood. Meanwhile Catholic bishops and a

---

* Margaret Erskine showed genuine affection for the King, but probably had several lovers; she was the model for Dame Sensuality in the play by Sir David Lindsay of the Mount, *A Satire of the Three Estates* (1540).

new hierarchy of lay commendators drawn from the nobility enjoyed an opulent and sometimes dissolute style. They milked church lands by capitalising short-term rental agreements into long-term feus. Their impoverished tenants, who could not meet the capital sum demanded to remain *in situ*, were displaced, resulting in about one-third of church tenants being forced out amid renewed Reformist criticism.

Henry VIII's anti-Catholic stance brought him up against his sister, Margaret Tudor, who managed to recover control of the government. Despite her ardent Catholicism, she divorced Angus and, in 1528, gained papal consent to remarry Henry Stewart, younger brother of Andrew, 1st Lord Ochiltree, her junior by six years. He was created Lord Methven, and, with the young James's blessing, they controlled the government with support from Archbishop Bethune and his up-and-coming nephew, David Bethune, the lay Abbot of Arbroath.

Henry VIII's second line of diplomacy was to offer James his daughter Mary Tudor in marriage in the hope of uniting Scotland with England. This was opposed by both the French party, who preferred a French marriage, and the great majority of the Scottish nobility, who mistrusted all things English. To reinforce his offer, Henry bribed the more influential Scottish nobles, including Arran, with pensions. Although they always accepted any largesse on offer, Henry was furious that he gained little practical support. He retaliated with a series of punitive attacks into southern Scotland. Yet his belligerence was counterproductive and his more long-standing supporters, such as Angus, temporarily turned against him. Bethune became determined to restore Albany's plan for James to marry a French princess to assure French support for the Scottish Crown against the English.

The loose affiliation of earldoms, upon which the Crown depended to maintain its authority, controlled their estates as fiefdoms, demanding allegiance and military support from lieges in return for protection and the right to graze cattle and sheep with occasional subsistence farming. It was no accident that the Scottish kings were known as the kings of Scots and not Scotland. The real power was with the earls, and the Crown's role was to settle disputes and coordinate matters of mutual concern. By 1536 its annual income, depleted by successive wars and poor administration, was reduced to between £10,000 and £17,500 Scots, collected inefficiently by hereditary sheriffs. Only once did Mary manage to raise taxes, when she demanded £12,000 to meet the costs of her son's baptism. Royal treasures, including the drinking cup of Robert Bruce, had to be sold, and she had insufficient resources for most of her reign to issue new coinage. To put her financial position into perspective, Elizabeth in England continually complained of

6

poverty, although she received at least £200,000 sterling annually, rising to £300,000 in her last ten years. (An English pound of the period can be tentatively valued at £1,000 today.) Both nations suffered from inflation, caused by the influx of precious metals from the New World and the debasing of coinage in Continental Europe.

Although royal marriages with princesses and daughters of wealthy families from Continental Europe helped to underpin the finances of Scottish kings, the Crown could not rely on continuous assistance from abroad, as even Marie of Guise discovered. As Queen Dowager of France, Mary was entitled to a French income of 40,000 livres, but she had difficulty in collecting it, especially during her captivity in England. She had a right on her twenty-fifth birthday to recover royal lands granted as perquisites during her minority. With most lairds holding their estates directly from the Crown, it is no coincidence that she was safely imprisoned at Lochleven by the recipients of her royal largesse before reaching this critical age.

Earls had gained their titles in various ways. Some were the direct descendants of the traditional *mormaers*, who had, in the Middle Ages, controlled their own fiefdoms. The measure of their power was not so much the area of land under their control, but the number of their adherents. These were not just their kin, but other supporters, who saw them as their friends or *kindness*. The earldoms of Angus, Mar, Huntly and Sutherland were in this landed category. Prior to the reign of James VI new earldoms were rarely created, and, when they were, it was often to provide a title for a younger royal son, or for the husband of a royal daughter. The Lennoxes obtained their earldom as the descendants of Murdoch, 2nd Duke of Albany, grandson of Robert II. Albany became Regent of Scotland and having married Isabel, heiress of Duncan, Earl of Lennox, passed the Lennox title down the junior branch of his family. Sir John Stewart of Balvenie was confirmed as the 1st Earl of Atholl in 1457, being the eldest son of Joan Beaufort, widow of James I and granddaughter of John of Gaunt. She had taken a new husband, Sir John Stewart, the Black Knight of Lorn. Marriage to a royal princess was the perquisite of a grateful king to a leading supporter, and was sometimes accompanied by the grant of an earldom. James Douglas, eldest son of the 2nd Lord Dalkeith, was granted the Earldom of Morton in 1458 before his marriage to the deaf and dumb Joanna Stewart, daughter of James I by Joan Beaufort. The new Earl's father had gone mad, and a streak of insanity was to be inherited by several of their descendants (see p. 81, footnote). Earldoms were also granted by a grateful king for services to the Crown. David Lindsay was created 1st Earl of Crawford in 1398 to recognise his military skills; he became Admiral of Scotland in 1403. William, Lord Sinclair, the

High Chancellor of Scotland, was created Earl of Caithness in 1455. His family had been the traditional Earls of Orkney, whose lands had been transferred to the Scottish Crown by the King of Denmark to underwrite the dowry of his daughter, Margaret, on her marriage to James III. In 1470, Caithness had obediently resigned the Earldom of Orkney to the Scottish king, in return for the incomplete Castle of Ravenscraig in Fife and other lesser estates. This rankled with the Sinclairs, who continued to interfere with affairs in Orkney. Sir William Hay, Constable of Scotland, became Earl of Erroll in 1457. Colin, 2nd Lord Campbell was created Earl of Argyll in the same year and was subsequently Master of the King's household. Thereafter the Crown could rely on the Campbells with their substantial standing army to control the west of Scotland on their behalf with a mixture of diplomacy and force, although their brutality caused great antipathy within the Highlands and Islands lasting for many generations. William Keith, whose family had for generations maintained military control of the north of Scotland from their stronghold at Dunnottar Castle in Kincardineshire, was raised to Earl Marischal in 1458 in thanks for his services to the Crown. Sir Alexander Cunningham, Lord of Kilmaurs, became Earl of Glencairn in 1488 after supporting James III to put down a rebellion at Blackness. Patrick Hepburn, Great Admiral of Scotland and Captain of Dumbarton Castle, was created Earl of Bothwell in the same year. Patrick, 3rd Lord Graham rose to Earl of Montrose in 1505 and Hugh, 3rd Lord Montgomerie was created Earl of Eglinton in 1508. Both had fought gallantly beside the young James IV when Duke of Rothesay at Sauchiburn in 1488, when James III was killed, and remained his confidants thereafter.

In addition to the powerful earls, Scottish lords held titles enabling them to sit as Lords of Parliament. Generally they did not have the wealth or authority of the earls, but were very often closer to the Crown, after fulfilling roles in the royal household or in government. Mary considered the Lords Seton, Livingston and Fleming as her closest friends and allies. (Seton at one point turned down an earldom considering that his family's status was such that he preferred to be Lord Seton, but his son ultimately accepted the Earldom of Winton from James VI.) Mary was accompanied to France for her education by daughters of each of these families, all coincidentally named Mary, making up three of her four 'Maries'. The Lady Fleming, who had been widowed when her husband was killed at Pinkie Cleugh in 1547, went with them as Mary's governess. She was the former Janet Stewart, an illegitimate daughter of James IV by Agnes Stewart, daughter of James, 1st Earl of Buchan. She was thirty-six when her husband died, but still exuded appeal. In addition to these confidants, there was John, Lord Erskine (soon

to become Earl of Mar), hereditary Governor of Stirling Castle and traditional protector of the heir to the throne, Lord Glamis, whose family fulfilled
a number of roles in the Royal Household or as justices, Lord Drummond,
whose family grew significantly in political importance during the period,
and a number of lords honoured for their military prowess. Many of these
were based in the Borders, where they were tasked with maintaining an
uneasy peace by policing both English and Scottish freebooters, who ter-
rorised the locality. Lord Home with his regiment of horse, Lord Herries,
and Lord Maxwell, Lord Lindsay of the Byres east of Edinburgh, Lord
Ruthven in Perthshire, Lord Ochiltree and Lord Boyd in Ayrshire and Lord
Gray in Forfar all fulfilled supervisory roles in their areas. There were a
number of others, but they played a lesser part in the events of the period.

There were also powerful lairds, not always ennobled, some of whom
undertook military roles particularly in the Borders. These included the Kers
of Cessford, their kinsmen the Kerrs of Ferniehirst, the Scotts of Buccleuch,
the Johnstons and the Armstrongs. Very often they were granted authority
by the Crown in the hope of making 'poachers turned gamekeepers', but the
temptation to plunder and pillage was often greater than the desire to serve
the monarch. The Borders remained extremely difficult to control, wracked
by family feuds, which often extended into England. This forced the Crown
into appointing lieutenants or wardens to maintain or re-establish peace.
During the early part of Mary's reign, it was often James, 4th Earl of Bothwell
who was given the task.* This did nothing to endear him to the English, who
considered him a scoundrel, or to the other Border families, against whom
he used every device to restore authority. Yet the acknowledged military
strategist of his day, despite his lack of political acumen, was Sir William
Kirkcaldy of Grange, a man of great integrity, who had learned his unrivalled
generalship in France. Others fulfilled roles as political advisers, as ambassadors, as administrators of the Household, and as lawyers. The Maitlands of
Thirlestane and Lethington had charm, wit and an extraordinary persuasiveness in political matters. Other officers of state included the Treasurer
Robert Richardson, the Clerk-Register James Makgill and the Justice-Clerk
James Bellenden. The reprehensible Sir James Balfour rose with undeniable

---

* The earls of Bothwell had made their name as professional soldiers, fulfilling roles policing the Borders, for
which they were granted Bothwell Castle in Lanarkshire. They had exchanged this for Hermitage, a forbidding
thirteenth-century citadel in Liddesdale, positioned to control the central Border region. This made them the
dominant Border magnates. They also owned Crichton Castle near Edinburgh. As hereditary Lords Admiral of
Scotland, they benefitted from treasure trove arising from any shipwreck on the Scottish coast, and this gave
them financial independence. Both as Border magnates and as Lords Admiral they came to distrust the
English.

ability through the legal profession to involve himself in many of the notorious events of Mary's reign, hoping for preferment. The five Melville brothers were often sent on diplomatic missions and became the great observers of the period. The Bethunes were an extended family of French origin. In addition to providing archbishops and a cardinal, they fulfilled roles at court. Robert Bethune accompanied Mary to France as head of her household with his French wife, allowing their daughter Mary to become the fourth 'Marie' despite being a couple of years older than the others. There were other families of influence, of course, but it was a tight little group at the centre of power.

At the time of Mary's birth on 7 December 1542, Scotland was a nation of 500,000 people, compared with 15,000,000 in both England and France. Unlike England and France, its population had failed to grow during the previous one hundred years, ravaged as it had been by military disasters against the English, which on each occasion resulted in losses on a scale of the First World War, decimating a generation of young men. This left many of the nobility succeeding to their titles and estates at an early age, short of both cash and parental discipline.

Wealth in Scotland tended to be in the form of land, although generating income from it in inclement weather and among feuding neighbours was haphazard. English and Continental observers alike considered Scottish farming methods on its poor and infertile land to be primitive. There was a little Ice Age from about 1560 to 1700, resulting in exceptionally cold winters and stormy summers, which exacerbated crop failures. The start of this period coincided with Mary's return to Scotland. By then, Scotland was almost treeless, except in remoter areas of the Highlands. There were con-tinuing efforts to require landowners to replant what was being cut for building and fuel. Far more of the land area was covered with water than is apparent today. Fife alone had twenty lochs of the size of Loch Leven. There were no enclosures, principally because leases to tenant farmers were granted for only four or five years at a time, so there was no permanence to holdings. Although there were areas of relatively better farmland particularly in Fife and Lothian, much was also in the Borders, exposed to the marauding English or feuds between rival clans. With the Crown having no standing army, there were no quick means of protection, and few towns other than Edinburgh were walled, leaving them open to attack. Most dwellings occupied by lairds were tower houses, built over the centuries to provide protection against feuding neighbours or the invading English. They stood as stark domesticated keeps fortified with defensive turrets, heavily barred doors and slit windows on the lower floors. The dormer windows above were high enough to be out of range of attack. At times of threat, women, children and livestock from the surrounding area were brought into the relative safety of the lower floors.

Roads were poor and ill-maintained. Randolph described his trip from Stirling in 1562 to join Mary and Lord James Stewart at Inverness, as 'a terrible journey both for horse and man, the countries are so poor, the victuals so scarce'.[2] Even the well-trodden route between Berwick and Leith was so 'deep and foul' that artillery had to be moved by sea. Carriages were unknown until 1561, when Mary brought one from France. They could not handle the rough terrain, and such bridges as there were across the myriad of streams and rivers were poorly maintained. Travellers had to pick their way past vagabonds on land and pirates at sea, causing much of Scotland to remain almost completely cut off from civilisation. The Gaelic-speaking north and west seemed a foreign country, only communicating with the rest of the nation during the movement of cattle to market in summer months. The Western Isles were almost completely isolated. Mary never visited them and none of the nobility held sway there. Even the Campbell dominions stretched no further north than Inveraray.

Despite Scotland's small size and economic shortcomings, the Auld Alliance with France gave it far greater significance than its remote location would suggest. Scots, who visited Continental Europe, spoke French, the language of diplomacy, even with the English, as there were sufficient dialectical differences between English and Scots to make conversation difficult. Yet Scots remained the language of the Scottish court. Scotsmen on the Continent had proved themselves as adept soldiers, perhaps a result of their experience in feudal disputes at home, and were in demand as mercenaries. The Scottish Gens d'Armes in Paris provided the Body Guard for the French Crown. The Scottish government, universities and Catholic Church all maintained links with their Continental counterparts, resulting in a regular transfer of personnel between them. Academics from the universities at St. Andrews, Glasgow and Aberdeen could hold their own at Continental centres of learning, where they often held senior posts. After the English Reformation, the Papacy saw Scotland and its Catholic Church as key to its efforts to achieve an English counter-Reformation.

Despite the lack of a strong Scottish manufacturing tradition, trade between the eastern seaports and Continental Europe remained active. Linen, wool cloth, skins, smoked and salted fish were exported to the Baltic and the Continent, with luxuries such as wine and salt being brought back in return. On the west coast there were few burghs, but Ayr maintained a flourishing trade with Ireland, and iron was landed in Kirkcudbright from

Spain. Glasgow, with its cathedral and university, was also beginning to grow in importance.

Very often the sons of prominent Scottish families were educated in Europe, with younger sons becoming mercenaries, fulfilling academic roles or training for the priesthood. This interchange helped to foster the Auld Alliance with France against the English. Many well-to-do Scots were influenced by French customs and architecture, with the principal royal castles being converted by James V into Renaissance palaces. Matthew, 4th Earl of Lennox spent most of his early years in France, and the junior branch of his family, the seigneurs d'Aubigny, made a living there as mercenaries. Glencairn was also educated in France, resulting in his close association with Mary's mother, Marie of Guise, when she became widowed, despite his conversion to Calvinism. George, 4th Lord Seton, when widowed, remarried a French lady-in-waiting, Mary Pyerres, and this encouraged him to send his daughter, Mary, to France as a companion for the young Queen. William Maitland, Cardinal Bethune, James Melville, George Buchanan, John Leslie, Lord James Stewart and many others completed their education in France. Perhaps surprisingly these links were not diminished by the Scottish Reformation. 'Earnest and brotherly' relationships and debates developed between scholars at Scottish and French universities despite opposing faiths.[3] As John Leslie explained, 'Of this comes, that so many of our countrymen, have such good success amongst strange Nations, some in the wars, some in professing of Sciences and some in merchandise.'[4] It was a willingness to travel that made Scots such natural pioneers when the British Empire started to extend itself about the world.

Those lords and other families surrounding the Crown needed to live by their wits and, as a result, were well educated. Yet this was not always true of those from remoter areas. It is said that Huntly, the most powerful man in northern Scotland, was almost illiterate. James, 4th Earl of Morton, who, as a second son of a second son, was not brought up with any aspiration to greatness, was a rough diamond of very little learning, despite becoming a most able, if unscrupulous, regent. Most nobles relied on being able to manage and no doubt milk valuable church lands to provide them with cash. They were seen as 'fairly shrewd, astute, and inconstant'.[5] They were open to bribery when it was offered, as the English knew only too well. It did not take much. De Silva, the Spanish ambassador in London, advised Philip II that a total payment of 8,000 crowns bought Elizabeth not only goodwill, but valuable information from all the principals of Scotland, regardless of their loyalties or religious persuasion. Even the Lords of the Congregation, a loose affiliation of the nobility, who were to use the banner of the

Reformation to oust French troops supporting Marie of Guise's regency from Scotland, were not connected by any bond of allegiance. When their objectives started to differ, they broke into opposing factions. There was no sense of honour or a concept of taking the long or altruistic view, and the nobility freely changed loyalties, making it difficult to gauge how they would react to a given situation. They were a world apart from the close-knit family units, such as the Guises, Montmorencys and Bourbons, of Mary's experience in France. They were only interested in *de biens et de grandeur* [wealth and status] and their own complex notions of kinship. It was often difficult for outside observers to understand the motives for an arranged marriage or to establish who was gaining loyalty from the other.

Despite their pride, clannishness and rivalries, lesser nobles dressed similarly to commoners, although, with their wives, they wore their finery in accordance with their rank at court. Their main extravagance was on horses to enable them to move around their estates. They did not generally aspire to a broader perspective by travelling elsewhere within Scotland, but remained in an isolated existence. This made them slow to join the tide of the Scottish Reformation, when it swept the populace at large. They took little interest in politics and only started to seek representation through the Lords of the Congregation and the Reformation Parliament of 1560.

Women were generally uneducated prior to the Reformation, and even nuns were often unable to read. The older Lady Huntly could not write and signed her name on documents with her hand 'led on the pen'. Lord James Stewart's mother, Margaret Erskine, signed her name almost illegibly with the letters barely linked. Yet the next generation of ladies wrote more proficiently. Despite educational shortcomings, the wives of the nobility tended to have all the mettle of their husbands and were certainly not a downtrodden breed kept in the background. They were obsessed with status, dressing, eating and with a retinue in accordance with their rank and not above it.

Superstition was rife. Witches were attacked by Reformers, anxious to eradicate the black arts, which they linked with aspects of the Catholic sacrament. Janet Bethune, widow of Scott of Buccleuch and a former mistress of Bothwell, was accused of enchanting Mary to enable Bothwell to seduce her. Margaret Fleming, the wife of the Earl of Atholl and one of Mary's ladies-in-waiting, cast spells in an unsuccessful attempt to transfer Mary's birth pains onto Lady Forbes of Reres. Mary's mistrust of Ruthven arose principally because he dabbled in sorcery.

There was no great air of culture until Mary imported French-style entertainments to court on her return to Scotland. Humour tended to be lewd, and Bothwell was not alone in enjoying smut. Visiting poets found themselves resorting to schoolboy obscenities to amuse their audiences. Although Mary appears to have shown personal decorum, there was a lascivious undercurrent not far below the surface. Although the French court may not have behaved much better, a gloss of respectability cloaked the worst excesses going on in the background.

Short of resources and weakened by continuing strife between rival factions, Scotland was never going to survive as an independent nation without help from abroad and was almost irrelevant in the cauldron of European politics except to create a bridgehead for an invasion of England. After spending three centuries trying to subordinate the Scots to its rule, England had succeeded only in forcing them into the arms of France. Its interference, both military and political, can be seen as the root cause of the tragic events of Mary's reign. Yet it was the fractured loyalties and self-interest of the Scottish nobility and Mary's failure to assert authority that allowed it to succeed to such devastating effect.

References

1. *Chronicles of the Families of Atholl and Tullibardine*, I, p. 32, cited in Antonia Fraser, *Mary Queen of Scots* p. 167
2. CSP Scottish, I, p. 649, cited in Antonia Fraser, p. 164
3. Ibid., p. 160
4. John Leslie, *The Historie of Scotland*, p. 116
5. An anonymous French Memoir of 1558, CSP Scottish, p. 205

2

James V's Marriages and Pro-French Policy

To cement a French alliance, Archbishop Bethune took on Albany's role as the French marriage broker. Having the offer of Marie de Bourbon available to him, James was able to sidestep Henry VIII's proposal of Mary Tudor, despite his mother's initial support for her. Bethune placed his astute, but unscrupulous, nephew David Bethune as Scottish resident in Paris to promote the French marriage. Yet Marie of Bourbon was not rumoured to have the charismatic appeal that might be desired by a man who had enjoyed a choice of beautiful women from an early age, and David Bethune persuaded Francis I to offer either of his daughters, Madeleine or Marguerite de Valois. Francis also bestowed the Order of St Michel on James, as a token of intent to welcome him as a future son-in-law. Yet James remained betrothed to Marie de Bourbon and, on 29 December 1535, signed the marriage agreement. He immediately left Stirling and, without advising the government, sailed for France with five ships. Yet he was driven back by a storm to St Ninians in Galloway. After returning to Stirling, he eventually left from Kirkcaldy in Fife on 1 September 1536, arriving at Dieppe nine days later. He borrowed clothes from his manservant John Tennant, so that he could catch a glimpse of Marie de Bourbon unrecognised. Being left unimpressed, he travelled to the court of Francis I at Lyon and immediately fell in love with the consumptive Madeleine, although Francis tried to promote his more robust, but less attractive, second daughter, Marguerite. James was not to be gainsaid and, on 25 November 1536, was betrothed to Madeleine at Blois. He was received in Paris with the status of Dauphin and was married at Notre Dame five weeks later. He worshipped his bride's fragile beauty. On 3 April, they reached Rouen on the long journey back to Scotland, arriving at Leith on 19 May. By July, she was dead, leaving James distraught.

David Bethune, who had so nimbly negotiated the change in marriage plans, had been groomed by his uncle, the Archbishop, to take on a pivotal role in Scottish politics and, in 1528, had been appointed Keeper of the Privy Seal. He had gone to Paris for the first time in 1510 to study civil and canon law and shared his uncle's Francophile loyalties. He was noted for almost unparalleled persuasiveness and, in recognition of his part in negotiating James's marriage to Madeleine, Francis I appointed him Bishop of Mirepoix in 1537 with an annual income of 10,000 livres. The Papacy also applauded the diplomatic coup of linking the two Catholic nations on either side of England. In 1538, Pope Paul III appointed him as only the second cardinal in Scotland's history and the first since 1387.

In early 1538 James sent the newly appointed Cardinal back to Paris to find a new French bride for him. Francis I chose Marie of Guise, born in 1515, daughter of the powerful Claude, Duke of Guise, and widow of the Duke of Longueville, Grand Chamberlain of France, who had died in 1537, by when they had produced two sons, although only one of them remained alive. She was 'of the largest size of women with dark auburn hair and creamy skin'. Always affable and generous, she gained many admirers with her regal confidence and intelligence. She had already been approached as a wife for Henry VIII after the death of Jane Seymour. Henry admired her dignified bearing, but the Guise family did not believe that marriage to the Protestant English king, an enemy of France, met their political interests. She herself claimed that, although her figure was big, her neck was small!

Marie of Guise's grandfather was René, Duke of Lorraine, an independent duchy between France and Germany. In addition to vast territories there, René also held substantial estates in France. These were left on his death in 1508 to his second son, Claude, who became a naturalised Frenchman. Claude was a close friend of the Dauphin, soon to be Francis I, a kinsman on his mother's side. In 1513, he married Antoinette, daughter of Francis, Count of Vendôme, the head of the Bourbon family, and they settled at Joinville, a turreted castle about 150 miles east of Paris on the border with Lorraine, where they raised a large family. Claude pursued a brilliant military career, accompanying Francis I to Italy, where he survived near fatal wounds at the Battle of Marignano. He also became a bastion against heresy and, in 1525, was created Duke of Guise. As ardent Catholics, the Guises had traditionally provided the Cardinal Archbishops of Reims, who crowned the French kings. This gave them a dominant position in the Catholic Church and provided their political influence with the French Crown. Claude's eldest son, Francis, Duke of Aumale, was another brilliant general, becoming Duke of Guise on his father's death in 1550. His next brother was the politically adept Charles, Cardinal of Guise, soon to be Cardinal of Lorraine and the most influential administrator at the French court.

Marie of Guise had met and married Longueville in 1534. On his death three years later, Francis I insisted on her marrying the widowed James V. She was required to leave behind her surviving son, Francis, to be brought up by her mother. It is rumoured that Francis wanted her out of sight as the Dauphin Henry had fallen for her and wished to repudiate the childless Catherine de Medici to marry her himself. Certainly they were always on close terms. Despite every effort, Francis could not be persuaded to change his mind. Her marriage to James took place on 18 May 1538, when Robert, 5th Lord Maxwell came to France to stand as proxy for the bridegroom at Notre Dame in Paris. Cardinal Bethune then escorted the new queen from France with a flotilla of ships and 2,000 men under Maxwell's command. She arrived with a household of 137 servants, landing on the Fife coast on 10 June, before travelling on for a second wedding ceremony with James at St Andrews, where Bethune crowned her as Queen of Scotland. There were pageants and plays performed in her honour and she tactfully expressed herself delighted with her surroundings, claiming that it was not the barbarous country destitute of comforts she had been led to believe. She set about updating the Scottish palaces in the French style, but her letters to her mother show that she was secretly homesick, pining for her son, the delicate three-year-old Francis, Duke of Longueville. James continued to entertain a succession of pretty mistresses, maintaining one at Tantallon, and 'set not much store by the queen'. Yet their first son, James, Duke of Rothesay, was born on 22 May 1539, followed by Arthur, Duke of Albany, on 27 April 1541. Tragically Arthur died two days after his birth at Stirling, and his brother, James, four weeks later at St Andrews. Despite their grief, Marie comforted her husband that they were young enough to produce more children, but she did not immediately conceive.

On his uncle's death in 1539, Cardinal Bethune became Archbishop of St Andrews, continuing with his policy of alliance with France. On his appointment, he also became *legatus a latere*, giving him sovereign powers in the Catholic Church independent of the King's authority. He was now the most influential man in Scotland after the King. He walked in procession from St Andrews Castle to the Cathedral and flaunted his status as a Prince of the Church rather than addressing religious reform. This made him a target for the Reformers, but he was sufficiently thick-skinned to follow his uncle's* arrogant and confrontational policy against them. After so much of his life spent in France, he had no rapport with the Scottish nobility or burghers in the towns, but lived in great opulence with his concubine

---

* The former archbishop had authorised the burning for heresy of the *proto-martyr* Patrick Hamilton. Hamilton had been the first Scotsman to preach Calvinist doctrines, which would later be adopted by the Kirk. As a bastion of the Church, the former archbishop had also ordered the execution of Henry Forest, Daniel Stratton and Norman Gourlay, all early Reformers.

Marion,* daughter of James, 1st Lord Ogilvy of Airlie, by whom he had at least nine children. In early 1546, their illegitimate daughter Margaret married David Lindsay, Master of Crawford, with the dowry of a princess in a magnificent ceremony at Finhaven Castle.

The Cardinal failed to provide the King with his uncle's balanced political advice. Although James continued to travel through his kingdom to gain allegiance, his approach was to assure subservience not support. In the north, he sought to 'exact the submission of the clans', but failed to gain Highland loyalty after annexing the Scottish Isles. His visits were too short for permanent effect and, when Bethune advised him to annex the Douglas, Crawford, Bothwell and Glamis estates in an attempt to stamp out heresy, he alienated the waverers. Far from being conciliatory, Bethune provided a list of 360 nobles and lairds deserving forfeit as Reformers, headed by his cousin (Janet Bethune's son), Arran. This was a fatal mistake, ultimately causing his downfall and a breach between James and the nobility.

Despite Henry VIII's success in fuelling the Scottish Reformation, he was losing the diplomatic battle. Even with the Cardinal's shortcomings, James had no political reason to turn against the Catholic Church, which provided financial support for the State and for himself, including £1,400 annually earmarked for the Court of Session, which he pocketed. He supported Bethune in his opposition to the heretics, backed by his mother and determined wife. Reformist books were prohibited and he refused even to open Calvinist tomes, which Henry provided for him. Yet he was powerless to take a military stand against England, even though he now had a modest number of French troops as part of Marie of Guise's dowry. Even if Bethune ignored it, the tide of Reformation was sweeping through Scotland, and James realised that the abuses of the Catholic Church needed to be brought under control.

With diplomacy having failed, Henry sent the 69-year-old Thomas, 3rd Duke of Norfolk for a Scottish campaign. Sir Robert Bowes, who had re-established his support from Angus and other dissident Scottish peers, plundered Jedburgh with an advanced guard of 3,000 men. On 24 August 1542, James sent Huntly with hastily gathered Scottish troops to face them at Haddon Rig. With Home's help, Huntly routed the English and captured Bowes. Angus was lucky to escape. With less than 10,000 men, Huntly then held his position on the Tweed against 30,000 English troops led by the

---

* To describe Marion (or Mariota) Ogilvy as a concubine is perhaps a little unjust. She had been his consort since the early 1520s before he had taken holy orders, and they may have in fact been married beforehand, but it suited those who opposed the Cardinal to see her in that light.

much feared Norfolk. Scottish euphoria was short-lived; three weeks later Norfolk invaded Lothian with 20,000 men, destroying villages and the harvest before retiring to Berwick. Huntly with his weaker force was in no position to face them. Yet the French party was buoyed up by his success and wanted to take a more aggressive stance. On 5 October 1542, a force was mustered at Haddington ready to advance into England, while James's main army under Oliver Sinclair, grandson of William, 1st Earl of Caithness, marched to Solway Moss near Carlisle. The scene was set for a major showdown.

3

The Death of James V and the Regency for the Infant Mary

James V died at Falkland on 14 December 1542, six days after the birth of his daughter Mary. He had suffered acute depression brought on by an unexplained malady* following the defeat for his Scottish troops by the English at Solway Moss, when many of his closest supporters were taken prisoner.

The planning was a disaster. James had collected 30,000 men with artillery at Burgh Muir, Edinburgh. Having advanced to Fala Muir at the western end of the Lammermuir Hills, his troops refused to cross the English border in fear of Norfolk's awesome reputation. On 3 November, he withdrew to Edinburgh, from where he set out for south-west Scotland. The Warden of the Western Marches was Maxwell, supported by Gilbert Kennedy, 3rd Earl of Cassillis, William Cunningham, 4th Earl of Glencairn and Malcolm, 3rd Lord Fleming, all experienced soldiers. On his arrival at Lochmaben where his army gathered, James was unwell, weak in both mind and body. He wrote to Marie of Guise, 'I have been very ill these three days past as I never was in my life; but god be thanked I am well.'[1] Yet he was far from recovered and rambled in and out of sanity. By rights, Maxwell, as Warden, should have taken command, but inexplicably James secretly appointed Oliver Sinclair as his General-Lieutenant. Sinclair was neither an experienced soldier nor the obvious leader of the nobility by birth. Yet, while at court, he had enthusiastically encouraged James, as the Pope's 'defender of the faith', to attack the heretic Henry VIII. Sinclair was no doubt encouraged by his brothers, Henry, Bishop of Ross and John, Dean of Restalrig (later Bishop of Brechin) with support from Bethune and the Scottish Catholic Church.

Even after giving the order for the Scots to advance, James had failed to

---

* James was not fit. He suffered from syphilis after years of living with a range of mistresses, even after his marriage to Mary of Guise. It could be that he caught cholera from the Earl of Atholl, who had recently died of the disease. He also showed symptoms of dysentery, suffering from diarrhoea, perhaps caused by drinking contaminated water.

say that he was not well enough to lead his 10,000 men himself and that he had handed command to Sinclair. Only on 25 November 1542, when his army crossed into Cumberland, did Sinclair produce his appointment. He was hoisted on spears and all men were ordered to obey him, but the nobility was indignant at having a commoner as their leader and would offer him only half-hearted backing. As they moved forward, laying waste the English countryside as they went, Cumberland farmers gathered 4,000 men to make a stand with a small nucleus of 300 hardened troops, provided by Sir Thomas Wharton, Sir William, 3rd Lord Dacre, and Sir William Musgrave.

Without an agreed chain of command, the Scottish army had no plan for attack. When Sinclair ordered them to advance, his men lacked heart and many of them were captured as they retreated into the bogs of Solway Moss. Their performance against the outnumbered and largely untrained English was inept. Henry VIII had given instructions for members of the Scottish nobility to be captured, so that he could seek their future allegiance as their price of freedom. Only twenty Scots were killed, but 1,200 were taken prisoner as they sank into the bog. These included Sinclair, Maxwell, Cassillis, Glencairn, Fleming, Laurence, 3rd Lord Oliphant, Patrick, 4th Lord Gray, Norman, Master of Rothes, Sir John Somerville and 500 gentlemen. According to John Knox, who strongly opposed this Catholic backed crusade, 'Every man called his own sloghorn [slogan] … Sinclair was without shot taken fleeing full manfully.'[2] Sinclair was brought to London, arriving on 19 December. To save his skin he agreed to support Henry and was paroled to Scotland. Six months later he was in Orkney and never regained influence.

Still at Lochmaben, James became completely incoherent, repeating, 'Oh fled Oliver! Is Oliver tane?'[3] From here he was taken back to Falkland, where he was inconsolable. Meanwhile, on 8 December, at Linlithgow, Marie of Guise gave birth to their third child, a daughter Mary, 'before her time'. According to Arran, she was 'a very weak child, and not likely to live as it is thought',[4] and she was a girl. Knox claimed that 'all men lamented that the realm was left without a male to succeed'.[5] Referring to the Stewart dynasty, James was no more sanguine, 'The devil go with it. It will end as it began. It came with a lass, and will go with a lass.'*[6] He died† six days later, a few days

---

* The Stewarts had gained the throne of Scotland through the marriage of Walter Stewart, 6th High Steward of Scotland to Marjorie, eldest daughter of Robert the Bruce.

† Much has been written about James's illness. There is no doubt that he was overcome by remorse for the failure at Solway Moss, but he was ill before the battle occurred. Like Mary, his daughter, he appears to have suffered from a nervous disorder brought about by stress. During these critical lapses he took erratic decisions, which were to prove just as fatal for Mary. It has been conjectured that their symptoms bore the hallmark of the inherited disease porphyria, later to afflict George III, and this will be discussed later.

short of his thirtieth birthday, having appointed Arran, heir to the throne after his infant daughter, as regent of his impoverished estate. Mary, at least, proved robust, but Arran, like his father before him, was ineffective as a leader.

With Cardinal Bethune's help, Marie of Guise, now Queen Dowager, took on the task of protecting her daughter's kingdom. The Guises had trained her well in statecraft, but little could have prepared her for dealing with the unreliable Scots. She had no confidant to turn to in Scotland and communication with France was slow. She had to hope that both France and the Catholic Church would continue to recognise Scotland's strategic importance. To assure this, she needed a marriage for her newly born daughter to an appropriate French prince. She was still young and attractive herself and had a number of suitors among the Scottish nobility, but could see the folly of being allied with one faction to the detriment of her relationship with the rest. With the Scottish government dominated by the French party, the English put about rumours that she was enjoying an affair with Bethune. This was certainly untrue, but he had quickly realised his error in trying to thwart the Scottish nobility – only they could provide military protection to back her small French garrison. Standing alone, the Scottish monarchy could only hope to maintain a balance between rival factions, a task that would absorb the next sixty years of Scottish history.

The nobles surrounding the Crown often held hereditary roles within the hierarchy of Scottish government, just as the Stewarts had done as grand stewards. They jealously guarded these status symbols, forming into allegiances when threatened or to promote themselves against rivals. During Mary's minority there were four factions, the Scottish Catholics led by Bethune; the court party led by the Queen Dowager, who promoted links with France; the English party, still supporting closer ties with England, and the Lords of the Congregation backed by the Reformers. The powerful families participating in government switched sides between these groups to suit their ambitions. With very few exceptions, they showed little in the way of loyalty or religious scruple and were motivated by political convenience rather than personal conviction. They could easily be swayed by financial hand-outs from England, or by any French, Spanish or papal bounty being proffered.

Arran's appointment as Regent reflected his position, following the death of Albany, as heir to the throne,* rather 'than to any commanding talents of

---

* He was the grandson of Princess Mary, sister of James III, who had married James, 1st Lord Hamilton. This couple had had two children, James, who obtained a charter granting him the lands and Earldom of Arran in 1503, and Elizabeth, who married Matthew Stuart, 2nd Earl of Lennox in 1494.

his own'. There was, moreover, some doubt about his legitimacy,* although this was almost certainly spurious, and had not prevented his appointment as Regent. He was a man of 'wealth and refinement' being both genial and tolerant, but 'indolent and vacillating in the extreme'. The Queen Dowager described him as 'a simple and the most inconstant man in the world, for whatever he determineth today, he changeth tomorrow'. [7] His principal objective was always his family's advancement.

Bethune became Lord Chancellor, but had no confidence in the dithering Arran, despite their kinship. He produced another version of James's will prepared from a piece of blank paper, which the King had signed for him before his death. This appointed a group of four, made up of Huntly, Archibald Campbell, 4th Earl of Argyll (who had inherited from his father in 1529 and died in 1558), James V's illegitimate half-brother, James, Earl of Moray (who died in 1544) and Arran, to act as a Council of Regency, with Bethune to be Governor of the young Queen. He then went to Fife and Angus to persuade George, 4th Earl of Rothes, and Gray with others to back him. This was a mistake as Rothes and Gray, both now Protestant, strongly mistrusted Bethune. In 1540, Rothes had been on his list of 360 Reformist lairds to be forfeited, as had Gray's uncle, Patrick, 3rd Lord Gray, who died in 1541. The list also included Sir James Kirkcaldy of Grange and Sir John Melville of Raith, Captain of Dunbar Castle. Despite the King having rejected Bethune's initial recommendation for their forfeiture, he had raised it again in 1542, shortly before the King's death.

Rothes and Gray approached Gray's brother-in-law, Huntly, who was not someone too bothered about legal nicety and a staunch Catholic. On learning that Bethune had forged the will, Huntly agreed that he had gone too far. Arran was reconfirmed as sole regent, and Bethune was warded at Dalkeith. When he blamed Rothes for divulging his plan, Arran had to step in to reconcile them.

With Bethune, the Queen Dowager and Moray all seeking continuing links with France, the issue for them was how to influence Arran, who had

---

* Bethune's contention that Arran was illegitimate was convoluted. His father's first wife, Elizabeth Home, had received a divorce from her former husband, Sir Thomas Hay, Master of Yester, to enable her to marry him on 28 April 1490. Fourteen years later, on 15 November 1504, the 1st Earl received the Pope's authority to divorce Elizabeth on the grounds that her original divorce from Sir Thomas Hay was invalid and she had not been free to remarry. This was reconfirmed on 11 March 1510. Despite this, Bethune now argued that Elizabeth Home had in fact received a valid divorce from Sir Thomas Hay and had thus been repudiated by the 1st Earl without cause. This invalidated the 1st Earl's second marriage to the Cardinal's 1st cousin Elizabeth Bethune, who was Arran's mother. He also argued (entirely against his own interest) that if papal authority were rejected because Scotland was becoming Reformist, then the Pope had no right to grant the divorce. This left Elizabeth Bethune's children illegitimate.

become a Reformer. Knox later recorded that at this time 'all men esteemed the Governor to have been the most fervent Protestant that there was in all Europe'. As a result 'the Papists raged against him', and his fame 'was spread in divers countries'.[8] Yet, when his religious commitment wavered, he frustrated his colleagues. To gain some support, Arran brought Angus back to authority, as the leader of a group of nobles, including Andrew Kerr of Ferniehirst, supporting renewed links with England. Having travelled to France after leaving Scotland in 1530, Angus now returned on terms negotiated by his brother Sir George Douglas of Pittendreich. Arran was given largesse by Henry VIII, in return for Angus, on 16 January 1543, being restored to his estates. With Henry's backing, Angus and Sir George now led the English party at court. It was as part of this arrangement that Sir George's second son, James, married Elizabeth, the third daughter of James, 3rd Earl of Morton, and became his heir. With Bethune imprisoned, Angus now became Arran's mentor, promoting Henry VIII's son, Prince Edward, as Mary's husband.

Everyone recognised that Mary's marriage was the key to Scotland's future and that those controlling her would influence the outcome. John, 5th Lord Lindsay of the Byres, a man of rugged integrity and an Extraordinary Lord of Session, was one of four nobles given custody of her on 15 March 1543 after Bethune's arrest. He had been present at her father's death and sought to shelter her from opposing factions. Erskine, Alexander, 5th Lord Livingston and the shy and retiring, but hugely wealthy William Keith, 4th Earl Marischal were her other protectors. The choice of a husband seemed to be between a foreign prince and a member of the Scottish nobility. While a foreign prince would pose the risk of subjugation to a foreign state, a Scottish noble would cause jealousy with the remainder. Francis, the future Dauphin of France, was not yet born, so this left the door open for Prince Edward, although Arran, in typical fashion, wanted to promote his eldest son, James.

In March 1543, Sadler arrived from England to hold secret talks with Arran for a marriage between the fifteen-month-old Mary and Prince Edward, now aged five, with an expectation that she should be brought up in England. Freed from Bethune's influence, Arran's only interest was to see how he would benefit and he offered to support Henry's break with Rome. Henry secretly proposed Princess Elizabeth in marriage to Arran's eldest son to cement a Protestant union between England and Scotland. He also offered to raise Arran to the Crown in the area north of the Forth, if the Scots failed to back the plan. Although this was highly satisfactory for Arran, particularly when Henry offered him 5,000 men, he really wanted £5,000 and, with his colleagues mistrusting all things English, he had little hope of gaining support for it.

Henry applied further pressure by offering to release the twenty-three prisoners from Solway Moss still held in the Tower, if they would back the English marriage. Not surprisingly they all agreed, but in most cases with little intention of honouring their undertaking. Yet Cassillis,* Rothes, Glencairn,† Fleming,‡ Gray and Maxwell remained for a considerable period loyal to the English. Moray and Argyll are thought to have been offered large bribes to support the union with England, so Arran was not completely without backing. On about 6 June 1543, a bond in favour of the English marriage was signed by Angus, Argyll, Crawford, Marischal, Cassillis, Glencairn and ten others. This was, of course, a complete anathema to the French party.

As usual Henry overplayed his hand and the Scots were determined that Mary's marriage should leave Scotland independent. When Henry insisted on Mary going to England for her education, they baulked. While it was recognised that she would live there once married, they would not agree to her leaving Scotland in advance. Henry was told very bluntly that this would be 'a right high and right great inconvenience to the realm of Scotland'.[9] While it was assumed that his 'high wisdom' would appreciate the sensibilities, it did not, but the Scots remained adamant.

The English marriage was never likely to find favour, even with those who were not members of the French party. After all the recent fighting, the Borderers feared closer links with their English rivals. Buccleuch, who had long since fallen out with Angus and remained in feud with the Kers of Cessford, strongly opposed it, despite persuasive efforts by the English Wardens. His opposition may have been influenced by the Cardinal, who had arranged his marriage to Janet Bethune,§ twenty-four years his junior. By agreeing to Buccleuch's divorce from Janet, daughter of Andrew Kerr of

---

* Cassillis's loyalty was sweetened by the offer of a pension. He had provided his brothers, David and Archibald, and his uncle, Thomas Kennedy of Crieff, as sureties, but appears to have failed to return to England to plead for their release.

† Glencairn had already shown himself as an ardent Reformer, retaining both George Wishart and John Spottiswood in his home, and he later joined Lennox in his military expeditions on the English behalf.

‡ Fleming played lip service to supporting the English, but remained secretly loyal to the Queen Dowager. With his son, James, Master of Fleming, left as surety in England, he was concerned for his safety.

§ Janet Bethune was the daughter of Sir John Bethune of Creich, a first cousin of the Cardinal and of Arran. She had a reputation for using witchcraft to maintain her beauty and to bond to her bidding 'the viewless forms of air', as celebrated by Sir Walter Scott in *The Lay of the Lost Minstrel*.[10] In 1559, after three marriages, numerous lovers and seven children, she entered into an affair with the twenty-four-year-old James Hepburn, 4th Earl of Bothwell, nineteen years her junior. After this she married on two further occasions. Her sister, Grizel, married Buccleuch's son, Sir William Scott.

Ferniehirst, the Cardinal opened up old sores between Buccleuch and Fer-niehirst, who was now supported by Cessford.

To hold the English marriage plan together, Arran tried to stop the Queen Dowager from communicating with France. Yet she managed to send warning of her plight to her mother, Antoinette de Bourbon, who advised the French government. The initial French plan was to send the Duke of Guise to Scotland with a sufficient force to distract Henry from making his proposed invasion of the Continent. In the end, they sent the young Lennox, a naturalised Frenchman, to escort Mary back to France. Having slipped the English fleet, he soon reached Scotland.

The Queen Dowager needed to remove Mary from Arran's direct control at Linlithgow and planned to take her to Stirling, which she had received as part of her dowry on marriage to James. She acted against Arran's instruction by sending coffers full of clothing and household goods on ahead. Linlithgow, where Mary had spent the first seven months of her life, had been rebuilt by James V round a quadrangle in elegant French style. The Queen Dowager likened it to a château on the Loire, but its small size made it difficult to accommodate both mother and daughter with their extensive entourages. Despite having magnificent royal apartments, Stirling was a keep, positioned precipitously on a rocky outcrop above the town. It offered security while Mary awaited transfer to Dumbarton and a ship for France.

In a brilliant game of double bluff the Queen Dowager enlisted the English ambassador Sadler to help her. Following his negotiation with Arran on the English marriage, he visited her at Linlithgow to see Mary, whom he dangled on his knee. He later confirmed to Henry that she was 'as goodly a child as I have seen of her age, and as like to live, with the Grace of God'.[11] He was uncertain how the Queen Dowager would react to his visit, but she charmed him with a story that, although she favoured Mary marrying Prince Edward, Arran had no intention of agreeing to it, as he wanted his son as Mary's husband. He was simply seeking an English bribe and, when Henry died, he intended to usurp the Scottish throne. Henry could prevent this by helping to move Mary to Stirling and by persuading Arran to release Bethune, who was maligned over the forged will, to enable him to gain the Regency. Sadler was amazed, but was taken in and promised not to reveal his sources to protect her. He sanctioned the move without realising her true intent, but for the time being Mary remained where she was.

On Lennox's arrival in Scotland, he went straight to Linlithgow to see the Queen Dowager. They agreed on the importance of Bethune's release to thwart the English marriage plan. Having his hand on the Catholic Church purse strings, Bethune was too influential to be left in the cold for long. He was being held at Blackness Castle under the ward of Seton, an Extra-ordinary Lord of Session. Seton was an academic, educated at St Andrews and in Paris, who had studied law after establishing himself as a surgeon. He was a close ally of the Queen Dowager, with his wife, Mary Pyerres, having been one of her French ladies-in-waiting. He was now approached by Lennox and a group of mainly Catholic lords, including Moray and Huntly, to allow Bethune to return under ward to St Andrews. Knox claimed that Bethune undertook to arrange favourable marriages for two of Seton's daughters, but he needed no such inducement. He was 'a wise and virtuous statesman', but died on 19 July 1549, a year after his youngest son, James, and daughter, Mary, had left for France as the Queen's companions. In mid-1543 Moray attended a Convocation at Perth to support Bethune's formal release from detention. On his arrival, Bethune called for Rothes, who was at the meeting, to be arrested and warded at Blackness. On 12 December, he organised an Act of Parliament to restore Castle Wemyss to Sir James Colville, although this had been in Rothes' control since its forfeiture. Rothes was not going to take these slights lying down.

Now that he was freed, Bethune 'began to rage as any lion loosed of his bond',[12] galvanising anti-English public opinion. He encouraged Arran's illegitimate half-brother, John Hamilton, Abbot of Paisley, to persuade Arran to drop the English alliance. Arran was told that, if he continued to abandon the Catholic cause, the question of his father's divorce would be reopened. He was offered French subsidies, which compared favourably with those from the English. Bethune became aware that Lennox had a personal agenda. If Arran were shown to be illegitimate, Lennox was the next in line to the Scottish throne. He planned to marry the Queen Dowager to claim the Regency for himself, allowing Mary to make a French marriage. He needed Bethune's assistance to progress this. Yet, despite Bethune wanting a French alliance, he stopped short of supporting a French marriage for Mary, fearing that this would result in Scotland being subsumed into France, thereby weakening the authority of the Scottish nobility and its Catholic Church. If he could persuade Arran to drop the English alliance, he would support his son, James, to become Mary's husband. Meanwhile Lennox continued to court the Queen Dowager.

Henry VIII was quick to react to Bethune's release and knew that Lennox was hoping to kidnap Mary to take her from Dumbarton to France. He *ordered* Arran to raise forces to bring her into the safety of Edinburgh Castle. Realising that there was no support for an English marriage, Arran used the excuse that Mary was suffering from the 'breeding of teeth',[13] and admitted to Sadler that Henry's terms for marriage to Prince Edward were not acceptable. Henry threatened war. He needed a quick resolution, as he was about to embark on his invasion of France. Arran compromised and, in the Treaty of Greenwich, signed on 1 July 1543, agreed to the marriage in terms, which guaranteed Scottish independence with Mary to be brought up and educated in Scotland. If she remained childless after her marriage, she was to be returned home as an independent queen. These terms allowed the Queen Dowager to retain Mary under her control and, when Sadler reported French ships being sighted off the coast, she at last had military support.

Lennox had Bethune's and Moray's backing to assist the Queen Dowager in moving Mary to Stirling and out of Arran's reach. On 24 July 1543, they signed a bond with Huntly, Argyll, Patrick Hepburn, 3rd Earl of Bothwell, John Gordon, 11th Earl of Sutherland and William Graham, 3rd Earl of Menteith, four Catholic bishops and thirty-six lords and lairds. They gathered 7,000 men at Stirling before marching to Linlithgow, still fearing that Arran would attempt to remove the infant Queen to Edinburgh. On his arrival, two days later, he had to capitulate. It was agreed that Mary should remain in the care of Marischal, Lindsay of the Byres, Livingston and Erskine, but, on 27 July, she was escorted with her mother to Stirling by 2,500 cavalry and 1,000 infantry, with a baggage train, which extended for almost a mile. She was to remain at Stirling for the next four years. The Queen Dowager had avoided signing Lennox's bond, and when Sadler visited her she reiterated her support for the English marriage and her need for protection from Arran. Sadler was again hoodwinked and reported that Mary 'would soon be a woman if she took after her mother. She was a right fair and goodly child'.[14]

Henry continued pressurising Arran to honour the English marriage plan. Despite being advised to act more moderately, the English fleet captured Scottish merchant ships en route for France, and Henry tried to take control of castles south of the Forth. He failed to appreciate the adverse effect of his bullying tactics. Even Angus and his pro-English colleagues seemed to turn against him, and marriage to Prince Edward became a lost cause. The pro-English policy was in tatters. Sadler found himself under surveillance and reported back to Henry VIII that he was isolated: 'I am not able to do his majesty the service where my poor heart would ... the whole body of the realm is inclined to France,' he wrote. He was surrounded by an angry mob in Edinburgh and was narrowly missed by a musket ball while walking in his garden. He asked Angus for protection at Tantallon and, in November 1543, was escorted across the border by Sir George Douglas with 400 horse. Safely on English soil, he reported, 'Nor do I think never man had to do with so rude, so inconsistent, and beastly a nation as this.'[15]

With Arran no longer in control of Mary, Bethune persuaded the General Council called at Stirling in June 1543 to depose him as Regent in favour of the Queen Dowager, and to appoint Angus, still apparently disaffected with the English, as Lieutenant-General. Arran realised that he had to compromise, but refused to surrender the regency. On 3 September, only a week after ratifying the Treaty of Greenwich, he held a secret meeting with Bethune at Falkirk, brokered by Moray. They embraced and rode on to Stirling, where Arran revealed the full extent of his secret plans with Henry for Mary to marry Prince Edward and for his son, James, to marry Princess Elizabeth. On 8 September, after threatening him with excommunication, Bethune persuaded him to repudiate the English alliance, after putting forward his proposal for Arran's eldest son to marry Mary rather than Elizabeth. He again threatened to reopen the question of Arran's legitimacy if he did not revert to Catholicism. John Hamilton, who was to succeed Bethune as Archbishop of St Andrews in 1546, again applied pressure. Arran seems to have blindly accepted the doubts over his legitimacy. On 8 September 1543, 'the unhappy man', as Knox disparagingly referred to him, received the Catholic sacrament with Argyll and Bothwell holding the towel over his head. He thereby lost any trust that Henry VIII had placed in him.

Although Arran retained the regency, Bethune stood as Chancellor at his side. Angus was confirmed as military commander, perhaps in an effort to assure his loyalty. Yet he remained in contact with Henry and was soon induced into rejoining the English camp. Lennox's loyalty to the regency was also doubted, when he claimed to be heir to the throne ahead of Arran. Arran and Bethune now appointed a council headed by the Queen Dowager and drawn from members of both the French and English parties. In the following May, Moray was put in command of a Scottish army to face Prince Edward's uncle, Edward Seymour, Earl of Hertford, but he died suddenly on 12 June 1544. With the Moray title becoming dormant, five years later its lucrative estates were granted by Arran to Huntly to confirm his support.

The Scottish nobles closed ranks behind Arran's regency. On 9 September, Mary was taken in procession to the Chapel Royal in Stirling, where she was crowned Queen. Arran carried the crown, Lennox the sceptre, and Argyll, militarily the most powerful of the Scottish lords, the sword of state. While the nine-month-old child howled, Bethune, dressed in the full panoply of a cardinal, held the crown over her head and used chrism to anoint her as Queen, a position which God alone could bestow and call to account. The bishops and nobles present swore allegiance, but the English party, including Angus, Gray, Glencairn, Cassillis and Maxwell stayed away. The ceremony lacked the pomp associated with coronations in England and France, and the

English ambassador reported it as having 'such solemnities as they do use in this countrie, which is not very costlie'.[16] Mary would quickly learn that ceremony gained prestige for the Crown, despite all its extravagance.

Although Arran was now supported by Bethune and the Queen Dowager, Lennox tried to usurp his position by proposing marriage to her. She was attracted by his assurances of loyalty, particularly if Arran should again oppose her. With Mary's coronation seen as a time to celebrate, she wanted some amusement and held a party at Stirling for her twenty-eighth birthday. She was still one of the most beautiful ladies in Scotland and it was 'like Venus and Cupid in the time of fresh May, for there was such dancing, singing, playing and merriness ... that no man would have tired therein'.[17]

The Queen Dowager already had another admirer in Bothwell and was not going to miss the opportunity to play Lennox off against him. On 16 June 1543, he had even divorced* his wife, Agnes Sinclair, to make way for his intended marriage. He used his close association with the judiciary as Sheriff of Edinburgh and his influence with Bethune, who signed the annulment as Papal Legate without referral to Rome, to ensure that his children's legitimacy was not prejudiced. Like Lennox, he had only recently returned to Scotland, after being exiled to the Continent for opposing James V's authority. Yet he was beginning to hold Reformist sympathies, which had resulted in his inclusion in Bethune's list of those to be considered for forfeit. As a soldier full of bravado, he was ready to participate in chivalrous pursuits such as duelling and jousting to promote his suit. In words resonant of comments on his son, Sadler described him as 'the most vain and insolent man in the world, full of pride and folly, and here nothing at all esteemed'.[18] Yet father and son had a charm which could captivate women.

Suddenly Bothwell found himself with a sophisticated rival. Lennox was aged twenty-seven, and, after living at the French court, was 'very pleasant in the sight of gentlewomen'.[19] He had been brought up in Provence† and

---

* The marriage was annulled on the grounds of consanguinity. Agnes Sinclair was the daughter of Margaret Hepburn, sister of Patrick, 1st Earl of Bothwell. Patrick, the 3rd Earl, was thus her first cousin once removed.
† The Lennox Stuarts had been mercenaries in France for several generations, and were traditional captains of the Scottish Gens d'Armes. The French title of Seigneur d'Aubigny had been granted by Charles VII on 26 March 1423 to John Stuart, grandfather of Sir John, 1st Earl of Lennox. When the Lennox earldom was granted in 1475 (although it was subsequently revoked and reconfirmed in 1488), the French title was carried by the junior branch of the family. Robert, 3rd Seigneur d'Aubigny had inherited from his cousin, Bernard, who died in Scotland in 1508. Bernard was an illustrious mercenary for the French, known as 'the father of war' and 'the prince of knighthood and the flower of chivalry', who had supported Henry VII against Richard III at Bosworth Field in 1485. This made the Lennox Stuarts historic allies of the Tudors. Robert had married Bernard's daughter, Anne, but had no children. On his death, Lennox's youngest brother, Robert, inherited as 4th Seigneur from his great-uncle and was the father of Esmé Stuart, later Duke of Lennox. Although the Earls

served as a soldier with his uncle, Robert, 3rd Seigneur d'Aubigny, becoming Captain of the Scottish Gens d'Armes.

Both Bothwell and Lennox recognised that, by winning the Queen Dowager's hand, they would be in a strong position to displace Arran as Regent and, in Lennox's case, to usurp his position as heir to the throne. They postured like peacocks before her, running up enormous bills on clothing, while they danced, sang and recited poetry, or engaged in shooting and jousting matches. She loved all the attention, but offered 'nothing but fair words'.[20] Bothwell resorted to subterfuge by circulating a rumour, which Lennox believed, that he was already secretly betrothed to her. Within a month of Mary's coronation, Lennox had retired to Dumbarton to lick his wounds determined on revenge.

In addition to sending Lennox from France, Francis I made every effort to restore traditional French links with Scotland by sending de la Brosse with six ships containing money and artillery to support the Queen Dowager. On arrival at Greenock on the Clyde in October, de la Brosse was met by Lennox and Glencairn. Assuming Lennox's continuing loyalty, de la Brosse handed over his precious cargo. Lennox and Glencairn took it back to Dumbarton Castle, but had no means of protecting themselves, and Lennox, who remained a French citizen, realised that his action was treasonable. They thus handed their prize back to de la Brosse for delivery to the Queen Dowager, enabling her to distribute 59,000 crowns as pensions to her adherents. This did much to buy support for her and the Pope also sent a subsidy. Bethune was exonerated by Parliament and took effective control. On 15 December, the Scots signed a treaty with France, which reconfirmed the Auld Alliance.

Lennox had no choice but to be reconciled with the Queen Dowager, but she made clear that she would not marry him. He needed another way to build his powerbase and, in fury, left for England. In a complete volte-face, he offered to support Henry VIII, if he were permitted to marry his niece, the beautiful but headstrong Lady Margaret Douglas, Angus's daughter. Although Bothwell continued to court the Queen Dowager, rumours of a liaison are probably unfounded and they did not marry.

Angus remained apparently loyal to the new regime and was sent to the Borders with the intention of making a raid into England, but nothing

---

of Lennox were based in Scotland, Matthew's father had been murdered there in 1526, and Matthew had gone to live in France while the dust settled. While there he had adopted the French spelling of the Stewart name, resulting in the royal family becoming Stuart on Mary's marriage to Lord Darnley, although Mary herself also adopted the French spelling of her name in France.

effectual took place, so that he was treated with continuing suspicion by his fellow Scots. This was not without justification and he continued to oppose Arran. He received English financial backing to sign a new bond with other members of the Douglas clan. In January 1544 he captured Leith, while his brother, Sir George Douglas, took Musselburgh. Lennox returned from England to Glasgow to support Angus, his future father-in-law, and the English party. The Queen Dowager retaliated, still having a modest number of French soldiers garrisoned around Scotland, but badly needed the Scottish nobility's assistance. Bothwell, who continued to have ambitions to marry her, drove Sir George out of Musselburgh. The Douglases were forced to submit and gave new sureties of loyalty to the Regency, while also writing to Henry to confirm their continuing support for him.

In April 1544, Arran used French troops to capture Glasgow, which Lennox had fortified. Sir George Douglas and Angus's father-in-law Maxwell, who had gone to Lennox's assistance, were taken hostage. When Angus went to intercede on their behalf, he was arrested and warded first at Hamilton Castle and later Blackness. Arran threatened Lennox, Glencairn, Fleming and Cassillis with forfeiture and forced them into a secret bond of loyalty to the Regency. From now on Fleming remained faithful to the Queen Dowager, even though his son remained a hostage in England. The rest wrote secretly to Henry, confirming their allegiance and seeking his military support. They provided him with a detailed invasion plan and Glencairn guaranteed safe passage for English troops from Carlisle to Glasgow.

On 17 May 1544, after visiting Henry VIII in England, Lennox and Glencairn agreed to kidnap Mary at Stirling and bring her to England. They were also instructed to gain control of the principal Scottish fortresses and impose Protestantism. In return, they were granted English pensions and Lennox was promised the Regency with Glencairn as Protector. Glencairn returned to Scotland a week later with 500 spearmen, but was met by Arran with double that number. In a fierce conflict, Glencairn lost many of his men including his second son, Andrew. He retired with a few remaining adherents to Dumbarton to await Lennox, while Arran took control of Glasgow. Lennox had led a naval expedition up the west coast and forced a number of Scottish lairds, who still had children held as hostages in England, into giving him support. After meeting Glencairn at Dumbarton, he immediately left to obtain further assistance from Henry. The Scottish lairds at Dumbarton took the opportunity to defect, and Lennox ordered that eleven of the child hostages should be slaughtered. This gained for him the undying enmity of the Scottish nobility. Although he returned in August after his wedding, he found Glencairn too demoralised to continue fighting, causing the new expedition to be abortive. Believing the English position was untenable, Glencairn defected to the Regency, although he temporarily rejoined the English at Coldingham Priory.

The Queen Dowager was soon at loggerheads with Arran, who wanted Mary to marry his son, and was furious with the untrustworthy Scots, who still accepted any largesse that Henry VIII offered. She had always favoured a French marriage for Mary, not least because it would promote Guise family interests in France. In November 1543, she and Arran had held rival Parliaments, with the French party meeting at Stirling and the Regency at Edinburgh. Bethune still doubted the merits of a French marriage and, overlooking any concern about Arran's legitimacy, again promoted Mary's betrothal to Arran's son. The Queen Dowager decided to play along with this and was persuaded by Bethune to realign with Arran, so that by 1546 she had gained parliamentary agreement to renounce the Treaty of Greenwich. This left Henry furious. Furthermore, after Bethune's assassination, the Queen Dowager sought to wrest the Regency from Arran and reverted to the French marriage plan as the only way to protect Scotland for her daughter. In 1544, Catherine de Medici had at last provided a son for the Valois dynasty and he became the prize on offer. This would assure the arrival of more battle-hardened French troops in Scotland. With continued bullying, the English had driven the Scots into the welcoming arms of France.

References

1. Agnes Strickland, *The Lives of the Queens of Scotland*, p. 402
2. John Knox, *History of the Reformation*, p. 88
3. Ibid., pp. 38, 89–90
4. Sadler to Henry VIII, 23 March 1543, in Antonia Fraser, p. 15
5. John Knox, *History of the Reformation*, p. 40
6. Robert Lindsay of Pitscottie, *History and Chronicles of Scotland*, p. 406
7. John Guy, *My Heart Is My Own*, p. 20 and Jenny Wormald, *Mary, Queen of Scots*, p. 55
8. Wormald, *Mary, Queen of Scots*, p. 55
9. Wormald, *Mary, Queen of Scots*, p. 55
10. Sir Walter Scott, *The Lay of the Lost Minstrel*, in Antonia Fraser, p. 303
11. Wormald, *Mary, Queen of Scots*, p. 43
12. Pitscottie, *Chronicles II*, p. 8
13. Guy p. 25, Antonia Fraser, p. 22
14. Sadler to Henry VIII, 10 August 1543, *The State Papers and Letters of Sir Ralph Sadler*
15. Sadler to Henry VIII, Sadler v. 355, *The State Papers and Letters of Sir Ralph Sadler*

16. Hamilton Papers II, p. 33, cited by Antonia Fraser, p. 24
17. Cited by John Guy p. 29
18. Cited by John Guy, p. 30
19. Pitscottie, *Chronicles*, cited by John Guy, p. 30
20. Cited by John Guy, p. 31

4

Lennox's Marriage and English Efforts to Restore its Influence

After failing in his suit to marry the Queen Dowager, Lennox's rapid defection to support the English was motivated entirely by his desire to be recognised as heir to the Scottish throne ahead of Arran. Marriage to Lady Margaret Douglas, Angus's daughter by Margaret Tudor, despite her head-strong reputation,* suited his plans every bit as well and provided her with a connection 'sufficiently gratifying to her ambition and followed by a mutual affection'.

Lady Margaret's upbringing had mainly been supervised by her father at Tantallon. Cardinal Wolsey was her godfather, and, when not with Angus, the Cardinal protected her by arranging a home for her with Thomas Strangeways at Berwick. In 1528, when she was thirteen and Angus had temporarily returned to authority in Scotland, she was considered of suffi-cient lineal importance to be brought to London to be educated as a royal princess with her cousin and contemporary Mary Tudor, and they both remained adamantly Catholic. She later became first lady-in-waiting to Anne Boleyn and lady-of-honour to Princess Elizabeth, being 'beautiful and highly esteemed'. Yet, when she became secretly betrothed to Sir Thomas Howard, Anne Boleyn's uncle, Henry VIII, on 8 June 1534, placed them both in the Tower. While there she suffered from an intermittent fever and, on her mother's intercession, was moved to the Abbey of Sion. She was eventually released on 29 October 1537, still only twenty-two, although Sir Thomas died in the Tower two days later.

---

* Lady Margaret Douglas was a very considerable catch for Lennox with her strong claim to be heir to the English throne after Henry's own children. Apart from being Catholic, her right was ahead of Lady Jane Grey, who was descended from Henry VII's second daughter, Mary. Her mother had not relinquished her claim to the English throne on her marriage to James IV in 1503, but Henry VIII had decreed that children born outside England could not inherit. This debarred James V and his heirs, but not Lady Margaret. Although, in his will, Henry preferred the Protestant descendants of his younger sister, Mary, Lady Margaret had the senior dynastic claim. While Mary Tudor was Queen, Elizabeth was considered illegitimate, so that, in the eyes of Mary Tudor at least, Lady Margaret was her heir.

Given doubts within the Catholic Church over Prince Edward's legitimacy, Henry barred Lady Margaret from the throne by declaring her illegitimate, on the grounds that her mother's marriage to Angus had been unlawful, as it lacked royal approval. He then returned her to favour by appointing her as first lady-in-waiting to both Anne of Cleves and Catherine Howard. Yet she formed another attachment, this time to Sir Charles Howard, Queen Catherine's brother, and was again disgraced to Sion. On 13 November 1541, she was moved to Kenninghall, Norfolk's country residence, to make way for Queen Catherine, who was by then in worse trouble. Yet Henry needed Douglas military support in Scotland and Angus was able to arrange for her to return to court, where she became a bridesmaid to Catherine Parr.

Notwithstanding his French upbringing, Lennox was quite prepared to adopt a Reformist stance to promote his marriage claim and to portray himself as a foil for Lady Margaret's Catholic excesses. With Arran having reverted to Catholicism, this commended Lennox as the Protestant claimant to the Scottish throne. He chose John Spottiswood, a Reformist cleric of growing reputation, to plead his cause. Spottiswood had travelled as a young man to England, where he was influenced by Cranmer. On his return to Scotland after Solway Moss, he had stayed with Glencairn, already a confirmed Reformer.

There were no doubts about Lennox's legitimacy, and Henry VIII was enthusiastic about a match for his niece, which could thwart Arran and link the Scottish and English royal families. He hoped also that Lennox's professed Reformist beliefs would temper his niece's Catholicism. Yet Lennox was always dominated by the astute Lady Margaret, who compensated for his political shortcomings. No one doubted his bravery as a soldier; he was well able to support Angus's military efforts to restore English influence in Scotland. Having confirmed his support for Henry, he remained steadfastly loyal to the English.

On 6 July 1544, Henry VIII and Queen Catherine Parr attended Lennox's marriage to Lady Margaret at St James's Palace. Henry provided the valuable Templenewsam estates in Yorkshire as a dowry. Mary Tudor gave her a selection of valuable gems including a gold brooch set with a large sapphire* and other enamelled jewels depicting stories from the Bible. Lady Margaret had never made any secret of her Catholicism and, with her husband away on military campaigns, she retired to Templenewsam. Out of sight of the English court, she became a catalyst for Catholic intrigue, causing Henry,

---

* It may well be this sapphire set in an enamel brooch which was to become known as the *Lennox Jewel*, given by Lady Margaret to Mary at the time of Darnley's arrival in Scotland.

when he learned of it, to exclude her under his will from the English succession. During Edward VI's reign, she remained in the north, but, as soon as the Catholic Mary Tudor became Queen, she returned to London.

Henry particularly blamed Bethune and the Catholic Church for the breakdown in negotiations for Mary to marry Prince Edward and hoped to rekindle the marriage by weakening Bethune's stranglehold on the Regency. This led him to infiltrate Protestant preachers into Scotland to support the Reformers, but left him uncertain of the loyalty of Angus, who remained Catholic. As a Protestant, even if out of convenience, Lennox seemed a more natural ally, despite his wife's Catholicism. Despite bribing his other Scottish supporters, Henry knew that they lacked the military muscle to gain control of Mary. He reverted to bullying tactics in retribution for Scottish broken promises and accused Bethune of inciting war against England. On 5 March 1544, he appointed Hertford as Lieutenant-General of the North; he was about to embark on his invasion of France and wanted to forestall any diversionary interference from Scotland. With Lennox's efforts having petered out in the west, Hertford was instructed to lead a lightning strike, which became known as the first of the 'Rough Wooings'. Hertford was given three weeks, during which he was to besiege Edinburgh and its castle, to destroy the port of Leith and ravish the lowland region between Edinburgh and Stirling. Having accomplished this, he was to devastate Fife, razing Bethune's Castle at St Andrews.

At the end of April, Hertford landed 15,000 men at Granton just west of Leith, where he overwhelmed Arran, Moray, Bethune and Bothwell, who had 6,000 men, and secured Leith to unload his provisions. When Sir Ralph Evers arrived from Berwick with 4,000 horse, they attacked Edinburgh, but ignored the Castle, which was well fortified. The Provost offered the keys of the town, if the residents were given free passage, but Hertford wanted unconditional surrender. After blowing in the Canongate, he looted and burned houses and churches in a fire that raged for three days. Holyrood and the adjacent Abbey Kirk were ransacked, and merchant ships were requisitioned in Leith to carry home the booty. He went on to Fife, where his troops ravaged and burned Kinghorn and the area round Kirkcaldy, but he had insufficient time to reach St Andrews. Instead he destroyed the area to within six miles of Stirling, resulting in Mary being moved north to the relative safety of Dunkeld. He returned to Leith, which he razed before departing south along the east coast route, burning market towns and flattening fortified towers as he went. He arrived in Berwick on 18 May, and, when his fleet reappeared from Leith, his crack troops were shipped to Calais to begin Henry's Continental campaign. Hertford personally went to London as

Lieutenant of the kingdom in Henry's absence. Yet such was his military reputation that he was recalled to France for the capture of Boulogne.

After fostering the English alliance, Arran was blamed for this Scottish disaster, but Bethune's confrontational policies were also criticised. The nobility started to believe that the Queen Dowager, who had gained respect with her prudent and cheerful disposition, should be involved in the Regency, and she sought control. To her disappointment, Parliament appointed her only as co-regent with Arran, leaving deadlock until Bethune again stepped forward to broker a compromise. Despite lacking control, she now sat regularly on the Privy Council, leaning them towards a French marriage for her daughter as the only means of combating the English. Yet the climate of Scottish opinion, progressively more Reformist, was not ready for this, and Bethune continued to back a marriage to Arran's son.

Henry's continuing aggression had whittled away any remaining loyalty to him from the English party. The Regency released Angus, Sir George Douglas and Maxwell from imprisonment after obtaining assurance of their support against the English. Angus was shocked at Hertford's wholesale destruction and, from now on, remained loyal to Scottish interests, while continuing to make conciliatory noises to Henry. He fought valiantly on Arran's behalf at the siege of Coldingham Priory on the Berwickshire coast, when Arran showed every sign of fleeing even before the relief force arrived. Although Glencairn had rejoined the English, he felt isolated and sought rehabilitation with the Regency. In December, Angus and his colleagues were absolved from treason and restored to their estates. The French recognised Angus's bravery at Coldingham by granting him the Order of St Michel, together with a gold collar and 4,000 crowns. Henry was furious with the Douglases and gave orders for Sir George's castles at Pinkie and Dalkeith to be destroyed. This resulted in his wife, Elizabeth, and sons, David (later 7th Earl of Angus) and James (later 4th Earl of Morton), being imprisoned for a short period. Yet when an English raiding party desecrated Melrose Abbey, the traditional burial place of the Douglases, a smaller Scots force ambushed them and took many prisoners. This greatly improved Scottish morale. Angus was also the key to Arran's victory over the English at Ancram Moor on 27 February 1545, although he was probably bribed by the Scottish government to assure his continued loyalty. Only Lennox among the Scottish nobility now supported the English and this destroyed his future standing in Scotland. In late 1544, Henry sent him to capture Dumbarton Castle, now held by French troops. With its almost impregnable fortifications, he failed to regain control, and Henry posted him to Ireland. In his absence, he was attainted by the Scottish Parliament for treason.

In May 1545, the French distributed another round of pensions in Scotland to assure Scottish loyalty. They also sent 500 more troops, but, with French resources depleted by their Italian campaign, they were paid in debased currency in the hope that the Scots would not realise. Copper and lead was added to 10,000 gold crowns to provide 150,000 debased coins, but the canny Edinburgh shopkeepers recognised the deceit, and the Queen Dowager fumed at this French lack of respect.

Having both Douglas and French support, the Regency moved onto the offensive. Angus and Sir George Douglas crossed the English border in July, but no great action resulted and Angus sent messages of goodwill to Henry, assuring him of his continued support for Mary's marriage to Prince Edward. He was no doubt seeking a restoration of his pension, as he was by then actively opposing the marriage in the Privy Council and signed the Act of Parliament revoking the Treaty of Greenwich.

Henry again tried to bludgeon the Scots into submission. By September 1545, Hertford had been able to leave Boulogne and mustered 12,000 troops at Newcastle before crossing into Scotland at Berwick. This time, he was more wary and limited himself to ransacking the locality of Jedburgh and Kelso, before returning to Newcastle after three weeks. He would not venture further north, fearful of the strength of the French reinforcements. France and England were both exhausted by war, and Hertford returned to France to broker a truce that was to include Scotland, but this was overtaken by events.

Henry continued to blame Bethune for Scotland's closer ties with France, having been advised by Sadler that it was he who was frustrating negotiations for Mary's marriage to Prince Edward. Henry linked up with the Reformist Fife lairds, still fearful that Bethune would arrange to attaint their estates. The lairds were being coordinated by Alexander Crichton of Brunston, supported principally by the Leslies, Kirkcaldys and Melvilles. On 17 April 1544, Norman Leslie, Master of Rothes,* had met Hertford at

---

* Norman, Master of Rothes, was Rothes' eldest son, born in about 1517, the child of Margaret, daughter of William, 3rd Lord Crichton, whom Rothes had married shortly before. On 27 December 1520, they obtained an annulment on the convoluted and probably doubtful grounds of their consanguinity, which had the effect of making both Norman and his brother, William, illegitimate. Despite this, Norman continued to be known as Master of Rothes, and was described by George Buchanan as 'a young man of such accomplishments that he has not his equal in all Scotland', although Buchanan was notoriously biased in his praise for fellow Reformers. After the annulment, Rothes married Elizabeth, daughter of Andrew, 2nd Lord Gray, but there were no children of this marriage. He then married Agnes, daughter of Sir John Somerville, the mother of Andrew and two other children. Margaret seems to have remained his mistress during his second and third marriages and, after the death of Agnes Somerville, he remarried her and they had three further children (including Agnes, who married Sir William Douglas of Lochleven). Yet Norman and William seem to have remained illegitimate in their father's eyes, and the Rothes title was eventually entailed to Andrew under his will.

Newcastle to propose raising a force of Scottish Reformers to support English invasion plans. He also offered to assassinate Bethune, if Henry would provide protection. Hertford sent Norman to discuss this in London, but Henry could not be seen to be implicated in Scottish domestic politics, when he was combating Continental infiltration at home. Yet he continued in secret communication through George Wishart, the most able and eloquent of the Protestant preachers infiltrated into Scotland. Henry had arranged for Cassillis, who still received an English pension, to provide protection for Wishart as he travelled around vilifying Bethune and the Catholic Church. Wishart had gained a following from those concerned at growing French influence and had been a formative influence on John Knox, a young St Andrews University graduate and Catholic priest, becoming a Reformer.

In February 1546, Cassillis encouraged Wishart to attend a provincial assembly called by Bethune at Blackfriars in Edinburgh. As he was in Dundee, Cassillis asked Knox to provide him with protection. Knox was at this time tutor to the sons of John Cockburn of Ormiston and Hugh Douglas of Longniddry, both of whom, as ardent Reformers, had been given the task of protecting Wishart. Knox duly appeared in Edinburgh with a two-handed sword. Bethune was warned that Wishart would attend the assembly and arranged for Bothwell, still a close confidant of the Queen Dowager, to arrest him at his lodging. Wishart told Knox to keep away and removed his sword, telling him, 'One is sufficient for sacrifice', but Knox was forced into hiding as his known associate.

Wishart was taken to St Andrews, where he was condemned for spreading heretical doctrine and, on 2 March 1546, was burned at the stake while senior members of the clergy, including Bethune, watched from the Episcopal Palace. Although Arran tried to stop his execution, Bethune dispensed justice as Papal Legate. Wishart died with great dignity, giving the Fife lairds the excuse they needed to assassinate Bethune. Although the older generation, including Brunston, stood back,* the conspirators included their younger kinsmen, Norman and William Leslie, their uncle, John Leslie of Parkhill, the young Sir William Kirkcaldy and the illegitimate John Melville.

On 29 May 1546, Bethune was dragged from his rooms at St Andrews, after spending a night with his mistress Marion Ogilvy. After her departure in the morning, the conspirators entered the castle dressed as workers

---

* This allowed them later to claim that they were not involved, and, although Rothes on 12 July 1547 was accused of being a part of the plan when with the army at Selkirk, he denied any involvement and was appointed the Regency's ambassador to Denmark in June 1550.

strengthening its fortifications. While Norman Leslie held the porter in conversation, Kirkcaldy lowered the drawbridge to provide access. The porter was killed after recognising John Leslie, known to be an enemy of the Cardinal and, having removed his keys, they threw his body into the fosse. They then evacuated 150 retainers without disturbing the 52-year-old Cardinal. When he woke, he tried to escape by the privy postern gate, but Kirkcaldy was waiting there. He then barricaded himself into his chamber. When John Leslie tried to force an entry, the Cardinal shouted for Norman, believing him to be more sympathetic than 'bloody-minded John'. The conspirators called for fire to burn down the door, but the Cardinal opened it and claimed protection as a priest. When John Leslie stabbed him, he earned a reproof from John Melville, who promptly followed suit to avenge Wishart's murder. The Cardinal's body was hung, drawn and quartered, before being strung up at the foot of the castle walls, where 'ane called Guthrie pisched in his mouth'.[1] The body remained in the Sea Tower, a notorious dungeon, salted, but unburied, for the next nine months, before being taken quietly to the convent of Blackfriars at St Andrews for interment. The conspirators took control of the castle and held Arran's seventeen-year-old son James, who was under Bethune's care for his education, as a hostage. Although Arran led French troops to besiege them, he did not call in their reinforcements, as they might have demanded Mary's marriage to the Dauphin in return for their help in trying to free his son.

Henry was euphoric at the Cardinal's death, but Bethune had been a conciliatory voice, and Scotland was pushed into the hands of France. The pro-French Huntly was appointed Chancellor and the nobility united behind Arran to regain control of St Andrews. Henry sent provisions by sea to support the 'Castilians', as they became known, enabling them to hold out with increasing English support for fourteen months. Yet Henry died in January 1547, followed by Francis I two months later.

The new French king, Henry II, was determined to end the siege. He sent a brilliant Italian naval officer, Leone Strozzi, a cousin of his wife, Catherine de Medici, with fifteen galleys to attack the Castilians. On 16 July, Strozzi sailed into St Andrews and eight days later began a massive bombardment. With guns placed on the ancient abbey roof to the east, and on the tower of the university chapel to the west, the siege was over in six hours. Arran's son was released. He had become a Reformer, which caused the Council, dominated by the Queen Dowager, to debar him from the succession to thwart any Reformist attempt to promote him ahead of Mary.

The Castilians were permitted to surrender with provision of their lives, but served eighteen months on French galleys. One of them was the young

Knox, who had entered the Castle during a period of armistice* over Easter 1547. He was persuaded to preach to the Castilians, developing the zeal for which he would become renowned. Having served his time, Knox was brought to England in February 1549† by Hertford, who had become Duke of Somerset and Protector for his nine-year-old nephew, now Edward VI. Here he met the young Cambridge graduate, William Cecil, Somerset's Secretary and Master of Requests, but, on Mary Tudor's accession, Knox escaped back to the Continent, eventually going to Geneva to train under Calvin.

Although Norman Leslie also served on the galleys, he escaped from France and returned secretly to Scotland, but, finding that the Queen Dowager was still looking for him, left for Denmark. From here he went to England, where Somerset gave him a pension. On Mary Tudor's accession, he returned to France as a mercenary, but, in 1554, was mortally wounded at Renti near Cambrai making a heroic charge, with his thirty horse against double that number. After being brought to Henry II's tent, the King acknowledged his exceptional gallantry by demanding that the Queen Dowager should restore the forfeited estates of Bethune's murderers.

Another Castilian was the young James Balfour, who served on the same French galley as Knox. Despite flirting with Protestantism during the siege, Balfour reverted to Catholicism. Knox, who always reserved his most cutting jibes for those deserting the Reformers, later referred to him as 'blasphemous Balfour and principal misguider of Scotland', seeing him, probably justifiably, as 'the most corrupt man of his age'. Balfour's family had a tradition as lawyers and, although trained for the clergy, he later studied canon law. After being released, he was appointed an official in the Archdeaconry Court in Lothian and sought advancement by supporting the

---

* There were several breaks in hostilities, and Pitscottie records that when matters were relatively quiet, the Castilians would ride out 'using their body in lechery with fair women'.

† Knox was initially sent as a preacher for two years to Berwick, where he did much to stop the feuding between the English in the town and Anglophile Scots, who had crossed the border to escape French influence. He also supported Thomas Cranmer in his attack on the mass, which he saw as idolatry, although he later annoyed Cranmer, by seeking a change to the draft 1552 Book of Common Prayer so that communicants were not required to kneel. It was at this time that he first met Elizabeth née Aske, wife of Richard Bowes. (They were the parents of both Sir George Bowes, who, as Lieutenant of the North, was instrumental in putting down the Northern Rising, and Sir Robert Bowes, later English ambassador to Scotland.) Elizabeth was Knox's contemporary and, having suffered a spiritual crisis after becoming a Reformer, became his ardent disciple. Knox was to marry her daughter Marjory in 1553 without obtaining Richard Bowes' consent. After moving to Newcastle, he was offered patronage by John Dudley, Duke of Northumberland, who had replaced Somerset as Protector for Edward VI. Cecil used his growing influence to have Knox appointed as one of the King's chaplains, but when Northumberland offered to appoint him as Bishop of Rochester, he caused offence by turning down the post, and later turned down the Privy Council's offer of the wealthy benefice of All Hallows, Bread Street.

Queen Dowager. He became chief judge of the Consistory Court of the Archbishop of St Andrews until it was disbanded in 1560. He then made his name clearing the backlog of cases within its jurisdiction. He was made a Privy Councillor and Extraordinary Lord of Session on 14 November 1561 and later transferred to the Commissary Court in Edinburgh as chief of four Commissaries handling the Church's uncompleted business. For this commendable work he was knighted in 1566.

Despite disliking Bethune, Angus was a Catholic and took no part in his murder. Yet on Bethune's death, he arranged to have his illegitimate son, George Douglas, appointed to the lucrative post of Postulate of the Abbey of Arbroath. George was to become better known as a principal in Riccio's murder.

In his efforts to reinstate the English marriage plan, Somerset conceded Scottish autonomy and offered a free trade agreement. Yet the French party was in the ascendancy and they had the promise of Henry II's support. Somerset decided on a two-pronged attack in a final round of Rough Wooings hoping to play on growing conflict between Catholics and Reformers. While Lennox led a force in the west, Somerset commanded the main English army of 15,000 men, which advanced along the Scottish east coast shadowed by the English fleet.

Arran moved hurriedly to defend the Scottish Crown, sending Mary north to the Erskine Priory at Inchmahone,* on the Lake of Menteith. On 10 September 1547, he moved out from Edinburgh with 12,000 hastily gathered troops and a further large contingent of poorly armed clergy dressed in black. Although they took up a well-entrenched position bristling with spears at Pinkie Cleugh near Musselburgh, they lacked discipline and Arran was unsure if his lieutenants were in receipt of English pay. Despite their strong defensive position, 4,000 Irish mercenaries on the left charged the English right, but were scattered by fire from the English fleet. Angus led the van on the Scottish right where his pikemen drove back the English horse, but when he attempted a flanking movement, his men were broken by a hail of English arrows and by fire from Italian musketeers. Sadler, as Secretary of the English Army, showed great resource in rallying his cavalry and their greater discipline won the day. The Scots panicked and failed to support Angus. Arran having lost control, his men retired from their strategic position to be

---

* It was at Inchmahone that Mary was joined for the first time by the four Maries, Mary Fleming, Mary Livingston, Mary Seton and Mary Bethune, with whom she was later to travel to France. Despite her mother being French, Mary was brought up in Scotland speaking Scots. It was only after they travelled to France that she and her companions started to converse in French.

picked off by English cavalry and guns. He fled the field 'scant with honour', leaving 10,000 Scots dead and 1,500 more as prisoners; the English had lost 200 men. This was a disaster on the scale of Flodden.

Although Edinburgh was open to him, Somerset failed to follow up on his victory despite burning Leith and, on 29 September, left Scotland. He had planned to build up a network of English forts, but Pinkie Cleugh caused a huge anti-English backlash. Mary was brought back to Stirling. Angus, who had retired to Calder, joined those infuriated with all things English. Although Lady Margaret was his only surviving legitimate child, he cut her out of her inheritance by limiting the entail of his earldom to heirs male. This promoted his brother, Sir George Douglas, and his sons despite her vigorous protests.

Fleming was one of the many killed at Pinkie Cleugh, and the Lady Fleming sought to have her son James, now 4th Lord Fleming, released from the Tower, where he was still being held hostage. He was now aged fourteen and had been in England for six years. He deserved better treatment than this. Sir John Melville was sent to London on the delicate mission to seek his freedom, even though Scotland was now irretrievably linked to the French. With his strong English sympathies, Sir John was considered the best man for the job. He had no problem negotiating Fleming's release, but was caught providing them with a complete disposition of Scottish and French troops. This resulted in his execution on his return. The main part of his attainted estates was granted to Arran's third son, David,* but was restored in 1563.

Arran took the blame for the disaster at Pinkie Cleugh and was now Regent in name only, while the Queen Dowager progressively gained control. She had no means of resisting the English, who, in April 1548, garrisoned Haddington with 2,500 men. She needed French support. Henry II offered to liberate Scotland, if Mary became betrothed to his son, the infant Dauphin. Arran was bought off with the French dukedom of Châtelherault in Poitou, which provided an annual income of 12,000 livres, a French marriage for his son, James now Earl of Arran,† to the eldest daughter of Louis de Bourbon, Duke of Montpensier, from whom the title had been usurped, and a further annual pension of 12,000 livres.

When the Scottish Parliament met in January 1548, it approved the Treaty of Haddington with France for Mary's marriage to the Dauphin, on terms

---

* No more is heard of David Hamilton, although he lived on until 1611 without marrying. It is reasonable to assume that, like two of his brothers, he suffered from insanity. See p. 81 footnote.

† Although Châtelherault's eldest son (now Arran) went to France, he was in effect a hostage, and the marriage never took place. The title and estates were eventually recovered by the Bourbons, but the Dukes of Abercorn continue to claim it to this day.

negotiated by the Secretary of State, Patrick Hepburn, Bishop of Moray. It needed only a minimum of discussion, and even Angus confirmed his support. Scotland was to retain its autonomy and was promised new French garrisons at Dunbar and Blackness. Mary was moved out of English reach to Dumbarton, which was still garrisoned by the French, in readiness to leave for France. Despite becoming dangerously ill with measles, she soon recovered. The Queen Dowager's brothers arranged an expeditionary force of 130 ships carrying 5,500 infantry and 1,000 cavalry, all well-trained veterans of the Italian campaign with their professional officers. The main force disembarked at Leith on 17 June 1548, and their commander, Andre de Montalembert, Sieur d'Essé, confirmed France's determination to protect Scotland.

The new French arrivals soon recognised Scottish shortcomings. D'Essé's colleague Jean de Beaugué recorded that they did not lack courage or the will to fight, but were plagued with factions. Despite an uneasy relationship with the Queen Dowager, Angus remained in command of the combined Scottish and French forces. In 1548, the English under Wharton were forced back to Carlisle after being defeated in the Western Marches. On 13 December, Luttrell, the English Captain, was pushed back at Broughly Castle. In early July 1549, the French besieged Haddington and placed Somerset's garrison of foreign mercenaries in fear of their lives. On 7 July, the Queen Dowager held a tented parliament outside the town, and it fell two months later. Although Somerset tried to counterattack, his unpaid Germans refused to move. By 1551, the English were ousted from Scotland and Mary's throne had been protected. Yet the agreement for her marriage to the Dauphin required that she should travel to France for her safety and education. Her mother was to be left behind to protect her Scottish throne.

References

1. Pitscottie, *Chronicles II*, p. 84

Part 2 The Young Queen

5

Mary's Arrival in France

Henry II sent his personal galley from France to collect Mary, accompanied by his ambassador, Artus de Maillé, Sieur de Brézé,* and a party of senior diplomats. The captain, Nicholas de Villegagnon, sailed up the North Sea and, to confuse the English patrols, travelled round northern Scotland and back through the Hebrides to Dumbarton on the Clyde. On 29 July 1548, aged five years and eight months, Mary stepped on board, carrying herself with regal deportment. She was

> 'one of the most perfect creatures that ever was seen, such a one as from this very young age with its wondrous and estimable beginnings has raised such expectations that it isn't possible to hope for more from a princess on this earth.'[1]

Mary travelled with an entourage of about thirty, including ladies' maids and menservants. This was headed as governess by her aunt Janet, the Dowager Lady Fleming, an illegitimate daughter of James IV. She was now aged thirty-seven, but still attractive with fair hair and perfect white skin. She brought her son, the young Fleming, newly released from imprisonment by the English, and her younger daughters, Agnes and Mary. Mary Fleming, who was a few months older than the young Queen, had been appointed as one of her four 'Maries',† all coincidentally called Mary, to accompany her to France. Although older, Agnes also became a maid-of-honour in France. Mary's Scottish nurse was Janet Sinclair, who went with her everywhere, travelling with her husband and a son and daughter of her own. The head of

---

* De Brézé was a member of the Guise faction.
† The nickname for Mary's four friends was apparently coined by Mary herself as a slightly irreverent play on a somewhat tedious French devotional book which they read, *Les Trois Maries*. This referred to Mary the Virgin, Mary Magdalene and Mary the wife of Clopas, who stood by the cross during Jesus's crucifixion. Yet *marie* was also a word for a maid-of-honour, and *maries* had accompanied the ill-fated Queen Madeleine on her journey from France. The word derives from the Icelandic *maer*, or virgin.

the household was Robert Bethune of Creich,* whose father, Sir John, was Keeper of the Palace of Falkland. Robert had married one of the Queen Dowager's French ladies-in-waiting,† Joanne de la Reyneville (or Gryssonier), and she now returned to France in the same capacity. They brought their young children, David, Mary and Lucretia, with them and another son, James, was born while they were in France. Their daughter Mary had been appointed as another of the Maries, while her sister Lucretia became a maid-of-honour on Mary's return to Scotland. The remaining two Maries were Livingston's daughter, who was accompanied to France by her father, and Seton's daughter, who came with her young brother James. These were the children of Mary Pyerres, also a former French lady-in-waiting to the Queen Dowager. After her husband's death in 1549, she joined them in France, perhaps to keep a watchful eye on her daughter, but also on the lookout for a new husband. Another Scottish maid-of-honour was Châtelherault's daughter Barbara Hamilton. She probably returned to Scotland with the Lady Fleming in 1550 and married the young Fleming in Scotland in 1553. Erskine and Livingston came as escorts to the royal party, which also included three of Mary's illegitimate half-brothers, Lord James, Lord John and Lord Robert Stewart. Lord James and Lord John were both seventeen, with Lord Robert a couple of years younger. They were being sent to complete their education, but Lord James and the young Fleming were back in Scotland by November 1549.

For the second time in her life, the Queen Dowager was separated from her child. To alleviate her anxiety, de Brézé wrote her a series of letters on the progress of the journey. She was understandably distraught when the royal party was forced to ride out a storm anchored at Lamlash on the Isle of

---

* The Bethunes of Creich were not ennobled, but Robert's grandfather Sir David Bethune had been Lord High Treasurer of Scotland, and his father Sir John was a first cousin of the Cardinal, and brother of Châtelherault's mother, Janet. Sir John's sister, Elizabeth, had been a mistress of James V and was the mother of Jean, Countess of Argyll. Sir John had married in unusual circumstances. Before becoming the keeper of Falkland Palace, he managed the family estates in Fife and this required him to visit Dundee. He became friends with the Constable of Dundee, and frequented an alehouse belonging to the laird of Naughton, brother of the Provost, John Hay. The Provost's comely daughter Jean spent time in the alehouse and Sir John and the Constable were both smitten with her. Eventually Sir John won her favour and, with the Constable's help, carried her off to St Andrews, taking with them a chest with 5,000 marks of gold belonging to the laird of Naughton. They set themselves up in the best inn, while Sir John went to explain the story to his uncle James, the Archbishop of St Andrews. The Archbishop visited them, taking one look at Jean and the chest of gold and called for a priest to marry them immediately. It is reported that the Bethunes had been dark-haired, but after marriage to Jean their progeny was thereafter fair and beautiful. There is no doubt that Mary Bethune had her grandmother's good looks.

† Ladies-in-waiting were all members of the aristocracy and were treated with great respect. It was entirely normal for their children to act as maids-of-honour, generally entering royal service in their teens and receiving a courtly education in return. Chamber women came from a lower order in the social hierarchy.

Arran, only fifty miles from Dumbarton, in the normally benign Clyde. Lady Fleming demanded to be put ashore 'to repose her',[2] but Villegagnon would have none of it, and she was told to go to France and like it, or to drown on the way! The weather must have been particularly bad, as a rudder was smashed, but, on 7 August, the flotilla finally set out for the open sea. They followed the west coast route through the Irish Sea passing to the west of the Isle of Man and round Cornwall, where de Brézé recorded that the 'weather was wondrous wild with the biggest waves I ever saw',[3] but by this means they avoided the English garrisons on the east coast and its shipping in the North Sea. On 15 August, after eighteen days at sea, twice as long as expected, they landed at St-Pol-de-Léon in north Brittany near the present-day Roscoff. According to de Brézé, Mary was 'less ill upon the sea than any one of her company so that she made fun of those that were'.[4]

On their arrival, Henry II was at war in Italy, but Mary's party was greeted at St-Pol-de-Léon by the town's *maître d'hôtel* and, surprisingly, by Francis I's erstwhile mistress, Anne de Pisseleu d'Heilly, Duchess of Étampes, who appeared out of curiosity. After resting from their journey, the party set out for Orléans to meet Mary's grandparents, the Duke of Guise and his wife Antoinette de Bourbon. They travelled with their luggage overland to Nantes, where they boarded a barge to travel up the Loire. On the way, the men, who were less careful about drinking the local water, all suffered from gastroenteritis. Erskine and Livingston were suspicious that they had been poisoned, and, tragically, 'le jeune Ceton',[5] Mary Seton's brother James, died of a 'flux of the stomach' (diarrhoea) at Ancenis on the Loire. Mary attended her first funeral Mass in his honour. When de Brézé was called away to deal with an uprising in the south, Antoinette de Bourbon travelled to meet them from Orléans. She greeted her granddaughter enthusiastically, reporting to her son, the Cardinal, that she was 'very pretty indeed and as intelligent as can be. She is a clear skinned brunette and, I think … will be a beautiful girl.'[6] She found the rest of the Scottish party, the Lady Fleming apart, less attractive and a bit scruffy. On reaching Orléans, Erskine and Livingston handed over their charges with some relief to return to Scotland.

At this time, Henry II used the château at St-Germain-en-Laye over-looking the Seine near Paris as his preferred residence, and the royal children were housed nearby in the medieval fortress at Carrières-sur-Seine. Despite her almost total inability to speak French, Mary and her retinue joined them there and were greeted, on 16 October, by the chamberlain Jean de Humières with his wife Françoise, who had charge of the royal nursery. Although Henry was still in Italy, Mary was immediately given the status of a French princess. Once she had settled, Antoinette returned to Joinville, but, as a lady-in-waiting to Catherine de Medici, regularly visited court and Mary signed letters to her as 'Your most humble and obedient daughter, Marie'.[7] It was through Antoinette's personal devotion that the beginnings of Mary's own undoubted faith can be traced.

The marriage between Henry II and Catherine de Medici had been arranged by his father, Francis I, and her great-uncle, Giovanni de Medici, Pope Leo X, to cement their alliance against Habsburg imperialism in Italy. Both husband and wife had been scarred by their upbringing, each having spent a part of their childhood as political prisoners, Henry in Spain and Catherine in Florence. Henry did not find Catherine attractive and she failed initially to become pregnant. He took Diane de Poitiers, nineteen years older than himself, and hitherto a chaste and highly intelligent widow at court, as his mistress, while Catherine managed to hide, but never to forget, the hurt that she felt, while treating Diane with unfailing courtesy. In need of allies, she cultivated a friendship with Francis I, showing her panache when out hunting with him and taking a detailed interest in his building projects at Chambord and Blois. Later, as Regent, she completed much of the work left unfinished at his death. She also became close to his mistress the Duchess of Étampes, Diane's political rival. Henry's wandering eye was not limited to Diane, and he demonstrated his potency by fathering a child by Filippa Duci, the hitherto virgin sister of one of his Piedmontese squires. Their daughter was named Diane,*after her godmother, Diane de Poitiers, who arranged her upbringing, while Filippa retired to a convent.

Catherine's failure to conceive brought her an unexpected ally in Diane de Poitiers. So long as she remained Henry's wife, Diane's own position was secure. If Henry should choose an attractive younger bride, she could be usurped. Diane ensured that Henry fulfilled his duty to achieve Catherine's pregnancy rather than repudiate her. This was a ménage à trois that bene-fited both wife and mistress, but the lack of an heir was a critical concern for the French government. Constable Montmorency was one of those who pressed for Catherine's repudiation to enable Henry to choose a more fertile bride. This gained for him Catherine's lifelong enmity. After prayers and offerings to the Almighty had seemed to fail, she resorted, in desperation, to every possible potion in the hope of becoming pregnant. She drank drafts of mule's urine as an inoculation against sterility. Poultices were applied to her

---

* Diane was later declared legitimate and granted the rank of Princess as Diane de France. She was graceful and sweet-natured, marrying Horace Farnese, Duke of Castro, as a child bride in about 1552, but he was killed at the siege of Hesdin a year later. In 1557 Henry arranged for her to remarry the Constable's eldest son, François, later 2nd Duke of Montmorency.

genitals during love-making. These included ground stag's antlers and cow dung, the smell of which was relieved by crushed periwinkle blended with mare's milk. These can hardly have been an aphrodisiac for the reluctant Dauphin. She admitted to Francis, in floods of tears, that she should be repudiated, but the King hated to see a lady crying and agreed to allow more time against the better interest of his dynasty, while Diane continued sending an unenthusiastic Henry to his wife on a regular basis. At last Catherine speculated that her technique was at fault. She arranged secretly for holes to be drilled in the ceiling of Diane's bedroom to watch her husband's love-making from above. Against her ladies' advice, she witnessed his unbridled passion through eyes full of tears, but was unable to see what was going on. Distraught, she called yet another doctor, Jean Fernel, for advice. He examined both Henry and her, and claimed apparently that both their organs showed slight physical abnormalities. No one knows what he said, but he proposed a technique to solve the problem said to involve a prescription of pills of myrrh. Whether by good luck or the doctor's sensible advice, Catherine almost immediately became pregnant after ten years of marriage.

Catherine's first child, Francis, suffered from respiratory difficulties, which stunted his growth. A succession of sisters and brothers followed, suffering a variety of childhood ailments. Yet their arrival brought security to the Valois dynasty. The children were placed in the Constable's care, leaving Catherine to be advised on their welfare by Diane, who maintained an interest in all aspects of royal affairs.

There has been much speculation on why Catherine failed to conceive, and why she subsequently produced, with the exception of the childless but abundantly healthy Marguerite (Margot), who later married and then divorced Henry of Navarre, a string of sickly children. Without medical evidence, it is only possible to speculate. It is probable that her menstruation started late, but as she did not conceive until she was twenty-four this is unlikely to have been her only problem. It has been suggested that the quack treatments used to make her pregnant led to defects in her children. From what is known of them, abhorrent though they may have been, there is nothing to suggest that they would have caused lasting damage. It has also been suggested that Henry suffered from syphilis, but this would have been unlikely at fourteen and would not have suited the fastidious Diane. Yet he could have been afflicted with it in later life. It is more likely that Catherine's lothario of a father, Lorenzo II de Medici, passed on congenital syphilis to his daughter, delaying her puberty and causing his early death. This could explain the abnormalities in her offspring. As will be seen, syphilis would become a much more certain factor in Mary's later difficulties.

Henry II at last returned from Italy on 9 November 1549 and, when he met Mary, he delightedly referred to her as his daughter, 'the most perfect child I have ever seen'. Catherine de Medici was similarly impressed, confirming that 'the little Scottish queen has but to smile to turn all French heads'.[8] She wrote to the Queen Dowager in Scotland saying that she was 'marvellously happy to have such a daughter who would, she hoped, be the support of her old age'.[9]

As the intended wife of the Dauphin and a queen in her own right, Mary took precedence over the other royal children. They frequently moved between palaces with their households, a necessity in large properties to allow the drains to be 'sweetened'. Yet for most of Mary's time in France, they stayed at the royal châteaux of Blois, Chambord and Fontainebleau. Henry had given Diane de Poitiers responsibility for their upbringing and she acted as the intermediary between the King and the children's household. She had passed on Henry's request that Mary should share a bedroom with Princess Elisabeth, who was nearly three years her junior. Mary always saw the gentle Elisabeth as her closest childhood friend and was distraught, in 1568, at her early death in childbirth, after becoming Philip II's wife. Nurses were trained at Diane's château at Anet,* some fifty miles north-west of Paris, rebuilt for her by Philibert de l'Orme as a monument to Diana the huntress. The royal children visited and dearly cherished Anet, an elegant property presided over by an unparalleled hostess with an acute political mind. Diane took Mary under her wing, recognising her political importance and her consequent need to ally with the Guises. She wrote to the Queen Dowager that she would look after Mary as if she were her own daughter, and, in 1555, Mary told her mother how well 'Madame de Valentinois'† cared for her. Mary also made regular visits to the Guise family, staying at Joinville with its gardens and parks that she came to love, and the palace of Meudon close to Paris, which was still being built on Mary's arrival. There was also the Hôtel de Guise in Paris on a huge site previously occupied by four substantial properties. Everything was on a hugely grander scale than Linlithgow, Stirling, Holyrood and Falkland. Although the four Maries travelled with her, they were educated separately, particularly to ensure that

---

* A Florentine visitor in the 1550s claimed 'that the golden house of Nero was not so costly or so beautiful'. Brantôme reported that it was 'for the king a terrestrial paradise – mysterious wooded nooks for the secret love, a vast carpet of verdure for the hunt or for riding and a barrier of hills against indiscretions and importunates – a veritable fairy castle.'[10]

† Diane was created Duchess of Valentinois by Henry II on 8 October 1548. In 1557, Mary even went so far as to suggest to her mother that Diane's granddaughter, Antoinette de la Marck, to whom she was devoted, should marry the young Arran. Diane had other ideas and Antoinette married the Constable's second son, Henry, Count of Damville in 1559.

Mary concentrated on learning French. They were sent to a Dominican convent for their schooling at Poissy. Without their constant attendance, Mary's French was soon fluent, becoming her first language both for conversation and correspondence. Yet she could still speak Scots.

In December 1548 shortly after Mary's arrival, her uncle Francis married Anne d'Este, daughter of the Duke of Ferrara and a granddaughter of Louis XII. They made a tall and handsome couple and, although the marriage had been arranged by Francis's brother the Cardinal, it became a true love match. Mary made her first public appearance in France to attend the wedding, wearing a heavily brocaded dress embroidered with jewellery. She was led onto the stage by Diane de Poitiers and the Lady Fleming to dance with the diminutive four-year-old Dauphin, to whom she was betrothed, and stooped down at the end to kiss him on the lips as royal formality required. Montmorency wrote to the Queen Dowager in March 1549

> I will assure you that the Dauphin pays her little attentions, and is enamoured of her, from which it is easy to judge that God gave them birth the one for the other.[11]

Mary learned to cosset the Dauphin despite his limited abilities, cherishing him like a younger brother, and she encouraged him in riding and other outdoor pursuits.

The Prior of Inchmahone had travelled with Mary from Scotland and stayed on unpaid as an act of devotion. The Queen Dowager received regular reports on the progress of her daughter's education. She insisted on her daily attendance at Mass with a French chaplain available at all times. Antoinette de Bourbon told her that Mary was extremely devout. At Easter 1550, when Mary was seven, her grandmother deemed it right for her to take her first communion and Mary wrote to her mother from Meudon to confirm her eagerness for this. Thereafter, she retained her own communion vessels to protect against infection.

Henry was soon concerned at the cost of maintaining Mary and her entourage. Living with the other royal children, she might have been expected to share their nursery staff, but the Guises insisted on a reigning queen having her own retinue. She had sixteen female attendants and fifteen indoor male servants, who included two masters of the household, valets, kitchen servants, a chaplain, tailor, dancing master and schoolmaster. The ways of Mary's Scottish retainers began to cause friction and seemed unsophisticated beside the more courtly French. Many of the male staff were sent home, but both the Lady Fleming and Janet Sinclair were retained after the intervention of Mary's mother, who was determined to retain a Scottish connection for her daughter. They now came under the direction of the Chamberlain, Jean de Humières. Neither lady was easy to please. The Lady Fleming made no effort to encourage the Scottish attendants to learn French or adopt French practices. She recommended a Scottish doctor for Mary, William Bog, who was adept at 'diagnosing Scottish temperaments'.[12] Without him, she would not be able to explain Mary's ailments, as she could not communicate with a French doctor. Janet Sinclair must have been a typical example of her profession. Her appeal to eat separately from Frenchwomen was to fail. She was made to live alongside the 'foreign' nursery staff, who patronised her Scottish manners. The Queen Dowager blamed her Scots blood, reporting, 'You know that nation, I need say no more!'[13]

The Lady Fleming had no difficulty in communicating her considerable charms. After their journey to France, De Brézé reported that she had

> pleased all this company as much as the six most virtuous women in this kingdom could have done. For my part I would not for all the world have had her absent, having regard not only to the service of the Queen but to the reputation of the Kingdom of Scotland.[14]

Her success continued on arrival at the French court. Knox believed that Mary had been 'sold to the devil', and he may have had a point. The court was certainly no haven of morality and Henry lived openly with Diane. The ladies solicited the men as much as the men solicited them. Mary must have become only too aware of the lascivious goings on. In 1550, the Guise brothers, who kept a proprietary eye on the royal nursery, heard that Montmorency had been paying the Lady Fleming undue attention. As he was Diane de Poitiers' principal rival for the King's ear, they quickly warned her. She provided a key to the Lady Fleming's apartment to enable Montmorency to be caught *in flagrante delicto*. To their horror, they found that he was acting as a blind for the sensual Lady Fleming to be courted by the King. The affair developed and Henry even wrote somewhat disingenuously to the Queen Dowager in Scotland, saying:

> I believe that you appreciate the care trouble and great attention that my kinswoman [she was Mary's aunt and he considered Mary to be his daughter] the Lady Fleming shows from day to day about the person of our little daughter the Queen of Scots, I must continually remember her children and her family.[15]

Diane thought that Montmorency had promoted the affair in an effort to topple her from her pre-eminent position next to the King. He certainly publicised rumours of the King having had a rift with her. Despite a broken leg after a fall from her horse, she returned to St-Germain from Anet to position herself outside the Lady Fleming's door. When the King appeared with Montmorency, she upbraided him for bringing the Queen of Scots into disrepute by sleeping with her governess, particularly as Fleming was known to have Huguenot sympathies. Henry made Diane promise not to advise the Guises (who had told her of the affair in the first place), while Catherine de Medici enjoyed Diane's discomfiture and played the outraged wife. Henry ignored them both, and the Lady Fleming unwisely, but certainly not ashamedly, became pregnant. Although Henry would have preferred her to show discretion about this, she flaunted her success and, in excruciating French with a strong Scottish accent, loudly pronounced, 'I have done all that I can, and God be thanked, I am pregnant by the King, for which I count myself both honoured and happy.'[16] Catherine saw to it that 'Madam de Flamin'[17] was shipped back to Scotland, travelling with her daughter Agnes, who was to marry Mary Livingston's brother, William, 6th Lord Livingston in 1553, while her daughter Mary remained behind in France as one of the Maries. Back in Scotland, the Lady Fleming gave birth to a son* named Henry, after his father, and Diane resumed her politically important position as royal mistress, but she was now aged fifty-one, and was beginning to find the 32-year-old King's sexually athletic overtures somewhat irksome. This allowed Catherine to develop her political authority by spending increasing time in the royal bed.

Only once was Mary's mother able to visit her in France. She was invited by Henry to be godmother to his newly born son, Charles (later Charles IX), and Henry sent six galleys to Leith to collect her. Mary was ecstatic at her mother's forthcoming visit and wrote to tell her grandmother the good news and of her hopes of impressing her. Unfortunately the Queen Dowager's departure was delayed by a quarrel among the Scottish nobility, so that she could not travel in the royal galleys and missed the baptism. Henry II arranged a passport for her to travel through England, and she crossed from Dover to Dieppe on 19 September 1550. Unlike her daughter, she was prone to seasickness. Her father Claude, Duke of Guise, had recently died at

---

* The Lady Fleming was determined that she should return with her son to France, but this was forbidden by the Queen Dowager. It was only after her death in 1560 that Elizabeth permitted her to travel through England with Lord 'Harry de Valois' and an escort of twenty-four horsemen. Both Francis and Mary were fond of her and appear to have received her graciously. Henry, Chevalier d'Angoulême, was thereafter brought up with the other royal children and his leaping agility on the dance floors at court was testimony to his Scottish ancestry. He became Abbé de la Chaise-Dieu and later Grand Prior General of the Galleys. Although he was noted for writing lyrical verse, he was a man of great cruelty, being associated with the St Bartholemew's Day Massacre. He was finally killed in a duel in 1586. The Lady Fleming died before 1564, probably in France.

the age of fifty-four, and she was greeted on arrival by a large family contingent led by her brothers. She travelled overland to Rouen to meet Henry II, who had come with Mary and the Duke of Longueville, now almost fifteen. Being in mourning for her father, she consulted Diane de Poitiers, the arbiter of fashion at the French court, to establish correct protocol. Henry used the Queen Dowager's visit as an excuse to celebrate the expulsion of the English from both Scotland and Boulogne,* while she sought more French support in her efforts to become the Scottish Regent. She had invited most of the pro-English party† to join her in France, both to impress them and to discourage any hostilities in her absence. Henry offered them generous pensions and, in October, arranged a spectacular celebration at Rouen with a royal procession through triumphal arches, and pageants, depicting Classical heroes and Valois victories. Dressed as Hannibal, he processed with a following of papier-mâché elephants on wheels. There were tableaux of the French royal family, highlighting the dynastic links of the Dauphin and Mary to the Crowns of France, Scotland and England. Mary and her mother were given pride of place in a blue-and-gold viewing pavilion.

Yet the situation in Scotland was not as rosy as Henry wanted everyone to believe, and the Queen Dowager needed more military support. No longer was it threatened by English invasion, particularly as Somerset was losing his grip on power, but the Reformers were gaining in authority to oppose French objectives. Her appeal for more troops was not what Henry hoped to hear. He had already raised 400,000 livres in taxation to pay his Scottish military costs and was anxious to cut expenditure. According to Sir John Mason, the English envoy, 'The King would fain be rid of her, and she as she pretendeth would fain be gone.'[18] She clearly overplayed her demands for money to repay her debts and to provide pensions for her entourage.

The Queen Dowager found herself having to deal with the embarrassment caused by the Lady Fleming's misalliance with the King and was instrumental in arranging her return to Scotland. A more serious problem arose when Robert Stewart, a Castilian from St Andrews, became bent on revenge against the French. Having changed his name, he joined the Scottish

---

* The English had captured Boulogne in 1544, and, although the French had laid siege to it, it was ceded back under their control only when peace was signed on 24 March 1550 after a payment of 400,000 écus. Montmorency had been responsible for the negotiations and was raised to a dukedom by a grateful French King.

† They included Alexander Cunningham, who had become 5th Earl of Glencairn on his father's death in 1548, Fleming (aged sixteen and no doubt anxious to see his mother and sisters), Cassillis, John, 11th Earl of Sutherland and the Master of Ruthven. This was an unashamed attempt to woo them towards the French alliance, although Ruthven complained at the paucity of his pay-off. They spent about a year in France, undertaking a royal progress round the country.

Gens d'Armes and gained access to the royal apartments at Amboise. He then bribed a cook to poison Mary's favourite dessert of frittered pears. Luckily someone talked and, although Stewart escaped to Ireland, he was ultimately caught by the English and brought back to France, where he confessed under torture and was executed. Although it was suggested that he was in English pay, this has never been established and appears unlikely as they still had hopes of Mary marrying Edward VI. A more poignant tragedy was the death of the sixteen-year-old Duke of Longueville, the Queen Dowager's surviving son from her first marriage. He contracted a mystery illness at Amiens, while escorting her to the coast and died in her arms. She had now lost all four of her sons and was heartbroken. She delayed her return to Scotland by six months, and even considered remaining in France to be near her daughter and family. Yet she was committed to governing Scotland on Mary's behalf and, after kissing her daughter goodbye, set off north soon after 18 October 1551. Mary never saw her again, but maintained a loving and intimate correspondence with her mother. The Queen Dowager stopped in London on her return, impressing the English court with the new French fashions for her ladies. She was greeted by Lady Margaret Lennox, who travelled from Templenewsam in Yorkshire to see her and to escort her to see Edward VI. Lady Margaret is thought to have used the opportunity to complain at being cut out of her father's will.

Mary was aged nine at her mother's departure, already fluent in French and well-versed in court etiquette. A drawing of her in crayon made at this time by François Clouet confirms her beauty and self-assurance. She had well-set golden-brown eyes, contrasting with her fair, almost ash-blonde, hair, and she retained a pale unblemished complexion. Her nose, which was later to lengthen and become more pronounced, was at this time well-proportioned. The drawing was a sketch for a painting in oils commissioned by Catherine in December 1552. When Henry II saw the finished work, he insisted on keeping it, although only the sketch survives. Mary was not only the linchpin to ensure continuing Guise prominence, but the key to Valois dynastic ambitions.

At this early period, less is known of the upbringing of the four Maries, although Claude de Pons, Demoiselle du Mesnil became governess for all the maids-of-honour. It can be conjectured that they lived a sheltered existence with simple pleasures at Poissy when away from the royal children, and they were to continue in a happily innocent environment on returning to Scotland. There was no whiff of scandal about any of them while in France. Although Mary married at fifteen, none of them contemplated a similar step. They were all older than their mistress, who was eighteen and a half when they left France (Mary Bethune was at least twenty, Mary Livingston and Mary Seton were more than nineteen, and Mary Fleming only a few months younger), and consideration of marriage might have seemed of paramount importance for attractive young ladies at court, surrounded by the most eligible blades in France in their finery. They had taken a vow of celibacy not to marry before their mistress and, despite very different personalities, remained single-mindedly unattached. Despite being the youngest, Mary Fleming, with her mother's royal blood, was deemed to be the senior of them. Having her mother's nubile good looks, Leslie considered her 'the flower of the flock'.[19] Mary Bethune may have lacked Fleming's fascination and flamboyance, but she probably stole the show for classic beauty. This was acknowledged on her return to Scotland, where she charmed even the dour Buchanan and Randolph, the English ambassador. She was more academic than the others and enjoyed romantic literature. Mary Livingston may not have had classic beauty, but she made up for it with vivaciousness. She was tall and became an energetic horsewoman and dancer, known as 'lusty' by her fellow Maries, meaning that she was athletic and active, rather than passionate. Mary Seton was of a similar height to Mary, but was more homespun and retained her vow of celibacy into old age. Yet she, more than the other three, who married with children, remained close to Mary, taking responsibility for dressing her hair even while in captivity in England. She only retired when her health broke shortly before Mary's execution, when she returned to spend her remaining years in a French convent in increasing penury.

As one of Catherine de Medici's ladies-in-waiting, Anne d'Este regularly met Mary at court. Her husband Francis was already recognised as the most brilliant of the French military commanders, and they regularly invited Mary to Meudon outside Paris, where she became one of the family with her younger but handsome cousins. It was here that she developed conversational skills, which for the rest of her life charmed all who met her. She saw the graceful and gentle Anne d'Este as her surrogate mother, resulting in great mutual affection. On a day-to-day basis, Mary was supervised by her uncle Charles, Cardinal of Lorraine, who visited regularly to inspect her household. He advised on her correspondence, and his maxim was 'discretion sur tout'.[20] Mary soon had her own secretaries, who converted sensitive letters into cipher. She wrote to her mother, 'I can assure you, nothing that comes from you will ever be disclosed by me.'[21]

In March 1553, Henry II arranged for the Dauphin, now nearly nine, to have his own household independent of the other royal children. At the same time Catherine de Medici arranged for her daughters to live with her and not in a separate household supervised by Diane de Poitiers. To maintain her status, the Guises also wanted Mary to have an independent household. This required grander clothing and more servants, adding to the cost of food and transportation. Jean de Humières had died on 18 July 1550 (although his wife continued to care for the royal children) and had been replaced by Claude d'Urfé, who allowed Mary's staff to expand. Her household was now supervised by the diplomat, Henry Cleutin, Sieur d'Oysel, with eight grooms, eight stable boys, thirty-six maids-of-honour, eleven honorary receptionists, eight secretaries, nine ushers, twenty-eight valets, four porters, four lodging directors, four wardrobe masters, the treasurer, Jacques Bochetel, two comptrollers-general, five doctors, three apothecaries, four surgeons and four barbers. There were fifty-seven kitchen staff and forty-two cellar men to 'the detriment of the general sobriety'. For amusement, there were also court musicians, poets, jesters, dancers, jugglers and acrobats. All these came at a price and Mary showered extravagant gifts on them.

Neither the Guises nor Henry were prepared to foot the bill for Mary's household. The Cardinal produced an estimate requiring an additional 24,000 *livres tournois* annually, excluding stabling for her horses to transport her possessions while following the court. They turned to the Queen Dowager, although the cost amounted to half the regular income of the Scottish Crown. After negotiations lasting nine months, a compromise was reached and she agreed to provide 50,000 livres per year, in part from Scottish revenues but mainly from the Longueville estates, while Henry proffered 30,000 livres. This extravagance did not help the Queen Dowager's popularity in Scotland. She was now seen to be milking Scotland to fund France. She also had to raise £60,000 in taxes to meet the costs of Mary's wedding to the Dauphin.

On 12 April 1554, the Cardinal arranged for the eleven-year-old Mary to claim the Scottish throne in her own right. This enabled her uncles to be appointed, in addition to Henry, as her French guardians, making them second only to the Valois kings in importance. It also empowered her to appoint her mother as Regent to replace Châtelherault, greatly enhancing Guise standing in Europe.

When Edward VI died of consumption on 6 July 1553, the Catholic Mary Tudor became Queen of England, signalling a counter-Reformation. Catholics were invited back to Court, and Lady Margaret Lennox* was

---

* Lady Margaret took precedence over Elizabeth, who remained illegitimate in Catholic eyes. They were showered with gifts. Lady Margaret received two cloth-of-gold gowns. Lennox was given a large pointed diamond, a gold belt set with rubies and diamonds and Edward VI's best horse. Darnley, already known to be musical, received Edward VI's lutes, and three suits of clothing. Such was the enthusiasm with which they were received that Lady Margaret had hopes that Darnley would be named as Mary Tudor's heir.

provided with luxuriously furnished apartments in the Palace of Westminster. Mary Tudor became betrothed to Philip, soon to become King of Spain, but eleven years her junior. This presented a renewed risk for French interests in Scotland, which needed the Queen Dowager's positive leadership to combat Châtelherault's shortcomings. When Angus, Huntly, Glencairn and Cassillis backed her for the Regency, she formally took control. Financial inducements were provided to Châtelherault and his family, and he was granted immunity from any prosecution relating to his period in office.

After the Lady Fleming scandal, the Guises appointed Françoise d'Estamville, Lady Parois, as Governess. This disappointed Mahanet des Essartz, Dame de Curel, who had been Antoinette de Bourbon's nominee and a former lady-in-waiting to the Queen Dowager in Scotland. She had taught Mary to speak French and, under Fleming, had been responsible for her clothing as lady of the bedchamber. Although Parois was energetic and capable and her incorruptible integrity found favour, she proved dull, nit-picking, greedy and tedious in the extreme. She improved Mary's deportment and regal posture, which only reverted to her more natural rounded shoulders when out of the limelight during her imprisonment. Yet she found the Cardinal's financial estimates woefully inadequate and many of Mary's staff remained unpaid, causing friction and absenteeism. Curel resigned after a row, complaining at being overlooked as governess. Parois produced a litany of complaints associated with money shortages. She wanted better transport for Mary's furnishings, which were being damaged during removal between palaces. In 1553, she wanted a hairdresser to tend Mary's hair, as she was dressing it herself and 'cannot do it as well as I would like'.[22] Mary seemed to delight in annoying her. She showed off by wearing Scottish dress, no doubt encouraged by her Scottish chamber women. This was not tartan at this early period, but wild animal skins draped strategically about the person. The poet Joachim du Bellay claimed that 'when in her Highland garb she resembled a goddess in masquerade'. It was clearly graceful deportment which carried the day!

To demonstrate her new status, Mary wanted the most fashionable designs in the most expensive materials. By 1551, she had sixteen dresses in a range of fabrics from cloth of silver to satin. She had six cotton aprons, three skirts, three caps, two farthingales, two overskirts, a cloak and a fur muff. She had 22-carat gold buttons enamelled in black and white, gold belts enamelled in white and red and assorted chains and collars. She wore sable and wolf skins. Parois complained to the Queen Dowager that she needed more money to meet the needs of the high-spirited thirteen-year-old, who remained ignorant of the financial difficulties. She wanted richly embroidered and professionally made monograms, then the vogue, on her finest garments. Sometimes these were worn as headdresses, sewn with jewels and enamels.

Mary faced a continuing battle of wills with Parois. If she wore more jewellery than Parois thought appropriate, she was reported to her mother for insubordination. She became almost hysterical that Parois was causing friction between her mother and herself and threw a tantrum. She had been instructed by her mother to give her old dresses with rich brocade to her aunts as vestments for their abbeys, but Parois saw these as her perquisites. Mary asked her *valet de chambre* to tell her if Parois tried to remove things. Worse still, Parois insinuated that Mary had been rude about Catherine de Medici to Diane de Poitiers.

Parois became a laughing stock at court, and many believed that she should have had enough money, if she were more economical. When she delayed settling with tradesmen, they demanded payment in advance. Money appeared to go missing, and Parois could not cope. She became ill, probably with dropsy, and temporarily took sick leave. At last the Cardinal arranged with Catherine de Medici to have her removed. From now on Mary's domestic arrangements were supervised by Anne d'Este, who appointed Jean de Beaucaire, Sieur de Péguillon and his wife Guyonne du Breüil from a dynasty of loyal royal servants* and they remained with Mary even after her return to Scotland. Harmony was restored, and with each passing year Mary became 'a child of the smooth land of France rather than of the rugged land of Scotland'.[23]

Mary's battle of wills with Parois had caused great stress to both of them. Parois's dropsy no doubt added to her irritation, but, as so often in later life, Mary also became ill. She suffered fits of depression, bursting into tears with abdominal pains, which caused her to vomit. She would recover as quickly as her illness began. These are not symptoms of the gastric ulcer which later afflicted her in Scotland, but may have been the 'Quartan Ague' or 'Sweat', a recurrent viral disease similar to malaria. This affected many during the summer months, including the Dauphin and the Duke of Guise's son, Henry. The Cardinal wrote to the Queen Dowager playing down her attacks by suggesting that she occasionally suffered heartburn and indigestion from overeating. He confirmed her doctors' view that she would outlive them all.

---

* Guyonne's daughter Marie became a lady-in-waiting in about 1553 perhaps to replace Barbara Hamilton. She remained closely associated with Mary on her return to Scotland and, as Madame de Martigues, was mentioned in Mary's will made before the birth of Prince James. Another French lady-in-waiting, who joined Mary in 1555, was Marie de Gagnon de Saint-Bohaire, much praised for her beauty. She left her service in 1560 after marriage, the year before, to the Duke of Rouannais and did not go with her to Scotland.

Even when she contracted smallpox, it had no lasting ill effect on her unblemished skin.

Mary had an unparalleled religious grounding and, despite the moral shortcomings of the French court, was brought up to a strict code of conduct. She excelled at calligraphy, needlework, drawing and dancing. Her education was meticulously planned, but, unlike Elizabeth in England, she had no great academic bent. She learned statecraft from the Cardinal, being given every opportunity to assimilate French politics with its factions and religious controversy. He encouraged an interest in Scottish affairs, and it was no doubt this that made her write to her mother at the beginning of 1557 complaining at the depletion of royal estates through grants of land to the Scottish nobility. Yet the Guises anticipated her remaining in France as the key to their continuing influence, while Scotland was ruled by others in her absence.

Catherine de Medici insisted on her daughters receiving an education similar to their brothers, and Mary followed an almost identical curriculum to the Dauphin. Following Francis I's love affair with the Renaissance, the French admired all things Italian, and Diane de Poitiers, herself a great patron of the arts, ensured that the royal children understood Classical design. They studied Latin and Greek,* with Mary reading histories by Plutarch and Livy, Ptolemy's *Geography*, Cicero, Plato, and Aesop's *Fables*, but she was not a brilliant classicist. It was perceived that 'the arts of speaking and of ruling well' were best acquired from studying the antiquities.[24] She learned rhetoric and at thirteen delivered an extemporary oration in Latin, no doubt learned by heart, before Henry II, Catherine de Medici and the entire court at the Louvre. Although she studied Italian and some Spanish, she preferred historical tales such as the story of Roland, the Arthurian legends, and the Spanish romance, *Amadis de Gaul*. Somehow the medicine seemed to work, and she developed a mind of her own, not always following the bidding of her uncles, even if her own judgements sometimes proved inept.

Mary was much happier studying modern writers. She read philosophical texts, often quoting from Erasmus's entertaining *Colloquies* and *In Praise of Folly*, his satire on monarchy and flattery. She wrote in French, generally in an epistolary style deemed to encourage oratory. Most of her schoolroom letters appear banal and record what her teachers wanted her to say, but they were not intended to be sent. She loved modern French poetry, particularly by Pierre de Ronsard, leader of a group of seven poets forming the Pléiade,

---

* By 1566, Mary's library of Latin and Greek books at Holyrood was of sufficient importance to be left to St Andrews University.

who believed that French stood on equal terms with Latin, Greek and Italian for clear and elegant writing. Ronsard had travelled to Scotland in the train of the tragic Queen Madeleine, and, in 1556, Mary became his patron, later helping him to publish the first edition of his works. She also read poetry by Joachim du Bellay, who had visited Scotland as part of her escort to bring her as a child to France. She wrote sonnets of her own (and the Casket Letters contained sonnets, although she is unlikely to have written them), but showed no particular poetic talent.

Mary undertook pastimes fashionable at the French court, influenced as it was by Italian fashion. She enjoyed singing, particularly works by Clément Marot, who had translated the Psalms into French with music by Claude Goudimel and Loys Bourgeois. She could accompany herself on the lute, singing in a Mantuan style, and also played the clavichord and harp. She could draw, but her forte was in rhythmically graceful dancing, following complex routines with simple gestures to depict musical emotions. To Henry II's delight, she danced with the Dauphin before an audience. She also performed for the court with the stately Anne d'Este, only twelve years her senior. The great connoisseur of female beauty, Pierre de Bourdeille, Abbe de Brantôme, could not decide which of the two was the more handsome. She gambled at cards with the Dauphin, beating him as often as not, and played dice, chess and backgammon. Catherine de Medici encouraged her in Italianate embroidery, and she worked with growing skill throughout her life in both *gross* and *petit point*, even sewing during Privy Council meetings after her return to Scotland. Some of her best work was done with Bess of Hardwick while captive in England. She embroidered wall hangings, valances, table and cushion covers and clothing, often as gifts. She developed monograms, with which to sign off her works, sometimes using the Greek *Mu* repeated upside down. This chosen *imprese* had a marigold in the centre facing towards the sun. Anagrams were then in vogue, and her motto, *Sa Virtu m'Atire* [Its virtue draws me], was a near anagram of 'MARIE STVART'.

Mary loved animals, particularly dogs and ponies, at one stage having sixteen dogs, generally terriers and spaniels, which scampered round her in typical French fashion. Shetland ponies were delivered from Scotland as gifts for the Dauphin and the other royal children. The royal nursery received two bears from the Marischal Jacques de Saint-André, giving rise to bills for the damage they caused. With royal hunting lodges on her doorstep, she became an expert horsewoman and went stag-hunting from the age of thirteen. Although protocol demanded that ladies rode side-saddle, Catherine de Medici, another brilliant horsewoman, encouraged her to ride astride, wearing serge breeches under her skirts. She also became an expert falconer, casting off the hawk and fearlessly collecting it again on her arm. She was also proficient at archery and pell-mell (croquet).

The French historian François-Eudes de Mézeray, writing a century later, summed up the general view of Mary:

> Nature had bestowed upon her everything that is necessary to form a complete beauty. And beside this she had a most agreeable turn of mind, a ready memory and a lively imagination. All these good natural qualities she took care to embellish, by the study of the liberal arts and sciences especially painting, music and poetry insomuch that she appeared to be the most amiable Princess in Christendom.

Yet marriage to the Dauphin was not a foregone conclusion. Despite her glamour, bearing and training to become Queen of France, this was fraught with political uncertainty. Would Henry II really be prepared to provide the ambitious Guise family with such an exalted connection to the Valois dynasty? As so often, Mary was a pawn in the complex game of chess being played out around her.

References

1. de Beaugué, cited by Antonia Fraser, p. 35
2. CSP Scottish, I, p. 157, cited by Antonia Fraser, p. 36
3. Jane T. Stoddart, *The Girlhood of Mary Queen of Scots*, pp. 411–412
4. Ibid.
5. Stoddart, p. 416
6. Prince Labanoff, *Lettres du Cardinal de Lorraine*, 116 and 116 n.4, cited by Guy, p. 45, and by Antonia Fraser, p. 45
7. Register House, Edinburgh, GD/97/3/ no. 7, cited by Antonia Fraser, p. 58
8. Hector De la Ferrière-Percy, *Lettres de Catherine de Medicis*, I, p. liv; cited by Guy, p. 46–47 and Wormald, p. 78
9. Hector De la Ferrière-Percy, I, p. 556
10. Leonie Frieda, *Catherine de Medici*, p. 144
11. Alphonse de Ruble, *La Première Jeunesse de Marie Stuart*, p. 30
12. J. H. Pollen, *Papal Negotiations with Mary Queen of Scots*, p. 414, cited by Antonia Fraser, p. 61
13. de la Brousse to Marie of Guise, Balcarres Papers II, p. 6; p. 32, cited by Antonia Fraser, p. 44
14. Stoddart, pp. 15, 22–3
15. Guy, p. 49
16. Antonia Fraser, p. 62

17. Bibliothèque Nationale, *Lettres de Catherine de Medici*, cited by Frieda, p. 114
18. CSP Foreign (*Edward VI*), p. 103
19. Leslie, cited by Antonia Fraser, p. 217
20. Cited by John Guy, p. 82
21. Cited by John Guy, p. 82
22. Labanoff, I, p. 199, cited by Rosalind K. Marshall, *Queen Mary's Women*, p. 46
23. Antonia Fraser, p. 63
24. Castiglione, Book of the Courtier

6

The Queen Regent's Efforts to Combat the Nobility and the Reformers

On gaining power, the Queen Regent's initial concern was to assess the impact on European politics of the marriage of Mary Tudor to Philip II. With England likely to be drawn into Spain's war with France, there were fears for French interests in Scotland. When Henry II encouraged her to make a diversionary incursion into England, her French troops moved artillery across the Tweed, but the Scots, with too many memories of military disasters, refused to support her and the advance was abandoned. This highlighted the fragility of her authority. She had to gamble that the Spanish were too committed on the Continent to open a new front on England's northern border. She could at least be sure that Philip II would not infiltrate Protestant preachers in support of the Reformist insurgents who were opposing her. She focused on dealing with the shortcomings of the nobility's feudal administration and, with Archbishop Hamilton's help, of the Catholic Church. Yet this allowed the Scottish Reformation to gather pace largely unchallenged.

The Queen Regent faced the nobility head on. Having traditionally operated as a loose confederation of magnates governing their own estates as petty tyrants, their motives seemed designed solely to feather their own nests. Feudal laws were unjust, and she now implemented order through the Court of Session. French administrators installed proper systems for collecting and delivering Crown rents and taxes to the Exchequer, but this was misinterpreted as back-door subjugation. In 1555, d'Oysel, the French ambassador and her senior adviser, who was later to head Mary's household in France, believed that the nobility were selfishly undermining her reforms.

Angus remained on uneasy terms with the Queen Regent, travelling about with a retinue of 1,000 ill-disciplined Douglas men. When she warded him in Edinburgh Castle, he arrived with all his supporters and was refused entry. When she suggested making Huntly a duke (duck), Angus said that he would be a drake. This jocularity made him popular with his fellow Scots, but he died aged sixty-eight at Tantallon in mid-January 1557. In accordance with the recent entail to his will, he was succeeded as 7th Earl by his nephew, David, son of Sir George Douglas of Pittendreich.* David only survived another five months, leaving his infant son, Archibald, as the 8th Earl. David's younger brother, James, already 4th Earl of Morton in right of his wife, became Archibald's guardian, thereby retaining the income of the Angus earldom for himself.

For a time, Châtelherault continued to support the Queen Regent, despite having reverted to be a 'fervent' Reformer after Bethune's assassination. Yet he was always more comfortable with less confrontational Lutheranism and its hope of ultimate reconciliation to the Catholic Church. More militant Calvinism, as espoused by Knox, offered no room for compromise, and Châtelherault started to have cold feet. The Queen Regent had long since lost faith in him and appointed a group of younger advisers to prominent positions. After being imprisoned in England as a boy, the eighteen-year-old Fleming became Lord High Chamberlain for life in 1553. Cassillis became Lord High Treasurer and, in 1554, she employed a new young Secretary, the twenty-six-year-old William Maitland, younger of Lethington, a man of great wit and learning from a well-connected, but not ennobled, Scottish family. He had been educated at St Andrews and the French court and was to become a profound influence on the succeeding period of Scottish history. He was converted by Knox to be a Reformer in 1556, but was not strongly religious. He was an archetypal civil servant, motivated to support the government in power. As a brilliant negotiator, he occasionally propounded objectives that differed from his personal views. This pragmatism caused him to be mistrusted.

The Catholic Church in Scotland was not blind to its shortcomings. Following initiatives at the Council of Trent, the first session of which ended in 1547, Archbishop Hamilton initiated reform in a series of councils between 1549 and 1559. He was later criticised for maintaining a mistress and suffering from syphilis, but at this time he was much praised for his religious learning even by Knox. The first of his councils called 'for the reformation of morals in the Church of Scotland and for the extirpation of heresy'. He attacked clergy taking concubines, or involved in trade and dressed as laymen. He insisted on the Church providing teachers in every diocese and required priests to preach on Sundays and feast days, while

---

* Lady Margaret immediately sent Darnley's tutor, John Elder, to France in an effort to gain from Mary restitution of her birthright and the release of her husband's Lennox estates from attainder.

bishops and rectors should do so at least four times per year. His reforms were generally implemented and, in 1558, the dean and chapter of Aberdeen told its bishop to rid himself of 'the gentill woman be quhom he is gretlie sclanderit'. In 1552, he published his Catechism, setting out, in clear vernacular language, the main tenets of the Church, including the Ten Commandments and the Creed. In 1559, common and evening prayers and litanies were introduced in Scots. Yet his work failed to deter church funds being plundered by both the Crown and the nobility. The priesthood was left underpaid, leaving incumbents academically and socially inadequate. The Queen Regent can be criticised for failing to give Hamilton's reforms her wholehearted backing until it was too late. Had she done so, heresy might have been nipped in the bud.

The growing power of the Reformers was triggered by the return of John Knox* to Scotland for a short period in 1556. After his departure, following the defeat of the Castilians in 1547, there had been no evangelical theologian of stature providing leadership. He now gained almost universal support in describing the Catholic clergy as a 'greedy pack'.[1] Yet the priesthood was greedy only because charges for baptisms, marriages and burials, together with the dispossession of excommunicates, were the principal sources of its meagre income. As early as 1547, Knox had espoused Calvinism in all its militancy, preaching to the Castilians of 'the abominable idolatry of the Mass, blasphemous to the death of Christ and a profanation of the Lord's Supper'.[2] This was ahead of his time, but he now used his evangelism to convert many to the Reformist faith. He stayed at Glencairn's house at Findlayston, where he became closely associated with Spottiswood, who he dominated, and Spottiswood did much to encourage other nobles to listen to him. Over succeeding years, he undertook missions for Knox, becoming, in 1558, Ecclesiastical Superintendent† of the Kirk for Lothian and Tweeddale.

Both Lord James Stewart and Argyll heard Knox preach at Calder in 1556, after which they joined a group of like-minded Reformers among the

---

* After the accession of Mary Tudor, Knox left England for Geneva with his new wife, Marjory Bowes, accompanied by her mother Elizabeth, who left her husband to be with her daughter and son-in-law. She was still with them in 1559, when Knox at last returned to Scotland with his wife and their two sons. Marjory died in 1560, but Elizabeth remained in his household until her own death in 1568. Although it was asserted that she did not 'live as flesh and blood' with Knox, there were strong rumours to the contrary, and she was always racked with guilt about leaving her husband. In 1564, Knox, by now aged fifty, remarried the seventeen-year-old Margaret Stewart, Ochiltree's daughter and a kinswoman of Mary, who 'stormed wonderfully' on hearing of it. This cradle-snatching union tarnished Knox's reputation.
† Within the Kirk, superintendents fulfilled the administrative role of bishops.

nobility, who were to form the Lords of the Congregation.* Although their faith was based on genuine personal conviction, the grouping conveniently offered a political platform from which to face the Queen Regent. Knox wrote to her, demanding that she should become a Reformer or face her 'dejection to torment and pain everlasting'.[3] She contemptuously treated the letter as a joke, when showing it to Archbishop Bethune of Glasgow. Her approach differed from her daughter, who was to burst into tears of frustration in dealing with Knox. Although he soon returned to Geneva, he was invited back by Lord James, Argyll and Glencairn in a letter dated 14 March 1557. Yet he overplayed his hand by producing a second version of his letter to the Queen Regent, three times longer and more vitriolic than the first. Wanting to avoid confrontation, they persuaded him to delay his return.

The Lords of the Congregation started to gather support, in part, because the Reformist faith was less financially demanding on its adherents than the Catholic Church, but, in the main, because of political concerns about French domination. It might have been thought that Huguenot influence in France now offered them a better prospect of backing than Catholic England, so it was political rather than spiritual concerns that more strongly influenced their supporters. Despite the Queen Regent's extraordinary diplomatic coup of negotiating Mary's French marriage and arranging the Crown Matrimonial for the Dauphin, in doing so she conceded freedom of worship to the Reformers.

Starting with Mary's marriage to the Dauphin in April 1558, a number of factors moved the Lords of the Congregation from a body concerned only with reform of the Church to one determined to oust French influence from Scotland. The Queen Regent's additional military strength and the security which Mary's marriage provided had made her more aggressive. On 28 April, she approved the burning of a former priest turned Reformer, Walter Myln, at the stake at St Andrews. This caused an inevitable backlash. The Reformers erected a pile of stones to mark Myln's burial place and, although the priests had them removed, they were always replaced. This *cause célèbre* provided the Lords of the Congregation with the motive to incite opposition, and she had a fight on her hands. When she admonished Argyll, he felt sufficiently secure to condemn the 'blood-letting and burning of poor men, to make your Lordship serve their wicked appetites'.

---

* The Lords of the Congregation were constituted in a bond signed in Edinburgh on 3 December 1557 by Argyll, his son Archibald, Lord Lorne, who inherited as the 5th Earl the following year, Glencairn, Morton, and the Lutheran Reformer John Erskine of Dun, who went on to become one of the first superintendents of the Kirk after 1560. Initially it was aimed entirely at reform of the Church, and, with Mary Tudor still on the English throne, without expectation of English support.

After Mary Tudor died on 17 November 1558, the Queen Regent again considered invading England to support Mary's claim to the English throne. This was no doubt on advice from the Guises in France, but was strongly opposed by Châtelherault, Huntly, Cassillis and Argyll, who would have had to provide troops, so that the plan was dropped. With Elizabeth's accession, the Lords of the Congregation had the prospect of English support. Yet, for a short time, there were doubts about her religious persuasion while she waited until April 1559 for the Treaty of Cateau-Cambrésis to be signed between France and Spain. She did not want Catholic powers combining against her in an attack on heresy. Yet when Elizabeth's Protestantism became clear, the Queen Regent was at risk of English attack, but, with France no longer at war in Italy, she received yet more French military support.

It was Maitland who first began to fear the increase in the Queen Regent's forces, not in terms of protecting the kingdom for her daughter, but in subjugating Scotland to French and Catholic domination. His concerns may also have been coloured by risks to his own position as Secretary when she was appointing so many French advisers. He started to persuade other Reformist nobles to share his views and, in 1559, resigned, so that he could oppose her. Robert Melville quickly joined him. More importantly, Arran, who had returned from France in September, persuaded his father to join the Lords of the Congregation, and Châtelherault also left court. He had by now lost credibility, but his move swung the balance in favour of the Reformers.

Châtelherault had traditionally relied for support on his daughter Jean's husband, Hugh Montgomerie, 3rd Earl of Eglinton. Although still a Catholic, Eglinton backed him against the Queen Regent. Yet he could not bring himself to join the Lords of the Congregation with the young Glencairn and Robert, 5th Lord Boyd, as his blood enemies, so prominent among them. His only motive was to stop Scotland being subjugated under France, and he fully supported Mary on her return to Scotland after her mother's death. Through his mother, Mariot Seton, Eglinton was a first cousin of George, 5th Lord Seton and shared the Seton family loyalty to the Stewarts.*

On Mary Tudor's death and Elizabeth's accession, Lady Margaret Lennox again retired to Yorkshire, but was closely watched by Elizabeth's advisers, who gathered evidence against her. With Châtelherault now a Reformer,

---

* Such were the close family links between the Montgomerie and Seton families that in 1840 William, 13th Earl of Eglinton, was able to lay claim to the Seton Earldom of Winton, which had been forfeited from George Seton, 5th Earl of Winton after the 1715 Rebellion. *From 1612 the earls of Eglinton were Setons.*

Lennox dropped any pretence of being Protestant and, although still in England, joined the French party to promote himself as the Catholic heir presumptive in Scotland. When Elizabeth heard this, he was thrown in the Tower, remaining there until 1564. Lady Margaret sent Darnley to France, but with her other children was confined to Sir William Sackville's home at Sheen, where she claimed that she should rightfully be Queen. She was again excluded from the succession based on unfounded questions over her legitimacy. Realising that this had ended her own political ambitions, she focused her considerable skills on promoting her son, Darnley, as heir to both the Scottish and English thrones.

While waiting at Dieppe in 1557, after delaying his return to Scotland, Knox wrote the document that gained him, for all time, his reputation as a political embarrassment. He produced his *First Blast of the Trumpet against the monstrous Regiment of Women*, a diatribe against the rule of both Mary Tudor and the Queen Regent published in early 1558. He saw it as 'a subversion of good order, of all equity and justice' for women to rule men.[4] His timing was unfortunate, as Mary Tudor died later in the year and Elizabeth also saw it as an affront. To make amends he wrote to her in July conveying his unfeigned love and reverence, but told her that she ruled by the will of the people and not by dynastic right. Elizabeth now saw him as an anathema and would never have his name mentioned. He remained insensitive to criticism and showed no Christian sympathy for his opponents, relishing any bloodthirsty brutality that brought about their end. Elizabeth's opposition forced him to return to Scotland, rather than to gain a more glittering Protestant post in England. On arrival, he quickly went onto the attack against the Catholic Church. Yet with the nobility benefiting from it financially, the Lords of the Congregation needed to steer him into addressing the political concern of ending the Queen Regent's 'tyranny of strangers'.

Reformist unrest initially started in Perth. Knox arrived to preach at St John's on 11 May, and his sermon caused a riot, leading to the sacking and looting of the nearby Catholic monasteries. Even he was shocked at the power of his oratory, referring to the mob as the 'rascal multitude'.[5] Yet the die was cast. When Ruthven returned there as Provost, he refused to help the Queen Regent's French garrison to suppress the insurgency. Glencairn and Andrew Stewart, 2nd Lord Ochiltree raised 2,500 troops to support Ruthven. The Queen Regent sent reinforcements, backed at first by Lord James and Archibald Campbell, 5th Earl of Argyll, who had succeeded his father five months earlier. Both later claimed to be trying to moderate her stance. Glencairn and Ochiltree were forced to withdraw and, on 29 May, her troops entered the town, deposing Ruthven as Provost. Two days later he signed a bond with Glencairn and Ochiltree for the 'liberty of the congregation' to oust the French from Scotland, and Lord James and Argyll quickly joined them.

With the Reformers at last having some military clout, the town councils of Edinburgh, Dalmellington and St Andrews appointed Reformist ministers. Knox went to St Giles' in Edinburgh, from where he galvanised them from the pulpit. Randolph claimed that he 'is able in one hour to put more life into us than five hundred trumpets continually blustering in our ears'.[6] He strongly backed military action against the Queen Regent, and had been furious at Lord James's and Argyll's initial support for her against Glencairn, Ochiltree and Ruthven. Together they presented formidable opposition. Patrick, Master of Lindsay, later 6th Lord Lindsay of the Byres, soon joined them, also encouraging his father to support them. The elderly Lindsay was not a vehement Reformer, but an honest churchman and mediator, and his military skills could be used to good effect.

The Lords of the Congregation had pockets of support in Edinburgh, Dundee, Perth, Ayr, and St Andrews, where the Reformation was already well established. They needed to demonstrate to the English that they could take on the Queen Regent and her newly reinforced French troops. On 4 June, Lord James and Argyll left Edinburgh with 300 men to link with other Reformist groups at St Andrews. Although she went after them, they remained one step ahead of her. Ruthven arrived at Cupar in Fife, bringing 100 horse and 800 men from Perth. Within a week 13,000 troops from further afield were encamped above the town at Cupar Muir.

When the Queen Regent learned of the Reformers' strength, she called an eight-day truce to avoid confrontation. On 13 June, Lindsay of the Byres was sent to negotiate, after the remainder refused her request for a private meeting with Lord James and Argyll. She agreed to their demand for her French troops to leave Fife. When she failed to call a promised meeting of the Commissioners at St Andrews, they demanded the French garrison's removal from Perth. Again she prevaricated and, although Huntly was in Perth to support the garrison, he left before the arrival of Lord James and Argyll, now backed by Rothes; Perth surrendered on 26 June. Despite his Catholicism, Huntly shared Scottish concerns about the Queen Regent's objectives. The Perth townspeople now sacked Scone and its abbey and, on 1 July, Kirkcaldy wrote to Sir Henry Percy, 'The manner of our reformation is this; pulling down friaries, and using the prayer book of the godly King Edward.' During July, Huntly received the Catholic treasures of Aberdeen Cathedral for safekeeping. Lord James and Argyll now marched to Stirling and then to Linlithgow to stop the Queen Regent gaining control of the

Forth. She retreated to the safety of the French garrison at Dunbar, and on 29 June the Lords of the Congregation entered Edinburgh unopposed.

Seton had been Lord Provost of Edinburgh since November 1557 and remained Catholic. When the Lords of the Congregation arrived, he sought to protect the Black and Grey Friars, who were being targeted by the Reformers but was unable to do so. Knox denounced him as 'a man without God, without honesty, and often-times without reason'. The Reformers set about suppressing 'all monuments of idolatry', and took control of the coining irons at the Edinburgh Mint, ostensibly to avoid the Queen Regent from debasing the coinage. This was merely an excuse to justify their actions. When Mary became Queen of France on 10 July, action against French troops could be seen as treasonable.

With her well-trained French forces, the Queen Regent counterattacked, and the two sides agreed another truce. Edinburgh was left to choose its religion, but Catholicism was not to be reinstated where already suppressed. Yet the Lords of the Congregation knew that they needed English support to defeat her French troops. On 19 July, they wrote an urgent letter to Cecil, sending Kirkcaldy in August to negotiate. This resulted in a breathing space and, in the autumn, Huntly persuaded Seton to reintroduce the Mass in St Giles 'to solicit all men to condescend to the Queen's mind'. Seton also attempted to arrest Knox. He pursued Knox's agent, Alexander Whitelaw, to Ormiston, mistakenly believing it was him. He was isolated and, with things going from bad to worse for the Queen Regent, he left for France. He arrived in Paris on 3 July 1560 to meet Mary and to enjoy a family reunion with his sister and widowed stepmother.

Lord James emerged as the leader of the Lords of the Congregation and adopted a façade of religious objectives to cloak his personal plan to oust the Queen Regent. He wanted to keep Mary safely out of the way in France and wrote carefully to Cecil hinting at her deposition to create a united Protestant Britain. Yet the Lords of the Congregation pulled back from this radical step. The Stewarts were entrenched as the rightful monarchs, and deposing Mary only opened the door for the discredited Châtelherault. Yet Knox was securely positioned to oppose a counter-Reformation, if Mary should return.

References

1. Antonia Fraser, p. 29
2. Guy, p. 39
3. Wormald, Mary, Queen of Scots, p. 88

4. Laing, Knox, IV, p. 373, cited in Antonia Fraser, p. 177
5. Wormald, Mary, Queen of Scots, p. 95
6. Wormald, Mary, Queen of Scots, p. 94

7

Dominant Forces among the Scottish Nobility

In addition to Châtelherault and Lennox with their competing claims to be heirs to the Scottish throne, there were four other powerful lords with sufficient strength to influence a weakened Stewart dynasty. These were Huntly with his power base in the north; James Hepburn, 4th Earl of Bothwell, with strength to the east of Edinburgh and in the Borders; Lord James Stewart, illegitimate half-brother of Mary, and later Earl of Moray, with the backing of the Lords of the Congregation; and Morton, also a Reformer and now leader of the powerful Douglas clans, representing both Morton (the 'black Douglas') and Angus (the 'red Douglas') in his capacity as guardian for his infant nephew. Morton generally acted in concert with Lord James with backing from Elizabeth and her ministers in England. Yet, by 1570, he had achieved sufficient personal status to assume Lord James's mantle following his assassination. With the exception of Lord James and Morton, the remainder had differing objectives and mistrusted each other.

Huntly was born in 1514, the grandson of James IV through his mother, the illegitimate Margaret Stewart, and was almost a contemporary of his uncle James V, becoming his close confidant. He was the most powerful magnate in northern Scotland, which he controlled as a personal fiefdom practically independent of the Crown. By Scottish standards, he was wealthy, generating income from his valuable farm lands outside Aberdeen and from the Church and Crown estates within his bailiwick which he administered. In 1530, he married Marischal's sister, the redoubtable Elizabeth Keith, described by Buchanan as 'a woman with the passions and purposes of a man'. She dabbled in witchcraft, which strongly influenced her husband's actions. He became a Privy Councillor in 1535, joining the Council of Regency when James V visited France to marry the frail Princess Madeleine. With a reputation as an able general, he became Lord of the North in 1540, and escorted the King to visit the Western Isles. On 24 August 1542, James chose him to captain the Scottish force which defeated Sir Robert Bowes at Haddon Rig, although his later military exploits were to prove less successful.

Huntly supported the Queen Regent and strengthened his own position by organising her removal with the infant Queen from Arran's clutches at Linlithgow to the relative security of Stirling. On 9 September 1543, he attended Mary's coronation there, again being appointed as Lieutenant-General of the North. After Bethune's murder, he became Lord High Chancellor on 5 June 1546 and a Privy Councillor. He led the van with Angus against Somerset's English troops at Pinkie Cleugh in 1547, dressed resplendently in white and gilt armour, but his hastily gathered men fled the field, being a principal cause of the Scottish defeat. He was captured and taken to London, where, to regain his freedom, he made a pact with Somerset to promote English policies in Scotland, although he soon forgot this and voted in favour of Mary's marriage to the Dauphin. After this show of support for the French, he was made a Knight of St Michel by Henry II on 13 February 1549, and was granted the benefit of the valuable Moray estates by Châtelherault as Regent. He continued to support the Queen Dowager, accompanying her when she visited Mary in France in 1550 and backing her to become Queen Regent in 1554. Yet she was nervous of his power and independence in the north, and when he failed to quell an uprising there in October 1554, she imprisoned him in Edinburgh Castle for five months. She also demoted him as Lieutenant-General, removed his governorship of Orkney, fined him, and took away his grant of the Moray estates received five years earlier (although it is not certain that this affected his practical use of them). Although he remained Lord High Chancellor, the great seal was handed to de Rubay, one of her French ministers brought in to provide better administration for her government, and de Rubay was appointed Vice Chancellor. Huntly never forgot this harsh treatment, even though he was restored as Lieutenant-General in 1557. With his cousin Sutherland,* he now shared Maitland's and Châtelherault's concerns that her objectives were to bring Scotland under French control, thereby weakening the power of the nobles. Despite his Catholicism, this led him to assist the Lords of the Congregation by failing to protect the French garrison at Perth in 1559.

Bothwell had many of the characteristics of his father, who he succeeded in 1556. He was Sheriff of Berwick, Haddington and Edinburgh, and inherited his father's lucrative position as Lord High Admiral, giving him access to a share of the treasure trove from all wrecks on Scottish shores. Despite this as a source of income, his efforts to support both the Queen Regent and Mary took their toll on his finances and he was severely in debt

---

* In addition to Sutherland, Huntly could rely on support from George Sinclair, 4th Earl of Caithness, also a Catholic. Caithness generally backed his political scheming, but never played a prominent part in Scottish politics, being preoccupied with his own chequered lifestyle in the north.

by the time of his marriage to Jean Gordon in 1566. He was a brave soldier and a good leader of men and, as a 'man of honour',[1] was always ready to fight duels to uphold his cause.

Bothwell had been well educated at Spynie in Inverness-shire by his kinsman* Patrick Hepburn, the Catholic Bishop of Moray, whose 'notoriously irregular' lifestyle rubbed off on his protégé. While history has no doubt made more of this than perhaps is justified, Bothwell was a man of strong language and sexual appetite, powerfully attractive to women, although by repute he was not averse to homosexual relationships and enjoyed anal sex. He later attended university in Paris, becoming fluent in French and writing in a well-formed italic script. He studied Latin and Greek, but his principal interests were mathematics, military strategy and chivalry.† Unlike his father, he became a Reformer, perhaps because Knox's family had been Hepburn dependants. He consistently refused to take Mass, insisting on both his marriage ceremonies, even to Mary, being conducted in accordance with Reformist rites. Yet his bawdy language and lascivious approach to life show no hint of any strong religious conviction.

Like his father, Bothwell was one of only a handful of Scottish peers who remained consistently supportive of the Queen Regent and he was later unfailingly loyal to Mary, despite their different religious persuasions, continuing to offer her assistance when it dwindled elsewhere. On 14 December 1557, he signed the betrothal for Mary to marry the Dauphin. With a rough band of freebooters, he maintained armed control over the Eastern Marches. On the Queen Regent's behalf, he took part in a swashbuckling raid into England at the age of twenty-one, causing great damage close to England's northern border. He was met by Sir James Croft, the English envoy, who was forced to treat with him for an armistice. Sir Henry Percy, an English adversary, was surprised to find him 'courteous and honourable',[2] despite him being steadfastly anti-English.

Lord James Stewart was the illegitimate son of James V by Margaret, daughter of James, 5ᵗʰ Lord Erskine. Although he had been brought up for the Church, being created Prior of St Andrews at an early age, he did not take holy orders. This did not deter him from milking the resources of his

---

* Being responsible for Bothwell's education, Patrick Hepburn is often described as his great-uncle. He was in fact a first cousin of Bothwell's great-grandfather the 1ˢᵗ Earl of Bothwell. He fathered at least five illegitimate children at Spynie and suffered from syphilis, pocketing much of the wealth of his bishopric during his tenure apparently to save it from falling into the hands of the Reformers.

† It was reported by Bertrand de Salignac de la Mothe Fénélon, the French ambassador in London, that he had spent much time in France studying magic, although this was probably a response to the claim that he used sorcery in his later seduction of Mary.

rich benefice. He became an astute political strategist and military tactician. With his dour commanding presence he was the true power in Scotland both immediately before and after Mary's return from France, managing to engineer a position for her that no other of her advisers could have achieved.

Having accompanied Mary to France in 1548 after her betrothal to the Dauphin, Lord James continued his own education there for about a year, and this no doubt contributed to his considerable intellect. Yet on returning to Scotland, he became an ardent Presbyterian and disciple of Knox, developing a religious conviction that conveniently matched his political ambitions. In May 1559, he became military commander of the Lords of the Congregation, which provided his political power base. Despite his Presbyterian faith, he had, up to then, used his backing of the Queen Regent to establish himself as her deputy. Yet leadership of the Lords of the Congregation offered more certain hope of advancement. With his regal manner and royal blood, his ambitions extended to the throne, an objective which suited Cecil in his efforts to achieve a secure Protestant government on England's northern border. Despite portraying himself as a man of principle, his methods were cool, calculating and insidiously self-promoting.

Morton started life with far less glittering prospects than the remainder of this elite power group, but he became Lord James's right-hand man, often carrying out his dirty work. As James Douglas, the second son of Sir George Douglas of Pittendreich, he was without great prospects and was seen as a man 'of most boorish calibre', being illiterate and lacking formal education. Mary considered him uncouth, cruel and unscrupulous. Yet he inherited Pittendreich from his mother and, in 1543, as part of a deal by Châtelherault to gain Douglas support, married Elizabeth, third daughter of James, 3rd Earl of Morton, and was appointed his heir. After being captured by the English during the Rough Wooings, he was taken to England, where he learned to speak with an English accent. Despite his imprisonment, he maintained the Douglases' traditional adherence to the English. He became a Reformer and, in 1557, subscribed to the original bond of the Lords of the Congregation, although he remained politically neutral, careful to hedge his bets, only confirming his allegiance to them when he realised that they would defeat the Queen Regent. On the death of his wife's father in 1550, James duly inherited as the 4th Earl of Morton,* although this was not put into

---

* As Châtelherault had married the 3rd Earl of Morton's eldest daughter, Margaret, he stood to lose by a deal designed to win him Angus's support. Yet the arrangement also overlooked the second daughter, Beatrix, who had married Maxwell. This rankled with the Maxwells, and their son, the hot-headed John, 8th Lord Maxwell later claimed the Morton title and was granted it after the 4th Earl's execution in 1581, although this was revoked in 1586.

effect until 1553. She became insane* in about 1559, and he was left to play a prominent role in the period without her support.

It was Morton who re-opened the plan for Châtelherault's eldest son, James, now Earl of Arran, to marry Princess Elizabeth on his father's elevation to the French dukedom. Arran was of course his wife's nephew. This was aimed at placing the couple on the Scottish throne. Yet he supported Lord James in his plan to return Mary to Scotland, while tolerating her Catholic worship in private, and he defended her against Knox, who continued to lambast her Catholicism. Whenever Lord James was abroad, it was always Morton who kept the Scottish nobility supportive of his policies. After Lord James's assassination in 1570, it was Morton who controlled the government as the most powerful man in Scotland, eventually becoming Regent himself.

In addition to Morton, Lord James initially had a powerful ally in Arran. While being held by the Castilians at St Andrews, Arran had been influenced by Knox's preaching to become a Reformer. After his release in 1550, he had travelled to France, taking command of the Scottish Gens d'Armes and distinguishing himself in the defence of St-Quentin. He met Mary, who was so impressed by his military achievement that she suggested to her mother that he should be created Duke of Arran. Her older and wiser mother paid no heed to this, but Mary was probably aware that he had been considered as a potential husband for her before she came to France. In early 1559, he reconfirmed his Calvinist faith and was forced to leave France for Geneva. On hearing this, Cecil, by now Elizabeth's Secretary of State, managed to spirit him back to England for a meeting to reconsider his potential as an appropriate husband for Elizabeth, and to compare him with Lord James as a potential successor to the Queen Regent. He arrived from France on 28 August 1559 and, although he met Elizabeth, he seems to have come up short. He quickly set off for Scotland and a fortnight later attended the meeting of the Lords of the Congregation at Stirling.

Prior to Mary's return to Scotland, Lord James's strongest military ally was Argyll, Arran's first cousin.† Argyll had been educated at St Andrews and was also an early Reformer. He held sway over the Gaelic-speaking west of

---

* There was a streak of inherited insanity among the Black Douglases, which seems to have affected all three of the 3rd Earl's daughters. Elizabeth, the youngest, was reported to have become deluded by 1559, but all three were certified to be insane at the time of the death of the 4th Earl in 1581, although this may have suited the scheming of Esmé, Duke of Lennox at the time. Perhaps most tragically, insanity also afflicted Châtelherault's children by Margaret, including his eldest son, James (Arran), his youngest son, Claud, and probably his third son, David, to the temporary detriment of the standing of the Hamilton clan at a crucial time. Even the actions of Beatrix's son, Maxwell, do not suggest someone, who was totally balanced.
† Argyll's mother was Châtelherault's sister, Helen Hamilton.

Scotland, with estates extending as far south as the Clyde and into Ulster. With the Campbell clan fulfilling its traditional role of policing the west of Scotland for the Scottish Crown, Argyll was the only Scottish lord to maintain a full-scale army. In the early days of the Lords of the Congregation, Lord James had linked with Argyll's father into a formidable military partnership against the Queen Regent. Despite suffering from epilepsy, the young Argyll was also a brave and competent soldier, and an ardent disciple of Knox. Although his political affiliations were to become less certain, he was, in this early period, strongly influenced by Lord James, marrying his illegitimate half-sister, Lady Jean Stewart.

Two other supporters of Lord James were Glencairn and Ochiltree, both of whom, coincidentally, had succeeded their fathers in 1548. Glencairn had accompanied the Queen Regent to visit Mary in France in September 1550. Yet he remained a strict Reformer like his father, having fallen strongly under Knox's influence, and did much to promote his return to Scotland in 1557. Ochiltree was also an early Reformer and his daughter Margaret was to marry Knox in 1564. They were the initial military leaders of the Lords of the Congregation, supporting Ruthven at Perth in 1559, when they were also backed by Robert, 5th Lord Boyd, who had succeeded his father before 1558 at the age of forty-one. This made him considerably older than Lord James and his other supporters, although he outlived them, only dying in 1590 at the age of seventy-three. The Boyds maintained a close affiliation with the Cunningham (Glencairn) family. This bond was already well established before they joined the Lords of the Congregation, united in their mutual hatred of the Montgomeries, with whom both families were involved in long-standing feuds.

Another of those to back Lord James was William Leslie, initially known as 5th Earl of Rothes, a strong Calvinist and early member of the Lords of the Congregation. He was the younger brother of Norman, who had been killed at the Battle of Renti in 1554. His father George, the 4th Earl, died at Dieppe four years later while returning from Mary's wedding in France. In his will, he had entailed his title to his third son, Andrew, the child of Agnes Somerville, on the grounds that Norman and William, his sons by Margaret Crichton had become illegitimate following the annulment of their marriage in 1520 (see p. 39 footnote). William disputed this* and claimed the Rothes title until Mary declared in Andrew's favour on 15 January 1566.

---

* This explains why 'Rothes' changed his allegiance on about 15 January 1566. Having been a staunch supporter of Lord James, by then Earl of Moray, he suddenly became a loyal ally of Mary. She confirmed that William was illegitimate during his exile after the Chaseabout Raid. This resulted in Andrew gaining the title

Yet another of Lord James's supporters was Sir William Kirkcaldy of Grange, whose father, Sir James, had been Lord High Treasurer under James V. Sir William had been forfeited after being involved in Bethune's assassination at St Andrews in 1546. During the subsequent siege of St Andrews, he took an active part in its defence and was sent to France after its surrender in July 1547. On arrival, he was imprisoned on Mont-St-Michel, but eighteen months later escaped to England, where he was given a pension by Edward VI. In February 1551, he was sent as a secret agent by the English to Blois, but, on Mary Tudor's accession, his activities were curtailed and he had little alternative but to join the French service as a captain of a hundred light horse. He distinguished himself against Charles V, 'both in valour in battle and skill in knightly pursuits', being described by Henry II as 'one of the most valiant men of our time'. Yet he too was nervous of growing French influence in Scotland. On 30 November 1556, he offered to become Mary Tudor's agent against both France and Scotland, but she did not take this up, although he resumed his English employment under Elizabeth.

In 1557, his forfeiture having been rescinded thanks to the heroics of Norman Leslie at Renti, Kirkcaldy returned to Scotland, where he was welcomed by the Lords of the Congregation with his unrivalled reputation as a military commander. Yet he too could be impetuous, and when his cousin John Kirkcaldy was severely treated by the English and imprisoned after a Border skirmish, Kirkcaldy challenged the English commander, Lord Rivers, to a duel. Perhaps unaware of his reputation from France, the challenge was accepted by Lord Rivers' brother, Sir Ralph, and Kirkcaldy unhorsed him after running him through the shoulder.

Kirkcaldy's mother, Janet Melville, was the daughter of Sir John Melville of Raith, who had been executed for supporting the English in 1548. Despite this, her five brothers were established at court in roles similar to the Bethunes and the Maitlands, as ambassadors, Lords of Session or as heads of the household as required. This sometimes caused them to have opposing loyalties. Like Kirkcaldy and Maitland, those of the Melvilles remaining in Scotland feared French subjugation, and initially backed Lord James and the Lords of the Congregation. Yet, following Mary's imprisonment at Lochleven, they all sought to restore her as Queen. The timing of their defection

---

and not unnaturally supporting her. It has been suggested that William was passed over in his father's entail because of the part that he had played in the murder of Cardinal Bethune. This seems highly unlikely, as it is clear that George tacitly approved of the action, and William obtained a remission for his part in it in 1548. William's claim to the title was based on the fact that his mother had subsequently remarried his father, and he claimed that this overcame their earlier annulment, but this was not upheld by Mary, who had no sympathy for him after his support for Moray.

from Lord James varied, leaving them on opposing sides at Langside. Robert, the second brother, initially served the Queen Regent as her agent at the French court. He returned to Scotland only in 1559, when he rejoined her service. Sir James,* the third brother, went to France aged fourteen in 1549 as Mary's page. This led him to follow a military and later diplomatic career in Europe, but he was recalled by Mary to Scotland for a role in her government. He became disaffected after her marriage to Bothwell and thereafter supported the Regency for James VI.

Alexander, 5th Lord Home followed a career very close to Kirkcaldy. After being captured at Pinkie Cleugh, where his father was killed in a skirmish on the day before the battle, he was motivated by his hatred of both the English and his family's hereditary enemies, the Hepburns, which led him into league with Lord James. He had backed the French against the English at the siege of Haddington in 1550, supporting the Regency by holding Home Castle for them. This resulted in him becoming Warden of the Eastern Marches on 19 April and Bailiff of Coldstream on 31 December 1551. With Morton and Ker of Cessford he was a Commissioner for the Treaty of Upsettlington with the English in 1559, where terms were discussed for freeing ransomed prisoners. Although not initially one of the Lords of the Congregation, he supported them at the siege of Leith, until the French again leaned on him for help and he returned home. Yet progressively thereafter he remained Lord James's ally.

Sir John Maxwell, born in about 1512, was another early ally of Lord James. A staunch supporter of Knox, he signed the Book of Discipline on 27 January 1561. Knox described him as 'a man stout and wittie'. He was the second son of Robert, 6th Lord Maxwell and, in 1548, had married Agnes, the Lady Herries of Terregles in her own right, against the wishes of Châtelherault, who was her guardian and had intended her for his second son, Lord John Hamilton. As a result, Maxwell was not confirmed as Lord Herries initially. He sided with Lord James more out of religious conviction than personal loyalty, becoming closely associated with Maitland's subsequent transfer of allegiance to Mary, supporting her at Langside and defending her during the Conferences at York and Westminster.

---

* Although he was not knighted until 1590, he is referred to as Sir James Melville to avoid confusion with James Melville, the academic and Presbyterian minister (who appears in volume II).

References

1. Guy, p. 221
2. R Gore-Browne, *Lord Bothwell*, cited by Alison Weir in *Mary, Queen of Scots and the Murder of Lord Darnley*, p. 16

8

The Rising Influence of the Guises and its Effect on Scotland

Determined to match his father's chivalrous and territorial achievements, Henry II's objectives in France were dominated by military ambition. Two families, the Montmorencys and the Guises, vied for influence. The Montmorencys were the traditional Constables of France, the most senior rank in its military hierarchy. Anne (pronounced Anné) de Montmorency, Grand Master of the Household, had been Henry's guardian, helping to rebuild his confidence after he returned from being a child hostage in Spain. Yet his standing was tarnished by military failure and his imprisonment by the Spanish after St-Quentin.

The Guises' extraordinary rise to pre-eminence over the previous fifty years had arisen from military prowess, political skill and shrewd marriages. Their military reputation had caused them to be placed in charge of French efforts to free Scotland from English domination. This had been a factor in the choice of Marie of Guise as James V's wife. In November 1552, her brother, Francis, Duke of Guise, had defended Metz with 6,000 men backed by a federation of Protestant German principalities against Charles V's Spanish troops. He had shown inspired leadership, personally wielding a shovel beside his men to shore up the defences; 'he was not seen to waste a single hour.' The longer he held out, so the Spanish were decimated by disease and cold. His name was made, not just in a defence against impossible odds, but by his humane treatment of the sick and dying enemy.

Guise's brother, Charles, Cardinal of Lorraine, was the politician of the family. He attracted huge audiences as a preacher and became the most gifted diplomat and negotiator at the French court. Family loyalty, a virtue almost entirely absent within the Scottish nobility, as Mary was to learn to her cost, led the Cardinal proudly to describe his brother after the siege of Metz as 'the most valiant man in the whole of Christendom'. Yet the Guises' rapid success brought them enemies and the Cardinal was financially inept. When they claimed descent from Charlemagne, it was suggested that they were tilting at the French throne. They were branded as foreigners and were feared for their determined persecution of the Huguenots. Although the Cardinal was Mary's principal mentor, she managed to remain admirably tolerant in her religious outlook and grew to stand up to more confrontational Guise advice. She always remained on closer terms with Francis and the gentle Anne d'Este. Despite the Cardinal's pluralistic acquisition of rich benefices, Guise interests absorbed copious funds, and he was not above embezzling parts of Mary's French income, particularly after her imprisonment in England.

As their power grew, the Guises began to challenge the Constable's traditional role as guardian of the royal children, particularly after Mary's betrothal to the Dauphin. They curried favour with Diane de Poitiers to take advantage of her influence as royal mistress. The third Guise brother, Claude, later Duke of Aumale, married Diane's daughter, Louise de Brézé, in 1547. Yet Diane became nervous of their growing influence and turned to the Constable, hitherto her rival. After Guise's victories at Metz and Calais, she arranged for her granddaughter Antoinette de la Marck to marry the Constable's second son, Henry, Count of Damville. The Guises, in turn, befriended Catherine de Medici, remaining her allies until well after her husband's death. She mistrusted the Constable for having encouraged Henry to repudiate her before she conceived and secretly detested Diane as her rival for her husband's favours.

After Guise had held Metz, the Constable encouraged Henry II, in 1566, [1556] to come to a truce with Charles V at Vaucelles. Both sides needed a respite from war, and Charles was planning to divide his vast dominions between his son Philip II, who gained Spain, the Low Countries, Milan and Naples, and his brother, Ferdinand, who was elected Holy Roman Emperor. Philip had already forged an alliance with the English by marrying Mary Tudor. Yet peace did not suit the ambitious Guises, particularly as the Cardinal had just spent six months in Italy establishing a military alliance with the new Pope, Paul IV of the belligerent Carafa family, aimed at thwarting Philip and his allies. The Pope had already excommunicated Philip for refusing to grant the see of Naples to his nephew, Cardinal Carlo Carafa, causing Philip to retaliate by sending the Duke of Alva, his viceroy in Naples, to attack Rome. Ignoring the truce arranged by the Constable, Henry sent Guise to protect the Pope and take Naples. Yet Guise's Italian allies failed to agree objectives or provide financial support and he became bogged down.

Buoyed up with success in Italy, Philip II brought England into his war against France, using an Anglo-Spanish force to besiege St-Quentin. In March 1557, the Constable, commanding a French relief force, made a disastrous attack. He was captured with 600 French nobles, including four of his sons. When St-Quentin fell, the way seemed open for Philip to march on Paris, but, inexplicably, he hesitated. With the Constable held prisoner, Henry recalled Guise from Italy as Lieutenant-General to restore French honour. Catherine, who was starting to show considerable political acumen, raised 300,000 livres from the terrified Parisians. Guise was able to halt Philip's advance and progressively pushed back the Anglo-Spanish forces. On 1 January 1558, despite appalling weather, he led a masterful attack on Calais to oust the English after 220 years. Henry arrived to make a triumphant entry into the town with the bands playing 'When Israel came out of Egypt'. The Italian setback was forgotten and the Guises were made. With the Constable still imprisoned in Brussels, they dominated French government and, on 19 April 1558, were rewarded with the announcement that their niece's marriage to the Dauphin would take place imminently. Henry arranged a sumptuous ceremony to highlight their achievements, positioning them to promote Mary's accession to the English throne.

Up to then, it had been no foregone conclusion that Mary would marry the Dauphin, despite their betrothal. She was a pawn in the wider arena of European foreign policy. If she served French interests better in some other marital alliance, Henry II would consider it. The Constable had done all he could to divert the French King from agreeing to such an advantage for his Guise rivals, but he was now imprisoned. He recommended coming to peace with Spain, cemented by the Dauphin's marriage to Philip II's sister, with Elisabeth de Valois being married to Philip II's son Don Carlos. Yet this lacked Spanish support. In July 1556, prior to St-Quentin, the French ambassador in Brussels had warned the Spanish that if Princess Elizabeth of England married the Archduke Charles of Austria to re-enforce an Anglo-Spanish alliance, Henry would arrange for Mary to marry the thirty-year-old
† Edward Courtenay, 20th Earl of Devon, a great-grandson of Edward IV,* and Plantagenet pretender to the English throne. Despite Guise opposition, he was more acceptable to the Spanish as a consort for Mary than the Dauphin, as the means of promoting her claim to the English throne, in the expectation that Mary Tudor would die childless. Together they would gain French and papal support to take the throne ahead of the illegitimate Elizabeth. Yet Devon had already been considered as a husband for

---

* Edward IV's fifth daughter, Katherine, sister-in-law of Henry VII, married Sir William Courtenay, later 18th Earl of Devon. Edward was their grandson and last descendant. He was thus a second cousin of Elizabeth and James V. His Yorkist connections had been in continuous trouble for supporting plots against the Crown, and he had spent most of his life in the Tower.

† 12th Earl by most reckonings (from 1556)   88

Elizabeth in a Protestant coup to oust Mary Tudor. On that occasion, as will be seen, he showed a lack of charisma and failed to cover himself with glory. The whole bizarre plan came to nothing when Devon died a few months later, so that Mary's betrothal to the Dauphin could be reinstated. The Guises breathed again. Even at her wedding, her cousin Antoine de Bourbon, King of Navarre (nephew of Antoinette de Bourbon), whispered to the Venetian ambassador that he had not expected it to take place, and it might not have done, if the Constable had been in Paris.

On 24 April 1558, Mary married the hapless and stunted Dauphin, in a ceremony full of spectacle. The wedding took place at Notre Dame and Mary was 'arrayed in her regal trappings, so covered in jewels that the sun itself shone no more brightly, so beautiful, so charming withal as never woman was.'*[1] Guise took charge of arrangements, acting as Grand Master in the absence of the Constable, still held in Brussels. The grand procession was led by the Swiss Guard, followed by Guise himself, the hero of Calais, ahead of Eustace du Bellay, Bishop of Paris. Behind them were troupes of musicians dressed in yellow and red, and a hundred gentlemen of the King's household escorting the royal party, all gloriously attired. The diminutive puffy-faced Dauphin limped along ahead of his household accompanied by his younger brothers, Charles and Henry. He hated public occasions, and the crowds had come to view his spectacular bride, who towered over him. She was radiant in a sumptuous white dress, which of itself was daring. White was traditionally the colour of mourning in France, but she knew that it complemented her pale skin and auburn hair. It was encrusted with diamonds with a long train carried by two young maidens. Her initial 'M' was embroidered on it in rubies and emeralds. Around her neck she wore the

---

* There can be no doubt that Mary was considered outstandingly glamorous at this time. At five foot eleven inches, she was seven inches above the height at which women were generally described as tall, and was already close to her full height at her wedding. With flawless pale skin and a fine figure, she was always a sought-after subject for court poets and artists, and this is borne out by pictures of her in childhood and adolescence. All the written evidence is unfailingly favourable. Even Knox described her as 'pleasing' and recorded that the people of Edinburgh called out, 'Heaven bless that sweet face.'[2] Sir James Melville saw her as 'very lovesome', and the poets around the court saw her as 'a true goddess'.[3] The Venetian ambassador described her as a princess who was 'personally the most beautiful in Europe'.[4] Yet it was her voice, her complexion, height, her lissome figure with perfect breasts, her hands and her grace of movement that tended to be singled out for praise. While Mary was always an attractive personality, as she reached maturity, she became less classically beautiful and her nose was to lengthen, but there are no remaining portraits of her made in the period immediately following her return to Scotland, so there are no visual means of judging her in her prime. When imprisoned in England, there were a number of portraits, which do not exude the glamour one might expect, but by then she was older and suffering from rheumatism and other ailments, and her nose seems to have become the dominating feature of a face, which shows signs of her putting on weight. These later portraits, originally painted secretly as miniatures while Mary was detained at Sheffield, were much copied as objects of Catholic veneration. They did not deter her many suitors and admirers, or detract from her contemporary aura as a romantic heroine.

Great Harry, a jewelled pendant given to her by her father-in-law to be, the King. It consisted of a gold letter 'H' set with diamonds with three huge diamonds above and a ruby the size of a pigeon's egg as a pendant on a gold chain below. On her head was a gold crown studded with diamonds, pearls, rubies, sapphires and emeralds surrounding a huge flashing 'carbuncle' said to be worth more than 500,000 crowns. She wore the crown with her hair down to show off her luxuriant tresses. On the wedding morning, she wrote to her mother, 'All I can tell you is that I account myself one of the happiest women in the world.'[5] The Dauphin thoughtfully wrote to the Constable in Brussels, regretting his absence, not a concern that was shared by the Guises.

The wedding was conducted by Charles de Bourbon, Cardinal Archbishop of Rouen, on a stage at the doors of Notre Dame. Henry II provided the ring, and, after a sermon by the Bishop of Paris, the royal couple withdrew for the nuptial Mass. Guise was cheered when he cleared everyone from the stage so that the throng outside could see through the west doors into the nave. Gold and silver coins, which were thrown by heralds as largesse, caused a riot as they rained down like confetti on the tight-packed crowd. Those at the front were crushed and had to beg the heralds to stop to prevent a fatality.

Afterwards, the couple walked round the stage outside in front of the cheering crowd before processing to the Archbishop's palace for a banquet that included dancing. Mary removed her heavy crown, although it was held above her head by one of the King's gentlemen while she ate. This enabled her to show off her hair while dancing with the King to applause from the invited guests. It was expected that she would dance with the Dauphin, but Henry led her to take the floor with his daughter Elisabeth to avoid it being seen that she towered above her clumsy stunted husband. At five o'clock, they moved on for the state banquet at the Palais, attended by city dignitaries and foreign ambassadors. The King and Dauphin went on horseback, while Mary and Catherine took a gold litter. There were masques, revels and breath-taking entertainments lasting two hours. Mary again danced with Elisabeth, and then six mechanical ships covered in cloth of gold with silver-gauze sails rocked their way across painted canvas waves. Each was captained by a Prince of the Blood, including the King, and each stopped to collect a royal lady. The King chose Mary, and the Dauphin took his mother. Louis de Bourbon, Prince of Condé (a nephew of Antoinette de Bourbon) escorted Anne d'Este. Mary's cousin, the handsome young Duke of Lorraine, escorted the eleven-year-old Princess Claude, who was to become his wife in a second Guise–Valois marriage in February 1559. The entertainment contained allegories depicting the dynastic importance of the union, by which the Crown of France was now linked with that of Scotland and England to create an empire that would dominate Europe. This was not a concept that pleased any Scots or English present. The festivities lasted all night and continued the next day at the Louvre, followed by a three-day tournament at the Tournelles, the Paris home of the royal family. By the end, Mary might be forgiven for being 'ill-disposed'. In Scotland, the celebrations were much more muted with bonfires and processions. Mons Meg, the great cannon at Edinburgh Castle, was fired and the shot reached to Wardie Moor two miles away.

The Queen Regent had sent nine Commissioners from Scotland to negotiate the marriage terms and to attend the celebrations. These included Lord James, Cassillis and John Erskine of Dun, all Reformers, as she wanted all factions to be represented. They were enthusiastic, not least because marriage would keep Mary in France, leaving Scotland to be governed by a regency, always lucrative for those in power. Lord James advertised his Protestantism by being accompanied by John Spottiswood. Others, who attended, included Reid, Bishop of Orkney, Rothes, Fleming and Seton. The Queen Regent's position in Scotland was too precarious for her to leave, but she appointed her mother, Antoinette de Bourbon, as her proxy to sign the marriage contract, which was finalised on 19 April. Nine days before the ceremony in a low-key negotiation conducted by Diane de Poitiers, Mary publicly confirmed the French guarantee of Scottish independence as agreed by the Treaty of Haddington. After some discussion it was agreed that Francis would not become King of Scotland, but their eldest son would inherit both kingdoms. If there were only daughters, the eldest would inherit Scotland alone, as Salic laws prevented female succession in France. If Mary died without issue, Châtelherault was confirmed as next in line to the Scottish throne. Mary was not required to provide a dowry on marriage, and there was no request for Scottish lands to be provided to members of the French nobility. Yet she became the Duchess of Touraine and of Poitou in her own right.

French acceptance of these generous terms arose because there was a second secret deal approved eleven days earlier, during which Mary signed three documents witnessed by the Cardinal, which contradicted her public undertaking. The first confirmed that, in the event of her death without an heir, the King of France would inherit Scotland, and succeed to her claim to the English throne; the second undertook that he should receive the revenue of the Scottish Crown until 1,000,000 pieces of gold had been repaid, deemed to be the amount expended by France on Mary's education and to defend her realm; and the third confirmed that these undertakings could not be revoked by either Mary or the Scottish Parliament. This last document was also signed by Francis. The documents were written in flowery language, and it is possible that the fifteen-year-old Mary did not read or understand the importance of what her uncles were asking her to sign. She expected to reside in France, leaving Scotland reliant on the Auld Alliance for protection against the English. To her own very French eyes these secret arrangements might have seemed a sensible precaution for an absentee queen, even if they were unenforceable without ratification by the Scottish Parliament. She believed that Scotland would be 'favoured, fed and maintained like an infant, on the breasts of the most magnanimous King of France'.[6] Yet the documents have the smell of a Guise-inspired deception, and Mary can be criticised for a lack of acumen in signing them without showing them to the Scottish Commissioners, who were conveniently in France. Luckily they came to light only a century later and there was never an attempt to enforce their terms.

Ignoring the public undertakings, Henry II lost no time in demanding the Scottish Crown Matrimonial for his son. This would make Francis the Scottish King, if Mary should die childless. The Scottish Commissioners offended him by refusing to confirm this without it being ratified by the Scottish Parliament, and it was surmised that some of them opposed it. After leaving Paris to return to Scotland several of them fell ill and died. There was an immediate suggestion of poison. Reid, Bishop of Orkney and President of the Court of Session, died on 6 September, Cassillis on 18 November, Rothes on 28 November, and the young Fleming, who had returned to Paris in the hope of recovery, died there on 18 December, aged twenty-three. His widow, Barbara Hamilton, Mary's former lady-in-waiting, was left with an infant daughter. She never remarried. Lord James also fell ill, but soon recovered, while Seton was unaffected. The hint of the use of poison gave the Reformers a pretext to counter French ambitions to subsume Scotland under the French Crown. Yet a sinister cause is improbable, and they are more likely to have suffered from typhoid. Mary thought that they had caught the plague, which was then prevalent.

Cassillis had been accompanied to France by his young son, Gilbert, who now became the 4th Earl of Cassillis. He remained in France after his father's death, and on 10 February 1559 was appointed a Gentleman of the Bedchamber of Henry II (which hardly accords with a theory that his father was poisoned). Unlike his father, he was at this time a Catholic and, on 27 December 1559, was condemned in his absence by the General Assembly of the Kirk as 'an idolater and maintainer'. On his eventual return to Scotland, despite a wayward nature, he became Mary's close ally.

When the surviving Commissioners returned to Edinburgh, they reported the request for the Dauphin to be granted the Crown Matrimonial, and it must be seen as surprising that the Scottish Parliament initially agreed, despite having a growing numbers of Reformers among its members. Henceforth the royal couple would be known as the King-Dauphin and Queen-Dauphine in recognition of their status. The Queen Regent could see this as her crowning achievement, which hugely improved her standing in France. Yet she had not bargained on the vacillating stance of the Hamiltons, who had most to lose by being demoted as Mary's heirs. As soon as Francis's claim was approved, they sided with the Lords of the Congregation. The Crown Matrimonial was neither confirmed nor revoked. The Scots never accepted that they were subordinated to France, and the Crown was never sent there.

Back in France, the Guises encouraged the confident young Queen-Dauphine, supported by twenty-five ladies-in-waiting and ten maids-of-honour, to dominate royal decisions by acting as her stuttering and sickly husband's spokesman. In addition to his continuously running nose, eczema and dizzy spells, he seems to have been impotent,* and Mary had no sexual expectation, despite their genuine affection. They made an incongruous couple. Although he grew considerably after their marriage, she still towered over him. He was prone to temper tantrums and, frustrated by his physical shortcomings, dressed in ridiculously ostentatious attire. His principal pleasure was taking Mary on ever more active hunting expeditions. For the time being, Henry II was still king, dominated by Diane de Poitiers in alliance with the imprisoned Constable, who made every effort to temper Guise influence.

By the summer of 1558, with France financially bankrupt,† Henry II shared a European desire for peace. He was wary of the Guises' hawkish ambitions against Spain and England, and wanted the Constable released from Brussels. Mary was sufficiently adept to move with the tide. She wrote to her mother that the French court was 'hoping for a peace, but this is still so uncertain, that I shall say nothing to you about it except that they [the Guises] say the peace should not be arranged by prisoners like the Constable

---

* Francis II's testicles were deformed. Regnier de la Planche, a close confidant of Catherine de Medici, recorded that he had 'genital organs all constrained and blocked making him unable to perform'.[7] It is now believed that Francis's stunted growth can be explained by *primary hypopituitarism*, a defect in the growth of the pituitary gland. This would also have resulted in his testicles failing to develop normally, causing sterility. The only reason for assuming that some kind of sexual union was achieved is Mary's belief in the autumn of 1559 that she might have become pregnant, but this is more likely to have been a misunderstanding arising from her irregular menstrual cycle, from which she was known to have been suffering.
† It is estimated that the French debt, as a result of continuous war, amounted to 40 million livres. As the income of the Crown was estimated at only 5 million livres, it was almost entirely absorbed in paying interest.

and the Marischal Saint-André.'[8] The Guises feared that it would restore lands, which they had made their name in conquering.

On 17 November 1558, Mary Tudor died childless in London. With deliberate provocation, Mary went into mourning for the loss of the English cousin she had never met. With Elizabeth illegitimate in Catholic eyes, the Queen-Dauphine was by blood the rightful successor. Encouraged by the Cardinal, Henry II claimed the English Crown for his daughter-in-law, thereby uniting France and Scotland with England and Ireland. Her arms at the French court were quartered with those of England. This was quickly reported by the English ambassador in Paris, Sir Nicholas Throckmorton,[*] to Cecil in London, and it soured Mary's future relationship with Elizabeth. The Queen-Dauphine was now Henry's most valuable commodity. The poets of the Pléiade waxed lyrical in celebrating her accession to the triple crowns. Even if Elizabeth were legitimate, and Mary herself never claimed otherwise, Mary was dynastically next in line, and would spend the rest of her life trying to demonstrate it.

The English government harboured no doubts over Elizabeth's legitimacy. She had been the focus of every Protestant plot to overthrow the Catholic Mary Tudor during her reign. She had been educated for her future role as Queen. She was now twenty-five, nine years older than her cousin, headstrong, academically capable and politically adept. Her tutor Roger Ascham recorded:

> Her study of true religion and learning is most eager. Her mind has no womanly weakness, her perseverance is equal to that of a man, and her memory long keeps what it quickly picks up. She talks French and Italian as well as she does English, and has often talked to me readily and well in Latin, moderately in Greek.[9]

She was an able student of scripture, history and classical literature, and a virtuoso on the virginals. Although attractive and witty, she lacked Mary's exceptional stature (she was five foot four inches), pale complexion and star quality.

England's ready acceptance of Elizabeth as Queen was a great blow for Henry. When he sought to have her declared illegitimate, the widowed Philip II immediately opposed him. Despite Mary's Catholicism, Philip did not

---

[*] Throckmorton had been one of Elizabeth's staunchest supporters during the reign of Mary Tudor, and his position as ambassador was a perquisite for his loyalty. He understandably overlooked that Elizabeth had been crowned Queen of France at her own coronation, a throwback to England's former control of Calais.

want the Queen-Dauphine on the English throne with the prospect of France and England combining to control both sides of the Channel. In an effort to maintain his Channel link between the two parts of his vast empire, he proposed marriage to Elizabeth, and she shrewdly strung him along. He pressurised the Pope not to confirm her as illegitimate, putting paid to Guise claims on Mary's behalf.

Henry II could not afford a war. Like Spain and England, France needed a respite and was facing rapid inflation. When the Constable was freed in October 1558, Diane de Poitiers quickly engineered his return to influence. He advocated a conciliatory policy towards Spain, and persuaded Henry that the Guises' imperialistic ambitions were counterproductive. This led to the Treaty of Cateau-Cambrésis signed on 2–3 April 1559 between France, Spain and England. This confirmed a 'strategic retrenchment that made France less vulnerable'. France gave up its claims to Savoy and northern Italy, surrendering all its conquests over the last eighty years, but recovered St-Quentin and its surrounding area. It was to retain Calais for eight years, after which an indemnity was to be paid. On 21 April, Mary and Francis, as Queen and King of Scots, wrote to Elizabeth, endorsing the treaty and vowing peace and friendship. Elizabeth was hugely relieved that Mary no longer claimed the English throne. With 20,000 French troops still being garrisoned in Scotland, a real threat to English security was removed. The Constable negotiated the Treaty of Upsettlington to confirm peace between Scotland and England, formally confirming Elizabeth, Mary's 'good cousin and sister', as the rightful Queen of England. Mary and Francis ratified this in France on 28 May 1559 with Henry and Catherine as witnesses. The Cardinal showed his contempt by doubting whether France should treat with anyone from England save the Dauphin and his wife. He saw the treaties as a sell-out, but the Guises had lost authority and retired to Joinville. Catherine, who had stoutly supported the Italian campaign in alliance with the Guises, implored Henry not to agree to the terms, even leaving court for a period in disgust. She blamed Diane, and told her that while reading the chronicles of France she found 'that from time to time, at every period, the affairs of Kings have been governed by whores'. Yet even she knew that France needed a respite from war.

Mary was left to make the best of her position. She was no longer addressed as Queen of England and had lost the Cardinal as her mentor. It was very stressful and, as always, she became ill. On 18 June, she had to be given wine in church to prevent her from fainting. This was no isolated incident and she seemed fragile, often vomiting after meals. Sir John Mason reported to Cecil, 'The Queen of Scots is very sick, and men fear that she will not long continue. God take her to him as soon as may please him.'[10] Despite suggestions of consumption, she is likely to have been suffering from chlorosis, or 'the green sickness', anaemia brought about by irregularities in her menstrual cycle. When Throckmorton attended for an audience, she was 'very ill on it, very pale and green, and withal short breathed, and it is whispered among them that she cannot live long'.[11] Maybe the wish was father to the thought. The English were well aware of the continuing threat that she posed. As always, she soon recovered and showed reckless courage out hunting; if she were ill, there was no sign of it during the chase. In December 1559, she was swept off her horse by a bough. Although badly bruised, she was quickly up again in the saddle. There is no doubting her bravery.

After Elizabeth had politely turned down Philip II's marriage offer, the new Treaty of Cateau-Cambrésis confirmed that he would marry Elisabeth de Valois, aged fourteen. On 15 June, Alva arrived in Paris, and six days later the delicate Elisabeth was married to the King of Spain by proxy amid great pomp. Alva placed his naked foot in her bed and their toes touched. As he replaced his stocking the courtiers present applauded and the marriage was deemed complete. Elisabeth, who had not yet reached puberty, did not depart for Spain until the autumn. On 27 June, a marriage contract was also signed between Philip's ally, Duke Emanuel Philibert of Savoy, newly restored to his duchy under the terms of the Treaty of Cateau-Cambrésis, and Henry's 36-year-old sister Marguerite, who had been overlooked by James V in favour of her sister Madeleine more than twenty-two years earlier. Yet the wedding itself was postponed by a tragedy three days later.

The death of Mary Tudor was not the only royal demise disturbing the balance of European politics. On 30 June 1559, Henry II arranged a spectacular jousting tournament at the Palais de Tournelles to celebrate the marriages. This was to be attended by the bridal couples and their assembled guests. Henry had been suffering from vertigo and Catherine begged him not to take part after having a premonition of his fate.* After several runs at the list, he insisted on one more ride. His opponent was a Norman with Scottish blood, Gabriel de Lorges, Count of Montgommery, Captain of the Scottish Gens d'Armes, a man of courage and skill. He also tried to excuse

---

* Catherine had dreamed that the King would be struck down by a lance. His mode of death had also been predicted in 1555 by Nostradamus, a well-known seer, who was also to predict the assassination of the Duke of Guise. Such was the public outcry, that there were calls for Nostradamus to be burned at the stake. Yet Catherine held great store by his predictions.

himself, apparently fearing the worst, but Henry commanded him to obey his Sovereign. As they met:

> the King was struck on the gorget and the lance broke, but the visor was not strapped down and several splinters wounded the King above the right eye. He swayed from the force of the blow and the pain, dropping his horse's bridle, and the horse galloped off to be caught and held by the grooms. Helped from his horse, his armour taken off and a splinter of a good bigness was removed.

Rosewater and vinegar were administered to revive him, but he was borne off with his face covered. Surgeons removed further smaller splinters and purged him with rhubarb and chamomile. They took twelve ounces of blood, purged him again, applied ice packs and fed him barley gruel. With the family gathered in vigil round his bed, he wavered in and out of consciousness, moving 'neither hand nor foot, and had a very evil rest, whereof there were great lamentations'.[12] The mortified de Lorges begged that the King should have his head or hand cut off, but the King told him that he had 'carried himself like a brave knight and a valiant man-at-arms' and had done nothing requiring pardon. On 8 July, the King ordered that his sister's wedding to the Duke of Savoy should take place. They were married at midnight in a nearby church amid great despondency. Only Catherine, in floods of tears, attended from the royal family. The King lingered on during the next day, managing to bless the Dauphin, but, early on 10 July, suffered a massive stroke, dying in agony. The Dauphin fainted and was carried from the room, leaving the assembled company including Catherine to go down on their knees before Mary, the new Queen of France.

By the splintering of a lance, the Constable and Diane de Poitiers were out, and Guise and the Cardinal of Lorraine supported by Catherine were back in. They took Francis, Mary and his brothers to the Louvre. Within three days they were in complete ascendancy. The Guises used Mary's ability to dominate her husband's decisions, and Catherine had no choice but to work with them. The Cardinal evicted Montmorency from his suite of apartments and Guise took his place at dinner. Although he remained Constable, Montmorency had lost authority and handed over his seals of office as Grand Master. Guise supporters were now placed in key government roles.

At last Catherine could take revenge on Diane de Poitiers, who had not been permitted to visit the dying King, and she retired to Anet. Crown jewels given by Henry to his mistress were now requisitioned for Mary and were returned with a detailed inventory. Many of these had been seized by Diane from the Duchess of Étampes following the death of Francis I. She was also required to exchange the exquisite château of Chenonceau* in Touraine, a gift from Henry, for Catherine's château of Chaumont,† a rather less spectacular alternative. Diane vacated it, but was allowed to retain Anet, her first husband's home, rebuilt for her by Henry, along with vineyards and other estates all over France. Yet she lost the tax on church bells‡ that had been another perquisite of her place next to the doting King. Catherine instructed the young King to write to her. On 12 July 1559, the Venetian diplomat, Giovanni Michiel reported his letter as saying:

> The King has sent to inform Madame de Valentinois that, because of her evil influence with the King, his father, she merited a severe punishment; but that in his royal clemency, he did not wish to disquiet her further.

Diane died at Anet seven years later, a mistress without a king and without authority. Yet she remained personally friendly with Mary, who visited her there. The unfortunate de Lorges was not treated so leniently. Catherine considered him responsible for her husband's death, and he was removed as a Captain of the Scottish Gens d'Armes. He later became a prominent Huguenot, and she personally watched him being beheaded and quartered after he was found guilty of treason in 1574.

Lady Margaret Douglas took the opportunity of the King's death to send her thirteen-year-old son, Darnley, with his tutor, John Elder, to offer his condolences. He delivered a letter from Lennox, who again petitioned to be

---

* Chenonceau on the banks of the River Cher had been bought by Francis I in 1535. Diane had improved the setting by building an elegant bridge from the château across the river and laying out gardens to stamp her personality on the property. Catherine in turn built a two-tiered gallery over this bridge and adding a garden in the Italian style to provide the finishing touch.

† Diane visited Chaumont only once. Catherine had used it as a place to study the occult and to establish the future for her children. Her astrologer, Cosimo Ruggieri, had visited her there, producing a mirror in a darkened room. In turn, each of her eldest three sons appeared in the mirror. He told her that the number of times their faces appeared would correspond to the years they would reign. Francis appeared once, followed by Charles who circled the mirror fourteen times, and then Henry made fifteen turns. After that the Duke of Guise flashed across the mirror, followed by Henry of Bourbon, Prince of Navarre, who appeared twenty-two times. Diane found numerous symbols of witchcraft, including pentacles drawn on the floor, which she found spooky. She remained living at Anet.

‡ This had allowed Rabelais to comment, 'The King had hung the chimes of his kingdom on the neck of his mare.'

restored to his estates in Scotland. Yet again this was turned down,* but Mary gave Darnley 1,000 crowns and invited him to attend Francis II's coronation.

The Guises' sudden ascendency caused disquiet at court. Clouet, the court artist, who had sketched and painted most members of the Valois and Guise families, set to work on a large allegorical painting, titled *The Bath of Diana*. (There are at least three versions of this picture still in existence, one of which is shown on the dust jacket.) In Ovid's *Metamorphoses,* Diana the huntress was disturbed by the hunter Actaeon, as she bathed in a forest stream. He was immediately turned by her into a stag, only to be killed by his own hounds. Clouet used this as a political satire showing a naked Mary as Diana being dressed by her nymphs in royal crimson, with the stag representing Henry II lying dead behind her. One of the nymphs, depicted as Catherine de Medici, also nude, sits in tears. They are surrounded by the Guise brothers as satyrs praising Diana's actions. In the background is a Roman emperor, supposedly Henri II riding away. In other versions this mounted figure is depicted as Francis II paying no attention to what is going on. Clouet† is certainly critical of the Guises' sudden rise to power, but it is not known who commissioned the pictures. He took a considerable risk in showing Mary and her mother-in-law in the nude with the Guises as satyrs, and it can be certain that they did not sit for their portraits!

With the Guises again in control, they provided the support so desperately needed by the Queen Regent in Scotland against the Lords of the Congregation. On 3 August, they sent money for distribution as pensions. They reintroduced their plan to subsume Scotland under France. The great seal of Scotland was redesigned to show Francis and Mary seated in Imperial Majesty. Throckmorton was invited to eat dinner at court off plate emblazoned with their new arms quartered with those of England. He wrote increasingly concerned dispatches to Cecil. The young King and Queen each confirmed to him that they would act in accordance with her uncles' advice. The Guises were now taking key decisions without consultation and encouraged Francis and Mary to enjoy their hunting.

The Guises' imperialistic ambitions were not limited to Scotland. They

---

* Lady Margaret seems to have developed a close rapport with the Guises as a result of these efforts. In February 1560 she confided to the Bishop of Aquila that, should Mary die without children, Lennox and she would be placed on the Scottish throne by the French.

† A second portrait in the style of the School of Fontainebleau and possibly by Clouet of *A Woman at her Toilette* shown naked from the waist up has less certainly been argued to be of Mary. This is now in the Worcester Art Museum in Massachusetts, and though the lady shows a passing resemblance to Mary's contemporary portraits, she is painted with blue eyes when Mary's were brown, and there are no symbols within the picture, which would identify her, as there are in *The Bath of Diana* painting.

had acquired lands in Normandy with ports suitable as naval bases to threaten England. These could also challenge the principal route through the Channel linking the two parts of Philip II's empire. In October, with Cecil and the English government pressing Elizabeth to send military support for the Lords of the Congregation, the Guises sent their youngest brother, René, Marquis of Elbeuf, with a fleet from Normandy to support their sister in Scotland, only to have it scattered by storms in the North Sea. At the beginning of December four of their ships were wrecked on the Dutch coast with the loss of 2,000 men and only a handful reached their intended destination. France now lacked the money for a new offensive, refusing to sanction further belligerence, and the Guises faced a growing tide of antagonism. Elizabeth realised that any slights arose from 'the ambitious desire of the principal members of the house of Guise'[13] and did not latterly criticise Mary, whom she saw as their puppet.

On 18 September 1559, with the court still in mourning, the Dauphin was crowned King Francis II at Reims by its archbishop, the Cardinal of Lorraine. It took four nobles to support the Crown of Charlemagne over his puny head. As a queen regnant, Mary was not crowned, but appeared in white, the traditional colour of mourning in France, conveniently the colour that suited her best. Catherine chose black, the mourning colour of Italy, but insisted on Mary taking precedence. Francis was soon exhausted, starting to yawn at the banquet afterwards, seated in accordance with tradition at a table by himself. This brought the event to a hasty conclusion.

As the official age of majority for kings in France was fourteen, there was no initial call for a regency, but, with Francis lacking any aptitude for government, the Guises retained control. Immediately after her husband's death, Catherine was bound up with her daughter Elisabeth's departure for married life in Spain, accompanying her from Blois to Châtelherault, where they parted amid great anguish on 25 November 1559. Despite her distress, Catherine retained her regal poise in severe black mourning clothes. Mary was similarly distraught to lose her childhood companion, sending her with a touching letter to Philip 'from the person who loves her most in the world'.[14]

After years of cultivating Catherine's friendship and providing her with support, the Guises no doubt expected to dominate her. Yet the 'Italian shopkeeper's daughter'[15] had been biding her time and progressively gained political influence. She was happy to leave the Guises to struggle with the financial consequences of continuous war, but was soon a force to be reckoned with. On 15 August 1559, Francis granted his mother 'the most opulent settlement that had ever been made to a queen dowager'. This included an annual pension of 70,000 livres, the Duchy of Alençon and other estates. She also received half the payments due on the confirmation of offices, fiefs and privileges at the start of the new reign. Francis began every letter, 'This being the good pleasure of the Queen, my lady-mother, and I, also approving of every opinion that she holdeth, am content and command that . . .' Mary wrote to the Queen Regent in Scotland, 'I believe that if the King her son were not so obedient that he does nothing but what she desires, she would soon die, which would be the greatest misfortune that could happen to this country and to all of us.'[16] Despite hints of a rift* between Mary and Catherine, there was no sign of it while Francis lived, and they displayed fondness and mutual respect. Catherine handed over the crown jewels to Mary, adding pieces of her own and they ate, shared sermons and sewed together.

Under French law, Mary as Queen had no shared rights of sovereignty with her husband, but the Guises ensured that she was the dominant partner. They maintained her status with ladies-in-waiting and maids-of-honour drawn from the great families of France, and she was always seen in public with an impressive entourage, many of whom had served under Catherine and even under her predecessor, Eleanor of Austria. Most were at least middle-aged, but all were experienced. They were headed by Antoinette de Bourbon and three of Mary's Guise aunts by marriage, Anne d'Este, Louise de Brézé, wife of Aumale, and Louise de Rieux, Elbeuf's wife. Others included Madeleine of Savoy, wife of the Constable. After Francis II's death, most rejoined Catherine's service on her restoration as first lady. Other than the four Maries, only two accompanied Mary back to Scotland.

About a month after Henry's death, Mary started to believe that she was pregnant. Given the accepted view that Francis was sterile, it is hard to envisage that she genuinely thought this. If true it would have placed her in an unassailable position at court. As the mother of a Valois heir, she would be positioned to stand behind the throne in the event of her husband's early demise. She adopted loose-fitting clothing, and arranged for the court to be moved from Fontainebleau to cooler surroundings at St-Germain. Yet by September she realised this was a false alarm. Although the Guises must have been disappointed, they made light of it, pointing out that a sixteen-year-old king and his young bride had plenty of time to produce children.

Yet Catherine and the Guises had great concerns about Francis's well-being. They will have been well aware of his sexual shortcomings, with such

---

* The Cardinal of Santa Croce, the Papal Nuncio in France, claimed that Mary had referred to her as nothing but the daughter of a merchant. If she did make such an unwise remark, Catherine was sensible enough to ignore it.

matters being common knowledge within the inner circle close to the Crown. He was also increasingly unwell. His face had become blotchy and his continuing running nose and dizziness were caused by an abscess developing behind his ear. He progressively deteriorated for about a year before he died, and Catherine positioned herself in the event of having to face the worst. Already an adept political intriguer, she remained at Mary's side showing her maternal kindness, while almost imperceptibly weaning her from her uncles' influence. Progressively she used their warm relationship to loosen the Guise grip on power, eventually becoming the principal force in government, Regent in all but name. Yet she too faced criticism. Pamphlets were describing her as a whore with a leper* for a son.

Mary began to disagree with the Cardinal's interference in Scotland. He advocated crushing the Reformers with an inquisitorial policy involving burnings at the stake, as employed by 'Bloody' Mary Tudor in England. Many of those facing persecution visited Mary in France, so she learned the shortcomings of this policy at first hand. With the Reformist banner now standing for independence from France, it was no longer patriotic for Scots to back the Auld Alliance. Catherine was a great comfort to Mary during the early part of 1560 with the Scottish news so dire, and she attended Mary's interviews with Scottish visitors, astutely offering more conciliatory guidance to counter the belligerent Guise approach, so that Mary started to criticise them for sidelining her.

The Cardinal's intolerant religious approach was not limited to Scotland. He was equally hostile to growing Protestant unrest in France. Royal garrisons protected the young King and Queen by using heavy-handed policing against dissenters. He arrested a number of leading Protestants including Admiral Coligny, already disowned by his uncle, the ardently Catholic Constable, for changing religion. The Guises faced opposition from their first cousin Antoine de Bourbon, King of Navarre and senior Prince of the Blood, who sought the Regency to counter their 'illegal' government. He argued that the King was still a minor and had no right to choose his own advisers. The Guises would have none of it, responding that kings came of age at fourteen and the Regency did not necessarily go to the senior Prince of the Blood. Antoine was a lacklustre vacillating man with no aptitude for leadership. While Henry II was still alive, Catherine had seen him as 'reduced to the position of a chambermaid'. He was pushed into seeking the Regency by his ambitious younger brother, Condé, but had no personal ambition for it and, faced with a showdown, retired from court without pressing his claim.

---

* Francis II's blotchy face with eczema and acne was often mistakenly thought to be leprosy.

Condé continued to scheme, and, in early 1560, Protestant rebels, led by his adherent, the Seigneur de la Renaudie, tried to gain control of the King while the court visited Blois. The conspirators had met at the port of Hugues near Nantes, giving rise to their Huguenot name. After gaining wind of it, on 21 February the Guises moved the court to Amboise, before the attempt could be made. Catherine took on the role as conciliator and arranged an amnesty, which led to the Edict of Amboise. A few religious prisoners were freed, but a request for freedom of worship was not agreed. She ordered Condé back to court and neutralised him by appointing him as chief of the King's bodyguard. Yet La Renaudie deployed Huguenots in the woods around Amboise, although no attack took place and troops searching the area found them confused about objectives. Eventually, on 15 and 16 March, most of the ringleaders were rounded up. La Renaudie was discovered three days later and was killed by a shot from a hackbut. The rest were brought to the château, where Guise arranged a public execution, determined to send shockwaves throughout the kingdom. The ringleaders were brought into the courtyard singing psalms before being beheaded in front of the King with his brother Charles, aged ten, and Catherine. Condé sat impassively, unable to do more than comment on their bravery in death. The remainder were tortured and hung before the château windows, where their rotting bodies decorated the battlements. Mary was considered too delicate to be a witness, but Anne d'Este cried out at the inhumanity, fearing vengeance on her family.

Catherine approved the executions at Amboise because the conspirators' actions were treasonable, but she sympathised with criticisms of the Catholic Church and was well aware that the hostility was as much focused against the Guises' 'illegal' grip on power. She listened to associates with Protestant leanings such as her sister-in-law, Marguerite, Duchess of Savoy, and her new Humanist Chancellor, Michel de l'Hôpital, appointed in May 1560. They persuaded her that Guise bloodlettings were counterproductive, and she brought her long alliance with them to an end.

Guise supremacy also suffered from France's financial difficulties. The Cardinal had failed to find a solution to the financial crisis, which he inherited. The public debt amounted to 40 million livres, a legacy of war in Italy and north-east France. Half of this was due immediately, and to cut expenditure he reneged on interest due on government debt, froze pensions, and stopped the salaries of government officials. Soldiers being demobilised after returning from Italy became rebellious when left unpaid. Yet he settled Guise family perquisites promptly and sent military support to his sister in Scotland. As the Cardinal himself said, 'I know I am hated.'

The Guises needed Catholic alliances to combat Huguenot unrest. They combined with their fellow military leaders, the Constable and Saint-André, to form the 'Triumvirs' as bastions of French Catholicism, although they were not formally constituted until 7 April 1561. They approached Philip II and the Papacy to assist in a holy war against heresy, insinuating that Catherine was being too conciliatory. They could rely on Philip to protect the Catholic world as he did not want a Huguenot threat on his borders. Alliance with Spain also offered the Guises backing if Francis should die, and explains their early attempt to arrange for the widowed Mary to marry his son, Don Carlos.

Despite Catherine's growing influence, the Bourbons still claimed the Regency, and Huguenot unrest continued to threaten civil war. When the Grand Council met at Fontainebleau on 21 August 1560, Coligny again demanded freedom of worship, but the Guises rejected this out of hand. Catherine's more conciliatory approach gained backing from a majority of the Council. Yet unrest continued and, in the autumn of 1560, she moved with the King and Queen from Fontainebleau to St-Germain-en-Laye for greater protection and later, with a strong guard, to Orléans. Coligny immediately called for the King to be seen by his people and demanded a meeting of the Estates. This was arranged for 10 December and was to be followed in January by a Church synod, causing Pope Pius IV to fear that France could break with Rome. With the Guises still clinging on to power, the Bourbons refused to attend and met with Huguenot sympathisers* at Nérac to plan a military confrontation.

In November, Catherine invited Antoine de Bourbon and Condé to meet the King at Orléans, where Condé appealed to her to sever Guise control. Despite wanting to bring them to heel, she could not undermine the Guises completely, as they provided royal military protection; replacing them with the Bourbons would cause chaos. On his mother's advice, the King had Condé arrested for levying troops illegally. On 26 November, Condé was condemned to death.

---

* It was rumoured that even the Constable backed them, but this seems unlikely given his alliance with the Guises as one of the Triumvirs. He remained ardently Catholic and later publicly disowned his nephew, Coligny.

References

1. S Jebb, *De Vita et Rebus Gestis Sereuissima Principis Marie Scotorum Reginae*, p. 671, translated in Strickland, VII, p. 499, cited in Antonia Fraser, p. 628
2. Antonia Fraser, p. 87
3. Antonia Fraser, p. 87
4. CSP Venetian, cited in Antonia Fraser, p. 88
5. Mary to Marie of Guise, 24 April 1558, cited in D. Hay Fleming, *Mary Queen of Scots from her birth till her flight into England*, p. 492
6. Estienne Perlin, 1558, cited in Wormald, *Mary, Queen of Scots*, p. 24 and Antonia Fraser, p. 80
7. Louis Regnier de la Planche, *Estat de France sous François II*, p. 75
8. Mary's letter to her mother, cited in Antonia Fraser, p. 95
9. Guy, p. 94
10. Antonia Fraser, p. 94
11. Hay Fleming, p. 29, p. 213 note, cited in Antonia Fraser, p. 94
12. Antonia Fraser, p. 100
13. Antonia Fraser, p. 98
14. De Ruble, p. 181, cited in Antonia Fraser, p. 105
15. Cardinal de Santa Croce, Papal Nuncio, cited in H. Forneron, *Les Ducs de Guise et leur Epoque*, p. 290
16. Labanoff, I pp. 71–2

9

Cecil's Influence on Changing the Balance of Power in Scotland

During Mary Tudor's reign, Elizabeth had always been the focus for Protestant revolt, despite most publicly attending Mass. Now, while she established herself as Queen, she carefully left her religious persuasion unclear, fearful of the hostile intentions of Philip II and the Guise-dominated French government. She encouraged Philip's overtures for marriage to ensure that France and Spain did not join forces against her. She could not allow Scotland to become a bridgehead for invasion in the north, where the English gentry was still mainly Catholic, and did nothing to provoke foreign opposition. It was only after signing the peace of Cateau-Cambrésis that her Protestantism* became clear. This unified her government behind her, and she was never threatened by militant minority groups in the same way as France and Scotland.

During Edward VI's minority, Cecil had been one of the architects of the English Reformation and, as a Cambridge-educated academic, provided both political and liturgical advice to help Elizabeth to develop her policies. While Mary Tudor was Queen, he had worked undercover to support Protestantism, but when this was discovered, he too was forced to take Mass at his Wimbledon home. Yet, by April 1559, with Elizabeth securely on the throne, he steered the Act of Religious Settlement through Parliament to confirm England as Protestant and was formally appointed Secretary of State. He saw Protestantism as the key to an English alliance with the Lords of the Congregation to protect the security of England's northern border, and they saw his appointment as their cue to take up arms against the Queen Regent, already vilified as an imperialistic Guise agent. They would destroy the Auld Alliance by ousting her French garrisons. Cecil's masterstroke was to avoid English troops invading Scotland, but to offer the Lords financial

---

* Elizabeth was brought up as a Lutheran and disliked more stringent Calvinist dogma. By insisting on ritual and ceremony, the puritans believed that she had Catholic sympathies, but her approach probably kept Catholic dissent at bay.

support. Invasion would have alienated the Scots and started a European war. He dropped reference to English suzerainty so that the disastrous impact of the Rough Wooings was soon forgotten.

As a Catholic, Mary Stewart had no place in Cecil's plan. He saw Guise ambitions as openly hostile. They were anti-Protestant, anti-English and had promoted their niece as the English Queen by quartering her Scottish and French arms with those of England. He knew the justice of Mary's dynastic claim, but she was politically unacceptable and militarily threatening. Yet Elizabeth strongly espoused a dynastic rather than a political succession, central to the Tudor philosophy of the divine right of kingship, while Cecil believed that monarchy should be accountable to Parliament.

Cecil's difficulties were compounded by the legal complexities of the English succession, which had been exacerbated by Henry VIII's efforts to nominate his successors. Parliament had agreed to this under the Third Act of Succession of 1544 empowering him to confirm his heirs by his 'last will and testament signed with the King's own hand'.[1] When his will was prepared, he was too ill to sign it, and it was completed with a metal stamp of his signature inked in afterwards by a clerk, causing doubts whether he had been conscious during its preparation. This called its validity into question. It nominated his three children, Edward, Mary Tudor and Elizabeth. This of itself was contentious as Elizabeth had been declared illegitimate by Act of Parliament in 1536, when his marriage to her mother, Anne Boleyn, had been annulled prior to her execution. She was also illegitimate in Catholic eyes, as Catherine of Aragon was still rightfully Henry's wife at Elizabeth's birth.

If his own line failed, Henry decreed that the throne should pass to the descendants of his favoured Protestant younger sister Mary, who had married his great friend Charles Brandon, Duke of Suffolk. This overlooked those of his Catholic elder sister Margaret, despite her prior dynastic right. In order to bar Margaret's heirs, Henry had ordained that no one born outside England could inherit the Crown, although at the time of her marriage to James IV of Scotland no such impediment had been put in place. While this barred the Scottish-born Mary Stewart, it did not debar Margaret's daughter Lady Margaret Douglas, who was born in the north of England. Yet Lady Margaret was steadfastly Catholic, and, although she had been invited to court, Henry had declared her illegitimate to protect the claims of his daughters.

The only straightforward part of the succession was that Henry was succeeded by his son, Edward VI, backed by a caucus of staunchly Protestant and powerful families, including the Seymours, Dukes of Somerset, the Dudleys, Earls of Warwick and later Dukes of Northumberland, and the Greys, Marquesses of Dorset and later Dukes of Suffolk. These were backed both by Parliament and the up-and-coming Cecil. Henry Grey, Marquess of Dorset had married Henry VIII's niece, Frances Brandon, now first in line after his own children, under Henry's will. When it became clear that Edward VI was dying of consumption, the Protestant caucus was determined to thwart the Catholic Mary Tudor from succeeding him. They persuaded Edward to change his will to appoint as his successor, Jane Grey, Dorset's fifteen-year-old eldest daughter. Despite rumblings of disquiet, Privy Councillors and leading judges were pressured into approval, cutting out not only Mary Tudor but also Elizabeth, in addition to Margaret's descendants. A somewhat bemused Jane was hastily married to Lord Guildford Dudley, Northumberland's fourth son (and a brother of Lord Robert), and, on Edward's death, she was proclaimed Queen, in what seemed a perfect coup with a semblance of legality to it.

Yet Mary Tudor also had herself proclaimed Queen, rallying support for her cause in Catholic East Anglia and from elsewhere in the shires, forcing Northumberland to lead an army out of London to face her as she came south. Freed from his dominating influence, the Privy Council did a volte-face declaring their support for Mary, as the proper dynastic heir. Not unnaturally, Elizabeth also backed her sister, thoroughly piqued that she too had been overlooked. They marched into London together and, to great acclaim, Mary was pronounced Queen. Northumberland was arrested and executed for high treason, while Jane Grey and his son, her husband, were thrown into the Tower.

By late 1553, Mary had become engaged to Philip, heir to the Spanish throne. England was now threatened with a Spanish invasion to restore Catholicism. Mary and Philip faced huge opposition and Sir Thomas Wyatt from Kent led a plot to install Elizabeth in her place to be cemented by marriage to Edward Courtenay, 20th Earl of Devon, her second cousin. He was a nervous participator, having already spent fifteen years in the Tower, generally in solitary confinement. When questioned, he revealed all he knew, implicating Dorset, who had raised a force in the north to back Wyatt. Yet Dorset garnered little support as he travelled south and, on reaching Coventry at the end of January, the gates were locked against him. The game was up and he paid off his men, but was betrayed by his gamekeeper, and, on 10 February, was executed for treason. Although Wyatt's Kentish men continued to advance on London, without Dorset's support they were defeated with Wyatt going to the gallows. Neither Jane Grey nor her husband was involved, but they remained a threat, and Mary Tudor ordered their execution two days later. She needed to establish if Elizabeth was implicated, but Devon was not sufficiently involved to know. He was exiled to Hungary, from where, as already recounted, he was considered as a husband for Mary Queen of Scots. Elizabeth was lucky to survive. No one broke ranks to give evidence against her, although she was certainly aware of the plot, but had been sufficiently astute to avoid any incriminating evidence being retained.

Cecil saw Mary Tudor as fulfilling his worst nightmare. Her Catholicism had not stopped her being recognised as Queen. If Elizabeth's legitimacy were doubted, Mary Stewart, as a Catholic and a Guise, was next in line. From now on every policy that he adopted towards Scotland was designed either to bring her down or to make her amenable to amity with England and the Protestant faith. He retained every scrap of evidence that could be used against her in the future and built relationships with those in influence in Scotland, who would either encourage her to follow his objectives or, failing this, would destroy her. His two earliest recruits were Lord James Stewart and Maitland. They were well educated, astute, discreet and arguably the most able men in Scotland. They gained positions of influence with him that Angus and Lennox had enjoyed with Henry VIII, although, after their demise, Morton became his champion.

On 31 August 1559, shortly after Mary became Queen of France, Cecil wrote himself a note, which remained the basis of his policy towards her for the rest of her life. It was entitled 'A memorial of certain points meet for restoring the realm of Scotland to the ancient weal', by which he meant that Scotland should return to being an English suzerainty. If she remained an absentee ruler, a council of nobles should be appointed 'to govern the whole realm'. If she disagreed she should be deposed. He supported Knox in propounding armed resistance to 'tyrannous [i.e. Catholic] rulers'. On 23 March 1560, he had still not changed his tune. He wrote to Elizabeth through the Privy Council:

> We do all certainly think that the Queen of Scots and for her sake her husband and the House of Guise be in their hearts mortal enemies to your majesty's person ... their malice is bent against her person and they will never cease as long as she and the Scottish Queen lives.[2]

Unlike Elizabeth, Cecil never believed that Mary, while in France, was a mere puppet of Guise policy. He saw her as the instigator of Catholic efforts to depose Elizabeth and place her on the English throne.

The Queen Regent in Scotland was still trying to stamp out heresy with additional French military support. Although the Scottish nobility had been kept at bay with a liberal distribution of French pensions, these dried up after the Treaty of Cateau-Cambrésis, and the Reformers gained increasing support to topple her. Following Mary Tudor's death, they could now expect English support. It is the tragedy of the Queen Regent that she was forced by her brothers into a confrontational course, with which she disagreed. Despite her Catholicism, she wanted conciliation, which might have saved the Auld Alliance. Yet she was given no choice, and Maitland pushed the Lords of the Congregation into allying with England to combat her French garrisons, while Cecil encouraged Lord James and Argyll to protect England's northern border by taking control.

Lord James must have assumed that the English would provide him with military help. Yet Elizabeth did not believe that the legitimate succession in Scotland should be overridden by religious preconditions. She also feared having to face a war with the French so soon after signing the Treaty of Cateau-Cambrésis. This could threaten English independence, and she needed time to recover from the financial turmoil and military disasters left by Mary Tudor. Despite wanting Protestant government in Scotland, she had to avoid being seen to be anti-French by offering the Lords of the Congregation overt support. Cecil took an opposite view and threw his weight behind them. When financial support alone proved insufficient to defeat the Queen Regent, he wrote lengthy reports to fellow members of the English Privy Council to justify military action even if it meant supporting rebels to oust a legitimate government. He hoped that Elizabeth would recognise England's security as more important than protecting Mary as an anointed Tudor queen on her Scottish throne. The Queen Regent was militarily dangerous. She had French troops garrisoned all over Scotland and a smattering of support among the Scottish nobility. The powerful Catholics feared that Lord James, the eldest son of James V, even though illegitimate, was tilting at the Crown.

The Queen Regent grouped her forces at Dunbar. She denounced Lord James and Argyll as rebels and accused Lord James of seeking the Crown. He hotly denied it, promising her his support, if the Reformers were tolerated. He told her that their only objective was 'to maintain and defend the true preachers of God's word'. She fortified Leith where a French garrison was stationed, forcing the Lords of the Congregation to withdraw from Edinburgh in search of more support.

Encouraged by Huntly's apparent neutrality at Perth, Lord James tried to gain support from the waverers among the nobility. In September 1559, he called a conference of Reformist nobles at Stirling, where he was joined by Châtelherault and Arran. On 21 October at a Convention at the Tolbooth in

Edinburgh, Châtelherault signed documentation to suspend the Queen Regent, although she paid no attention to it. Yet, as heir to the throne, he had a right to replace her, and this gave the Lords of the Congregation a semblance of legality.

Meanwhile Lord James sought help from Elizabeth, who was beginning to fear that Spain would join with France to place Mary on the English throne. Yet she preferred to blur her decisions in a manner that exasperated her advisers, but did much to protect her in the early part of her reign. She refused to invade Scotland to back a rebel cause, but provided more financial backing, while hotly denying any involvement to the foreign ambassadors in London, 'at which she was expert to the point of genius'. Her powers of dissimulation were such that the ambassadors had to admit, 'She is the best hand at the game living.' Although 4,000 foot and 2,000 horse were quartered at Berwick, she would not send them across the border. Instead, she sent the young and able Admiral William Winter with English ships from Berwick to harry reinforcements and supplies arriving in the Forth from France, but with instructions to say that he was seeking out pirates without her authority, if caught. He survived the severe storm in the North Sea, which had scattered Elbeuf's invasion force. On 31 October, she used Cecil's agent, Thomas Randolph, to send £3,000* secretly to Lord James, but the Queen Regent had warning of it and sent Bothwell, who with John, 5ᵗʰ Lord Borthwick and Seton were the only lords still loyal to her, to ambush the courier. Bothwell took his prize to Crichton hotly pursued by Lord James and Arran with two hundred horse, one hundred foot and two pieces of artillery. On 9 November, after fleeing with his booty, he offered to fight Arran in a duel. Ever the coward, Arran refused, but Bothwell was now Lord James's implacable enemy.

By 21 October, Lord James had the backing of 15,000 men and re-entered Edinburgh. Yet the Castle Governor, John, 6ᵗʰ Lord Erskine, who had succeeded his father in 1552, was housing the Queen Regent, now suffering from dropsy, in the Castle and would not desert her. Although Ruthven presided over a meeting of the nobility to appoint a Council of twenty-four to replace her as Regent, she still took no notice. Yet her doctors were unhelpfully advising rest and a warmer climate. She was moved to Leith, now well-fortified and garrisoned with 3,000 French troops. Lord

---

* This money in support of the Lords of the Congregation was delivered by Randolph, using the assumed name of 'Barnabie'. He took bags of untraceable gold coin to Lord James's adherent Captain John Cockburn, Laird of Ormiston. Cockburn carried the first instalment of £1,000 across the border, but was waylaid by Bothwell in East Lothian.

James's occupation of Edinburgh had achieved nothing in military terms, and negotiations with her proved fruitless.

Despite the loss of Elbeuf's reinforcements, the Queen Regent used the French garrison in Leith to good effect. On 6 November, Lord James and Arran sent a force out from Edinburgh to protect a convoy of provisions stuck in the marshes between Holyrood and Restalrig. The French sallied out, pushing them back into Edinburgh at the Canongate with the loss of more than 1,000 men. It was only Kirkcaldy's timely intervention that prevented a worse outcome, when, with help from Lord Robert Stewart, he pursued the French back to Leith.

The Lords of the Congregation knew that they lacked the military skills and artillery to face the French without English support. Once more, they withdrew from Edinburgh to Stirling, but on condition that Parliament was called to meet on 10 January 1560. Randolph paid grudging tribute to the Queen Regent's 'craft and subtleties'[3] during this negotiation, and Throckmorton admired her 'queenly mind'.[4] He wrote to Cecil, for the love of God 'to provide that she were rid from hence, for she hath the heart of a man of war'. Ochiltree was sent to Glasgow for more support and to gain assurance of Châtelherault's and Huntly's backing, if she should fail to keep to the deadline.

At last, on 27 December 1559, Cecil persuaded the English Privy Council to intervene, after citing the unique opportunity to establish Scotland as a dependency. Two thousand more troops were sent to Berwick, and, on 23 January, Winter arrived in the Forth to cut French supply lines by blockading Leith. The Queen Regent demanded an explanation, refusing to believe that he was acting without authority. The Lords of the Congregation remained on the defensive until Elizabeth's troops were positioned. They took half their men to Fife, where they were joined by Ruthven, allaying concerns over his loyalty after a period as a mercenary in France. The remainder went to Glasgow to protect the west of Scotland. In a skirmish in Fife, one hundred French troops under Captain le Battu burned Kirkcaldy's home at Grange to the ground. The Master of Lindsay helped Kirkcaldy to surround them, killing fifty and capturing the remainder. Lindsay then killed le Battu in single combat.

Bothwell took command of the Queen Regent's Scottish and French troops and, on 24 November 1559, took Linlithgow and regained control of Edinburgh, which was undefended. He went on with 800 men to capture Stirling and advanced into Fife to attack Lord James and Arran at Cupar Muir. Buoyed up by a sermon on the field from Knox, the Lords of the Congregation, with an inferior force, kept the French at bay for twenty-one days, giving Winter the opportunity to capture two French men-of-war and vessels carrying military supplies. Some remaining barques were driven ashore to be destroyed by Lord James's men. Without provisions the French were forced back through Stirling to Leith. When Kirkcaldy tried to slow their retreat by destroying the bridge over the River Devon at Tullibody, they rebuilt it with roof timbers from the church. Although the Queen Regent encouraged James Macdonald, the strongest of the western chiefs, to bring her support with his 700 men, Argyll persuaded him to join the Lords outside Leith trying to prevent the French garrison from sallying out again.

At last, Maitland arranged a meeting at Berwick to negotiate a military alliance with the English. Lord James went with Ruthven, Sir John Maxwell, the Master of Lindsay and Maitland to agree terms with the young Thomas Howard, 4th Duke of Norfolk, who commanded the English troops. The English agreed to protect the Scots 'in their old freedoms and liberties' while Mary remained in France.[5] The Scots in turn proffered their help against the Irish. Mary's quartering of the English coat of arms with those of France and Scotland had persuaded Elizabeth to intervene. Mary angrily wrote to her mother promising undying love and more French troops, but the Guises were isolated and could not deliver them. Although she begged her to take care of her health, the Queen Regent was now dangerously ill. She wrote to d'Oysel:

> I am lame and have a leg that assuageth not from swelling. If any lay a finger upon it it goeth in as into butter.

On 2 April 1560, Norfolk's troops crossed into Scotland, joining Lord James and Glencairn with their forces at Prestonpans ready to advance on Edinburgh.

On 17 April, when the Queen Regent failed to call the promised Parliament, the Lords of the Congregation joined in a bond to expel the French. This had forty-nine signatories including seven earls, and a week later Châtelherault and Huntly reaffirmed their support, after Huntly was promised continued control of the north. Home and Ker of Cessford, both Catholic, signed a second bond three days later. Cessford was no doubt encouraged by his able younger brother, Mark Kerr, Commendator of Newbottle, now a Reformer.

Even now it was not plain sailing. Elizabeth's earlier prevarication had left Norfolk with inexperienced and underfunded troops. Although Boyd and Ochiltree joined them to attack Leith on 7 May, they were soundly rebuffed by the French garrison. A group of Scottish whores, determined not to lose their regular French clientele, caused considerable injury to the attackers by throwing burning coals on them from the Leith battlements. With Seton's help, Bothwell had earlier ambushed and captured the English commander. The French remained in control of Leith and, although Parliament met outside its walls three days later, the disappointed Commissioners could do no more than ratify the Treaty of Berwick, hoping that Elizabeth would send more men. Knox reported that Lord Robert Stewart was so distraught that he 'renounced papacy and openly professed Jesus Christ'.

By holding the port of Leith, the Queen Regent was still positioned to receive reinforcements and dispatched Bothwell to France for help, unaware that her brothers' hawkish policies had been rejected. Given their plight, he sailed to Denmark, hoping to transport 5,000 German mercenaries with Frederick II's fleet, while he went on to France over land. At forty-five, the Queen Regent was now terminally ill and died at Leith on 11 June, swollen and in great pain. Shortly beforehand, she wrote to Argyll regretting the hostilities and blaming Huntly, probably unjustifiably, for his poor advice. Such was their personal respect for her that Lord James, Argyll and Glencairn called a ceasefire to visit her on her deathbed. She asked them to believe that she wanted to protect Scotland as much as France, proposing, as a compromise, the removal of both French and English troops. Buchanan in his *History* recorded that 'she possessed an uncommon genius, and a mind strongly inclined to justice [but] was much under the influence of the Guise clan who marked out Scotland as the private property of their family.' Knox was less charitable when he claimed that 'her belly and loathsome legs [did] ... swell, and so continued till that God did execute his judgment upon her.'[6] She was one of that 'monstrous regiment', for whom the wearing of a Crown was 'as seemly a sight ... as to put a saddle upon the back of an unruly cow'. He showed none of the moderation which guided her in maintaining Scotland for her daughter. The Reformers even opposed the shipment of her body back to France in a lead-lined coffin, concerned at the prospect of a Catholic burial. It was only in July 1561, more than a year after her death, that she was at last laid to rest at her sister Renée's convent of St-Pierre-des-Dames in Reims.

News of the Queen Regent's death reached France on 18 June, but Mary was not told for ten days while negotiations over Scotland's future were hammered out. She then withdrew weeping to her rooms for a month, suffering another physical collapse. She adopted the *deuil blanc,* the mourning headdress that she would wear until she married Darnley five years later. Her mother's portrait remained a cherished possession and was among those found after her execution at Fotheringhay. Yet, after her mother's death, from the distance of France, she failed to assert her authority over Scotland, and the Guises could not help her. The Lords of the Congregation were left to govern unmolested, and sought closer ties with England.

Bothwell learned of the Queen Regent's demise while in Denmark and decided to lie low. He had been graciously received by the King and entered into a misalliance with Anna, daughter of a Norwegian nobleman, Christopher Throndssen, an admiral in the Danish navy. He seduced her with a promise of marriage, and she sold her jewellery to finance their travel to Flanders. Still short of funds, he set off alone for the French court, arriving there in September. He was well received after his support for the Queen Regent, but was described by Throckmorton, whom he met in Orléans, as 'a [vain]glorious rash and hazardous young man'.[7] Francis made him a Gentleman of the Bedchamber and Mary gave him 600 crowns to restore his finances. He later admitted that she 'rewarded me much more liberally and graciously than I deserved, which angered my enemies to the greatest degree'.[8] She respected his vitality and, before his return to Flanders, she appointed him as a Commissioner for her Estates. Anna* returned to Scotland with him on 17 November 1560, but he unceremoniously dumped her, despite her being pregnant. He now flitted between Scotland and France, never spending long enough in any one place for the Lords of the Congregation to catch up with him, but, as Lord High Admiral, he arrived in Calais to transport Mary's baggage on her return to Scotland.

Lacking reinforcements, the French were forced out of Scotland. Châtelherault was appointed Regent with Lord James as his Deputy. The French government instructed their ambassador, Charles, Sieur de Randan, to achieve peace before their Scottish costs brought 'the ruin and desolation of France'. The Guises swore revenge on Elizabeth for backing the Scottish rebels, but they were in no position to do so. With Mary in fear of losing her throne, they asked Philip II to mediate to defend Catholicism in Scotland. Yet it suited him to be pragmatic,† and his main interest was in retaining England as an ally. He did not want Mary, the Queen of France, also as Queen of England, threatening his means of communication through the Channel. Without consulting Mary, Spanish and French representatives

---

* Anna Throndssen reappeared in Scotland in 1563 to seek recompense from Bothwell, but he does not appear to have assisted her, although she was still alive in 1607. The Throndssen family claimed that she had married Bothwell, after they had offered a dowry of 40,000 silver dollars, but she never claimed to be the Countess of Bothwell and there is no record of the marriage. It has been suggested that his only known child, William, was Anna's son and certainly Bothwell's mother left her estate to him.

† Philip managed to prevent Elizabeth being excommunicated by the Pope for twelve years after her accession to the English throne.

began negotiating with Châtelherault and Lord James in Edinburgh and Cecil was sent by Elizabeth from London.

The Spanish saw the negotiations as a natural follow-on from the Treaty of Cateau-Cambrésis, while the Guises considered them a French sell-out. After a month's negotiation, the Treaty of Edinburgh was signed on 6 July 1560. Elizabeth was recognised as the rightful English Queen, and Mary's claims were dropped. All French and English troops were to leave Scotland, except for sixty French soldiers at Inchleith and Dunbar, with their other forts and garrisons being razed to the ground. Châtelherault and Lord James were reconfirmed as Governor and Deputy, heading a Council of twenty-four Scottish nobles to govern so long as Mary remained abroad. Catholic services were banned. It was even confirmed that Elizabeth's role had been that of an impartial umpire to create the conditions for a negotiated treaty, and not that of ally to the Lords of the Congregation. Always with an eye to personal benefit, Châtelherault saw to it that he was restored to his French estates, which in the meantime had been attainted. Finally, if Francis and Mary failed to ratify the terms, England could intervene to uphold the Presbyterian faith. Mary still had her throne, but at a price. It is hard to imagine how the negotiators expected Francis and Mary to endorse it. Yet the agreement cemented lasting friendship between Lord James and Cecil. On 1 August 1560, it was ratified by the Scottish Parliament. Maitland spoke as 'harangue maker', confirming the abolition of Papacy, and Knox agreed to prepare a new Confession of Faith based on Calvinist doctrine. Christmas and Easter festivities were banned as being Papist, although the pagan festival of Hogmanay was allowed to survive.

On returning to London, Cecil fully expected a reward both for the Scottish negotiators and for himself, but Lord Robert Dudley, his political opponent, had the Queen's ear. He received nothing, despite facing considerable personal expense, and his request for pensions for the key Scottish lords was turned down. Elizabeth claimed she had spent £247,000, more than a year's revenue, providing men and equipment to free the Scots from France and they had benefited enough. Cecil could only brood on Elizabeth's folly in favouring Dudley, whom he disliked intensely.

From the safety of France, Mary refused to ratify the Treaty of Edinburgh, which she had played no part in negotiating, and she failed to endorse the subsequent Reformation Parliament. Both would severely compromise her position on the Scottish throne. As a Catholic, she could not accept the banning of Papacy and had no intention of forgoing her claim to the English throne. On 9 August, Throckmorton visited her to gain approval. She was no longer relying on her Guise uncles to script her replies, but leaned on

Catherine de Medici. She spoke to Throckmorton in Scots, a possible indication that she knew Francis was dying and she faced the prospect of returning to Scotland. She responded:

> My subjects in Scotland do their duty in nothing, nor have they performed their part in one thing that belongeth to them. I am their Queen and so they call me, but they use me not so ... They must be taught to know their duties.[9]

When pressed to approve the treaty, she replied, 'What the King my husband resolves in this matter, I will conform myself unto, for his will is mine.' At least Francis would not take a decision without consulting her. She reminded Elizabeth's ambassador of her Tudor lineage, and went on: 'I pray her to judge me by herself, for I am sure she could ill bear the usage and disobedience of her subjects which she knows mine have shown to me.' She called for 'amity' with her 'sister Queen'.[10] This will have struck a chord with Elizabeth, and Throckmorton, so long scathing in his faint praise of her, was impressed. In a clear shot at Elizabeth, he reported:

> For my part, I see her behaviour to be such, and her wisdom and kingly modesty so great, in that she thinketh herself not too wise, but is content to be ruled by good counsel and wise men (which is a great virtue in a Prince or Princess, and which argueth a great judgment and wisdom in her).[11]

Mary promised Elizabeth a gift before the year-end of a new portrait of herself wearing the *deuil blanc*, to be reciprocated with a portrait of Elizabeth. Otherwise, Throckmorton came away empty-handed, and Mary's refusal to approve the treaty started a battle of wills that would last for the rest of her life.

The Scottish Parliament did not wait for royal approval of the Treaty of Edinburgh and met to dismantle the Scottish Catholic Church.* Presbyterianism became the standard religion, with the General Assembly as its highest court, empowered to criticise Catholics and Reformers alike. On instructions from Parliament, Knox arranged a committee of Reformers including John Spottiswood to draw up a Book of Discipline 'learnit in the

---

* The financial structure of the Catholic Church remained untouched. There was no suppression of the monasteries as in England, but they were left to decline through a lack of support, and the Catholic clergy and bishops continued to receive their stipends. Church funds were already controlled by the Crown, and no one wanted to upset the lucrative benefices enjoyed by members of the nobility. In 1562, it was at last agreed that two-thirds of the income should remain with them, with the balance being provided to finance the Court of Session and the Kirk.

mysteries of the new testament'. This provided a structure for lairds (landowners), the Kirk and the burghs to be represented in the General Assembly. Superintendents were appointed to act as presidents of assemblies, fulfilling the administrative role previously undertaken by bishops. Links were provided between national and local congregations, offering more immediate communication with outlying areas. Local congregations were to elect a committee, or 'session', to appoint their minister and a schoolteacher to offer a liberal range of subjects. This gained the backing of the burgesses of the towns and the people at large. Knox's most laudable objective was to establish a morally upright community with universal schooling for women as well as men, with secondary and university education for those who would benefit. The office of the diaconate was set up to provide healing for the sick and help for the poor. All this was to be financed by confiscating Catholic Church revenues. As most of these were received by lay members of the nobility, the financing received no support, despite universal praise for the concept. Even Erskine baulked at it, benefiting as he did as Commendator of Inchmahone, although Knox blamed his lack of enthusiasm on his Catholic wife, Annabella. The Book of Discipline also provided a Scottish Confession as a clear statement of faith, following Calvinist doctrine braced against a counter-Reformation. It opposed the Mass and considered ordination of clergy to be superstitious, but accepted the possible need to restore this after a decent interval. It carefully differentiated its nomenclature from Catholic worship, hence 'kirk' and 'congregation' not 'church' and 'parish'. All 'monuments of idolatry' were to be destroyed. This was carried out at Paisley, Fulford, Kilwinning and Crosraguel, but was more difficult to achieve in the Catholic north. It was only good sense that prevented civil strife.

Knox wanted to give the General Assembly power to challenge the secular authority of both Crown and government. To achieve this he tried to insist on the nobility signing the Book of Discipline as a key test of the Kirk's future authority. The issue was whether Scotland should be governed by the Crown supported by its political leaders, or by the General Assembly. Only the most extreme Reformers among the nobility were going to concede their personal political authority to the collective dictates of the Kirk. Argyll and Arran signed, and Lindsay of the Byres claimed that he would be the oldest to support it, when he signed with his son, Patrick,* on 17 January 1561, but

---

* Patrick, later 6th Lord Lindsay of the Byres, remained vehemently Reformist, but lacked his father's rugged charm. He was 'a raging, furious, rude, ignorant man, nothing different from a beast',[12] as Mary was to discover.

he lived only another three years. Glencairn, Ochiltree, Boyd, Rothes, Sir John Maxwell and William, 5th Lord Hay of Yester* signed ten days later. Yet most of the nobility avoided doing so and the Crown never ceded its authority.

After the July Parliament, Maitland, who had become its Speaker, set out to London on 11 October with Morton, Glencairn and Robert Melville as ambassadors to seek help in the event of a French invasion. To underline their desire for an English alliance they reopened the possibility of Elizabeth marrying Arran to replace Mary on the Scottish throne. Although both Morton and Maitland had become lukewarm about this, Arran wrote to Elizabeth on 18 July 1560. When Mary learned of the plan in France, she had to trust that her sister Queen would not countenance it. Being at the height of her romance with Dudley, Elizabeth made clear that she was 'indisposed to marry'. On 3 January 1561, the ambassadors returned to Edinburgh empty-handed. Arran was not too disappointed. He had become far more attracted by the prospect of marriage to Mary, following Francis's death on 5 December 1560. There was now a real prospect of Mary returning to Scotland, and the Scottish negotiators became extremely nervous of the treasonable nature of their proposals in England.

With Mary widowed, the stage was set for a power struggle between Lord James and Huntly. Lord James could expect backing from the Lords of the Congregation, while Huntly looked for Catholic support. It was difficult to judge Châtelherault, now apparently a Reformer, as he had changed sides once too often, but it was certain that Lennox would take the opposite stance. Bothwell was the joker in the pack. Despite being a confirmed Reformer, he had steadfastly supported the Queen Regent, and was looking for the main chance to promote his own position. Being strongly anti-English, Lord James considered him an enemy, particularly after his successful skirmishing on the Queen Regent's behalf. Yet he was no natural ally of Huntly.

References

1. Guy, p. 279
2. Guy, p. 116
3. Antonia Fraser, p. 115

* The signature of Hay of Yester is surprising. He was brought up in France as a Catholic, and returned to Scotland only after obtaining a passport to travel on 20 June 1559. He also signed the Treaty of Berwick on 14 February 1562, but was soon mistrusted as 'a great papist'. On Mary's return he supported her faithfully.

4. Sir James Melville of Hallhill, *Memoirs of His Own Life*, p. 51; CSP Foreign, II, p. 511; III, p. 73, cited in Antonia Fraser, p. 115

5. Antonia Fraser, p. 112

6. Knox, I, p. 319, p. 116, cited in Antonia Fraser, p. 114

7. CSP, Foreign, III, p. 409, cited in Guy, p. 220 and Antonia Fraser, p. 149

8. H. Cockburn and T. Maitland (eds), *Les Affaires du Conte de Boduel*, p. 7, cited in Guy, p. 222 and Antonia Fraser, p. 149

9. CSP, Foreign, III, p. 394, cited in Antonia Fraser, p. 117

10. Guy, p. 115–6

11. Antonia Fraser, p. 130

12. Adam Blackwood, *History of Mary Queen of Scots: A Fragment*, cited in Weir, p. 39

10

Negotiation with Mary in France

The death of Francis II on 5 December 1560 left the lingering hopes of the Guises in tatters. In mid-November, after hunting near Orléans, he had complained of his recurring dizziness and a buzzing in his ear. On the following Sunday, he collapsed in church and had a swelling 'the size of a large nut'[1] from an abscess behind his ear, causing stabbing pains in his head. When the doctors lanced it, puss was discharged through his mouth and nostrils, providing temporary relief, but he was gravely ill.

With Condé still imprisoned, Catherine summoned Antoine de Bourbon. In a masterstroke, she accused him of treacherously inciting rebellion. Fearing that he would be condemned like his brother, he protested his innocence, but, as a mark of good faith, offered to cede to her his claim to the Regency in return for her protection and agreement to release Condé. After he confirmed this in writing, she promised to appoint him Lieutenant-General of the Kingdom if Francis should die and persuaded the ailing King to affirm that he had personally authorised Condé's arrest, so that she could not be accused of it. Catherine thus assured herself the Regency, if the King did not survive.

By late November, the King was suffering seizures and was unable to move or speak. Mary and Catherine nursed him between them and sought divine aid by walking in procession with his brothers to nearby churches. The doctors bled him, purged him with enemas including rhubarb and considered boring through his <u>scull</u> to relieve the pressure. This was averted when the discharge appeared to stop, only to be followed by another substantial eruption of puss from his ear, nose and mouth, which made him delirious. On the morning of his death, he was completely debilitated and, after lying prostrate all day, died in the late evening. He had not reached his seventeenth birthday.

Throughout this tragic episode, Condé's fate hung in the balance. If the King lived, the Guises would ensure that he was executed. If he died, Francis's brother, the ten-year-old Charles, would become King, allowing Catherine as Regent to free him. Calvin wrote triumphantly to Sturm on

r. Not hitherto notable as an oarsman.

121

hearing the news, 'Did you ever read or hear of anything more timely than the death of the little King?'[2] The Huguenot cause seemed destined to take centre stage. Despite her acute grief, Catherine moved with consummate political speed. She recalled the crown jewels from Mary, not wanting them available to fund the Guises. She barred any access to the palace. She called a meeting of the Privy Council to proclaim Charles as King. She then claimed the Regency, gaining immediate support from the Bourbons. The Guises then met with Catherine in Antoine de Bourbon's presence for a discussion which she herself had scripted. They blamed any past errors on following the dictates of the dead King, which Catherine sagely confirmed. Everyone, in turn, professed their loyalty to her. She sweetened the bitter pill for the Guises by confirming that Mary would receive an annual dowry of 60,000 livres from her estates as Duchess of Touraine and Poitou. On 21 December, Catherine called a *conseil privé*, where at the age of forty-one she was proclaimed Governor. She was in effect more than Regent; she was the absolute monarch of France. Condé was freed. Bourbon became Lieutenant-General, but she would not confirm him as her deputy should she be ill, pointing out that 'the case you foresee will never arise'.

Mary was suddenly an expensive inconvenience. A count of her personal staff showed that, in addition to the four Maries, she employed 286 courtiers and servants. Only those close to her were now permitted in attendance and she left her royal apartments for the seclusion of a private chamber, undertaking forty days of mourning with windows blackened. She gained much sympathy. She had lost both her mother and husband within six months of each other, and her other close confidante, Elisabeth de Valois, had left in the previous year to become Queen of Spain. She had undoubtedly been fond of her husband, despite his physical shortcomings, and was no longer Queen. With the Guises diminished in authority, she needed allies. She was joined by her grandmother, Antoinette de Bourbon, and, despite her grief, had time to think. By the end of her seclusion, she was sufficiently in control of her emotions to attend a requiem Mass for her husband in the Greyfriars church in Orléans.

Catherine's patience had been rewarded, and she took up the government for Charles IX. Although none of her male offspring was in robust health, she had two other sons and was determined to protect their interests by acting as conciliator between Catholic and Huguenot, balancing power between the factions around the throne. The Constable was restored to his former status, but Guise continued in command of the army. She was determined not to drive his family into open hostility. Yet they retired to Joinville in April 1561 and about 700 of their adherents left court. She now relied heavily on L'Hôpital, her Humanist Chancellor, and he persuaded her that France was financially bankrupt and was in need of peace both at home and abroad.

Although Mary contemplated a return to Scotland, she faced a dilemma in religious matters, and it was not the Guise family's first choice for her. If she tried to return as a Catholic queen, flaunting her religion as the Papacy and European Catholics expected, she faced immediate conflict with the Lords of the Congregation, who were likely to retain support from the English. Although large parts of Scotland were still controlled by the powerful Catholic nobles, she would need significant additional military strength to achieve a counter-Reformation. This would require marriage to a powerful Catholic ally. This presented two problems. Firstly, there was a danger of Scotland becoming subsumed into her chosen spouse's homeland. Secondly, she was likely to live with her spouse outside Scotland. Yet, if she returned unmarried, accepting the religious status quo, as Lord James was to suggest, she could promote her dynastic claim to the English throne. It was her dynastic ambition that motivated her return.

Mary's Guise uncles had other ideas. They saw Mary's remarriage as the means of restoring their flagging influence, and suggested that she should marry the new king. According to Brantôme, the ten-year-old Charles gazed at her portrait with longing and expressed his desire to espouse his glamorous sister-in-law, with whom he had been brought up. This was quickly scotched by Catherine, who had no desire to see a return to Guise supremacy, and in any case marriage to a brother-in-law would require papal dispensation. In a flurry of diplomatic activity, the Guises approached Philip II, their secret ally as Triumvirs, to propose her marriage to Don Carlos, his son by the Infanta Mary of Portugal. The Infanta had died in childbirth, and Don Carlos had physical and mental shortcomings that might have seemed even more deterring than those of Francis II had they been more generally known. He was a hunchback with twisted shoulders and never weighed more than six stone. He was also a sadist, who roasted live rabbits and tortured horses to hear them scream. He became brain-damaged after fracturing his scull falling downstairs while chasing a servant girl whom he enjoyed flagellating. Although his life had been saved by a trepanning operation, he was left epileptic and remained homicidal. Yet all of this appears to have remained hidden from the diplomatic community.

On 10 January, Throckmorton reported that the Guises were making every effort to promote the Don Carlos marriage, and Philip played along with the negotiations. His envoy arrived at the French court at the end of January to hold lengthy meetings with Mary and her uncles. Although not officially aware of the discussions, Catherine opposed the plan and wrote to Elisabeth in Spain to be extremely wary of the objectives of 'le gentil-homme', their coded reference to Mary. She feared that Mary's marriage to the Spanish heir could threaten her daughter as Queen. Elisabeth played her part in discouraging her old confidante's suit. Elizabeth in England also wanted to prevent the potential heir to the English throne from forging another powerful Catholic alliance. Faced with the prospect of open hostility from both France and England, Philip pulled back. He also knew that the marriage would involve military intervention in Scotland, which he could ill-afford. He had no wish to upset the English so soon after brokering the Treaty of Edinburgh to destroy the Auld Alliance and he wanted to curb Guise imperialistic ambitions. Elisabeth de Valois reported to her mother that the negotiations had come to nothing. With a general desire for peace, Catherine proposed that Don Carlos should marry her daughter, Marguerite, then aged seven. Yet Philip had no enthusiasm for a second Valois connection, with Catherine showing such conciliation towards the Huguenots.

Negotiations did not stop there. The Guises approached Ferdinand I, the Holy Roman Emperor, to propose Mary's marriage to his third son, the Archduke Charles,* who was seen as a moderate. This offered an alternative link to Habsburg power. Although the Archduke controlled the Austrian Tyrol, Mary considered that he lacked the financial and military clout to assist her in Scotland. Furthermore he was already Elizabeth's suitor and Mary did not want her cast off.

The wily Lady Margaret Lennox passed on her condolences through her good-looking fourteen-year-old son, Darnley, who was still in France. She plied Mary with the advantages of a marriage which would combine their close claims to both the Scottish and English thrones. She even suggested that they should replace Elizabeth.† Yet Mary was still intent on marrying Don Carlos at this point, and knew that Elizabeth would see the Darnley marriage as hostile. She had no wish to be confrontational, and Lady Margaret's hope of Mary falling for her handsome young son fell flat.

Less controversially, Arran put forward his suit, but Mary gave this little

---

* Catherine de Medici was no more enthusiastic about Mary's marriage to Archduke Charles than to Don Carlos. She wrote to her ambassador in Austria, to discover what he could, so that she could plan how to oppose it.
† Elizabeth got wind of Lady Margaret's 'secret compassing of marriage betwixt the Scottish Queen and her son', and Lady Margaret had to use all her guile with flattering letters to redeem her mistrust. She denied any treasonable intent, claiming 'it was the greatest grief she ever had to perceive the little love the queen bears her'. Yet there was no concrete evidence and Elizabeth eventually rehabilitated them back to court, where she 'made much' of Darnley for his proficiency on the lute and kept him in daily attendance, presumably to ensure that the scheming was dropped.[3]

serious attention, in the main because of his strong Reformist conviction, but also because he was Elizabeth's cast-off. Perhaps she was aware of early signs of his insanity.* Whatever the reason, she formally turned down his proposal before returning to Scotland, making him a bit of a laughing stock for failing to gain either Elizabeth or Mary.

Throckmorton continued to admire Mary's determination to make a political marriage. This was so different from Elizabeth, still at the height of her romance with Dudley, whose wife, Amy Robsart, had died in suspicious circumstances. He reported:

> As far as I can learn, she more esteemeth the continuation of her honour and to marry one that may uphold her to be great than she passeth to please her fancy by taking one that is accompanied with such small benefit or alliance, as thereby her estimation and fame is not increased.[4]

One of those tasked by the Guises to promote Mary's marriage was Sir James Melville, already established as a diplomat at the French court. Having arrived in France aged fourteen in 1549 as Mary's page, he joined the retinue of John de Montluc, Bishop of Valence for three years, before service with the Constable, during which he was wounded at St-Quentin in 1557. In 1559, Henry II sent him to Scotland to establish whether Lord James was really seeking the Scottish Crown as the Queen Regent suggested. On his return, he withdrew to the court of the Elector Palatine, where he was tasked with commending the Elector's second son, Duke John Casimir, in marriage to Elizabeth. It was Melville who acted for the Guises in promoting Mary's marriage to the Archduke Charles, and he later proposed the marriage of Charles IX to the second daughter of Emperor Maximilian. None of his negotiations succeeded, but when Mary returned to Scotland, she needed his diplomatic experience and recalled him to become a Privy Councillor and Gentleman of the Bedchamber with a pension for life. On arrival on 5 May 1564, he was immediately involved in her marriage negotiations.

One by one, dynastic marriage negotiations came to nothing. Mary could remain comfortably in France as Queen Dowager and Duchess of Touraine in her own right, where she might make a noble if not a royal marriage, or she could seek to return as a widow to Scotland, from where the opportunity of the English throne might come her way. Her gambling streak plumped for

---

* Arran was beginning to demonstrate episodes of erratic behaviour during which he had absurd fantasies. He had left camp outside Leith in April 1560 because of mental illness.

the high-stake challenge of Scotland. She knew that to be accepted as Elizabeth's heir, the choice of her husband was crucial. When Cecil wrote to Randolph,* now English ambassador in Scotland, the third item in his memorandum was 'the menace of a foreign marriage by the Scottish Queen'.[5] He advised the Scottish Lords 'to persuade their sovereign to marry at home or else not to marry without some great surety', advocating deferment of any decision until her return. Candidates acceptable to Cecil included the kings of Denmark and Sweden and the dukes of Ferrara and Bavaria, but they offered little advantage to Guise family interests.

Mary went against her uncles' wishes by taking an early decision to return to Scotland. With her mourning over, she withdrew from court at Orléans and was escorted by Antoinette de Bourbon to Fontainebleau, where she reorganised her household to include those with recent Scottish experience. The most senior was d'Oysel, her mother's chief adviser, who was appointed a Knight-of-Honour. Yet he had recently married in Paris and did not wish to return to Scotland. He briefed her on the factions within the Scottish nobility and was her principal mentor before her return. He advised her to trust Lord James, despite his part in bringing down her mother, believing that only he could hold the Scottish nobility together, allowing her to return to her throne. She also appointed Jacques de la Brosse, who had mistakenly delivered the Queen Regent's supplies to Lennox, after Lennox had sided with the English. He was a long-standing Guise adherent, having been in de Brézé's entourage escorting Mary to France in 1548. She could rely on charisma to attract support on her arrival, but, to establish what was going on beforehand, she developed an intelligence network through her mother's former servants.

Elizabeth sent Francis Russell, 2nd Earl of Bedford, a close ally of Cecil, to deliver her condolences to Mary, and, in February 1561, Throckmorton accompanied him for an audience with her at Fontainebleau. She asked them to thank Elizabeth 'for her gentleness in comforting her woe when she had most need of it' and confirmed her desire to begin their relationship afresh.[6] D'Oysel escorted them back to their lodgings, but they returned a few days later on their true mission, which was to seek ratification of the Treaty of Edinburgh. If Bedford thought he could cajole her, he was mistaken. Mary balked, just as Elizabeth would have done. She claimed politely but firmly

---

* Randolph was a protégé and close confidant of Cecil, who had been educated in Paris, where he had met both Lord James and Knox, and had studied under George Buchanan, becoming a staunch Calvinist. As will be seen, his reports to Cecil as Scottish ambassador provide a fascinating insight into Mary and her court after she returned from France.

that she was 'without counsel', the Cardinal of Lorraine being absent, and the Scottish nobility not yet arrived. She made clear that she did not rely on her uncles in Scottish matters, 'being of the affairs of France',[7] but, if her Council were here, she would give such an answer as would satisfy him. When Throckmorton pressed her, she changed the subject, complaining of Elizabeth's failure to send her promised portrait as a symbol of their new beginning. She still hoped to avoid ratifying the treaty by fostering a warmer relationship. Despite Bedford making a second attempt on the following day, she continued to plead her youth and her need for advice from the Scottish Council. If she failed to listen to them, she could only expect them to treat her as badly as they had her mother. There was no answer to this, and the ambassadors left empty-handed, making Cecil all the more convinced that she was the prime mover in a Catholic conspiracy to usurp Elizabeth's throne.

In mid-March 1561, Mary left Fontainebleau with Antoinette de Bourbon for farewell visits to her Guise relations at their estates, but her uncles did not understand or approve of her plan to return to Scotland. Antoinette's reaction is not known, but they remained on good terms and continued to correspond through all Mary's tribulations until Antoinette's death in 1583. After calling at the Guise château of Nanteuil, she went to Reims for three weeks to see her aunt, the Abbess Renée, at the convent of St-Pierre-des-Dames, where her mother's body would soon be buried. Renée provided a shoulder to cry on, while she rebuilt her composure. Mary then set out for Nancy to visit the Duke of Lorraine and his new young wife, her sister-in-law, Princess Claude. The journey was interrupted by emissaries wanting to see her. Throckmorton sent agents on two occasions, still seeking ratification of the Treaty of Edinburgh, but without success. At Vitry-le-François in Champagne, she was met by the Scottish priest John Leslie,* who had travelled overland from the Netherlands. Lord James arrived at St-Dizier a few miles further on. Both had been sent to negotiate her return to Scotland and they met her separately.

John Leslie was acting for Huntly and other Catholic earls, including Cassillis, Caithness and David Lindsay, 10th Earl of Crawford, who formed a

---

* Born on 29 September 1527, Leslie was the illegitimate son of the Rector of Kingussie, Gavin Leslie, and was now aged thirty-three. As an exceptionally able child he was educated at King's College, Aberdeen, but, as a bastard, had required dispensation to enter the priesthood. In 1549, he had been sent to France, where he studied canon and civil law at the universities of Paris and Poitiers, only returning to Scotland in April 1554. He first came to attention as a Catholic priest in January 1561, when he debated with Knox in Edinburgh on the subject of the Mass. This resulted in his imprisonment in Edinburgh to ensure that he listened to Reformist preachers at the Kirk. Huntly was so impressed with his persuasiveness and fluency in French that he chose him to put forward his proposal to Mary.

strong and united group. Leslie promised Mary a warm reception if she would land at Aberdeen to be escorted by 20,000 troops on a wave of Catholic popularity to Edinburgh. Mary was too well aware of the military power of the Lords of the Congregation to fall for this romantic idea. She knew the broader political difficulties of attempting a Catholic revival and turned down the proposal out of hand. Even the Catholic John Stewart, 4th Earl of Atholl, failed to offer Huntly his backing on political grounds. Mary's only concession was to confirm the appointment of two Catholic bishops to vacant sees. Leslie tried to rekindle concerns about Lord James's personal ambition for the throne, but she had already decided to trust her half-brother.

Despite the failure of his mission, Leslie gained Mary's respect. She retained him in France to seek help for the Scottish Catholics from both the Pope and her uncle, the Cardinal. He accompanied her back to Scotland and, in 1562, became Professor of Canon Law at King's College, Aberdeen. On 19 January 1565, he also became an ordinary judge in the Court of Session, ultimately being appointed Bishop of Ross and the principal adviser to Mary in her captivity.

Lord James came as representative of the Regency and the Scottish Parliament. He was the dominant force in the Council, and had been sent to 'grope the young Queen's mind', well aware of the broader political implications of her return. Since negotiating the Treaty of Edinburgh, he had remained in contact with Cecil, who was closely monitoring events from an English viewpoint. Cecil had no rapport with the vacillating Châtelherault, but respected Lord James and Maitland, whose objectives for Scotland were similar to his own for England. Although Elizabeth was determined that Mary should ratify the Treaty of Edinburgh, thereby confirming Elizabeth as the rightful English Queen, Lord James's objective with Cecil was to establish a basis, acceptable to both the Scottish Parliament and the English, for Mary, as a Catholic, to return to her throne. So long as she aspired to the English throne, she would find alliance with France less appealing.

Despite their common interest in maintaining the Protestant status quo, Lord James, Maitland and Cecil each had slightly differing agendas. Lord James wanted to become Regent and political adviser for his young half-sister, thereby ousting Châtelherault. If she faltered as Queen, he would be positioned to promote himself, as the eldest illegitimate son of James V and leader of the Lords of the Congregation. Maitland, as Scotland's most able politician and diplomat, wanted to negotiate a Protestant marriage for Mary to underscore her dynastic claim to be heir to the English throne. Cecil supported Maitland in seeking an appropriate Protestant marriage. He wanted Presbyterianism maintained in Scotland and expected Mary to suborn her personal religious beliefs to those of her future husband. Yet he wanted her claim to the English throne to be taken on trust, until she demonstrated her Protestant affiliation. He would never accept a committed Catholic as English Queen, unless cloaked in a politically Protestant exterior. He could not discuss such sensitivities with Elizabeth, still hoping that she would solve his problem by marrying and having children of her own.

Yet for now Lord James, Maitland and Cecil shared a common goal. They needed to persuade Mary, a member of the militantly Catholic Guise family, that her return to Scotland as Queen was dependent on her accepting the religious status quo, with Lord James as head of her government. This was not the time to identify a suitable Protestant husband. Without admitting it publicly, both Philip II and Catherine de Medici secretly approved. The Spanish, French and English had lost the stomach for war and had developed an understanding that would last for the next fifteen years to keep Guise aspirations under control.

Given his leading part in bringing down the Queen Regent, Lord James's visit to France involved personal risk, and there was no great enthusiasm in Scotland for Mary to return. Randolph reported to Cecil that 'some care not though they never saw her face'. Lady Huntly consulted her 'familiars' (her private coven of witches), who convinced her that Mary would 'never set foot on Scottish ground'.[8] Lord James began his meeting with Mary by laying out the official terms offered by the Scottish Parliament and asked her to become a Reformer. She responded by offering him a cardinal's hat and rich benefices in France, if he would foreswear Presbyterianism. He then reverted to his more realistic plan developed with Maitland and Cecil, spending five days in building his rapport with her. If she accepted the religious status quo, he would arrange for her to receive the Catholic sacrament in private. This of itself was abhorrent to Knox and his ultra-Protestant supporters such as the Master of Lindsay. Yet, by limiting the threat of a counter-Reformation, Lord James was confident that he could win them over and he already saw Knox's ranting as politically unhelpful.

Heeding d'Oysel's advice to be guided by her half-brother, Mary pragmatically accepted the proposal. Lord James's dour gravitas made him a natural choice as adviser, both reliable and incorruptible; she mistrusted Châtelherault and Arran, particularly after the proposal for Arran to marry Elizabeth to usurp the Scottish throne. She envisaged Lord James as her *eminence grise* when she eventually came to govern on her own. It was only his close association with Cecil that prevented her, on d'Oysel's advice, from appointing him as Regent immediately. She was naive in failing to realise his

+ presumably Cecil's subventions did not count. 129

ambition for power. He promoted his hope for the wealthy Earldom of Moray, still attainted from Huntly, and asked for £20,000 in pensions to guarantee allegiance from his supporters. He now had to persuade the English to accept the basis he had negotiated for Mary's return, and gamble that Elizabeth would not see Mary's personal Catholicism as unacceptable for the heir to the English throne.

Lord James returned to Paris to gain Throckmorton's backing for his discussions, explaining the advantages for both Scotland and England. The fickle nature of the Scottish nobility made the plan dependent on English support. Throckmorton, who was trusted by Elizabeth, agreed to promote it, seeing him as 'one of the most virtuous noblemen'.[9] Elizabeth saw the advantage of allowing her cousin's return, despite holding Catholic services in private, but would not recognise her as her heir. She wanted the Treaty of Edinburgh ratified, while Mary wanted to reopen its decision to ban Catholicism with her ministers after returning to Scotland. Elizabeth knew only too well the danger of having the heir to the English throne with a faith different from her own after all the Protestant intrigue to oust the Catholic Mary Tudor. She did not need Mary turning the tables on her.

After her meeting with Lord James, Mary went on to Nancy for a Guise family gathering with hunting and banquets, despite developing a 'tertian ague' (a form of malaria where the fever recurs every third day). She had to go to Joinville to be nursed by her grandmother and could not attend Charles IX's Coronation in Reims on 15 May. Guise and his fellow Triumvirs were pressured into being there by the Pope, who feared growing Huguenot sway in France. The Cardinal of Lorraine, who officiated, warned that 'anyone who advised the King to change his religion would at the same time tear the crown from his head'. When it was placed there by his brother, Henry, Charles nearly collapsed under its weight.

On 10 June, Mary returned from Joinville to Paris, again breaking her journey at Reims. She stayed at the Louvre, where Throckmorton visited her eight days later, still demanding ratification of the Treaty of Edinburgh, while she reiterated her need to discuss it with her Council. He argued that these were the same lords who had negotiated it in the first place, but she believed they might take a different view if she were among them. She now planned an early return to Scotland, sending d'Oysel to London to obtain a passport for safe passage through the North Sea and shelter, if needed, at an English port. Piqued at Mary's obdurate refusal to ratify the treaty, Elizabeth refused this routine request. Mary imperiously criticised Throckmorton, although he had more sympathy for her than his headstrong mistress, and she received his backing to send her equerry Arthur Erskine of Blackgrange, Erskine's

† If accurate this speaks humbly for all the rest,

younger brother, with the Lord of St Colme* to London to make a final request for the safe conduct. Meanwhile she planned to travel without it. The row shocked Maitland in Scotland, who wanted the two queens 'as near friends, as they were tender cousins'.[10] With the melodrama of a tragic heroine, Mary told a highly embarrassed Throckmorton:

> I trust the wind will be so favourable as I hope I shall not need to come on the coast of England, and if I do, Monsieur l'Ambassadeur, the Queen your mistress shall have me in her hands to do her will with me and if she be so hard-hearted as to desire my end, she may then do her pleasure and make sacrifice of me, peradventure that casualty might be better for me than to live.[11]

With this she embraced him.

On 20 July, Mary joined a four-day fête in her honour at St-Germain, where Ronsard read verses extolling her beauty. She then set off for Calais with her uncles, aunts and a large retinue, arriving on 10 August. Although Elizabeth at last sent the passport, false reports of Mary's whereabouts had been issued to confuse the English and they could not find her. She thus went to sea without it.

As hereditary Lord High Admiral, Bothwell arrived at Calais with the Bishop of Orkney, also an experienced sailor. They joined the Catholic Hugh, 3rd Earl of Eglinton, who had arrived in France in February to await the Queen's return. The Eglintons were the traditional deputies as Admirals of Scotland, with a reputation for piracy after numerous skirmishes with English merchant ships. Together they took command of the Dutch merchantmen chartered for Mary's baggage.

Before leaving, Mary provided Anne d'Este with a magnificent collar set with seven cabochon rubies, four emeralds and four clusters of little diamonds and rubies. She gave Throckmorton's wife a magnificent washing set of silver gilt. At about midday on 14 August, they set sail with an impressive entourage, including three of her Guise uncles, Aumale, Elbeuf and the Grand Prior Francis, and the four Maries. Michel de Castelnau,† Sieur de Mauvissière, travelled as diplomatic escort. Even the Constable's son, Damville, went with them, as did Brantôme. These travelled in the main

---

* This was almost certainly James Stewart, soon to be created Lord Doune, then Commendator of St Colme.
† Castelnau was later to fulfil a prominent role as French ambassador in both Scotland and England. In his memoirs he described Mary as a 'naturalised Frenchwoman ... not just the most beautiful, but the most elegant of all her sex, both in speech and good manners'.[12]

galley, captained again by Villegagnon, with a second vessel for servants. There were a dozen baggage vessels, carrying quantities of gowns, furnishings, plate and a hundred horses and mules. As they left harbour, a fishing boat sank with the loss of all hands after colliding with one of her vessels. Despite this bad omen, Mary remained steadfast and faced the elements by sleeping on deck. Yet she broke down as she left the French coast, saying, 'Adieu France, adieu France, adieu donc ma chère France.'[13] It is perhaps disappointing that the more romantic words

> 'Adieu, plaisant pays de France!
>   O ma patrie,
>   La plus cherie!
> Qui a nourri ma jeune enfance.'[14]

have been discovered to be an eighteenth-century forgery!

References

1. Dr. Potiquet, *La Maladie et La Mort de Francois II*; in M. H. Armstrong-Davison, *The Casket Letters*, Appendix A
2. Forneron, p. 327, cited in Antonia Fraser, p. 124
3. Kim Schutte, *A Biography of Margaret Douglas, Countess of Lennox, 1515–1578*, pp.161–2; cited in Marshall, p. 114
4. CSP, Foreign, III, p. 423, cited in Fraser, p. 133, and Wormald, *Mary, Queen of Scots*, p. 106
5. Calendar of Manuscripts at Hatfield House, I, p. 258, cited in Antonia Fraser, p. 135
6. Guy, p. 124
7. CSP, Foreign, IV, p. 201, III, p. 565, cited in Antonia Fraser, p. 129, p. 136
8. Antonia Fraser, p. 224
9. Antonia Fraser, p. 142
10. Antonia Fraser, p. 146
11. Hay Fleming, p. 246; cited in Marshall, pp. 196–7
12. Guy, p. 132
13. Pierre Brantôme, 'Discours de la Reine de d'Escosse', from *The Lives of Gallant Ladies*; cited in Antonia Fraser, p. 151, and Guy, p. 133.
14. Meusnier de Querlon, *Anthologie Françoise* of 1765.

11

Establishing Mary's Status and Government on her Return to Scotland

On 19 August 1561, after only five days at sea, the two galleys carrying Mary and her entourage anchored off Leith in a thick Scottish haar (mist). Knox reported that 'scarce could any man espy onother the length of two pairs of boots'. They waited for it to clear before tying up to the wooden jetty. The baggage vessels were making their own more cumbersome way, well behind. There had been a scare when the galleys were intercepted by the English, who only confirmed Mary's safe passage and delivered a friendly message from Elizabeth. They had no plans to detain her and were without a fleet in the North Sea to do so. Yet they arrested Eglinton and his baggage ship – carrying her furniture and horses, including her fine State palfrey – in connection with an earlier suspected act of piracy. They were detained at Tynemouth for a month before being allowed on with her furniture. By then her horses had been moved to Edinburgh overland.

Being ahead of schedule at Leith, there was no official welcoming party, but Villegagnon fired his guns to announce Mary's arrival and a crowd soon gathered on the quay. She was given a meal at a nearby house, before riding with her party on borrowed horses through pouring rain to Holyrood. Brantôme considered the 'nags' a come-down from France, believing she had exchanged paradise for hell. As she approached Edinburgh, she was met by a mob on its knees, seeking a reprieve for a tailor, John Gillon,* whom they had rescued from the Tolbooth prison earlier in the day. She had no idea what to do. At last, Lord James, Argyll, Arran and Erskine arrived at Holyrood to greet her and Lord James advised her to grant Gillon a reprieve. By evening, the townspeople were celebrating with music and bonfires,

---

* A month previously Gillon had acted as Lord of Misrule in a festival, which gave him licence to be involved in petty pilfering for a day. It was soon out of hand with drinking and casual sex, and he was sentenced by Knox to death. He had expected to be let off with a whipping in accordance with custom, when most of the stolen goods were returned, but Knox remained adamant.

shouting the praises of their beautiful and merciful Queen. Even Knox
admitted that they were rejoicing, and 'honest musicians gave their saluta-
tions at her chamber window'.[1] The French were less impressed and, when
Mary wanted to go to bed, Brantôme complained that five or six hundred
'knaves of the town' played fiddles, rebecs (stringed instruments) and sang
psalms 'so badly and out of tune that nothing could be worse!'[2] According to
Knox, she showed absolute tact when she did 'will the same to be continued
some nights after'.[3] She thanked them in colloquial Scots,* having made a
point of speaking it with her entourage in France, even occasionally writing
in it. Yet French was her language for correspondence.

Mary had never visited Holyrood as a child, but her father had employed
French masons to rebuild it in the French style for Madeleine as the most
magnificent palace in Scotland. It echoed, in miniature, parts of Chambord,
and was positioned outside the walls of Edinburgh next to Holyrood Abbey
Church with a deer park beyond. It was approached over an iron drawbridge, but, although the windows of the State rooms were secured with iron
gratings, it remained unfortified. Mary's mother had occupied the royal
apartments while in Edinburgh, completing the private chapel, which was
linked to an anteroom with a heraldic ceiling, and laying out the parterre
gardens. Yet the Queen Regent's furniture was in store and Mary's had not
yet arrived.

It did not take Mary's French staff long to initiate the service she
expected, and they quickly grew to a complement of more than 170. Yet by
comparison to France the weather was inclement and, despite the existence
of a small bourgeoisie in the towns, there was a huge gulf between the
nobility in their castles or tower houses and the rural peasantry in their
bothies.

It was only on 31 August, a fortnight after their arrival, that the Provost of
Edinburgh welcomed Mary and her party with a civic banquet at the former
Edinburgh home of Cardinal Bethune. On the following day, Villegagnon set
off for France with those of the escort party, who had fulfilled their mission.
Everyone was overawed by her glamour, and she arranged a pageant to mark
her triumphal entry into Edinburgh. Arran persuaded his father not to
attend, sharing Presbyterian concerns at all the display. Knox dismissed it as
idolatrous with the words, 'Fain would fools have counterfeited France.'[4]

---

* Scots was a dialect of English. An educated Englishman could understand correspondence written in Scots,
but there were significant variations in both usage and spelling of words. Gaelic, the language of the Highlands,
was not spoken elsewhere, and Mary could not understand it.

Dressed in her finery, Mary made up for her tawdry appearance at Leith by processing on horseback with her leading nobles for a state banquet at the Castle, where the guns fired a salute. She stopped every few hundred yards for a presentation from the townsfolk. This followed the pattern of earlier festivities arranged by the Queen Regent and included people dressed as Turks and Moors, because the costumes happened to be available. Yet it had a strong Presbyterian bias, and Huntly intervened to stop the burning of an effigy of a priest taking Mass. In one tableau, a choir of children sang to a 'godly prince', an accepted euphemism for a Protestant one. A 'bonny bairn' descended from a mechanical cloud to present the keys of the city to Mary together with a Bible and psalter, symbols for her to adopt a Reformist religious policy. She discreetly passed them to the Catholic Arthur Erskine of Blackgrange, now Captain of the Guard. Well lubricated with wine flowing from one of the fountains, the crowd welcomed her and was certainly not put off by her Catholicism.

Mary relied on her charm to prevent religious conflict and, although Catholic services remained officially banned, she sought tolerance. She approved an Act of the Privy Council to prevent religious intervention against her Reformist government. Yet Knox kept anti-Catholic propaganda to the fore by preaching for two hours each Sunday as a prophet of doom against Papacy and, with Arran, Glencairn and Patrick, Master of Lindsay, opposed Mary taking Mass privately. This upset Lord James, who needed all his powers of persuasion, with support from Argyll, Morton, Lord Robert Stewart and Maitland, to honour his pledge to her. Even before Mary's return, the Master of Lindsay had shown 'more faithfulness than discretion' by trying to fulfil the General Assembly's request to destroy 'idolatrie and all monuments thereof'. On Mary's first Sunday in Scotland, he heckled her at Mass with her French guests and servants in the Chapel Royal. With a group of fellow extremists, he shouted out that the 'idolater priest should die the death'. The chaplain carrying the altar furniture and candles was 'trodden in the mire' and had to be rescued by Lord Robert Stewart.[5] He was so traumatised that he had difficulty in lifting the host for the Elevation. Lord James stood sentry at the door to provide protection, and Lindsay, who was married to Lord James's half-sister, Euphemia Douglas, held back from trying to disrupt the proceedings only out of devotion to his brother-in-law. To try to calm matters, Lord James invited Mary and Lindsay to stay with him at St Andrews, where she tried to work her charms on Lindsay while playing archery, making him 'enamoured with her at the butts'. Yet he remained discourteous and she came to despise his treatment of her. The ultra-Reformist Rothes (William Leslie) was another who needed to be won over. In September 1561, she went with her entourage to stay with him, but Randolph reported that the visit was marred when Rothes found that some of his plate had gone missing. Randolph implied that her royal party was sponging off the locality as it moved around.

The Catholic peers were equally strident in their attempts to defend their religious freedom and were determined on a crusade to restore Papacy. With his dominance in the north, Huntly infuriated Lord James by claiming he could 'set up Mass in three shires'. Despite lacking authority in the north, Lord James hoped to wean him away from attempting a counter-Reformation and Mary alienated the Catholics by backing Lord James and reconfirming that she sought Catholic services only for herself in private.

Seton was one Catholic who supported Mary and Lord James. After falling foul of Knox in Edinburgh, he had visited her in France, where he was rewarded with a generous pension for his loyalty to her mother. He confessed to Throckmorton that he had been evilly used at home, but intended to return 'to live and die a good scotchman'. Mary granted him a passport to travel home on 10 November 1560, and on her own arrival he was returned to favour.

Church revenues had started to be collected by James V as early as 1535, when the Pope granted him the formal right to nominate Catholic bishops (although, given the distance of Scotland from Rome, this had been in practical effect since 1487). With Catholicism banned, the Crown continued to control Church income without the need to follow England in making a formal break from Rome. Matters were left well alone. Like her father, Mary still had access to Church funds to benefit loyal supporters and supplement royal coffers. When the Kirk was established by the Act of Reformation of 1560, even Reformers among the nobility prevented Knox from establishing control of Church wealth, with so much of its income already being received by them. It was not until February 1562 that Mary bowed to Reformist pressure by providing one third of Church income for their impoverished clergy. Neither Archbishop Hamilton of St Andrews, who had granted significant benefices to members of the Hamilton clan, nor Archbishop Bethune of Glasgow, who in 1560 had moved to live in Paris, was by then in a position to oppose her.

Mary played her part with Lord James by refusing to disturb the religious status quo that she found on her return. Yet she was determined that no one should molest her guests or servants taking Mass with her in private. She handled this tactfully, while building respect and popularity. Melville reported that she behaved 'so princely, so honourably and so discreetly, that her reputation spread in all countries'.[6] Castelnau confirmed that the Scots were delighted with her. Although the Pope tried to persuade her to follow Mary Tudor in taking action against the heretics, this conflicted with her hope for recognition as Elizabeth's heir. When Nicholas Gouda, the Papal Nuncio, arrived with the Pope's letter in the summer of 1562, she made clear that she could not guarantee his safe conduct and advised him to stay indoors as much as possible unless he sought a violent death. She told him that it was 'impracticable' to send Scottish priests to the Council of Trent, but he was able to confirm the absolute strength of her personal faith.

Mary recognised that she needed to establish her prestige. The effectiveness of her government in Scotland much depended on her being recognised as heir to the English throne. This would make it treasonable for her subjects to appeal to England against her religious persuasion. Although she hoped to gain Elizabeth's favour by accommodating the Reformers, she encouraged Catholics among the nobility to join her privately at Mass. Arran objected that she was taking advantage of a concession granted only to her. He accused those attending of 'idolatry' and frightened off Home, when invited, from attendance. From the pulpit of St Giles', Knox declaimed that 'one Mass was more fearful to him than ten thousand armed enemies being landed in any part of the realm'. Mary had recognised his pivotal role in providing anti-Catholic propaganda even before returning from France and warned Throckmorton that he was the most dangerous man in her kingdom. This 47-year-old architect of the Scottish Reformation was now a profound irritant and had composed a prayer to be said after Grace with his family: 'Deliver us, O lord, from the bondage of idolatry. Preserve and keep us from the tyranny of strangers.' She summoned him to Holyrood, where he faced the eighteen-year-old Queen, believing that she threatened all that he had achieved. He was not about to pull any punches on grounds of her youth and sought only to present her in a malevolent light. She challenged his comments in *The First Blast of the Trumpet against the Monstrous Regiment of Women,* those 'weak, frail, impatient, feeble and foolish creatures'.[7] She objected to his incitement of armed revolt against an 'idolatrous ruler', especially a female ruler, which conflicted with the Tudor view of the divine right of monarchy. He admitted that his particular complaint was with Mary Tudor, who had repealed Protestant legislation in England, but Mary pointed out that his book referred to all women rulers. When she asked whether subjects should have the power to resist princes, Knox was clear that it was an act of 'obedience' to resist those who opposed the true faith 'until that they be brought to a more sober mind'. As a Tudor monarch, Mary was stunned at the inference that she was subject to her people. Knox magnanimously agreed to tolerate her for the time being, claiming backhandedly 'to be as well content to live under your grace as Paul was to live under Nero'.[8] Mary was left in tears of frustration. Yet he respected her conviction in her own faith, writing to Cecil:

> Her whole proceedings do declare that the Cardinal's lessons are so deeply printed in her heart that the substance and the quality are likely to perish together ... If there be not in her a proud mind, a crafty wit and an indurate heart against God and his truth, my judgment faileth me.[9]

This was not what Cecil was hoping to hear.

Knox sought another interview with Mary to persuade her to the true path of the Reformers. As soon as they met, she again attacked him for undermining her position by opposing women rulers. He conceded that he would not disallow her rule on the grounds of her femininity alone. Yet they came to at an impasse over religion and her absolute right to govern. Mary confirmed to him, 'Ye are not the Kirk that I will nurse. I will defend the Kirk of Rome, for, I think, it is the true Kirk of God.' Knox retorted, 'Conscience requireth knowledge, and I fear right knowledge ye have none.' She quickly replied, 'But I have both heard and read.'[10]

Maitland was embarrassed at Knox's outbursts. He wrote to Cecil that Mary 'doth declare a wisdom far exceeding her age'. He went on:

> The Queen my mistress behaves herself so gently in every behalf as reasonably we can require. If anything be amiss, the fault is rather with ourselves. You know the vehemency of Mr. Knox's spirit, which cannot be bridled, and yet doth sometimes utter such sentences as cannot easily be digested by a weak stomach. I would wish he would deal with her more gently, being a young princess unpersuaded.[11]

Yet Cecil was also corresponding with Knox and may well have encouraged him to test the strength of her faith. Maitland saw these showdowns as unhelpful, fearing that she might be provoked into a less conciliatory religious stance. In an effort to limit Knox's more controversial demands, he managed to withdraw the requirement for the nobility to sign the Book of Discipline. When, on 2 October, the Edinburgh Town Council issued a proclamation that placed Catholic priests in the category of prostitutes and whoremongers, Mary was able to have it suppressed and have the Council members deprived of their privileges.

In contrast, Mary's working relationship with Lord James started well, particularly as he was left to manage the government on her behalf. He installed able military leaders to settle petty feuding between local lairds in the Border region, creating an environment for peace with England. On 4 September 1561, Sir John Maxwell became Warden of the Western Marches, with its long-standing history of local bloodletting, and Ker of Cessford, one of the more powerful local magnates, became Warden of the Middle Marches.

Before arriving in Scotland, Mary had already agreed the make-up of her Privy Council with Lord James, although she may have had little choice in the matter. There were to be sixteen, representative of all factions, of which six would be in attendance at any time with full executive powers. Lord James took control to facilitate the transition from the former Council of twenty-four. This augured well for a period of settled government. He appointed Maitland and Morton as his two closest advisers. Maitland had already established a close bond with Cecil, after steering the legislation for the Scottish Reformation through Parliament. He stayed with him when in London, where they shared a love of Classical literature. Despite his rough manner, Morton was an outstanding administrator, notwithstanding a propensity for feathering his own nest. The Council had eight Reformist nobles, Lord James, Erskine as Lord Treasurer, Morton, Argyll, Châtelherault, Glencairn, Bothwell, and Marischal; and four Catholics, Huntly as Lord Chancellor, George Hay, 7th Earl of Erroll, Atholl, and William Graham, 2nd Earl of Montrose. The remaining four were the Officers of State, who had previously served under the Queen Regent: Maitland as Secretary, Robert Richardson as Treasurer, James MacGill of Rankeillor as Clerk-Register, and James Bellenden of Auchnoul as Justice-Clerk. In practice, William, Lord Keith took the place of his sickly father, Marischal. Despite having returned from Paris, Seton did not sit on the Council. He became Master of the Household, but Mary's efforts to restore him as Provost of Edinburgh met with resistance. Henry Sinclair, Bishop of Ross* became Lord President of the Court of Session.

Lord James and Maitland held sway in the Council, and the practice of having six nobles present soon lapsed. Mary attended meetings only rarely, spending her time cocooned in her apartments with a close circle of courtiers, such as the Setons, Livingstons, Flemings and Bethunes. Her failure to

---

* Henry Sinclair was the brother of Oliver Sinclair, who had led the Scottish army at Solway Moss. He appeared to be a neutral with regard to the Reformers, resulting in Knox describing him as 'ane perfect hypocrite, and conjoined enemy of Christ Jesus', despite him voting an absolution for Knox. He went to Paris for his health in early 1564, dying there a year later.

become involved in government is in marked contrast to her mother and to her son James, when he came of age. When the Council met, it was generally only the Reformers who attended. All the Officers of State backed Lord James and would continue to support him through most of the upheavals of the next six years. He treated Mary in a bluff, dominating manner, although Maitland was more obsequious. The lack of any opposition made them extremely powerful, particularly as statutes of the Privy Council had the force of Acts of Parliament. Parliament remained remote from government and its business was delegated to a committee, the Lords of Articles. When Parliament sat, its role was to sanction its committee's actions. Being chosen by those in power, the Lords of Articles were in effect the Privy Council's rubber stamp. The issue for Lord James was not in gaining approval for new legislation, but in implementing it. This had previously been the responsibility of the great magnates, fulfilling their hereditary roles, but the Queen Regent had appointed a new class of civil servants to execute government and to administer the courts, thus circumventing the nobility's despotism and corruption.

While Lord James and Maitland managed her government, Mary established her position at court, captivating those around her and showing all the surefootedness that she lacked in politics. In addition to her Scottish cronies, there were a number of her mother's former French officials such as Bartholomew de Villemore, her Comptroller, and Jean de Bussot, Seton's deputy as Master of the Household. None of these were involved in government, but they seemed suspiciously pro-French and Catholic, while the majority of the Council was pro-English and Reformist. Mary exuded charisma, and Buchanan reported, 'She was graced with surpassing loveliness of form, the vigour of maturing youth, and fine qualities of mind.'[12] Even Knox grudgingly admitted that she held 'some enchantment whereby men are bewitched'.[13] Yet by now her attraction lay in her elegance and charm rather than classic good looks. Enjoying the revenues of the Duchies of Touraine and Poitou as Queen Dowager of France and the inheritance from her mother's estates as Duchess of Longueville, she was financially secure. She indulged in an agreeably cultivated existence, sharing her most intimate thoughts with her servants, in absolute reliance on their discretion. She was always generous, often paying for their wedding dresses and marriage celebrations, which she made a point of attending.

Soon after her arrival, Mary visited Stirling, where she had been christened, staying for two days at her birthplace at Linlithgow on the way. Despite an alarm caused when an upset candle set her bed curtains alight as she slept, she had a nostalgic time at the place, which her mother had considered as her Scottish home. Despite planning to take Mass in the chapel there on the Sunday, this was barred by Lord James and Argyll, still trying to constrain criticism of her Catholic services, which were only permitted at Holyrood. Despite Lord James's efforts to placate the Reformers, they 'so disturbed the quire, that some, both priests and clerks, left their places with broken heads and bloody ears. It was a sport alone for those that were there to behold it.'[14]

Knox continued to rant about her 'devilish opinions', but holding services in private soon met with the approval of the majority of the nobility. Mary travelled on to Perth, making a triumphal entry to public acclaim. The townspeople presented her with a golden heart filled with more pieces of gold, but she faced a sermon condemning the errors of the Catholic Church. She found herself being heckled and the stress caused her to faint, so that she had to be carried indoors from her horse. Randolph described this as one of those 'sudden passions' to which she was 'prone after any great unkindness or grief of mind'.[15] She was soon well enough to continue to Dundee, from where she took the ferry back across the Tay to Fife. After a short visit to Falkland, she spent a week in St Andrews before returning to Holyrood.

By this time, Mary's transport ships had arrived with Bothwell, and her palaces could be bedecked in splendour, although she never indulged in rebuilding work. Ten cloths of state provided canopies over thrones with five more for use out of doors. More than 200 magnificent tapestries depicting Classical scenes were carefully unpacked to decorate the state rooms and royal apartments. There were twenty complete sets of between seven and twelve pieces, each of which would fill the walls of a room. Some moved with her to decorate her accommodation for the rest of her life, even going with her to Fotheringhay. Thirty-six Turkish carpets were rolled out on the floors. Forty-five beds were re-assembled, of which fifteen were trimmed with gold or silver lace or furnished with richly embroidered valances and bed curtains. Her throne was gilded and upholstered in crimson and cloth of gold. Low stools covered in velvet were set out for the four Maries, and eighty-one embroidered cushions were placed around the rooms. Buffets displayed gold and silver plate with glass and other ornaments. For banquets Mary had two white linen tablecloths forty feet long. These were rare luxuries.

Mary's household was supervised by her French chamberlain, Servais de Condé. Her nine ladies-in-waiting took precedence. These included the four Maries, promoted from their positions in France as maids-of-honour. Two others were Mary Seton's and Mary Bethune's mothers, the former Marie

Pyerres and Joanne de la Reyneville, who had been ladies-in-waiting to Mary's mother. Marie Pyerres was now Madame de Briante,* having returned to France to remarry Pierre de Clovis, Seigneur de Briante in 1554 following Seton's death in 1549. Briante also held a position in the household. The remaining three were aristocratic French ladies, who had arrived in Scotland with Mary: Guyonne de Péguillon, who came with her husband and son, the unmarried Isabelle Camp, Demoiselle de Cobron, and Suzanne Constant, Demoiselle de Fonterpuys. They may well have been on the hunt for aristocratic Scottish husbands, but returned to France unattached well before the murder of King Henry (Darnley). When ladies-in-waiting left Mary's service, new ones were appointed. One replacement was Mary Fleming's older sister, Margaret, Countess of Atholl, now in her early forties, and, judging from her remuneration of £500 per year, she became the senior of them. Another was Mary Erskine, Mar's daughter, who would marry the young Angus in 1573, but died two years later. A third was Jeanne Piédefer, Madame de Bettoncourt, from a long-standing family of French courtiers. She had also served the Queen Regent and had married the widowed Alexander, 5th Lord Livingston, thus becoming Mary Livingston's stepmother. On his death in 1553, she remarried Pierre de Joisel, Seigneur de Saint Rémy-en-Bouzemont and de Bettoncourt, later Master of the Queen Regent's Household. They appear to have gone back to France on the Queen Regent's death in 1560, but returned to serve her daughter.

Mary also had seven maids-of-honour with their new governess, Mademoiselle de la Souche, to replace Mesnil, who was by then about sixty and did not come from France. Two were Scottish, Mary Livingston's sister, Magdelene, and Mary Bethune's sister, Lucretia. In 1562, Magdelene† married Arthur Erskine, Mary's equerry, and was in high favour with Mary, who provided them with lands at Cromar in Aberdeenshire. Lucretia‡ was still in Mary's service at the time of Carberry Hill. Others were French, one being the much favoured Mademoiselle Rallay, who appears to have been promoted from chambermaid. Rallay seems to have gone back to France in about 1567, but returned to join Mary in her captivity in England with a

---

* She returned to France widowed for a second time in 1574 to take her brother to court over payment of her jointure. Mary asked Archbishop Bethune to do all he could to help her. She died in France in 1576.

† Magdalene remained in Mary's household until 1567, but had no children. When Arthur Erskine died in about 1570, she remained a widow for seven years before remarrying Sir James Scrymgeour. Mary was upset by this remarriage, deeming Scrymgeour to be to beneath her. She said, 'The marriage of Magdelene Livingston displeases me greatly,' and withheld providing a wedding present from England.

‡ Lucretia later married her father's second cousin David Bethune of Melgund, the Cardinal's illegitimate son. It does not seem that this was an ideal match as David had divorced his first wife and was more than twenty years her senior.

younger relation, Renée Rallay, known as 'Beauregard'. The elder Rallay was 'one of the principal consolations of my captivity', but she either retired or died in about 1585. Beauregard stayed on, and was still with Mary at Chartley.

There were fourteen ladies of the bedchamber when Mary returned from France, but staff came and went. One was Mary's dwarf, Nicole La Jardinière, 'la Folle' (the fool), who accompanied her everywhere. La Jardinière had her own governess, Jacqueline Critoflat, and they were still at Holyrood after Carberry Hill, only returning to France in 1570, when Lennox generously arranged a pension for them and paid for their travel. Margaret Carwood* entered Mary's household in 1564, becoming a favourite chamber woman. There were many others, often French, in addition to grooms, butlers, cooks, upholsterers, furriers and jewellers. Those with special roles included Margaret Asteane, the midwife, Margaret Tweedie, Mary's nurse, and Jane Colquhoun, who was a second fool dressed in royal livery, a red-and-yellow gown, hose and coat.

Being dressed as a widow in her *deuil blanc,* it might be assumed that Mary cut a less spectacular figure than in France. Yet white and black provided a dramatic foil for her pale complexion, golden eyes and light-auburn hair. The inventory of her extensive wardrobe shows that many of her dresses were white, explaining why she was known as *La Reine Blanche* well before leaving France. Unlike Elizabeth, who sometimes bedazzled like a peacock, Mary, with innate good taste, believed more simple clothing suited her best, but she never stinted on quality. Her underwear included silk doublets, and there were *brassières* of black and white silk. She wore silk stockings coloured gold and silver with garters adorned with fancy buttons to show off her legs when dancing. She had hats and caps of embroidered black velvet or taffeta often set off with white veils and embroidered handkerchiefs and scarves. There were numerous shoes in velvet, leather or buckram, and an ample supply of gloves. Outdoors she wore velvet, damask or Florentine serge. She also wore 'highland dress', donning loose woollen twill mantles, generally embroidered and reaching to the ground. Neither tartan, as we know it today,† nor kilts then existed. On grander occasions, she wore velvet cloaks

---

* Margaret and her sister Janet Carwood had become wards of John Fleming, illegitimate half-brother of Mary Fleming. Rather than find them suitable husbands, Fleming held them captive for several years at their deceased father's home, Carwood House, near Biggar, until in 1554 they were able to sue him in the Court of Session. Mary arranged the wedding of Margaret to John Stewart of Tullipowreis. This took place on 11 February 1567, the day after King Henry's murder.

† At this period tartan was used to refer to any multi-coloured material, often of velvet and sometimes used to make waistcoats and trews. The first plaid cloth did not start to appear until the late seventeenth century.

and mantles, some trimmed with ermine. Despite her *deuil blanc*, she understood the importance of cutting a dash at state functions with glittering gowns of cloth of gold or silver, and embroidery so rich that it was often passed from dress to dress and between times was stored with her jewellery.

Mary greatly prized her enormous jewellery collection valued at 491,000 Scots crowns. This was worn as adornments, provided as gifts or pledged (and even sold) to raise money. She suffered great heartache if pieces were stolen or seized by her enemies. On arrival in Scotland she redeemed a jewelled cross pawned by her mother and bought Scottish pearls from an Edinburgh merchant, no doubt to complement some white attire. Scottish pearls were recognised as the best in Europe, and Mary was famed for her fine collection. She was also particularly fond of rubies, which suited garments of crimson velvet.

Mary Seton was acknowledged as Mary's favoured hairdresser having learned her skills in France. Despite the luxuriant hair of Mary's youth, she often wore perukes (false hairpieces) as a fashion statement in a variety of colours. Yet as her hair thinned and became prematurely grey from age and imprisonment, these became necessities, and were among the first items sent from Lochleven on her arrival at Carlisle.

Mary imported courtly entertainments from France. She introduced equestrian masques, which included mock tournaments where participants, including court ladies in costume or wearing masks, 'ran at the ring'. Teams competed on Leith sands and other places. The object was to see who could score the most points spearing a ring suspended above posts in an agreed number of turns. To Knox's horror, Mary's pastimes also included music and dancing. He found this 'offensive in the sight of god'[16] and she again asked him to discuss his complaints. He agreed to tolerate her dancing, if she did not behave as a Philistine. Yet she was always artistic and expressive, and certainly not unseemly as he implied.

Mary's mood of exuberance was broken on 5 December 1561, the anniversary of Francis II's death, with a requiem Mass held in the Chapel Royal at Holyrood. This was a solemn and private occasion, when Mary lit a great candle trimmed with black. None of the lords attended and very few of her servants, as there were fears that the Reformers would interfere. Even the French ambassador, Paul de Foix, stayed away. The court returned to an atmosphere of 'joyousity for Christmas', with music, dancing and glittering hospitality. Overcoming his Calvinist scruples, Randolph reported, 'The ladies be merry, leaping and dancing, lusty and fair ... My pen staggereth, my hand faileth farther to write ... I never found myself so happy, nor never so well treated.'[17] He had taken a shine to Mary Bethune, which perhaps accounted for his euphoria. Knox still saw dancing as an invention of the devil, complaining that when 'her French fillocks, fiddlers and others of that band got to the house alone, there might be seen skipping not very comely for honest women'.[18] Yet his was a lone voice and Mary was becoming much loved.

Knox's vitriol was not just aimed at Mary personally. He jumped on any scandal affecting those around her. He heard that a French serving lady had 'played the whore' with Mary's apothecary, becoming pregnant. On the child's birth, the couple sought to do away with it 'not far from the Queen's own lap'. He reported that they were condemned to be hanged, but did not say that it was Mary, with her abhorrence of immorality, who had insisted on it. The four Maries were also fair game for Knox's tongue, as he searched vainly for a scandal with which to tarnish the Queen. He referred to a ballad going round the court casting doubt on their morals, the wording of which he must 'for modesty sake omit'. (Sadly no verifiable version of it is known.) Yet their behaviour seems to have been faultless,* and Randolph was captivated by them. When they rode with Mary to Parliament in 1563, he wrote:

Virgins, maids, Maries, demoiselles of honour,
Or the Queen's mignons, call them what you please, your Honour.[19]

When Mary Livingston became engaged to the Catholic John Sempill, with whom she particularly enjoyed dancing, Knox implied that her marriage to 'The Dancer' was hastened by 'shame'.[20] Yet despite Mary's initial misgivings that John Sempill was beneath Livingston's social status, they married to universal approval at a long-planned ceremony, and their first child was not born until at least a year later. Livingston remained in favour, retaining responsibility for Mary's jewellery. Progressively, people ignored Knox's ranting. The Council formally confirmed Mary's right to hold Mass with her household in private, but drew the line at it being sung. Knox complained that they were seduced from extremism by the gentle and civilising influence of the court. Scandals, such as they were, fell on him. In 1563, at the age of forty-nine, he married Ochiltree's daughter, the seventeen-year-old Margaret Stewart, seriously damaging his credibility.

---

* Although it is known that Mary Bethune was admired by Randolph, there is no suggestion of an illicit affair between them. Randolph was seventeen years older than her, and any suit that he may have played appears to have fallen on deaf ears. Mary Fleming conducted a two-year flirtatious courtship before agreeing to marry Maitland, having him twisted round her little finger by all accounts. Their children were born at a decent interval after their marriage, and there is no suggestion of any improper liaison beforehand. Mary Seton remained committed to her vow of chastity given in France, and was indisputably without taint. She never married, despite proposals later in life, devoting her best years to her mistress.

Dancing at court required music, with minstrels and musicians being retained as lute and viol players. Mary herself sang well and accompanied herself on the lute, seeing it as a means of showing off her elegant long fingers. Although she played the virginals, her performances did not bear comparison to those of Elizabeth, and praise was more muted. She enjoyed pipers and retained a shaum (an early form of oboe) player. Her domestic staff sang part songs and played instruments. When short of a bass singer among her *valets de chambre*, they were joined by David Riccio, a young Piedmontese of good but impoverished family, who also played the lute. He was visiting Edinburgh in the suite of the Duke of Savoy's ambassador, Robertino Solaro, Count Moretta, and left his post to enter Mary's service. During Mass at Easter in 1565, Randolph complained that 'she wanted now neither trumpets, drum, nor fife, bagpipe or tabor'.[21]

Mary also took an interest in literature. She set aside time to read in Latin with the scholarly Buchanan, who was captivated by her, and she even took instruction from him in Calvinist doctrine. They studied Livy's *History of Rome* for an hour or so each afternoon. Yet she had never been an avid Classical student in France, and preferred their mutual enjoyment of French vernacular poetry, which he had some reputation for writing. He prepared theatrical entertainments, some performed by puppets, and wrote a series of masques normally with a Classical theme. The scripts were often in French verse full of classical metaphor. Performances were often followed by music and dancing. The first was staged at the banquet to honour Mary's departing Guise uncles, when she and the Maries with senior nobles played the main parts, although thereafter roles were played by her staff or professional actors. Buchanan wrote verses to honour Mary Fleming, who was chosen as 'Queen of the Bean' on Twelfth Night in 1564 after finding a hidden bean in her slice of a specially baked Twelfth Cake. She was now queen for a day wearing a crown and seated in state on the throne. As Queen Flaminia, she was draped in cloth of silver covered with jewellery.[22] Randolph reported that 'the fair Fleming' was chosen by Fortune to be a queen. He compared her to 'Venus in Beauty, Minerva in wit and Juno in worldly wealth'.[23] On Valentine's Day, it was Mary Bethune who was singled out for Buchanan's praise in *Valentiniana*, a masque created in her honour. Another poet was Alexander Scott, who composed '*A New Year gift to Mary when she come first home. 1562.*' This included the words:

Let all thy realm be now in readiness
With costly clothing to decoir thy Court.[24]

Even the puritanical Scots were joining in on the glamour.

Despite enjoying the trappings of royalty, Mary loved playing pranks. She would walk through the streets with the four Maries wearing male clothing. Her height of course helped her disguise. She even joined her Maries in wearing men's clothing at a dinner for the French ambassador. In St Andrews they dressed as burgesses' wives, keeping house and doing their own shopping. In Stirling, they went through the streets in disguise begging for money, noting who was prepared to give and who refused. Mary tried this again with Darnley in Edinburgh, three weeks before their marriage.

When travelling on state occasions, Mary had a litter slung between mules covered in velvet, trimmed with gold and silk, and a luxurious coach drawn by horses. This looked like a four-poster bed on wheels and was the first of its kind in Scotland. Mary enjoyed being outdoors and was never happy unless she had plenty of fresh air and exercise. As an expert horsewoman, she would ride out alone for up to three hours at a time and travelled on horseback to new destinations. She went hunting and hawking as she had in France, sharing her interests with Darnley and Lennox. She went regularly to Falkland, rebuilt by her father in 1531 as a hunting lodge, and visited other lodges with their deer parks and forests. Hunting deer involved beating in as on a present-day pheasant shoot to push the herd towards the participants, who laid chase with barking dogs, often Irish wolfhounds, accompanied by men with arrows, javelins and clubs. To ensure ample sport, deer were imported by litter beforehand and wild boar had to be brought from France. The protection of royal deer required stringent anti-poaching laws, and they were rounded up to be moved on again after each hunt. Mary stayed for hunting parties with both Argyll, her brother-in-law, and Atholl, who had married, as his second wife, her senior lady-in-waiting, Margaret Fleming. On one occasion in 1564, Mary camped with the Atholls on the shores of Loch Lochy. Two thousand Highlanders had been employed for two months to gather in two thousand red, roe and fallow deer, which stampeded, only narrowly missing the royal party. Later, when Mary let her dog loose after a wolf, the herd ran into a group of Highlanders, resulting in two or three men being killed, despite throwing themselves flat in the heather.

Although fearless in the hunting field, she showed a feminine love of dogs, both for hunting and as pets. Her small dogs milled around her in blue velvet coats, as she wandered through her homes and gardens. Food scraps were retained for them in the kitchens with two loaves of bread set aside each day. Trained hawks were highly prized by royalty as presents and were among gifts sent to Elizabeth in 1562 in anticipation of their meeting. Mary was proficient at golf, pell-mell (croquet) and archery, for which she wore a velvet glove, but was often content walking in her palace gardens, which typically did not surround the residence, but were in secluded areas nearby. At Stirling, the gardens and archery butts were on level ground below the outcrop that supported the castle walls. Indoors she played chess,* back-gammon, cards, dice and 'biles' (billiards).

When Bothwell returned to Edinburgh, he was singled out for his loyalty to Mary's mother with a gift of land, despite opposition from Lord James. He did not attend Privy Council meetings regularly, and after falling out with Arran was barred from court. Their antipathy stemmed back to his capture of the English money sent to the Lords of the Congregation in October 1559. He would never take any slight lying down, and, with Arran increasingly eccentric, took amusement in baiting him. His sister Jean had become engaged to Mary's half-brother, Lord John Stewart, and Bothwell hosted their wedding reception at Crichton. He also arranged a stag party for Lord John in Edinburgh, inviting Mary's uncle, Elbeuf, who had delayed his departure for France. Late at night and dressed in masks, they escorted Lord John on a drunken sortie through Edinburgh in hope of catching Arran *in flagrante* with his mistress, Alison Craik, 'a good handsome wench'.[25] Although they gained access to the home of Alison's stepfather, where she was staying, Arran was not there. On the following evening they tried again, but, after being refused entry, they broke down the door, ransacking the house. Arran, who was now with his mistress, managed to escape by a back entrance, but the General Assembly lodged a complaint with Mary. They particularly blamed Elbeuf, as a Catholic 'degenerate'. Despite Mary issuing a stern rebuke, this did not stop them trying once more. By the next evening, the Hamiltons had assembled 300 men to guard the Market Place armed with spears and jacks to oppose Bothwell, who arrived with 500 supporters. The common bell was sounded and, from the safety of Holyrood, Elbeuf declared that ten men could not hold him back from the battle about to break out. Randolph, who remained at his lodging, reported to Cecil, 'I thought it as much wisdom for me to behold them out of a window as to be of their company.' It was only the last-minute intervention of Lord James, Argyll and Huntly which calmed matters down. Mary saw it all as a joke that had gone badly out of hand. She again reprimanded Bothwell and banished him to Crichton for a fortnight, hoping that all would soon be forgotten. When Lord James persuaded the General Assembly to demand a trial, Mary refused. A month later Bothwell hosted Lord John's marriage to Jean, attended by Mary and Lord James, and the couple were granted Dunbar

---

* Her library contained *The Rules of Chesse* translated by William Caxton from the French in 1474.

Castle by Mary as a wedding gift. Randolph was impressed by the sporting and other pastimes that took place. Yet it took Knox until February to arrange a meeting at Châtelherault's new mansion at Kirk o' Field to persuade Bothwell and Arran to be formally reconciled.

Arran, who was beginning to appear deluded, claimed that Bothwell was encouraging him to rekindle his suit to marry Mary. In all probability Bothwell had been ridiculing him, and this caused more feuding. Mary was by now extremely wary of Arran, despite his association with Lord James, but again insisted on Bothwell being reconciled to him. He had become a man possessed, calling for a saw to cut off his legs and for a knife to slash his wrists. In March, he claimed to Knox that Bothwell had told him to murder Lord James and Maitland and to carry off the Queen to Dumbarton* to marry her. He wrote to Mary and Lord James, who were at Falkland, claiming that Bothwell was trying to implicate him in a plan to share power. All this was treasonable and there had to be an investigation. It is hard to judge whether Arran's story was told in spite to get even for the attack on his mistress, or whether Bothwell had put him up to it in jest. Yet he was now undoubtedly insane. Randolph claimed that he was

> so drowned in dreams and so feedeth himself with fantasies, that either men fear that he will turn into some dangerous and incurable sickness or play some day some mad part that will bring him into mischief.[26]

Châtelherault was distraught, restraining his son at his house at Kinneil near Bo'ness, from where Arran smuggled out a second letter in code to Randolph, telling a similar story. This was shown to Mary, but his kinsman, Gavin Hamilton, told her it was false and to ignore it. Yet Lord James wanted any excuse to bring Bothwell to book.

Arran and Bothwell were arrested for conspiracy and, on 4 May, were brought to Edinburgh Castle. With nothing to hide, Bothwell came forward willingly. Arran was interviewed by Erskine and Morton, both of whom found him apparently mentally fit, but he relapsed and was handed back to his father's care. He promptly escaped half-naked in his underclothes down knotted sheets from his window. He went to the Stirling home of Kirkcaldy of Grange, where Knox interviewed him and reported that 'he began to rave and speak of devils, witches and such like, fearing that all men about came to kill him'.[27] He was taken to St Andrews, where Lord James kept him

---

* At this stage, Dumbarton was in the control of Arran's father, Châtelherault, who was in tears of distress over the whole incident, but Lord James insisted that the castle should be handed over to Mary as a precaution.

confined to await a confrontation with Bothwell before Mary and the Privy Council. When it took place, Arran accused Bothwell of treason, and Bothwell challenged him to a duel, but Arran was in no state to take part. Despite his obvious lunacy, Lord James treated Arran harshly, imprisoning him in Edinburgh Castle, although he was 'ill-bruited for the rigorous entertainment he faced there'.*[28]

Bothwell was exonerated without trial. Yet Lord James, now in complete ascendancy, gained Mary's approval to retain him in Edinburgh Castle on the unlikely pretext that he was intriguing with the English. Lord James needed to stop him making mischief, while he and Mary were on a planned trip to the north to deal with Huntly. When, on 28 August 1562, Bothwell escaped after bribing a guard, he hoped that Mary would recognise his three months of imprisonment as unjust. He went to his mother, Agnes Sinclair, at Haddington, where he asked Knox to intercede for him. On 23 September, he submitted to Mary, but she was still in Lord James's thrall and was not amused at his escape. Randolph, who had also been involved in the transfer of English money three years earlier, reported gleefully, 'Anything that he can do or say can little prevail . . . her purpose is at the least to put him out of the country.' In late December, Bothwell sailed for the Continent without consent. Although Mary was reportedly furious, she had some sympathy for his plight, but, unluckily for him, his ship was wrecked in a storm off the Northumberland coast near Holy Island, where he was arrested. He was handed over to Thomas Percy, who had been restored as 7th Earl of Northumberland. Although Northumberland offered to return him to Scotland, Lord James wanted Bothwell to be tried in London, knowing that the English hated him. Randolph reported that he was 'a blasphemous and irreverent speaker both of his own sovereign, and the queen my mistress', and one whom 'the godly of this whole nation have cause to curse forever'.[29] On 24 January 1563, he was taken to the castle at Tynemouth, from where he was sent by Elizabeth to the Tower.

Despite Mary's friendship with Seton, his position as Master of the Household proved difficult. He too had had a row with Bothwell, and Mary had had to insist on a bond between them to keep the peace. More unfortunately, he also fell out with Maitland, indispensable to Mary's marriage negotiations, and she forced him into exile. In March 1565, he went to

---

* Arran was released on a caution of £12,000 on 2 May 1566, by which time he was completely insane and could no longer speak. He retired to the care of his mother at Craignethan Castle living on in confinement and unmarried until 1609. Eventually James VI was to allow his next brother, John (later Marquess of Hamilton), to take the Arran title, before his elder brother's death.

France and was still there when Mary married Darnley. Yet such was their close friendship that he provided Seton Palace for her honeymoon, despite remaining abroad. When he was recalled in August 1565, he became her devoted supporter through all her tribulations.

Although a Reformer, Argyll supported Lord James in tolerating Mary's private Catholic worship. This resulted in Knox denouncing him for protecting her at a service in the Chapel Royal on 14 September 1561. He was unhappily married to Lady Jean Stewart, illegitimate daughter of James V by Elizabeth Carmichael of Crawford. Although he chose to live on his own estates, she preferred life at court. Despite him having several illegitimate children, she failed to provide him with an heir, and when she took lovers of her own, he ordered his clansmen to hold her prisoner, seeking a divorce. With a roving eye, he became intoxicated with Mary. Although his interest was not reciprocated, she could manipulate him to her beck and call thereafter. He generally supported those opposing Atholl, who had failed to restore Argyll estates controlled by him during Argyll's attainder.

Atholl gives a first impression of changing sides at will to promote his position. As a Catholic, he initially supported the Queen Dowager's French party against the Lords of the Congregation, but, when he started to share fears of her attempting French subjugation of Scotland, he backed Arran's marriage to Elizabeth. Recognising the strength of the Lords of the Congregation, he failed to support Huntly in his planned counter-Reformation to restore Mary on her return to Scotland and, as a Privy Councillor, joined Lord James's expedition against him. Yet on Huntly's demise he found himself as leader of the Catholic party, causing Lord James to mistrust him. He supported Lennox's plan for Darnley to marry Mary, but, having developed a close association with Maitland, when he became his brother-in-law, he soon became disillusioned with the young King. This caused him to fall out with Lennox and, although he was not involved in the conspiracy for the King's murder, he was not averse to the outcome.

Erskine found himself in the midst of increasingly polarised Presbyterian and Catholic factions. As a third son, he had joined the Church as Abbot of Dryburgh and Commendator of Inchmahone, without expecting to inherit. Yet when his elder brothers predeceased their father, he became Lord Erskine in 1555. He was no intellectual match for Mary's political advisers, but she recognised his integrity, and he held both Edinburgh and Stirling Castles with impartiality at a time when honesty was in short supply.

It was Lord James who held sway. He had engineered Mary's return to Scotland, and throughout this early period she deferred to him. As Cecil's close friend, he seemed to offer her the best hope of recognition as

Elizabeth's heir. Once achieved, Mary could relax and enjoy her privileged existence surrounded by her court, while he managed her government.

References

1. Knox, *History of the Reformation*, I, p. 8
2. Hay Fleming, p. 246
3. Knox, *History of the Reformation*, I, p. 8, cited in Antonia Fraser, p. 160
4. T. Thomson (ed), *Diurnal of Occurrents*, p. 67, Knox, II, p. 21, cited in Antonia Fraser, p. 179
5. Guy, p. 140
6. Weir, p. 34
7. Laing, Knox, IV, p. 373, cited in Antonia Fraser, p. 177
8. Knox, II, p. 13 et seq., cited in Antonia Fraser, pp. 177, 178
9. CSP, Scottish, I, p. 551; Knox, II, p.20, Laing, Knox, VI, p. 132, cited in Antonia Fraser, p. 178
10. Knox, II, p. 13 et seq., cited in Antonia Fraser, p. 178
11. Cited in Guy, p. 148 and Wormald, *Mary, Queen of Scots,* p. 127
12. George Buchanan, *The Tyrannous Reign of Mary Stewart*, ed. Gatherer p. 53, cited in Antonia Fraser, p. 219
13. Weir, p. 31
14. Cited in Graham, p. 143
15. *Diurnal of Occurrents*, p. 69, cited in Guy, p. 144, and Antonia Fraser, p. 180
16. Weir, p. 29
17. Guy, p. 149
18. Knox, II, p. 43, cited in Antonia Fraser, p. 209
19. Hay Fleming, p. 490, cited in Antonia Fraser, p. 218
20. Knox, II, p. 102, cited in Antonia Fraser, p. 216
21. CSP, Scottish, II, p.148, cited in Antonia Fraser, p. 209
22. J. Robertson (ed), *Inventaires de la Royne d'Ecosse*, p. xlix, note 3, cited in Guy, p. 153 and Antonia Fraser, p. 218
23. Antonia Fraser, p. 218
24. Wormald, *Mary, Queen of Scots*, p. 133
25. CSP, Scottish, I, p. 582, cited in Antonia Fraser, p. 196
26. CSP Scottish, I, p. 609, cited in Antonia Fraser, p. 198
27. CSP Scottish, cited in Weir, p. 41
28. Antonia Fraser, p. 199
29. State Papers in the Public Record Office, cited in Guy, p. 224

12

The Diplomatic Efforts to Establish Mary as Elizabeth's Heir

Mary's initial preoccupation on returning to Scotland was to gain acceptance as Elizabeth's heir, wanting this to be resolved before considering marriage. As early as 1559, Elizabeth had told Parliament that she did not intend to marry, although this may have been a political manoeuvre to hold Philip II's suit at bay while negotiating the Treaty of Cateau-Cambrésis. This resulted in her being dubbed even then as the Virgin Queen. Yet in 1560, she contemplated marrying Dudley,* with whom she enjoyed a fling lasting eighteen months, all the more scandalous because he was already married to Amy Robsart. The Spanish ambassador reported, 'Lord Robert has come so much into favour that he does whatever he likes with affairs and it is even said that her Majesty visits him in his chamber day and night.'[1] Despite the innuendo, it seems unlikely that her virginity was compromised. When Amy Robsart died after falling downstairs, Elizabeth reluctantly decided not to marry him and tore up the grant to make him an earl. Cecil had threatened to resign if she did.

---

* Lord Robert Dudley had been a childhood friend of Elizabeth. His father, Northumberland, had failed in his attempt to install Lady Jane Grey on the English throne, resulting in his attainder and execution (see p. 179 footnote), leaving the family in a parlous financial position. Yet by selling land they had helped to support Elizabeth in captivity during Mary Tudor's reign. Elizabeth had fallen passionately in love with the attractive Dudley, resulting in a rumoured affair between them. Despite his father's position as Protector for Edward VI, Dudley was associated with the conservatives in English politics, including Norfolk and some of the powerful Catholic families in the north, who wanted to break Elizabeth's close association with the 'low-born' Cecil. Cecil feared that his carefully planned efforts to secure a Protestant succession in England would be jeopardised if Elizabeth married this fifth son of the attainted Duke, and it would open up petty jealousies within the English nobility. He initiated a rumour that Dudley was offering to restore Catholicism in England, if Philip II would support his marriage to Elizabeth. Yet he had been married for ten years to Amy Robsart, who, by September 1560, was extremely ill, probably suffering from breast cancer. Cecil hinted that Dudley was poisoning her, but she died after breaking her neck in a fall downstairs at the home of friends. With Dudley at the height of his romance with Elizabeth, the natural question, no doubt fuelled by Cecil, was to ask if her fall was an accident. Had she committed suicide or was she pushed? Although the investigation exonerated Dudley, the rumours persisted and Elizabeth realised that she could never marry him. She needed the love of her people, and this marriage would bring only dissent. When faced with a similar choice, Mary would fail to show such political sensitivity.

While in France, Mary had refused to ratify the Treaty of Edinburgh, the terms of which obliged her to forgo her claim to the English Crown. It had been hoped by Lord James and Maitland that, once back in Scotland and away from Guise influence, this unacceptable condition might be dropped. Although she was the lineal heir, she was barred under Henry VIII's will, having been born outside England, and reinstatement required Elizabeth's approval.

Having promoted Arran's marriage to Elizabeth to enable them to usurp the Scottish throne, Maitland was extremely nervous before Mary's return. He wrote to her in France offering her 'faithful service', and, on 29 June 1561, she replied, making clear that she knew exactly what he had been doing, but that she would forget the past and judge him only by his future loyalty, but, as the 'principal instrument' of the 'practices' attempted against her, she told him to curtail his 'intelligence' with Cecil.[2] She wrote:

> Nothing passes among my nobility without your knowledge and advice. I will not conceal from you that if any thing goes wrong after I trust you, you are the one that I shall blame first. I wish to live henceforth in amity with the Queen of England and am on the point of leaving for my realm. On arriving I shall need some money for my household and other expenses. There must be a good year's profit from my mint . . .[3]

This was imperious stuff from an eighteen-year-old, and he was quickly reinvented as a faithful servant, despite him sending a copy of her letter to Cecil.

As Buchanan later pointed out, Maitland was 'chameleon'-like, and he now worked on regaining Mary's trust by renegotiating the unacceptable terms of the Treaty of Edinburgh. Even before her return, he and Lord James had agreed to approach the English with a 'middle way'. Lord James wrote to Elizabeth, and Maitland to Cecil, carefully constructed and coordinated letters. Lord James regretted Mary having claimed the English throne while in France, blaming the Guise family's bad advice. He proposed 'a perpetual quietness', with Mary renouncing her immediate dynastic claim in return for being 'allured' with recognition as Elizabeth's heir. If Elizabeth agreed, he would try to bring Mary 'to some conformity' in religion.[4] Maitland argued that, as soon as Mary set foot in Scotland, she would win hearts. Her Catholicism was unlikely to detract support, with the Reformation insufficiently established and many lords remaining Catholic. Even Reformist nobles were unlikely to oppose her and, being 'inconstant' and 'covetous', could be bought off. If Mary actively pursued a Catholic policy, it could be disastrous for the Scottish Reformation. He did not say so, but Lord James was implying that, if Elizabeth would accept her as her heir, Mary could be persuaded to maintain the politically Protestant status quo in Scotland.

In September 1561, only thirteen days after the Queen's return from France, Maitland, now aged thirty-three, went to London to offer Mary's ratification of the Treaty of Edinburgh in return for acceptance as Elizabeth's heir. On arrival, he met Elizabeth in company with Cecil and Dudley. He pointed out that Henry VII had not debarred Margaret Tudor's heirs from the English throne on marriage to James IV. He then made his offer, while admitting that it would require modification of the treaty's terms, under which Mary had to surrender her present and future claim. Elizabeth was sympathetic, but explained her predicament frankly. While admitting that there was no claim she preferred to Mary's, she could not acknowledge her as her heir. 'Think you,' Elizabeth asked,

> that I could love my winding-sheet, when as examples show, princes cannot even love their children who are to succeed them? ... I know the inconstancy of the English people, how they ever mislike the present government and have their eyes fixed upon the person that is next to succeed ... They are more prone to worship the rising than the setting sun.

She admitted being the focus for plots against Mary Tudor, sometimes without knowledge of them, and, as the second person in the realm, was at their mercy. 'There were occasions in that time I stood in danger of my life ... so never shall my successor be.'[5] If Mary was acknowledged as her heir, there was no going back; it was a right. Yet she agreed to appoint Commissioners to modify the treaty, so that Mary's claim was foregone only during her lifetime, upholding the dynastic succession, which both queens held so dear. She told Maitland to correspond with Cecil to confirm this, and he came away feeling that this had been a good opening.

Elizabeth was offering benevolent neutrality in return for Mary's friendship. By admitting that there was no claim that she preferred to Mary's, she was not threatening to debar her under the terms of Henry VIII's will. She seemed to expect Mary to succeed her, if she gave certain assurances. She should confirm Elizabeth as the rightful Queen, should give up any league with France, remaining friendly towards England, and should make an acceptable marriage with ultimate conversion to Protestantism. Maitland, who did not see Mary's Catholicism as inviolable, told Cecil, 'Surely I see in her a good towardness, and think that the Queen, your sovereign, shall be able to do much with her in religion if they once enter in a good familiarity.'[6] They should hold a meeting, as even Mary's Guise uncles in France recognised. Yet, if Mary remained a Catholic, neither Cecil nor the English Parliament would ever countenance her claim.

In Elizabeth's eyes, the rival claimants to the English Crown all had shortcomings which weakened their position. If Mary were debarred for being born outside England, the next in line was Lady Margaret Lennox, Margaret Tudor's daughter by marriage to Angus, followed by her two sons, Darnley and his brother Charles Stuart. Although she had been born in England, Henry VIII had vetoed Lady Margaret as a Catholic, making her equally unacceptable to Parliament. The next in line, dynastically, was 23-year-old Catherine Grey, sister of the ill-fated Jane, and grand-daughter of Henry VIII's younger sister Mary. Being both Protestant* and born in England, she was first in line under Henry VIII's will. Yet she had incurred Elizabeth's enmity. Having married and divorced the Earl of Pembroke's son and heir, Henry Herbert, she clandestinely escaped from court for long enough to marry and hurriedly bed Edward Seymour, Earl of Hertford, without Elizabeth's consent, as required by the Royal Marriage Act of 1536. The only known witness had been Hertford's sister, Jane, who died of consumption shortly after. By early 1561, Catherine was obviously pregnant and, after confessing to the marriage, was thrown with her husband into the Tower. When cross-examined, neither would name the priest who had married them, claiming that he had been hauled in off the street. If there were other witnesses, they wisely failed to appear. Hertford was fined £15,000 by the Court of Star Chamber and the marriage was annulled, making them guilty of 'fornication'. On 24 April 1561, Catherine gave birth to a son and, while still in the Tower,† had three more children, although all were declared illegitimate to debar them from the throne. Their jailer, Sir Edward Warner, was removed from his post and imprisoned for his leniency.

---

* Catherine's Protestantism was fairly pragmatic, and the Spanish ambassador had considered her as sufficiently compliant to be used to restore England to the Catholic faith, even contemplating arranging her kidnap for marriage to Don Carlos. Elizabeth had always kept a close eye on her, retaining her as a Lady of the Bedchamber to enable her to do so.

† The couple spent nine years in the Tower. Despite their children's illegitimacy, Edward, their heir, was reconstituted as Earl of Hertford, and his son, William, was restored by Charles II as 2nd Duke of Somerset, later being created Marquess of Hertford in his own right. He too made an unwise alliance in 1610, when he secretly married Arabella, daughter of Charles Stuart, Lady Margaret's son. With so much Tudor blood coursing through their veins, James VI, like Elizabeth before him, considered them hostile to his position on the throne.

Catherine eventually started a hunger strike to gain sympathy and died on 26 January 1568 aged twenty-seven. Her sister Mary Grey was never seriously considered for the succession. She was almost a dwarf with a curvature of the spine and may have been mentally deficient. In 1565, she secretly married the Sergeant-Porter, Thomas Keyes, a giant of a man, and their disparity in size caused wry amusement. When this came to light, she too was placed in the Tower, remaining there until her husband's death in 1572. They had no children, but she lived on in some poverty until 1578.

Following Devon's death, the leading Plantagenet claimant was the 25-year-old Henry Hastings, Earl of Huntingdon, a descendant of the Countess of Salisbury, niece of Edward IV. He happened to be Dudley's brother-in-law. Yet with the Tudors well established, his claim was remote. When Elizabeth was ill with smallpox in the spring of 1562, Parliament identified Mary Queen of Scots, Lady Margaret Lennox, Lady Catherine Grey and Huntingdon as the four serious contenders. The Spanish ambassador, Alvares de Quadra, Bishop of Aquila, reported that there was no certainty about the outcome, but no one wanted Mary, and she would need Elizabeth to recognise her senior dynastic position.

Finally, and fairly implausibly, there was the Infanta Isabella of Spain born in 1566, daughter of Elisabeth de Valois and a descendant of John of Gaunt. The Spanish Armada was launched in 1588 to support her claim, and she was again promoted in 1594 by the Jesuit Robert Persons in his book, *Conference about the next succession to the Crowne of Ingland*. This was aimed at gaining papal support and the English never took her claim seriously.

Regardless of dynastic entitlement, the English Parliament wanted a Protestant monarch. Elizabeth would be acting against their wishes if she favoured Mary, who was always mistrusted as a member of the Guise family. In January 1563, Sadler spoke against her in the House of Commons, arguing that 'our common peoples and the very stones in the streets should rebel against it'.[7] With English Catholic intrigue always near the surface, a Catholic heir would fuel continuing doubts over Elizabeth's legitimacy. This would come into even greater focus in 1570, when Elizabeth was excommunicated, although by then Mary was imprisoned in England. While Maitland believed that Mary should be recognised as Elizabeth's heir, if she accepted the amended terms of the Treaty of Edinburgh, Elizabeth wanted her to take it on trust while she demonstrated her political Protestantism. A meeting of minds would never be reached.

Although Cecil was determined on a Protestant succession, he strung Mary along. She would hardly adopt a Catholic policy in Scotland with the prize of the English throne, as she assumed, within her grasp. In his eyes, her acceptability depended on her renouncing Catholicism, but this was not an option she would contemplate. Maitland hoped for Cecil's blessing if he negotiated an acceptable Protestant marriage for her, but in this he was to be mistaken. Yet Elizabeth recognised Maitland's worth, providing him with a pension to assure his loyalty.

Despite Elizabeth's undertaking to renegotiate the terms of the Treaty of Edinburgh, this did not happen. Six weeks after Maitland's return to Scotland, she changed her mind, demanding ratification in its original form. Mary had nothing to gain and everything to lose by agreeing. Cecil no doubt saw that renegotiation would focus attention on Elizabeth's doubtful legitimacy. Elizabeth needed Philip II's continued goodwill, but, with Mary's stock rising, there were fears that he might support her.

Needing a new tack, Maitland tried to engineer a meeting between the two monarchs. He had initially hoped that Mary would return to Scotland via London to conclude terms to become Elizabeth's heir. With Elizabeth still seething that Mary had not ratified the treaty, she would not meet her. Once back in Scotland, Mary approached Randolph to try again. By talking to her, Mary believed that she would so inspire her that any differences would melt away. As she told Bedford while still in France, 'We are both in one isle, both of one language, both the nearest kinswoman that each other hath, and both Queens.'[8] By reaffirming their kinship, Elizabeth would be persuaded to recognise her dynastic claim. Mary wrote to her:

> We will deal frankly with you, and wish that you deal friendly with us; we will have at this present no judge of the equity of our demand but yourself ... If God will grant a good occasion that we may meet together, which we wish may be soon, we trust that you shall more clearly perceive the sincerity of our good meaning than we can express by writing.[9]

While Elizabeth felt an affinity with male company, Mary preferred to be with women and told Elizabeth, 'It is fitter for none to live in peace than for women, and for my part I pray you think that I desire it with all my heart.'[10] Elizabeth was receptive and, in January 1562, promised to send her agreed portrait. Yet the English Privy Council was divided. Although Mary's religious tolerance had been well received, Cecil followed Henry VIII's will by promoting Catherine Grey, despite her being out of favour. Yet Elizabeth considered making Mary her de facto heir without officially nominating her. She was a respectable widow who had not put a foot wrong.

Mary was encouraged by the promise of Elizabeth's portrait and sent another of herself, a miniature in a heart-shaped diamond frame, as a token to a royal lover. She joked that she would have no husband other than Elizabeth, and later sent a heart-shaped ring, accompanied by Latin verses composed with Buchanan's help. When Elizabeth replied with lines in Italian, she reciprocated in verse with her hopes for an early meeting.

Despite Scottish Catholic opposition, Mary persuaded her Council to approve her English visit. On 25 May, Maitland went back to London, where he remained until July to finalise details for a meeting at York in August or September. The planning was well advanced with masques written as entertainments for three evenings. Cecil redoubled efforts to stop the meeting, complaining at the expense, estimated at £40,000. Then bad news came from France. On 1 March 1562, while travelling with his men from Joinville to Paris, Guise had attacked a group of Huguenots holding an unauthorised service in a barn at Vassy in Champagne. He claimed that, when he tried to stop it, his men had been pelted with stones. Thus provoked, they left twenty-three dead and more than one hundred wounded. Cecil saw this as the start of a Guise-inspired religious crusade, which could spread to England. In France, Catholics and Huguenots took up arms. Trying to curb Guise power, Catherine de Medici showed sympathy for the Huguenots, now led by Condé. Although Spain seemed likely to support the French Catholics, Throckmorton told Elizabeth that, by backing the Huguenots, she could gain Calais, Dieppe or Le Havre, and perhaps all three. With England poised for war against her Guise relations, Mary called in Randolph to dissociate herself from her uncles' 'unadvised enterprise'. Although Elizabeth still wanted the meeting at York to go ahead, Cecil advised postponement to the English Council, when it met in early June, citing wet weather and a shortage of 'wine and fowls' at York.[11] Without telling Elizabeth, he sent Sir Henry Sidney to Scotland to cancel it.

By 25 June, fighting in France seemed to have come to nothing. Maitland had continued to lobby Elizabeth, who was at Greenwich, and to his relief she overruled Cecil, confirming her visit to York, despite the Council's universal opposition. 'It is both groaned at and lamented of the most and the wisest,' wrote Sir Henry Sidney to Throckmorton. Mary was given safe conduct to meet sometime between 20 August and 20 September with 1,000 attendants and provision for Catholic worship in private. Although she had to pay her share of the cost, Scottish coin could be exchanged on arrival. Through gritted teeth, Cecil arranged for an elephant to participate in the pageant. Maitland returned home in triumph and Elizabeth sent her long overdue portrait. News of the meeting received a muted reception among the Scottish nobility; Châtelherault claimed that a poisoned arm would prevent him from travelling and Huntly reported a sore leg. They were suspicious of Elizabeth's motives, but Mary remained highly excited. When she quizzed Randolph on Elizabeth's looks, he diplomatically confirmed that she could soon judge for herself and she 'would find much more perfection than could be set forth with the art of man'.[12] Yet, on 12 July, the day of Maitland's return, Elizabeth in London prevaricated. Fighting had again broken out in France, and she feared that she would have to intervene. She knew that the meeting would greatly strengthen Guise standing, helping their efforts to be restored to power in France. This could lead to a Catholic league against Protestant England. With Elizabeth now committed to supporting the Huguenots in the French wars of religion, the meeting would have to wait, and Cecil could return the elephant. When Sir Henry Sidney went to Mary to postpone it until the following year, she received him with 'great grief ... divers manifest demonstrations ... and watery eyes'. She 'fell into such a passion as she did keep her bed all that day'.[13] Although she continued to ask Randolph to rearrange it, she was beginning to mistrust Elizabeth's good intentions.

In an effort at conciliation in France, Catherine de Medici permitted Huguenot worship in private, and, sensing that they were gaining ground, Condé sought to hold services in public. He captured Orléans, Angers, Tours and Blois. When Lyons fell, Catherine had to act. With growing Huguenot influence at court and in the country, the dismayed Catholics needed the Guises to recover lost ground. Yet Catherine turned to the Constable, who, with Guise assistance, sought help from the Papacy and Catholic powers. The Huguenots turned to the English, promising to restore Calais, but Elizabeth prevaricated over sending Dudley with an invasion force.

Mary was caught in the middle. By supporting her family, she would be on the opposite side to Elizabeth. By backing Elizabeth, she would support heretics against her family and their lawful sovereign. She kept her head down and, with time on her hands, was persuaded by Lord James to face Huntly and the overly powerful Gordons in northern Scotland. It was only on arrival in Aberdeen that she received Elizabeth's letter justifying sending her army to France. 'Necessity has no law,' she said, 'We have no choice but to protect our own houses from destruction when those of our neighbours are on fire.'[14] She argued that Charles IX would see her as a good neighbour in preserving the Huguenots and destroying tyranny. She set out graphic stories of Catholic butchery of Huguenots, confident that Mary could not ignore her uncles' terrible crimes. Despite claiming that her uncles would have acted out of duty, Mary assured Randolph of her neutrality. Elizabeth ended by saying, 'I would write more, but for the burning fever that now holds me in its grip.'[15] She had contracted smallpox, which could be fatal, and Mary readied herself to claim the English throne. Yet when the English Privy Council discussed the succession at the height of Elizabeth's illness, only a single voice favoured Mary, and Elizabeth recovered.

Despite failing to arrange a meeting with Elizabeth, Mary recognised Maitland's efforts by formally appointing him as her Secretary of State and she provided him with the Abbacy of Haddington. After Huntly's defeat, he continued his efforts to rearrange the meeting with Elizabeth, complaining to Cecil that Mary was 'perplexed', and caught in the middle of a conflict between her uncles and England. She required a more secure interest in the succession than relying on Elizabeth's trust after bringing down the leading Scottish Catholic. When Mary assured Randolph that she 'never more heartily desired the Queen's Majesty's kindness and goodwill than she now doth', he took her side, telling Cecil that, despite her love for her uncles, 'yet she loveth better her own subjects'. The 'amity' meant more to her than a 'priest babbling at an altar'.[16] Yet Cecil was unyielding.

The war in France was a disaster for the English. In October 1562, Guise captured Rouen from the Huguenots after a long siege, and the English were pushed back to Le Havre. Mary showed a lack of tact by holding balls to mark Catholic victories. These were hardly likely to placate the Reformers, and Knox showed disgust at her celebration of Protestant deaths and voiced disapproval when 'the dancing began to grow hot'. The English feared a Guise attempt to place Mary on the English throne. This caused Elizabeth's correspondence with her to dry up. Cecil had to counter the threat posed by Mary and, when Parliament met on 11 January 1563, he tabled a Bill of Exclusion to debar her from the English throne. When Mary was told this, she retired to bed for six days, but, on 13 February 1563, sent Maitland to London in a last-ditch effort to stop Cecil's Bill from becoming law. He carried a letter from Lord James, seeking to re-ignite a 'love once kindled'.[17] Mary had told him that, if the parliamentary debate went against her, he should demand an audience for her with Elizabeth. Yet she faced vociferous opposition as a woman, a Guise, a Catholic and a foreigner, so that the Bill was passed. Although Maitland tried to deflect this by offering her as an arbitrator with France, he had no real hope of this being taken up. The English remained committed to the Huguenots, and the Catholics at last thought they had them on the run.

Mary was understandably distraught, realising that Lord James's 'middle way' had failed. She needed a new approach and decided to secure her dynastic rights with a suitable husband, even one lacking Guise approval.

Maitland was sent on from London to open negotiations in France, while Mary became preoccupied with breaking the Gordon stranglehold in the north.

References

1. Guy, p. 156
2. Guy, pp. 129, 255
3. Guy, p. 129
4. Guy, p. 146
5. Mortimer Levine, *Early Elizabethan Succession Question from Tudor Dynastic Problems*, pp.117–8, cited in Antonia Fraser, p. 186
6. Guy, p. 148
7. Antonia Fraser, p. 188
8. CSP Foreign, III, p. 573, cited in Antonia Fraser, p. 189
9. 5 January 1561, Labanoff, I, p 123, cited in Antonia Fraser, p. 190
10. CSP Scottish, I, p. 559, cited in Marshall, p. 200
11. Guy, p. 160
12. Philippson, *Marie Stuart*, III, p. 457, cited in Guy, p. 161
13. Sidney to Cecil, 25 July 1562, CSP Scottish, 1547 – 1563 p. 641
14. Guy, p. 166
15. Guy, p. 166
16. Guy, p. 168
17. Guy, p. 168

13

The Destruction of Huntly and the Gordons

While diplomatic efforts to find Mary a husband continued, she busied herself with domestic issues. It was Lord James who married, choosing Agnes Keith, Marischal's eldest daughter and a Reformer. Lord James's mother, Margaret Erskine, had originally arranged his marriage to the orphaned Christina Stewart, Countess of Buchan in her own right, despite her being sixteen years his junior. Their betrothal gave him temporary possession of the Buchan estates, but, well before she was old enough to marry,* he fell for Agnes. On 10 February 1562, Mary hosted their well-attended wedding celebration at Holyrood with feastings and masques over three days. Knox preached at the ceremony at St Giles', but considered the 'vanity used thereat offended many godly', and Arran demonstrated his growing insanity by 'falling sick from misliking the ostentation'.[1]

In recognition of Lord James having masterminded her return to Scotland, Mary sealed the celebrations by granting him the lucrative Earldom of Moray, a title he had always coveted, having sought it from the Queen Regent after forgoing his father's plan for him to take holy orders. She had roundly advised him to follow this chosen career, offering him a bishopric, but, as a Reformer, this had no interest for him. The grant of the earldom presented a complexity as its estates had previously been given to Huntly by Châtelherault when Regent. In 1555, the Queen Regent had attainted Huntly, but, with his absolute control in the north, he continued to occupy the Moray lands. Although the grant to Lord James was dated 30 January 1562, he agreed that it should not immediately be made public and, on 7 February, it was announced that he had been created Earl of Mar. Yet the rights to this earldom were also disputed. Lord James's uncle Erskine† claimed the title

---

* Nothing daunted, Margaret Erskine arranged for Christina to marry her youngest son, Robert Douglas, who duly became 4th Earl of Buchan.
† The Erskines claimed the Earldom of Mar through the female line from Gratney, one of a long line of Mormaers (or Earls) of Mar, and this had been confirmed by a charter from Robert III in 1395. Sir Robert Erskine had adopted the title in 1438, having been created a Lord of Parliament on 23 May 1429 as Lord

and successive generations of his family had sought in vain to prove their hereditary right. By granting it to Lord James, the Erskine claim seemed to have fallen on deaf ears. Yet he had no desire to thwart his uncle, and it was never intended that he should hold both titles in the longer term. He simply wanted a powerbase in the Catholic north from where to combat Huntly, complementing his backing in the south from the Reformers in the burghs and more clandestinely from the English. He wanted the announcement of his grant of the Moray earldom to cause the maximum provocation to Huntly.

It was not only Lord James who wanted Huntly's stranglehold on the north weakened; Mary had good reasons of her own. Huntly had led the Catholics in opposing her efforts at conciliation with Elizabeth. Furthermore the 26-year-old Sir John Gordon, Huntly's third son, seemed to consider himself above the law, despite being described by Buchanan as a man 'in the very flower of youth'.[2] He had been given cynical encouragement by Lord James and Maitland that he would make a suitable husband for Mary. Yet he was a rogue and in 1561 was involved in a brawl in Edinburgh with James Ogilvy of Cardell, Master of Mary's Household, who in 1558 had married, as his second wife, Mary Livingston's sister, Marion. A plausible version of events can be pieced together, based on the known genealogy.* Following the death of Cardell's father, Alexander Ogilvy of Deskford in July 1544, his widow, his second wife Elizabeth Gordon, daughter of the Dean of Caithness, continued to live at Findlater Castle. In about 1561, Sir John Gordon, aged twenty-six, wooed Elizabeth, now aged at least fifty-two, with a promise of marriage, to gain control of the Castle, in the hope of usurping Cardell's inheritance. No marriage took place, and, by the time of the brawl, she was being held there as Sir John's prisoner in a 'close chamber'.[3] Cardell was now

---

Erskine. Yet, four years after his death in 1453, James II arranged an assize of error against the grant, and Sir Robert's son Thomas was debarred on grounds of illegitimacy. There was no justification for this, but the title carried with it valuable estates, which devolved to the impoverished Crown. It then passed to successive younger sons of the Scottish kings, remaining their perquisite for the next hundred years.

* The recorded version of the story found in a number of sources is completely absurd, and seems to be a Gordon-inspired attempt to mitigate Sir John's actions. It suggests that it was Alexander Ogilvy of Deskford who was wounded by him in the brawl in Edinburgh, furious that he had run off with his wife. Yet genealogical tables show that Deskford died in July 1544 and he would have been sixty-six at the time of the brawl, not an age to confront a 26-year-old 'in the very flower of youth'. The story states that Elizabeth Gordon claimed that her stepson, the apparently upright Cardell, at least six years her junior, had made sexual advances to her. This had persuaded her husband to disinherit his son in favour of his 'kinsman' Sir John. She then apparently ran off with the dashing young man at least twenty-six years younger than herself. Although Sir John was Ogilvy's kinsman, their relationship was remote. Deskford's mother Agnes was the illegitimate daughter of the 2nd Earl of Huntly. This made Sir John his half first cousin twice removed. If Deskford wanted to disinherit his son, he had several closer Ogilvy kinsmen including Cardell's son, his grandson. It is also difficult to explain, if it was Deskford who took part in the brawl, why Findlater had already been passed to Sir John during his lifetime.

about forty-six, twenty years older than Sir John, and was badly wounded. He seemed to have no practical means of regaining Findlater and freeing his stepmother. The young Queen was incensed and arbitrated to ensure his reinstatement. Sir John was arrested and taken to Stirling, but promptly escaped back to Findlater, leaving Mary all the more determined to put matters right.

Together Mary, Lord James and Maitland engineered a plan to bring the Gordons to heel and to enable Lord James to gain control of the Moray estates. On 11 August 1562, they set out from Stirling with a well-equipped force. Their main objective was to see how the overweight and unfit Huntly, now aged forty-eight, would react. In addition to Strathbogie and numerous other castles, he held Inverness and Inverlochy for the Crown. Since 1549, he had also administered the Moray estates despite their later attainder. Strathbogie was rich in treasures and furnishings, including the church ornaments from Aberdeen Cathedral held for safekeeping until Catholicism could be restored.

The royal party insisted on Randolph travelling with them to witness Mary facing up to the most powerful of the Scottish Catholic magnates. Kirkcaldy was given command of their army with support from his old comrade the Master of Lindsay. They travelled through appalling weather via Perth, Coupar Angus, Glamis and Edzell, to arrive, on 27 August, at Aberdeen, where they were greeted by the Countess of Huntly, the redoubtable Elizabeth Keith, aunt of Lord James's new wife. She made a plea on behalf of her son, Sir John, but Mary insisted on him returning to captivity in Stirling. Although he returned there, he soon escaped again, raising 1,000 horse to harry the royal party, intending, as he later admitted, to abduct the Queen. Mary was enraged and refused Huntly's invitation to visit Strathbogie, despite his reputation for 'marvellous great' hospitality.*[4] This was a wise precaution, as he seems to have been planning a Catholic coup to capture her, forcing her into marriage with Sir John, after arranging for Lord James, Maitland and Morton to be killed. The strength of the royal army with Kirkcaldy in command made this impracticable, but Sir John continued his harassment as it moved on to Darnaway Castle, the Moray stronghold, which Randolph reported as 'very ruinous'.[6]

From the relative safety of Darnaway, Mary and Lord James announced his grant of the Earldom of Moray, and she issued a proclamation accusing

---

* Randolph was impressed with Huntly when they first met, stating that 'his house is fair, best furnished of any house that I have seen in this country; his cheer is marvellous great, his mind then such as it appeared to us, as ought to be in any subject to his sovereign.'[5]

Sir John of trying to 'break the whole country, so far as is in his power', and for failing to return to ward.[7] By 11 September, they had reached Inverness Castle, held on the Crown's behalf by the sheriff, another of Huntly's sons, Alexander. He committed the treasonable offence of refusing Mary entry until he had his father's agreement, forcing them to lodge in the town for the night. Huntly, who was still at Strathbogie, became rattled on hearing that the Highland clans were siding with the Queen, and he confirmed entry to the Castle on the following day. Moray (as Lord James was now known – or by the English as Murray) stormed in and arranged for the hapless Alexander to be hung from the battlements.

Mary had used all her guile to gain local support. She wore Highland dress, and felt strangely at home with the Gaelic people in their skins, speaking a language that she did not understand. Leslie recorded that they often slept out in the heather. They appeared in their numbers from the glens to see the beautiful young Queen. She met the seventeen-year-old Hugh, 5th Lord Fraser of Lovat, who offered his clan's services against the Gordons, although, perhaps to his embarrassment, some remained in Gordon ranks at Corrichie. Mary turned down his loyal offer, wanting to limit future feuding.

With Sir John still dogging them, the royal party travelled on to Spynie to visit Patrick Hepburn, the Catholic Bishop of Moray. On reaching Findlater, they called out for Sir John to surrender, but there was no reply and they lacked cannon to force an entry. Sir John was further north with his 1,000 troops hidden in the woods, planning to separate Mary from Moray as they crossed the Spey. When Mary was warned of this, she appeared with an escort of 3,000 men, which forced him to retire. Randolph had 'never seen her merrier, never dismayed, nor never thought that stomache to be in her that I find'. He was completely caught up in it all, reporting to Cecil, 'It may please you to know that in good faith where so many were occupied, I was ashamed to sit still, and did as the rest.'[8] On 22 September, she returned to a great welcome at Aberdeen, having again seen Gordon troops at Cullen. With lodgings in short supply, Randolph had to share a bed with Maitland and was horrified later to discover that Huntly had intended burning their hostel to do away with his companion.

Moray persuaded Mary to summon Huntly to Aberdeen, and, on 25 September, he was ordered to surrender the Crown's cannon, which he held at Strathbogie. Although this was promised within forty-eight hours, the cannon did not appear and he was denounced as a rebel. When Mary repeated her instruction, he could not decide what to do. His eldest son George, Lord Gordon, was sent to persuade his father-in-law, Châtelherault, to raise the south against Moray, and he even contacted Bothwell, who had by then escaped from Edinburgh Castle. Yet Huntly lost his nerve and offered troops to help to capture Sir John. As Mary did not want any untrustworthy Gordons in her midst, she refused them. To avoid capture, Huntly now led a will-o'-the-wisp existence, sleeping at different locations each night and visiting Strathbogie by day. Mary instructed Kirkcaldy to capture his castle and he ordered up 120 hackbutters and cannon. He set out with twelve men hoping to surprise Huntly at his midday meal. The plan was to hold the entrance until reinforcements arrived. Timing was of the essence, and, while he negotiated with the gatekeeper, his back-up force appeared and gave the game away. Huntly escaped over a back wall onto a waiting horse without his sword or boots. Despite his weight, his fresh horse outdistanced his pursuers and he disappeared into Badenoch. Meanwhile Sir John had succeeded in capturing fifty-six of Mary's hackbutters near Findlater. On 16 October, father and son were outlawed and, although they offered to hand over Findlater and Auchendown, they refused to give up Strathbogie.

Lady Huntly was left at Strathbogie to handle royal emissaries, but, when Mary refused her an audience, she rejoined her husband. Her witches had advised her that his unmarked body would lie in the Tolbooth at Aberdeen the next evening, and she persuaded him to attack the royal forces and apprehend the Queen. With his cousin, Sutherland, and 800 men, he took up position on the hill of Fare at the field of Corrichie, fifteen miles from Aberdeen, expecting Mary's troops raised locally to defect to him. Yet Moray arrived from Aberdeen with 2,000 men supported by Argyll and Morton. Although Huntly was hopelessly outnumbered, he was too unwell to withdraw and could only appear on parade at ten o'clock the next morning, 1 November, by when his forces were committed. Kirkcaldy and the Master of Lindsay took command of the royal army, exhorted by a speech from Maitland. Having raked Huntly's elevated position with fire, they forced him into attack, but his men were trapped in the swampy ground below. Huntly, Sir John and his younger brother Kenneth were captured, but, at this critical moment, Huntly 'burst and swelled' after suffering a seizure, falling dead from his horse.[9] His unmarked body was slung over a pair of fishing creels to be taken to the Tolbooth, thus fulfilling his wife's prophecy. It was then disembowelled and embalmed to prepare it for a treason trial in Edinburgh.

Although Kenneth Gordon was reprieved, Mary witnessed Sir John's execution in Aberdeen on the following day. Moray had insisted on her attendance to show that his infatuation was not reciprocated. Yet Sir John made her distraught by announcing from the block his hopes of marrying her and, when the executioner made a clumsy job, she fainted. She remained for the next day in her chamber, but was sufficiently recovered to take furnishings from Strathbogie, including elaborate tapestries, beds covered with velvet worked in gold and silver thread, and the ornaments from Aberdeen Cathedral. Some of these were given to Moray for Darnaway.

On 26 November, Châtelherault handed over Gordon, who was convicted of treason on 8 February 1563 and transferred to Dunbar. Moray persuaded Mary to defer execution, while Châtelherault, who reconfirmed his Reformist allegiance, worked on Knox to gain him a reprieve. Gordon was forced to attend the proceedings against his father, whose embalmed but unburied body was brought to Edinburgh from Aberdeenshire. 'The coffin was set upright, as if the Earl stood on his feet.'[10] As Randolph had said of Huntly, 'Were it not that no man will trust him either in word or deed', he would have been capable of a great deal of mischief.[11] Mary always saw him as a traitor, and Maitland shared her feelings in saying, 'I am sorry that the soil of my native country did ever produce so unnatural a subject as the Earl of Huntly hath proved in the end against his Sovereign.'[12] On 28 May, all the Gordon estates were attainted, and Sutherland retired to Flanders. Gordon remained at Dunbar from where he was released in 1565, with Mary needing support for her marriage to Darnley. Huntly was replaced as Lord Chancellor by Morton.

On their return from the north, Mary formally reconfirmed Lord James as Earl of Moray, and appointed him Sheriff of Elgin, Forres and Inverness. By breaking Gordon dominance in the north, Moray was now the most powerful figure in Scotland. In addition to spoils from Strathbogie, Mary gave him a further annual income of 1,000 marks. Yet she recalled the Earldom of Mar, making way for it to be available for Erskine with his undoubted integrity and neutrality. Although he had become a Reformer in 1560, his wife, Annabella Murray, daughter of Sir William Murray of Tullibardine, remained Catholic, and Knox saw her as 'a verry Jesabell'.[13] As a close confidante of Mary, she continued to promote the Erskine claim to the Mar earldom as opportunity arose. Mary had provided Moray and the Reformers with unassailable power. Despite having irretrievably weakened the Scottish Catholics, in January 1563 she reconfirmed the strength of her personal faith to both her uncle, the Cardinal, and the Pope.

References

1. Knox, II, p. 32, cited in Antonia Fraser, p. 215
2. Buchanan, p. 79, cited in Antonia Fraser, p. 221

3. Antonia Fraser, p. 221
4. Wormald, *Mary, Queen of Scots*, p. 125
5. Guy, p. 163
6. Antonia Fraser, p. 225
7. Antonia Fraser, p. 225
8. Randolph to Cecil, 18 September,1562, CSP Scottish 1547–63, p. 651, cited in Antonia Fraser, p. 226
9. *Diurnal of Occurrents*, p. 74, cited in Antonia Fraser, p. 230
10. Guy, p. 165
11. CSP, Scottish, I, p. 513, cited in Antonia Fraser, p. 221
12. Keith, II, p. 182, cited in Antonia Fraser, p. 233
13. Knox, cited in Antonia Fraser, p. 526, and Weir, p. 71

14

The Question of Marriage

With Moray dominating her government, Mary settled down to her introspective court life, every inch the model queen in her mourning clothes. Unlike Elizabeth, she made clear that she wanted to marry, but Moray preferred others to take the lead on finding her a husband who might weaken his own position, and the negotiations proved slower than she had hoped. She was beginning to find his moralising demeanour irksome, and his 'middle way' to gain for her acceptance as Elizabeth's heir had come to nothing.

By comparison, Maitland was amenable and Mary began leaning on him for advice. She relied on his diplomatic skills to find her a husband, seeing marriage as the means of providing the 'fortification of her estate' and reinforcing her dynastic claim to the English throne.[1] She would not necessarily subordinate herself to her husband, but believed the nobility would be more compliant if dealing with a man. In January 1563, Maitland took charge of her marriage negotiations, in effect replacing Moray as her leading minister. Yet he did not have Moray's authoritative personality and immediately sought broader representation on the Council. In February 1563, he appointed Ruthven, known as an extreme Reformer and capable soldier. On 22 September 1563, Ruthven was used to expel the clan Gregor from Strathearn and, on 8 May 1564, was reappointed Sheriff of Perth. Yet his history of taking sides for personal benefit and his reputation for sorcery caused mistrust and, according to Randolph, Moray disapproved of his appointment. Even Mary found him a man 'I cannot love', and Ruthven blamed this on his use of enchantment. Her concerns were to prove justified with his leading role among the conspirators involved in Riccio's murder.

On 15 August 1562, while Mary was in the north, a priest celebrating Mass in her private chapel was threatened by a mob led by two Presbyterians, Patrick Cranstoun and Andrew Armstrong. Mary ordered their arrest, citing 'forethought, felony, hamesucken [an attack on a householder in his home], violent invasion of the palace and spoliation of the same', but Knox summoned a 'Convocation of the Brethren', to call on his more militant colleagues to attend their trial to liberate them.[2] Mary saw this as incitement to armed resistance and to take the law into their own hands, and a majority of the Privy Council agreed that he was acting treasonably. Mary was looking for an opportunity to bring him down and, against Maitland's advice, sent him for trial before Parliament, attending herself. When he arrived with his cap off, Mary derided him, saying, 'Yon man made me weep and shed never a tear himself. I will see if I can make him weep.'[3] He was charged with conspiracy to 'raise a tumult by convoking' his colleagues to free the offenders.[4] Yet he came with a substantial following including his new brother-in-law, Ochiltree. Ruthven defended him by saying, '[He] makes convocation of the people to hear prayer and sermon almost daily.'[5] Knox argued that he had acted lawfully as a minister of the gospel and had Kirk approval. He also asked for help from Moray, who was infuriated at his loss of influence. When Moray supported Knox, Maitland whispered a warning to Mary that she was losing the argument and told Knox, 'You may return to your house for the night.' Knox was acquitted and Mary was left fuming, while he continued to lambast her. Although humiliated, she realised that she needed Moray and, swallowing her pride, reinstated him beside Maitland as joint chief minister.

The choice of Mary's husband, whether Protestant or Catholic, would inevitably disturb the careful balance between her private Catholic and public Protestant affiliation. Any overt Catholic would also jeopardise negotiations for the English succession. She needed a man of appropriate status, but a powerful prince with his own dominions would be seen as a threat by the English. Yet, if he lacked influence, she gained nothing. A Scottish or English subject would be seen as demeaning unless he promoted her claim to the English throne and would cause jealousy with his peer group. There was a limited choice of suitable candidates and overcoming the issues would not be easy. Her principal objectives were to choose someone to promote her claim to the English throne and to avoid having to leave Scotland permanently to reside with a less powerful husband, thereby placing her throne at risk.

Widows were not generally the first choice for royal husbands, but, at twenty, Mary had youth, beauty and a crown in her favour. She knew that her dynastic claim to the English throne was more of an attraction than her assured possession of the Scottish one. Cecil feared that, if Mary chose a Catholic husband, the Pope would declare Elizabeth illegitimate, causing English Catholics, still in a majority in the shires, to rise in Mary's favour. He saw that a Scottish royal family siring children would win English hearts and pass allegiance from the childless Elizabeth to Mary and her family, who could unify the two kingdoms. He sent advice that, if Mary married without

Elizabeth's consent, it would be seen as hostile. He did what he could to delay Mary choosing a husband in the hope that Elizabeth would marry before her.

Mary's initial plan was to seek marriage to a powerful foreign prince. Yet there were only a handful of suitable candidates and, as she pointed out to Randolph, they were not falling over themselves to seek her hand. While in London, Maitland met de Quadra to reopen negotiations for her to marry Don Carlos, while carefully citing her religious tolerance in Scotland to protect her claim to the English throne. These negotiations had been continued since Mary left France through the secret intercession of Anne, Duchess of Arschot, daughter of Antoine, Duke of Lorraine, a close friend of Philip II's chief minister in the Low Countries, Antoine de Perrenot, Cardinal Granvelle. This marriage suited Moray, as Mary would become an absentee ruler in Spain, leaving him to reassume the Scottish government on her behalf. Maitland argued that Philip II was a religious pragmatist, who had permitted Protestantism to develop in the Low Countries and had shown only reluctant support for Mary Tudor's burning of English heretics. Yet he was probably wrong in concluding that Philip would accept the religious status quo in both Scotland and England. De Quadra was enthusiastic, and wrote to Philip, 'Not only would you give your son a wife of such excellent qualities ... but you also give him a power which approached very nearly to [Pan-European] monarchy.'[6] Maitland saw it as 'such a marriage as would enable her to assert her rights'. He reported from London that the eighteen-year-old Don Carlos, whose physical and mental shortcomings seem to have remained hidden from the diplomatic community, was 'very far in love with her'.[7]

When Knox heard rumours of the marriage negotiations, he managed to rake up just a whiff of sexual scandal against Mary. In 1561, she had been accompanied to Scotland by Pierre de Bocosel, Seigneur de Châtelard, a poet on the fringes of the Pléiade who was part of Damville's train. Châtelard wrote elegant verses in her honour, claiming that there was no need of lanterns on their galley, 'since the eyes of this Queen suffice to light up the whole sea with their lovely fire'.[8] In the tradition of courtly love, Mary had responded with verses of her own. Much later Knox suggested that, while dancing together, she rested her head on his shoulder, 'and sometimes privily she would steal a kiss of his neck'.[9] Although Châtelard had fallen hopelessly in love with her, he returned to France with Damville. Yet, in the autumn of 1562, he rejoined her at Aberdeen, where he presented Damville's compliments and a book of his own poetry. She was flattered and gave him a sorrel gelding and money for clothing. After their return to Edinburgh, while Mary held a late meeting with Moray and Maitland, he crept into her bedroom to hide under her bed. When the room was routinely searched by two grooms before she retired for the night, Châtelard was ejected, still wearing his sword and dagger, and on the next morning Mary ordered him to leave court. Yet he followed her to St Andrews, where he again burst into her room, while she was with two serving ladies and, according to Randolph, made 'audacious' advances. When she screamed for help, Moray appeared, and she called on him to stab Châtelard with his dagger. Although Moray drew his sword, he cautioned her:

> Madam, I beseech your grace, cause me not [to] take the blood of the man upon me. Your grace has entreated him so familiarly before that you have offended all your nobility, and now if he is secretly slain at your own commandment, what shall the world judge of it? I shall bring him presently to the presence of justice, and let him suffer by law according to his deserving.[10] Mary was taken aback, 'Oh, you will never let him speak?' 'I shall do, madam, what in me lieth to save your honour.'[11]

Moray's cooler advice prevailed. Châtelard was tried at St Andrews and, on the scaffold, recited Ronsard's *Hymn of Death*, calling out, 'Adieu, the most beautiful and the most cruel Princess in the world.'[12] Mary may have led him on, but she was clearly sufficiently terrified to install Mary Fleming to sleep in her room thereafter. His motives are hard to comprehend, although he was known to have been a Huguenot.* Was he just a lovesick swain?

In September 1562, Knox called a Reformist meeting in Ayr, which was attended by Glencairn, where a bond was signed to protect the Kirk against Mary's rumoured marriage to Don Carlos. He told a large congregation at St Giles' that, if Mary married a Catholic, the realm would be betrayed and she would have 'small comfort'. 'In vehement fume', she demanded, 'What have ye to do with my marriage?', and 'What are ye within the Commonwealth?' He was ready with his answer:

> A subject born within the same, Madam. And albeit I be neither Earl, Lord nor Baron within it, yet has God made me (how abject however I was in your eyes) a profitable member within the same.

He then repeated his sermon, rendering her speechless until she 'howled'. When she had dried her eyes, he told her it was the truth. 'She had no

---

* Maitland reported that Châtelard had been sent by Huguenots in France to wreck the Don Carlos marriage proposal by sullying her honour. Yet would he have risked his own life for this?

occasion to be offended', and he would endure her tears rather than sully his conscience. She ordered him to leave, but as he went he told her ladies that their 'gay gear' would help them little in the inevitable coming of the 'Knave Death'.[13] She had again been made to look foolish.

Rumours of the Don Carlos marriage plan resurfaced in Scotland over Easter, and Archbishop Hamilton unwisely celebrated Mass, forcing Mary temporarily to imprison him. On 17 April 1563, Maitland arrived in France to seek French support for it, but Catherine still had no desire to allow such an axis of power against France. Despite wanting Philip's help against the Huguenots, she was not going to hand him the English throne in return. The Guise family was in no position to assist Maitland. Two months earlier, while making a routine inspection of his army at Orléans, Guise had been shot three times in the back of his shoulder by a Huguenot. Mary learned this devastating news in St Andrews and, on 15 March 1563, heard that he had died.* She 'was marvellous sad, her ladies shedding tears like showers of rain'.[14] When another of her uncles, the Grand Prior Francis, died of natural causes shortly after, Mary Bethune, 'the hardiest and wisest of the Maries', was delegated to break the news. When it was rumoured that the Cardinal had been captured by Huguenot forces, Mary's Court was forced into a state of depression. Randolph reported: 'Here we have not a little ado ... I never saw merrier hearts with heavier looks since I was born.' Mary felt alone. She confided in Randolph that she needed a husband, both personally and politically. She had been widowed for more than two years and was destitute of confidants except the four Maries, who knew Scotland no better than she did. Randolph persuaded Elizabeth to write a much cherished letter of condolence after Guise's death.

Despite de Quadra's encouragement, Philip II only played along with the Don Carlos marriage negotiations to ensure that Mary did not marry the twelve-year-old Charles IX. Yet Catherine de Medici was still vetoing Mary's marriage to her second son. With the Guises trying to strengthen their alliance with her, when she was at last focusing against the Huguenots, the Cardinal wrote to Mary in August, strongly criticising the Spanish marriage and trying to rekindle the suit of the Archduke Charles. Without telling Mary, the Cardinal went to Innsbruck to negotiate with the Archduke, arrogantly presuming

---

* The Guise family were extremely affronted when Anne d'Este quickly remarried Jacques de Savoie, Duke of Nemours. He had been involved in a scandal in 1556 when Françoise de Rohan, one of Catherine de Medici's maids-of-honour, became pregnant and named Nemours as the father. He denied this when interviewed by the Cardinal of Lorraine, who did not believe him. The Cardinal told Anne d'Este that he strongly disapproved of her remarriage, but Nemours won over the Guises by making handsome provision for her children and herself, and Mary continued to correspond with the new couple from imprisonment in England.

that Mary would follow his will when pressed. Yet Mary did not believe that the Archduke offered her sufficient clout in her hopes for the English succession. As she later told the Duchess of Arschot, 'Not that I don't consider it great and honourable, but less useful to the advancement of my interest, as well in this country, as in that to which I claim some right.'[15] By 15 June, Philibert du Croc had arrived in Edinburgh to gain her approval, remaining closeted with her for days, but, to Randolph's relief, nothing came of it, and she concluded that the Cardinal 'careth not what becometh of me'.[16]

Elizabeth disapproved of Mary marrying the Archduke Charles as much as Don Carlos and told Maitland that Mary would become her enemy if she chose a husband from the Austro-Spanish Empire. She feared it would result in her being excommunicated, causing English Catholics to back a foreign invasion to place Mary on the throne. She implied that she would not reject a suit from the Archduke herself. Maitland classified English views on Mary's marriage into three categories: Elizabeth wanted Mary's husband to give her the 'least cause to stand in fear';[17] the Papists wanted a Catholic to put Elizabeth under maximum pressure; and the Protestants wanted a man to defend their cause. Maitland knew that Knox and the hard-line Reformers in Scotland would oppose a Catholic husband. On his return he tried to neutralise their bigotry by denying any marriage plans. Yet Mary was not diverted from diplomatic efforts to gain Spanish approval for Don Carlos. When ambassadors arrived on 24 June 1563 from Eric XIV of Sweden promoting the suit of his son Gustavus Vasa, it was peremptorily rejected.

During 1563, to placate the Reformers, Mary allowed ministers to occupy manses and glebes of former Catholic priests. In April, she visited Moray's mother, Margaret Erskine, at Lochleven, where Knox was invited for another meeting. For once, this was a relatively less vitriolic encounter. When she asked him to end his Catholic persecution, which was particularly fierce in the west of Scotland, he reminded her to administer the law, which had made Papacy illegal. The next day, when hawking in Kinross, she asked him to intercede with Argyll, who still wanted to divorce the wayward Lady Jean Stewart, her half-sister. Although Lady Jean was one of her closest confidantes, Mary admitted that she 'was not so circumspect in all things as that she wished her to be'.[18] Knox was asked to write a stern letter, but Argyll paid little attention to it.

Knox dredged up another scandal. In June 1563, Parliament passed an Act making adultery a capital offence. On the same day, one of Mary's French chaplains was found in bed with another man's wife. Knox immediately preached on the moral deficiencies of the Mass and licentiousness at court:

> The Queen's idolatry, the Queen's mass, will provoke God's vengeance
> ... Her House ... is become the haunt of dancing and carnal con-
> cupiscence ... Dancing is the vanity of the unfaithful, which shall cause
> the people to be set in bondage to a tyrant.[19]

There was no stopping him. He equated Catholicism with unbridled sexual
lust, and Mary was flaunting her sexuality with dancing and banquets,
making her unfit to be Queen. He claimed that, as a Catholic, she ruled from
the heart, but Elizabeth, as a Protestant, ruled from the head. Elizabeth was
one of those special women 'raised up by divine authority to be the nursing
mothers' of the Protestants.[20] Yet in reality Elizabeth was still at the height of
her dalliance with Dudley, whose wife was still alive.

A crisis blew up when Sir Thomas Smith, the new English ambassador in
France, reported that terms for marriage to Don Carlos had been agreed.
This was completely untrue, as Philip was contemplating locking his son
away and he ended any thought of him marrying in August 1564, although
Mary did not come to accept this until March 1565. Smith reported that the
Cardinal of Lorraine had negotiated with the Pope for Mary to offer England to Don Carlos as a dowry. When Condé was captured in March 1563
during the Huguenot defeat at Dreux, a Catholic invasion of England
became a realistic threat. The Huguenots sued for peace at Amboise and
were forced to combine with the Catholics in pushing the English from
France. Despite being dug in at Le Havre, plague* and bad weather forced
Dudley, in July, into ignominious surrender, under the terms for which Calais
was finally ceded to France. Elizabeth now had to be on the defensive,
protecting England as an island fortress. She needed to dictate Mary's choice
of husband and to make her sever links with France and Spain.

Catherine de Medici had also heard the false rumour of the Don Carlos
marriage agreement. She immediately suggested that Charles IX, now aged
thirteen, should marry Elizabeth, who was thirty, and that his brother Henry,
who was twelve, should marry Mary, now twenty-one. Castelnau was sent to
London to propose this, but Elizabeth had no desire to be an absentee ruler
and politely turned down Charles IX, as being both too big (in terms of
power) and too small. Mary believed, incorrectly as it turned out, that Henry,
as the second son, provided no advantage, after she had been married to his
brother, the King. She also feared the consequences of leaving Scotland.

Elizabeth stepped up diplomacy with her sister Queen. On 1 September,

---

* When the Garrisons returned to England, they carried the plague with them, causing a major outbreak
during the winter of 1563, with 3,000 dying in a week in London.

Randolph told Mary that, if she married the Archduke Charles, the 'amity' with England would be at an end. Although Mary had already rejected the Archduke, Randolph bore the full brunt of her fury. She demanded to know what husbands were 'sortable'. Elizabeth knew that she had to clarify 'whom we can allow and whom not; secondly what way we intend to proceed to the declaration of her title', and Mary realised that she had to listen.[21] She had no expectation of European support and could not afford conflict. Southern Scotland was economically dependent on trade with northern England. To maintain control and to stop Knox's insubordination, she needed recognition as Elizabeth's heir.

On 17 November, Randolph at last delivered Cecil's words defining a husband acceptable to the English. Ideally he should be 'some fit nobleman within the island' committed to the 'amity'. If no one met these conditions, she could seek English consent to marry a foreigner, provided that he resided in Scotland after their marriage. He must be 'naturally born to love this isle', and 'not unmeet'. No one from France, Spain or Austria would be acceptable. Elizabeth had intended that, if Mary followed this advice, her dynastic claim would be reinstated. Yet Cecil changed the drafting to say:

> We do promise her, that if she will give us just cause to think that she will in the choice of marriage show herself conformable ... we will thereupon forthwith proceed to the inquisition of her right by all good means in her furtherance.[22]

Although Mary was a foreign head of state, her claim to be Elizabeth's heir would be tried in an English court. This was of course outrageous, but shows Cecil's paranoia following the surrender at Le Havre.

Knowing that Mary would see Cecil's letter as a bitter pill, Elizabeth sent her a diamond ring as 'a token of affection'. Randolph delivered this first and reported that it was 'marvellously esteemed, oftentimes looked upon, and many times kissed'.[23] Yet when Mary received Cecil's letter, she was confused by the mixed messages. She was not going to allow the English to nominate her husband and privately renewed her search for someone suitable. Yet she decided to appear compliant in front of Randolph, while taunting him with help from members of her court. When she told him that she was expected to marry an Englishman, others asked if Elizabeth had become a man. When asked to suggest a name, he gave no answer, being under instruction not to do so, but said rather lamely, 'Whom you could like best.'[24] When pressured to be more specific, he recommended sending a delegation to ask Elizabeth.

The strain was telling on Mary and, as so often, she became ill from depression, weeping without apparent reason. Having danced late into the night on her twenty-first birthday, she stayed in bed all the next day. Officially she was suffering with a cold, 'being so long that day at her divine service'.[25] Yet she was suffering an abdominal pain in her left side, which is the first record of her gastric ulcer, and her medicines did not initially bring relief.

To promote herself in marriage, Mary continued to maintain the grandeur of her court. On Shrove Tuesday 1564, she held a celebration lasting three days. This began with a sumptuous banquet, offering every sort of delicacy. She and her Maries wore costumes in black and white, and these were echoed by her guests and staff. A boy dressed as Cupid led in the first course to the sounds of an Italian madrigal. This was followed by a radiantly beautiful girl as Chastity, who accompanied the second course, reciting Latin verses to denote a pure mind, symbolic of Mary herself. The third course was ushered in by a boy dressed as Time, with verses extolling the enduring mutual love and affection of Mary and Elizabeth. Randolph told Cecil that it was the grandest such event ever staged in Scotland, and he shed his puritanical shell to enter into the spirit of it all. He reported that the Scottish court 'did nothing but pass our time in feasts, banqueting, masking and running at the ring and such like'.[26] Yet Mary had still not replied to the letter setting out the English conditions for her marriage.

Maitland began the marriage debate with Elizabeth by suggesting a private meeting with Mary to discuss alternatives. Although Elizabeth continued to pay lip service to it, a meeting was a non-starter with the English Parliament. Moray and Argyll argued that, as Elizabeth's letter mentioned no specific candidate and was 'only general', Mary's reply could only be 'uncertain'. They wanted Elizabeth to nominate someone. Mary made clear that, although 'princes at all times have not their wills', she wanted 'nothing more' than Elizabeth's love and was 'without evil meaning' towards her. Randolph affirmed that 'the word of a prince' was to be trusted, but, although her love was genuine, it was not to be presumed upon.[27]

Realising that she had to name someone, Elizabeth concluded that she should offer Dudley. She had decided not to marry him herself and was determined to remain a virgin queen. As an ambassador had said to her:

> Madam, I know your stately stomach; ye think if ye were married, ye would be but Queen of England, and now ye are King and Queen both; ye may not suffer a commander.[28]

Marriage could only breed discord, as Mary was to discover. Elizabeth had already proposed Dudley's name to Maitland in an off-the-cuff aside in the previous year, but he had not taken this too seriously. He replied tongue in cheek that she 'had better snap him up herself', but used all his diplomacy in saying that it was proof of the love she bore Mary, 'as she was willing to give her a thing so dearly prized by herself'.[29] He believed that Mary, who had described him as 'Elizabeth's groom' [he was Master of the Horse], would be gravely affronted at the offer of Elizabeth's cast-off. Dudley was still under a cloud following the unexplained death of his wife, was only the fifth son of the attainted Northumberland,* was not of royal blood, lacked estates or titles and had not redeemed himself in a successful campaign supporting the Huguenots in France. There was a second problem. Dudley was very unenthusiastic at the thought of being put out to grass in Scotland, even in marriage to Mary, and worked behind the scenes to scupper the plan without offending Elizabeth. This suited Cecil, who saw the negotiation as a delaying tactic, knowing that it would come to nothing.

In September 1563 Randolph was told to advise Mary that Elizabeth wanted her to marry an Englishman, without officially mentioning Dudley's name. Randolph visited her at Craigmillar as she returned from a trip to the west. She knew he had Dudley in mind, and responded:

> Monsieur Randolph, you have taken me at a disadvantage ... Do you think that it may stand with my honour to marry my sister's subject?'[30]

Randolph replied that this was 'the means of whom she may perchance inherit such a Kingdom as England is'. Mary asked why this improved her dynastic claim. She argued that she had no expectation of the English throne, as Elizabeth 'may marry and is likely to live longer than myself', but she made clear:

> My respect is what presently be for my commodity, and for the contentment of friends, who I believe would hardly agree that I should imbase my state so far as that.

The 'commodity' of princes was their honour and reputation.[31] She believed that she would gain the Scottish lords' respect, as she desired, only if her

---

* John Dudley, Earl of Warwick, had been created Duke of Northumberland in the reign of Edward VI following the attainder of Sir Thomas Percy, who would otherwise have been heir to the Percy Earldom of Northumberland. The Duke was attainted and beheaded in 1553, after his ill-fated attempt to place Lady Jane Grey, married to his fourth son Lord Guildford Dudley, on the English throne. In 1557, Sir Thomas Percy's son, Thomas, was restored as 7th Earl of Northumberland, but was later attainted following the Catholic-inspired Northern Rising in 1569, after which the Northumberland earldom passed to his brother.

dynastic right to the English throne were recognised. After telling her advisers to leave, she asked Randolph, in the presence of the four Maries, 'Does your mistress in good earnest wish me to marry my Lord Robert?'[32] He confirmed this, and she asked if this meant that she would be recognised as Elizabeth's heir. He said that he thought that she might. 'How would it look', she asked:

> if Elizabeth married and had children and I had chosen a commoner as King of Scotland. Would it not be better for England to match me where some alliance and friendship might ensue?

Randolph replied that Elizabeth's chief objective was 'to live in amity with Scotland', but Mary claimed she had demonstrated her continuing loyalty and should be permitted to marry whom she liked.[33] She made clear that she would choose for herself, but did not rule out completely a member of the English nobility. After dining, the lords rejoined them, and Moray asked Randolph why the English were so anxious to arrange Mary's marriage when they should be focusing on Elizabeth's. Dudley's name was not made public, but Moray privately favoured him, seeing him as a friend, and he wanted to act as his sponsor for the Scottish Crown. Maitland suggested a conference at Berwick, perhaps with Bedford present, to progress it.

Elizabeth believed she could always rely on Dudley, and was initially happy at the thought of him marrying Mary, but, being ambitious and arrogant, he would never have remained her puppet. In November, Randolph reconfirmed her opposition to 'the children of France, Spain or Austria'.[34] Then, in March 1564, the Emperor Ferdinand came forward with another offer of his son, the Archduke Charles, undertaking to provide 2 million francs on marriage with a further 5 million after his death. He also agreed that he should live with Mary in Scotland, but wanted an answer by the end of May. The Scots warned Randolph of this offer in confidence. Randolph concluded that they were trying to force Elizabeth to commit herself. He made Dudley's suit public, but this made her realise that she could lose him and she suggested nonsensically that they should live as a *ménage à trois* in an extended royal family in London. This was not a good example of her ruling 'from the head' as Knox expected, and Mary saw it as unworkable.[35] She needed her husband with her in Scotland to maintain control.

With marriage negotiations temporarily deadlocked, Mary spent the first part of 1564 working to assure strong government at home. To broaden her activity away from 'courtly frippery', she reorganised the Court of Session to assure the poor of a proper hearing. Many judges, even those associated with Knox, were giving biased judgments in favour of rich and powerful friends. She increased their stipends so that they sat on at least three days per week in both morning and afternoon, and even attended hearings herself. She took another summer progress to the Gaelic-speaking Highlands, listening to the harp, bagpipes and bardic poetry. She won hearts and minds by ordering the court into Highland dress.

In February 1563, Elizabeth had asked Mary to allow Lennox to return to his estates, ending his long exile in England. Her apparent motive was to destabilise government in Scotland while Mary was negotiating to marry Don Carlos. Although only recently released from the Tower, Lady Margaret remained as a focus for Catholic intrigue, and Elizabeth kept her under virtual house arrest at court, where her son, the seventeen-year-old Darnley, sang and performed on the lute in the evenings 'as indeed he plays very well'.[36] Lennox's repatriation was not initiated by Elizabeth as a means of promoting his son as Mary's husband, but the advantage of marrying her male contender for the English throne was not lost on Mary. His mother had furnished him with courtly graces and, although apparently Catholic, he did not seem vehemently so, regularly throwing his critics off guard by attending Protestant services, which made him seem less threatening in Scotland than Don Carlos. As soon as Elizabeth had proposed Lennox's return, she regretted what she had begun. She asked Maitland and Moray to block the passport that she had so recently requested, but they wryly advised Mary, who immediately granted it. Even Kirkcaldy realised the inevitable outcome of Lennox's return, when he suggested that Mary's 'meaning is not known, but some suspect she shall at length be persuaded to favour his son'.[37]

Meanwhile Mary played along with the Dudley suit, while secretly trying to revive negotiations with Spain for Don Carlos, but she also planned to meet Darnley. When the English Parliament met again in October, she sent Sir James Melville back to London to renew her claim to the succession, but with instructions to encourage Lady Margaret to seek a passport for Darnley to visit his father. Elizabeth liked Melville, who was a good linguist, allowing her to practice her French, Italian and indifferent German with him, but she was bitter at some of Mary's recent letters. She showed him the draft of an acid reply she had prepared. When Melville explained Mary's frustration at not knowing whom Elizabeth preferred for her husband, she tore up the draft and again suggested Dudley. Yet she also showed him Dudley's portrait miniature kept in her bedroom, and he saw that it was inscribed 'My Lord's Picture'. She then showed him a 'great ruby, as big as a tennis ball'.[38] When he suggested that she should send it to Mary as a token of her love, Elizabeth was taken aback, but then said that, if Mary did as she wished, she could have both the ruby and the man. In the meantime, she provided him with a diamond for Mary. To reinforce Dudley's cause, she created him Earl of Leicester, but Melville saw her tickle his neck during the ceremony. She was again having cold feet at the prospect of losing him and jealously questioned Melville on Mary's beauty.* She was determined to show off her own virtues. One evening Hunsdon took Melville in secret to Elizabeth's chamber, where he heard her playing 'exceedingly well' on the virginals. When she saw him she feigned surprise, but he was ready with his answer, 'I heard such melody, which ravished and drew me within the chamber, I wist not how.' On his final evening in London, he watched Elizabeth dancing and tactfully assured her that Mary 'danced not so high and disposedly as she did'.[39]

Darnley carried the sword of state at Dudley's ennoblement, and Melville had to answer Elizabeth's questions on Mary's interest in him. She had already told him that 'ye like better yon long lad', and he replied, 'No woman of spirit would make choice of such a man that was more like a woman than a man, for he was very lusty,† beardless and baby-faced.'[40] Despite his veneer of polish, Darnley was seen as reckless, proud and stupid. He was sexually promiscuous, which had left him with syphilis, although this may not then have manifested itself. He was described as a 'great cock chick', which denoted his homosexuality.[41]

Melville returned to Scotland on the day after the ennoblement ceremony carrying the diamond sent by Elizabeth for Mary, and Cecil had given him a gold chain. Lady Margaret sent him with other valuable gifts, a 'fair diamond' for Mary, an emerald for her husband, a diamond for Moray, a watch set with diamonds for Maitland and a ring with a ruby for Melville's brother, Sir Robert. He considered her a very wise and discreet matron, but Randolph described her as 'more feared than beloved of any that know her'.[42]

Mary kept her marriage intentions to herself and, in July 1564, arranged another royal progress to see and be seen by her subjects. Her route to the west and south-west of Scotland included Argyllshire and Ayrshire. Maitland did not go with her, explaining, 'In the place I occupy, I cannot be spared for voyages, nor do I like it (for it lacks not peril) unless to some good end.' The

---

* Melville claimed that he offered 'to convey her secretly in Scotland by post, clothed like a page disguised, that she might see the Queen', a suggestion that Elizabeth 'seemed to like well'. There is no doubt that Melville was on good terms with her.

† It is not quite clear what Melville meant by referring to Darnley as lusty, but in the context of being beardless and baby-faced it is reasonable to assume that he was hinting at his homosexuality.

Court again wore 'Highland apparel' with Randolph fitted 'in outward shape ... like unto the rest'.[43] The trip involved hunting, hawking and archery with visits to Invarary in Argyll and to Eglinton in Ayrshire. From here she went on to Dumfries and Drumlanrig before returning to Edinburgh via Peebles. Knox complained that she took Mass wherever she went and, to Elizabeth's annoyance, Luis de Paz, de Quadra's agent, visited her in Argyllshire to continue the Don Carlos marriage negotiations.

On 22 September 1564, Lennox made an impressive entrance into Edinburgh after an absence of nearly twenty years, riding to Holyrood magnificently attired, supported by twelve velvet-clad horsemen in front and thirty attendants in grey livery behind. Mary received him graciously and, after making their peace, he was offered some of the best rooms. On 16 October, to Moray's great annoyance, all his estates around Glasgow and the Clyde were restored. Mary had needed all her persuasion to induce Parliament to agree to this, but she claimed it was 'at the request of her dearest sister Elizabeth'.[44] Although Mary was only permitted to attend Catholic services alone, Lennox celebrated Mass with her at the Chapel Royal, only adding to his mistrust among the nobility. Even Mary was suspicious despite the provision of yet more valuable gifts from Lady Margaret. She received a valuable jewel, almost certainly the magnificent Lennox Jewel,* still in existence. This is a pendant which opens to reveal enamels depicting tokens of affection. For assisting in his return, Maitland and Atholl each received large diamond rings and the four Maries were given 'pretty things'.[45] Lady Margaret was also seeking Darnley's passport, but Elizabeth initially refused it, while still actively promoting Leicester as Mary's husband.

With Moray, Maitland and Knox all favouring Leicester, Moray worked assiduously to achieve terms to assure Mary's recognition as Elizabeth's heir, while forgoing her immediate Catholic claim to the English throne. She would indisputably have married Leicester if the English had agreed. In November, Randolph and Bedford met with Moray and Maitland at Berwick as Commissioners to discuss the terms. Moray and Maitland became furious when it was explained that Elizabeth would never willingly consent to Mary marrying anyone but Leicester, but was unable to confirm her as her heir. They told Cecil that she had backtracked, and that marriage to Leicester was 'no fit match' unless the right to the succession was agreed.[46] Cecil could not

---

* It has already been suggested that the Lennox Jewel had been a wedding gift from Mary Tudor to Lady Margaret, then her close confidante. The jewel is of the type generally given as a love token at marriage, and it is not unreasonable that the inscription reading 'Death shall dissolve' initially related to Mary Tudor's undying friendship with Lady Margaret, but was now used to promote Darnley's suit.

drag out the suit any longer and had influenced Elizabeth not to confirm Mary's future rights to the succession, knowing that she would not marry Leicester without them. Cecil needed to put forward an alternative. When Maitland suggested Norfolk, whose second wife, Margaret Audley, had recently died, Norfolk politely turned down the offer.

On 23 September 1564, Elizabeth wrote to Cecil that she could not decide how to handle Mary's marriage: 'I am at a loss to know how to satisfy her, and have no idea what to say.'[47] Cecil was aware of Throckmorton's argument that Mary posed no threat as heir to the English throne if married to an Englishman, and he lobbied for Darnley to replace Leicester as her suitor. In one sense, this would make Mary's dynastic claim unassailable, avoiding the need for parliamentary consent, and it was a face-saving solution to allow Elizabeth to retain Leicester. Yet Cecil was entirely cynical about Darnley's suit. Darnley was already parading his dynastic claims to both the Scottish and English thrones with arrogance and overbearing conceit.* He was a 'political lightweight', insufferably spoilt by doting parents, making him much less dangerous than a foreign Catholic Prince. The Cardinal of Lorraine described him as a 'gentil huteaudeau' [agreeable nincompoop].[48] If Cecil were to overlook Mary as Elizabeth's heir, he faced Darnley as next in line. He was male, was born in England and was not debarred under Henry VIII's will. Yet to Cecil he remained as much of an anathema. Despite a thin veneer of Protestantism, he was at heart a Catholic. His mother had never compromised her faith by attending Protestant services and had endured house arrest for her intransigence. Cecil gambled that Darnley's marriage to Mary would kill off two birds with one stone, destroying her credibility. Elizabeth would then realise that they were inappropriate as her successors, despite their unrivalled dynastic claim. Cecil shared the English view that, if Mary 'take fantasy to this new guest, then shall they be sure of mischief'. He probably considered Darnley as another temporary diversion to delay Mary's more serious marriage opportunities, never expecting that she would tolerate his bisexual and boorish character for long. He may even have persuaded Moray that he posed no real threat.

With Leicester still harbouring ambitions to marry Elizabeth, he assisted

---

* Darnley's dynastic position was extremely strong. Through his mother he was the grandson of Margaret Tudor and great-nephew of Henry VIII. As Mary was Margaret Tudor's granddaughter, they were half first cousins. His mother also claimed the Earldom of Angus, although his grandfather had debarred her to thwart Lennox, who had become Henry VIII's pro-English ally. Through his father, Darnley was the great-great-great-grandson of James II, making the Lennoxes heirs to the Scottish throne after the Hamiltons. With continuing doubts over the Hamiltons' legitimacy (although it has already been suggested that these were unfounded), Darnley could claim to be heir to the Scottish throne after his father. With such a pedigree, he was brought up by his mother at Templenewsam in Yorkshire expecting to become King.

Cecil in promoting Darnley as Mary's consort, and they both encouraged Elizabeth to permit his visit to Scotland. On 12 February 1565, a passport was granted for Darnley to visit his father. Darnley always recognised Leicester's part in providing it, and Elizabeth later told Guzman de Silva, the Spanish ambassador, that Leicester had himself turned down the marriage opportunity. By then, she had decided to pull back from letting him go.

Cecil's mistake in promoting Darnley was his failure to appreciate that the marriage would destroy Moray's authority, upon which the 'amity' with England depended.

References

1. Guy, p. 170
2. Guy, p. 187
3. Guy, p. 187
4. Guy, p. 187
5. Guy, p. 187
6. Guy, p. 174
7. Guy, p. 174
8. Châtelard, cited in Antonia Fraser, p. 88
9. Knox, cited in Guy, p. 178
10. Knox
11. Cited in Weir, p. 45
12. Brantôme, cited in Guy, p. 178, Antonia Fraser, p. 236 and Wormald, *Mary, Queen of Scots*, p. 147
13. Knox II, p. 82, cited in Guy pp. 176–7, Wormald, *Mary, Queen of Scots*, p. 148, Antonia Fraser, pp. 247, 248, and Marshall, p. 155
14. CSP Foreign, VI, p. 211, cited in Antonia Fraser, p. 237
15. Guy, p. 181
16. Guy, p. 183
17. Guy, p. 175
18. Knox, II, p. 73, cited in Antonia Fraser p. 247
19. Guy, p. 180
20. Guy, p. 177
21. Guy, p. 182
22. Guy, p. 183
23. Guy, p. 185 and Antonia Fraser, p. 191
24. Guy, p. 186
25. Guy, p. 186
26. CSP, Scottish, II, p. 8, cited in Antonia Fraser, p. 216
27. Guy, pp. 189–90
28. Wormald, *Mary, Queen of Scots*, p. 134
29. Antonia Fraser, p. 245

30. Randolph, 5 March 1564, Cotton MMS; Caligula B X f. 265
31. Randolph, 5 March 1564, Cotton MMS; Caligula B X f. 265
32. Guy, p. 192
33. Guy, p. 192
34. Antonia Fraser, p. 245
35. Guy, p. 193
36. Schutte, p. 182; cited in Marshall, p. 114
37. Guy, p. 194
38. Guy, p. 197
39. Cited in Wormald, *Mary, Queen of Scots*, p. 134, and Antonia Fraser, p. 209
40. Melville, p. 35, cited in Wormald, *Mary, Queen of Scots*, pp. 150–1, and Antonia Fraser, p. 254
41. Guy, p. 198
42. Melville, p. 40, cited in Marshall, p. 115
43. Knox, II, p. 85, note 6, cited in Antonia Fraser, p. 248
44. Guy, p. 198
45. Guy, p. 199
46. Guy, p. 200
47. Guy, p. 202
48. A. Teulet, *Papiers d'État Relatives a L'Histoire de l'Ecosse au 16e siecle*, II, p. 42, cited in Antonia Fraser, p. 256

15

Mary's Efforts to Take More Personal Control of her Government

In the early years of Mary's return to Scotland, Moray and Maitland held such a stranglehold over her government that it was perhaps inevitable that she would seek to spread her own wings. She gibed at Moray's constraining influence, but when she grasped the reins of government, she took decisions of which he strongly disapproved. Whatever else may be concluded about her, when left on her own, she showed political naivety and a misjudgement of people hard to reconcile with someone apparently so well groomed to govern.

With Moray the power behind the throne, Maitland mentored Mary to follow his advice. With his charm and persuasiveness, she saw Maitland as the person most likely to gain for her the succession to the English throne. This was his focus in the early part of her reign and, so long as it concurred with Moray's objectives, they remained closely associated. They had a taste for power, and neither would willingly relinquish authority. Yet, starting in 1564, several things started to weaken their dominant position in guiding Mary, not least because the choice of Mary's husband would soon be resolved. As their influence declined, their own close working relationship was irretrievably undermined.

Moray strongly opposed Lennox's restoration to his estates after leading English forces into Scotland during Mary's mother's regency. It was inevitable that Lennox would promote Darnley as Mary's spouse, undermining Moray's position as her principal adviser and undoing his considerable achievement in uniting the nobility behind her. Mary was also wary of Lennox, but recognised the dynastic advantage of marriage to his son. To counter Moray's opposition, Mary sought to rehabilitate Bothwell, who was still being held by Elizabeth in the Tower. In early 1563, she instructed Randolph to demand his release, saying, 'I do desire that he may be sent hither again into Scotland. So shall the pleasure be great and I will gladly requite the same.' She told Randolph, 'Whatever they say against him, it is rather from hate of his person and love that they bear otherwise than that he has deserved.'[1] Mary had just learned that her dynastic right to the English throne would be subject to trial and did not want Bothwell or any other Scottish lords held in England against her will. Elizabeth was bombarded with letters, two from Mary and one from Mary Fleming, who also persuaded Maitland to write. Even Randolph wrote, probably being pushed into it by Mary Bethune.

Mary was still angry at Bothwell breaking out of Edinburgh Castle and arranged a summons for his return to prison in Scotland. Yet Randolph reported that she wanted him to be 'reserved, though it were in prison, in store to be employed in any kind of mischief that any occasion may move.'[2] He knew that Bothwell could threaten both Moray and the 'amity', and told Cecil that his opinion of him had not changed. 'One thing I thought not to omit', he reported, '[is] that I know him as mortal an enemy to our whole nation as any man alive, despiteful out of measure, false and untrue as a devil.'[3] It was from Randolph's agent, of course, that Bothwell had waylaid the English money transfer four years earlier.

In April, Mary was still questioning the delay in Bothwell's release from the Tower, but was told that he imminently awaited trial over a legal dispute. By the end of June, he was freed on parole, but was not permitted to leave England. Randolph told Cecil, 'Lock up your wives and daughters!'*[4] By then, Mary was busy with her marriage negotiations, but Bothwell was short of money and petitioned her for help. In December, he wrote to Randolph from Northumberland seeking Mary's consent to leave England for France. The passport was granted, but he did not leave immediately. Randolph reported to Cecil that Bothwell had met up secretly with Mary at Dunbar in February 1564, and he believed that she planned to repatriate him. Yet for once Bothwell's mission was an act of kindness. Mary and he both visited his sister Jean on the death of Lord John Stewart after only two years of marriage.† It was not the start of a romance between them, as Buchanan later suggested. After consoling his sister, he honoured his pledge to go to France, where Mary arranged for him to become Captain of the Scottish Gens d'Armes.

In February 1565, after a year on the Continent, Bothwell again petitioned Mary to be allowed home, humbly offering to accept reasonable conditions.

---

* This was no doubt a reference to Bothwell having taken Anna Throndssen as a mistress in Denmark, before dumping her after his return to Scotland.

† Mary was the godmother to their son, Francis Stewart, named after Francis II. Francis was later to become the 5th Earl of Bothwell, after changing his name to Francis Stewart-Hepburn. ~ *queried the aims of rebellion,*
but did not change his name.

Randolph reported, 'Of herself, she is not evil affected towards him, but there are many causes why he is not so looked upon as some others are.'[5] Bothwell did not wait for Mary to reply, but arrived in Scotland a month later without her parole. He went to Hermitage Castle, sending William Murray* to plead his cause. Mary declared that 'she could not hate him', but Moray demanded his arrest and attainder.[6] The theft of the consignment of English money still rankled. Bothwell kept on the move to prevent Moray catching him, but managed to visit his mother Agnes Sinclair at Haddington. Randolph reported that he 'followeth the matter so earnestly that Scotland shall not hold them both'.[7] Tullibardine's brother, James Murray of Pardewis, and Bothwell's former servant, Dandie Pringle, were persuaded to tell Mary that he had spoken dishonourably of her in France. Bothwell had apparently claimed that she and Elizabeth 'would not make one honest woman', and that Mary had been the whore of her uncle the Cardinal.[8] It was also claimed that he had threatened to kill Moray, Maitland and Cecil. Genuinely shocked, Mary agreed that he should be tried for his treasonable remarks. According to Randolph, his return was 'altogether misliked and she had sworn upon her honour that he shall never receive favour at her hands'.[9]

When Bothwell was charged for his escape from Edinburgh Castle, Mary insisted on bail with a surety of £200. Although she tried to avoid a treason trial, it was set for 2 May and Moray nominated Argyll as the presiding judge and brought between 5,000 and 6,000 armed men to Edinburgh. Mary probably warned Bothwell not to appear. Despite being ably defended in his absence by his cousin, Alexander Hepburn of Riccarton, the jury found him guilty of treason, but Mary allowed him to leave for France before the verdict. She then stopped the Justice-Clerk from confirming sentence, although it was left on the record lest he should transgress again. Moray was even more furious when she refused to forfeit his estates. 'It is to be believed', wrote Randolph, 'that the Queen's Majesty would [do] him good, but I trust her Grace will not declare the same at this present.'[10] In return, Bothwell backed her marriage to Darnley.

It has been suggested that the real purpose for Moray having troops in Edinburgh for Bothwell's trial was to thwart Mary's marriage to Darnley. He apparently planned to kidnap the couple, taking Mary to St Andrews and

---

* There is some confusion as to whether this was Tullibardine, who later opposed Bothwell's marriage to Mary. It may have been Bothwell's chamberlain, who later travelled with him to Denmark. It seems unlikely that Tullibardine would have helped Bothwell, when his brother, James Murray of Pardewis, was reporting what Bothwell had been saying behind Mary's back.

Darnley to Castle Campbell while seeking Elizabeth's help. Yet Mary and Darnley had left Edinburgh to go hunting before their appearance.

After Lennox's arrival in Scotland he had gone to stay with his kinsman,* Atholl, to whom he confided his ambitions for Darnley to marry Mary and became 'well friended of Lethington'. Despite them having opposite faiths, Mary Fleming had persuaded Maitland to form a league with Atholl, her brother-in-law. Maitland recognised that Darnley met all his objectives to achieve for Mary a dynastic union strengthening her claim to the English throne. He was by then doubtful that Leicester's suit would come to anything. Yet marriage to Darnley would open the old factions within the Scottish nobility.

Lennox and Darnley needed other allies and gained support from Eglinton, Caithness, Seton (from France), and Livingston among others. Eglinton had been a long-standing Lennox associate in his feuding against Glencairn and Boyd. He now took Mass with Darnley at Holyrood. Darnley also became friendly with Riccio and John, 5th Lord Fleming, who had succeeded his brother in 1558.

Riccio was already one of Mary's closest confidants. He had a good bass voice and played the lute in a quartet made up of her *valets de chambre*. He also loved extravagant clothing, and Melville described him as a 'merry fellow', but 'hideously ugly', being deformed (probably a hunchback). Buchanan claimed spitefully that 'his appearance disfigured his elegance'.[11] Yet he was both loyal and discreet, and an amusing raconteur. In December 1564, Mary dismissed Augustine Raullet, her French secretary, ostensibly for accepting English bribes. Yet Raullet was a Guise adherent and was feeding the Cardinal with details of her diplomatic initiatives. Although he was later reinstated, he now returned to France with his wife, who had been Mistress of Mary's household, with his trunk containing his books and papers being confiscated as he boarded ship at Leith. His departure opened the door for the appointment of Riccio, whose inability to write good French did not seem to deter Mary, despite her regular redrafting of the correspondence. He now controlled access to her and freely accepted bribes, which no doubt financed his extravagant wardrobe. After his murder £2,000 was found among his possessions and this could not have been amassed from his salary of £80 per year. Scottish courtiers considered him a 'sly crafty foreigner', referring to him derogatorily as 'Seigneur Davie', when he grew arrogant and greedy in his new role.[12] It was even suggested that he was a papal spy, but no evidence for this has been established among the Vatican archives.

---

* Lennox was the grandson of Sir John Stewart, 1st Earl of Atholl, who was the present Atholl's great-grandfather.

Melville tried to warn him to be more circumspect and, with Mary spending so much time with him, gently reminded her of the stir caused when Châtelard was caught in her bedroom, but she would not be restrained from showing Riccio favour.

Facing general hostility, Riccio's friendship with Darnley blossomed out of mutual self-interest. He believed that Lennox and Darnley would protect his position, while he did what he could to promote the marriage. He was admitted to Darnley's 'table, his chamber and his most secret thoughts'. They would even 'lie in one bed together', which must be construed as evidence of a homosexual relationship between them.[13] With Riccio gaining in influence with Mary, he encouraged her to wrest control of her government from Moray and Maitland, seeing an opportunity to usurp Maitland's position as Secretary of State. According to Buchanan, who was close to the Lennoxes, Riccio 'was also assiduous in sowing seeds of discord' between Darnley and Moray.[14]

Those opposing the marriage became shocked by the triangular relationship developing between Mary, Darnley and Riccio. They saw it as a Catholic conspiracy to undermine the Kirk. At the beginning of April, Moray withdrew from court in disgust at the Catholic ceremony planned for Easter. He needed to assess what backing was available to him from the English, before taking a more hostile step. Mary used his absence as an opportunity to act independently.

After supporting Lennox in his plan for Darnley to marry Mary, Atholl became the focus for opposition to Moray and helped to defeat his ambitions to gain the throne, particularly as Argyll, Moray's most powerful supporter, was also declining in influence. With Moray and Argyll losing authority, Atholl progressively took control of government, and Mary neutralised Maitland by sending him on embassies abroad. From about 15 April to 13 May, he was in London to sound out approval for the marriage. Being friendly with both Atholl and Lennox, he could be relied upon to promote it in the best possible light. When Moray opposed it and developed his ambitions to replace Mary on the throne, Maitland began to mistrust him, and their relationship was irretrievably weakened. Yet Moray was quicker than either Maitland or Atholl to realise that Darnley's arrogant priggishness would eventually alienate them all.

Being away from Scotland, Maitland could not see Darnley's shortcomings at first hand or realise that Riccio was usurping his role. Yet he remained nominally as Secretary of State and was astute enough initially to retain a foot in both the Moray and Atholl camps while he judged how the wind blew. He progressively began to realise that Moray was right to oppose

Darnley and he became almost schizophrenic about the marriage plan. Professionally he favoured it because it met the diplomatic objectives of assuring Mary's succession to the English throne, but personally he opposed it because it threatened his authority.

Although Maitland was practically superseded in his absence by Riccio, he was completely engrossed in courting the fascinating Mary Fleming, fifteen years his junior. Their age disparity caused some mirth and Randolph reported that 'wise as he is he will show himself a fool'.* With Maitland preoccupied, Riccio was able to use Darnley's influence to fulfil the role of Secretary of State (although he was never formally confirmed in it) after Maitland had left court. Mary can be blamed for lacking judgement in allowing a court musician of doubtful integrity to usurp her most trusted and experienced adviser's position. Maitland may have thought that he could return to influence when he wanted, but, if so, he reckoned without her growing infatuation for Darnley.

Maitland would never accept his demotion as Secretary of State without a fight. He became devious in the extreme, resorting to every subterfuge to gain reinstatement. It was he who planned the murder of Riccio and the removal of Darnley from the throne. Yet he carefully avoided being in the vicinity when crimes were committed. As a master at hiding his feelings, he was soon mistrusted on all sides.

References

1. Guy, p. 225
2. Guy, p. 224
3. Gore-Browne, cited in Guy, p. 225
4. Guy, p. 225
5. Guy, p. 227
6. Cockburn and Maitland; CSP Scottish
7. Guy, p. 228
8. CSP, Scottish, II, p. 139, cited in Guy, p. 228, and in Antonia Fraser, p.270
9. Guy, p. 228
10. Guy, p. 228
11. Buchanan, p. 93, cited in Antonia Fraser, p. 272
12. Cited in Weir, p. 51
13. Buchanan; cited in Edith Sitwell, *The Queens and the Hive*, and Guy p. 211
14. Buchanan, cited in Weir, p. 62

---

* This was a bit rich as Randolph, who was born in 1523, was still playing court to Mary Bethune, some seventeen years younger than himself.

Part 3 The Darnley Marriage

16

The Complex Scheming that Led to Mary's Marriage to Darnley

Despite the combined persuasion of Lady Margaret, Cecil and Leicester, there has been much debate on why Elizabeth granted Darnley a passport to visit Scotland when she knew that the Lennoxes wanted to promote his marriage to Mary. She knew this would make the couple's claim to be her heir irresistible and, in Catholic eyes, both had a better claim to the English throne than she did. She knew that they would galvanise Catholic opposition to her, particularly as they could unite Scotland with England. Yet, despite the public opposing the match, she agreed to Darnley's visit with its inevitable consequences. She seemed to believe that he would not agree to marry Mary while his mother was under her control, threatened with the loss of the family's substantial English estates. That was to reckon without Lady Margaret's astute acceptance that the prospect of the Scottish and English thrones for her son was a prize worth any personal inconvenience for herself. Perhaps the consolation for Elizabeth of keeping Leicester for herself was too important to her.

Born on 7 December 1546, Darnley was four years younger than Mary. He and his brother Charles, nine years his junior, were the only two of the Lennoxes' ten children to survive infancy, making it understandable that they were indulged by doting parents. He was named Henry after his godfather, Henry VIII, but was brought up as a Catholic. His mother saw to it that he was schooled as a royal prince, completing his education in Paris and studying French and Latin to a high standard. He learned courtly pursuits, being a capable poet, lute player and dancer. He was an excellent horseman, loving the chase and hawking, and was trained in swordplay, shooting, running at the rings, tennis, golf and pell-mell (croquet). As the son of handsome parents, there can be little doubt that he was exceptionally, if effeminately, good-looking with a slim athletic physique. He was about six foot two inches tall, comparing well with Mary, who was only about three inches shorter, so that they towered above their contemporaries at a time when few men stood more than five foot six inches. At first sight, he made a favourable impression as Mary's suitor.

Yet beneath the outward gloss, Darnley was an objectionable and self-opinionated boor. Despite his careful education, he lacked common sense. Unable to hold his tongue, he revealed everything he was told to his friends and servants, who themselves were not always discreet. He was arrogant and idle and, when thwarted, could be petulant and uncouth with a violent temper. He was tactless and failed to keep his word. He was also selfish, vain and extravagant, spending substantial sums on food and clothing. He often became drunk and his openly homosexual* liaisons continued unabated. One of many adverse comments described him as 'mentally and morally weak, and his imbecility was conjoined with reckless courage ... and fatal obstinacy'. Yet his parents seemed blind to his shortcomings and failed to guide him to a more moderate stance. It is not difficult to understand that he alienated most of those with whom he came into contact. Melville sum-marised him as being 'haughty, proud, and so very weak in mind as to be a prey to all those that came about him'. He went on:

> He was inconstant, credulous and facile, unable to abide by any resolutions, capable to be imposed upon by designing men, and could conceal no secret, let it be either to his own welfare or detriment.[3]

Randolph, who had done so much to promote Mary's match with Leicester, did not relish Darnley's arrival and had heard 'bad things' about him. These appear to have been common knowledge in England at least.

Elizabeth granted a passport for Darnley to join Lennox in December 1564, and he left London on 3 February 1565, arriving in Edinburgh ten days later. With Mary away hunting in Fife, he spent three days in Edinburgh meeting Randolph, who lent him horses until his own arrived from England, and he developed a close friendship with Mary's wayward half-brother, Lord Robert Stewart, who entertained him at Holyrood. He then set out for Fife, where, on 17 February, he met Mary at the home of Sir John Wemyss of Wemyss. Lady Margaret had sent her son with further generous presents, this time for Mary, Maitland and Moray. Mary was more impressed than on

---

* Knox wrote that Darnley 'passed his time hunting and hawking, and other such pleasures as were agreeable to his appetites, having in his company gentlemen willing to satisfy his will and affections'.[1] In his *Historie of James the Sext*, Melville recorded that Darnley was 'much addicted to base and unmanly pleasures'.[2] In February 1566, when Mary was pregnant, Drury wrote to Cecil of a matter that had taken place at Inchkeith too disgraceful to be named in a letter. Such practices were very much the vogue among pleasure-loving males associated with the French court, which Darnley had visited as part of his upbringing.

her first meeting with him as a baby-faced fourteen-year-old in France more than four years before. He spent two nights at Wemyss before joining his father, who was with Atholl at Dunkeld. Yet he came back to take the ferry with her across the Firth of Forth on her return to Holyrood.

Mary gave no initial sign that meeting Darnley was more than a courtesy to her cousin, but she described him to Melville as 'the lustiest [most vigorous or athletic-looking] and best proportioned long man that I have ever seen'.[4] On first impressions he went down well, but Moray saw him 'rather as an enemy than a preferer of Christ's true religion'.[5] When the court returned to Edinburgh, Darnley tried to allay Moray's fears by accompanying him to St Giles' to hear Knox preach. He would happily display Reformist sentiments to help his cause, but also attended Mass with Mary privately. After hearing Knox, he dined at Holyrood with Randolph and Moray, who suggested that he should partner Mary in a galliard. Even Randolph saw them as outwardly well-suited and described him as 'a fair jolly young man'. He reported, 'A great number wish them well – others doubt him, and deeply consider what is fit for the state of their country.'[6] Violent snowstorms in Edinburgh made travel impossible, and, confined to Holyrood, Darnley enjoyed cards and dice with Mary and charmed her with his lute playing. This brought him into contact with Riccio, and their friendship developed. Darnley was present at banquets and masques, which Mary arranged, but she did not show him undue attention.

Despite Lady Margaret's capacity to scheme, no one expected the match to prosper. It seemed clear that Elizabeth would never countenance it, although Mary may have interpreted her grant of a passport as tacit approval. With Randolph still promoting Leicester, he played down any signs of a romance with Darnley, reporting that her interest 'arose rather from her own courteous nature than that anything is meant, which some here fear may ensue'. Yet he knew Mary's unpredictability, 'seeing she is a woman and in all things desires to have her own will', and he soon had to admit that Darnley's behaviour was 'well liked, and hitherto he so governs himself that there is great praise for him'.[7] Buoyed up by his success, Darnley lost no time in proposing marriage, which Mary just as quickly turned down. Yet Melville reminded her that it would 'put out of doubt their title to the succession' and Riccio was also persuasive.[8] Mary was enjoying Darnley's company with his love of hawking and hunting, and his courtly skills as a musician, poet and dancer.

In early February, Mary took Randolph aside to make clear that she intended to remarry: 'Not to marry, you know it cannot be for me. To defer it long, many incommodities ensue.'[9] At this stage, she would still have chosen either Don Carlos, remaining unaware of his incapacity, or Leicester, if she were proclaimed as Elizabeth's heir, and, as late as 24 March 1565, she tried unsuccessfully to revive the Don Carlos marriage negotiations. On 16 March, Randolph had been forced to advise her that, if she married Leicester,

> Elizabeth would advance her title to the succession in every way that she could, but could not gratify her desire to have her title determined and published, until she be married herself, or determined not to marry.[10]

This of course might never happen. Although Randolph confirmed Elizabeth's continued friendship, Mary realised that negotiations to marry Leicester had been a waste of time. 'To answer me with nothing,' she replied, 'I find great fault, and fear it shall turn to her discredit more than my loss.'[11] She walked out of their meeting and went hunting. In reality, Elizabeth had no choice; neither Cecil nor the English Parliament relished Leicester, his political opponent, as consort for the Catholic heir to the English throne. Yet she knew this made Mary's marriage to Darnley inevitable, despite what she might say in public. Moray was 'almost stark mad' with rage, seeing that his position was in danger, as was Maitland.[12] Randolph blamed Leicester, who had never even met Mary. He could not believe that he would forgo such a woman of 'perfect beauty'. He wrote to his friend Sir Henry Sidney, 'How many countries, realms, cities and towns have been destroyed to satisfy the lusts of men for such women.' Leicester had spurned a kingdom and the chance to lie with her 'in his naked arms'.[13]

With Don Carlos and Leicester no longer available, Mary decided to choose a husband for herself. On the day following her discussion with Randolph, she rode to Leith sands to watch Darnley and a group of companions running at the ring. Randolph went with her and she asked him to seek a passport for Maitland to travel through England to France. She did not explain his purpose, but Randolph inferred that she wanted to discuss her marriage options with her Guise relations. She had been encouraged by Riccio to believe that marriage would free her from Moray and Maitland. Yet she failed to appreciate its impact on her relationship with Elizabeth, the English government and the Reformers.

Love was already in the air at court where Mary Livingston sought to marry John Sempill, the illegitimate son of Robert, 3rd Lord Sempill,* who

---

* Lord Sempill held lands in Refrewshire, but had a well-established reputation for lawlessness, generally taking sides with his mother's family, the Montgomeries, in feuds against the Boyds and Cunninghams. In 1549, Archbishop Hamilton had to intercede to save him from execution for slaying William, 5th Lord Crichton at Châtelherault's house. John Sempill was one of several illegitimate children by Elizabeth Carlile, an Englishwoman, which resulted in Randolph describing him as 'a happy Englishman'.[14] There was also a substantial family of legitimate children by Lord Sempill's wife, Isabel, daughter of Sir William Hamilton of Sanquhar. One of these, Grizel, lived openly as the Archbishop's mistress, providing him with at least three children, whom he later legitimised, and the Sempills acted as his bailiffs at Paisley Abbey.

was a Catholic, 'a man sold under sin, an enemy to god and all godliness' according to Knox. Mary Livingston was known as 'Lusty' by her fellow Maries, but this had no sexual connotation as when applied to Darnley, and indisputably referred to her energy. The Livingstons approved of Sempill, despite rumblings about his illegitimacy, perhaps recognising Mary's wholehearted support for the couple. Despite the Maries' undertaking not to marry before their widowed Queen, Mary became bound up in all the arrangements. Randolph, who still had an eye for Mary Bethune, reported, 'at least she will have compassion on her four Maries, who for her sake have vowed never to marry if she be not the first.' The planning went on for two months beforehand, and Mary paid for the rich silk to make the wedding dress and for the banquet, which took place at Forfar on 6 March 1565. She provided them with estates worth £500 per year, including Auchtermuchty in Fife and lands at Strathbogie forfeited from Huntly (although these had to be swapped for Little Cumbrae Island in the Clyde when the Huntly estates were restored). John's father promised him property at Beltries out of his grandfather's estate. His uncle William Sempill had received lands at Auchinames from Archbishop Hamilton for services that he had provided and, having no children, promised these to his nephew on his death. John duly inherited them in 1576. The French ambassador wrote to Catherine de Medici that Mary had 'begun to marry off her Maries, and says that she wishes she herself were of the band'.[15]

Despite Randolph's admiration for Mary Bethune, this seems to have been unrequited on her part, although Mary was well aware of his interest. When Elizabeth would not permit him to attend her marriage to Darnley, Mary tried to entice him by keeping Bethune away from him for a fortnight beforehand, while promising that, if he came, she would allow him to dance with her. Despite this attractive offer, Randolph would not disobey his Queen. Mary Fleming was still being courted my Maitland to much incredulity. Kirkcaldy considered her about as suitable for him 'as I am to be pope'.[16] Yet Maitland was obsessed, telling Cecil that his passion brought him at least one 'merry hour' in the day despite the difficulties of state matters, averring 'that those that be in love be ever set upon a merry pin'.[17]

Moray was soon openly opposing Mary's plan to marry Darnley, whose veneer of charm was starting to crack. It was unfortunate that when Lord Robert Stewart showed Darnley a map outlining his half-brother's extensive estates, Darnley unwisely commented that they were 'too much for his needs'.[18] Lord Robert appears to have warned Moray, who complained indignantly to Mary. Darnley was made to apologise, but Moray knew that his former authority would be lost if Darnley became King. He was almost certainly behind a Reformist mob that abducted a Catholic priest from Holyrood during Easter 1565, while the court was at Stirling. The priest was taken to the Market Cross where he was pelted with eggs (the Catholic symbol for Easter) and beaten up. Although the Provost rescued him, he had to interrupt his supper to stop a Catholic mob from retaliating. The Scottish lords became polarised over the marriage, rejoining the factions that Moray had worked so hard to dissipate. Initially, Moray had support from Argyll, Glencairn and other Protestant lords, who mistrusted Darnley's Catholicism, and from Châtelherault and the Hamiltons, who hated the Lennoxes and saw that any resulting children would demote their claim to be heirs to the throne.

Robert Melville, whose family estates had been restored only two years before, also opposed the marriage, despite accepting the gift of a ruby ring from Lady Margaret Lennox. Mary neutralised him by sending him with his brother Sir James to seek Elizabeth's consent in London, relying on them to promote it in the best light. Robert stayed on as Mary's envoy in London and was still there at the time of Darnley's murder and Mary's subsequent marriage to Bothwell, whom he also strongly disliked. He eventually returned to Scotland in May 1567, when he retired to his estates at Murdocarney in Fife.

On 5 April 1565, the court moved for Easter to Stirling Castle with Mary and Darnley in the early stages of courtship. He partnered her at billiards against Randolph and Mary Bethune. It was agreed that, whoever won, the ladies would share the stake. When Randolph and Mary Bethune triumphed, Darnley settled the debt and presented Mary with a ring and brooch set with two agates worth fifty crowns. He could ill afford such extravagance, and Lennox had to borrow 500 crowns from Maitland to keep the suit alive.

By some quirk of fate, Darnley became ill at Stirling, suffering a cold followed by skin eruptions. He then developed a measles-like rash,* accompanied by 'sharp pangs, his pains holding him in his stomach and in his head'.[19] These are the symptoms of secondary syphilis, which he must have contracted in England before his arrival. Mary insisted on nursing him herself and any formality in their relationship evaporated. He was given rooms in the royal apartments, where he remained for a month, and Mary visited him at all times of the day and night, even after midnight. As he

---

* Darnley seems to have been treated for measles, and it may well be that Mary's doctors failed to diagnose syphilis at this stage. There is no record of the use of 'salivation of mercury' as a cure, nor of halitosis, which was its side effect. Yet, when he suffered a renewed bout of syphilis at the time of James's baptism, this treatment was applied with resultant reports of his bad breath.

slowly recovered, royal decorum disappeared, and she was overwhelmed with sensations that she cannot have known she possessed. In the words of a poem of the period it was, 'O lusty May, with Flora Queen.'[20] She did not realise that his temperamental character was not just that of a fractious invalid, but a symptom of his disease. She had become enthralled with a 'fantasy of a man, without regard to his tastes, manners or estate'.[21] Concerns about Elizabeth's approval and Mary's need to make a powerful connection were suddenly irrelevant. When warned that his shortcomings would cause discord with the Scottish nobility, she was in no mood to listen. She refused to travel even to Perth while he remained ill, but showered gifts on him and, by nursing him at night, compromised her reputation.

With Darnley four years her junior, Leslie later confirmed that there was a strong maternal element to Mary's feelings, causing her to overlook his adolescent shortcomings. Darnley was delighted with the attention, and the success of his family's plan, but was too narcissistic to become infatuated himself, seeing her only as a trophy. Everyone was caught out by the model queen falling in love out of unbridled passion. The Privy Council was split, with Maitland, who was under pressure from Mary Fleming, Atholl, Ruthven and Riccio, supporting the marriage, and Moray, Châtelherault and Argyll against it. Mary later claimed that Moray had encouraged the suit to annoy Châtelherault and the Hamiltons, thinking that he could change her mind when he needed to. This would explain why he seemed slow in trying to stop the relationship from developing, and implies that he accepted Cecil's assumption that she would soon realise Darnley's shortcomings. Randolph wrote to Cecil belittling his 'behaviour, wit and judgement', and considered Mary 'in contempt of her people'.[22] After all the favour she had shown to Moray, she expected him to back her marriage. When he opposed it, she let it be known that it confirmed his ambition for the Crown.

The true purpose of Maitland's diplomatic mission became clear on his arrival in London. He had no intention of going to France and demanded Elizabeth's approval for Mary to marry Darnley, who was both a member of the English royal family and an English subject. Elizabeth was suddenly alarmed, realising that the Scottish Protestant nobles, with whom she had formed such a good working relationship, were in great jeopardy. She told the Privy Council that the marriage was 'unmeet, unprofitable and perilous to the sincere amity between the two queens'.[23] She refused her consent, claiming that she was offended at Darnley's failure to seek her permission before leaving England. On 20 April, Lady Margaret was placed under house arrest at Whitehall and the Templenewsam estates were confiscated. Their contents included an ornate bed canopy bearing the royal arms. Two months later, she was moved to the Tower with her confinement made 'hourly more severe' and was released to Sheen only in March 1567 after her son's murder.[24] Elizabeth signed letters recalling Lennox and Darnley, but then countermanded them, not wanting to be accused of having promoted the marriage by sending them north in the first place. On 24 April, she sent Throckmorton to Scotland to convey her disapproval and to tell Mary that, if she married Leicester, the succession could be arranged. Cecil spent the whole of 1 May in the Privy Council debating how to stop the marriage. Yet Mary ignored the English bluster and sought approval from European Catholic heads of state. Maitland followed his brief by meeting de Silva, the Spanish ambassador in London, to promote it with Philip II, who saw it as assuring the 'success of her claims and the quiet of her country'.[25] Slightly to Mary's relief, Catherine de Medici also signalled approval, hoping that Elizabeth would seek closer links with France, if the 'amity' with Scotland broke down. She then hedged her bets by telling Elizabeth that she opposed it. Mary also gained support from the Papacy, hitherto disappointed at her tolerance of the Reformers. On 22 May, she sought a dispensation needed because she and Darnley were cousins. This had the Cardinal of Lorraine's support, despite his earlier disparaging comments.

On 3 May, Mary received a letter from Maitland warning her of Elizabeth's fury. She did not waver and advised him to tell her sister Queen that 'she did mind to use her own choice in marriage'.[26] He had already left London before receiving her reply and thought better of returning to deliver it, not wanting to risk the 'amity'. He was so angry with her that he showed it to Throckmorton, whom he met at Alnwick, while both were on their way north. Mary was furious at him failing to deliver her letter and dismissed him from court. This left him time to be with Mary Fleming, whose influence was such, that he was 'blinded to further and prosecute this marriage' out of love for her.[27]

Mary tried to win over Moray by confirming that, as a minor, Darnley would not be offered the Crown Matrimonial. She summoned him to Darnley's sickroom, but he still refused his support, 'because he feared that the Lord Darnley would be an enemy to true religion'. 'Hereupon between them rose great altercation, [and] she gave him many sore words.'[28] Although Mary hoped for Argyll's backing, he retired to his estates 'indignant at the overwhelming insolence of Darnley'.

If anyone believed that the marriage would founder out of lack of support, they bargained without Lady Margaret's scheming from imprisonment. She bought Morton's important backing by agreeing to cede her claim to the Angus earldom. Although he generally supported Moray, he would not turn down any rich pickings arising out of his decline in favour. His infant nephew, Archibald, was already established as the 8th Earl of Angus in accordance with the entail to the 6th Earl's will and, as his guardian, Morton received the income for himself. He brought with him the support of his close associates, Glamis and the unattractive Lindsay of the Byres, who had succeeded his father in December 1563. Lindsay was Atholl's uncle by marriage and Glamis was the grandson of Janet Douglas, Morton's aunt. Ruthven, who had married Lady Margaret's illegitimate half-sister, Janet, also offered support. Mary overlooked her concerns at his use of sorcery by visiting him at Ruthven Castle for two days starting on 25 June, and he became the chief councillor to promote the marriage. She could not afford to be too particular in her allies.

Erskine was persuaded that the marriage was a true love match by his wife Annabella, Mary's close confidante. Mary at last arranged a Royal Charter on 23 June 1565, fulfilling his long-held family ambition to be confirmed as Earl of Mar.* Home gave his support out of loyalty to Mary, despite being threatened by the English under Bedford. Even Glencairn, who disliked Darnley and supported Moray, overcame his Protestant scruples to attend the ceremony.

On 15 May, while at Stirling, Mary formally asked the Scottish lords to support the marriage in the face of Elizabeth's opposition. Although they were not enthusiastic, they closed ranks behind her, being affronted by Elizabeth's blatant interference. 'Many consented on condition that no change was made to the established state of religion.'[29] Only Ochiltree, Knox's father-in-law, now opposed it on religious grounds, but Moray left before the vote and Argyll refused to attend. On 21 May, Moray was forced to withdraw from court and joined his mother at Lochleven. He now shunned Council meetings and Atholl took formal control of the govern-ment. Mary had demonstrated four years of religious tolerance. She was popular, and the Scots did not consider it a bad match. It would not take Darnley long to undo their goodwill.

On 15 May, Throckmorton arrived at Stirling Castle, but, with the gates locked, he was obliged to find lodgings in the town. When Mary saw him, he handed over Elizabeth's letter and a 'determination' from Cecil signed by a

---

* Mary's lawyers confused the grant by reinstating the original title, which passed through the female line, and then passing on to him the new one originally offered to Moray, which did not. In 1875 the House of Lords upheld the view that the entail of the original title had been replaced by the new one, allowing the Earls of Mar and Kellie, represented by the male Erskine line, to hold both grants. However, this decision was amended in 1885 when the female line was granted the original title to become Earls of Mar, but leaving the newer one with the Earls of Mar and Kellie.

majority of the English Privy Council advising her to drop Darnley in favour of Leicester or another English nobleman. As Leicester had not signed it, its impact was diminished, and Mary advised that she would marry Darnley. She had taken Elizabeth's advice in rejecting Continental candidates, choosing an Englishman, who was Elizabeth's 'near kinsman'. Yet she agreed a delay for three months.

Throckmorton reported back to Leicester that Mary was 'seized with love in fervener passions than is comely in any mean personage'. Having witnessed her passionate embraces, he commented, 'I cannot assure myself that such qualities will bring forth such fruit as the love and usage bestowed on Darnley shows,'[30] and concluded that their marriage was 'irrevocable otherwise than by violence'.[31] Randolph confirmed all this, saying, 'Shame is laid aside, and all regard of that which chiefly pertaineth to princely honour removed out of sight.'[32] They were even rumoured to be in bed together, but this seems unlikely, and was later denied by Randolph, who would have been only too keen to report such a scurrilous titbit, but he noted pessimistically that she

> was so altered with affection towards the Lord Darnley that she hath brought her honour in question, her estate in hazard, her country to be torn in pieces ... The queen in her love is so transported, and he is grown so proud, that to all honest men he is intolerable, and almost forgetful of his duty to her already, that hath ventured so much for his sake. What shall become of her, or what life with him she shall lead, that taketh so much upon him to control and to command her, I leave to others to think.[33]

Despite love tokens being exchanged every day, Darnley became progressively more objectionable and hot-headed: 'He spareth not, in token of his manhood, to let blows fly.'[34] Immediately following the vote by the lords at Stirling, he was knighted and created Earl of Ross. Yet when the grant was delivered, he threatened Bellenden, the Justice-Clerk, with his dagger, because he was not appointed Duke of Albany as he expected. Mary had held this back while awaiting Elizabeth's reaction. On 23 May, Châtelherault came to make his peace with him while he convalesced at Stirling, but Darnley threatened to 'knock his pate'. 'His pride was intolerable and his words could not be borne except where no man speak again.'[35] He associated with court reprobates, particularly Lord Robert Stewart, and was often found drunk in Edinburgh bars and brothels. Unable keep his mouth shut, he leaked the marriage terms before the Council had approved them.

Maitland and Moray saw this as calamitous. It was clear that he saw the marriage merely as a necessary step on his way to becoming King of both Scotland and England.

When the Guises in France heard of Darnley's behaviour, the Cardinal cautioned Mary against the marriage, despite having supported the papal dispensation. Even the four Maries caused a rift by expressing concerns, perhaps coloured by Maitland's rapidly changing opinion. Darnley's allies would no longer defend him. By June, Randolph reported that, 'being of better understanding' of Darnley's shortcomings, Mary was trying 'to frame and fashion him to the nature of her subjects', but with little success as he was 'proud, disdainful and suspicious', and she became ill.[36] Randolph told Leicester, 'Her majesty is laid aside, her wits not what they were, her beauty another than it was, her cheer and countenance changed into I wot not what.' She had become 'a woman more to be pitied than any that I ever saw', and he was 'the most unworthy' to be matched with her.[37] Randolph wrote prophetically, 'What shall become of him I know not, but it is greatly to be feared that he can have no long life among these people.'[38]

Mary would not be diverted from the wedding plan and, on 10 June, summoned a Convention of the nobility to meet at Perth to gain formal approval for a Catholic ceremony. Leslie dissuaded her from being more confrontational and using the opportunity 'to take the final order of religion'. Moray did not go to Perth, claiming that he was ill with diarrhoea at Lochleven, and spread a rumour that the Lennoxes were planning to assassinate him. They in turn claimed he planned to kidnap Darnley and his father to return them to England. There is no evidence that this was contemplated, but, on 2 July, Elizabeth summoned them back. Mary retired to her rooms in tears. If she defied Elizabeth, she risked her hopes of the English succession. If she capitulated, Darnley would be charged with treason. After delaying her decision for a fortnight, she defiantly instructed them to stay. She told Randolph that Elizabeth had sent Darnley north believing him unworthy of her, but she would choose her own husband and would 'snap her fingers at all who opposed' her marriage. Randolph suggested that Elizabeth would like her better if she became Protestant. This made Mary furious that she was expected to barter her religion to gain Elizabeth's approval. She told him that, if the 'amity' were now lost, it would be an 'incommodity' as much for Elizabeth as for her.[39]

Cecil threatened war, but, with Darnley being so much despised, he favoured a marriage that might destroy Mary's credibility. Randolph was now aware of Cecil's objective and saw it as a great benefit for Elizabeth, as English Catholics would never support her with Darnley at her side. In June, the English Privy Council secretly agreed to finance Moray, and Elizabeth sent him £3,000 'to uphold the true religion and to support their queen with good advice'. He met with Randolph, Châtelherault, Glencairn, Argyll and Boyd at Lochleven, resulting in Cecil being approached for troops and artillery, but Elizabeth could not be seen to provide overt support against an anointed queen. Moray had the support of Knox and other Reformist ministers, who condemned Mary from the pulpit, and he tried to kidnap the couple before their wedding, as they travelled from Perth to Callendar for the christening of Livingston's eldest son, Alexander. Having been tipped off, Mary left Perth at five o'clock in the morning, escorted by Atholl and Ruthven with 300 horse. They completed the thirty-mile journey without a break, arriving at Callendar an hour before they had been expected to leave Perth.

On 9 July, Mary and Darnley spent two nights at Seton, although Seton himself was still in France. Randolph reported to Elizabeth that they had been secretly married* beforehand in Riccio's apartments at Holyrood 'with not above seven persons present', and they consummated their union at Seton.[40] Yet Randolph later reported that these were merely rumours and 'the likelihoods are so great to the contrary'. His later retraction may have been based on knowing that Darnley was homosexual, but it seems realistic that they would have taken the opportunity away from prying eyes at Court to sleep together. It would have been too much of a temptation for such a besotted couple. Much later when Mary 'was at variance with her husband', Moray wrote to Giovanni Correr, the Venetian ambassador in Paris, 'that the King had boasted to him of having had intimacy with her before she was his wife'.[41] When Mary heard this, she challenged Darnley, but he denied saying it. This only added to Moray's antagonism of him.

On 22 July, the wedding banns were read at St Giles'. On the following day, Darnley was at last made Duke of Albany and, before the wedding on 29 July, Mary confirmed that he would be crowned as King Henry. She did not have parliamentary consent for this and later had to attend the vote to assure agreement. She told Parliament that she had 'previously been married to one of the greatest kings in Christendom and therefore intended to wed no one unless he were a king'.[42] Yet she refused Darnley the Crown

---

* It has been suggested that this was a form of betrothal ceremony, after which it was normal for a couple to have sexual relations. This could explain why Mary brought forward the formal wedding ceremony ahead of receiving the Pope's dispensation and ahead of the three-month delay promised to Throckmorton, so that she limited the risk of becoming pregnant beforehand. Although the papal dispensation had been requested on 22 May, such was the communication difficulty with Rome that it was not granted until early September. Yet by their wedding day on 29 July, Mary hoped that it would have been approved. The grant, when given, was in fact backdated to the time of the request, so Prince James's legitimacy was never in doubt.

Matrimonial, which would have allowed him to succeed if she died childless, on the grounds that he was a minor. Yet he was well aware that Francis II had been granted this status at a younger age, and it remained a bone of contention thereafter. He had damaged his cause by claiming that he cared more for English Catholics than Scottish Reformers, and Parliament would never have ratified it.

The wedding took place in a Catholic ceremony on 30 July at between five and six o'clock in the morning. Mary still wore 'a great mourning gown of black with the great white mourning hood', and was escorted by Lennox and Atholl, who then attended Darnley, who was wearing a magnificent jewelled outfit.[43] After exchanging vows, he provided Mary with three rings for the fingers of her right hand as was then the custom, the middle one a 'rich diamond'.[44] Other than Moray, Châtelherault and Argyll, almost all the nobles attended. John Sinclair, Dean of Restalrig and Lord President of the Council, officiated with prayers over the kneeling couple and was appointed Bishop of Brechin soon after. The couple parted with a kiss while Mary attended a nuptial Mass to symbolise that she could replace her widow's weeds with wedding finery, and King Henry remained in his chamber not wishing to give offence to the Protestant lords. Each of her ladies then removed one pin as she changed out of her mourning clothes. Although Randolph did not attend, he reported that they did not immediately retire to bed 'to signify unto the world that it was not lust moved them to marry, but only the necessity of the country, if she will not leave it destitute of an heir'.[45] At noon they began a magnificent marriage feast served by Atholl and Morton, the only two lords other than Lennox prepared to offer them unreserved support. This was followed by music and dancing and, before retiring, there was a supper followed by a Latin masque written by Buchanan. Celebrations continued for three days with three more of Buchanan's masques on different aspects of love. Knox saw it as nothing but 'balling and dancing and banqueting'.[46] Largesse was thrown to the crowds, before the couple returned to Seton for their honeymoon.

On the day after the wedding, Darnley was again proclaimed King, making him as proud as a peacock, but only his father echoed support, shouting out, 'God save his grace!' On Mary's instruction, the King's name was given precedence over hers on state documents and on coinage struck to mark the occasion. Yet he remained objectionable, and Randolph reported that 'he looketh now for reverence to many that have little will to give it to him'.[47] Mary seemed blind to his shortcomings, being 'given over unto him her whole will to be ruled and guided as himself best likes, but she can as little prevail with him in anything that is against his will'.[48] She asked Melville to wait upon the King, who was but young, and give him my best counsel, which might help him to shun many inconveniences, desiring me also to befriend Riccio, who was hated without cause.[49]

Melville seems to have gained the King's respect.

After their honeymoon the couple returned to Edinburgh and the King arranged for an ostentatious throne to be positioned above the rest of the congregation at St Giles', from where he listened to Knox's sermons for the next two months. Yet Knox supported Moray and, not being one to mince his words, referred to Mary as 'that harlot Jezebel' and claimed that God had set boys and women to rule over them.[50] The King grimaced under Knox's invective and stormed out. He refused dinner and went hawking. Knox was suspended for fifteen days, during which he published his sermon.

Elizabeth was furious on hearing of the wedding, particularly after Mary's undertaking not to marry for three months. She feared that Catholicism would be restored in Scotland as a prelude to Mary seeking the English throne. On 30 July, she sent John Thomworth, a Gentleman of her Privy Chamber, to Scotland to interview Mary, but with instructions to ignore the King. He was to remonstrate over her 'very strange' and 'unneighbourly' conduct. She was to be told that 'she forgets herself marvellously to raise up such factions as is understood among her nobility'. Knowing that Moray was about to start his rebellion, which she had financed, Elizabeth told Mary to be reconciled to him, 'who has so well served her'. Mary would have none of it. She moved with admirable speed to isolate Moray and his fellow rebels. She refused to call Parliament to meet in July to avoid giving them a platform to oppose the marriage. She portrayed Moray as petulant at losing power. Her show of tolerance weakened his criticism of her and gained her the moderates' support. Yet she was determined to gain freedom of Catholic worship, and Randolph estimated that Papists outnumbered Reformers in Edinburgh. When the General Assembly tried to abolish the Mass, she refused to risk losing the friendship of the King of France, the ancient ally of this realm, and of the other great princes, her friends and confederates, who would take it in evil part, of whom she may look for support in all her necessities.[51]

Marriage gave Mary the confidence to stand up to Elizabeth. She told Thomworth that she did not 'enquire what order of government her good sister observed within her realm' and that princes of a realm were 'subject immediately to God'. She warned Elizabeth 'to meddle no further with private causes concerning [Moray] or any other subjects of Scotland'.[52] Otherwise she would interfere on behalf of her mother-in-law, Lady

Margaret, who had been unworthily imprisoned. She offered a deal; she and the King would do nothing to enforce their immediate dynastic claim to the English throne and would not assist English rebels allying with foreign princes against her or seek to change the religion, laws or liberties of England. In return, they expected Elizabeth not to ally with foreign princes or Scottish rebels against her rule and to settle the English succession in her favour by Act of Parliament. She now felt more secure than at any time since leaving France, but her supporters, particularly King Henry and Riccio, were woefully inadequate as substitutes for Moray and Maitland in government and she had to deal with Moray's rebellion.

When Mary had returned to Scotland, the Crown's traditional supporters were initially in disarray, after all the opposition to Bethune and later to the Queen Regent. Yet now there was a clearly formed group who would back her against Moray, if their interests diverged. They were initially open-minded about Darnley, but he quickly alienated many of them. Support has to be seen to be for Mary alone, although, after the King's murder, even this almost evaporated until her imprisonment at Lochleven. As the senior Catholic among the nobility and head of government, Atholl led Mary's supporters with Maitland's clandestine assistance. They were not all Catholic and were not close-knit.

Mary could always rely on blind allegiance from traditional courtiers like Seton, Livingston and Fleming. Seton returned from France only in August 1565 and was not an enemy of Moray, but would always support her against him. Livingston, who had inherited from his father in 1553, was Mary Livingston's brother, who had married Mary Fleming's sister, Agnes. This made them close confidants, whom she visited regularly at Callendar. Fleming was a friend of the King, and, as Atholl's brother-in-law, became Great Chamberlain on 30 June 1565.

The powerful Catholic families also supported Mary against Moray. In addition to Atholl, these included Erroll, David Lindsay, 10th Earl of Crawford* and Eglinton, who, like the Gordons, saw her, even when imprisoned, as the means of restoring Papacy against an increasingly dominant and dogmatic Kirk. Crawford acted as the cupbearer at her

---

* Born in 1527 Crawford had inherited from his kinsman and guardian, David Lindsay of Edzell in 1558. His father, Alexander, Master of Crawford, known as 'The Wicked Master', had been stripped of his titles after seizing and imprisoning his own father, the 8th Earl. This had resulted in Edzell being appointed as the 9th Earl. The Wicked Master came to an untimely end in Dundee in 1541, and the 9th Earl, whose own son became the 1st Lord Lindsay of Balcarres, rehabilitated The Wicked Master's son to restore the dynastic Crawford bloodline. Yet the 10th Earl was also lawless and violent, and was treated with caution by his colleagues. He had been reconverted to Catholicism by the Jesuit William Crichton and married Cardinal Bethune's illegitimate daughter Margaret.

wedding and remained loyal until his death in 1578, when his son, David, the 11th Earl, took over his Catholic mantle. She could also rely on Sir Thomas Kerr of Ferniehirst, who had succeeded his father, Sir John, in July 1562. He had married Janet, daughter and heir of Sir William Kirkcaldy of Grange, and their second son changed his name to William Kirkcaldy to inherit his illustrious grandfather's estates. Ferniehirst was a 'stout and able warrior', who continued his family's feud with the Scotts of Buccleuch and more intermittently with his mother's family, the Kers of Cessford, despite efforts to settle matters by intermarriage between the three groups. He was secretly Catholic, but, in December 1564, was warded in Edinburgh for non-payment of *teinds* [tithes] to the Commendator of Jedburgh. On Mary's marriage, he joined the Privy Council, providing her with protection when travelling in southern Scotland. He brought the support of his brother-in-law, Hay of Yester, who was also on the Privy Council. Cassillis was not much more than twenty on Mary's return to Scotland, but, despite a lawless lifestyle, remained loyal, and until the end of 1565 took Mass with her as a Catholic at Holyrood. In 1566, he married Glamis's daughter, Margaret Lyon, and, according to Knox:

> By her persuasion became a protestant, and caused to reform his churches in Carrick, and promised to maintain the doctrine of the evangel.

This did nothing to diminish his support for Mary. Although mercurial, Sempill, Mary Livingston's father-in-law, was another Catholic supporter, having traditionally allied with the Lennoxes against the Hamiltons, particularly in disputes over Paisley Abbey. He had become Governor of Castle Douglas in 1533 and had supported the Queen Regent, although more out of dislike* for Châtelherault than loyalty to the French party. He also brought the support of his son-in-law, James, 4th Lord Ross, and initially of his nephew and ward, Alan, 4th Lord Cathcart. Yet, as a Reformer, Cathcart later defected to Moray and Morton.

The Hamiltons followed Châtelherault's lead in supporting Moray, but as soon as King Henry with his Lennox connections had been removed, they reverted to Mary and backed her during her captivity in England, both

---

* In the autumn of 1559, Sempill had attacked Châtelherault, resulting in the Hamiltons retaliating by besieging Castle Sempill. Leaving his son, Robert Master of Sempill, in command, he managed to escape unnoticed to the French garrison at Dunbar. On Castle Sempill's surrender, the Hamiltons discovered the deception and sought him out at Dunbar, but the French refused to hand him over. The Queen Regent relaxed him from his attainder in March 1560.

against Moray's Regency and James VI, when he took up the reins of government. This was principally because James recognised the Lennox Stewarts as his heirs, but also because he was to usurp the Hamilton title of Earl of Arran for his favourite, Captain James Stewart. Châtelherault's second son, Lord John Hamilton, born in 1532, had been granted the benefice of the Abbey of Arbroath* in 1541. On 10 May 1560, he ratified the Treaty of Berwick at Leith and supported his elder brother Arran's suit to marry Elizabeth. He was also implicated in the story of Bothwell inciting Arran, by now insane, to abduct Mary to Dumbarton to marry her. In March 1563, Châtelherault had to advise him to return to court to make his peace with Mary. He appears to have remained in favour with her thereafter. In 1564, he went to Italy, and was not in Scotland at the time of her marriage, only returning in late 1566. His brother, Lord Claud Hamilton, eleven years his junior, was only twenty-two when Mary married and had been detained by the English in Newcastle as a hostage to assure the ratification of the Treaty of Berwick, but was freed in February 1562. He received a grant of Paisley Abbey from his illegitimate uncle, Archbishop John Hamilton, who always supported Mary, despite having become another worldly prelate, plundering church benefices for his kinsmen and maintaining Grizel Sempill as his mistress at Paisley.

Another of Mary's most influential Catholic supporters was John Leslie, who had visited her in France. Although a priest, he had become an ordinary judge in the Court of Session. On 18 October 1565, he became a Privy Councillor and was her principal adviser during her captivity.

A number of Protestants placed loyalty to their Catholic queen above their Reformist scruples, but most of these despised the King. Sir John Maxwell was one of those who supported her, or perhaps more particularly opposed Moray, once she was dissociated from King Henry and later Bothwell. His allegiance followed a pattern not dissimilar to Maitland.

Despite the considerable power of Mary's supporters, only Lennox could boast acknowledged military skills. She needed to foster the loyalty of Moray's traditional enemies. This meant rehabilitating Bothwell and George Gordon.

---

* His rights to the abbacy have resulted in Lord John being known as Lord Arbroath in many references, but this was not a peerage.

References

1. Knox, II, p. 174, cited in Antonia Fraser, pp. 275–6, and Weir, p. 101
2. T. Thomson (ed), *Historie and Life of James Sext*, cited in Weir, p. 57
3. Melville, cited in Weir, p. 57
4. Melville, p. 45, cited in Antonia Fraser, p. 256, and Marshall, p. 116
5. Randolph to Cecil, 8 May 1563, CSP Scottish, II p. 156
6. CSP, Scottish, II, p. 126, cited in Antonia Fraser, p. 257
7. Guy, p. 205, Antonia Fraser, p. 258, and Weir, p. 59
8. Melville, cited in Weir, p. 59
9. Guy, p. 203
10. Weir, p. 60
11. Guy, p. 206
12. Guy, p. 206
13. Guy, p. 207
14. Antonia Fraser, p. 258
15. Teulet, II, p. 32, cited in Antonia Fraser, p. 258
16. CSP, Scottish, II, p. 75, cited in Antonia Fraser, p. 257
17. CSP, Scottish, II, p. 129, cited in Antonia Fraser, p. 257
18. R. Keith, *History of the Affairs of Church and State in Scotland*, cited in Weir, p. 60
19. Guy, p. 208
20. Bannatyne MS; Oxford Book of Scottish Verse, p. 176, cited in Antonia Fraser, p. 261
21. CSP Scottish, cited in Weir, p. 63
22. CSP Scottish, cited in Weir, pp. 63, 65
23. CSP Scottish; Keith, cited in Weir, p. 64
24. CSP Spanish, cited in Weir, p. 77
25. Guy, pp. 208–9
26. CSP Scottish, cited in Weir, p. 66
27. Guy, p. 209
28. CSP Scottish, cited in Guy, p. 209, and Weir, p. 66
29. Cockburn and Maitland, cited in Weir, p. 67
30. CSP Scottish, cited in Weir, p. 68
31. Cited in Guy, p. 213
32. CSP Scottish, cited in Weir, p. 68
33. Guy, p. 211, Wormald, *Mary, Queen of Scots*, p. 155, and Weir, p. 68
34. CSP Scottish, cited in Weir, p. 69
35. CSP Scottish, cited in Weir, p. 69
36. Weir, p. 72
37. CSP Scottish, cited in Guy, pp. 211–2, and Weir, p. 69
38. Cited in Antonia Fraser, p. 263, and Weir, p. 72
39. CSP Scottish, cited in Guy, p. 214
40. Weir, p. 72
41. CSP Venetian, cited in Weir, p. 280
42. CSP Spanish; Klarwill, *Queen Elizabeth and Some Foreigners*, p. 251, cited in Weir, pp. 73–4

43. Randolph to Leicester in CSP Scottish, cited in Weir, p. 75
44. J. Robertson, cited in Guy, p. 215
45. Randolph to Leicester in CSP Scottish, cited in Guy, p. 217, and Weir, p. 75
46. Knox, II, p.158, cited in Weir, p. 76
47. CSP Scottish, cited in Weir, p. 76
48. CSP Scottish, cited in Weir, p. 76
49. Melville, cited in Weir, pp. 76–7
50. Knox, cited in Weir, p. 77
51. Cited in Wormald, *Mary, Queen of Scots*, p. 157
52. Teulet, cited in Guy, p. 217 and Weir, p. 78

17

Moray's Rebellion

Moray may have been illegitimate, but he was James V's eldest son. Unlike Châtelherault and Lennox, he was well respected and had powerful backing from the Reformers. In 1536, James V had sought a papal dispensation to marry his mother, Margaret Erskine, requesting an annulment of her 1527 marriage to Robert Douglas of Lochleven. This would not necessarily have legitimised Lord James, who was already aged four. She had six more children after returning to her husband when her lengthy royal liaison petered out, and Lord James was left at court to be educated with the King's other illegitimate sons. He was technically legitimised in 1551 to enable him to pass property on to his children, and, being so tantalisingly close to being heir to the throne, he tried unsuccessfully to promote his claim retro-spectively. He was well suited to be king with his regal bearing and intellect.

Despite his obvious qualities, Moray needed general support from the nobility to grasp the Crown and, as Mary's brother, could not marry her himself. If he could not be king, he wanted to remain the power behind the throne, but he feared that the intolerable King Henry, who now stood in his way, would undo all his good work. Although the Scottish nobility came to recognise the King's shortcomings, there was initial enthusiasm for the royal couple. This left Moray with limited support, despite English monetary backing.

When Moray tried to build Reformist opposition to the marriage, Mary isolated him politically by exposing the flaws in his propaganda. She had already allayed suspicions by reissuing her 1561 proclamation in the name of both the King and herself to confirm the maintenance of the religious status quo. When she heard that people were celebrating Mass in northern Scot-land, she told them not 'to do anything as was feared by the Protestants'. She forwent normal Catholic mores by eating meat for the first time in Lent. She attended the Protestant baptism of Alexander, Master of Livingston and heard sermons from approved Reformist preachers. Most Reformers did not believe that their religion was under threat, and even Knox did not back

Moray's attempt to gain the Crown for himself. He thus lacked vehement anti-Catholic support.

Moray reverted to inciting the traditional feudal divisions among the Scottish nobility, which he had spent so long trying to heal. He made a personal attack on the Lennoxes by seeking help from their traditional enemies. With Mary so popular, this was never likely to succeed, and it seems that, for once, he allowed self-interest to override more realistic objectives. Despite his covert English support, he did not realise that taking up arms against Mary was doomed to failure.

On 18 July, while at Stirling, Moray called a second meeting with Argyll, Châtelherault, Kirkcaldy and Rothes. They sent a plea to Elizabeth to provide military support for an armed rebellion. Mary needed to act fast. On 24 July, she wrote to the Pope of her intention to restore Catholicism in Scotland in the hope of him providing a subsidy. On 1 August, she ordered Moray to appear before her within six days and, when he did not come, he was 'put to the horn'. She warned Châtelherault and Argyll that they would suffer a similar fate if they supported him. By 14 August, the estates of Moray, Rothes and Kirkcaldy had been seized and Mary began converting members of the court to Catholicism.

On 15 August, Moray, Châtelherault and Argyll left Edinburgh for Ayr, having summoned Glencairn, Rothes, Boyd, Ochiltree and Kirkcaldy to join them there in arms within five days. Although still at court, Maitland was regarded with suspicion. From Ayr, Moray called 'all good subjects to join them in resisting tyranny, for a king had been imposed on them without the assent of parliament'.[1] Although still supporting him, Maxwell remained in the south-west. This left Moray to set out against Mary with only 600 horse, although probably more than double that number arrived in Edinburgh.

Mary was ready to take him on. By 19 July, ten days before her wedding, she had quietly pledged her jewellery to fund a royal army of between 6,000 and 7,000 men. On 22 August, she announced that she would face the rebels and, within four days, her troops were mustered from around Edinburgh. The Catholic Sir Simon Preston of Craigmillar was appointed Provost to protect the capital in her absence and he joined the Privy Council. On 28 August, she set out with between 8,000 and 10,000 men, wearing a steel cap and with a pistol in her saddle holster; King Henry, resplendent in gilt armour, was beside her. They had the support of Lennox, Atholl, Crawford, Eglinton, Caithness, Cassillis, Erroll, Montrose, Lord Robert Stewart, Fleming, Livingston, Home (entirely out of loyalty to Mary), Kerr of Ferniehirst, Hay of Yester, Sempill (who held a command in the van), Ross and Cathcart, with Morton (although she was suspicious of his loyalty), Lindsay of the Byres, Ruthven and Glamis all still backing Darnley as Douglas kinsmen. Many of the rank and file rallied behind her. Atholl was appointed Lieutenant of the North to deal with Argyll, while Lennox became Lieutenant of the West and later of the South-West. Even Knox could only admire her, writing: 'Albeit the most part waxed weary, yet the Queen's courage increased man-like, so much that she was ever at the foremost.'[2]

When Charles IX and Catherine de Medici sent their special ambassador, Castelnau, to Scotland to congratulate Mary on her marriage, she had to explain that Moray and his allies were seeking to depose her on behalf of the Reformers and had sought English help. If Elizabeth supported them, there would be no order in the world. She saw them as republicans wanting to usurp her government by killing both the King and herself, just as they had deposed her mother. If they succeeded in Scotland, their anarchy would spread to England, the Netherlands and France. She needed French help to nip the rebellion in the bud. Castelnau was not expecting a plea for assistance, having been briefed to persuade her to be reconciled with Moray to avoid a civil war and to assure her claim to the English succession by protecting the 'amity'. Yet Mary would not compromise and told him:

> It is incompatible with my honour and with the safety of my person and that of the King my husband, because these rebellious subjects of their bad faith and evil will have decided to kill us both.

She ignored his advice that 'utility, prudence and expediency' obliged her to make concessions. The King was even more determined to risk everything by fighting. Castelnau noted that the grandeur he had seen earlier had turned to defiance.

Although Mary's efforts to gain French support fell on stony ground, she had better success with the Papacy. With Moray justifying his attack on religious grounds, Mary portrayed herself as a champion for the Catholic cause. Although she had confirmed the religious status quo in Scotland and had failed to launch a counter-Reformation since leaving France, she was defending her Catholic throne and, in September, sent an emissary to Rome seeking a subsidy.

In what has become known as the Chaseabout or Roundabout Raid, the two opposing armies never met. Mary set out towards Ayr through wind and driving rain, pushing Moray's troops ahead of her and giving them no time to rest. Moray was hopelessly outnumbered, and Mary had hackbutters with her. In an effort to gain more support, Moray bypassed her army to reach Edinburgh on 31 August, where he awaited Argyll. Although Châtelherault, Glencairn and Rothes came with him, the combination of Sir Simon Preston with the townspeople and Mar at the Castle held Edinburgh for Mary. When Mar brought its guns to bear, Moray was forced to leave on the following day. Meanwhile, Mary waited in Glasgow for her northern levies, which were due at Stirling by the end of September. She was now ready to face Moray in battle and doubled back to Edinburgh, but Moray again managed to avoid her by heading south-west to Dumfries.

Mary knew that the English were likely to support Moray. On 7 September, she sent Elizabeth a strongly worded message through Randolph warning her not to help him. Although furious, Elizabeth feared a French counter-invasion and had cold feet. She could still not be seen supporting rebels against a fellow monarch, but she promised Moray asylum. Lennox and Atholl pursued Argyll back to the Highlands, although he retaliated by ravaging their lands as he went. When, on 6 September, they captured Castle Campbell, Moray sent Maxwell from Dumfries to mediate, claiming rather lamely that his actions were true to God, the Queen, and the 'Commonwealth'. He was still complaining at Darnley being proclaimed King without parliamentary consent, but Mary did not listen.

During September and October, Mary went to Fife, Kinross and Perthshire to gather more support, cutting Moray's lines of supply to Dumfries from his traditional powerbase in Fife. On 6 September, she summoned Glencairn, Ochiltree and Boyd to appear at St Andrews within six days and, ten days later, issued a manifesto attacking those who 'under pretence of religion' had raised 'this uproar' so that they might 'be kings themselves'.[3] When Glencairn and Ochiltree failed to appear, they were, on 1 December, found guilty of treason in their absence. Glencairn left for England, but returned home early in the new year. Boyd had appeared on 29 October, but he too was found guilty of treason, although, in an effort at unity, on 6 March 1566, King Henry pardoned him and ordered him back to court. Mary travelled to Lochleven, which was being used by Moray as a store for munitions, and threatened his mother and half-brother Sir William Douglas with sequestration if they would not support her. When she later told Sir William to surrender the Castle, he feigned sickness but agreed to make it available to her at twenty-four hours' notice. Mary returned to St Andrews and then on to Dunfermline Abbey, Perth, Innerpeffray Abbey and Ruthven Castle to impose a bond of obedience on the Fife lairds. She crossed the Tay, but Dundee refused her request for money and demanded £2,000 Scots to buy their loyalty. She was short of funds and, with her popularity in Reformist burghs wavering, she doubled back to Edinburgh, where she borrowed 10,000 marks (£6,667 Scots) and asked Elizabeth for 3,000 troops. Elizabeth ignored this, but suggested a truce, if she would pardon Moray and the rebels.

Mary had turned to Moray's traditional enemies for support and, having the upper hand, was in no mood to compromise. On 19 July, ten days before her wedding, Cecil had noted, 'The Earl Bothwell is sent for.'[4] Bothwell's journey from France involved taking a fishing boat from Flushing in an attempt to evade English warships under the command of Wilson, a well-known privateer. On 17 September, Wilson caught up with him at Eyemouth, north of Berwick, but he managed to escape with six or eight men in rowing boats with the loss of most of his equipment. With some remaining armour and pistols, he joined Mary in Edinburgh. This ended any hope of a compromise with Moray, and Maitland immediately retired to Lethington, leaving the post of Secretary of State vacant.

Mary gave Bothwell a great welcome, and even the King was 'very gracious and polite' to him.[5] On 28 September, he was reappointed to the Privy Council and restored as Lieutenant-General of the Borders. From his base at Hermitage Castle, he re-established himself with the Border lairds and gained Mary's special trust by bringing many of them into her camp. He had the military skills to deal effectively with lawlessness in the Borders and to provide secure defence against English incursions. Yet his peer group still mistrusted him. Randolph reported, 'His power is to do more mischief than ever he was minded to do good in all his life,'[6] but took wry delight when Mary upset the King by putting him in command of the royal army in place of Lennox. This caused their first open row. Yet she believed that Bothwell, with his deep-seated hatred of Moray, would display the greater drive. Although Bothwell retained command, they compromised, so that Lennox was to lead the van in battle.

Soon after her wedding, Mary released George Gordon from Dunbar after two years of imprisonment. He presented himself at Holyrood, where Mary restored him as Lord Gordon. Although he was soon affirmed as Earl of Huntly, she did not immediately return his estates. He justifiably blamed Moray for his family's ruin and became Bothwell's close associate. He quickly went north to raise troops and returned on 4 October. Although he had made a show of becoming a Reformer at Dunbar and refused to take Mass with Mary in the Chapel Royal, this was probably an expedient, and he was soon back in the Catholic camp. His father's body was at last returned for burial in the family tomb at Elgin Cathedral. On 8 October, he joined the Privy Council, and his estates were freed. Mary had ensured that they were sufficiently dissipated to prevent him becoming a magnate on his father's former scale. Both the Dowager Lady Huntly and her daughter, Jean, returned to court, and Mary was soon on remarkably good terms with them. Bothwell, Huntly and Atholl now became Mary's chief advisers. Despite supporting her devotedly, they lacked Maitland's statecraft and Moray's ability to coordinate the nobility. Although Lennox remained a powerful ally, as soon as Moray had gone into exile he started to promote his son at Mary's expense.

On 8 October, Mary set out with her forces for Dumfries. Lennox and King Henry had delayed their departure to go hunting and appeared a week late. This allowed Moray to escape, causing them lasting antagonism with Bothwell. On their arrival, Dumfries was deserted, with Moray, Kirkcaldy and Rothes having crossed the border to Carlisle, from where they reached Newcastle eight days later. Although Maxwell had instructions to arrest them as they went south, he failed to do so and was accused of treason. Yet Mary absolved him after he confirmed his allegiance to her and became her most loyal supporter. Meanwhile, Bothwell garrisoned Dumfries with 1,500 men to prevent the rebels' return.

Still not prepared to offer Moray overt support, the English again sent him money secretly. Randolph provided 3,000 crowns to Lady Moray, and Bedford gave £1,500 to Moray himself. Yet Mary still had the whip hand and would not listen to Elizabeth's pleas for clemency. Moray and his allies were summoned to appear before Parliament on 12 March 1566 'to hear and see the doom of forfeiture orderly led against them'.[7] Argyll went into hiding in the western Highlands, but the remainder stayed in England. When the King went on another hunting trip, Châtelherault used the opportunity to apologise to Mary for his family's part in the revolt. On 2 January, she pardoned him on condition that he went into exile to France for five years. The Lennoxes did not approve of her leniency, but she was starting to mistrust their motives and needed the Hamiltons held in reserve.

Moray was bitter with Elizabeth for failing him, but she faced a dilemma on how to avoid provoking the French. Initially, she refused to allow him to come to London, but relented and 'in a piece of refined deceit' derided him on his knees before the French and Spanish ambassadors. Having made clear that she would never support him against Mary, she secretly granted him a further £3,000 to restore English influence with instructions to find a way to return to Mary's favour. Despite telling him to leave England, he was permitted to return to Newcastle. Elizabeth asked Robert Melville to intercede on his behalf, but Mary would not barter Lady Margaret's release from the Tower for his pardon. Yet Mary was taken in by the public humiliation meted out to him and agreed to negotiate a new treaty with England. She recalled Bothwell from Dumfries to act as one of her Commissioners, causing the English negotiators to withdraw in anger.

With Bothwell now dominant at court, it was agreed that he should wed

Huntly's sister, Jean Gordon. By signing the marriage contract, Mary confirmed that this was on her 'advice and express counsel'. They had to wait for papal dispensation, as Bothwell and Jean were third cousins,* placing them within the fourth degree of consanguinity, but the necessary documentation was signed by Archbishop Hamilton. Huntly provided £8,000 as a handsome dowry, which enabled Bothwell to redeem Crichton from his creditors, but Jean astutely retained a jointure over the estate. Mary gave eleven ells [an ell is forty-five inches] of cloth of silver and a taffeta lining for her stunning wedding dress. Bothwell insisted on a Protestant marriage service, which took place on 24 February 1566 at the Canongate Church. Mary attended and paid for the banquet and celebration at Holyrood, including jousting and 'running at the ring'.

The marriage was no love match. Jean Gordon had 'a masculine intelligence', but was 'a cool detached character' lacking beauty and softness.[8] With Seton back from France, he provided his home with its romantic associations for their honeymoon. This did not prove idyllic. Within a week Bothwell had returned alone to Edinburgh after Jean caused friction by wearing black in mourning for the loss of her sweetheart, Alexander Ogilvy of Boyne. Two months after their wedding Mary arranged for Ogilvy to marry Mary Bethune, who had broken off her long-running attachment to Randolph. Yet, in 1599, Jean eventually married Ogilvy, by when her second husband, Alexander, 12th Earl of Sutherland, and Mary Bethune had died. Although Bothwell and Jean were reconciled and lived together 'friendly and quietly', there were no children of the marriage.[9] Yet the new axis formed between Bothwell and Huntly was extremely disturbing for Moray's supporters. Many shared Maitland's view that Mary and King Henry were trying to weaken the Reformist nobility, and Moray soon regained the support of Morton, Ruthven and Lindsay, concerned at this new threat.

References

1. Keith, cited in Weir, p. 78
2. Knox, II, p. 162, cited in Guy, p. 230 and Antonia Fraser, p. 269
3. Guy, p. 230
4. Guy, p. 220
5. Weir, p. 83
6. Guy, p. 231

* Patrick Hepburn, 1st Earl of Bothwell had married Margaret Gordon, daughter of George, 2nd Earl of Huntly.

7. Guy, p. 254
8. Gordon; cited in Antonia Fraser, p. 285
9. Sanderson, p. 38, cited in Weir, p. 102, and Marshall, p. 131

18

Mary's Efforts to Govern Without Moray and Maitland

After their marriage, Mary quickly became disillusioned with King Henry, who arrogantly and unnecessarily fell out with those that the Crown needed for support, and their relationship proved a disaster. In September 1565, while trying to focus opposition against Moray, she was embarrassed by her husband's very public visits to bars and male brothels in Edinburgh. When she went herself to try to curb his drinking at an Edinburgh merchant's, he was so abusive that she left in tears. A lady of the court became pregnant by him and Randolph reported that he was unworthy to be Mary's consort. His performance in government was no better. Although he was required to sign all state documents, he could not keep his mouth shut, so that confidential papers could not be shared with him. If he showed an interest, his plans were extravagant and beyond the means of the royal purse. Instead of being concerned with his duties and obligations, he was pre-occupied with his rights and privileges, but Mary continued to delay offering him the Crown Matrimonial, which he demanded obsessively, until he proved himself, knowing that Parliament would be unlikely to ratify the grant. He spent most of his time hawking and hunting, irritating her with his absences.

Mary became pregnant in September, so that she was not always able to work herself and could not join the King's hunting trips. She had initial doubts about the date of her conception, but it was before 25 September, when the papal dispensation for their marriage arrived from Rome. For-tuitously, this was backdated to the time of its request on 22 May. There were rumours even then that the King was not the father, but there is no doubt that he was and, as a young man, James bore him a striking resemblance. Her pregnancy was of huge dynastic importance. The child would provide immeasurable support for her claim to the English Crown and would stand ahead of King Henry, with or without the Crown Matrimonial, as her heir. Mary was still suffering from the recurring pain in her side and, in

November, took to her bed, but the King paid her little attention and went to Fife for nine more days of hunting. On 1 December, she was sufficiently incapacitated to travel to Linlithgow in a litter, rather than on horseback as usual.

Lennox seemed blind to his son's worst excesses. On 19 December, he wrote to Lady Margaret in the Tower:

My Meg, we have to give God most hearty thanks for that the King our son continues in good health and liking, and the Queen great with child, God save them all, for the which we have great cause to rejoice more. Yet of my part, I must confess I want and find a lack of my chiefest comfort, which is you ...[1]

The Spanish ambassador concluded that the King would not have been led astray if his mother had been with him, as she could control him. Much to Mary's annoyance, in December he joined his father for another long hunting trip at Peebles. Although he returned to Edinburgh for Christmas, he then rejoined his father for further hunting until mid-January.

The King's hunting trips with his father may well have been a cover for their Catholic scheming. He was never a devout Catholic, but his parents encouraged him to parade his religion to promote his personal claim to the Scottish and English Crowns. To cultivate European Catholic heads of state, he pushed the Scottish court into openly celebrating Mass. The Chapel Royal was like a Catholic parish church. At Christmas 1565, he ostentatiously attended midnight Mass, followed by matins and high Mass, praying 'devotedly on his knees'. He was behaving as if he were above the law, as he had no authority to attend Catholic services as approved for Mary. Yet he was positioning himself as the focal point for a British counter-Reformation. Philip II had sent the trusted Alva to Bayonne in May and June 1565 to reconfirm the terms of the Treaty of Cateau-Cambrésis with France. European Protestants feared that this would result in a Catholic league to crush them, but there is no evidence of an attempt to form one. After the Chaseabout Raid, King Henry sought French help to outlaw the Reformers, but Mary played no part in this. He used Castelnau to seek for him the Order of St Michel, the highest badge of chivalry in France.

With Moray's revolt now over, by 19 October Mary was back in Edinburgh, but the majority of her Council remained Reformers. She and the King generally mistrusted them and started to appoint middle-class advisers into positions around the Crown. This upset the nobility, who considered such roles as their perquisites. New appointees included Sir James Balfour,

Leslie, Riccio, David Chalmers and Francis Yaxley, all Catholic and, initially at least, friends of King Henry. Yet none of them had the experience of Moray and Maitland. The principal need was to appoint a new Secretary of State, and the two obvious candidates were Balfour and Leslie, both trained in canon law.

Balfour had proved a successful Lord of Session. Yet he was treacherous and corrupt, cynically using his experience as a church lawyer to further his own ends. Knox saw him as a notorious blasphemer, claiming that he 'neither feared god nor loved virtue', having reverted to Catholicism after becoming a Reformer at St Andrews.[2] Yet, after the King visited him at his wife's home at Burleigh, he became his right-hand man. In July 1565, he joined the Privy Council as Clerk-Register, from where he advised Mary to keep Moray in exile.

Leslie was now thirty-eight and became a conscientious and hard-working Privy Councillor, despite showing impulsiveness and a lack of sound judgement. Although the King signed his appointment to become Secretary of State, as the better Catholic, Mary countermanded it, but, on 24 February 1566, he was appointed Abbot of Lindores, becoming Bishop of Ross two months later. He continued to remain close to Mary, advising and defending her during her later imprisonment.

Mary had a third candidate for Secretary of State in her French Secretary, Riccio, who had become the King's 'only governor', and the man who 'works all' in his counsels.[3] With the King away so often, Riccio arranged a steel imprint of his signature, which he could use on his behalf. Mary trusted Riccio, who had done much to clear the obstacles for her marriage, and, when the King was absent, enjoyed his company. He was sociable, playing cards or making music with her late into the evening. As her relationship with the King deteriorated, that with Riccio grew. He was soon acting as Secretary of State, but was never formally confirmed as such. Randolph became extremely concerned at his Catholic and anti-English influence, writing:

> How she, with the chief of her nobility, can stand and prosper, passes my wit. To be ruled by the advice of two or three strangers, neglecting that of her chief counsellors, I do not know how it can stand.[4]

While Mary may have been misguided in promoting Riccio, it is unlikely that there was anything improper in their relationship. She was pregnant and quite unwell during the autumn of 1565 and spring of 1566, and he was no Adonis, being a hunchback nearly a foot shorter than herself with an 'ill-favoured' face. Yet it suited Mary's enemies to imply that there was more to it than met the eye, and both Randolph and Maitland saw it as dynamite, if the King should hear of it. Randolph, who later described Riccio as 'a filthy wedlock breaker', implied something much darker in Moray's defection from Mary than his personal ambition and hatred of the King, but would not put his thoughts in writing.[5] It has been construed that Moray believed that Mary was having an affair with Riccio, but there is no evidence to support this, and it is far more likely she was merely seeking companionship. Maitland also promoted the story, seeing that Riccio had usurped his rightful position as Secretary of State. Yet Mary took no notice of criticism and opened herself to scandal by favouring him over more experienced advisers.

David Chalmers was a lawyer and had been Balfour's colleague in the Court of Session and in the Admiralty court, over which Bothwell presided as Lord High Admiral. Both were later implicated with Bothwell in King Henry's murder, but carefully covered their tracks. Yet, for now, Chalmers was advising the King.

Francis Yaxley was another shadowy Catholic claiming Scottish descent, who arrived from England as the protégé of Lady Margaret Douglas to provide the King's communication link with English Catholics. He was an erstwhile employee of Cecil and, having full diplomatic credentials in Europe, was trusted with the names of his secret agents. Although he became the King's Secretary, Mary was unaware of the diplomatic initiatives he was conducting purportedly on her behalf. On 13 October, the King sent him to Brussels to tell Philip II that she had lost confidence in her Guise relations and needed Spanish support for a Scottish counter-Reformation. He claimed that English Catholics 'of good power' would support a Spanish coup to place her on Elizabeth's throne.[6] Yet Philip would have needed the Pope to ratify her claim, before he could support the plan. His idea was to invade Ireland, where Spain was conducting an active trade, as an obvious bridgehead for an attack on England. As it remained predominantly Catholic with many Gaelic chiefs in revolt, Philip discussed with Yaxley his hopes of gaining their support to make Mary their queen in Elizabeth's place.

Mary was unaware of any of these negotiations, but both the Pope and Philip II believed that, with King Henry at her side, she was sincere in seeking to restore Catholicism in Scotland. On 10 January 1566, the Pope wrote to her:

> We congratulate your Highness on having by this notable fact commenced to dispel the darkness which has brooded for so many years over that kingdom and to restore it to the light of true religion – complete what you have commenced.

Yet Philip needed a delay until after his invasion of the Netherlands, as he could not risk the English interfering with his supply lines through the Channel. He sent 20,000 crowns for Mary with Yaxley, but he was shipwrecked off Holy Island on the Northumbrian coast while returning from Brussels. When his body and document case were washed up, Elizabeth claimed the bounty as treasure trove.

After being chastened by Elizabeth and told to find a means to return to Scotland, Moray wrote to Riccio from Newcastle offering him £5,000 if he would obtain for him a pardon. Riccio, who was seeking Parliament's agreement to prosecute Argyll for treason and to sequester all the dissident nobles' estates, demanded £20,000. Moray then approached King Henry, who had never been his friend, sending a fine diamond and signing an obligation to be 'his loyal servant'. These overtures again failed and, although Mary's attitude towards the rebels had started to soften, she was still being encouraged to proceed against them by the newly elected Pius V and by James Bethune,* Archbishop of Glasgow, now her ambassador in Paris. The King was determined to punish them and arranged for their moveable possessions, confiscated by the Crown, to be auctioned off. On 1 December, Glencairn, Ochiltree and Boyd were found guilty of treason in their absence and, in desperation, considered trying to kidnap the King and Queen.

The strongly Catholic bias among Mary's new advisers seemed particularly suspicious at a time when her Guise relations were stepping up their persecution of French Huguenots. The King was no longer attending St Giles' to hear Knox's sermons and provocatively persuaded Mary that the status quo was not equitable. At Parliament in the spring, Mary sought to restore 'liberty of conscience', saying 'she will have the mass free for all men that will hear it'.[7] This might have seemed reasonable, but Knox, having masterminded the Scottish Reformation, faced the prospect of all his hard work being undone. When the Kirk would not give ground, religious persuasion became polarised.

Mary's approach to religion changed very rapidly. As late as 10 December, she had reconfirmed freedom of Reformist worship and, at Christmas, refused to attend Mass with the King, while deliberately sitting up at cards

---

* Bethune was the nephew of the Cardinal, born in 1517. In 1531, he went to France for his education and was later sent on a mission by Francis I to the Queen Dowager. After the Cardinal's death in 1546, he succeeded his uncle as an adviser to the Queen Regent and in 1552 was appointed Archbishop of Glasgow. He supported her loyally and was in Leith with her during the siege. On her death, he returned to Paris, taking with him the Catholic muniments from Glasgow Cathedral for preservation, passing them to the Scots College in Paris for safekeeping. Mary met him before returning to Scotland. As a man of unimpeachable integrity, he became her ambassador to the French court and remained her mentor and closest confidant.

until late. This enabled him to prick her Catholic conscience by implying that his faith was the more devout. Pushed by her Catholic advisers, Mary resiled from her policy of only attending Mass in private and seemed to stop at nothing in her attempts to charm her most intractable advisers into becoming Catholic. Randolph reported that she was 'bent in the overthrow of religion'.[8]

On 7 February 1566, the King was invested with the Order of St Michel, which Castelnau had obtained for him. He saw this as recognition for his pro-Catholic stance. He celebrated with a Catholic festival over Candlemas, which had begun on 2 February. Ambassadors from both the French King and the Cardinal of Lorraine arrived for his investiture, with praise flooding in from Catholic sources abroad. The Cardinal sent a letter from Pius V, congratulating both Mary and the King in glowing terms on the 'brilliant proof of your zeal by restoring the due worship of God throughout your realm'.*[9] This was of course premature, but the Pope was encouraging Mary to weed out the 'thorns and tares of heretical depravity'. With so many foreign dignitaries hoping to see progress in restoring Papacy, Mary had to be seen to support her husband, with her pregnancy giving her a greater sense of security. She wanted to diffuse the perception that it was the King who was taking the lead. On 31 January, she wrote to the Pope buoyantly promising to restore 'religion in splendour' in Scotland and later in England. 'In an evil hour' in February, she signed a bond sent by the Cardinal of Lorraine to endorse a new Catholic league between France, Spain and the Empire. She also sent William Chisholm, Bishop of Dunblane as her emissary to Rome seeking spiritual and financial aid.

The King's investiture at Candlemas was shunned by the Reformers. This made him abusive, and he caused a scene by locking Bothwell and Huntly into a room, threatening to throw away the key. Mary tried a different tack, leading them by the hand into Mass, but they refused to attend, preferring to hear Knox at St Giles'. Despite his loyalty, even Livingston refused an order to attend Mass. Yet there were 300 people at the services for the King's investiture.

Insensitive as ever, the King would not let matters rest and threatened to restore Mass at St Giles' Kirk and in the Council. Randolph reported that Mary was preparing to renew her immediate Catholic claim to the English

---

* It is known that the Pope had been led to overstate the position as a result of Yaxley's diplomacy while in Brussels. He had promoted King Henry as the man who would achieve the counter-Reformation in Scotland. As a result of the Pope's letter, Mary believed that the Papacy would now support her claim to be the rightful Queen of England.

throne. Yaxley had led her to believe that her support among English Catholics was 'never so great'.[10] Cecil seemed to have been right; the English were attracted to her and away from Elizabeth on her producing an heir. At the banquet for the foreign ambassadors after the King's investiture, she pointed to a conveniently positioned portrait of Elizabeth and announced that 'there was no other Queen of England but herself'.[11]

Despite Mary's public show of support for her husband's pro-Catholic stance, their relationship was not harmonious. They had already argued over Bothwell's appointment to replace Lennox in command of their forces, and the King was furious when she pardoned the Hamiltons after the Chase-about Raid. During Christmas 1565, there were further spats in their apartments, and Mary cancelled the understanding that they ruled jointly. State documents that had placed the King's name ahead of hers, now placed hers first. Coinage struck at the time of their marriage, showing Henry and Marie by the Grace of God King and Queen of Scotland, was changed on the issue to celebrate victory over Moray to show Marie and Henry, Queen and King. At his investiture of the Order of St Michel, the King was not permitted to bear royal arms. He reduced Mary to tears when she tried to temper his debauchery at parties with members of the French ambassador's suite and again denied him the Crown Matrimonial.

The King was not playing his part in government and failed to provide Mary with the support she needed with royal papers. He showed her no affection, preferring liaisons in male brothels in Edinburgh or with ladies of the court. He continued his ostentatious displays of devotion to imply that he was the stronger Catholic. Mary may have become aware of his under-hand diplomacy in Europe, on which she was not being consulted. They were growing apart. Her pregnancy was another factor. Having sired her child, she no longer required him to sleep with her. As he showed no enthusiasm for visiting her bedroom, she saw no reason to go to his, and by all accounts they lived separately.

Regardless of religious persuasion, the Scottish nobles now ganged up against the upstarts in government. The prospect of Moray and the other rebels in exile being attainted at the forthcoming Parliament on 13 March was seen as precedent for future forfeitures. With the Reformers among them having every reason to fear a counter-Reformation, they looked to Maitland for a solution.

Mary began to feel threatened by her husband's plotting, and Randolph was aware of a scheme by Lennox and the King 'to come to the crown against her will'.[12] It was almost certainly Maitland, who encouraged Lennox into proposing a deal to Argyll. Moray and the other exiled lords would be recalled and pardoned, and the King would reverse his religious policy by reconfirming the status quo, if, in return, he was granted the Crown Matrimonial. Moray was being asked to agree to the Crown being given to the person against whom he had rebelled only five months before. Everyone would benefit at Mary's expense, and Moray cynically agreed. Yet this required Riccio's removal, as he was blocking Moray's recall and keeping Maitland sidelined.

Having played on the King's ambition to be granted the Crown Matrimonial, Maitland implied to him that it was Riccio who was blocking Mary from granting this coveted status. He also suggested that Mary's close friendship with Riccio was more than that of Queen and Secretary, and even questioned the paternity of her unborn child. Rumours reached Catherine de Medici that the King had returned to Mary's apartment late one evening to find the door locked. After shouting to gain entry he had found Riccio in a nightshirt quailing in a cupboard. This seems highly unlikely, as Riccio would never have survived such an encounter, and the King did not report it, even when needing justification for Riccio's murder. Randolph and Bedford, who wanted to make the most of any scandal, claimed 'that David had more company of her body than he, for the space of two months'. Although a sexual liaison seems unrealistic, there is no doubt that the King was inordinately jealous of their close friendship. He believed that Riccio had usurped the position of influence that should have been his.

The Reformers needed a scapegoat to blame for the move towards Catholicism, and Riccio was their obvious target. Melville was not alone in believing that he 'had secret intelligence with the Vatican'. Yet, as Mary became isolated, she relied on Riccio all the more. He had 'the whole guiding of the queen and country'.[13] Maitland had long feared the effect of the Queen having a Catholic circle of ministers round her and knew that his own rehabilitation depended on breaking it. That would require Moray's reinstatement, but he had begun to despair of achieving it. Riccio's removal was also an essential step in his restoration as Secretary of State and in stopping further deterioration in the power of the Protestant nobility. On 9 February 1666, he wrote to Cecil saying:

> All may be reduced to the former estate if the right way be taken ... I see no certain way unless we chop at the very root – you know where that lieth, and so far as my judgement can reach, the sooner all things be packed up the less danger there is of any inconveniences.[14]

He was seeking Cecil's blessing to arrange Riccio's murder.

There has been much debate on precisely what Maitland meant by chopping 'at the very root'. Given his close association with Mary Fleming, it is unlikely that he sought at this stage to topple Mary from her throne. Yet it is more certain that the King had his father's support to use the murder of Riccio as a means of bringing down the Queen. When the plot was put together, Randolph wrote to Cecil:

> I know that there are practices in hand contrived between father and son to come by the Crown against her will. I know that if that take effect which is intended, David, with the consent of the King, shall have his throat cut within these ten days. Many things grievouser and worse than these are brought to my ears, yea, of things intended against her own person.[15]

With Châtelherault in exile, it was, of course, an ideal time for the Lennoxes to remove Mary and her unborn child, and to claim the Crown for themselves. All the later actions of the conspirators imply that the Queen's downfall was also an objective.

As soon as the King had been hooked into the plan to remove Riccio, he looked to his Douglas kinsmen to manage matters for him, with Morton and Ruthven designated to make the arrangements. Morton saw this as his opportunity to achieve a powerful position, and Maitland persuaded him to play on the apparent slur against Douglas honour caused by the Queen's friendship with Riccio. Morton also realised that they would need Moray's rehabilitation to garner more general support among the nobility. Both Randolph and Bedford, who were well aware of the planning, kept Cecil closely briefed. Randolph was in trouble with Mary, who had learned of his part in funding Moray's revolt by smuggling untraceable coin to his wife. When he was accused on 19 February, he hotly denied it, but was given a safe conduct to depart from Scotland at Berwick. Yet with Riccio's assassination still being planned, he remained in Edinburgh until 2 March, a week beforehand, to keep Cecil informed. He was by then able to advise that Moray and the exiled lords would leave Newcastle for Berwick on the next day, planning to reach Edinburgh on the day following the murder. Elizabeth wrote to Mary to complain at Randolph's dismissal. She was still objecting to Mary's treatment of Moray, despite his all too obvious treasonable activities which she had financed, and she now sent him a further £1,000.

Most people seemed to know of the plan to murder Riccio. Other than Mary, the exceptions included Bothwell and Huntly, who were bound up in arrangements for Bothwell's marriage to Jean Gordon on 24 February and would never have welcomed Moray's return. As a Catholic, Atholl was also kept in the dark, despite his close association with Maitland, but he also mistrusted Riccio and was not averse to his death. Cecil knew every detail. This was not simply a plan to remove Riccio, but to discredit the King and restore Moray and Maitland. It might even fulfil his objective of bringing down the Queen along with the wayward King.

References

1. Cecil Papers, cited in Weir, p. 91, and Marshall, p. 117
2. Weir, p. 82
3. Guy, p. 237
4. Wormald, *Mary, Queen of Scots*, p. 161, and Weir, p. 86
5. Weir, p. 88
6. Guy, p. 238
7. Guy, p. 240, and Weir, p. 94
8. John Guy, p. 243
9. Wormald, *Mary, Queen of Scots*, p. 160, Antonia Fraser, p. 280 and Weir, p. 93
10. Guy, p. 243
11. Guy, p. 243
12. Guy, p. 244
13. Weir, pp. 90, 94
14. CSP, Scottish, II, p. 255, cited in Guy, p. 245–6, Antonia Fraser, p. 283, and Weir, pp. 99–100
15. P. F. Tytler, *History of Scotland*, V, p. 334, cited in Guy, pp. 244, 247, and Antonia Fraser, pp. 283–4

19

Riccio's Murder

Failing to see his own shortcomings and 'infatuated by his own arrogance', the King blamed Riccio for freezing him out of government. He wanted revenge and the Crown for himself. The disaffected nobility were only too willing to encourage him to plan Riccio's murder by pampering to his ambitions. 'His youth and inexperience would render him as wax in the hands of the ruthless, power-hungry men who were closing in on him, and as such he would prove their most dangerous weapon.'[1] He believed that the Crown Matrimonial would enable him to dominate Mary. Even without it, the Lennoxes were positioned to claim the Crown for themselves should Mary die without an heir. With Châtelherault in exile, they had only to cite his illegitimacy. The conspirators' objective was to bring down Mary's Catholic advisers, thereby regaining liberty of religion and the return of their estates. They needed the King involved to provide immunity from prosecution, but he would never be allowed to govern.

Having supported the King's marriage, Morton could claim to be affronted at Mary's infatuation with Riccio, but his principal motive was to obtain Moray's rehabilitation. He also made his support conditional on the King withdrawing Lady Margaret's claim to the Earldom of Angus, which he still administered for his nephew. He was one of the many nobles who, like Moray, faced sequestration of parts of his estates on Riccio's recommendation at the forthcoming Parliament. This required the murder to take place beforehand. Although Maitland had orchestrated the plan, his involvement evaporated. He made a point of dining at Holyrood with peers from the Queen's party including Atholl, Huntly, Caithness, Bothwell and Sir James Balfour that night. This of itself can be seen as suspicious and implies an attempt by him to keep them out of the way. The other conspirators, particularly the King, all confirmed his intimate involvement afterwards, resulting in his attainder.

Morton formulated the murder plan during January and February 1566.

With Ruthven* and George Douglas 'the Postulate',† he gathered together other Douglas connections bent on family advancement. In the main, they were those who had supported the King's marriage to Mary. Ruthven continued as their ally, despite the death of his first wife, Janet Douglas (Lady Margaret's illegitimate half-sister), and his remarriage to Janet Stewart, eldest daughter of John, 2nd Earl of Atholl. Others included Ruthven's son William, later to become Earl of Gowrie, and Sir William Douglas‡ of Lochleven, no doubt out of loyalty to Moray, his half-brother. He had made a miraculous recovery from his apparent sickness during November when threatened with the sequestration of Lochleven with its store of munitions. Lindsay of the Byres, who had supported the marriage and was close to Morton, also joined them. His wife, Euphemia Douglas, was Sir William's sister and a half-sister to Moray. Glamis was the only Douglas kinsman supporting the marriage who does not appear to have taken part in the murder. They had the backing of the Officers of State on the Council, who felt threatened by Riccio's shift towards more Catholic government. There was a group of henchmen, including Andrew Ker of Fawdonside (a cadet branch of the Kers of Cessford), Patrick Bellenden, brother of the Justice-Clerk, and two Ruthven retainers, Thomas Scott, under-sheriff of Perth, and Henry Yair, a former priest. In all there were about eighty conspirators.

The conspirators, other than the King, were seeking to remove the threat of a counter-Reformation by restoring Moray and his fellow exiles. Lady Antonia Fraser has pointed out that, if they were only seeking to murder Riccio, there were ample opportunities away from Edinburgh, and it was Morton's original plan to seize him more clandestinely in his quarters at Holyrood. Yet it seems that the King was not averse to the consequential death of the Queen and her unborn child.§ By murdering Riccio in her presence, there was a realistic expectation of shock causing a miscarriage

---

* Ruthven was already crippled from inflammation of the liver and kidneys, which resulted in his death in Newcastle three months later. His involvement was conditional on the King solemnly swearing not to reveal the plan to the Queen, which he unhesitatingly agreed.

† George Douglas was an unsavoury character, who had been involved in Cardinal Bethune's murder. He was Lady Margaret's illegitimate half-brother, the son of Archibald, 6th Earl of Angus. He joined the Church as a young man, having 'seized the lucrative office of Postulate of Arbroath, despite being a lacklustre preacher, a fornicator, and a devious and violent ruffian'.[2] Melville claimed it was he who incited the King by putting into his 'head such suspicion against Riccio'.

‡ Sir William Douglas of Lochleven was always close to Morton. By the obscure entail to the 3rd Earl of Morton's will, he was to become heir to the Morton title, later becoming the 5th Earl.

§ John Guy takes an opposite view. He argues that the King had no motive to seek the Queen's death unless he had the Crown Matrimonial, as Châtelherault would be her heir. Yet the bond for Riccio's murder promised him this and it also mentions the possible presence of the Queen at the murder. If the King's motive were to gain the throne for himself, he needed both the Queen and their unborn child to die, as the child would stand ahead of his own claim, even with the Crown Matrimonial.

and, in mid-pregnancy, this invariably led to the mother's death. Even Randolph understood that this was an objective. Given Maitland's close association with Mary Fleming, he may have been unaware of this after pulling back from the detail, but Mary came to believe that she was an intended victim and undoubtedly some of the conspirators tried to terrify her. It was the King who arranged for the murder to take place at a private supper party held by the Queen at Holyrood, in expectation of being offered the throne if Mary should die. The other conspirators played along with his treasonable plan, as it provided grounds for his future deposition to allow Moray to be swept to power.

The conspirators did not trust the King and insisted on a bond to prevent him from denying knowledge of the plot afterwards, or to 'allege that others persuaded him to the same'.[3] On 1 March, he signed a deed acknowledging that he was the chief author of a plan to murder the 'wicked, ungodly' Riccio, even though 'the deed may chance to take place in the presence of the Queen's majesty'.[4] He assumed full responsibility for this, despite the apparent concerns of Morton and Ruthven. The deed was signed by all those taking an active part, including Morton, George Douglas, Ruthven and Lindsay. They were not to 'spare life or limb in setting forward all that may bend to the advancement of his [the King's] honour'.[5] It confirmed that the King would be offered the Crown Matrimonial in return for pardoning and protecting the other signatories and permitting the exiles to return to their estates. He gave assurance that Protestantism would be maintained, despite his very public show of Catholicism at Candlemas only a month earlier. Although it was also signed by Ochiltree, Boyd, Glencairn and Argyll, they were not actively involved, and there were other supporters who backed it but do not appear to have signed. These included Lennox, Kirkcaldy, Knox and Archibald Douglas (brother of William Douglas of Whittinghame and the probable murderer of the King at Kirk o' Field) and, of course, Maitland. A second copy was sent to Newcastle for signature by Moray, Rothes* and the other exiled lords, but not every conspirator may have known this. Despite approving it, Moray was permitted to keep his hands clean and did not sign it.

If Mary survived, the conspirators had decided to imprison her at Stirling to await her child's birth. After his failure in the Chaseabout Raid, her detention offered Moray an outcome that was probably just as satisfactory. It would certainly suit Cecil if Moray were invited to take the throne, and he

---

* More correctly he should now be referred to as William Leslie, as Mary had already transferred the Rothes earldom to his younger brother, Andrew, on the grounds that William was illegitimate. (See p. 82, footnote.)

hoped to engineer this. The Douglases had not in the main supported his rebellion and may have believed that there were richer pickings from promoting King Henry under their close supervision, but Morton knew that only Moray had the authority to take control. On 8 March, the day before the murder, the King granted Moray a passport to return to Scotland, not realising his intention to usurp control. Home was to escort him, so that he arrived in Edinburgh immediately following the murder. Yet they reckoned without Mary's quick-wittedness.

Randolph kept Cecil, Bedford and the English Privy Council abreast of the plan as it developed. On 13 February, he sent Leicester full details, including rumours of plans to engineer Mary's death, but told him to keep it to himself for fear of word reaching Elizabeth, who might warn her. Randolph and Bedford advised Cecil of the King's involvement four days beforehand, and Elizabeth was advised that the removal of Mary's pre-eminently Catholic and anti-English adviser was a political necessity. The plan also fitted well with Cecil's efforts to bring down the King and Queen. If implicated, the King could be charged with treason and Mary might die from a miscarriage. If she survived, she would be imprisoned with the King, allowing Moray to become Regent for her unborn child. If she died, he could aspire to be King. On 8 March, Cecil went to the Tower to advise Lady Margaret, perhaps hoping to allay any suspicion that he disapproved of her son. It can be no surprise that the plan leaked and, although Mary told Sir James Melville that she was aware of rumours, she dismissed them, claiming 'our countrymen were well-wordy' and asked 'What can they do? What dare they do?'[6] Melville also warned Riccio, 'but he distained all danger and despised counsel, claiming: "They are but ducks, strike one of them and the rest will fly." '[7] Yet he raised a bodyguard of Italian mercenaries for his protection.

Mary later recorded that there was a wider plan, which miscarried, to murder her close advisers, including Bothwell, Huntly, Livingston, Fleming and Sir James Balfour, but there is no evidence for such a scheme. Although Bothwell, Huntly and Balfour dined with Maitland that evening and tried to reach the Queen, they were told that harm was intended only to Riccio. Sir James Balfour's inclusion in her list is surprising, as he was still a close associate of the King, and there may have been doubt of his loyalty, as he was threatened with being 'hanged in cords' if he revealed the King's involvement.

The plot was brought to a head by the opening of Parliament on 7 March, when Mary was attended by Bothwell carrying the sceptre, Huntly the crown, and Crawford the sword of state. Still piqued at not being granted the

Crown Matrimonial, the King was not present. Despite being nearly six months pregnant, Mary proposed the dissident nobles' attainder, setting the hearing for 12 March. On the morning of 9 March, the King played tennis with Riccio presumably to allay any suspicions, and in the evening Mary held a private dinner in a small room (twelve feet long by ten feet wide) next to her bedchamber at Holyrood. She was joined by her half-brother and sister, Lord Robert Stewart and Jean, Countess of Argyll, Robert Bethune of Creich, Master of the Household, Arthur Erskine of Blackgrange, her Equerry and Master of Horse, and Riccio, bedecked in a gown of furred damask over a satin doublet and russet velvet hose. He also wore a cap, which he failed to remove, as he should have done in her presence. Fleming, as Great Chamberlain, Anthony Standen, Mary's page, Leslie, an apothecary and groom were in attendance. Although it was Lent, meat was being served in deference to Mary's pregnancy, and the party looked forward to an evening of music and cards afterwards.

The King was not expected at the dinner, as he now rarely ate with Mary, but he admitted Ruthven and an accomplice to his apartment below. They climbed the privy staircase leading to the Queen's bedchamber. From here the accomplice went to unlock the outer doors of her presence chamber beyond to provide access to the remaining conspirators, led by Morton, from the main staircase. Much to the surprise of the party, the King joined them after they had begun eating, and sat down beside Mary. He was affable enough and well received, but suddenly Ruthven appeared wearing a helmet with armour under his cloak. He was extremely pale and feverish,* but demanded that Riccio, who by now was cowering for protection behind the Queen, should be handed over. Mary, who had always mistrusted Ruthven, with his reputation for sorcery, demanded to know his offence. He told her, 'He hath offended your honour, which I dare not be so bold as to speak of.'[8] He also accused him of hindering the King's grant of the Crown Matrimonial and banishing many of the lords with a plan to forfeit their estates at the present Parliament. Mary replied that, if he had done wrong, he should be tried before Parliament. She asked the King if Ruthven was acting at his bidding, but he denied this. The Queen then told Ruthven to leave or face arrest for treason. Lord Robert, Bethune, Erskine, the apothecary and the groom tried to seize him, but he drew a pistol, warning them off, and advanced with his dagger on Riccio, who was still hiding behind Mary in the window recess.

---

* He was gravely ill with liver and kidney failure and died on 13 June 1566 in Newcastle, but as one of the organisers he was determined to play his part.

236

The door again opened and Lindsay burst in, followed by six more heavily armed men, George Douglas, Bellenden, the Master of Ruthven, Ker of Fawdonside, Scott and Yair. There was a violent struggle and the table was overturned, with its contents knocked to the floor. The Countess of Argyll managed to save a single candle, which, in addition to the fire in the hearth, provided the only light. Ruthven manhandled the Queen out of the way, saying that he had the King's assent, and told the King, 'Sir, take the Queen your sovereign and wife to you.'[9] The King gripped her arm, while Lindsay rammed a chair into her stomach, and Fawdonside held his loaded pistol to her womb. She later claimed he would have killed her, if his gun had not 'refused to give fire'. 'One of Ruthven's followers offered to fix his poniard in the Queen's left side', but Standen grabbed it, and was later knighted for saving her life, as he recalled to James VI.[10]

George Douglas seized the King's dagger and thrust it at Riccio, coming so close to the Queen that she could feel the cold steel at her throat. Melville claimed that it was left 'sticking in him'. On his knees and clawing at the queen's skirts, Riccio cried out, 'Justice! Justice! Save me, my Lady! I am a dying man. Spare my life!'[11] The King bent back his fingers, so that others could drag him from the room. Ruthven gave orders for him to be taken down the privy stairs to the King's bedchamber. Yet he was dragged through the Queen's bedchamber to her presence chamber, where armed men waited. They were 'so vehemently moved against David that they could not abide any longer',[12] and Lindsay, Morton and more than a dozen of their supporters stabbed him to death, showing all the hallmark savagery of a ritual killing, with between fifty-three and sixty wounds left in his body, and the King's dagger left embedded in his side. One of the attackers was wounded in the blood lust, and Yair was so fired up with anti-Catholic sentiment that he stabbed to death a Dominican friar, Father Adam Beck, in his bed. Beck, who had been one of the Queen Regent's chaplains, was the only other casualty. The King continued to restrain the Queen, who later claimed to have been in 'extreme fear of her life'.[13]

After hearing the war cry, 'A Douglas! A Douglas!', Bothwell and Huntly ran with their servants from dinner with Maitland to investigate. They were intercepted by Morton, who had posted twenty men on the stairs to the Queen's apartments. Ruthven explained that Riccio had been murdered on the King's command. They were told to return to Bothwell's rooms, but, smelling danger, escaped by a back window 'through the little garden where the lions were lodged', riding first to Crichton and then on to Dunbar.[14] Huntly's mother stayed behind to tell Mary that they would plan a rescue. Mary's servants also came to her aid with staves, but they too were warned off. Morton placed an armed guard round Holyrood and, after seizing the keys from the porter, secured all the gates and doors. Later that evening, Atholl, Tullibardine, Maitland, Fleming, Livingston, Balfour and Leslie were permitted to leave 'in fear of their lives', and Atholl went home to Dunblane.[15]

King Henry was still with Mary in the supper room when Ruthven returned with Lindsay of the Byres and others. Ruthven was feverish and collapsed into a seat, demanding wine, which he downed at a single gulp. In their presence, Mary asked the King how he could betray her so shamelessly. He recited his concerns that Riccio had had too much of her company and even her body, and had persuaded her not to treat him as her equal. She asked what had happened to Riccio. Ruthven explained that he was dead and advised her to pay more attention to her husband and the nobility. Mary later recalled that they

> were highly offended with our proceedings and tyranny, which was not to them tolerable, how we were abused by the said David ... in taking his counsel for the maintenance of the ancient [Catholic] religion, debarring of the Lords which were fugitive, and entertaining of amity with foreign [Catholic] princes and nations with whom we were confederate; putting also upon Council the Lords Bothwell and Huntly, who were traitors and with whom he [Riccio] associated himself.[16]

The Queen rounded on Ruthven, saying that he had been one of her Privy Councillors throughout and blaming him particularly for her rough treatment. She promised that, if she died in childbirth, her friends would take their revenge, but he merely confirmed having followed the King's orders.

Mary turned to the King, demanding: 'Why have you caused to do this wicked deed to me, considering I took you from a low estate and made you my husband? What offence have I made you that you should have done me such shame?'[17] He baulked at being treated as inferior and replied: 'Suppose I be of the baser degree, yet am I your husband and your head, and you promised me obedience on the day of our marriage and that I should be participant and equal with you in all things.' She retorted:

> For all the offence that is done to me, my Lord, you have the weight thereof, for the which I shall be your wife no longer nor sleep with you any more, and shall never like well until I have caused you to have as sorrowful a heart as I have at this present.[18]

Still believing that she had been involved in an affair with Riccio, the King complained that Mary had not 'entertained' him since Riccio had come into favour.[19] According to Ruthven, the King said that she 'used to sit up at cards with David till one or two after midnight' and no longer came to his chamber. When he went to her, she 'either would not or made herself sick'.[20] He asked if she found him sexually inadequate, 'Am I failed in any sort?' 'What distain have you of me?' The Queen retorted that, under royal protocol,

> it was not a gentlewoman's duty to come to her husband's chamber, but rather the husband to come to the wife's. Her duty was to be chaste, loyal and obedient.[21]

A messenger then knocked at the door to report that Bothwell and Huntly had escaped. The King immediately left with Ruthven, and Mary was left alone to make a plan. She feared that she would be held captive or worse, but remained extraordinarily calm, saying: 'No more tears. I will think upon a revenge.'[22] She had the presence of mind to send a lady to Riccio's room to recover ciphers used for her correspondence, but she could not communicate with her household, as Douglas men guarded her door and the palace gates. Yet the indomitable Lady Huntly managed to deliver Bothwell's message that he would attempt to free her. She also knew Moray was about to return and, being unaware of his part in the conspiracy, hoped for his assistance.

When the King returned, he arranged for Riccio's lacerated body to be removed from the presence chamber. It was thrown down the stairs and laid across a wooden chest in the porter's lodge. The porter removed the King's dagger and stripped off the rich clothing. On the following day, his remains were quietly buried in the Canongate cemetery near the door to Holyrood Abbey.

After so much disturbance, the 'common bell' had been sounded, resulting in a crowd gathering in the forecourt outside Holyrood. The Provost, Sir Simon Preston, arrived with 400 members of the watch armed with spears. The King dispersed the crowd by confirming from a window that a papal agent had been punished, but Mary was unharmed. When she tried to be seen, Lindsay threatened 'to cut her in collops' if she showed herself.[23] She was later furious with Sir Simon for not investigating further.

The conspirators had agreed that Mary should be sent to Stirling 'under safe keeping' for her confinement and intended retaining her there afterwards.[24] Lindsay claimed that she would find plenty of time to nurse her baby and sing it to sleep, or shoot with her bow in the garden and do her fancywork. The King was assured that he would receive the Crown Matrimonial and would share the management of the government with the nobles, so long as liberty of religion was confirmed. Yet Ruthven warned:

> If you wish to obtain what we have promised you, you must needs follow our advice, as well for your own safety as for ours. If you do otherwise we will take care of ourselves, cost what it may.[25]

The King was told not to talk to the Queen without other conspirators being present. Lennox and the King were suddenly in fear of their lives, and Ruthven warned that, if anyone tried to help Mary escape, they would 'throw her to them piecemeal'.[26] The conspirators now awaited Moray's arrival with William Leslie (formerly Rothes), in the expectation of Moray's return to power.

Mary knew that the conspirators' weak link was the King. She needed to separate him from them to establish who was behind the plot and to help her to escape. She asked him to spend the night with her. Yet Ruthven insisted on him remaining under guard in his own bedchamber. The King now realised that the conspirators had no intention of giving him authority. They had cynically 'made use of him, only that they might involve him in the disgrace and infamy of an act of such atrocity'.[27] During the night, he approached the Queen's bedroom by the privy staircase, but the door was locked. He shouted out that he needed to discuss their safety, but the guard would not allow him in. From this, Mary surmised that she had every chance of persuading him to save her and to confirm the child's legitimacy. On the next morning, he was at last permitted to join her, 'having passed that night in perplexity, in terror for his own life'. He admitted having signed a bond with the conspirators, which promised him the Crown Matrimonial, being 'young and imprudent and blinded by ambition', but claimed he never thought they would murder Riccio. He told her he was taking a great risk in talking to her and 'that if it were ever known that he had done so he would be a dead man'.[28] He showed her the passport he had granted to allow Moray's return. Mary knew this was not the whole story, and witheringly told him that she would never forget his part in what had happened. She then forced every detail out of him, and warned that the conspirators would never allow him authority and would place his life in danger, which he already realised. She concluded: 'Since you have placed us on the brink of the precipice, you must now deliberate how we shall escape the peril.'[29] He agreed to escape with her, but they quarrelled for two hours on how to do so, until he stormed out. Although it has been suggested that she had difficulty

ocs inimici mei convertantur & er=

ubescat valde velociter · Gloria ·

Francis II and Mary as King and Queen of France. Mary, who was four years the elder, towered over her diminutive and stunted husband, dominating him in political matters. This allowed her Guise uncles to take control of French Government. *Bibliothèque Nationale, Paris/White Images/Scala Florence.*

Left - right:

Catherine de Medici, wife of Henry II and Mary's mother-in-law. During her husband's lifetime she remained in the shadow of Henry's powerful mistress Diane de Poitiers, but after his death positioned herself to out-manoeuvre the Guises. She took control of Government following the death of Mary's husband, Francis, leaving Mary with little choice but to return to Scotland. *Clouet/Bibliothèque Nationale, Paris/©RMN.*

Charles de Guise, Cardinal of Lorraine, Mary's uncle and mentor in France. With his brother, Francis, Duke of Guise he took control of French Government when Mary became Queen of France. *Clouet/Musée Condé, Chantilly/©RMN.*

Henry II, King of France and Mary's father-in-law. He was delighted at their first meeting on her arrival in France, describing her as "the most perfect child I have ever seen". *Primaticcio (attr.to)/Chateau d'Arnet/Bridgeman Art Library.*

Main image:
Mary's French Coat of Arms as Dauphine of France quartered with that of England. This caused a furore with English diplomats, giving the implication that Mary was claiming the English throne as Elizabeth was illegitimate. *©The British Library Board/ Caligula B X f18.*

Marie of Guise, Mary's mother, who remained in Scotland to oversee the Government after her husband James V's death and while Mary was safely in France. "She possessed an uncommon genius, and a mind strongly inclined to justice." *Corneille de Lyon/Scottish National Portrait Gallery.*

Above left:
Lord James Stewart, Earl of Moray, Mary's illegitimate half-brother. When she was first widowed, he arranged her repatriation from France, despite her Catholicism, with him managing her Government. Yet when she sought to curtail his authority, he worked with Cecil to depose her as Queen. *Private Scottish Collection.*

Above right:
William Maitland of Lethington, Mary's Secretary of State and a brilliant diplomat. He became so bound up in the plotting to depose her from the Scottish throne that, despite his personal loyalty, he believed himself at risk of his life if he failed to provide falsified evidence to incriminate her and justify her detention. *©Lennoxlove House Ltd/ Scran.ac.uk*

Main image:
James Douglas, 4th Earl of Morton, leader of the powerful Douglas clan, a man "of most boorish calibre", cruel and unscrupulous, but he was loyal to the English and acted as Moray's lieutenant, holding the Confederates together while Moray was in exile. *Arnold Bronckorst/Scottish National Portrait Gallery.*

Top left:
Matthew, 4th Earl of Lennox, was thwarted in his suit to marry the widowed Marie of Guise, and turned to Henry VIII, who approved his marriage to his beautiful niece, Lady Margaret Douglas, to form a connection which was "sufficiently gratifying to her ambition and followed by a mutual affection". *©Crown Copyright/ Historic Scotland.*

Middle left:
The handsome Henry Stuart, Lord Darnley. Mary fell hopelessly in love with "yon long lad". She married him in 1566, despite his dissolute and reckless character and the disapproval of Elizabeth and her senior advisers. *Scottish National Portrait Gallery.*

Top right:
Lady Margaret Douglas, the daughter of Henry VIII's elder sister Margaret, Mary's grandmother. Many English Catholics regarded Lady Margaret as the rightful claimant to the English throne. *The Royal Collection ©2012 Her Majesty Queen Elizabeth II.*

Right:
The magnificent Lennox Jewel was almost certainly a wedding gift from Mary Tudor to Lady Margaret Douglas on her marriage to Lennox. Lady Margaret later gave the jewel to Mary Stewart at the time of her marriage her son. *The Royal Collection ©2012 Her Majesty Queen Elizabeth II.*

Lord Robert Dudley, Earl of Leicester. Despite being Elizabeth's favourite, she promoted him to become Mary's husband, but he was reluctant, still hoping that he might gain the greater prize of Elizabeth herself. *Waddesdon/The Rothschild Collection/The National Trust.*

Elizabeth I, wearing pearls and carrying a sieve to symbolise her virginity. Her determination not to marry made Mary's dynastic right to the English throne, despite her Catholicism, appear unavoidable. *Zuccaro/Pinacoteca Nazionale, Siena/Bridgeman Art Library.*

Top left:
Mary in a feathered hat embroidered in pearls, probably painted shortly after her marriage to Darnley. ©*National Portrait Gallery, London.*

Left:
William Cecil, Elizabeth's Secretary of State, who was determined to prevent Mary as a Catholic from succeeding to the English throne, despite Elizabeth's desire to achieve the correct dynastic Tudor inheritance. ©*National Portrait Gallery, London.*

Top right:
James Hepburn, 4th Earl of Bothwell, from a miniature painted at the time of his first marriage to Jean Gordon. He was described as "a vainglorious, rash and hazardous young man". *Scottish National Portrait Gallery.*

Above:
The matching picture of Bothwell's wife Jean Gordon, "a cool detached character" but a woman of "masculine intelligence". *Scottish National Portrait Gallery.*

persuading him to help her, he knew he had been duped. She cannot be accused of causing his murder by persuading him to disassociate himself from the other conspirators; he took the decision himself. Yet she did persuade him to let her gentlewomen return, giving her a conduit to communicate with her supporters, particularly Bothwell and Huntly. Although Morton and Ruthven quickly removed them, she had already had time to send messages. She warned Argyll, whose wife had been at the dinner, of her predicament and, despite having signed the bond, he set out for Edinburgh to support her and to be returned to favour. She acted cool-headedly, just as in the planning of her marriage and before the Chaseabout Raid.

Mary's first objective was to sow discord between the returning exiles and the murderers, hoping to divide and rule. Never again should she allow her advisers to dominate her as Moray had done 'and so become enslaved', but she should balance rival factions. She would pardon the exiles not directly involved in the murder, but would punish those who had taken part, replacing Morton as Chancellor with Huntly. She could not fathom Maitland, but, having warned him that she would hold him to account for any actions against her, she decided to attaint him.

Mary's escape plan involved feigning labour pains so that her guards would be removed. When the King returned in the afternoon, she asked for her gentlewomen to return to assist her. The conspirators nominated a midwife, but Mary's ladies primed her to verify the seriousness of her condition and, with the backing of Mary's French physician, she confirmed, conveniently but inaccurately, that Mary was gravely ill, and needed to be released. The conspirators remained suspicious and redoubled the guard. No one was permitted to leave with their face hidden or whose identity was suspected.

Mary told the King to be reconciled with the other conspirators to allay their suspicions. When he asked her to pardon them, she initially refused out of conscience, but then told him to offer anything he pleased in her name. Having rejoined them, he issued a proclamation dissolving Parliament, telling its members to leave Edinburgh within three hours. The exiled lords were unaware of this and, on 12 March, when Moray and his colleagues appeared for trial at the Tolbooth, it was deserted. With the conspirators protected from immediate attainder, they agreed to reduce Mary's guards.

Meanwhile, the Dowager Lady Huntly worked on an escape plan. She was grateful to Mary for restoring the Gordon estates and titles and was no doubt an expert at intrigue after life at Strathbogie. She received a message from her son suggesting that she could smuggle in sheets or a rope ladder under a lidded serving dish. In view of her pregnancy and the presence of guards looking down at her windows from above, Mary vetoed this plan. When Lady Huntly made other suggestions, Lindsay became suspicious and had her removed. Fortuitously, she had by then hidden a message scribbled by Mary in her chemise and, although she was searched, it was not found. This instructed Bothwell and Huntly to bring a troop of armed horsemen to Seton on the next evening to escort her to Dunbar, the nearest impregnable royal fortress, which Bothwell's sister still occupied. She also instructed Mar to hold Edinburgh Castle on her behalf. Sir John Stewart of Traquair, the Captain of the Guard, was to come on the next evening with Arthur Erskine and Anthony Standen bringing horses outside the walls. In the meantime she continued to feign labour pains.

Moray, William Leslie and Kirkcaldy had arrived secretly in Edinburgh shortly before Riccio's murder, but remained in hiding until the King could confirm it. They then came to him at Holyrood, where he greeted them thankfully, before they went on to the Canongate to dine with Morton at his home. Mary had refused to see Morton and Ruthven all that day, but, on hearing of Moray's arrival, she summoned him. He was still eating with Morton when her message arrived, but hurried to her for an emotional reunion. He expressed shock at Riccio's murder, and denied being the 'chief promoter of the atrocities', as was rumoured.[30] She seemed to accept this, and told him she knew that, if he had been there on the previous evening, he would have protected her. She agreed to his reconciliation, claiming that, but for the King, she would have recalled him much earlier. Yet, when he made an emotional plea for the conspirators to be pardoned, she refused. He then advised her to be reconciled to the King.

Mary tried to gain the King's confidence, appealing to his masculinity by offering to sleep with him. After Moray had returned to Morton, she again invited him to her bedchamber. This must have raised the conspirators' suspicions that her labour pains were a sham, and she was seeking his help. As they still held the bond in which he had authorised the murder, they were not unduly concerned, but, without this, the coup lost its semblance of legality. To stop the King joining the Queen, they seem to have nobbled him by making him hopelessly drunk, causing him to pass out in a stupor in his bedchamber. At midnight, George Douglas took Ruthven to see him spread-eagled across his bed. Neither Randolph nor Bedford, in their reports to Cecil, could understand why he failed to go to her. At dawn, Ruthven woke him to reprove him for not keeping his assignation, although he had almost certainly played his part in preventing it. The King now climbed the privy stairs to seek a pardon for them.

The King sat beside Mary's bed for an hour while she slept or feigned to do so. When she awoke, she was understandably off-hand. 'Why did you not come up yesternight?' she asked. He claimed to have overslept, but replied: 'Now I am come, and offer myself to have lyen down by you.'[31] She said she was too unwell for love-making and started to dress, while he sought a pardon for the conspirators to protect his position with them. To give them a false sense of security, Mary sent him back 'very merrily' to confirm that she would grant their pardon, if they came to her.[32] Despite their scepticism, he swore on his life that she was serious, but, when she sent the midwife and physician to plead for her removal to 'some sweeter and pleasanter air', they saw her offer as 'but craft and policy', and asked for her offer to be put in writing.[33] When he returned, she set out for him the facts of political life. If she pardoned them, they would not need to give him the Crown Matrimonial, and Parliament would need to be recalled for its ratification. If he became a Reformer, he would lose any credibility with European heads of state, and, if not, the conspirators would topple him. Realising she was right, he agreed to escape with her that night.

In the late afternoon, Moray came with Morton, Ruthven and Lindsay, and they knelt down before Mary, but she would not agree to pardon them. When Moray lectured her to show clemency, she scathingly replied that

> ever since her earliest youth, her nobility and others of her people, had given her frequently opportunities of practicing that virtue and becoming familiar with it.

To justify her 'blotting out the past', they needed to demonstrate good conduct.[34] Each in turn grudgingly begged forgiveness. When Morton's hose became blood-stained after he had knelt where Riccio had died, he claimed: 'The loss of one mean man is of less consequence than the ruin of many lords and gentlemen.'[35] Mary replied: 'I was never bloodthirsty nor greedy upon your lands and goods since coming into Scotland, nor will I be upon you.'[36] She used her threatened miscarriage to bring the conversation to an abrupt end, but left word with the King that she would 'put all things in oblivion as if they had never been', if they produced written pardons for her signature.[37] Although these would be highly incriminating if left unsigned, they agreed to prepare them, after the midwife again confirmed the seriousness of her condition.

Mary sent one of her ladies to Melville to ask Moray not to join the other lords for dinner. He came to see her alone with the King, and they walked hand in hand for more than an hour. Being doubtful that she would sign the pardons, he took the line that the other conspirators were traitors, so that he could make his peace with her. He knew that the King would not protect them, but believed he could arrange their rehabilitation, once back in power. Although the conspirators feared that he was turning his back on them, despite what they had done for him, Morton understood his objective.

At six o'clock, the King collected the pardons from the conspirators for Mary's signature, but she instructed him to delay his return by taking his supper before delivering them back. When Archibald Douglas returned to collect them, it was already late and the King claimed she was unwell, but would sign them in the morning. He then arranged for her remaining guards to be removed, as he would stay with her. Maitland seems to have advised them 'that it would not avail them in law if there were the least appearance of restraint upon her'.[38] Given all that had passed, it is hard to see how this would have improved their legal position, but Randolph believed Maitland wanted to help her, as his own objective of removing Riccio had already been achieved. Ruthven warned the King: 'Whatever bloodshed follows will be on your head'.[39] The conspirators now retired for dinner at Morton's home, unwisely leaving their unsigned pardons behind.

Mary and the King now had the chance to escape. At midnight, they were led by Standen and Margaret Carwood down the privy staircase and by the back stairs to the servants' quarters, where her French staff would not give her away. They emerged from the back door of the wine cellar into the Canongate cemetery. On seeing Riccio's newly dug grave, the King exclaimed: 'In him I have lost a good and faithful servant. I have been miserably cheated.'[40] Traquair and Arthur Erskine were waiting outside the wall of the cemetery, while Bothwell and Huntly had summoned 'their best friends and most loyal of Her Majesty's subjects' to Seton to await her.[41] At the last minute the King asked that Lennox should go with them, as he feared for his life if left behind. Mary angrily refused, as he 'had been too often a traitor to her and hers to be trusted'.[42]

Mary rode pillion behind Arthur Erskine, while Traquair carried one of the Maries, probably Mary Seton, and King Henry rode Standen's horse, with Standen up behind, but he shook so much that Standen had to steady him. They set off for Dunbar, a distance of twenty-five miles, planning a break at Seton. They trotted through the silent Edinburgh streets, but, as soon as they were out of earshot, they cantered the ten miles to Seton, stopping only when Mary vomited. When the King saw a group of horse-men ahead, he feared it was Morton and Ruthven. He spurred on his horse and whipped up Mary's, shouting, 'Come on! Come on! By God's blood, they will murder both you and me if they can catch us.' Exhausted and in pain, Mary told him 'to have some regard for her condition', but 'to push on and take care of himself'.[43] He disgusted everyone when he did so, but the horsemen turned out to be Bothwell, Huntly, Seton, Fleming, Livingston and Sir James Balfour.

At Seton, the royal party switched horses and rode their own to Dunbar, arriving at five o'clock in the morning. Despite exhaustion and sickness after five hours in the saddle, Mary was cock-a-hoop. Atholl, Rothes (Andrew Leslie), Marischal, Glencairn, Home and Sir John Maxwell arrived with a strong force. Glencairn needed to rely on the King not revealing his signature on the murder bond. There were soon 4,000 men pledged to restore Mary to her throne, and she consulted John Leslie on how to avenge the murder.

References

1. Weir, p. 96
2. Weir, p. 96
3. Weir, p. 102
4. CSP Scottish; Lord Ruthven, *The Murder of Riccio, being Lord Ruthven's Own account of the Transaction*; Keith; Buchanan; Knox, cited in Weir, p. 102
5. Keith, III, p. 265, cited in Antonia Fraser, p. 284
6. Melville, p. 113, cited in Antonia Fraser, p. 161, p. 286
7. Melville, cited in Weir, p. 101
8. Ruthven; Claude Nau, *Memorials of Mary Stewart*, cited in Guy, p. 249
9. Ruthven, cited in Guy, p. 249
10. Nau, cited in Weir, pp. 107, 106
11. Robert Birrel, *Diary 1532–1605, from Fragments of Scottish History*, p. 5 footnote, cited in Antonia Fraser, p. 290, and Weir, p. 107
12. Randolph and Bedford, cited in Weir, p. 107
13. Mary to Archbishop Bethune, cited in Weir, p. 107
14. Melville; Cockburn and Maitland; Teulet; cited in Weir, p. 109
15. Melville, cited in Weir, p. 109
16. Nau, cited in Guy, p. 251, and Weir, p. 109
17. Nau, cited in Guy, pp. 251, 252
18. Weir, p. 108
19. Guy, p. 251
20. Ruthven, cited in Guy, p. 252, and Weir, p. 89
21. Nau, cited in Guy, p. 252, and Weir, p. 89
22. Nau, p. 4, cited in Antonia Fraser, p. 292
23. Mary to Archbishop Bethune; Nau, cited in Antonia Fraser, p. 292
24. Nau, cited in Weir, p. 110
25. Nau, cited in Weir, p. 110
26. Nau, cited in Weir, p. 110
27. Nau, cited in Weir, p. 110

28. Nau, cited in Weir, p. 111
29. Nau, cited in Weir, p. 111
30. Weir, p. 113
31. Guy, p. 256
32. Guy, p. 256
33. Ruthven, cited in Weir, p. 114
34. Nau, p. 16, cited in Antonia Fraser, p. 294 and Weir, pp. 114–5
35. Nau, cited in Weir, p. 114
36. Guy, p. 258
37. Weir, p. 115
38. Ruthven; Melville; cited in Weir, p. 115
39. Ruthven, cited in Weir, p. 116
40. Nau, cited in Antonia Fraser, p. 295, and Weir, p. 116
41. Cockburn and Maitland, cited in Weir, p. 116
42. Nau, cited in Weir, p. 116
43. Nau, p. 17, cited in Antonia Fraser, p. 295, and Weir, p. 117

20

A Time for Compromise

On the morning of 12 March, the conspirators returned to Holyrood to find that Mary and the King had escaped. Without their promised pardons they were doomed. Furious at being left behind, Lennox galloped to Dunbar to take his son to task. Moray, who had distanced himself from the other conspirators, went to the Tolbooth to announce that they would answer any charges in Parliament (where no one would accuse them). Morton, Ruthven and Lindsay sent Sempill, who had not been involved in the plot, to Dunbar to ask the Queen to fulfil her promise to sign their pardons. Mary refused, keeping Sempill with her for three days. Despite being wary that Elizabeth was behind the murder, Mary dictated a graphic letter to her explaining her ordeal:

> Some of our subjects and council by their proceedings have declared manifestly what they are ... having slain our most special servant in our own presence and thereafter held our proper person captive treasonably.[1]

She warned that it could happen to her, but apologised for being too tired to write herself. She told both Bethune in Paris and Charles IX that she was not 'in robust health after the bodily indisposition of our person'.[2]

With the King still terrified, Mary forced him to list the conspirators' names. He named Maitland, but not Moray, Argyll or Glencairn. As Moray had not signed the bond, it is possible that the King could not verify his complicity. He was now shunned by most of Mary's supporters, with Fleming, a former confidant, being particularly critical. When Mary tried to intercede, it was clear that he was regarded with ill-concealed contempt. Their loyalty was to Mary alone.

On 15 March, Mary rewarded Bothwell with the ward-ship of Dunbar, replacing Sir Simon Preston, after his failure to rescue her at Holyrood. Five days later, Huntly became Chancellor in place of Morton, and Balfour took over from MacGill as Clerk-Register. Mary also confirmed Sir John Maxwell to his wife's inheritance at Terregles. She mustered troops at Haddington with a week's provisions to escort her back to Edinburgh. She thanked

Melville for his loyalty, when he brought a letter from Moray, who was desperately seeking rehabilitation. The King asked whether Moray had sent him a similar letter, but Melville claimed diplomatically that he considered the King and Queen to be as one. The King was in great fear of the other conspirators, but Melville said that they had fled.

After arriving at Haddington, on 17 March Mary confided in Melville her bitterness towards the King. Melville blamed his youth and the bad counsel he kept with George Douglas among others, but he could see the 'great grudges which she held in her heart'.[3] The next day, she made a triumphant return into Edinburgh, acclaimed on all sides. She was supported by Bothwell, Huntly, Home, Seton, Marischal, Archbishop Hamilton and 8,000 men. She refused to go to Holyrood, fearing that some of the conspirators might still be there, but lodged instead at Sir John Maxwell's home in the High Street with cannon positioned outside, and later at the Bishop of Dunkeld's larger house in the Cowgate. Bothwell policed the streets with trained bands, supplemented by Hamilton adherents.

Morton, Ruthven, Lindsay, Ker of Fawdonside, George Douglas and sixty-three others were denounced as rebels in their absence by the Privy Council. On 29 March, they were attainted, with their homes stripped of chattels. Atholl took control of Tantallon, temporarily becoming the young Angus's guardian, which entitled him to the income of his estates. Mary particularly blamed Morton, because Ker of Fawdonside, who had levelled a pistol at her, was his adherent.

Morton and the other conspirators had headed for England. Morton stayed at Alnwick, while the Master of Ruthven went on to Newcastle with his sick father. On arrival, they wrote a grovelling letter to Cecil protesting that they had acted on the King's orders and 'for the preservation of the state and the Protestant religion'. Embarrassed at their failure to detain Mary, Elizabeth witheringly advised Morton to find 'some place out of this realm' where he might hide.[4] Although he tried to go to the Netherlands, Mary had already written to prohibit his entry, and he returned into hiding in England. In May, Elizabeth again told the conspirators to leave, but, as so often, this was for public consumption and they remained unmolested in the north. Before Ruthven's death in Newcastle on 13 June 1566, he wrote for her benefit his 'Relation', which justified the murder on the grounds of Riccio's adultery with Mary.

On 21 March, Knox, who had approved the murder, left for Ayrshire, where he wrote his history of the Reformation in Scotland, beseeching God to 'destroy that whore in her whoredom'.[5] Although Maitland remained behind, he was denounced to Mary by both the King and Bothwell. He was warded in Inverness, but preferred to hide with Atholl at Dunkeld, in the hope of him interceding for him. Although Atholl attempted this, Bothwell had been granted Maitland's attainted estates and blocked his rehabilitation, and, although Maitland tried to buy himself a pardon, Randolph had little hope of him succeeding.

Moray was not convinced that Mary believed his assurance that he was not a party to the murder conspiracy. He and Argyll retired to Linlithgow, where they worked with Cecil to gain the conspirators' rehabilitation. Mary had to be pragmatic; most of the nobility was implicated, and she needed a government. She absolved those who did not appear to have played an active part, sending Balfour to Linlithgow with a pardon for Moray and the former exiles. She undertook to restore their estates, if they returned home and did not intercede on the conspirators' behalf. Argyll and Glencairn were back at court in ten days.

Although Randolph spread a rumour that Mary had sent emissaries to Rome seeking a divorce from the King, she would not have considered this before her child's birth. She had to confirm his innocence, as any treasonable action would prejudice her child's legitimacy. On 20 March, the King signed a declaration before the Privy Council 'upon his honour, fidelity and the word of a prince' that he 'never counselled, commanded, consented, assisted nor approved' Riccio's murder. When this was publicly proclaimed at the Mercat Cross the next day, it was 'not without laughter'.[6] Mary was contemptuous of his disloyalty to his fellow conspirators, but had to deflect rumours that he had acted out of revenge, particularly after she had arranged to rebury Riccio's body in 'a fair tomb' at Holyrood Abbey Church.[7]

The King still denied any part in the 'conspiracy whereof he is slanderously and sakelessly traduced', only admitting to having rehabilitated the exiled lords from England without authority. He gave orders for the henchmen to be arrested, resulting in Henry Yair, Thomas Scott, Sir John Mowbray of Barnbougle and William Harlaw being condemned to be hanged and quartered. Bothwell stepped in to reprieve Mowbray and Harlaw, who were Lothian lairds, at the scaffold. The conspirators in exile were so furious with the King that they sent Mary the bond he had signed authorising the murder to take place in her presence. If they returned, he would face a blood feud. Moray provided Mary with the bond signed in Newcastle. This disclosed the King's offers to pardon the exiles and to maintain the religious status quo in return for them granting him the Crown Matrimonial. She now knew he had betrayed Riccio, her unborn child, his fellow conspirators and herself. She kept him out of her bed and state affairs, but he remained in residence with her in the High Street, where he could be watched, and to keep up appearances. He was caught trying to go to Stirling to rebuild bridges with Moray and Argyll, but they were already travelling to Edinburgh to see Mary. He was isolated and Randolph reported that he planned to visit Flanders 'to move his case to any prince who' would listen. Although Lennox was banned from court, he remained at Holyrood, 'sore troubled in mind' and still ill,[8] but the King visited him only once.

With Mary about to move to the royal apartments at Edinburgh Castle to await the birth of her child, she realised it was politically expedient to tolerate Moray and remained socially on good terms with him and his wife. Yet she did not trust him, and Bothwell 'now began to be in great favour', becoming in effect her chief adviser and the most influential member of the Privy Council.[9] She praised his administrative 'dexterity', which was 'so acceptable to us that we could never to this hour forget it', particularly after masterminding her escape.[10] The captaincy of Dunbar brought him the income from its surrounding lands and he still held the fertile lands of Haddington Abbey from Maitland's attainted estates.* As a soldier he combined resource, dependability and the leadership to muster Borderers to his command. Although a Reformer, he had always supported Mary and her mother, despite his imprisonment in both Edinburgh Castle and the Tower.

Bothwell's strongly Reformist stance brought the government's swing towards Catholicism to an end. By an Act of Council, benefices worth less than 300 marks annually were automatically granted to Presbyterian incumbents, and some were taken up. Stipends for ministers were much greater than the pittance previously offered to the priesthood. The Kirk received £10,000 from the Crown out of church revenues. Yet with Mary dependent on papal funding, she could not allow the Catholic powers to think that she was abandoning them. She sent the Bishop of Dunblane to Rome to advise the Pope of Riccio's murder, and asked her uncle, the Cardinal, to seek further Vatican aid for her. She hoped that the Pope would understand the delicate balance she had to follow, but he sent the fanatical Nicholas de Gouda as his Nuncio, accompanied by Father Edmund Hay, Rector of the Jesuit College in Paris, to assess her situation. Philip II was shocked, not only at Mary's rapidly changing religious stance, but that the fervently Catholic King had joined with heretics in a murder conspiracy.

Mary's more conciliatory religious stance, coupled with Riccio's removal, encouraged Elizabeth to renew her correspondence with her. Elizabeth had been genuinely shocked at the manner of Riccio's murder, sending warnings to both the King and Moray never again to betray Mary. The King feared

---

* At this time, Maitland's father still resided at Lethington, but Bothwell ravished the estates.

reprisals on his mother in the Tower and wrote to confirm that she was in no way involved. With Elizabeth having sympathy for Mary, she refused to receive his letter. She told de Silva, 'Had I been in Queen Mary's place, I would have taken my husband's dagger and stabbed him with it!'[11] Robert Melville came north to assure Mary of her support, and, to the King's chagrin, on 4 April Mary invited Elizabeth to become a godmother to their unborn child. When he delivered the message, Melville suggested to Elizabeth that it was an opportunity for them to meet, 'whereat she smiled'. The King asked Charles IX to be a godfather, but Philip II was ignored, perhaps because of his recent coolness, although Mary invited his close ally, the Duke of Savoy.

Despite his administrative skills, Bothwell was not an ideal political adviser and was hated by the English. He lacked Moray's and Maitland's diplomacy, and was out of his depth with Cecil's subtleties. He lacked the patience to use persuasion, preferring to settle differences with a duel. In Mary's memoirs, written in England, Nau recorded, 'He was a man whose natural disposition made him anything but agreeable or inclined to put himself to much trouble or inconvenience to gain the goodwill of those with whom he was associated.'[12] Yet, at her confinement in June, his influence was greater than all the other lords together, according to Sir Henry Killigrew, who had replaced Randolph as English ambassador.* This made him 'the most hated man in Scotland'. Despite being a Reformer, he enjoyed 'a cup too many' with the Bishop of Ross, who, as Mary's ecclesiastical adviser, was writing his *Actis and Constitutionis of the Realme of Scotland from the Reigne of James I* as part of his reform of Scottish law.

Bothwell was now aged thirty and, at five feet six inches, was not handsome, despite having a string of female conquests. In May 1566, while visiting Haddington with his wife, he enjoyed a fifteen-minute liaison in the steeple of the abbey with her serving maid, twenty-year-old Bessie Crawford, a blacksmith's daughter. On a second occasion, Bessie's black hair was in disarray after a tryst in a chamber within the cloister, and he needed help to rebutton his trousers. Jean dismissed Bessie in fury and appears to have received the lands of Nether Hailes from her husband as a peace offering. Mary was not immune to his appeal. As Sir John Maxwell (later Herries) explained:

He was high in his own conceit, proud, vicious and vainglorious above measure, who would attempt anything out of ambition. His reckless daring appealed to her romantic sentiments, while his strong character

---

* Sir Henry Killigrew was Cecil's brother-in-law, and was privy to his scheming with Moray and Maitland. He always came to Scotland when matters of extreme delicacy needed to be handled.

and resolute purpose contrasted forcibly with the weakness of her husband Darnley, and his inability to control or protect her.[13]

Yet there is no realistic evidence of impropriety between them prior to King Henry's death, or that they were contemplating marriage. Historians have been unjustifiably coloured by the flawed evidence provided in 1568 for the Conferences at York and Westminster, designed to blacken Mary's name.

References

1. Labanoff, I, p. 351, cited in Antonia Fraser, p. 296, and Weir, p. 119
2. CSP Venetian, cited in Weir, p. 119
3. Melville, cited in Weir, p. 120
4. Guy, pp. 260, 261
5. John Prebble, *The Lion of the North: One Thousand Years of Scotland's History*, cited in Weir, p. 123
6. Mary to Archbishop Bethune, cited in Guy, p. 260; *Diurnal of Occurrents*; Teulet; Gatherer, Buchanan, cited in Weir, p. 123
7. CSP Spanish; Teulet; CSP, Foreign; Keith, cited in Weir, p. 122
8. Teulet; CSP Scottish; cited in Weir, p. 127
9. Melville, cited in Weir, p. 122
10. Gore-Browne, cited in Weir, p. 122
11. CSP Spanish, cited in Weir, p. 128
12. Nau, p. 41, cited in Antonia Fraser, p. 303
13. Gore-Browne, p. 351; Herries, p. 80, cited in Antonia Fraser, p. 302

21

James's Birth and its Aftermath

While awaiting her child's birth, Mary was under the protection of Mar, hereditary Keeper of Edinburgh Castle and Governor of Stirling. She could not face Holyrood with the nightmare of Riccio's murder fresh in her mind.

After Riccio's death, Mary regularly presided over the Privy Council. This was now made up of Bothwell, Huntly, Atholl, Seton, Livingston and Fleming. She wanted sound government during her confinement, but, with Bothwell proving politically inept, needed Moray's reasoned political leadership and close English ties. On 21 April, she recalled him with Argyll to Edinburgh, where they were formally reconciled, but she kept them with her at the Castle to keep her eye on them. Their rehabilitation had been opposed by Bothwell, Huntly, the Bishop of Ross and the King. Yet, on 29 April, Mary formally reappointed Moray, Argyll and Glencairn to the Privy Council.

Mary tried everything to achieve accord. She used Castelnau to appease rivalries, and he gained respect for his impartiality in brokering the return of Moray, Argyll and Glencairn. At the end of April, she held a feast to reconcile them with Bothwell, Huntly and Atholl, and they joined hands as a symbol that they would work together. Yet Bothwell used his influence to keep Maitland sidelined at Dunkeld, but when he offered to hunt him down and kill him for his part in Riccio's murder, Moray had to protect Maitland. Despite their lack of cohesion, the Council was united in its disaffection for King Henry, who was almost without friends. Among the nobility, only Atholl and Lennox would talk to him, and Lennox, who had moved to Dunbar, was much offended with him. His one supporter of influence was Balfour, who had fallen out with the Queen, but even he was soon of doubtful loyalty. The King seemed oblivious of his precarious standing,* but, like Bothwell, wanted Maitland kept away from court, lest he should reveal

---

* Randolph reported: 'He is neither accompanied for, nor looked for by any nobleman, attended by certain of his own servants, and 6 or 8 of his guard, he is at liberty to do or go what or where he will.'[1] Although he was cold-shouldered, he was being given enough freedom to plot, but was being carefully watched. He was a marked man.

253

his part in the murder. He again suggested appointing the Bishop of Ross as Secretary of State, and was furious when Mary turned this down. He sent a message that he had two pistols hanging on the back of his bed, primed and ready to shoot himself. She coolly went to his bedchamber, where he lay in a drunken stupor, to retrieve them. Despite trying to improve his standing by stirring up old factions, he was universally shunned. Although Melville attempted to mediate, Mary told Moray to reprove him for associating with the King.

With Lennox banned from court, the King did not 'seem bad personally, or in his habits'. He passed his time 'mostly in warlike exercises, being' commended for his horsemanship.[2] Mary made a show of marital harmony, and it was reported they again lived as husband and wife, although this is uncertain. With Mary being conciliatory to the Reformers, the King again tried to improve his flagging image abroad with letters to foreign heads of state to show he was the more ardent Papist, in the hope of being accepted as the Catholic pretender to the English Crown. He denied involvement in Riccio's murder, writing to Charles IX and Catherine de Medici that he had been 'greatly wronged by a rumour that makes me guilty of such a horrible crime'.[3] He signed his letter as King of Scotland, sealing it with the royal arms. He corresponded with de Alava, the Spanish ambassador in Paris, with whom he became 'an intimate friend',[4] and, on 29 April, de Silva informed Philip II that he was hearing Mass every day. He wrote to Philip and the Pope that Scotland was 'out of order', criticising Mary for failing to restore Catholicism. Philip acknowledged it, which the King interpreted as encouragement. He received 2,000 crowns from English Catholic sources, as part of a wider plot hoping for Spanish support to make him King of both Scotland and England. Cecil heard that he claimed to have at least forty English supporters involved in a scatter-brained plan to gain control of both the Scilly Isles and Scarborough Castle, as bridgeheads for a Spanish invasion. Yet there is no evidence that Philip would have supported such a plan, as he was relying on Guise assistance for his military objectives in the Netherlands. It was Mary, not the King, who remained the focus of English Catholic intrigue to replace Elizabeth. Just as Cecil had feared, her pregnancy had caused her stock to rise.

One adverse outcome of the King's diplomacy after Riccio's murder was that Philip became wary of supporting Mary. Yet she remained the papal focus of hopes for a counter-Reformation. On 12 May, the Pope promised her 150,000 crowns, but wanted to be sure that it would be used to restore Catholicism. He sent the hard-line Jesuit Vincenzo Laureo as his Nuncio to confirm this. Laureo, who had recently been appointed Bishop of Mondovi, left Rome on 6 June, planning to visit his new see, before travelling to Savoy and then on to Scotland.

With so much rumour of Catholic plotting, Cecil wanted to test Mary's loyalty to Elizabeth, and, without telling his mistress, used an agent provocateur, Christopher Rokesby, to entice her into a plot to gain the English throne. Rokesby arrived in Scotland in May, posing as a Catholic fleeing English persecution. He ingratiated himself with Bothwell, who arranged for him to meet Mary. He presented her with an ivory crucifix and, after confirming the strength of Catholic support for her in England, asked her to back an English plot for Elizabeth's assassination. Mary became suspicious when he suggested that she should discuss it with her Privy Council. Being eight months pregnant, she was in no mood for intrigue, but Rokesby returned to England to build a dossier of purported supporters. On his return, Mary had him arrested and seized his papers. Among them were Cecil's highly incriminating instructions in cipher. Killigrew, who knew what was afoot, wrote immediately to warn Cecil of trouble. With Mary preparing for her confinement she did not react immediately, but later wrote to Cecil:

> Since our first arrival within our realm of Scotland, We ever had a good opinion of you, that you at all times had done the office of a faithful minister. Yet these were shaken by the strange dealings of an Englishman named Rokesby, ... [and] began a little to suspend our judgement, until we receive further trial therein.[5]

She knew that Elizabeth would not tolerate his underhand approach, and he would be embarrassed if she were told. She was trying to buy his loyalty by saving his bacon. When Melville met him in London, he reported that Cecil was 'nothing altered' in his 'good inclination' towards her, to which Mary smugly confirmed, 'of the which we were not a little rejoiced'.[6] Rokesby remained imprisoned at Spynie until she was sent to Lochleven.

Although Bothwell and Huntly remained her most influential advisers, Mary refused their request for Moray to be imprisoned during her confinement to stop him trying to usurp authority. Despite their warnings of his intimate involvement in Riccio's murder, she gave him charge of the government. He promptly refused them lodgings in Edinburgh Castle, forcing Mary to bar them all from dining with her for a period to keep the peace. She then riled them all by appointing Riccio's eighteen-year-old nephew, Joseph (Giuseppe), who had come to Scotland in Castelnau's train, as her new French Secretary.

Before her confinement, Mary asked the Bishop of Ross to prepare three copies of her will, one for her Guise relations, one for herself and one for her chosen Regents. The Regency document has not survived, but it is known that she appointed a committee of three, made up of Argyll, Mar and probably the King. The King resented Argyll and Mar's inclusion, but she wanted to maintain a conciliatory voice in government with absolute loyalty to the Stewarts. Neither Bothwell nor Moray would have been acceptable, but the lords all signed an undertaking to be bound by it, although she no doubt avoided divulging it to them.

The principal part of Mary's will dealt with bequests of her jewellery. An inventory of 250 lots was compiled on sixteen folio pages by Mary Sempill (Livingston) and Margaret Carwood, who were responsible for it. They signed each page, although Carwood's signature is laboriously drawn and she was probably illiterate. Mary annotated her wishes for each item in the margins. If she died, everything except a few specified items was left to her child. If her child also died, there were a range of bequests for those close to her. Her finest gems were to be added in perpetuity to the Scottish crown jewels. These included 'The Great Harry', Henry II's gift on her marriage to the Dauphin. Other principal items were to go to her Guise relations, with a gift of rubies and pearls to pass through successive generations to the first-born of their family. The murdered Duke's children were each to receive rich jewels, particularly his youngest son, Francis, her godson, who was named after her first husband. Anne d'Este was to receive other fabulous items and the Abbess Renée was the beneficiary of several chattels including a portrait of Elizabeth. The Aumale and Elbeuf children were each remembered and the Cardinal was to receive an emerald ring. There were twenty-six bequests for King Henry although these seem to have been the return of gifts he had made to her. One was a diamond ring enamelled in red, against which Mary wrote, 'It was with this that I was married; I leave it to the King who gave it to me', hardly a show of affection.[7] There were smaller items for both Lennox and Lady Margaret. She remembered her Scottish relatives including Jean, Countess of Argyll, Moray and his wife, and her godson Francis Stewart,* son of Lord John Stewart and Jean Hepburn. Gifts for her household included her equerry, Arthur Erskine, her ladies-in-waiting, including the four Maries, Margaret, Countess of Atholl, Marie Pyerres (now Madame de Briante) and Joanne de la Reyneville (wife of Robert Bethune of Creich), her French Secretary, Joseph Riccio, and other servants. She remembered members of the nobility, including Bothwell, Huntly, Argyll,

---

* He later became Francis Stewart-Hepburn, 5th Earl of Bothwell, and would gain a place in history as the principal thorn in the side of James VI. *meant of a new creation (b.b.1581, the last heir dying in England after the battle of Worcester 1651 - the Bothwell and Hailes titles were limited to heirs male.*

Atholl and the Dowager Lady Huntly, although none received special treatment. The notable exclusions were Maitland and the Hamiltons, then out of favour. The University of St Andrews was to receive her Greek and Latin books.

By 3 June, Mary had withdrawn for her confinement, still depressed at her husband's shortcomings. On 18 May, she had told Castelnau that she would have preferred to convalesce in France for three months afterwards, but would resist the temptation to return there permanently. Being concerned for her security, she placed Argyll in an adjacent room to protect her night and day. Margaret Asteane was appointed as midwife and was given a new black gown. It was another fifteen days before she began her labour, which proved difficult and protracted. The Countess of Atholl used sorcery to cast the pains onto Lady Forbes of Reres,* who suffered magnificently without providing the Queen with any apparent relief. She was 'so handled that she began to wish that she had never been married', praying for the baby to be saved rather than herself.[8] After twenty hours, a son was born between ten and eleven o'clock on the morning of 19 June. Although she was exhausted, James, Duke of Rothesay's abundant health caused great rejoicing, with artillery being fired from the Castle and 500 bonfires lit in Edinburgh alone. Mary Ogilvy (Bethune) gave the news to Sir James Melville, who, within the hour, set off to tell Elizabeth in London.

On hearing of the birth, Elizabeth, with understandable jealousy, complained, 'Alack, the Queen of Scots is lighter of a bonny son, and I am but of barren stock.'[9] Far from weakening Mary's claim to the English throne, the King had immeasurably strengthened it by siring a male heir. Yet he could no longer claim to be heir to the Scottish throne and she treated him with distain. During her lying in, he had 'vagabondised every night' with his young male friends.[10] He would ride off alone along the coast, stripping to swim in secluded places, paying no attention when she told him to avoid such risks. He visited her to see the child and she tried to stop any lingering rumours by making a solemn oath to him before Sir William Stanley that James was 'begotten by none but you'. With James's obvious Lennox looks, as confirmed by his early portraits, she reportedly said, 'He is so much your son that I fear it will be the worse for him hereafter.'[11]

On the day after the birth, Killigrew joined the nobility to give thanks at St Giles' for the delivery of an heir. He reported continuing disquiet among rival factions, but went on to visit the Queen, still weak from her ordeal. She

---

* Margaret, Lady Forbes of Reres, also a Lady-in-Waiting, was a member of the ubiquitous Bethune family. She had married Sir Arthur Forbes of Reres and was Mary Bethune's aunt.

excused a lengthy interview, speaking faintly with a hollow cough, but he saw the Prince suckling at Helen Little, his wet nurse* and 'afterwards as good as naked ... well proportioned, and likely to prove a goodly prince'.[12] Although James remained with his nurse by day, at night he slept in a cradle by Mary's bed, as she still feared an attempt by the King to kidnap him in the hope of ruling on his behalf.

The birth of a son made Mary more confident in promoting her claim to the English throne. She communicated with Catholics both in England and on the Continent and wrote to the Pope welcoming Mondovi's forthcoming visit on 17 July. There was rejoicing in Paris, where Patrick Adamson,† a Scottish Presbyterian minister, wrote verses referring to James as the most serene Prince of Scotland, England, France and Ireland. This brought furious English protests, and he spent six months imprisoned for his indiscretion. All this strained Mary's relationship with Moray, who was still seeking the repatriation of Morton and his fellow exiles, and she continued to mistrust him.

Mary recovered only slowly, and the pain in her side recurred, leaving her depressed. In late July, with her doctors advising a change of air, Moray and Mar escorted her by sea down the Firth of Forth, where, as Buchanan reported ,'she joyed to handle the boisterous cables.'[13] She recuperated at Alloa Tower, Mar's home near Stirling, in company with her intimate friends, the Countesses of Mar, Argyll and Moray. As Lord High Admiral, Bothwell had arranged the sea trip, but did not travel with them.‡ The King had not been told of it in advance, but, when he learned where Mary had gone, rode

---

* There are records that Lady Forbes of Reres was the wet nurse. Buchanan described her as a 'woman very heavy, laith by unwieldy age and fatty substance'. While she had charge of nursery arrangements, it is unlikely that she suckled the Prince.

† Adamson was much later to become Archbishop of St Andrews and supported the appointment of bishops on James VI's behalf.

‡ Both Buchanan in his *Detectio* and Lennox later claimed that Mary was already involved in an affair with Bothwell at Alloa and encouraged the King's departure, so that the liaison could continue. This was a complete fabrication as Bothwell was not there and it contradicts Buchanan's later assertion that their affair began in September 1566 (which was equally untrue). With Moray present, he would have done all he could to avert it, and Mar was extremely strait-laced, having trained for the Church, and would not have condoned it. When Bedford reported the King's jealousy at the Queen's intimate friendship with the Countesses of Argyll, Moray and Mar, he did not mention any concerns over a liaison with Bothwell. Yet Buchanan insinuated, 'What her usage was in Alloa need not be rehearsed but it may be well so said that it exceeded measure and all womanly behaviour ... but even as she returned to Edinburgh ... what her behaviour was, it needs not be kept secret being in the mouths of so many; the Earl of Bothwell abused her body at his pleasure, having passage in at the back door ... This she has more than once confessed herself ... using only the threadbare excuse that the Lady Reres gave him access ...'[14] The pun was deliberate, to confirm Bothwell's taste for anal sex. Although a Lady-in-Waiting, Lady Forbes of Reres was not at Alloa, as she was supervising the nursery arrangements for Prince James. She was one of Bothwell's discarded mistresses, and there were unfounded reports of her acting as a go-between with Mary on later occasions. According to Drury, she was so jealous when Bothwell later married Mary that she was replaced at court by his widowed sister Jean. This makes her promotion of an affair between Mary and Bothwell extremely unlikely.

to Alloa to join them. Yet she could not abide him near her, and he left in a few hours, after a massive row. Castelnau had also joined them, having been briefed by Catherine de Medici to reconcile the royal couple. He reported the King's arrival, but barely saw him.

Mary relaxed at Alloa for several days, and Mar arranged dancing, masques and sports, which she enjoyed with the court ladies. John Spottiswood, who had retired to his parish at Calder, was deputed by the General Assembly to visit her to congratulate her on her son's birth and to request a Reformist baptism. Not surprisingly Mary refused. She also received Maitland, who tried to negotiate his rehabilitation, but she would not agree to it. Despite Lady Moray's opportunity to plead for her husband's return to favour, Bothwell remained in authority, and, on 30 June, Mary granted him the Priory of North Berwick. Kirkcaldy claimed that he 'hath now of all men greatest access and familiarity with the Queen, so that nothing of importance is done without him.' This made him

the most hated man among the noblemen of this realm, and it is said that his insolence is such that David was never more abhorred than he is now disliked on every side.[15]

Yet, at this time, there was no hint of him conducting an affair with Mary.

The King's relationship with the Queen continued to deteriorate. Bedford reported:

The Queen and her husband agree after the old manner, or rather worse. She eateth but very seldom with him, but lieth not nor keepeth no company with him, nor loveth any such as love him ... It cannot for modesty nor the honour of a Queen be reported what she said to him.[16]

She 'fell marvellously' out with Melville for giving the King an Irish water spaniel, saying 'she could not trust him who would give any thing to such one as she loved not'.[17] Later, when travelling back to France, Castelnau claimed to Bedford that they were reconciled, but this was either wishful thinking or an attempt to deceive him. One of Bedford's own spies reported, 'He cannot bear that the Queen should use familiarity either with men or women, and especially the ladies of Argyll, Moray and Mar.'[18] If she failed to pay him due attention, he stormed out in a tantrum.

Mary warned Moray of a threat by the King to kill him and, on her return to Edinburgh, deliberately humiliated her husband before the whole court by telling him that 'she would not be content that either he or any other should be

259

unfriendly to Moray'. She asked him to admit that his hatred arose from hearsay 'that Moray was not his friend, which made him speak that which he repented'.[19] The King told his father of this lack of respect and her refusal to sleep with him. Yet his plotting against Moray continued, and he was still being watched. Bothwell also wanted Moray out of the way and proposed that George Douglas should be offered a pardon if he would give evidence to incriminate Moray and Maitland in Riccio's murder, but Mary knew their importance in government. Moray retaliated by inciting border lairds including Home, Scott of Buccleuch and Ker of Cessford into a confederacy with English support against Bothwell, who was forced to leave Edinburgh to deal with it. Moray is thought to have instigated a story that William Ker, Abbot of Kelso, who was under Bothwell's protection, had revealed Glencairn's involvement in Riccio's murder with 'infamy and words of dishonour'.[20] Despite being the Abbot's godson, Cessford promptly sent two kinsmen to sever his head and arms, so that, on 28 July, Bothwell arrived in Kelso to apprehend Cessford.

On 3 August, Mary paid another five-day visit to Alloa. She was continuing to suffer from the pain in her side and remained depressed. Except on social terms, she no longer trusted Moray, although he remained at court, but there were no other able advisers to help her to re-establish her authority. She wanted religious tolerance, but, with Bothwell controlling the Council, the Catholic nobility remained marginalised. She could see his political shortcomings and increasingly took advice from Atholl, who was guided behind the scenes by Maitland. It was on this second visit that Atholl and Moray again requested Maitland's rehabilitation, and he formally submitted to her at Stirling on 4 August. The only evidence of him having masterminded Riccio's murder was the King's increasingly unreliable word, so that, after dining with him alone, she reappointed him as Secretary of State. He immediately advised Cecil and, by 11 August, was back in Edinburgh for an official reconciliation with Bothwell. He could now use his persuasion to gain the exiled conspirators' rehabilitation, but Mary was still not ready to forgive them. His reappointment also heralded the growing prominence of Atholl, whose long-term enemy, Argyll, was left in the wilderness.

Maitland's reappointment shows that Bothwell did not have things all his own way, and he had to relinquish the Abbacy of Haddington, but remained for a considerable period in occupation, leaving them at daggers drawn. There were unverified rumours of Maitland attempting to poison Bothwell, 'who had grown so hated that he cannot long continue', particularly because he opposed the exiles' return.[21] He certainly combined with Moray to use his influence against him.

While in Alloa, Mary received word that Mondovi was waiting in Paris before visiting Scotland, but she replied that this would cause 'great tumults', and she could not receive him with the honour he deserved.[22] Despite her earlier encouragement to the Pope, a counter-Reformation was now impossible and Moray had persuaded the nobility to refuse him entry. John Bethune, Master of the Household, was sent to Paris with her apologies, but Mondovi sent a stern rebuke, instructing her to restore the Catholic faith, and Bethune returned with a proportion of the promised subsidy as an inducement. On 21 August, Mondovi wrote to the Cardinal of Alessandria in Rome that Mary's difficulties

> might be obviated if the King of Spain should come, as it is hoped, with a strong force to Flanders ... If justice were executed against the six rebels, who were leaders and originators of the late treason against the Queen, [their] deaths would effectually restore peace and obedience in the kingdom.

He named them as Moray, Argyll, Morton, Maitland, Justice-Clerk Bellenden and former Clerk-Register MacGill, 'a man of no family and contriver of all evil'. This confirms that it was now the general view that Moray had been behind Riccio's murder. Mondovi described the King as 'an ambitious and inconstant youth, [who] would like to rule the realm'.[23] Yet with Mary lukewarm, he saw him as the only means of restoring Catholicism and of bringing the lords involved in Riccio's murder to book. From the distance of Paris he had not seen matters for himself, but the Pope naively approved of what he was proposing.

Following Maitland's reappointment, the King was increasingly ostracised at court and went hunting. Mary always feared that he was planning a conspiracy, when on rare occasions he was seen in conversation with any of the nobility. He seems to have remained in touch with Philip II, now in the final stages of his planned invasion of the Netherlands. Anthony Standen (father of Sir Anthony, who had protected Mary during Riccio's murder) left Scotland to assist his Catholic plotting at this time and remained abroad until 1605.

It was quite probably the need to keep tabs on the King, which persuaded Mary to resume sexual relations with him. On 13 August, she made him a large payment from her Treasury, and provided cloth of gold to furnish caparisons for his horse and a magnificent upholstered bed that had belonged to the Queen Regent. Although this implies a reconciliation, he was still frequenting Edinburgh brothels. In mid-August, she joined him for stag-hunting at Meggetland, south of Peebles, accompanied by Bothwell, Huntly, Moray, Atholl and Mar. This does not suggest very harmonious company, and by then Buchanan claimed that she was behaving 'capriciously, arrogantly and disdainfully' towards him. On 19 August, she visited Traquair on the Tweed, where the King joined them unexpectedly.[24] The hunting had been disappointing, and at supper he asked Mary, who remained unwell, to accompany him for a chase on the following day. Mary later told Nau, 'Knowing that if she did so, she would be required to gallop her horse at a great pace, she whispered in his ear that she suspected that she was pregnant.' Although this seems to confirm a resumption of sexual relations, it was only two months since James's birth, and she could not have known if she had conceived. Yet it makes Buchanan's suggestion of her conducting a relationship with Bothwell at this stage even less likely. The King's infamously brutal response was, 'Never mind, if we lose this one, we will make another.' Traquair, who had been closely allied to the King, after being knighted by him at the time of the royal marriage, 'now rebuked him sharply', saying 'he did not speak like a Christian'. The King retorted, 'What! Ought we not to work a mare well when she is in foal?'[25] It is no surprise that the *rapprochement* failed.

On 22 August, Mary interrupted her hunting to return to Holyrood for two days after hearing that the King was plotting to kidnap James to force her to grant him the Crown Matrimonial. The Prince was still in the care of Mar and his wife at Edinburgh Castle. Mary decided to move him to the safety of Stirling, the traditional childhood home for royal children. She took no chances and, on 31 August, Lady Forbes of Reres set out with the Prince in a litter, escorted by four or five hundred hackbutters. The Queen supervised the security arrangements for the royal nursery at Stirling, appointing Bothwell to captain his bodyguard. To maintain appearances, she then rejoined the King to hunt at Glenartney near Loch Earn in Perthshire, going on to Drummond Castle near Crieff before returning to Stirling. Her health had not improved, but she was not pregnant.

On 6 September, Mary returned to Edinburgh to plan James's christening celebration. Although she stayed initially at the Exchequer House* in the

---

* Buchanan records that Bothwell continued his illicit affair with Mary at the Exchequer House, whose secluded gardens backed onto the home of David Chalmers, shortly to be appointed by Bothwell as Common Clerk of Edinburgh. According to Buchanan, the 'dissolute' and portly Lady Forbes of Reres assisted Bothwell in visiting Mary from Chalmers' house. The Queen and Margaret Carwood apparently let her 'down by a sash over the wall into the next garden. But behold! The sash suddenly broke! Down with a great noise tumbled Lady Reres. But the old warrior, nothing dismayed by the darkness, the height of the wall or her unexpected flight to earth, reached Bothwell's chamber, opened the door, plucked him out of bed – out of his wife's embrace – and led him, half-asleep, half-naked, to the arms of the Queen.'[26] There is no other evidence to corroborate this, and at the time she was supervising the royal nursery at Stirling. Buchanan claimed that the King threatened to leave Scotland on hearing of it, but, if so, he never mentioned it during the next few weeks, despite ample opportunity. He had not, of course, been reticent in accusing Riccio, when similarly implicated with the Queen. The story is yet again unthinkable.

Cowgate, by 12 September she was back at Holyrood. The King remained at Stirling, apparently in a foul mood at Maitland being reappointed Secretary of State. He was visited by Lennox, who wrote to Mary of his son's humiliation and intention to go abroad, as he felt unsafe in Scotland. Morton was keeping tabs on the King's movements from England and reported a ship waiting for him in the Clyde. He apparently intended going to France in the hope of supporting himself on Mary's dowry, but, as he remained in touch with Philip II, Alison Weir has suggested that he may have planned to visit him in Flanders. When Mary visited Stirling to talk through his concerns, he refused to return with her to Holyrood. Back in Edinburgh, she showed Lennox's letter to the Privy Council, who resolved to talk to the King. His scheming from abroad would be even more dangerous than at home. Yet, to everyone's surprise, he appeared in Edinburgh a week later, but refused to visit Holyrood until the Council members had been dismissed, only embarrassing Mary and offending them. She tackled him privately about his plans, but, despite admitting to having a ship in the Clyde, would not confirm his plan for departure. This resulted in *'une forte belle harangue'* [a big slanging match],[27] witnessed by the new French ambassador, Philibert du Croc, who had replaced Castelnau. She

> took him by the hand, and besought him for God's sake to declare if she had given him reason for this resolution; and entreated he might deal plainly, and not spare her. [She had] a clear conscience, and that all her life she had done no action which could anywise prejudice either his or her honour.[28]

When pressed, he denied that she had given him any justification to leave, complaining only at not being adequately recognised as King. As he left, he whispered theatrically, 'Adieu, Madame. You shall not see my face for a long space.'[29] She was visibly upset, but both the Council and du Croc advised her to continue her wise and virtuous existence. Du Croc reported to Catherine de Medici that the Scots were

> so well reconciled with the Queen as a result of her own prudent behaviour, that nowadays there was not a single division to be seen between them.[30]

If there were any hint of an affair between Mary and Bothwell at this time, the King would surely have cited it to gain sympathy. After leaving for Glasgow with his father, he wrote to Mary that he was planning to sail, but

263

complained only at his lack of authority. Mary showed the letter to the Council, who confirmed they would not give him control of public affairs. Melville told Archbishop Bethune in Paris that the King was using his threat of departure to gain the dismissal of Maitland, MacGill and Bellenden. Yet Mary told him he had only himself to blame and he should learn to regain the nobility's respect. She told Lennox that the King had no cause for complaint. The Council took no chances; they wrote to Catherine de Medici with a full account of his behaviour, in case he should seek to set up a royal court in exile. Although du Croc reported to both Archbishop Bethune and Catherine that his ship remained in readiness, he stayed out of sight in Scotland, hunting and fishing. Du Croc reported:

> It is vain to imagine that he should be able to raise any disturbance, for there is not one person in all the kingdom, from the highest to the lowest, that regards him any further than is agreeable to the Queen. And I never saw her majesty so much beloved, esteemed and honoured.[31]

In late September, Moray again persuaded the Council to refuse Mondovi's written request to visit Scotland, but Mary did not tell him, and he remained in Paris awaiting his invitation. By now, Pius V believed that the threat of Philip II's delayed invasion of Flanders would be needed for the mission to succeed, and, by mid-October, Mondovi realised that Mary was stalling, resulting in the Pope recalling him to his see. The Cardinal of Lorraine tried to discourage Mondovi from doing 'something signal for the service of God in Scotland'[32] and half-heartedly agreed to intercede, but was in no hurry to do so.

References

1. Nau, p. 7, cited in Antonia Fraser, p. 299
2. CSP Spanish, 18 May 1566, cited in Weir, p. 130
3. Egerton, MSS, cited in Weir, p. 131
4. CSP Spanish; cited in Weir, p. 141
5. Guy, p. 266
6. Guy, p. 266–7
7. Cited in Guy, p. 269, and Antonia Fraser, p. 305
8. Melville, cited in Antonia Fraser, p. 307
9. Melville, p. 56, cited in Wormald, *Mary, Queen of Scots*, p. 163, and Antonia Fraser, p. 308

10. Nau, p. 28, cited in Antonia Fraser, p. 300
11. Herries, p. 79; cited in Wormald, *Mary, Queen of Scots*, p. 163, and Antonia Fraser, pp. 309–10
12. Bannatyne's Memorials, p. 238; CSP, Scottish, II, p. 289, cited in Guy, p. 267
13. Antonia Fraser, p. 311
14. George Buchanan, *Detectio Mariae Reginae*, cited in Guy, p. 389
15. Weir, p. 145
16. CSP Foreign, VIII, p. 114; Keith, III, p. 349; Hay Fleming, p. 136, cited in Guy, p. 270, and Weir, p. 146
17. Guy, p. 271; Cotton MSS; Caligula, Selections from Unpublished Manuscripts; CSP Foreign; Keith, cited in Weir, p. 146
18. CSP Foreign, VIII, p. 118; Hay Fleming, p. 411, cited in Guy, p. 270, and Antonia Fraser, p. 312
19. CSP Foreign, cited in Weir, p. 146
20. Weir, p. 143
21. Weir, p. 147
22. Pollen, pp. 282 et seq., cited in Antonia Fraser, p. 316
23. Weir, p. 149
24. Weir, p. 148
25. Nau, p. 30, cited in Antonia Fraser, p. 312, and Weir, pp. 148–9
26. Buchanan, *Detectio*, cited in Weir, p. 152
27. Keith, II, p. 447, p. 450, cited in Antonia Fraser, p. 314
28. Privy Council to Catherine de Medici; du Croc to Archbishop Bethune; cited by Keith; Teulet; cited in Guy, p. 272
29. Le Croc to Catherine de Medici, 15 October 1566; Keith II, p. 451, cited in Guy, p. 272, and Weir, p. 155
30. Antonia Fraser, p. 315
31. Weir, pp. 158–9
32. Weir, p. 159

22

Mary's Illness at Jedburgh and Convalescence at Craigmillar

To demonstrate her involvement in government, Mary agreed to attend assizes in Jedburgh to deal with the petty offences postponed during her pregnancy. Before leaving Edinburgh, she told Moray, Bothwell, Argyll and Huntly to subscribe to a bond offering each other mutual support, but to ignore the 'King when his orders conflicted with the Queen's wishes'.[1] On 1 October, she ordered the Border lairds to meet her at Melrose. Although the King was invited, he was still threatening to go abroad and did not appear. On 7 October, she left for Jedburgh with an entourage of forty men, including Moray, Huntly, Atholl, Livingston, Seton, Caithness, Rothes, Maitland and the Bishop of Ross together with judges and court officials. They stayed with Home *en route* at his castles at Home, Wedderburn and Langton.

As Lieutenant of the Borders, Bothwell had set out for Liddesdale three days earlier, taking 300 horse to round up offenders for trial. Melville later claimed that Bothwell and Huntly had a plan to murder Moray at Jedburgh, although Bedford told Cecil that Home would protect him. On arrival at Hermitage, Bothwell imprisoned some of the notorious Armstrongs and Johnstones, before going after the Elliotts, who had eluded him. When he caught up with them, he was severely wounded by Jock Elliott of the Park, but managed to shoot him before passing out from loss of blood. He was brought unconscious back to Hermitage with stab wounds to his forehead, thigh and left hand, giving rise to rumours of his death. If Moray's murder had been planned, it was now forgotten, and when the Armstrongs and Johnstones gained control of Hermitage, Bothwell's officers had no choice but to release their captives.

On 9 October, Mary arrived at the fortified house in Jedburgh, which still stands just off the main street. She was greeted with the news of Bothwell's injuries at Hermitage, twenty-five miles to the south-west. Although the assizes lasted six days, there were fewer cases without the Armstrongs,

Johnstones and Elliotts in custody. Moray considered Mary over lenient in her sentencing, after fining those found guilty, rather than seeking their execution.

On 16 October, with the assizes over, Mary rode with Moray and her party to visit Bothwell at Hermitage, believing that he was dying. She wanted a briefing from him as Governor of this border district, but, after meeting him for two hours with Moray and others,* she set off back to Jedburgh. Despite the round trip of fifty miles in a day, Hermitage was considered too forbidding for the Queen and her attendants to spend a winter night. As she returned, she fell from her horse when it slipped in a bog, losing her watch, and had to stop at a farmhouse near Hawick to dry herself and repair her clothing.

On the next day in Jedburgh, Mary became feverish and the pain in her side was now so acute that she vomited blood 'more than sixty times'. This resulted in convulsions and she lost consciousness. Although physical and mental stress was blamed, she had lost so much blood and became so cold that it seemed unlikely she would recover, horrifying her entourage. The gastric ulcer causing her pain seems to have haemorrhaged.† Matters were made worse by a message from Stirling that the Prince was also ill 'and that his life was despaired of'.[3] He at least recovered quickly after being made to vomit, but the Queen 'had a very severe fit of convulsions', losing her vision and ability to speak.[4] Despite his injuries, Bothwell arrived on a horse litter from Hermitage, determined to be on hand should the worst happen. He had made a remarkable recovery, despite the legacy of a scar on his forehead, and was determined to stop Moray regaining authority. If Mary were to die, he wanted to hear her final wishes.

When at last the Queen seemed to rally, it proved short-lived. On 24 October, she relapsed and 'all her limbs were so contracted, her face was so distorted [with pain], her eyes closed, her mouth fast and her feet and arms stiff and cold'.[5]

She slipped into a coma and again seemed close to death with funeral

---

* Buchanan asserts that Mary went to Hermitage out of lust to see Bothwell, attributing her subsequent illness to 'having gratified her unlawful passions' with him and to 'her exertions both day and night'.[2] Nothing could have been further from the truth.

† There has been much speculation as to the true cause of Mary's illness, but there can be little doubt that it was the result of internal bleeding from a gastric ulcer, which also caused the recurrent pain in her side. Although there are also suggestions that she was suffering from porphyria, the hereditary disease that later afflicted George III, she never suffered the bouts of delusion that are its general symptom. One reason for assuming that Mary suffered from porphyria is that it could also explain her father's fatal collapse after Solway Moss. Yet no further symptoms of it recurred during her captivity in England, when her illnesses were well documented. Whatever the cause, there can be little doubt that her illness was exacerbated by acute depression at her predicament of being married to the King.

arrangements being discussed. Her servants opened windows to release her spirit, while Moray gathered up her plate and jewellery. Yet her French doctor, Charles Nau, 'a perfect man of his craft', arranged for her to be 'handled by extreme rubbing, drawing and other cures'.[6] He bound her limbs tightly and forced wine down her throat, causing her to vomit an amount of corrupt blood, which gained some relief. According to his brother Claude Nau, Mary's French Secretary during her captivity in England, he suspected poison, with the implication that Moray was involved. An enema given as a purge produced 'suspicious results'.[7] Yet, after three hours, she had recovered her sight and speech, and started to sweat. Prayers were said in Edinburgh, and she made a new will to ensure that the throne passed to James and not King Henry, who she blamed for her illness, and she made a plea for religious tolerance. Despite Bothwell's hopes, Moray was given 'the principal part of the government'.[8] She placed 'the special care of the protection of our son' in the hands of Elizabeth[9] so that his father was kept out of the picture. This was a masterstroke designed to make Elizabeth adopt him as his mother. As it now seemed that she would remain childless, Mary expected him to be brought up by her in England to inherit the English throne as a Protestant. Although Elizabeth's reply is missing, on 20 November she acknowledged this obligation, and Mary thanked the English Privy Council for the 'good offers' from her 'dear sister'.[10] On 6 November, while travelling from Paris, Father Edmund Hay wrote:

> Although she confirmed her desire to die in the [Catholic] religion ... she frankly admitted that she had been neglectful not only in government of the realm, but also, and chiefly, in promoting the Catholic religion.

Although a message was sent to recall the King from hunting in the West of Scotland, he could not be reached immediately. On 27 October, he set out in haste, arriving the next day, when the worst was over. He was not invited to attend a meeting of the Council and, being unwelcome, returned on the following day, furious, to Glasgow. His absence and the delay in his arrival concerned the diplomatic circle in Edinburgh. Du Croc told Bethune that this was 'a fault that I cannot excuse', and it led the Venetian envoy to speculate that he had poisoned her. Mary herself believed poison had caused her illness, but this was not shared by those around her. Maitland considered that:

> the occasion of the Queen's sickness is thought and displeasure ... and the root of it is the king. For she has done him so great honour,

contrary to the advice of her subjects, and he, on the other part, has recompensed her with such ingratitude and misuses himself so far towards her that it is a heartbreak for her to think he should be her husband, and how to be free of him she sees no outgait.[11]

Maitland already knew she wanted to be freed from her marriage.

Mary recovered quickly. On 30 October, two days after the King's departure, fire destroyed part of her Jedburgh lodging,* but she was well enough to be moved to a nearby fortified tower belonging to Ker of Ferniehirst, paying forty pounds in rent. On 9 November, she had sufficiently recovered to move by easy stages towards Edinburgh in a litter. On passing Berwick, the English deputy governor, Sir John Forster, crossed the border to pay his respects, but his horse reared when his guns fired a salute, kicking her in the thigh. She was in pain for two days, and he had to beg forgiveness, despite her making light of it. After three weeks she reached Sir Simon Preston at Craigmillar, just south of Edinburgh.

During her illness, European politics had not stood still, and Philip II was preparing for war against the Dutch Protestants. Elizabeth wanted to avoid Scotland becoming a bridgehead for a Catholic invasion of Britain and told Cecil to seek a Scottish alliance, hinting that she would confirm Mary as her heir. On 7 November, she sent Bedford to propose terms by which her rights to the English succession might be secured. She told the Scots:

> Our meaning is to require nothing to be confirmed in that treaty but that which directly pertains to us and our children, omitting anything in that treaty that may be prejudicial to her title as next heir after us and our children, all of which may be secured to her by a new treaty betwixt us.[13]

Each would recognise the other as lawful queen with Mary's English claim being deferred only behind Elizabeth's descendants. Elizabeth argued that 'this manner of proceeding is the way to avoid all jealousies and difficulties betwixt us, and the only way to secure the amity.' Yet this was subterfuge as, two days beforehand, she had told the English Parliament that any recognition of a successor would bring 'some peril unto you and certain danger

---

* Yet again Buchanan's version of events bears no relation to the facts. He records that Bothwell returned to Jedburgh, where Mary moved him 'from his accustomed lodging to the Queen's house in the chamber directly under her own'. There they apparently carried on their sordid affair notwithstanding that both had been at death's door. The news was reported to the distraught King, who 'delayed not but with all speed came to Jedburgh'.[12]

unto me'. Yet she offered to retract the demand for ratification of the Treaty of Edinburgh, if replaced with a new 'treaty of perpetual amity'.[14]

For once Cecil did not interfere with Elizabeth's efforts to avoid a Spanish-led invasion of Britain. He wanted a secure Protestant government in Scotland and worked assiduously to have Morton and his fellow conspirators repatriated, knowing that they would trigger a blood feud against King Henry. Despite their estrangement, it might still be possible to implicate Mary in any action taken against the King, thus impairing her claim to the English throne. Cecil avoided becoming personally involved, but pulled all the strings.

Mary recalled Robert Melville to Edinburgh to find a way to overcome the hurdle of her exclusion from the English throne under Henry VIII's will, the validity of which was in doubt (see p. 107). This nominated Catherine and Mary, the younger sisters of Jane Grey, whom Elizabeth opposed for marrying without her consent, as required by the Royal Marriage Act of 1536 (see pp. 156–7). She preferred the blameless Scottish Queen, if she would agree to the 'perpetual amity'. Confirmation of this was overtaken by events.

Elizabeth needed to develop an understanding with Mary, who was under increasing pressure from the Papacy to restore Catholicism in Scotland. Mondovi was using the threat of Philip II's military presence in the Netherlands to insist on the execution of Moray and the other Protestant leaders. Yet Mary considered 'the perpetual amity' and her acceptance as Elizabeth's heir to be of overriding importance. She told Mondovi that 'she could not stain her hands with the blood of her subjects, and dared not risk offending Elizabeth'.[15] Cecil tried to solve the succession by recalling Parliament to persuade Elizabeth to marry the Archduke Charles, but she was furious at him raising such a personal matter. Mary's request for her to act as James's guardian was thus well-timed.

King Henry used the Spanish invasion of the Netherlands as another opportunity to champion his Catholicism. While Mary was being moved from Jedburgh to Craigmillar, she was warned that he had written to European Catholic heads of state of her lack of Catholic commitment. This was Mary's first concrete evidence of his duplicity. If she wanted peace in Scotland, the restoration of Catholicism had to be deferred. Although the King's objective was to improve his own standing, she was mortified at being accused of lacking faith. She immediately wrote to de Silva, and, on 14 November, he reported to Philip II:

The Queen has heard that her husband has written to your Majesty, the Pope, the King of France, and the Cardinal of Lorraine that she was dubious of the faith and asked me to assure your majesty that as regards religion she will never with God's help fail to uphold it with all the fervour and constancy which the Roman Catholic Christian religion demands.[16]

Yet again Philip's trust in her was being nibbled away and neither he nor Catherine de Medici offered her further tangible support. The Pope sent Father Edmund Hay to advise her to carry out Mondovi's instructions. This made her furious with the King, and it was in this mood that she discussed ways of ending her marriage at Craigmillar.

On arrival at Craigmillar on 20 November, Mary was still being tended by her doctors and was heard to say she 'could wish to be dead'.[17] Eventually on 2 December, 'she vomited a great quantity of corrupt blood, and then the cure was complete'.[18] Much to her chagrin, the King arrived a few days later hoping to restore marital relations, but she would have nothing to do with him. She told him to return to Stirling, warning Bethune in Paris that they were beyond reconciliation. He had never apologised for his part in Riccio's murder, and du Croc again reported her paranoia that he was involved in plotting, whenever he was seen speaking to a member of the court. When he left on 3 December, he asked du Croc to ride out from Edinburgh to see him. When asked to intercede for him, du Croc said there was nothing he could do. King Henry again threatened to leave Scotland, reopening doubts over the Prince's paternity, but it was another idle threat and he returned to Stirling for the baptism.

Mary spent almost a fortnight convalescing at Craigmillar. All her senior advisers, other than Atholl and Glencairn, who were not in Edinburgh, were with her. They blamed her recent illness on her disaffection with the King, and they persuaded her that their separation was a political necessity for Scotland's security. She had originally aired this with Maitland at Jedburgh, and he had been considering how to achieve it. Mary always saw divorce as her preferred means of separation, but it presented difficulties that needed investigation. Maitland was well aware that the only acceptable grounds for a Catholic divorce were adultery or an annulment. Although there was ample cause for separation on grounds of the King's adultery, neither party would be permitted to remarry, and Mary wanted more heirs to protect her succession. An annulment could only be permitted on grounds of non-consummation, which could not be argued in this case, or because the couple was within the fourth degree of consanguinity (third cousins or closer). Yet, as annulment meant that the marriage had never taken place, any child of the union would become illegitimate. There was precedent

271

for children remaining legitimate, if the couple was unaware of their consanguinity when they married. Yet the King and Queen had applied for a papal dispensation beforehand. Their only hope was to argue that the dispensation was invalid as it had arrived only after their marriage.

A second problem with divorce was how to control the King afterwards. Far from it improving the security of the realm, it would make him the focus of every Catholic scheme against Mary. Lennox believed that the lords at Craigmillar planned to imprison the King after the Prince's baptism. Yet there is no evidence for this, and, if so, the idea must have been dropped. By holding him in custody, Mary would alienate English Catholics, some of whom preferred his claim to the English throne to hers.

The more certain solution was to bring about the King's death, and Maitland considered arranging his prosecution for treason. Yet, under Scottish law, a king could not be found guilty of treason. The Bishop of Ross believed that this could be overcome, as he was a consort subject to the Queen, but, even so, a treason trial based on Riccio's murder would implicate Morton and his fellow exiles and bring to light Moray and Maitland's involvement. With so many foreign dignitaries due to arrive for the Prince's baptism, the prospect of a trial involving the King and the principal Scottish lords was too scandalous to contemplate and, if the King were found guilty, Prince James's legitimacy would again be in doubt. This left murder as the only sure option, although Mary would never agree to it and could not be told. There was a simple means of achieving it, without involving anyone at Craigmillar. If the conspirators in exile returned, they would inevitably arrange for the King's death in a Douglas blood feud.

Maitland's plan at Craigmillar thus focused on gaining the Queen's agreement for the exiles to be rehabilitated, and he glossed over the difficulties of obtaining a divorce. He took Moray to broach it with Argyll, Huntly and Bothwell, requesting each of them to assist in persuading the Queen to repatriate the exiles. They all supported this, provided it did not offend her, but Bothwell and Huntly's only reason for supporting the return of Moray's allies was to enable them to arrange the King's murder. Maitland then suggested that they could gain Mary's agreement, by offering to arrange her divorce from the King. When Argyll, who had long wanted a divorce from Lady Jean,* said that he 'knew not how that might be done', Maitland assured him that a way could be found 'to make her quit of him, so that you and my Lord of Huntly will only behold the matter, and not be offended

---

* In 1567, when Mary was in Lochleven, Jean retired from Edinburgh to Argyllshire, but she could not tolerate being with her husband and soon left again. Yet, when he tried to persuade her to divorce him, she refused.

thereat'.[19] This careful reply does not necessarily imply divorce. Bothwell also requested that, in return for offering assistance, they should have all their estates restored, but, despite Buchanan's later claim, Bothwell did not originate the divorce plan to promote his own marriage to Mary, and Moray and Maitland would never have allowed it. Yet he shared the general outrage at the King's behaviour, and was not averse to his death.

As their spokesman, Maitland now approached the Queen, offering to arrange matters 'as well for her own easement as for the realm' in return for her agreeing to pardon the exiles for their part in Riccio's murder and for restoring all their attainted estates.[20] Despite mistrusting Morton, Mary agreed to him being rehabilitated to Tantallon. She accepted the proposal for a divorce on two conditions: one that the divorcement were made lawfully; the other that it was not prejudicial to her son; otherwise Her Highness would rather endure all torments and abide the perils that might chance her.*[21]

With the English succession in mind, she could not countenance an impediment to her son's legitimacy. Yet, like Argyll, she did not know how to overcome this. Bothwell reassured her that his father had divorced his mother, without prejudicing his legitimacy, when hoping to remarry Mary of Guise. In that instance, Cardinal Bethune had confirmed that he was unaware of their consanguinity at marriage, and, as *legatus a latere,* did not refer it to Rome.

Although Maitland tried to reassure Mary that they would use legal means to be rid of the King, he stated rather obliquely that Moray was as scrupulous a Protestant as she was a Catholic and 'I am assured he will look through his fingers thereto, and will behold our doings, saying nothing of the same'. [23] This can be interpreted only to mean that Moray would be allowed to keep his hands clean while a nefarious plot was undertaken. He was still seen by the nobility, other than Bothwell and Huntly, as their natural leader. Mary was given similar assurance that she would be involved in nothing which tarnished her reputation. Yet she came to realise that, in the process of removing the King, the Protestant lords tried to sully her honour and even to make her son illegitimate, so that Moray could take the Crown. When, in

---

* Buchanan claimed that Mary initiated the plan to be rid of her husband by saying, 'About the fifth day of November, removing from Jedburgh to Kelso ... she said that unless she were quit of the King by any means or other, she could never have one good day in her life, and rather that she should fail therein, she would rather be the instrument of her own death. Returning to Craigmillar ... she renewed the same purpose ... in an audience with my Lord of Moray, the Earl of Huntly, the Earl of Argyll and Maitland, propounding that the way to be rid of the King and make it look best was to begin an action of divorce against him ... whereunto it was answered how that could not goodly be done without hazard, since by the doing thereof the Prince her son 'should be declared bastard ... which answer, when she had thought over it, she left that conceit and opinion of the divorce and ever from that day forth imagined how to cut him away.'[22]

1569, Moray was challenged on reports that he had taken part in the discussions at Craigmillar, he denied any involvement 'tending to any unlawful or dishonourable end'.[24] This, of course, was not a denial of his knowledge of the plans, only that he had not discussed them. His objectives will be discussed later, but if he were allowed to 'look through his fingers', his personal agenda, even then, was to regain control of government.

Although the lords at Craigmillar contemplated the King's murder, they knew Mary would not agree to it, and she was kept aloof from the plan. Two of the depositions made for her defence in England show that she knew that means other than divorce were being contemplated but vetoed them. In the first of these,* she told them, while still at Craigmillar:

> I will that you do nothing by which any spot may be laid to my honour or conscience, and therefore I pray you rather let the matter be in the estate as it is, abiding till God in his goodness put remedy thereto, than you, believing to do me service, may possibly turn to my hurt and displeasure.[25]

Maitland had smoothly replied, 'Madam, let us guide the matter among us, and Your Grace shall see nothing but good and approved by parliament.'[26] The second deposition was prepared in 1568 by her Scottish supporters, including Huntly and Argyll. It implies that she was aware of all the options discussed at Craigmillar, as it states that they had contemplated 'other ways [from divorce and treason] to dispatch him; which altogether Her Grace refused, as is manifestly known.'[27] Despite her veto, she knew murder had been contemplated and that the Douglases would want revenge on return from exile. If she were aware of the full deliberations at Craigmillar, as the depositions suggest, the Lords had to be sure that she would not demand a proper investigation afterwards. When the time came, she was as anxious as they were to huddle up the evidence. She had to have known that the King's murder was the only safe way to restore her security, but was not involved in it.

To confirm their agreement, the Lords at Craigmillar will have signed a bond similar to that for the murder of Riccio with the precise objective left ambiguous. Although no such document has survived, there is evidence of it from several sources. Mary later told Nau that, when Bothwell left her at Carberry Hill, he gave her a paper and told her to guard it well, as it was the

---

* This document, known as the 'Protestation of Huntly and Argyll' and dated 5 January 1569, was prepared by Mary in captivity in England and sent to them for signature. It was intercepted by Cecil en route, and he ensured that they never saw it.

evidence of the complicity of the other lords in the murder. If this were the bond, as seems likely, it was quickly removed from her and destroyed.* If Casket Letter II is to be believed (and it is the one part of the Casket Letters that appears plausible), the King told her in Glasgow that he was aware that a bond for his murder had been prepared at Craigmillar. In the admittedly suspect deposition of Bothwell's henchman James 'Black' Ormiston before his execution in 1573, he recalls the bond as saying:

> It was thought expedient and most profitable for the Commonwealth, by the whole nobility and Lords underscribed, that such a young fool and proud tyrant should not reign or bear rule over them: and that for divers causes therefore, that these all had concluded that he should be put off by one way or another: and whosoever should take the deed in hand, or do it, they should defend and fortify as themselves.[28]

It has to be unlikely that the bond would so overtly have contemplated the King's murder, but the names of the signatories mentioned sound plausible. These were Huntly, Argyll, Bothwell, Maitland and Balfour, who was said to have drafted it. Admittedly, by this time, they had all fallen foul of the government, but, as they include names other than Bothwell and his henchmen, they retain a ring of authenticity, particularly as they exclude Moray, by then deceased, who was allowed to 'look through his fingers'. Yet the names may have been edited by those taking the deposition, as Morton is thought to have signed it at Whittinghame after returning from exile. As the King's ally, Balfour's involvement may seem surprising, but as a lawyer he was closely associated with Bothwell, then Sheriff of Edinburgh. His signature denotes one of the many changes in his loyalty during his political career.† With the King isolated, he now hoped for advantage by backing his enemies.

---

* John Guy does not believe that a bond was signed at Craigmillar. He argues that the decision to murder the King was not taken until the meeting between Morton, Maitland and Bothwell at Whittinghame on about 14 January. Certainly the detailed plan could not have been made until it became clear that the King would move to Kirk o' Field at the end of January. Although it was reported that Bothwell gave a document to the Queen at Carberry Hill only to have it removed by her captors, John Guy argues that there was no contemporary evidence for it or that it was a bond. He claims that Mary would not have needed to ask for a copy to enable her to provide evidence at the Conferences at York and London, if she had already seen it. This does not seem convincing. It is more likely that she wanted the written evidence of a document she had already seen. He contends that Balfour concocted a story of a bond after the event to incriminate those who were then his enemies. Yet there are several pieces of evidence for the bond's existence and it seems unthinkable in a conspiracy for the King's murder between doubtful colleagues that they should not have felt the need for mutual protection.

† There are suggestions that Balfour was playing a double game as a friend of the King, by trying to lure the Protestant nobility into a murder plan which would incriminate them. While his movements over the next few weeks are obscure, we know he was part of the plot himself. With the King isolated, he seems to have chosen this moment, as so often, to change sides.

Just as Morton retained the bond for Riccio's murder, so Bothwell, the soldier among them, agreed to become involved by briefing the returning exiles and offering them assistance; he kept the bond as his security. Yet it is unlikely that Mary saw it until Carberry Hill.

References

1. Archibald Douglas to Mary, cited by Keith, cited in Weir, p. 157
2. Buchanan, *Detectio*, cited in Weir, p. 161
3. Nau, cited in Weir, p. 161
4. Nau, cited in Weir, p. 161
5. Guy, p. 274, and Antonia Fraser, p. 318
6. Cited by Tytler; Nau; Leslie; cited in Guy p. 274, and Weir, pp. 162, 163
7. Nau; Leslie; cited in Weir, p. 163
8. Nau; CSP Spanish; see Archives of Edinburgh University, cited in Weir, p. 163
9. Guy, p. 276
10. Guy, p. 277
11. Tytler, new enlarged edition, II, p. 400, cited in Guy, pp. 275, 282, Antonia Fraser, p. 318, and Weir, p. 162
12. Buchanan, *The Tyrannous Reign of Mary Stewart*, ed. Gatherer p. 169, cited Guy, p. 391
13. Guy, p. 278
14. Sir J E Neale, *Elizabeth I and her Parliaments*, cited in Guy, p. 278
15. Weir, p. 170
16. CSP Spanish, I, p. 597, cited in Antonia Fraser, p. 328, and Weir, p. 165
17. Le Croc to Catherine de Medici, 2 December 1566, Keith II, p. 474, cited in Antonia Fraser, p. 320, and Weir, p. 170
18. Nau, p. 32, cited in Weir, p. 170
19. Cotton MMS, *The Protestation of Huntly and Argyll*; Keith; W Goodall, *Examination of the Casket Letters said to be written by Mary Queen of Scots to James, Earl of Bothwell*; Mumby; cited in Weir, p. 172
20. Weir, p. 172
21. Guy, p. 283, and Weir, p. 173
22. Buchanan, *Book of Articles*, 1568, cited in Guy, p. 391
23. Guy, p. 283, Wormald, *Mary, Queen of Scots*, p. 164, and Antonia Fraser, p. 321
24. Written by Moray and Cecil in London, and pasted to back of Protestation; cited in Weir, p. 175
25. Protestation of the Earls of Huntly and Argyll, Keith II, p. 475, cited in Guy, pp. 283, 391, and Weir, p. 174
26. Keith, III, p. 290, cited in Wormald, *Mary, Queen of Scots*, p. 164, and Antonia Fraser, p. 321
27. Goodall; cited in Weir, p. 175
28. Hosack, I, p. 532, cited in Antonia Fraser, p. 322, and Weir, p. 177

23

The Baptism of Prince James

On 7 December 1566, the Queen left Craigmillar for Holyrood to finalise arrangements for the Prince's baptism at Stirling ten days later. This was to be a celebration not only for the heir to the Scottish throne, but for a future King of England. Three days later, she travelled to Stirling over two days. The King was already there, but she gave Bothwell responsibility for the arrangements and for greeting visiting dignitaries. Sir John Forster reported to Cecil, 'All things for the christening are at his appointment and the same scarcely well liked of with the rest of the nobility as it is said.'[1] By giving Bothwell such prominence, Mary again showed a lack of tact with so many English being present, and Sir James Melville reported afterwards that he 'had a mark of his own that he shot at', strutting about full of self-importance.[2]

Mary was so concerned at rumours of the King's scheming that the Privy Council issued an edict to stop firearms being brought into the Castle, and she dismissed the majority of his servants. Although he replaced them with Lennox dependants, she remained disconcerted at their number. She warned their leader, Robert Cunningham, not to cause trouble and told the King that, if any of them left the Castle, they would be banned from returning. Du Croc reported that she kept a wary eye out 'for further contrivances', forbidding the King from meeting foreign dignitaries unless she herself were present.[3] There was good reason for this. The town clerk of Glasgow, William Hiegait, had sent a warning, through Archbishop Bethune's servant William Walker, of a rumour that the King was seeking help to kidnap the Prince and crown him, so that he could claim the Regency.* Hiegait had heard that the King was threatening to kill Mary's close advisers and was so jealous that either they or he had to go. Yet, even with Lennox's support, he would have needed overseas help to face Mary's allies.

---

* William Hiegait proved an unreliable witness and when confronted by the Privy Council to confirm his allegations lost his nerve, admitting only to hearing a rumour that the King was in danger. It was said that he later warned the King that, if he went with Mary to Edinburgh, she would imprison him.

According to Melville, Mary was 'still sad and pensive', fearing that the exiles' rehabilitation would lead inevitably to a blood feud. 'So many sighs would she give that it was a pity to hear her, and few there were to endeavour to comfort her.' Despite encouragement from both Moray and Mar, she would not eat. She walked in the park with Melville, who tried to console her by saying that 'her friends in England would soon help her to forget her enemies in Scotland'. Yet he too commended clemency for the exiles 'to best gain the hearts of the whole people, both here and in England'.[4]

Mary had obtained support from both Catholic and Protestant Council members to make the Prince's christening a spectacle to rival anything seen in France. There was to be a three-day fête modelled on that organised in the previous year by Catherine de Medici at Bayonne to mark French and Spanish reconciliation. She borrowed £12,000 from Edinburgh merchants, and raised taxes to pay for it. This was not just a celebration of a baptism, but of Moray and Argyll's reconciliation with Bothwell. Although they would not attend the Catholic ceremony, she provided them with new clothing for the events afterwards. Moray wore green, Argyll red and Bothwell blue, while many others were magnificently attired 'some in cloth of silver, some in cloth of gold, some in cloth of tissue, every man rather above than under his degree'.[5] Banquets with fine wines were prepared to match the magnificence of the costumes, with the food delivered by an elaborate mechanical *engine* on a moving stage, which eventually collapsed as the final course was being served. Each course was accompanied by satyrs and nymphs, or by a child lowered from a golden globe reciting verses. A stage was built for Buchanan's masques, which extolled Mary's virtues, hardly according with his later *Detectio.* Mary's valet, the witty Sebastian Pagez, an accomplished musician from Auvergne, prepared entertainments including a ballet, which caused great offence by depicting the English as satyrs with their tails held in their hands to make obscene gestures! The Scots roared with laughter, but Bedford had to step in to restore order when an Englishman named Hatton threatened to stab Pagez through the heart. Yet he allowed the English in his train to join in the dancing, despite his Puritan outlook. Even a bull hunt was organised. The Comptroller of the Royal Artillery prepared a spectacular firework display for the finale with cannon from the arsenals at Edinburgh and Dundee being hauled up the sides of the Castle rock to maximise the effect.

The King was highly offended that foreign dignitaries in attendance would see his fall in status. Du Croc had already reported that he was unlikely to be at the baptism 'as his pride could not brook the insulting neglect'. Even Catholics were generally disillusioned with him. He was shunned both by Bedford, who had instructions from Elizabeth not to recognise him as King, and by du Croc, who was advised from France not to allow him an interview as he was not 'in good correspondence' with Mary.[6]

James was carried at his christening by Charles IX's proxy, the Count of Brienne, while the Protestant Countess of Argyll represented Elizabeth, after Bedford refused to attend the Catholic service. With his mother still held in the Tower, the King again objected to Elizabeth being chosen, but Mary overruled him. The Duke of Savoy's proxy, Robertino Solaro, Count Moretta, was expected on 17 December, but was inexplicably delayed and failed to arrive for the ceremony. Mary could wait no longer, and it was only on 1 January that he reached Paris to confer with Mondovi and de Alava before pressing on towards Scotland. Even then he made slow progress, only reaching London on about 18 January. It was suggested that his delay arose from negotiations to provide the King with assistance in restoring Catholicism.

The Duke of Savoy sent a bejewelled and feathered fan as a christening gift, while Charles IX provided a necklace of pearls and rubies. On the day before the ceremony, Bedford presented Mary with an enamelled gold font from Elizabeth, richly encrusted with gems and weighing twenty-eight pounds. He only narrowly avoided being ambushed with it by thieves near Doncaster, as he travelled north. It was too small for a six-month-old child, but he was instructed to play down its opulence by suggesting it would be suitable for Mary's next baby. The King did not attend its presentation, piqued at Elizabeth telling him to be obedient to Mary in all matters. When Bedford confirmed that she wanted a conference to discuss Mary's claim to the English throne, Mary promised to send councillors to finalise arrangements.

The Catholic baptism service was conducted by Archbishop Hamilton, but Mary would not let him spit into the child's mouth, as was the custom, knowing that he suffered from syphilis. The Prince was christened Charles James, taking his first name from the King of France. Catholics attending included Seton, Fleming, Atholl and Eglinton, but the Protestants waited outside. According to Knox, never slow to belittle Catholic ritual, Seton carried 'the salt, grease and such other things', when others refused and 'brought in the said trash'. Although a Reformer, Sir John Maxwell became 4th Lord Herries of Terregles, the title of his wife's family, in further thanks for his loyalty.

The Queen seemed to put aside her problems and presided in style over the three days of celebration. Yet she was privately 'pensive and melancholy'. On the next day, when du Croc came for an audience, he found her weeping on her bed. Bedford had at last persuaded her to repatriate the exiles, although Morton also recognised the part played by Bothwell and Moray in winning her agreement. On Christmas Eve, Mary formally pardoned

Morton and seventy-six other conspirators, provided that they stayed away from court for two years. Only George Douglas 'the Postulate' and Ker of Fawdonside were not reprieved, as they had risked the lives of her unborn child and herself. She saw this pardon as another step in appeasing Elizabeth so as to gain recognition as her heir and, on 2 January, wrote to thank her for reviewing Henry VIII's contentious will.

The King caused great embarrassment by remaining in his apartments at Stirling. Although his absence seemed to be designed to imply doubt over the Prince's paternity, in reality he did not want the lesions and suppurating pustules over his face and body to be seen, after another outbreak of his secondary syphilis. His affliction has been confirmed by scientific examination of his scull at the Royal College of Surgeons in London. Du Croc reported that, even at Stirling, he was already being treated with salivation of mercury and medicinal baths, the standard remedy at the time. He told Archbishop Bethune:

> His bad deportment is incurable, nor can there be ever any good expected from him for several reasons which I might tell was I present with you. I can't pretend to foretell how all may turn; but I will say that matters can't subsist long as they are without being accompanied by several bad consequences.[7]

The King was unhappy at being cold-shouldered, and was in mortal fear of the exiles' restoration. They saw him as the direct cause of their banishment and loss of their estates. Mary asked Bothwell to speak with Morton to prevent the King's assassination, and she refused to allow the exiles' return to court. Yet with Bothwell set on organising them to arrange it, he was not the ideal conciliator. The King tried to ingratiate himself by personally authorising a pardon for Fawdonside in return for his help to gain the Scottish Crown. Yet Fawdonside was soon part of the conspiracy for his assassination.

With the celebrations over, Mary left Stirling without the King for Christmas, staying as Lord Drummond's guest at Crieff. Bothwell was one of several Councillors to accompany her, leading to further speculation in Buchanan's *Detectio* of his 'filthy wickedness' with her.[8] Yet none of those present reported anything to corroborate this later tale.* Mary went on to stay with her Comptroller, Sir William Murray of Tullibardine, brother of

---

* According to Buchanan, it was at this time, while in bed as lovers, that Mary and Bothwell arranged the plot to kill the King choosing as the murder location the house at Kirk o' Field. Yet as will be seen all the credible evidence shows that it was the King, while returning from Glasgow, who chose to recuperate at Kirk o' Field.

Annabella, Countess of Mar. Tullibardine had been knighted by the King, so Mary may have been hoping to build bridges with him. Although Bothwell went with her, it would have been quite impolitic for her to conduct an affair with him on this visit, as Buchanan later alleged. She remained at Tullibardine until 31 December before returning to Stirling. Bedford spent Christmas as Moray's guest at St Andrews, where he was lavishly entertained for several days before they both rejoined the Queen.

Despite the doubts of those surrounding her at Craigmillar, Mary still hoped to arrange a divorce from the King and, on 23 December, temporarily restored Archbishop Hamilton in an attempt to seek a way to achieve a nullity without prejudicing her son's legitimacy. Although a Catholic divorce could only be granted by the Pope, Mary hoped that the Archbishop would mediate on her behalf. As his consistorial role had been removed in 1560, his reappointment was illegal and he was unlikely to succeed. Yet Mary tried to placate the Kirk and, on 20 December, gave the General Assembly a further £10,000. Despite her efforts, they could see his reappointment only as an attempt at a Catholic revival, and Moray advised her to comply with their demand for his removal. Hamilton stood down on 9 January, but before this had given her advice that a Catholic divorce could not be achieved on acceptable terms. The Kirk was in no mood to be conciliatory and required the Countess of Argyll to do penance for attending the Catholic baptism as Elizabeth's proxy. On 13 December, with unfortunate timing, Father Edmund Hay arrived in Edinburgh with the Bishop of Dunblane on the Pope's behalf. They went immediately to see the Queen at Stirling, but she claimed to be busy with the christening arrangements and probably did not meet them. She knew that they would demand the execution of the senior Protestant lords, but such a step would have been politically disastrous, if not practically impossible. Realising that he would not succeed, on 23 December Hay wrote to Mondovi that he would shortly leave Scotland.

Thoroughly disaffected, the King crept away to Glasgow before Christmas without taking his leave, hoping for a cure and intending yet again to go abroad. His affliction only gradually became public knowledge, and it was initially reported that he had been poisoned, and later that he had 'the Pox', which was assumed at the time to mean smallpox. As soon as he was on the road, his condition could no longer be hidden. Buchanan reported:

> Hardly a mile out of Stirling, a violent disorder struck every part of his body. Livid pustules broke out accompanied by much pain and vexation in his whole body. [He had] black pimples all over his body, grievous sweat in all his limbs, and intolerable stink.[9]

A white taffeta mask covered his disfigured face. By 2 January, he was too ill to contemplate going abroad and needed proper treatment. He sent a message to Mary that he needed to see her, but she did not go to him immediately. She had just left Stirling for Edinburgh, going on to Seton, where she was reported to have been thrown from her horse, and used this as a pretext not to go to Glasgow. Yet she sent her physician to continue an eight-week course of salivation of mercury. This involved sweating the patient and applying mercury both orally and to anoint the gums. As the gum tissue died, the teeth were loosened, causing bad breath and copious flows of saliva. The treatment was then completed with a series of sulphurous baths.

Despite his predicament, the King continued his scheming to gain the throne in place of Mary. She still believed that his plot for Riccio's murder was directed against herself and, if Hiegait's rumour is to be believed, he may also have considered crowning Prince James and claiming the Regency. He was still demanding the dismissal of Mary's closest Protestant advisers, particularly Maitland. As late as 20 January, she wrote to Bethune in Paris that she knew of the King's scheming, 'but God moderates their forces well enough, and takes the means of execution of their intentions from them'.

With so much rumour of plotting, it is hardly surprising that Mary deferred visiting Glasgow, despite the King's continued requests for her to join him. Before going, she moved the Prince from Stirling to Edinburgh where he would be out of reach of a kidnap plan launched from Glasgow. Given Tullibardine's friendship with the King, it has also been suggested that she feared leaving the Prince in the care of his sister Annabella, Countess of Mar. If this were a consideration, Mary had no grounds to suspect her loyalty. Despite being a Catholic, Annabella proved the most loyal and caring guardian of James and, even in due course, of James's son. He always considered her as his surrogate mother. On 6 January, Mary was able to attend Maitland's marriage to Mary Fleming in the Chapel Royal at Holyrood, but the newly-weds had little time for a honeymoon. Maitland remained at court and, four days later, accompanied Mary to Stirling to collect the Prince. He was still with her on about 12 January, while they returned with the Prince to Holyrood, after a night on the way with the Livingstons at Callendar.

With divorce not an option, Mary decided to make a new start with the King, while maintaining sufficient supervision over him to limit his plotting against her. The King's assassination, even without her involvement, could only prejudice her hopes of being recognised as Elizabeth's heir. It was to achieve his return with her to Edinburgh, where she could keep an eye on

him, that she now set out to Glasgow. This was in keeping with her rehabilitation of Moray after the Chaseabout and of the exiles involved in Riccio's
murder, despite their treasonable actions. Restoring the King to her bed
could provide more heirs once the symptoms of his syphilis had subsided. It
also assured her son's legitimacy, and enhanced her claim to the English
throne. Yet it was a blow to everyone else, who had seen Mary's dis-
illusionment as justification for his removal with the prospect of immunity
from prosecution.

Mary instructed Bothwell to travel to Dunbar to meet Morton as he
returned from England. She wanted assurance that the exiles would not start
a blood feud against the King, which might prejudice her intentions. Morton
crossed the border on 9 January, after writing from Berwick to thank Cecil
for arranging his rehabilitation and offering to do him 'such honour and
pleasure as lies in my power'.[10] Cecil probably understood what this meant.
The King was a Catholic and a political embarrassment, and would remain
so as long as he lived. The returning exiles in feud with him feared for their
lives if he came back to authority. Having arrived at Dunbar, Bothwell
suffered a haemorrhage, a legacy from his wounds received in Liddesdale,
and was laid low for a week. By then, Morton had reached Sir William
Douglas's home at Whittinghame about six miles west of Dunbar, where he
met Sir William's brother, Archibald, who had acted as the communication
link for the exiles. On 19 January, Bothwell was sufficiently recovered to
meet them there, and Maitland appeared from Lethington six miles further
on, having arrived there for his honeymoon from Stirling two days earlier.

References

1. Guy, p. 285
2. Guy, p. 286 and Weir, p. 261
3. Labanoff, I, p. 395, cited in Antonia Fraser, p. 328
4. Melville, cited in Weir, pp. 125, 180, 181
5. J Robertson, p. 61, p. 63, p. 69, cited in Antonia Fraser, p. 324
6. Du Croc to Archbishop Bethune, cited in Keith, and Antonia Fraser, p. 325
7. Du Croc to Archbishop Bethune, cited in Keith, Guy, p. 285 and Weir, p. 184
8. Weir, p. 188
9. Knox; Buchanan, cited in Weir, p. 190
10. Guy, p. 288

24

Mary's Visit to Glasgow to Persuade the King to Return to Edinburgh

Details of the King's plotting against the Crown are at best shadowy. Yet his plan, however fanciful, was to encourage Catholics in Scotland and northern England into supporting invading troops, who would install him on the English throne. This shows the deluded grandeur of an unrealistic man, but was extremely dangerous both for Mary, in her efforts to be recognised as Elizabeth's heir, and for Elizabeth and Cecil, well aware of strong Catholic sentiment in the north. He also seems to have hoped that, by kidnapping James, he could claim the Regency. With little support from among the Scottish nobility, he would have needed foreign assistance, but there is no evidence of either Catherine de Medici or Philip II offering it, despite their continued correspondence with him. Yet there is evidence of secret communication with Philip II and the Papacy, which was being kept from Mary, although its objective is not known. This can be pieced together from apparently unrelated information.

Following Yaxley's death, Killigrew had reported that his former servant Henry Gwynn had arrived in Edinburgh with letters for King Henry from Philip II in Flanders. It is not clear what they said but the King appears to have found them encouraging. Killigrew appears to have employed William Rogers to spy on the King, and Rogers managed to gain the confidence of Sir Anthony Standen, through whom he was invited to go hunting and hawking with King Henry. Rogers learned that Gwynn had also brought the King 2,000 crowns from an English merchant, together with letters from Lady Margaret and from Arthur and Edmund Pole, Yorkist pretenders to the English throne, who were in the Tower. Arthur Pole had apparently offered to resign his claim to the English throne in favour of Mary and her husband, although Mary does not seem to have been made aware of it.

The King also seemed to be plotting to gain the Scottish throne for himself. When Ker of Fawdonside returned from England, he was claiming 'that within fifteen days, there would be a great change in the court, that he would soon be in greater credit than ever, and then he inquired boldly how the Queen was'.[1] Although Mary was warned of this, she did not understand what was being planned, but it alarmed her at a time when she was having such hopeful negotiations with Elizabeth. Although the Pope was impressed by the reports of James's lavish Catholic christening, he had heard that Hay's mission had failed and that Mary lacked the zeal to restore Catholicism. With the King so well informed of discussions at Craigmillar and elsewhere, she was sure he had spies at court and she intercepted his correspondence to stop him granting passports to his messengers to go abroad. Yet the King's spies in Edinburgh continued in communication with him behind her back. Two possible candidates for them are Joseph Riccio and an Italian Catholic in Mary's service, Joseph Lutini, who also carried Mary's papal messages. On 6 January, Lutini was granted a passport to travel from Edinburgh to Paris. Although this was signed by the Queen, Riccio had forged her signature and gave Lutini money to take a message to Moretta at Berwick. As this was without the Queen's authority, he must have been travelling for the King, who was then in Glasgow and seems to have used Lutini and Moretta as his conduit to communicate with Mondovi, the Vatican and the European Catholic powers.

When questioned on Lutini's departure, Riccio claimed that he had absconded with money he had lent to him. Although Lutini had agreed to leave his horses and clothing in Edinburgh as security, he had taken them as well. It was then found that he owed money to other servants including Sebastian Pagez. When Mary realised that some of her bracelets were missing, Riccio again blamed Lutini. She immediately instructed Maitland to write to Sir William Drury at Berwick to apprehend him, although Drury was temporarily absent. Unaware of these accusations, Lutini remained in Berwick awaiting Moretta's arrival.

On 23 January, Drury returned to Berwick to find Mary's letter awaiting him. He arrested Lutini, who claimed to be travelling to France on the Queen's affairs, but was currently too ill to continue. Drury realised that the passport was counterfeit and sent it with a copy of Maitland's letter to Cecil in London. Riccio needed to divert attention from his forgery, as its discovery would be a capital offence. When Moretta arrived in Berwick, he was permitted to see Lutini, who told him that he was travelling on Riccio's instruction. Furious at having his cover blown, Riccio sent Lutini precise instructions on what to say, if he returned to Edinburgh, but Drury intercepted them, and they too ended up in Cecil's papers. When Lutini eventually returned to Edinburgh, the King was dead and Bothwell dismissed him with enough money to return abroad. By then Riccio had also left, after being branded, quite unrealistically, as one of the King's murderers.

On 24 January, Moretta moved on from Berwick towards Edinburgh, but met his old friend, du Croc, who rode back with him as far as Dunbar so that they could talk. He reached Edinburgh on 25 or 26 January, lodging at Balfour's house.* As Mary was by then in Glasgow, he was greeted by Moray and Maitland. Although they were uncertain of the purpose of his visit, he seems to have been assessing the feasibility of placing the King on the Scottish throne. There is no evidence of military support being offered by the Papacy, but there were continuing rumours from the Continent of a plan to assassinate Mary. If these were true, it foundered with the King's murder, after which Moretta quickly left Edinburgh. Spanish rumours that she was in danger had reached de Silva in London during December. He had heard from Philip II's aunt, Margaret, Duchess of Parma, in Brussels of a report from de Alava in Paris that there was a plot for Mary's assassination. As King Henry remained de Alava's close confidant, it is reasonable to assume that he was behind it. On about 25 January, de Alava also warned Archbishop Bethune that 'there be some surprise to be trafficked to the Queen's contrary'.[2] His delay in telling the Archbishop has been seen as suspicious, but he would have been waiting for Philip II's sanction to divulge the story. Philip was always well briefed on King Henry's deluded ambitions and must have disapproved of them if he agreed to Mary being warned. De Alava gave Bethune no hint of his sources or the nature of the plot, and Mary remained in the dark. Bethune asked Catherine de Medici if she knew of anything, but was not entirely convinced by her denial. He sent an urgent warning for Mary to tighten her security and be reconciled with the King, but his letter arrived only on the day after the King's murder.

Even though Mary was unaware of the King's plotting from Glasgow, he was too dangerous to be left on the loose and she wanted him back under her control. On 20 January, she at last set off for Glasgow on her own initiative to persuade him to return with her to Edinburgh. His removal from Glasgow would, of course, assist any assassination plan, but Mary's objective was to rehabilitate him. She was escorted for the first part of her journey by Bothwell and Huntly with a company of mounted hackbutters. She came with a horse litter on which to transport the King back to Edinburgh.

---

* The fact that Moretta stayed with Balfour has been taken to suggest that Balfour was another party in the King's plot against Mary. Yet this implies a level of deviousness that, even by Balfour's standards, seems implausible, as he was indisputably part of the plot to rid Mary of the King. During Moretta's visit, Balfour was purchasing gunpowder and arranging its transfer to Kirk o' Field. As he moved out of his home in the latter part of Moretta's visit, it is more likely that Moretta was there as his lodger.

Although she stopped for the night with Livingston at Callendar, he was not involved in any conspiracy against the King. From here, Bothwell returned with Huntly to Edinburgh, as he had pressing business in the Borders, and Mary arranged for a party of about forty Hamiltons to escort her on to Glasgow, including Archbishop Hamilton and Sir James Hamilton of Luss. As long-standing Lennox opponents, they were not the most conciliatory group with which to enter Glasgow on 22 January, but she needed protection and would require all her guile to persuade the King to return with her.

The King had a Gentleman of the Bedchamber in Glasgow, Captain Thomas Crawford of Jordanhill, who had been a distinguished mercenary on the Continent before returning with Mary in 1561. He later provided evidence both to Lennox and the Commissioners at the Conferences at York and Westminster of Mary and the King's conversation in Glasgow. He claimed to have heard rumours* of the discussions at Craigmillar from Lord Robert Stewart, who later denied divulging anything. Fearing a trap, he advised the King not to return with Mary, but later confirmed that he went voluntarily.

On Mary's arrival, Lennox sent Crawford to apologise for not coming personally to greet her, as he was unwell. Casket Letter II confirms that he was suffering from nose bleeds, an indication of fear in sixteenth-century France. On hearing this, Mary retorted that 'he would not be afraid if he were not culpable', but Crawford assured her that Lennox's only fear was to know what she might have planned for him.[4] Mary curtly told him to hold his peace. The King also asked to defer meeting her until the following day, as he was still suffering skin eruptions on his face. Doubtful of her security at Lennox Castle, she stayed in Glasgow for the night, probably at the Episcopal Palace, where she had Hamilton protection.

It was now that Mary was said to have written the first of the so-called Casket Letters to Bothwell. Their origin and intent to incriminate her in her husband's murder will be discussed in detail later, but the individual letters are dealt with in the period of the text to which they apply. They were numbered I to VIII for their use as evidence at the Conferences, placing

---

* There is no doubt that the discussions at Craigmillar had leaked. On 18 January, de Silva reported from London, 'The displeasure of the Queen of Scotland with her husband is carried so far that she was approached by some who wanted to induce her to allow a plot to be formed against him, but she refused. But she nevertheless shows him no affection.'[3] Mary had surmised that there must be a spy at court and it has been conjectured that she thought this was Balfour. His possible role as a double agent has been discussed in footnotes on pp. 275 and 286. Yet he was already a key member of the plot for the King's murder. The more likely candidates for spies are Lutini and Joseph Riccio.

them in rough chronology. In addition to the letters, there were two purported versions of Mary's marriage contract with Bothwell, and a long love poem made up of twelve sonnets. Together these amounted to twenty-two documents. As none of the originals now exist, their content is known only from French or English language transcripts made for the Conferences and, in a few cases, from translations included as Appendices to the Scottish edition of Buchanan's *Detectio*, where the first sentence only is in the original French. Without originals, the handwriting cannot be authenticated. Yet most of them seem to have been genuine letters, but either taken out of context or manipulated with false additions, although at least one seems a complete forgery. None of the transcripts is dated, addressed or signed. Yet Mary's letters were always addressed and included a carefully constructed phrase before her signature. Each has textual shortcomings, suggesting inexpert and hurried manipulation. A great deal of ink has been expended on them over succeeding centuries and the purpose here is to outline only the most plausible outcome of this research.

Casket Letter I was almost certainly written from Mary to Bothwell and may be a postscript to an official letter. At the top of the transcript there is an annotation in an English hand reading, 'Proves her distain against her husband'. Although it is headed 'From Glasgow this Saturday morning' it is much more likely that it was written from Stirling on Saturday 11 January, a fortnight before. In this context it is clear that Mary was unaware of Bothwell's haemorrhage at Dunbar and was annoyed that he had not confirmed Morton's undertaking not to seek revenge against the King. As she had been in Stirling with the infant James, whom she had not seen for some while, she mentioned him to Bothwell. She wrote:

It seemeth that with your absence forgetfulness is joined, considering that at your departure you promised to send me news from you; nevertheless I can learn none. And yet did I yesterday look for that [i.e. Prince James] [which] shall make me merrier than I shall be. I think you do the like for your return, prolonging it more than you have promised. As for me if I hear no other matter of you according to my commission, I bring the man [i.e. James] [on] Monday to Craigmillar, where he shall be upon Wednesday; and I go to Edinburgh to be let blood, if I have no word to the contrary. He [i.e. James] is the merriest that ever you saw, and doth remember unto me all that he can to make me believe that he loveth me. To conclude, you would say that he maketh love to me, wherein I take so much pleasure that I never come in there but my pain of my side doth take me: I have it sore today. If

Paris doth bring back unto me that for which I have sent, it should much amend me. I pray you send me word from you at large, and what I shall do if you be not returned when I shall be there; for if you be not wise, I see assuredly all the whole burden [i.e. protecting the King from a vengeful Morton] fallen upon my shoulders. Provide for me and consider well. First of all I send this present to Lethington to be delivered to you by Beaton,* who goeth one day of law of Lord Balfour. I will say no more unto you, but that I pray God send me good news of your voyage.[5]

If from Stirling, Casket Letter I is an innocent message mildly rebuking Bothwell for not keeping her informed. It is certainly not a love letter to him. Her description of the 'man' only makes sense as a reference her son and his apparent affection for her. This was a common description for a male child used by the Guise family, and Mary always referred to her husband as the King. She plans to move James from Stirling to Craigmillar, a favourite retreat, to provide security close to Edinburgh while she is being let blood, and we know that James arrived there with her on Wednesday, 15 January. Yet there is strong evidence that the letter was manipulated by adding the words, 'From Glasgow, this Saturday morning' (implying it was written on 25 January, the only Saturday that Mary was there). As James never went to Glasgow, the immediate implication is that the 'man' being discussed is the King and Mary is bringing him to Craigmillar as part of her plot with Bothwell to murder him. Yet the King was still extremely unwell and could not have left Glasgow for Craigmillar two days later, and he arrived at Kirk o' Field only after a further week's rapid recuperation. To describe the King as 'the merriest you ever saw', when he was sulking in Glasgow and covered with pustules is absurd and conflicts with Casket Letter II.

The timing of Paris's† journey with Mary's letters is also problematic. We know that she arrived in Glasgow only on 22 January and that Casket Letters I and II were purportedly written during the next three days. Thus Paris could not have reached Edinburgh, a hard day's ride away, with packages for Maitland and Bothwell until the evening of 25 January at the earliest. Yet

---

* According to Alison Weir, this is either Archibald Bethune, a long-standing member of her household, or John Bethune, Master of her household.
† Paris, also known as 'French' Paris or Joachim, was a French servant whose real name was Nicholas Hubert. He had been in the Queen's service for about a year having previously been employed by Bothwell, who continued to pay him. Before that he had worked for Seton. He later claimed under torture that Bothwell had bullied, kicked and beaten him. Yet they were on close terms while he worked for Mary, and he is known to have carried messages between them.

Moray's journal recording Bothwell's movements confirms that he left Edinburgh for Liddesdale on the evening of 24 January. This is corroborated by Henry, Lord Scrope, who kept a watching eye on his activities* from Carlisle. Neither Paris nor Bethune would have had time to follow Bothwell to Liddesdale and, as Paris went straight back to Glasgow, he could not have met him. Yet a fortnight earlier, on 13 January, he could easily have ridden from Stirling to meet Bothwell at Dunbar, near Maitland at Lethington. By suggesting that Casket Letter I was written from Glasgow, it implies that Mary thought Bothwell should have been planning the King's murder, or she would find 'all the whole burden fallen upon my shoulders'.[6] Yet at that time he was actively involved in policing Liddesdale.

On 23 January, the morning after arriving in Glasgow, Mary met up with the King. The gist of their conversation is recorded in Casket Letter II. In its English translation this amounts to 3,132 words purportedly written by her on 23 and 24 January, although the transcript is undated and unsigned. It is annotated by the English, 'The long letter written from Glasgow from the Queen of Scots to the Earl of Bothwell'.[7] Mary's official record of her meeting with the King, which forms the principal part of this document, is almost certainly genuine and may have been the one letter originally found in the silver casket, and we know that Paris did carry a letter from Glasgow on her behalf. In the Scots version, Bothwell is referred to in the third person and in other parts so are Moray and Maitland. This implies that it was originally addressed to several of her advisers, including Bothwell. This official report is corroborated by Crawford's evidence prepared in late 1568 for the English Commissioners at the Conferences at York and Westminster. He claimed that the King had told him of the conversation immediately afterwards, but, as his report is almost word for word identical to Mary's, he must have copied it. It was important to keep both pieces of evidence consistent, and, although their similarity may seem suspicious, the content appears plausible.

According to Crawford (and to a great extent to Casket Letter II), the King claimed to have been cruelly treated by Mary, who would not accept his repentance for having 'failed in some things, even though such like greater faults have been made to you sundry times, which you have forgiven. I am but young ...' He used the excuse that they were not living as man and wife,

---

* According to Scrope, Bothwell went as far as Jedburgh on the first evening from Edinburgh and from there moved into Liddesdale with about eighty men. They captured a dozen brigands including their leader, Martin Elwood, an associate of the Elliots. Elwood managed to warn his followers, who arranged a rescue, during which one of Bothwell's men was killed and five more captured. Bothwell went in pursuit, but despite a furious chase failed to catch up with them, and returned to Jedburgh empty-handed.

which 'bringeth me in such melancholy as you see I am in'. When she asked why he had a ship waiting to take him abroad, he blamed his lack of money. She queried Hiegait's report of his plot to imprison her, so he could rule in James's name. At first he denied knowing of it, but then admitted being told of Hiegait's story by John Stewart of Minto, Provost of Glasgow and that 'the Council had brought me a letter to sign to put him in prison, and to kill him if he did resist'. He told her that he was aware of a bond prepared at Craigmillar that she had refused to sign. He again asked her to 'bear him company, for she found ever some ado to draw herself from him to her own lodging, and would never remain with him past two hours together at once'. She seemed to doubt his assurances of loyalty, and did not reply immediately, but was 'very pensive, whereat he found fault'.[8]

The conversation then moved into safer territory. The King said he had heard that Mary had come with a litter, and she replied that she hoped he would use it to travel with her to Edinburgh, as he did not appear well enough to ride. He complained 'that it was not meet for a sick man to travel that could not sit on a horse, and especially in so cold weather'. She explained that she had arranged for him to convalesce at Craigmillar, 'where she might be with him and not far from her son'. He agreed to go in the litter, if 'he and she might be together at bed and board as husband and wife, and that she should leave him no more'. Realising that his principal objective was to renew sexual relations, she confirmed that this was why she had come, but insisted that before they could get together, he must be purged and cleansed of his sickness, which she trusted would be shortly, for she minded to give him the bath [for his cure] at Craigmillar.

She told him not to divulge their discussion, as 'the Lords would not think good of their sudden agreement considering he and they were at some words' before, and he accepted their need to placate them.[9]

The wording of the official letter confirms Mary's intention to be rehabilitated with the King. Whether she was genuinely prepared to live with him again as man and wife once his cure was complete may seem unlikely, but their later conversations at Kirk o' Field show that she had led him to believe this. She remained disillusioned with him and probably intended to keep him under house arrest in Edinburgh to prevent him from trying to usurp the throne or from kidnapping Prince James to gain the Regency. There is no hint that she was bringing him to Edinburgh to facilitate his murder, as both Cecil and Moray would imply, and she was trying to gain Morton's assurance that he would be protected.

Although Mary was able to persuade her husband to return with her to Edinburgh, he did not divulge details of his scheming against her. His rather meek agreement to go with her suggests that he hoped his objectives would prove more practicable, if they were reunited. Yet his decision to go was taken against the advice of both his father and Crawford, who objected to Craigmillar being used for his recuperation. It was well fortified and seemed better suited as a prison or a murder location. If Mary genuinely sought his rehabilitation, Crawford believed that she should have brought him to Holyrood.

Surrounding the official report, which forms the main part of Casket Letter II, there is evidence of manipulated insertions. These are principally at the end, but also where there may have been spaces in the original text. In Cecil's transcription, there are two double-lined gaps in the printed text and John Guy has suggested that these mirrored those in the original. At both these points further incriminating words seem to have been added, which perhaps failed to fill the available space, and result in *non sequiturs*. In the middle of the document there is a list of headings, presumably to remind Mary of matters to report. All these are covered in the text. Yet immediately before and after it, the letter becomes absurdly personal and incriminating. The traditional view had been that the letter was written over two days and the headings were at the break between two sessions. Yet, as Mary records that she was short of paper, it is more likely that the original report spanned the headings with a gap on either side, later filled with falsified additions. In some instances these are in Mary's idiom, perhaps culled from earlier passionate letters to the King. Others seem to be drawn from letters written by Bothwell's lovers, suggesting that the perpetrator had access to all their correspondence. The second section is followed by another list of headings:

> Remember you of the purpose of Lady Reres, of the Inglishman, of his mother, of the Earl of Argyll, of the Earl of Bothwell and of the lodging in Edinburgh,

but they are not covered in the preceding text and seem to be incriminating falsifications.[10] If the letter were addressed only to Bothwell, it is unlikely that Mary would have referred to him in the third person. The lodging in Edinburgh is assumed to refer to Kirk o' Field, although it had not by then been chosen as the King's residence. It has already been seen that Lady Reres is depicted as a go-between in the purported romance between Mary and Bothwell, although this is hardly probable.

The official report begins, 'Being gone from the place where I have left my heart', hardly the way to open a document for general consumption.[11] If there were space at the top of the opening page, someone could have added these words to imply Mary's infatuation for Bothwell, but, if genuine, they probably apply to the infant James. Immediately before the first list of headings are the words:

> We are tied to each other by two false races. The good year untie us from them. God forgive me and God knit us together for ever for the most faithful couple that ever he did knit together. This is my faith. I will die in it.[12]

This implies that Mary is tied to the King and Bothwell to Jean Gordon, whose families are each acting 'falsely' against them. Yet, at this stage, Huntly was still loyal to Bothwell, only turning against him after his sister's divorce. It also implies that Mary was already involved in a relationship with Bothwell. Perhaps the words came from a letter that she wrote after their marriage, but they are more likely to be from one of Bothwell's former mistresses distraught at his arranged marriage to Jean Gordon. Immediately afterwards, the letter continues:

> I am ill at ease and glad to write unto you when other folk be asleep, seeing that I cannot do as they do, according to my desire, that is, between your arms my dear life ...[13]

This could also have been written by one of Bothwell's former mistresses. The letter continues:

> Cursed be the pocky fellow that troubleth me thus much ... I thought I should have been killed with his breath, for it is worse than your uncle's breath ...[14]

If not written by Mary, this shows an intimate knowledge of what was happening. The perpetrator knew that the King was receiving 'salivation of mercury' for his syphilis with its side effect of bad breath, and was aware of Bothwell's 'uncle's' similar affliction. This is assumed to refer to Bothwell's kinsman, Patrick Hepburn, Bishop of Moray, who was known to have syphilis.

Immediately after the first headings, the letter refers to Livingston teasing Mary about Bothwell's infatuation for her while drinking her health at Callendar in the presence of Lady Forbes of Reres. Yet again the perpetrator seems to have known all the circumstances, but the wording does not imply that Mary was already involved in an affair with Bothwell. It is then claimed that she was secretly sewing her lover a bracelet, 'In the meantime take heed that none of those that be here do see it, for all the world will know it.'[15] Again, this could have been written by one of Bothwell's former lovers, and the wording is inconsistent with the previous section, where the writer has confirmed that Bothwell's infatuation has been noticed by Livingston. The letter then says:

> You make me dissemble so much, that I am afraid thereof with horror, and you make me almost to play the part of the traitor. Remember if it were not for obeying you I had rather be dead.[16]

Although this is incriminating, it is not consistent with the surrounding wording, which reverts to her agreement to resume sexual relations with the King. In the next apparent gap, the letter states:

> To be short he will go anywhere upon my word; alas! And I never deceived anybody, but I remit myself wholly to your will ... Think also if you will not find some invention more secret by physick, for he is to take physick at Craigmillar and the baths also. And shall not come forth of long time ... but I shall never be willing to beguile one that putteth his trust in me. Nevertheless, you may do it all, and do not esteem me the less therefore, for you are the cause thereof. For my own revenge I would not do it.[17]

This implies that she is encouraging Bothwell to poison the King, as she cannot bring herself to deceive him after he has put his trust in her. Yet it is unthinkable that Mary would append a murder proposal onto an official account of her discussion with her husband to be shown to others. If these are her words taken from another letter, then the original source would surely have been submitted. Although Buchanan had access to the Casket Letters to enable him to write his *Detectio*, he does not refer to the proposal to use poison. He would surely have done so if it were in the version shown to him, and it would seem that the original evidence had to be modified to make it less ambiguous and more incriminating.

The letter continues in an implausibly intimate manner, again referring to Mary secretly sewing a bracelet. It then says:

> Burn this letter for it is too dangerous, neither is there anything well said in it ... Now, if to please you, my dear life, I spare neither honour, conscience nor hazard, nor greatness, taking it in good part ... Love me always as I shall love you.[18]

Yet she would hardly have put such an instruction in writing, and the letter was not burned. As Lady Antonia Fraser has reasoned, although Casket Letter II offers the only incriminating evidence against Mary, the authenticity of the incriminating parts is very doubtful.

Although parts of Mary's correspondence used in evidence seem to have been forged, this does not of itself show her as innocent of the murder. Yet we know that, when divorce could not be achieved on acceptable terms, she would have preferred to have the King rehabilitated. Despite the risk of his continued plotting and her distaste at resuming sexual relations with a syphilitic, he strengthened her claim to be recognised as Elizabeth's heir, as now seemed so tantalisingly close. As late as 8 February, the day before the King's murder, Mary sent Melville to London to renegotiate the Treaty of Edinburgh and wrote to Cecil asking him to accept her good opinion of him, despite their differences. On the evening of the murder, she was showing the King great affection, hardly likely if she were a party to it. Yet rehabilitation overlooked two crucial matters. It assisted those wanting the King's demise and was unacceptable to the Scottish nobility and the English government led by Cecil.

References

1. Nau, p. 31; corroborated by Drury to Cecil, 13 August,1575, cited in Antonia Fraser, p. 331, and Weir, p. 202
2. Keith, I, p. ciii, cited in Antonia Fraser, p. 329
3. Keith, I, p. ciii, cited in Antonia Fraser, p. 329
4. Weir, p. 214
5. CSP, Scottish, II, Appendix II, p. 722; R H Mahon, *Mary Queen of Scots, A Study of the Lennox Narrative*, p. 111; J Robertson; Cotton MMS, Caligula; CSP, Foreign; cited in Guy, p. 401, and Antonia Fraser, p. 454
6. CSP Scottish II, cited in Weir, p. 196 and Guy, p. 401
7. CSP, Scottish, II, Appendix II, p. 722
8. Crawford's Deposition, Cambridge University Library, ed. in CSP Scottish, cited in Weir, p. 208
9. Crawford's Deposition, Cambridge University Library, ed. in CSP Scottish, cited in Weir, p. 209
10. Antonia Fraser, p. 459
11. Guy, p. 404, and Antonia Fraser, p. 455
12. Guy, p. 406, and Antonia Fraser, p. 456
13. Guy, p. 406
14. Antonia Fraser, p. 458
15. Guy, p. 407
16. Guy, p. 407
17. Guy, p. 407, and Antonia Fraser, p. 458
18. Guy, p. 408

25

The Planning of the Murder of the King

If Moray were to be permitted to 'look through his fingers' without being implicated in the King's murder, it was even more important for those planning it to keep Mary in the dark, as she would have to call for an investigation afterwards. She had consistently affirmed that she did not want her name to be sullied. Although one of Bothwell's kinsmen, John Hepburn of Bolton, confessed under torture that he believed Mary had consented to the murder, her passionate behaviour with the King at Kirk o' Field beforehand makes it highly unlikely that she knew of it.

Bothwell saw the King's murder as a political necessity. Although he hoped to discuss it with Morton at Dunbar, his haemorrhage prevented their meeting. He knew the exiles would want revenge on the King for failing to protect them after Riccio's murder, and, as their leader, Morton was the obvious man to organise it. As soon as he had sufficiently recovered, he came to meet Morton at Whittinghame, hoping to pass responsibility for it onto the planner of Riccio's murder. Morton certainly wanted the King dead, but was in no position to arrange it. In accordance with the terms of his rehabilitation, he was not permitted within seven miles of the court at Holyrood. He had also been told by Moray to persuade Bothwell into organising it himself. Cecil and Moray wanted Bothwell as the scapegoat, so that they could perhaps implicate Mary with him in a crime of passion. This involved engineering a tale of a romance between them, when none existed. They had three objectives; Moray would be restored as Regent of Scotland; Cecil would remove two unacceptable claimants to the English throne; and England's northern border would be protected by an anglophile Protestant government in Scotland. This may sound like being wise after the event, but there is evidence of these objectives being pre-planned. Even Mary came to accept this herself. In Nau's *Memorials*, written on Mary's instruction, while in captivity in England, he records that the Queen's enemies 'having used [Bothwell] to rid themselves of the King, designed to make [him] their instrument to ruin the Queen'. They thus signed a bond to induce her to

296

marry Bothwell 'so that they might charge her with being in the plot against her late husband and a consenting party to his death.'

When Bothwell realised that he would have to organise the King's murder himself, he was determined to cover his tracks so completely that he could not be implicated. The complication of any investigation of the murder is in sifting through all the concocted depositions particularly of Bothwell's movements to show that the evidence of his presence at the murder is unrealistic. Immediately beforehand, he was residing at Holyrood with his wife, where arrivals and departures would have been noted by the Guard. He remained in the Queen's company for the whole of the day of the murder, for much of it attired in fancy dress. He was at the palace shortly before it took place, holding a late meeting with the Queen and Stewart of Traquair, Captain of the Guard, almost certainly to discuss the Prince's future protection. He was in his bed at Holyrood with his wife, when woken to be told of the explosion, although in reality it is inconceivable that he could have slept through such a blast. There is no plausible evidence that he left Holyrood to involve himself in the murder after his late meeting with the Queen, and the Guard was never asked to verify his movements. He slept at Holyrood to demonstrate that he had remained in his bed.

Yet Bothwell was deluded to think he could avoid being implicated. Too many of his enemies knew he was involved. Moray's allies could plant rumours without infringing their bond, and they fanned them to good effect. Within a week, the public learned from placards posted in Edinburgh that he had organised the murder, and the Queen was implicated with him in a crime of passion, despite there being no hint of impropriety between them beforehand.

There is little doubt that the detailed murder plan was conceived by Bothwell, Morton, Balfour and Douglas with a few trusted henchmen. In his deposition, John Hay of Talla, another Bothwell associate, claimed that, on 7 February, two days beforehand, Bothwell said to him:

> John, this is the matter. The King's death is devised. I will reveal it unto you for if I put him not down, I cannot have a life in Scotland. He will be my destruction![1]

Morton, Maitland and Balfour later admitted becoming aware of the detailed plan on about 7 February as did Moray. It was probably only then that it was finalised, and it is known that the gunpowder was moved into position only on the evening of 9 February, shortly before the explosion. Yet they all knew well before this that murder was contemplated.

On 19 January, the day before escorting the Queen as far as Callendar, Bothwell arrived at Whittinghame to meet Archibald Douglas. Although he was a Lord of Session and minister of the Kirk, Douglas was a devious character, having been on the fringes of Riccio's murder plot. He had already agreed to assist with the King's assassination, and was associated with Bothwell through the courts, and later married his sister Jean, widow of Lord John Stewart.* It is often suggested that it was Morton who persuaded his 'cousin' Archibald to take his place in the conspiracy. Yet he was only a remote connection, being a second cousin of his wife's grandfather the 2nd Earl of Morton. He was there because he had acted as the communication link between the Craigmillar bond signatories and the exiles in England, and had been invited to take part by Bothwell.

Morton arrived at Whittinghame to find himself at a meeting with Bothwell, Douglas and Maitland, who had arrived from Lethington. The official purpose was to ensure, on the Queen's behalf, that he would not reopen old scores with the King. Yet Bothwell briefed him on the murder objective and privately asked him to arrange it, 'seeing it was in the Queen's mind that the King should be taken away'.[2] Morton later claimed that Douglas and Maitland added their persuasion (although Douglas denied this and Maitland was then out of favour). In all probability, Maitland was trying to assist Morton in persuading Bothwell to arrange it himself. Morton testified that he asked to see the Queen's warrant approving it, but they became evasive. He claimed that, even if it had had the Queen's sanction, he would have preferred to return to exile. This, of course, was a blatant attempt to demonstrate his innocence. Although he later implied that he could not become involved, after being so recently pardoned, he certainly provided henchmen. John Hepburn of Bolton's deposition says that the original plan was for each of the nobles to send two of their servants 'to the doing thereof in the fields' (meaning some out-of-the-way place).[3] Paris implied the use of a ritual blood feud, similar to that devised for Riccio. He claimed under torture that Maitland was Bothwell's chief accomplice,† supported by Argyll, Huntly, Morton, Ruthven and Lindsay among the nobility. When asked if Moray was involved, Paris claimed he was neutral. Given the careful manipulation of the depositions, it is surprising that these names were not expunged, but each could probably demonstrate that he was not present, and there is no other evidence of Argyll, Huntly, Ruthven and Lindsay's

---

* After the death of Lord John Stewart, Jean Hepburn remarried John Sinclair, Master of Caithness from whom she was divorced in 1575, at which point she married Archibald Douglas.
† At the time of this deposition, Maitland was out of favour with Moray.

involvement. Although Douglas and Balfour are known to have taken part, Paris did not mention them. It was Bothwell and Morton, who were the principal organisers, but they avoided being there on the night. Bothwell was with the Queen, where his absence would have been noticed, and Morton faced arrest if seen within seven miles of Edinburgh. To cover their tracks completely, they arranged to blow up the Kirk o' Field at night, having encircled the building to prevent the King's escape.

As Moray intended to leave Edinburgh beforehand, he wanted Morton to organise the nobility in his absence. Morton was told to ingratiate himself with Bothwell, so that they could share the government afterwards. Although they were never natural allies, he might be able to entice Bothwell into setting his cap at the Queen, which could implicate her in a crime of passion. To return to power, Moray needed Bothwell destroyed and the Queen discredited. He would then arrange for Morton, Maitland and Balfour's involvement to be airbrushed out, although Maitland avoided being involved in the detailed arrangements. Balfour did not come to Whittinghame, but he bartered olive oil to acquire a barrel of gunpowder and arranged its positioning in the cellar of the Old Provost's Lodging. Although his movements remained shadowy, he later sought a pardon, which he would have needed only if he were involved. By 9 February, he had left his Edinburgh home, where Moretta was staying, and was busy unnoticed at Kirk o' Field. Yet it was Douglas who coordinated the arrangements on the night, relying on Moray and Cecil's protection in return for his silence. He was ultimately found innocent of a crime, for which several others were executed. Without realising it was happening, Bothwell became isolated with his henchmen, allowing Moray, who had always hated him, to claim that he had organised the murder alone. Morton told the truth in 1581, when he admitted under oath that he knew of the plot, but had not taken part in it. Yet he will have signed the Craigmillar bond with Douglas at Whittinghame and took no steps to warn his kinsman, the King, of the plan to murder him.

Bothwell and Morton soon had enough adherents to 'take the deid in hand'. With Bothwell 'ruling all at court', there is evidence of him recruiting help by claiming that the murder had the Queen's approval.[4] There is a report that, after meeting at Whittinghame, Bothwell and Maitland went with Douglas to Holyrood to obtain the Queen's sanction, which she refused. Douglas, who was apparently acting only as a messenger, was instructed 'to show to the Earl of Morton that the Queen will have no speech of the matter'.[5] This story seems a fabrication conveniently devised to implicate Maitland and Bothwell and to exonerate Morton and Douglas. It also suggests that Mary was aware of the murder plan, even if she did not approve it.

As she failed to arrange a full investigation afterwards, any foreknowledge would have implicated her. Yet in all probability there was no such meeting. If the conspirators wanted her kept in the dark, they would hardly have asked for her approval.

To give credence to a crime of passion, Buchanan's *Detectio* recounts numerous liaisons between Mary and Bothwell before the King's murder, but none of them stand up to critical examination. Both had been at death's door, hardly an aphrodisiac for a romance. In a court full of rumour, the ambassadors' grapevine would have jumped at any juicy impropriety. With Mary actively seeking recognition as Elizabeth's heir, she would not have wanted any scandal prejudicing her hopes. The King with his close bloodline to both thrones was far more appropriate as a consort than the unacceptable Bothwell.

Even though the *Detectio* can be shown to be fabricated, it has been suggested that Bothwell undertook the King's murder as part of a personal agenda to marry the Queen. From the doubtful evidence of Casket Letter II, we have seen that Livingston hinted at Bothwell's infatuation at Callendar before Mary's visit to Glasgow. Yet Bothwell had no reason to believe that she would agree to marriage if freed from the King, and he was already married. If marriage were his motive, he would have sought assurance of support from the other signatories of the Craigmillar bond. There is no verifiable evidence of a rumoured discussion at Dunbar at which the nobility bargained with him for personal benefit in return for their backing. They hated him and would hardly promote him to replace the King. It was Moray that they wanted as the power behind the throne. If Bothwell married the Queen, Moray would be left out in the cold. Yet with the King dead, Morton cynically enticed Bothwell into a marriage for Scotland's security. It was only then that the crime of passion became plausible.

References

1. R. Pitcairn, *Ancient Criminal Trials in Scotland*, I, pt. 1, p. 496, cited in Antonia Fraser, p. 340, and Weir, p. 265
2. Weir, p. 199
3. Pitcairn, *Criminal Trials*, pt. 1, p. 498, cited in Antonia Fraser, p. 340
4. Weir, p. 201
5. Gore-Browne, p. 293, Holinshed; cited in Antonia Fraser, p. 330, and Weir, p. 201

26

The Demise of the King

Although Mary remained depressed and unwell, she had been able to persuade the King to return from Glasgow. She reasoned that Edinburgh offered him protection, and she could keep watch on his plotting. The returning exiles were not permitted within seven miles of court, and she believed that Bothwell had gained Morton's undertaking not to harm him.

On 27 January, the royal party left Glasgow with the King in Mary's litter. They spent a night at Callendar followed by one or two nights at Linlithgow, before heading for Craigmillar. Bothwell returned from the Borders, reaching Edinburgh on 30 January. He could not have been planning the murder while in the Borders as Buchanan claimed, and the lodging at Kirk o' Field had not yet been chosen.* He arrived in time to escort Mary and the King to Craigmillar, but, shortly beforehand, the King announced that he would not stay there, perhaps heeding Crawford's concerns that he could be imprisoned. Instead, he chose to recuperate at Kirk o' Field, just inside the Town Wall, where he would make a rapid recovery in fresh air on a hill overlooking the Cowgate. This location was undoubtedly chosen at the last moment by the King himself. One of his servants recorded:

> It was devised in Glasgow that the King should have lain first at Craigmillar, but because he had no will thereof, the purpose was altered and the conclusion taken that he should lie beside the Kirk o' Field.[2]

He did not want to be seen with his taffeta mask at Holyrood three-quarters of a mile to the north-east. With Châtelherault still exiled in France, he seems to have assumed that he could occupy his new mansion there. Yet Archbishop Hamilton was in residence and, with the Lennoxes as traditional

---

* Buchanan recorded, 'In the meantime, the Earl of Bothwell, according to the device [plan with the Queen] appointed between them, prepared for the King the lodging where he ended his life. In what place it stood enough know and enough thought even that it was a ruin unsuitable to have lodged a Prince into, standing in a solitary place at the uttermost part of the town, separate from all company.'[1] As will be seen, this is all patently untrue.

Hamilton enemies, it was not made available. Balfour then proposed the Old Provost's Lodging nearby, as it was available for lease from his brother.

To gain a full understanding of events at Kirk o' Field, it is necessary to understand its layout. The Old Provost's Lodging faced onto a small quadrangle measuring eighty-six by seventy-three feet with a well at its centre, just within the Town (or Flodden) Wall in the south-east corner of Edinburgh. Until the Reformation the quadrangle had been surrounded by the collegiate buildings of the church of St Mary-in-the-Fields further to the west. This church was now in ruins, damaged first by the English in 1544 and then by the Reformers in 1558, and the buildings in the quadrangle had been converted into residences. The old Friars' Hospital outside the quadrangle to the north-west had been rebuilt as the three-storey Hamilton House. To the east, there were gardens with orchards sloping downhill, and beyond these, about 200 yards to the north-east, was the ruined Blackfriars Monastery with its gate through the Town Wall.

Sir James's brother, Robert Balfour, had taken a lease over three of the buildings in the quadrangle in the previous year. He occupied the New Provost's Lodging himself and let out the Old Provost's Lodging for short-term rent, employing John Hepburn of Bolton as its warden. The Old Provost's Lodging was adjoined by the single-storey Prebendaries' Chamber, built over a cellar to provide a *salle* of forty-five by fifteen feet, where tenants could entertain their guests. Robert Balfour held several properties for rent, and the lodging had been used by Bedford in the previous month, before attending the Prince's baptism at Stirling.

The New Provost's Lodging was on the west side of the quadrangle, with an adjoining wall running from its southern end to the Town Wall, which ran at right angles behind the southern side. This adjoining wall completed the quadrangle's enclosure, but it had a gateway through it providing its main access. The south side of the quadrangle to the right of this gateway housed the Prebendaries' Chamber and, beyond that, the Old Provost's Lodging, which backed onto the Town Wall, with a door on its east side at cellar level, opening onto the gardens and orchards sloping away beyond. The narrower Prebendaries' Chamber had a secluded little courtyard behind it, backing onto the Town Wall.

The Old Provost's Lodging was on three floors. On each of the upper two levels, there was a bedroom measuring sixteen by twelve feet, with a window facing north onto the quadrangle, and with a *garde-robe* behind measuring seven by twelve feet. The two bedrooms were connected by a turnpike stair in a turret. At the rear, there was a galleried staircase area that extended over the top of the Town Wall to provide sleeping quarters for servants. The drop from the galleried area to the ground on the far side of the wall was about fourteen feet. The wall was six feet thick at its base, tapering to one foot at the top. The lodging's main entrance was from the quadrangle to the lower of the two bedroom floors, which also provided access at the same level to the *salle*. The cellar, reached by a stone stairway, was a vaulted stone undercroft, in which there was a kitchen with its door opening onto the garden to the east. On the kitchen's west side, a second door opened into a passage, leading back through the Town Wall, where there was a postern gate opening into an alley known as Thieves Row. The passage must have had access on its opposite side to both the cellar under the Prebendaries' Chamber and to the little courtyard behind. The cellar of the Prebendaries' Chamber started at head height by the passage, but tapered to two feet high at its west end. Outside the Town Wall to the south of Thieves Row were further gardens, next to which there were two small cottages.

There is no plausible evidence that Kirk o' Field was chosen as a suitable place to murder the King, although this was to be alleged by Buchanan. The detailed murder plan could not have been developed until his arrival on 1 February, and there is evidence that it was not finalised until a week later. Neither Bothwell nor Morton was involved in choosing it, although they could only have approved of its layout and location, as it could be approached almost unnoticed through the postern gate from Thieves Row and from the side door to the kitchen.

Although adequate by the standards of the time, the King was disappointed at the accommodation's lack of grandeur, and 'in no wise liked of'. It took all Mary's persuasion for him to agree to occupy the rooms, which were 'more easy and handsome'. She explained that there was 'a privy way between the palace and it, where she might always resort to him till he was whole of his disease'.*[3] This ran outside the Town Wall from Holyrood to the gate at Blackfriars Monastery, from where there was access through the east garden. To make the Lodging more amenable, Mary improved the interior by arranging for six tapestries, confiscated from Strathbogie, together with a turkey carpet and furniture, to be brought from Holyrood. Further tapestries depicting 'the hunting of the conies' were hung in the *garde-robes*. The King

---

* In fact, there was no known cure for syphilis. The treatment being administered cleared up the skin rash which affected the whole body, including the inside of the mouth, during which the patient was highly infectious. There were then periods of remission during which the patient was less infectious, until the rash broke out again. Irrational behaviour, particularly delusions of grandeur, was a recognised symptom of the disease. Eventually tertiary syphilis would develop causing insanity, paralysis and congenital deformity for unborn children. There is no evidence that the King had become permanently disfigured or had reached the stage of tertiary syphilis, and Mary still seems to have been attracted to him at Kirk o' Field, despite knowing of his affliction.

The murder scene at Kirk o' Field drawn by one of Cecil's spies. Note the courtyard area behind the rubble of the destroyed buildings where deliveries could be made relatively unnoticed. The National Archives/Photolibrary.com.

305

agreed to sleep in the upper bedroom, but did not consider the black velvet bed, which Bedford had used, as adequate. His own bed,* hung with violet-brown velvet and richly decorated with cloth of gold and previously belonging to the Queen Regent, was brought in, and a bath was placed beside it for his medicinal treatment. This was covered by the door taken off the upper entrance to the internal turnpike staircase. Mary was to occupy the bedroom on the floor below, from where she could nurse him and keep a watchful eye on what he was up to. Her bedroom was also elaborately furnished with a bed, covered in yellow-and-green damask with a furred coverlet, and a leather chair of estate on a dais upholstered with watered silk of red and yellow. Five more of the Strathbogie tapestries were hung on her bedroom walls.

Mary slept at Kirk o' Field on 5 and 7 February after administering the King's medicinal baths. She also considered staying there on the night of the murder, again demonstrating that she was unaware of the detailed plan. She visited him daily and, by all accounts, good relations were restored. They would sit up playing cards until midnight or listening to music. Knox wrote that 'everyman marvelled at this reconciliation or sudden change'.[4] This has been seen as a deception by Mary to avoid suspicion, but, if she were to rehabilitate the King, she needed to regain his confidence. Such was their apparent rapport that he warned her of efforts being made to sow discord between them. In a tone of injured innocence, he even reported that there were claims that he planned to take her life. She was not taken in and, despite her outward showing of affection, was aware of his continued plotting. On 7 February, she again wrote to Drury in Berwick to demand Lutini's arrest, and on the next day forbade Moretta from coming to visit the King. She must have enjoyed using the excuse that she feared his master the Duke of Savoy's resentment at the King's part in the murder of his former servant, Riccio. Despite her mistrust, the King appears to have accepted her friendly overtures, writing to Lennox that she 'doth use herself like a natural and loving wife'.[5]

It was about now that Mary is purported to have written Casket Letter III, for which a transcript survives in the original French. It is annotated by an English clerk, 'To prove the affections'. It starts:

Monsieur, if the displeasure of your absence, your forgetfulness, the fear of danger so promised by everyone to your so-loved person may

---

* To implicate Mary in her husband's murder, Moray claimed that she had arranged for this bed to be returned to Holyrood on the pretext of saving it from damage by soiled bathwater, but in reality to save it from the explosion. Yet this was another of his fabrications, as both the bed and the rich tapestries were in the inventory of items destroyed.

give me consolation, can console me, I leave it to you to judge, seeing the unhap that my cruel lot and continual misadventure has hitherto promised me, following the misfortunes and fears, as well of late as of long time by-past, the which ye do know.

It carries on in this uncharacteristically submissive vein, saying:

I will in no wise accuse you ... of the coldness of your writing, since I am so far made yours that that which pleases you is acceptable to me ... and to testify to you how lowly I submit me under your commandments, I have sent you, in sign of homage, by Paris, the ornament of the head [probably a locket of hair] ... In place whereof, since I have always left it unto you, I send you a sepulchre of hard stone [thought to have been a memento mori – a jewel designed to remind the wearer of his mortality], coloured with black, strewn with tears and bones ... The enamelling that is about is black, which signifies the steadfastness of her who sends the same. The tears are without number ... of your absence, that I cannot be in outward effect yours ... My only wealth receive therefore in all good part the same, as I have received your marriage with extreme joy, the which shall not part forth my bosom till that marriage of our bodies shall be made public ... I have shown unto the bearer that which I have learned, to whom I remit me, knowing the credit that you give him, as sure does that will be for ever unto your humble, obedient, lawful wife ...[6]

The reference to Paris (although Mary generally referred to him as Joachim and this could of course be a forged addition) is really the only evidence that this is a passionate message from Mary to Bothwell when she cannot be with him. The letter's humble tone with its grammatical inconsistencies makes it quite implausible as one she would have sent to him. He was purported to have been making suit to her, not her to him. Although he could be cruel, there is no evidence of any unkindness to her before her abduction from Almond Bridge to Dunbar. If written by Mary, it is much more likely to be a letter to the King before their official marriage. As Paris was Bothwell's servant before entering royal employment, it is also possible that it is a copy, forged in Mary's writing, of a letter to Bothwell from a former mistress, perhaps Anna Throndssen. It is quite unrealistic as a love letter from Mary to Bothwell. She could not claim to be his lawful wife, as neither of them was free to marry and, as both were for most of this time at Holyrood, she could hardly complain of his absence. Also it is difficult to envisage, during her recent hectic schedule, that she would have had time to commission an elaborate jewel for him.

When the King arrived at Kirk o' Field, Mary appears to have tried to arrange for the nobility to be reconciled with him as part of his rehabilitation. Yet they would have none of it, warning her that he would put a knife to her throat and theirs. According to Buchanan, only Bothwell made any show of friendship, apparently to deflect suspicion from his involvement in the murder plan. Yet the King used the friendlier atmosphere to discuss Maitland privately with Mary, warning that he 'was planning the ruin of the one by the means of the other, and meant in the end to ruin both of them'.[7] Maitland certainly wanted the King's ruin, but, as Mary Fleming's husband, it is unlikely that he also sought to destroy the Queen. Yet he supported Moray, who wanted them both brought down.

The King had several of his own servants at Kirk o' Field. His valet William Taylor slept on a pallet in his room, with Taylor's page, Alastair (or Andrew) McCaig, sharing the galleried anteroom outside his *garde-robe* with two other chamber servants, Thomas Nelson and Edward Symonds. There were up to six others, supervised by Hepburn of Bolton, provided by the lodging. They slept with the King's four grooms, including Master Glen, on the floor below. Bonkil, the cook, returned home at the end of each day, as did Sandy Durham, Master of the King's Wardrobe. There were no guards, indicating that the King was oblivious to rumours of plotting against him.

Melville recalled that 'many suspected that the Earl of Bothwell had some enterprise against' the King, although he did not personally believe this and said nothing.[8] On 8 February, Lord Robert Stewart came to warn the King that 'if he retired not hastily out of that place, it would cost him his life'.[9] The King immediately told Mary, who interviewed Lord Robert with Moray and Bothwell in front of the King. When Lord Robert denied giving the King a warning, the King drew his sword and started a fight, so that Mary had to ask Moray to intervene. By now, both Moray, as he subsequently admitted, and Bothwell knew that the story was true, but said nothing. This again confirms Moray's intimate knowledge and approval of the murder plot. By arranging for Bothwell and Moray to interview Lord Robert, it could be implied that Mary also knew of it, but she would have needed her two most senior advisers to question her half-brother.

At the Conference at York, a letter was produced in Mary's 'own hand', placing a different slant on Lord Robert Stewart's row with the King. Far from Mary asking Moray to stop the fight, it showed that she incited it to provoke Lord Robert into killing her husband to save Bothwell having to do so. Yet it was quickly withdrawn and was not seen or mentioned again.

Perhaps it was too obviously a forgery. If genuine, it would surely have provided compelling evidence for her prosecution. Casket Letter IV, purportedly written to Bothwell on 7 February, two days before the murder, seems to corroborate the missing letter's assertion that Lord Robert was incited by Mary to murder the King. Yet it is completely implausible as one written by Mary to Bothwell, and is so long that it is unimaginable that she would have taken the time to write it, when she was seeing him every day. There is a French transcript and an English translation made for the Conference at Westminster, for which it was annotated somewhat obscurely, 'Letter concerning Holyrood House'.[10] It seems to be an amalgamation of at least two letters with a forged addition. It contains an obscure metaphor from Greek mythology and a quotation from an early version of a sonnet from *"Le Second Livre des Amours"* by Ronsard. Mary, the King, Maitland, Buchanan and Cecil might reasonably be expected to have understood the analogy, but, despite his having some Classical learning, it would surely have been over Bothwell's head. Yet it is known that the King employed reference to the sonnet in his own verses. In this instance, its use in confirming that Mary incited Lord Robert into killing the King is entirely conjectural, as neither is mentioned by name. Furthermore, it only takes on its intended purpose in the English version used at Westminster, which mistranslates what is recorded in the French transcript. Cecil, who knew the poem, spotted the error and corrected his copy, but did not draw attention to the obvious shortcoming. It is more likely to be a letter written from Mary to the King, using an analogy with which he was familiar. In that context, she is jealous at some new mistress, and threatens a separation if he does not return to her. A more detailed analysis is given as a footnote.*

---

* Casket Letter IV begins, 'I find the fairest commodity to excuse your business that might be offered. I have promised him to bring him tomorrow. If you think it, give order thereunto.' Although this was deemed to refer to Lord Robert, it does not mention him by name and the suggestion that she is inciting Lord Robert to undertake Bothwell's dirty business by killing the King is conjectural. The remainder of the letter appears to be a rebuke by a loving writer to a wayward recipient and makes no other reference to Lord Robert being involved in the murder It continues, 'the thing of this world that I desire the most ... is your favour or goodwill ... Otherwise I would think that my ill luck, and the fair behaviour of those that have not the third part of the faithfulness and voluntary obedience that I bear unto you, shall have worn the advantage over me of the second lover of Jason. Not that I do compare you so wicked, or myself so unpitiful a person.' In Greek mythology the second wife of Jason was Glauce, who was murdered by his vengeful first wife, Medea. The letter has been taken to infer that Mary feels the same jealousy for Bothwell's first wife, Jean Gordon, as Medea did for Glauce. Yet, as Medea was the first wife of Jason and Mary would become the second wife of Bothwell, the analogy seems the wrong way round. The letter then moves into a different theme, suggesting that it comes from a different source. It refers to the Ronsard sonnet. The English translation presented at Westminster states, 'Watch well if the bird shall fly out of the cage, or without his father make as the turtle [dove] shall remain alone for absence, how short soever it be.' This would imply that Mary thought the King might try to escape from Kirk o' Field, not wanting to be absent from his father with so much plotting afoot; by implication Bothwell should take steps to prevent him leaving. Yet the word 'father' in the English translation is a

On 8 February, Lennox left Glasgow to visit his son at the end of his convalescence. He wanted to use the King's warmer relationship with the Queen to seek his own reconciliation with her. It was reported that he was attacked in a Glasgow street before leaving and was saved only by Sempill's intervention, but Lennox never mentioned it and arrived safely at Linlithgow. It has also been suggested that his visit was timed to congratulate the King on a successful coup against Mary. Yet it is not known how this would have been achieved.

With the murder imminent, on the morning of Sunday 9 February Moray came to the Queen, who gave him consent to leave Edinburgh to see his wife, who had suffered a miscarriage at St Andrews. This seems to have been an excuse, as he did not return immediately his wife had recovered. As he later admitted, he knew that the King was to be murdered that night.

Mary is reputed to have taken time out of an almost impossibly busy schedule on Sunday 9 February to write Casket Letter V to Bothwell. This concerned the dismissal of an 'unthankful' servant, and is endorsed, 'Anent the dispatch dismissal of Margaret Carwood; which was before her marriage; proves her affection.' Yet the letter itself does not refer to Margaret Carwood by name and she was certainly not the servant that Mary dismissed. She had been granted a handsome pension on the previous day in contemplation of her marriage, which Mary attended, and Mary paid for her wedding dress and reception, which took place on 11 February, despite the King's murder the day before. For Mary to attend this service was thus a mark of signal favour. The letter begins:

My heart, alas! Must the folly of one woman whose unthankfulness to me ye do sufficiently know, be occasion of displeasure unto you, considering that I could not have remedied thereunto without knowing

---

mistranslation of the French 'per' as shown in the French transcript, and Cecil corrected his copy to 'mate' without saying anything. A more accurate English translation of the Ronsard original should read, 'Beware lest the bird flies out of its cage, or like the turtledove without its mate lives alone to lament its absence, however short that may be.' The corrected translation makes no sense as a letter from Mary to Bothwell, but could well have been one she wrote to the King, while she was contemplating divorce. As the King referred to the turtledove in his own poetry, he would have understood that she was threatening separation, if he stayed away, even for a short time, with some new mistress. The letter ends, 'That that I could not do [ie ask Bothwell to his face to murder the King], my letter should do it with a good will, if it were not that I fear to wake you, for I durst not write before Joseph, Bastien and Joachim, who were but new gone from I began.'[11] Written immediately after the original French wording, this cannot be construed as an admission that she cannot bring herself to ask Bothwell to murder the King. It can only be a falsified addition to corroborate the English mistranslation, showing that she encouraged her bedfellow, Bothwell, to prevent the King's escape (and to explain why she needed to write to him, when they were in bed together). Her bedroom servants are named simply to imply that she is writing to Bothwell, her bed-companion at Holyrood, while the King is recuperating at Kirk o' Field.

it. And since that I perceived it, I could not tell you, for that I knew not how to govern myself therein.

This seems to refer to an unnamed servant, known to have become pregnant out of wedlock. While this did not happen infrequently, it was much frowned upon by both the Kirk and Mary. Margaret Carwood was certainly not unthankful and was not pregnant before marriage. The only known slur against her is Buchanan's dubious assertion in his *Detectio* that it was 'Margaret Carwood, who was privy and helper of all their [Mary and Bothwell's] love'. She was never called to give evidence of a proper understanding of the letter, which indicates that Mary is just as angry with the servant as the recipient. Without knowing the context in which it was written, its meaning is ambiguous, but it can be conjectured that the recipient has blamed Mary for continuing to employ a servant against his will. Mary is responding that she only wants to do as he wishes. If he can find an alternative she will be rid of her, as soon as she has been married off. She says:

For neither in this, nor in any other thing, will I take upon to do anything without knowledge of your will, which I beseech you let me understand; for I will follow it all my life more willingly than you do declare it to me.

He seems particularly angry at the servant gossiping about his unfaithfulness to Mary. The French transcript continues:

And if ye do not send me word this night, what ye will that I shall do, I will unburden myself of it [dismiss her], at the risk of making her attempt [reveal] something that could be harmful to what we are both aiming at [the English throne].* And when she shall be married, I beseech you give me one [a new servant], or else I shall take such as shall content you for their conditions; but, as for their tongues, or faithfulness towards you, I will not answer [for them].

---

* This sentence has been maliciously mistranslated in the English version and, taken out of context, becomes very sinister. It reads, 'And if ye do not send me word this night, what ye will that I shall do, I will rid myself of it, and hazard to cause it to be enterprised and taken in hand, which might be hurtful to that whereunto both we do tend.'[13] This implies that Mary is planning the King's murder with Bothwell, despite it making no sense in a discussion about the servant.

If she is to choose the new servant, she cannot be responsible for them being loyal to the recipient. She then denies complaining about his lack of fidelity, by continuing:

> I beseech you that [the alleged infidelities] are opinion of other person, be not hurtful in your mind to my constancy. [You now] mistrust me, but when I shall put you out of doubt and clear myself, refuse it not my dear love, and suffer me to make some proof of my obedience, my faithfulness, constancy, and voluntary subjection, which I take for the pleasantest good that I may receive, if ye will accept it, and make no ceremony at it, for ye could do me no greater outrage, nor give me more mortal grief.[12]

This is clearly a letter from Mary to the King, who is concerned at gossip about their marital difficulties at a time when they are being reconciled. She is trying to dissuade him from causing a scene when they are both hoping for her recognition as Elizabeth's heir. It is the King who is referred to as 'my heart' and 'my dear love' in a spirit of reconciliation, although this may be a forged addition. It is hard to imagine that Bothwell would have been concerned with the dismissal of Mary's servant, and, as they were together all that day, a letter would have been unnecessary.

On the morning of Sunday 9 February, the King attended Mass before taking his last medicinal bath. Mary attended the wedding in the Chapel Royal of her French valet, Sebastian Pagez, who married another favourite servant, Christina (or Christily) Hogg. Mary provided the richly embroidered wide-sleeved wedding dress made from thirteen and three-quarter ells of black satin, with a velvet lining. She also gave thirty-two ells of green ribbon to make her skirt and hood. At noon, she attended the wedding breakfast as guest of honour. The guests wore carnival clothes with masks, and Pagez had prepared a masque for the evening, which the Queen had promised to attend. As a Reformer, Bothwell will have excused himself from the Catholic marriage service, but in carnival clothes he attended the wedding lunch at noon. At four o'clock, without changing, he came with the Queen to a dinner for Moretta at the home of John Carswell, Bishop of the Isles (or Argyll) on the Canongate, with most of the nobility, other than Moray and Maitland, in attendance. It is not known why Maitland was absent, as he joined the Queen at Kirk o' Field later and was not involved in the detailed murder plan.

With their dinner over, at about seven o'clock members of the court still in costume rode with the Queen to Kirk o' Field, where she was joined by 'the most part of nobles then in this town', including Bothwell, Huntly, Argyll, Maitland and Cassillis.[14] It was later claimed that she intended spending the night there on the last day of her husband's convalescence, and he certainly tried to persuade her to stay. Yet she had always planned to return to Holyrood for the wedding masque and her horses remained at Kirk o' Field for the purpose. The King entertained her with music, and she chatted to him 'more cheerfully than usual for a few hours' and 'often kissed him'. Before leaving, she gave him a ring as a token of her promise to be permanently reunited by sleeping with him on the following night. Moray, who was not of course there, later claimed to de Silva that she 'had done an extraordinary and unexampled thing on the night of the murder in giving her husband a ring, petting and fondling him after plotting his murder', which was 'the worst thing' about the deed.[15] This is yet more of his scurrilous rumour-mongering. The guests at Kirk o' Field showed no apparent concern at the royal embraces, with Bothwell, Huntly, Argyll and Cassillis playing dice. It was after eleven o'clock when the Queen was reminded to leave to attend the masque. To the King's disappointment, she immediately set out for Holyrood with her entourage, telling him she would stay there for the night, as it would be too late to return afterwards. Bothwell had reminded her that she was going to Seton the next morning and would want an early start and it is alleged that Maitland also discouraged her return. It had been a long day and there was a light frosting of snow. As she mounted her horse to leave, she saw Paris with his face all blackened, saying, 'Jesu, Paris, how begrimed you are!'[16] He did not respond, but she would hardly have drawn attention to him, if she had known that he had been moving gunpowder into the cellar under cover of the babble above.*

When the Queen arrived at Holyrood, she saw the end of the masque and attended the bawdy ceremony to put the bride and groom to bed. At around midnight, she held a private conference with Bothwell and Stewart of Traquair, the Captain of the Guard. After fifteen minutes, Traquair left, but Bothwell stayed with her 'for a considerable time'.[18] It has been conjectured that Traquair and Bothwell were reporting knowledge of the King's alleged plot against her, implying that she saw this as the last straw for her marriage, but there is no evidence that she faced imminent danger requiring such an urgent discussion. With the gunpowder already packed into the cellars of the

---

* Buchanan made the most of this, recording: 'As soon as she saw [him] she knew that the powder was put in the lower house under the King's bed, for Paris had the keys both of the front and back doors of that house, and the King's servants had all the remaining keys of the lodging. And so with feigned laughter she said: "I have given offence to Bastian by not attending the masque in honour of his marriage tonight, for which purpose I will return to Holyrood." '[17]

Old Provost's Lodging and Prebendaries' Chamber, it was too late to abort the explosion. It has also been argued that Bothwell needed Mary's blessing to light the fuse. Yet it would have been unrealistic to seek it when they were already committed, particularly as neither she nor Traquair were aware of the plan. Yet Traquair knew the King's shortcomings, and might have had sympathy with the conspirators. Given the late hour, their lengthy conversation must have had another urgent purpose, perhaps the arrangements for the Prince's security while Mary was at Seton. Bothwell may have prolonged the discussion to demonstrate his non-attendance at the murder scene, particularly as Traquair, as Captain of the Guard, could be asked to confirm his movements.

Apart from some extraordinarily dubious depositions taken from Bothwell's henchmen under torture, there is no evidence of him leaving Holyrood that evening to supervise the explosion, and the guard was never asked to confirm his movements, as there would have been none to report. Without being involved in the movement of the gunpowder, he could hardly light the fuse. If he had wanted to give his final authority, with or without the Queen's sanction, it would have been less conspicuous to send Paris or another servant. As Sheriff of Edinburgh, he would be woken immediately after the explosion and needed to be in his rooms. If he only returned to Holyrood afterwards, he would have some explaining to do. When he went to investigate on the next day, he did not seem to know what had happened. This again suggests that he was not there.

After the Queen had left Kirk o' Field, Sandy Durham also retired for the night. It was later suggested that he seemed over-anxious to depart and may have been a spy for the conspirators, but this seems unlikely. The King arranged for his 'great horses' to be ready to leave for Seton with the Queen at five o'clock the next morning. He then ordered wine and sat up for about an hour with the remaining servants, playing his lute before retiring. They had no forewarning of what was to happen.

At about two o'clock in the morning there was a huge explosion, resembling a volley from twenty-five or thirty cannon, which woke people all over Edinburgh. According to Herries, 'The blast was fearfull to all about, and many rose from their beds at the noise.' It was followed by 'the confused cries of the people'.[19] Paris was later to say that every hair on this head had stood on end. The Old Provost's Lodging and adjacent Prebendaries' Chamber were destroyed,

> not only the roof and floors, but also the walls to the foundation, so that no one stone rests on another.[20] It was said that great stones, of

the length of ten foot and of breadth of four foot, were found blown from the house far away.[21]

Mary recorded that all was 'either carried far away or dashed in dross to the very groundstone'.[22]

Several depositions were taken on 11 February, the day after the murder, from those in the vicinity of the explosion. Barbara Martin in Blackfriars Wynd testified that she had heard running footsteps passing immediately beforehand. She looked from her window to see thirteen armed men emerging from Blackfriars Monastery to the south and hastening up the High Street. Her neighbour, Meg Crokat, who had been in bed with her two children, ran naked to the door of her cottage to see eleven men, one wearing silk, emerging from Blackfriars Gate, where they split into two groups as they hurried away. She asked them what the 'crack' was and, after hearing Barbara Martin calling them traitors, concluded that they were up to no good. Women lodging in cottages by the south garden and orchard outside the Town Wall heard a plaintive voice crying, 'Pity me, kinsmen, for the love of him who had pity on all the world!'[23] This was followed by silence.

The town watch arrived and arrested Captain William Blackadder, the first man they saw. He happened to be a friend of Bothwell, but came running after hearing the explosion, while enjoying a drink with a friend. A large crowd gathered at the scene of devastation, some with lanterns. They found an empty barrel of gunpowder by the side door to the east garden and spotted the blackened figure of Nelson crying for help from the top of the Town Wall. He was only superficially injured, either being thrown clear by the blast or, more likely, escaping beforehand by climbing out from the gallery. People started digging franticly, knowing that the King was staying there, but it was dark and cold with intermittent snow.

At Holyrood, Mary was also woken by the explosion and sent messengers to establish the cause. They returned to report that Kirk o' Field was destroyed. Bothwell, as Sheriff of Edinburgh, was woken by his servant George Halket, who told him that the King was believed to have been killed. He shot up shouting, 'Fie! Treason!'[24] He sent men to investigate before returning to bed with his wife to await news.

Two bodies were found in the rubble; one was McCaig, but two more servants survived (probably including Symonds, who like Nelson was on the upper floor). There was no sign of Hepburn of Bolton or the lodging servants, suggesting that they had all been involved in moving the gun-powder and had left before the explosion. There was still no sign of the King or his valet, Taylor, but, at about five o'clock in the morning, a search of the south garden and orchard beyond the Town Wall revealed their nearly naked, but unmarked, bodies more than fifty yards from the lodging. There was no gunpowder on their clothing or evidence of strangulation. It was later established that one of the King's ribs was broken, but that was the only sign of a struggle. Beside them, laid out in a row, was a chair, a piece of rope, a dagger, the King's furred nightgown and a quilt. These were carefully positioned, and the king's hand modestly covered his genitals. A backless velvet slipper, thought to have belonged to a conspirator, lay nearby.

A surgeon, John Pitcairn, was called to remain with the King's body. A message was sent to tell the Queen that the King was dead, and Bothwell, who was still in bed, was woken by Huntly. He dressed quickly and, with Huntly, Argyll, Atholl, Maitland and the Countesses of Atholl and Mar, went to console the Queen. He reported that she was 'greatly afflicted by it all'[25] and Clernault, the Cardinal of Lorraine's agent, wrote that she was 'one of the most unfortunate Queens in the world'.[26] Moretta added that she was 'in great fear of a worse fate'.[27] She seemed unable to deal with her correspondence, but sent Bothwell with men to make a diligent search. He held several suspects, until they could provide alibis for their movements. He also arranged with Sandy Durham for the King's body to be laid out in the New Provost's Lodging with a guard of honour, before it was carried back to Holyrood to be embalmed. The Court was ordered into mourning and, in accordance with French custom, Mary retired into forty days' seclusion.

Huntly suggested calling the Privy Council to 'deliberate about the means of apprehending the traitors who committed the deed' and it met at the Tolbooth shortly after noon with Argyll, as Lord Justice-General, presiding.[28] Many of its members were parties to the conspiracy, but Tullibardine represented Lennox interests. To bring some order to all the rumour, they prepared a detailed account to be sent with Clernault to Catherine de Medici. This stressed that they were

> engaged in an enquiry and, having once uncovered the matter, Your Majesty and all the world shall know that Scotland will not endure that such a cause for shame should rest upon her shoulders.[29]

They reported Mary's belief that it was only good fortune that prevented her and a great many of the nobility being killed with her husband. They offered a reward of 2,000 crowns for information, but professed their own ignorance. They interviewed Thomas Nelson, but when asked who held the key to the building, he replied that it was the Queen. Realising his state of shock, Tullibardine asked for an adjournment until the next day.

References

1. Buchanan, *Book of Articles*, cited in Guy, p. 392
2. Guy, p. 293, and Weir, p. 228
3. Weir, p. 228
4. Weir, p. 233
5. Darnley to Lennox, 7 February 1566, Nau, p. 34; Mahon, p. 115; cited in Guy, p. 296, Antonia Fraser, p. 339, Wormald, *Mary, Queen of Scots*, p. 164 and Weir, p. 234
6. CSP, Scottish, II, p. 728, cited in Guy, pp. 418–9 and Antonia Fraser, p. 460
7. Nau, cited in Weir, p. 235
8. Weir, p. 235
9. Melville, cited in Weir, p. 236
10. Calendar of manuscripts at Hatfield House, I, p. 376, cited in Antonia Fraser, p. 461
11. Calendar of manuscripts at Hatfield House, cited in Guy, pp. 421–423, and Antonia Fraser, pp. 461–2
12. CSP, Scottish, II, Appendix II, p. 722, cited in Guy, pp. 423–4, and Antonia Fraser, p. 462
13. Guy, p. 424
14. Labanoff, II, p. 3, cited in Guy, p. 301, Antonia Fraser, p. 343, and Weir, p. 244
15. Guy, p. 298
16. Nau, p. 34, cited in Guy, p. 298, and Antonia Fraser, p. 344
17. Buchanan, *Detectio*, cited in Guy, p. 393
18. Buchanan, *Detectio*, cited in Weir, p. 247
19. Pitcairn, *Criminal Trials*, I, pt. 1, p. 502; Herries, p. 84: cited in Antonia Fraser, p. 350, and Weir, p. 249
20. Sloane MMS, cited in Weir, p. 250
21. Weir, p. 250
22. Sloane MSS; Keith, cited in Antonia Fraser, p. 353 and Weir, p. 250
23. Labanoff, VII, p. 108, from a letter from Mondovi to Cosimo de Medici, cited in Guy, p. 307, and Antonia Fraser, p. 352
24. Deposition of William Powrie, in Pitcairn, cited by Antonia Fraser, p. 354, and Weir, p. 251
25. Cockburn and Maitland, p. 13; cited in Weir, p. 252
26. CSP Scottish; Clernault in State Papers in Public Record Office; cited in Weir, p. 252
27. CSP Venetian, cited in Weir, p. 252
28. Cockburn and Maitland; Knox; cited in Weir, p. 253
29. Privy Council to Catherine de Medici, Sloane MMS; cited in Weir, p. 256

27

A Review of What Happened

The henchmen involved in the King's murder were provided by Bothwell, Morton, Archibald Douglas and probably Balfour. They included Bothwell's relative, Hepburn of Bolton, the warden of the Old Provost's Lodging, who is likely to have provided the duplicate keys. Other Bothwell men included John Hay of Talla, whose mother was a Hepburn; James 'Black' Ormiston, Bothwell's bailiff; Robert 'Hob' Ormiston, Black Ormiston's uncle; James Cullen, a captain of the Royal Hackbutters and explosives expert, who had been a mercenary in France, Denmark and Poland, but was now a 'creature of Bothwell's';[1] Patrick Wilson, a merchant who had arranged Bothwell's tryst with Bessie Crawford, and who provided a barrel of gunpowder; and three of Bothwell's servants, who were to move it into position, William Powrie, his porter, George Dalgleish, his tailor, and the reluctant Paris. It is probable that some of them were seconded as the lodging's 'downstairs' servants. Archibald Douglas, Bothwell's close associate, came with a dozen or so Douglas adherents provided by Morton and himself. Ker of Faw-donside, forgetful that he owed his return from exile to the King, was outside Kirk o' Field with a detachment of mounted men. There were probably about thirty men involved, but the depositions vary.

Balfour's name was linked with Bothwell's on bill boards in Edinburgh shortly after the murder. He purchased and supervised the movement and packing of the gunpowder, and presumably arranged its storage close to Kirk o' Field, possibly at the New Provost's Lodging. He may not have been involved thereafter as there were enough servants to heave it into position, but his movements on the day of the murder are not known. He was closely associated with Bothwell (but not a kinsman as is sometimes suggested) and several of the depositions link him to the plot without identifying his role. There is also a reference implicating Huntly, Bothwell's closest ally among the nobility, but this is not corroborated and appears unlikely.

Archbishop Hamilton, who had accompanied Mary to Glasgow, was much later accused of being part of the conspiracy, perhaps because the Hamiltons were the Lennoxes' traditional enemies. He was staying at

Châtelherault's house from where a light was seen in an upper window before the murder. After the explosion the light had been extinguished, hardly surprisingly, but this was deemed to be a signal.*

There is no doubt that Bothwell masterminded the murder plan, even though he was not present. While in captivity in England, even Mary came to accept (if she did not already know it) that he was 'one of the murderers of the King'. He detested King Henry, but also seems to have developed an infatuation for Mary in the weeks beforehand. This was mentioned by both Melville and Livingston, not people with reason to falsify it. Yet it is very unlikely that he arranged the murder hoping to marry her, as he was already committed to Jean Gordon. Nevertheless, once undertaken, Morton seems to have given him encouragement.

Most of the evidence for the murder arrangements comes from the manipulated depositions of Bothwell's associates, almost all taken under torture. Not unnaturally each was trying to protect himself, but there is a common thread implicating Bothwell and, where possible, the Queen. They almost completely erase the involvement of Morton, Balfour, Douglas and other conspirators, except where they had fallen foul of Moray at the time of preparation.

The manipulators went to great lengths to avoid unhelpful depositions being made available. Paris was only most reluctantly involved and admitted going to the docks at Leith beforehand to find a boat on which to escape, but none was ready to sail. As he had carried messages between Bothwell and the Queen and had helped in the movement of the gunpowder at Kirk o' Field, his evidence might have seemed crucial. He later escaped with Bothwell to Denmark, where the lords asked Captain John Clark, a Scottish mercenary working for the Danish King, to extradite him. This was not as one might expect to procure him as a witness, but to make certain he kept his mouth shut. Clark arrested him on 30 October 1568, but it was only three weeks later, shortly before the Conference at Westminster, that Cecil was told. No urgent effort was made to repatriate him to give evidence, and he was not brought back to Scotland until June 1569. He was then imprisoned at St Andrews until, on 9 and 10 August, he secretly made two

---

* After Carberry Hill, there was a strong rumour that Archbishop Hamilton was implicated, but this is likely to have been malicious propaganda from the Confederates against one of the Queen's supporters. As late as 6 February 1568, Archbishop Bethune in Paris reported that Moray was determined to prosecute Archbishop Hamilton in Parliament, 'on the plea that he had had a hand in the murder'.[2] If Moray considered doing so, it was not progressed, although Lennox and his supporters, no friends of the Hamiltons, continued to believe in his guilt. When the Archbishop was eventually arrested after the fall of Dumbarton, he was again accused on the flimsiest evidence of taking part. He was by then more justifiably implicated in Moray's murder, so that Lennox, who had become Regent, arranged his immediate execution without trial.

conflicting depositions under torture before Thomas Buchanan, George Buchanan's nephew, and George Wood, Moray's private secretary. It is clear that these had been manipulated. In the first, he claimed that, while acting as the Queen's messenger, he had tracked Bothwell down at Kirk o' Field on 25 January 1567. Yet at that time Bothwell was indisputably in the Borders. He also claimed that Bothwell said to him, 'Commend me to the Queen and tell her that all will go well. Say that Balfour and I have not slept the night, that everything is arranged, and that the king's lodgings are ready for him.'[3] Yet we know that Kirk o' Field had not been chosen by 25 January, and the murder plan had not by then been agreed. The deposition implies that Balfour, who was by now out of favour, knew of the plot before 25 January. Yet he was much later to confirm that he learned of it only on 7 February, the most likely date for it to have been finalised. Paris claimed that Maitland, also by then out of favour, had told him to advise the Queen to use Kirk o' Field as the King's lodging. Yet we know that Maitland was not involved in the choice of location. In his second deposition, Paris slightly contradicts his earlier one. He says that he came to Edinburgh on 25 January and found Bothwell dining with Balfour (although we know that Bothwell was still in the Borders) and Bothwell told him to tell Mary that he was sending her a diamond in place of his heart (although there is no plausible evidence of a romance between them before the King's death). He then visited Maitland, who told him that the King would be better off at Kirk o' Field (still highly unlikely as at that time Craigmillar had been chosen for the King's recuperation). On 27 January, he arrived back in Glasgow, just as Mary and the King were leaving for Craigmillar. According to his deposition, he accompanied them as far as Linlithgow, from where he was sent off by the Queen with two bracelets for Bothwell, now apparently returning from Liddesdale (and not in Edinburgh as stated earlier in the deposition). Reference to the bracelets seems designed to corroborate Mary's gift as reported in Casket Letter II, prepared two years earlier. In addition to Balfour and Maitland, the deposition also implicates Huntly and Argyll in the murder plot. By then all four were seeking Mary's restoration, and Moray was using every means to try to discredit them. Paris had to be silenced as he knew too much and his depositions were never published. He was not brought to trial, but was taken straight to the gallows to be hung, drawn and quartered. From the scaffold, he bravely shouted out denying having carried letters between Bothwell and the Queen as was recorded. Buchanan never included Paris's evidence in updated versions of his *Detectio*. It conflicted with what he had already tabled.

It was Bothwell who developed the plan to use gunpowder to blow up Kirk o' Field and its occupants. With the King having several loyal servants on the premises, Bothwell did not believe he could maintain secrecy, if he were stabbed or poisoned. By blowing them up, he hoped to destroy the evidence. The claim that the lodging had been undermined before the King's arrival can only be a fabrication. John Hay of Talla recorded, probably correctly, that Bothwell did not finally decide on using gunpowder until 7 February and it was delivered only on the evening of 9 February. By then, Bothwell could not have supervised its positioning as he was with the Queen and in costume.

All the depositions confirm two sources of supply of the powder. The main part appears to have come from the arsenal at Dunbar, while a second delivery came in a barrel purchased from Patrick Wilson in Edinburgh. According to Drury, this was valued at £60 Scots and appears to have been acquired by Balfour in a barter transaction for olive oil. During his imprisonment in Denmark, Bothwell recorded that the gunpowder went to 'Sir James Balfour's house', where a mine was prepared.[4] With Moretta staying there, it is quite unlikely that Balfour would have received it at his main residence, but it could more logically have been taken to the New Provost's Lodging, from where it was a short step to the little courtyard behind the Prebendaries' Chamber giving access to the cellars below the King's accommodation. Yet Robert Balfour would not have agreed to the destruction of his letting accommodation without compensation. Little is known about him, but he was one of several younger brothers of Sir James, without the means to bear its loss, and it is suggested that Sir James acquired his leases shortly before the explosion. If so, the New Provost's Lodging could justifiably be described as Sir James's house. The propaganda afterwards accused Sir James, not Robert, of involvement in the conspiracy. An almost complete absence of evidence against either of them demonstrates Sir James's part in putting the official story together.

The depositions weave very different and sometimes conflicting stories to show how the gunpowder arrived at Kirk o' Field. They are all totally unrealistic, but were designed to involve Bothwell and his men in every stage of its movement and to implicate the Queen. If accepted at face value, there was insufficient powder, inadequately contained, to achieve the explosion that occurred. Paris claimed that Bothwell told him of his intention to use gunpowder on 5 February, while they were attending the Queen at Kirk o' Field. Bothwell had been suffering from 'the bloody flux' (dysentery) for some time and sought his old servant's help for a place to relieve himself from his 'usual illness'.[5] Paris helped him to undress and stayed with him at a place between two doors, while Bothwell divulged his plan and Paris reluctantly agreed to help him. Two days later Bothwell apparently asked him to provide a key to the Queen's room, but, as he did not have one, Paris arranged for a copy to be made. When he produced it on the next day, Bothwell already had a complete set and told him to retain it. Bothwell could presumably have obtained the set of keys from Hepburn, who was later to drop them down a hole in a quarry. The need to access the Queen's bedroom fits with the unlikely story that the powder was placed under her bed, implying that she knew of the planned explosion.

According to the depositions, the main gunpowder supply left Dunbar on 7 February. Paris reported that it arrived on the evening of 9 February, packed in 'polks' (leather bags) in two trunks, one of leather and one of wood, to be stored in the back hall of Bothwell's lodgings at Holyrood. This implies that Bothwell had arranged its delivery and perhaps that the Queen knew about it. Yet we know that Bothwell was not available to receive it at Holyrood on 9 February, and it is implausible to suggest that such dangerous material should have been brought to a royal palace full of candle lights and open fires, and risking discovery by the guard on arrival. It would have been delivered to an agreed location close to Kirk o' Field. Yet every deposition is consistent on it going to Holyrood and from there to Kirk o' Field. John Hay of Talla confirmed the second source of supply. His servant went to Patrick Wilson to collect the barrel, estimated to be the size of a 54-gallon cask. If so, the servant would not have been able to move it by himself. Yet he apparently brought it openly through the Edinburgh streets to Holyrood.

According to Hay's deposition, from four o'clock in the afternoon until dusk on 9 February, he attended a two-hour meeting at Holyrood with Bothwell and Hepburn. As soon as it was dark, they walked to Black Ormiston's house in Blackfriars' Wynd to discuss final details with Black and Hob Ormiston. Then, from about half past eight to ten o'clock at night, Bothwell stood in the Canongate to supervise the gunpowder's movement from Holyrood to Kirk o' Field. Yet we know that from four o'clock Bothwell was with the Queen at the dinner for Moretta, and the idea of his involvement in moving gunpowder wearing carnival costume in the very public Canongate is unthinkable. If it was being brought from Holyrood, his men were all aware of the shorter more secluded route through the old Blackfriars Monastery gate.

Hepburn's deposition claims that Bothwell remained at the banquet held for Moretta until a quarter to eight. From here he apparently went with Paris to visit his mother and then walked to Black Ormiston's lodging, leaving there at half past eight to join the Queen at Kirk o' Field. While this timing may seem more plausible, his absence from the Queen for this forty-five-minute period would not have gone unnoticed. Paris claimed to have walked with Bothwell from the dinner for Moretta to join the Ormistons, going on with them to the Cowgate to meet Hay and Hepburn. After discussing the murder plan, Bothwell and Paris came on to Kirk o' Field. This is largely corroborated by Black Ormiston, who claims to have met Bothwell in the Cowgate, walking from the dinner to Kirk o' Field. They then agreed to move the gunpowder by the secret way, and he apparently went to open the old Blackfriars Monastery gate to let it in.

Between half past eight and ten o'clock, Powrie, Dalgleish and Wilson apparently moved the trunks and the barrel containing gunpowder openly through the streets from Holyrood to the Blackfriars Monastery gate about 200 yards from Kirk o' Field. Powrie originally claimed that they completed the task with two horses in one journey, but later amended this to using one horse on two journeys, with the trunks carried on the first and the barrel on the second trip. Whichever version is accepted, it is estimated that only two hundredweight of powder could have been moved, insufficient to achieve the explosion that occurred, and it would have seemed extraordinarily suspicious to the guards at Holyrood. Black Ormiston and two others (not recognised by Powrie, Dalgleish or Wilson) wearing cloaks and velvet slippers, met them at the gate. (This unsubstantiated reference to their footwear seems designed to explain that the single velvet slipper found near the king's body belonged to one of Bothwell's men.) Both Hepburn and Powrie claimed that Bothwell came to the gate to tell them to hurry (which is unlikely, but it gives the impression that the powder was being moved at his instruction). The depositions are consistent that the powder was delivered to the side door of the kitchen, but do not make it clear how it arrived. The obvious way from the Blackfriars gate would have been through the east garden, a distance of 200 yards. Hepburn claimed that Powrie was sent to buy candles and, by the light of one of them, the polks were unpacked from the trunks and were carried with the barrel by Powrie, Dalgleish and Wilson to a wall surrounding the east garden. From here, Hepburn, Hay and Black Ormiston heaved them over it to the side door. Yet there does not seem to have been anything more than a low wall in the east garden (none is shown in the drawing sent to Drury immediately after the murder) and there would have been access through any garden wall, as it formed part of the secret way from Holyrood mentioned by the Queen. Another version says that the polks were taken by Powrie, Dalgleish and Wilson outside the Blackfriars gate and round the back of the Town Wall into Thieves Row. At a point opposite the east garden Hepburn, Hay and Black Ormiston lifted them over the fourteen-foot wall (although the barrel would have been too heavy to lift). To move them this way seems nonsensical and risked making a noise.

A much more probable and less obtrusive route would have been to use either the postern gate from Thieves Row or the little courtyard behind the Prebendaries' Chamber. These both led to the cellar passage, giving hidden access to the kitchen and the cellar below the Prebendaries' Chamber. As the empty barrel was found by the side door to the east garden it has been assumed that it was too wide* to go through it, suggesting that it could have arrived there only from the Blackfriars gate. The manipulators certainly tried to show that the gunpowder arrived in the east garden and that Paris provided access by unlocking the side door (although it had no lock and needed to be unbolted from the inside). There are two reasons for them wanting to demonstrate that it came in by the side door. The kitchen had access by stone steps to the floor above, where the Queen's bedroom was located. To implicate the Queen, it was claimed that the powder was placed under her bed. If it came in this way, it could hardly have come from the New Provost's Lodging, making Balfour's involvement less likely. From there, the shorter and more convenient route was into the little courtyard behind the Prebendaries' Chamber with its access to the cellar passage. Whichever route was chosen, it was only the lodging servants who could have transported it unobtrusively.

Once inside the lodging, the Ormistons positioned the gunpowder. This could only have been after Bonkil had gone home for the evening and the kitchen embers had been extinguished. The royal party, arriving from the dinner for Moretta, was not in need of food. Powrie and Wilson seem to have become worried and were apparently sent back to Holyrood with the empty trunks. Yet this also seems nonsense, and the trunks were more likely to have been destroyed in the explosion.

The depositions claim that loose gunpowder was piled under the Queen's bed. This is also nonsense. Any of the guests could have visited her bedroom, which was on the same level as the *salle* to leave coats or use the *garderobe*. This would have disturbed those moving the powder. Loose powder would have covered the room in dust, risking ignition from a naked light, and, if not contained, powder would burn rather than explode. An explosion in the bedroom could never have destroyed the lodging and Prebendaries' Chamber completely. Yet the depositions all confirm that, after positioning

---

* There is no absolute evidence that the barrel was too large to go through the door to the east garden, and this is only assumed because it provides an explanation for it being found there. It could have been emptied, perhaps to fill a mine, within the cellar, after which it could have been moved through the side door out of the way.

the powder, Paris locked the Queen's bedroom giving the key to Hepburn, even though Hepburn had his own set.

The only realistic way to achieve the damage that occurred was for the gunpowder to be packed into mines in the cellars under both the Old Provost's Lodging and the Prebendaries' Chamber. These were accessible from the passage to the postern gate and to the little courtyard, where its movement would have been concealed from view. Yet Bothwell apparently again found it necessary to appear to tell them to make less noise.

With the gunpowder in place, Paris apparently left the side door unbolted and the cellar door unlocked. The Ormistons went home after establishing that others would prepare the fuse. Although access was apparently to be provided through the side door, they would have had to rely on the King's servants not bolting it before they retired. It is more likely that those lighting the fuse entered through the postern gate. It was claimed that George Dalgleish acquired a yard of lint to make a fuse from the guard at Holyrood. Perhaps this information was intended to implicate Traquair and even the Queen, or to corroborate the gunpowder being moved from Holyrood in the first instance. When the Queen was leaving for Holyrood from Kirk o' Field late in the evening, she saw Paris all 'begrimed' as he went to advise Bothwell that all was ready. He claimed that Argyll patted him on the back, implying that Argyll was also in the know. By the time of Paris's deposition, Argyll had only recently submitted to Moray after supporting Mary.

With everything apparently prepared, Bothwell returned to Holyrood with the Queen. After holding their late meeting, it is alleged by Buchanan that he 'passed to his chamber and there changed his hose and doublet and put his side cloak about him and passed up to the accomplishment of that most horrible murder'.[6] His alleged movements then become absurdly public for a soldier expert in covert operations. Carrying his sword and with at least eleven men, including Paris, Powrie, Dalgleish and Wilson, they apparently walked to Kirk o' Field, making themselves known to the guard, before taking the open route down the Canongate. They woke the porter to open the Netherbow Port 'to friends of Lord Bothwell's'[7] (although elsewhere it is implied that they crossed through the wall only at the Blackfriars gate), but when asked why they were out so late, they did not reply. They then marched openly up the High Street and into Blackfriars Wynd. This conveniently explains why Barbara Martin saw a party of men shortly before the explosion. Although they stopped at Ormiston's lodgings, he was not apparently there and later claimed to be drinking with a friend, Thomas Henderson, no doubt a convenient alibi. They then took the secret way through the monastery grounds to gather in the east garden. It is reported that Bothwell told them not to stir, while he and Paris went forward with Cullen. Cullen had apparently advised Bothwell to strangle the King, as it was more certain than powder, and he scaled the Town Wall to hide in the south garden to block the King's escape. This implied that it was Cullen, acting on Bothwell's instruction, who suffocated the King, explaining away any Douglas involvement. If Cullen did scale the wall, it is more likely, as an explosives expert, that he entered the lodging by the postern gate in Thieves Row, from where he lit the fuses in the cellars before joining the Douglases.

All the plausible evidence shows that Archibald Douglas and about a dozen followers were hiding in the cottages near the south garden, where they were joined by Cullen to block the King's escape route. Douglas's servant, John Binning, testified under torture in 1581 that his master was 'art and part' of the murder and 'did actually devise and perpetrate it'.[8] It is known that the Douglas men wore clothing over their armour and slippers to deaden the sound of their boots. This would explain the find of a velvet slipper. As a voice was heard shouting: 'Pity me my kinsmen!', it can be implied that the King recognised his Douglas assassins, and they were seen afterwards leaving by Blackfriars Wynd. None of the depositions suggest that Bothwell's men went that way.

The depositions tell a different story. When Bothwell and Paris allegedly returned to the east garden, Paris escorted Hay and Hepburn to the side door (still apparently unbolted) and opened the door to the Queen's bedroom for them to light the slow-burning fuse. They then locked all the doors to prevent the King's escape (although the side door only bolted from the inside), and returned to the east garden. The depositions all report a long delay. Fearing that the fuse had failed, Bothwell apparently pulled Hepburn behind him to investigate, but Hepburn held him back from looking through the Queen's bedroom window (which faced onto the quadrangle at the front of the building). At this moment there was a flash from a window apparently facing the garden, followed by a violent explosion. The lodging lifted behind them as they scrambled back to rejoin Dalgleish and Powrie. From here they ran through the old Blackfriars Monastery into the Cowgate.

There are shortcomings in all this evidence. Although a flash was reported from a window before the explosion, there was no window facing the east garden. The explosion was too great for the powder to have been in the Queen's bedroom, and the conspirators could not have hoped to light a fuse there without disturbing the sleeping occupants. A seasoned soldier like Bothwell would never have returned to check the fuse by looking through a window. The only purpose of this evidence is to demonstrate Bothwell's part in lighting it.

The reported route taken by the conspirators on leaving Kirk o' Field is also ridiculous. Having allegedly returned down the Cowgate to the Netherbow Port, they again had to wake the porter, despite the explosion. They could just as easily have gone through the old Blackfriars Monastery gate or climbed over a broken down piece of wall further on. It is claimed that they split into two groups, with Bothwell and Paris continuing down the very public Canongate to Holyrood, while the remainder took St Mary's Wynd. Only Bothwell needed to return to Holyrood, but they all apparently gave his name when challenged by the guard, by when the palace was in a state of alarm. Neither the porter at the Netherbow Port nor the guard was ever asked to confirm these movements.

With the plans to destroy Kirk o' Field already finalised, Bothwell had no reason to return to supervise the lighting of the fuse. His only justifiable motive would have been to bring the Queen's sanction, but she would not have been aware of the plan and it was too late to abort it. If he did return, he did not need eleven men with him. He could have gone alone or perhaps with Paris, who knew the interior. There is no evidence that his other companions helped in lighting the fuse, but they could have been there to block the east garden as an escape route. Only Cullen of Bothwell's party crossed the Town Wall, but could not have sealed off the south garden and Thieves Row alone. Although they must have seen them, neither Hepburn nor Hay mentioned the presence of Douglas men. This evidence can only have been expunged.

Bothwell apparently lost patience with Paris, who was reportedly panicking as he returned to Holyrood. Hay had to threaten him with a pistol to shut him up, but claimed to have taken him to his house for the night. It seems nonsensical that Hay and Paris should have returned to Holyrood, where their movements would be recorded, only to leave again. A claim that the Queen saw Paris and told him 'not to worry' can only be seen as another effort to incriminate her.

The final twist is that the gunpowder did not kill the King. His servant Nelson, who had been sleeping in the gallery, was calling for help after the explosion from the top of the Town Wall. The King must have been disturbed, probably by those lighting the fuse and, with his valet Taylor, tried to escape. The servants who survived seem to have been in the upper gallery, from where they scrambled onto the Town Wall with the King, who had grabbed his dagger, a nightgown and quilt before leaving. He and Taylor lowered themselves on the far side with a rope and chair, but the King seems to have fallen and cracked a rib. They ran through the south garden and orchard, but were accosted by Archibald Douglas and his henchmen, now including Cullen, who emerged from the cottages. The King pleaded for his life, before both he and Taylor were suffocated. Cullen, who admitted being there, said 'the king was a long time a-dying, and in his strength made debate for his life'.[9] With the explosion imminent, they had no time to move the corpses nearer to the lodging, but laid them out with their possessions, before escaping up Blackfriars Wynd, leaving behind a velvet slipper. When Bothwell arrived the next morning to inspect the bodies, he was unaware of how the King and Taylor had died. Having assumed that they had been killed in the explosion, he was amazed to find their bodies unmarked. Although Douglas was eventually charged with the murder, the trial was so arranged that he was found not guilty.

References

1. Mahon; CSP Scottish; Cecil's description, cited in Weir, p. 271
2. Weir, p. 427
3. Paris's 1st deposition, Public Records Office; cited in Weir, p. 262
4. Cockburn and Maitland; cited in Weir, p. 289
5. Antonia Fraser, p. 341, and Weir, p. 264
6. Buchanan, *Detectio*; cited in Weir, p. 271
7. Weir, p. 271
8. Weir, p. 273
9. Reported by Drury in CSP Scottish, cited in Weir, p. 296

28

The Immediate Aftermath to the King's Murder and Mary's Reaction to it

On the morning after the murder, Bothwell visited Kirk o' Field in his capacity as Sheriff of Edinburgh. He arranged for the King's body to be moved to the New Provost's Lodging for examination and stopped the public from searching for clues in the rubble. Having returned to Holyrood, he went with Huntly to see the Queen. He told Sir James Melville that 'the thunder came out of the sky and had burnt the King's house' and that the Queen was 'sorrowful and queet'.[1] She also went to see the body, but showed no emotion. In the afternoon, it was brought on a board to Holyrood to be embalmed, before lying in state at the altar in the Chapel Royal. There was no state funeral,* but the body was interred in the tomb of the kings in the old Abbey Kirk at Holyrood 'quietly in the night without any kind of solemnity or mourning heard among all the persons at Court'.[3]

Although Mary was extremely shocked and no doubt frightened at her husband's death, she was expected to face up to it cool-headedly. In her letters written immediately afterwards to Elizabeth and her French relations, she confirmed her belief that she was also intended as a victim to make way for a regency for her son. This implied that she thought that Moray sought the Regency or even planned to usurp the throne for himself. Nau later recorded her belief that Moray had left Edinburgh after finalising his plan to gain the Crown by ruining her. Either he had arranged the murder himself, or it had been done on his behalf by the returning exiles as a blood feud against the King. Mary never varied from her view that the returning exiles

---

* Cecil noted that the King's private burial caused great indignation in London, where it was felt that a state funeral would have been more appropriate. Buchanan's *Book of Articles* (the English translation of his *Detectio*) later claimed that the body was 'without any decent order, cast in the earth without any ceremony or company of honest men'.[2] Yet the location was magnificent and the quiet ceremony was ill-attended principally because it was conducted with Catholic rites. In accordance with normal custom for a consort, the Queen did not attend. Lennox, who had been in Linlithgow, returned to Glasgow without being present, probably concerned for his own safety or in fear that his part in his son's plotting might be leaked.

wanted her dead. It was to be expected that she would deal severely with their treasonable actions.

Mary's initial reaction to her husband's murder was identical to that following Riccio's death eleven months before. It was only by chance that she had not slept that night at Kirk o' Field. She wrote to Elizabeth and her French relations:

> We hope to punish the same with such rigour as shall serve for example of this cruelty to all ages to come. Always who ever have taken this wicked enterprise in hand, we assure our self it was dressed always for us as for the King.[4]

On 11 February, Clernault left for Paris with the Council's letter to Catherine de Medici and one from Mary to Archbishop Bethune. She told him, 'The matter is so horrible and strange, as we believe the like was never heard of in any country.'[5]

Yet Mary seemed too distraught to take control. Although she wrote to Lennox promising justice for the King, she took no immediate action to set up an enquiry, and the Council's efforts were half-hearted. A reward of £2,000 Scots was offered for information with 'an honest yearly rent' and a pardon to anyone giving evidence, but no one came forward. A proclamation signed by Argyll was affixed to the Mercat Cross confirming that

> the Queen's majesty, unto whom of all others the case was most grievous, would rather lose life and all than it should remain unpunished.[6]

No proper investigation was undertaken. On 11 February, Barbara Martin and Meg Crokat became intimidated when cross-examined and were dismissed as fools by the judges. They may have said too much as their evidence was suppressed. Pitcairn, the surgeon, was also interviewed, but could add very little.

While the Council was involved in its investigation, Mary went into seclusion in darkened rooms and, on the Council's advice, moved for security with Prince James into Edinburgh Castle. One hundred mules were required to transport her clothing, furnishings and papers from Holyrood. Yet, on 11 February, she attended the wedding ceremony of Margaret Carwood to John Stewart of Tullipowreis, honouring a pledge to her faithful retainer. Although she was not at the banquet afterwards, her involvement drew scathing comments from Buchanan for leaving her mourning chamber so soon. Otherwise she remained in her rooms, apparently too upset to see anyone. Believing that she was endangering her health, her physicians advised the Council that she needed fresh air. Yet again she chose to go to 'Seton to repose there and take some purgations', arriving on 16 February with Maitland, Livingston, Archbishop Hamilton and about one hundred attendants.*[7] Although Bothwell, Huntly and Argyll escorted her there, Bothwell and Huntly immediately returned to act as James's official guardians at Holyrood. She also needed to return to Edinburgh after three days, as will be explained, but was still distraught and, by 21 February, was back at Seton, this time with Bothwell in attendance. By now her grief seemed illusory. On 26 February, she dined with Thomas, 1st Lord Wharton, at Trenant, where, according to Drury, she partnered Bothwell to beat Huntly and Argyll at archery with the losers paying for dinner. Although other reports claimed that she was too unwell to play, the damage was done.

From Mary's viewpoint, the one person who could hardly have been involved in the King's murder was Bothwell. Although he remained a loose cannon politically, he had been her saviour after Riccio's death, and she could always rely on him. She knew at first hand that he could hardly have murdered the King, as he had been with her for the whole of the day beforehand, and she had seen him, until he assuredly went to bed with his wife at Holyrood, shortly before the explosion. Yet his attitude afterwards was unexpected. While it would be thought that he too would want his archenemy, Moray, and the returning exiles investigated, he was advising her, like everyone else, not to investigate too thoroughly. Even more surprisingly, there were rumours of his involvement, and Lennox was telling her that he was the culprit. On 16 February, only a week after the murder, the first placards appeared which accused Bothwell and quite absurdly implicated her.

Despite Bothwell's name being mentioned as the likely perpetrator of the crime, only he, in Moray's absence, had the prestige to manage the government, and Mary pinned her hopes on his guidance by putting him in charge. Unlike King Henry, he could not be treated as a wayward youth of twenty, and, at thirty-two, he soon dominated her with his assuredness and vigour, becoming the virtual ruler of Scotland with command of the Royal Bodyguard. After Argyll, he was the most powerful Scottish magnate with his own Border militia; he had an apparently close alliance with Morton,

---

* By breaking her mourning so quickly Mary was severely criticised by Buchanan in his *Book of Articles*. He claimed that her visit to Seton with Bothwell 'had so many conveniences that they had gone back there to the detriment of their reputations'.[8] Yet Bothwell did not arrive until the second visit on 21 January and it was the Council who had encouraged the trip for her health.

leader of the powerful Douglases; and he also had the availability of military support from the Gordons. He negotiated with a German mercenary to provide Mary with 3,600 crack troops, although it is not clear that they ever reached Scotland. As hereditary Lord High Admiral, he received the proceeds of treasure taken from all wrecks on the Scottish coast. As Sheriff of Edinburgh, he maintained a close association with the legal profession, holding coveted preferments in his gift. He could be suave, despite a rough and lawless nature and an uncontrollable temper. Although Mary feared him, his attraction was in being Moray's deadly foe.

To the shock of the Guise family and European heads of State, Mary's European correspondence dried up and she seemed completely distraught and dazed, retiring to a darkened room to cry. It has been argued that her lacklustre demeanour was caused by illness. Yet, she had always been courageous in a crisis, even when unwell. Only eleven months earlier, when five months pregnant, she had shown extraordinary resource after Riccio's murder to save her throne. She had been to Glasgow since her haemorrhage at Jedburgh and with considerable guile had single-handedly persuaded the King to return with her to Edinburgh, writing a detailed and logical report of their conversation to her advisers. After marrying Bothwell, she would again show great bravery in escaping from Borthwick Castle and in trying to garner support for their cause. Yet now she collapsed. This was not out of remorse for her husband, who, as she knew, was continuing to plot her overthrow, but she did not want him dead. Regicide was an unpardonable crime, and his death weakened her hopes of being accepted as Elizabeth's heir. If she had sought a proper investigation, she would have retained her Crown, and the King's murder would have been seen as the necessity it was for her security.

If illness were not the cause of Mary's indecisiveness, it can only be assumed that she had come to realise that the King's murder did not just involve Moray, Morton and the returning exiles. Perhaps the lords at Craigmillar, including Argyll, Huntly, Bothwell and Maitland, had taken the law into their own hands to free her from her husband. When divorce and a trial for treason could not be achieved on an acceptable basis, her options were either to make the best of her marriage, perhaps with the King under some form of house arrest, or to condone a plan for his assassination. We can be sure that she never gave approval for his death, but the nobility would never accept their reconciliation. Perhaps she felt guilty at them having to take action to remove a man, over whom she had made a complete fool of herself. She knew murder had been discussed, and was aware from the King in Glasgow of a bond prepared at Craigmillar. If they had acted collectively, none of them would want a detailed investigation, and Bothwell would have been best suited to have organised the deed.

Like Mary, the Privy Council was making very little serious effort to seek out the murder culprits, and there were concerted efforts at a cover-up. Almost all the depositions used as evidence were taken under torture and are hardly credible, even though corroborated from several sources. They were not made public at the time and were attested by Justice-Clerk Bellenden, who was not present when they were taken. When their evidence was eventually tabled, it implied that Bothwell and his henchmen had undertaken the King's murder unassisted by the rest of the nobility, and even that the Queen had enticed him into it. Her motive for wanting her husband's death was being explained by her being involved in a passionate romance with Bothwell.

Bothwell relied on the Craigmillar bond for protection, and only Lennox and his close allies were showing any remorse at the twenty-year-old King's death. To assure that his accomplices kept quiet, Bothwell provided them with bribes and promises of future protection. Hay and Hepburn were rewarded with fine horses. Powrie, Dalgleish and Wilson were promised positions at Hermitage and were assured, if they held their tongues: 'they should never want so long as he had anything'.[9] Paris remained for a time in Mary's employment, carrying confidential messages between her and Bothwell. Sir James Cockburn of Skirling became Governor of Edinburgh Castle. This alienated Mar, the former Governor, with his vital control of Prince James. Skirling also became Comptroller of the Household to replace Tullibardine.

Although Bothwell's power was growing, he needed a guard to travel through the streets and 'held his hand on his dagger' when meeting opponents.[10] Yet he brazened it out and, on 14 February, attended King Henry's funeral. On 7 March, he arranged Morton's formal rehabilitation. After making a humble apology for his part in Riccio's murder, Morton was restored to his estates and returned to court as Lord Chancellor. Bothwell tried to assure his loyalty by agreeing to share the government with him, but was not above circulating rumours that Morton had arranged the murder, leading Drury to believe he had been involved. In late April, Drury advised Cecil:

Morton is noted to have assured friendship with Bothwell, which, to be the thankfuller now for his favour showed him in his absence and trouble, he intendeth to continue.

Sir James Melville also confirmed that Bothwell had 'packed' up a quiet friendship with Morton.[11]

On 16 February, the first of a number of placards appeared. This accused Bothwell, Balfour, David Chalmers and 'Black' John Spens, the Queen's Advocate, who was described as 'the principal deviser of the murder, the Queen assenting thereto, through the persuasion of the Earl of Bothwell and the witchcraft' of Janet Bethune (Bothwell's former mistress and widow of Sir Walter Scott of Buccleuch). It went on to say, 'And if this is not true, [ask] Gilbert Balfour [another brother of Sir James].'[12] Chalmers was Bothwell's recent appointee as Common Clerk of Edinburgh and, according to Buchanan, had provided his garden for trysts between Bothwell and the Queen. Although Spens was later arrested, any part that either he or Chalmers played in the murder is unknown. Balfour kept out of sight and, on 26 February, returned home with an escort of thirty men by a secret way, remaining there with armed protection. On the next night, the placards accused Mary's foreign servants, Pagez, Joseph Riccio and Francisco Busso. It was to scotch this unlikely tale that Mary temporarily returned from Seton. Bothwell threatened to wash his hands in the blood of the placards' creators, if he could find them, but they were not silenced and, after a few nights, voices in the streets were shouting out that he had murdered the King.

By dawn on 11 February, the day after the murder, the news had reached Drury at Berwick some sixty miles away, and he forwarded a message to Cecil, inadvertently reporting that Lennox's body had been found beside his son. By then Drury knew from his spies in Edinburgh that the King had not been killed in the explosion, but had been suffocated. He organised agents to establish what had happened. One of them prepared a narrative drawing of the murder site, which Drury forwarded to Cecil in London. By the end of February Drury had heard that Hepburn of Bolton was one of the murderers and had lit the fuse, that Balfour had purchased the gunpowder, that it had been Cullen's idea not to rely on gunpowder alone* but to strangle the King for greater surety and that Fawdonside was with a group of horsemen in a nearby alley ready to help if called. Fawdonside later carried messages for Bothwell and was still with him at Carberry Hill.

On 14 February, Cecil was able to advise Elizabeth. The French ambassador in London immediately sent an express messenger to du Croc, who was in Dover awaiting a ship for France, asking him with all speed to advise the French court. Still believing that Lennox had been a victim, Lady

---

* As an explosives expert Cullen was almost certainly responsible for positioning the gunpowder and preparing the mine on Balfour's behalf. Although he apparently confessed to his part in the crime, he was never brought to trial, presumably because he knew too much. He took refuge in the Orkney Islands, where he remained for four years. When he unwisely returned south, Morton had him arrested and hanged.

William Howard (Margaret née Gamage), wife of the Lord Chamberlain, and Lady Cecil (Mildred née Cooke) went, on Elizabeth's instruction, to advise Lady Margaret in the Tower. She was inconsolable, and Elizabeth sent her physician with the Dean of Westminster to comfort her. On 21 February, Elizabeth asked her cousin, Sir Richard Sackville, to take Lady Margaret into his care at Sheen and eventually released her to the run-down royal palace of Coldharbour. Although Elizabeth maintained control of Templenewsam, the Lennoxes were permitted to draw on its revenue.

With the King dead, Moretta's mission (whatever it had been) could be forgotten. He quickly left Edinburgh, travelling with Father Edmund Hay to Paris to advise Mondovi. He provided two differing reports. In the first, he claimed that the King had heard a noise and looked out to see a group of armed men attempting to enter the lodging, but they found the doors locked with the keys on the inside. Having run downstairs to escape, he was intercepted and strangled on reaching the garden. The fuse was then lit to hide the evidence. Moretta changed this report when it became known that the King had climbed over the Town Wall. His second version claimed that

> the King heard a great disturbance, at least so certain women who live in the neighbourhood declare, and from a window they perceived many armed men round about the house. So he, suspecting what might befall him, let himself down from another window looking on the garden, but he had not proceeded far before he was surrounded by certain persons.[13]

After being strangled with his nightshirt, his body was dragged into the garden. This suggests that he climbed out of the window in the servants' antechamber opening onto the far side of the Town Wall. Clernault reported that the King and Taylor were found *mort et étendu* [dead and laid out], as if they had been moved from where they died.[14] He also said that McCaig's body was found dead nearby (and not in the rubble of the building as reported elsewhere). It thus seems that all the servants in the upper antechamber escaped the blast.

On 17 February, de Silva sent a report from London to Philip II in the Low Countries. He had delayed it for three days in the vain hope of hearing that the perpetrators had been arrested. On 18 February, Sebastian Pagez left Edinburgh with letters from Mary to Archbishop Bethune and Mondovi in Paris and to Elizabeth in London. Dolu, the treasurer of Mary's French dowry, went with him. She acknowledged the Archbishop's warning of a plot against her, which had arrived after the King's death. Pagez must have overplayed the strength of Mary's faith to Mondovi, who reported to Rome that she was now ready to execute the six leading Protestant lords. Yet there is no other evidence that she contemplated this. Robert Melville heard the news while travelling to London to negotiate Mary's claim to the English succession. He immediately returned to Edinburgh, but she was too distressed to receive him and 'ordered him to continue his journey as he had been previously instructed'.[15] He returned to London with the Council's official account of the murder for the English government.

The news was greeted with horror across Europe. By March, Moretta had told Giovanni Correr, the Venetian ambassador in Paris, who reported:

> It is widely believed that the principal persons of the kingdom were implicated in this act, because they were dissatisfied with the King ...'[16] This assassination is considered to be the work of the heretics, who desire to do the same to the Queen, in order to bring up the prince in their doctrines and thus more firmly establish their own religion to the exclusion of ours.[17]

Suspicions fell on Moray. Mondovi reported from Paris that he

> has always had the throne in view although he is a bastard. He is persuaded by the [Protestants] that it is his by right, especially as he maintains that his mother was secretly espoused by the King his father.[18]

Following the arrival of Moretta and Father Hay in Paris on 15 March, Mondovi added that Moray

> desires upon this occasion to murder the Earl of Bothwell, a courageous man much trusted and confided in by the Queen, with the intention of being afterwards able to lay snares for the life of Her Majesty with greater ease.

He also claimed that Moray sought

> the governorship of the Prince and, by consequence, the whole realm. If he should gain this, which may God avert, he may be able to accomplish the wicked end he has set before himself, and herein the favour of England will not be wanting. The English Queen is jealous of the Prince as the legitimate heir of both those realms, and will not omit to favour the said Moray, being bound to her by many obligations as well as religion.[19]

Although his insight into Scottish affairs was not always reliable, on this occasion he seems to have been fairly close to the truth. Yet the Edinburgh propaganda soon took effect, and Bothwell became the most likely perpetrator with Mary seen to have connived in it. Melville reported that 'everyone suspected the Earl of Bothwell and those who durst speak freely to others said plainly that it was he.'[20] Yet de Silva realised that no one would dare to accuse him openly.

Rumours of Mary's involvement in the murder continued to grow. Even the Cardinal of Lorraine ignored her, believing what he had heard in France. He wrote secretly to Moray, suggesting that they should unite to restore order and decency in Scotland. Unaware of Cecil's scheming, on 24 February Elizabeth wrote in the strongest terms to advise Mary to seek

> to preserve your honour [having heard that] instead of seizing the murderers, you are looking through your fingers while they escape ... if it be the nearest friend you have, to lay your hands upon the man who has been guilty of the crime.[21]

She knew of the rumours that accused Bothwell and wanted to avoid the ugly precedent of a queen being deposed. When faced with a similar situation, she had insisted on a proper investigation after Leicester was implicated in the death of his wife, Amy Robsart. Although he was exonerated, she gave up all thought of marrying him to avoid further political embarrassment. If Mary failed to distance herself from Bothwell, Elizabeth could never confirm her to the English succession. Renegotiation of the terms of the Treaty of Edinburgh was now forgotten; Elizabeth wanted its ratification in full. Mary was too insulted to reply. Catherine de Medici told her, through her ambassador, to 'do such justice as to the whole world may declare your innocence'.[22] Although privately she believed Mary was well rid of her foolish husband, she recognised that culprits needed to be brought to justice. When Mary failed to take action, Catherine wrote again, on behalf of both Charles IX and herself, to confirm that

> if she performed not her promise of seeking by all her power to have the death of the king their cousin revenged, and to clear herself, she should not only think herself dishonoured, but to receive them for her contraries, and that they would be her enemies.[23]

Even Archbishop Bethune, her most loyal supporter, told her 'to preserve that reputation in all godliness you have gained of long' by prosecuting those who committed the crime.[24]

In the light of all this forthright advice, Mary's failure to arrange an independent investigation was inexcusable. Yet she seemed to believe that she was at personal risk if she probed too far and chose to gloss over what had happened, fearing she could be next. She forgot that, unless justice was seen to be done, rumours of her involvement would continue to grow. The lords realised this and, as soon as they gained power, were quick to appease public opinion by bringing Bothwell's henchmen to book.

On the Continent, opinion of Mary's involvement was mixed. Some thought that she had acted out of revenge for Riccio's murder. De Alava in Paris reported to Philip II that many believed she had acted in self-defence before the King killed her, although he did not personally believe this. As he had initiated the warning of the King's scheming to Bethune, he was in a position to judge whether this posed a serious threat. He was inclined to Archbishop Bethune's view that the murder was controlled from England and aimed against the Queen as well. Cecil faced a lot of awkward criticism and, after suffering Lady Margaret's strident demands for vengeance, confessed to Drury that he wanted nothing more than to resign.

Lennox wrote to Cecil offering to collaborate with him to avenge his son's murder. Although the King had repudiated his allegiance to Elizabeth and had opposed her appointment as James's godmother, Lennox assured Cecil that he had always been her most loyal subject and 'acquaintance'. Lennox did not come to Edinburgh 'on account of the overweening power and licence of Bothwell', but he bombarded Mary with letters.[25] Despite her protestations to the contrary, he complained that she was not doing enough to bring the murderers to book and asked her to cross-examine those mentioned in the placards. As she was unaware of any evidence that would stand up to examination in court, on 1 March she wrote to him from Seton that there were so many names

> that we wot not on what ticket [placard] to proceed. But if there be any names mentioned in them that you think worthy to suffer a trial, upon your advertisement we shall stand with the cognition taking, as may stand with the laws of this realm; and, being found culpable, shall see the punishment as rigorously executed as the wickedness of the crime deserves.[26]

She was telling him that, if he brought a private prosecution, she would punish anyone found guilty. Yet Lennox had no evidence. Disillusioned, he asked Cecil for Elizabeth's help to press for a trial. He told Mary to prosecute those on the first two placards, which included Bothwell, Balfour and her foreign secretaries. Perhaps he hoped to disassociate himself from their part in his earlier plotting.

References

1. Melville, cited in Weir, p. 254
2. Weir, p. 302
3. Guy, p. 318
4. Keith, cited in Antonia Fraser, pp. 353–4, and Weir, p. 257
5. Labanoff, II, p. 3, cited in Guy, p. 300, Antonia Fraser, p. 353, and Weir, p. 257
6. Sloane MMS; CSP Spanish, cited in Weir, p. 300
7. Robert Melville to Cecil, 26 February 1567, CSP Scottish, cited in Weir, p. 307
8. Weir, p. 307
9. Weir, p. 276
10. Weir, p. 311
11. Guy, p. 304, 313
12. Keith, cited in Weir, p. 303
13. CSP Venetian, cited in Guy, p. 302 and Weir, p. 273
14. Guy, p. 303
15. CSP Spanish; cited in Weir, p. 301
16. CSP, Venetian, VII, p. 389, cited in Antonia Fraser, p. 356, and Weir, pp. 280, 324
17. CSP Venetian, VII, p. 388, cited in Antonia Fraser, p. 353, and Weir, p. 307
18. Pollen, cited in Weir, pp. 280, 320
19. Pollen, cited in Weir, p. 323
20. Melville, cited in Weir, p. 312
21. State Papers in the Public Record Office; CSP Scottish, cited in Weir, p. 308
22. Guy, p. 310
23. CSP Foreign, Drury to Cecil 30 March 1567, cited in Weir, p. 322
24. Weir, p. 318
25. Buchanan; cited in Weir, p. 306
26. Labanoff; cited in Weir, p. 314

Part 4 Playing the End Game

29

The Game of Chess

Mary and Bothwell failed to appreciate that they were pawns in a much more sophisticated game of chess being played out around them. Although Moray organised it, Cecil did everything he could to support him without becoming personally involved. Elizabeth was facing a build-up of Catholic hostility fuelled by Philip II, and Mary was the focus of every Catholic plot against her, whether from home or abroad. Cecil urgently needed secure Protestant government to be re-established in Scotland as a protection for England's northern border. Mary's marriage to King Henry had reinforced her dynastic claim if Elizabeth died childless, and, although Elizabeth had advised Parliament, immediately before the King's murder, that she would not recognise the Scottish Queen, she was still dangling the English throne before her, despite it being an anathema to Cecil.

Cecil had supported Moray in repatriating Mary from France in 1561, but she had not proved as compliant as he had hoped. Since then, her threat to English security had only increased. Moray had not been able to mould her into following his Protestant leadership. Despite showing tolerance, she remained determinedly Catholic. The English Parliament had become vociferous in its view that it would never accept a Catholic monarch, even on terms that permitted freedom of Protestant worship, and Mary had chosen a Catholic husband against English advice. Most importantly, Elizabeth had failed to resolve the succession by marrying and producing heirs of her own and was now unlikely to do so.

Cecil needed a more drastic solution. If Mary could be implicated in the plot to kill her husband, she would lose prestige as a Catholic icon, and Elizabeth would find her unacceptable as her heir. Cecil's role was to protect his mistress and secure her government. Elizabeth was unaware of his scheming and initially took steps that contradicted his objectives. She wanted the appropriate dynastic succession, even if that meant a Catholic queen, and played no part in his underhand game of chess. Yet she was eventually persuaded of the danger posed by Mary and supported her astute and loyal Secretary.

Cecil was always fully informed on events in Scotland and his detailed records are the principal source of evidence for the King's murder. He had to stop a Scottish counter-Reformation. He had persuaded Elizabeth to fund Moray's rebellion in the Chaseabout Raid and to approve Riccio's murder. He continued to see Moray, his close confidant, as the obvious choice for Scottish Regent: trustworthy, shrewd, Protestant, a proven leader and an Anglophile. When an anonymous letter arrived in Scotland reporting that Archbishop Bethune believed Moray was 'the author of the king's death', Moray admitted to Cecil, 'I am touched myself' (meaning that his involvement was being mentioned in rumours). His letter was carried south by Killigrew, Cecil's closest associate. Moray ended it by saying that 'he hath heard and seen more than I can write'.[1] This implies that Cecil and Killigrew both had an intimate understanding of Moray's plan and trusted him. Archbishop Bethune was also well informed; he 'affirmed that the assassination was controlled from England, where the intention had been to kill the queen as well'. With great prescience he wrote from Paris, 'I fear this to be only the beginning of the tragedy, and all to run from evil to worse, which I pray God of his infinite goodness to avoid.'[2]

Moray had spent much time with Cecil in England after the Chaseabout Raid making a plan for his restoration to authority. Following the Prince's birth, he could not claim the throne, but the Regency met his thirst for power just as well. After Riccio's murder, he had hoped to use the King's involvement to justify Mary's arrest, if she did not die from a miscarriage. With James yet to be born, he may then have hoped for the Crown. It was only her resourcefulness that had put paid to this. When it came to the King's murder, he advised Morton and Maitland to ensure that Bothwell organised it, so that he became the scapegoat. If he could then persuade him to become the Queen's protector by marrying her, he might be able to develop a crime of passion scenario to implicate Mary as well. If he had not thought this through at Craigmillar, this plan was fully formulated by the time of the King's death, when it was put into effect. Cecil's close involvement in the scheme can be inferred because he did nothing to discourage the hated Bothwell from taking control of government or from contemplating marriage to Mary. On the face of it, their marriage could only be to Moray's disadvantage.

Maitland supported Moray in seeking the King's removal and in wanting Bothwell out of the way. Yet they did not always see eye to eye, and Mary Fleming, who by all accounts continued to twist her husband round her little finger, might have been expected to keep him loyal to the Queen. Immediately after the murder, Maitland continued to follow his official brief of gaining for Mary the English succession. On 13 March, he wrote to Cecil accepting that this would only be realistic if she became Protestant. He promised to discuss this with her, believing that she could be persuaded after her recent financial support for the Kirk and coolness to Mondovi. Yet he had been so involved in the plan for the King's murder that for a fatal period, starting in late March 1567, he was blackmailed by Moray into helping him and later claimed that he would have been at great personal risk if he had not. He single-handedly persuaded Mary to marry his arch-enemy, Bothwell, to make the crime of passion story seem plausible, although he knew that Bothwell would be unacceptable to the English as Mary's consort on the English throne. Perhaps he hoped that later he would be able to dissuade her from the marriage, as he was to try to do at Dunbar. He also manipulated their correspondence to provide the Casket Letters as evidence of the crime of passion. He was as much the cause of Mary's downfall as Moray and Cecil, despite his later support for her in captivity. His position was impossible and, although he initially remained at court, he kept a low profile. Moray's allies doubted his loyalty, even after he left Mary's service to join them at Stirling.

Despite Morton sharing the government with Bothwell, he was never his natural ally, but was under instruction from Moray, and at the same time told Cecil that he would do 'anything in my power to gratify you as your assured friend'.[3] Moray gave Morton the task of marshalling the Scottish nobility to enable him to 'look through his fingers' from abroad as events unfolded. He had learned during the Chaseabout Raid that he could not be seen to promote himself and had to wait to be called. Although Morton had sent henchmen to assist Bothwell at Kirk o' Field, he personally kept his hands clean. His job was to entice Bothwell into believing he should marry the Queen for the security of Scotland. If this brought Mary down, Moray would become Regent. Moray and Cecil did not have to promote a crime of passion story themselves, as it was fed to the Lennox faction. It was almost certainly Tullibardine who initiated the placard campaign in Edinburgh with help from his brother, James Murray of Pardewis. He had always remained loyal to the King and was one of the few seeking justice for him.

Argyll, who remained close to Mary, provided stability by helping Bothwell in government. He too may have been acting on Moray's instruction as the means of squeezing out Atholl, with whom he remained at loggerheads. Yet Argyll's loyalty was to Mary alone and, when Bothwell sought to marry her, he temporarily joined those seeking to oust him. As soon as Bothwell was out of the way, he alienated Moray and Morton by reverting to his support for Mary. Atholl is an enigma, as he had been kept in the dark by the conspirators and was likely to seek a proper enquiry. After initially backing her marriage to the King, he had fallen out with Lennox over his son's shortcomings. Yet as a leading Catholic he was distressed by his death and, on the night afterwards, heard sounds as if the foundations of his Holyrood apartment were being undermined. After a sleepless night, he moved with his family into the town and Tullibardine went with him. Buchanan claimed that Bothwell thought they were probing too far, so 'it behoved them, for fear of their lives, to leave the court'.[4] On 26 February, Melville reported that they had been recalled to Edinburgh under penalty of rebellion.

Moray had to play his game most carefully. He had to carry the factious Scottish nobility with him and to provide incontrovertible evidence against Bothwell and Mary, when none existed. Mary remained popular despite her Catholicism. Although most of the lords at Craigmillar wanted to be rid of the King, neither Bothwell nor Huntly and the Catholics would have seen advantage in Moray replacing the Queen. Knowing that he lacked support, he gave no hint of his intentions to the bond's signatories. His failure to overthrow her in the Chaseabout Raid and her escape after the murder of Riccio had been calamitous for him. Her Catholicism alone did not provide acceptable grounds for her deposition, but her involvement in a crime of passion to murder her husband fitted the bill.

Given Bothwell's part in the King's murder, it might have seemed logical for Moray to encourage a detailed enquiry, by feeding into it sufficient information to accuse him. Yet this would incriminate most of Moray's allies as signatories of the Craigmillar bond, which Bothwell held. Other than the bond, there was very little verifiable evidence against him and none against the Queen. If Bothwell were accused, she would protect him. He had always been loyal, and it was Moray and his allies whom she mistrusted. To give veracity to the crime of passion story and to airbrush out the part played by others, he needed to demonstrate Bothwell's involvement in every stage of a murder plan that had Mary's blessing. He had to show that Bothwell and his henchmen had organised the provision of gunpowder, the lighting of the fuse and the suffocation of the King with his servant outside the Town Wall. He also had to provide incontrovertible evidence to prove it. His allies resorted to torturing witnesses to manipulate their depositions, but, despite all efforts, they often conflicted or did not follow the required line, making them implausible as evidence.

It was only in anticipation of the English Conferences more than a year after the murder that Moray and his allies began to put together the evidence they would use to back their assertions of the Queen's part in a crime of passion. While she was being held without trial at Lochleven, he had been able to avoid producing evidence on the apparent grounds of protecting her honour, but, after her escape to England, there had to be an enquiry. It was only on 27 May 1568, more than fifteen months after the King's murder, that Buchanan, now aged sixty-two, was commissioned by Moray to prepare his *Detectio*, a highly fanciful but damning account written in Latin, designed to colour public opinion against Mary. Buchanan followed the line of the Edinburgh posters that she had formed an attachment out of lust for Bothwell, such that they had worked together to bring the King back from Glasgow to Edinburgh, where Bothwell could murder him and leave them free to marry. He provided page after page of scurrilously readable tittle-tattle against the Queen written in a vitriolic style. As he had not been present, he relied on 'closed writings', which Moray sent to him. His first version became available only in early June 1568, when he referred to its hasty preparation.

At first glance, Buchanan seems an unlikely choice to be the author of a condemnation of Mary and Bothwell. He was a Classical scholar, poet and Calvinist, educated in Paris. He had helped Mary with her Latin when she returned to Scotland, assisting her in composing poetry as part of her correspondence with Elizabeth, and had written masques to entertain the court. Having eulogised on the beauty of the Maries, he had most recently written a masque extolling Mary's virtues for Prince James's christening celebrations. Yet he was brought up near Glasgow of impoverished parents, owing his education to Lennox philanthropy. While he would support Mary as the wife of a Lennox son, the King's murder made her his deadly enemy. He also owed a favour to Moray, by whom he had been appointed Principal of St Leonard's College at St Andrews University. He now used his platform as Moderator of the General Assembly to back Moray and his adherents. He was also a political theorist who advocated the republican ideals of a free state as espoused by Greece and Rome. He linked Classical ideas with Calvinist doctrine to develop a far more sophisticated thesis than Knox's *Monstrous Regiment of Women* for opposing the divine right of monarchy. Rulers were chosen to fulfil defined roles and were not above the law. If they failed in them, they could be replaced, even by tyrannicide.

Buchanan trusted Moray and may genuinely have believed that Bothwell had arranged the King's murder with Mary's connivance. In mid-1568, without close examination, people grasped at his *Detectio* as the evidence needed to incriminate her. Yet, on publication, he described it only as 'an information of probable and infallible conjecture and presumptions'. Obvious errors have been cited, but he believed the ends justified the means.

He painted the King as a saintly paragon to match the Lennox image of him and cunningly blended fact with scurrilous gossip to create a tissue of lies. It would never stand up to scrutiny to find Mary guilty of conspiracy, and it provided no credible evidence of her having advance knowledge of the plot to kill her husband.

Moray needed incontrovertible evidence. It was only in the summer of 1567, with Mary already imprisoned at Lochleven, that there is the first mention of a letter written by her being found in a silver casket in Edinburgh. This rapidly grew to a total of twenty-two documents. The lords argued that it was these that justified them rising against their anointed Queen. Yet there is conflicting evidence for the timing of the discovery. In November 1567, the lords confirmed in Parliament that they took up arms against the Queen on 15 June, as a result of seeing 'divers her privy letters'.[5] Yet in his sworn statement to Elizabeth and Cecil, Morton says that the letters were found only on 19 June, four days too late to justify them in taking action at Carberry Hill. While Moray was returning to Scotland from France in early July, he told de Silva in London of a single letter written by Mary to Bothwell from Glasgow implicating her in the murder. De Silva was also aware from du Croc of the lords' assertion that Mary was an accomplice to her husband's murder 'proved by letters under her own hand'. The casket became the purported source of all the falsified correspondence used to justify Mary's detention in England.

Modern research shows that there are obvious shortcomings in the Casket Letters, but, at the time, they seemed sufficiently plausible to keep Mary under arrest, and they have fooled generations of later historians. The English Commissioners, who knew they were flawed, never permitted their cross-examination. The limited objective was to justify retaining Mary under house arrest in England, without finding her guilty of her husband's murder, which Elizabeth wanted to avoid. The result was that Mary was indisputably wronged.

After being openly hostile to King Henry and with rumours linking him with the murder, Moray went to great lengths to clear his own name. On 13 March, he advised Cecil that he had been in St Andrews when the blast occurred. Yet Mary became very suspicious when he asked her for a passport to visit England, apparently en route for France. If innocent, he had no reason to leave. Yet he had to avoid taking part in the struggle for power that was ahead. He would not challenge Mary for the throne for a second time. As her half-brother, he could not make the perfect political alliance by marrying her. Yet he was of royal blood, had held the reins of power before and had English support. He was not walking away, but would wait to be called as regent for James. He knew only too well that, without general support, this role was a poisoned chalice. If his departure allowed Bothwell to gain control by marrying the Queen, he had evidence of his part in the King's murder with which to bring him down later. He countered rumours of his own involvement by isolating Bothwell and his henchmen as the perpetrators of the crime and by orchestrating the crime of passion story to implicate the Queen.

Moray did not leave Scotland immediately, but stayed away from Edinburgh, despite Mary's requests for assistance. He used the excuse of his wife's miscarriage to remain at St Andrews, but she was not too ill to prevent him, on 26 February, travelling to meet secretly with Morton, Lindsay of the Byres, Caithness and Atholl at Dunkeld, where they will have focused only on a mutual desire to bring Bothwell down. With Atholl present, Moray will have glossed over the Craigmillar bond and Mary's future. Morton's attendance demonstrates that his friendship with Bothwell was illusory. The meeting agreed to form a coalition of Protestant and Catholic 'Confederate' lords working for the good of Scotland. Yet, when rumours against Mary mounted, Moray had to be seen to be supportive. He did not need her brought down before Bothwell had sought to marry her. He returned to Edinburgh for a short period before 8 March to provide a steadying hand. More importantly, he was able to meet Killigrew.

Elizabeth had reappointed Killigrew as her ambassador in Scotland, ostensibly to express her concern at Mary's loss. He arrived in Edinburgh on 7 March and delivered Elizabeth's stinging letter of 24 February demanding a thorough investigation into the murder. After returning from Seton, Mary received him at Holyrood in a darkened room. Yet his main purpose was to establish from Moray how the crime of passion story was developing. After dining with Moray and his allies, he provided an official report indicating that every effort was being made to find the murderers. 'Despite great suspicions, there was no proof.' Yet he was probably trying to ensure that the Scottish lords would rebel against Mary, who was favouring Bothwell, England's enemy. Until her abduction on 24 April, the only evidence of an amorous relationship between them was in the placards, and news of her abduction could not have reached London before his departure. In all probability, he brought Cecil's sanction for Mary's deposition, but this would only be justifiable if she married Bothwell. With Cecil maintaining such detailed records, the lack of explanation for Killigrew's visit is suspicious, and Moray told Cecil that he 'hath heard or seen more than I can write'.

Jean Gordon had been so ill at the end of February that one ambassador reported her death and Bothwell began to think that he might be free to remarry Mary. By 20 March, Jean had recovered and took the first step in seeking a divorce. It is not clear what prompted her to this, although Buchanan's *Detectio* alleges that her agreement formed part of the negotiation for the return of Huntly's estates. Yet, as these were not formally restored by Parliament until 19 April, it would be surprising if she jumped the gun and, according to Drury, Huntly was reluctant to agree to the divorce (although this may not have been correct). It has also been suggested that Jean was in fear for her life, believing that her illness had been caused by poison. She had never loved Bothwell and, whatever her motive, the documentation cited his adultery with Bessie Crawford in May 1566, ten months earlier. Her action only added to speculation that Mary would marry Bothwell. Rumours of it started to circulate among Edinburgh stallholders, and when Mary rode past the Lawnmarket women cried out, 'God save your Grace if you be innocent of the King's death.'[6] Drury could soon tell Cecil that 'the judgement of the people' was that they would marry, and even the English ambassador in Paris had heard the story.[7]

The campaign of placards in Edinburgh gathered pace and focused against Bothwell. There were crude portraits of him with the words, 'Who is the king's murderer?' or 'Here is the murderer of the king', with Murray of Pardewis still believed to be behind it.[8] If Mary were not involved in a crime of passion with Bothwell, an explanation is needed on why it could have been rumoured on placards only five days after the King's murder, when there was no evidence by then of any amorous attachment between them. It is believed that Tullibardine, who had recently left Edinburgh, arranged the placards for the Lennox faction assisted by his brother, Murray of Pardewis, who was accused of it by Bothwell. Yet they were not close enough to verify the crime of passion story, and it must have been fed to them by someone who wanted to implicate Mary in the King's death. The only realistic candidates are Moray and Cecil, with assistance on the ground from Morton and Maitland. This implies that they had a well formulated plan to promote this scenario well before the King's murder. There was also a second more sophisticated source of propaganda. Both Maitland and Buchanan are plausible candidates for initiating it, but it was more realistically Cecil, who was, at the same time, employing Sir Francis Walsingham in anti-Papist propaganda in England. This new campaign was meticulously planned and, as each placard appeared, those involved made sure that the content was fed to Lennox, while Drury kept Cecil closely advised of its impact. On 1 March, Mary was depicted as a mermaid, a well-recognised synonym for a prostitute, next to a hare, which was the Bothwell crest. It is full of scurrilous Classical metaphor. In her right hand, Mary holds a large sea anemone, the symbol for female genitalia. In her left is a folded net with which to snare her prey. The hare is surrounded by swords to denote Bothwell's military standing, with one suggestively positioned as a phallic symbol. Mary was mortified and, with Bothwell, tried to establish who was behind it. They interviewed the minister of Dunfermline, who could give no help, but made Bothwell laugh by suggesting that it must have been a Papist canon who had sired three children in adultery!

The Placard of the Mermaid and the Hare. The NationalArchives/Photolibrary.com

Bothwell asked the Council to silence the propaganda. On 14 March, a warrant accused Murray of Pardewis of having 'devised, invented and caused to be set up certain painted papers upon the Tolbooth door of Edinburgh, bending to her majesty's slander and defamation'.[9] Pardewis fled to England, but offered to return to defend himself. Although he seems to have been behind the initial campaign, which aimed at having Bothwell brought to book, it is unlikely, as a Catholic, that he would have provided the smutty innuendo of the mermaid.

As criticism grew, Mary became increasingly concerned. On 19 March, with Bothwell's agreement, she arranged for James to be escorted by Argyll and Huntly to Stirling, where Mar had been newly reconfirmed as Governor. She had earlier discussed with Killigrew the possibility of sending him for his upbringing to England. Yet Elizabeth believed that this would cause Mary 'anxiety, as any little illness it might have would distress her'.[10] Elizabeth's only concern was to avoid the potential heir to the English throne being sent to France. Although Mary had considered returning there, Catherine de Medici wanted her to clear her name.

On 12 March, at the end of her mourning period, Mary was in tears while attending a requiem Mass for the King at Holyrood. She was completely distraught at a further requiem Mass on Palm Sunday, 23 March. On 30 March, Drury reported: 'She has been for the most part either melancholy or sickly ever since [the murder], and ... often swooned ... the Queen breaketh [weeps] very much.'[11] She was too stricken to correspond herself, with her letters being in Scots not French, which confirms that she did not draft them. Although she replied to Elizabeth's letter of 24 February demanding action to clear her name, this is lost. According to de Silva, who discussed it with Elizabeth, it 'contained only lamentations for the troubles she had suffered in her life, and a request that the Queen would pity her'.[12] This was no way to impress her sister Queen. Her extraordinary show of sorrow continued, when, accompanied by two of her Maries, she prayed for four hours on Good Friday, 28 March. Yet by Easter, she was back to her old self again, returning to Holyrood for dancing and banquets. It was now that Bothwell started to court her, and no one was discouraging him.

If the public was beginning to believe that Bothwell had murdered the King to marry Mary, there is no evidence that Mary even remotely considered it until her abduction. He was the one person she trusted and, without his help, she believed the Reformers would arrange for Moray to replace her. Yet the Lords were encouraging Bothwell into marriage with her. This would make a crime of passion appear plausible, but it was important that he should not be provoked. A trial for murder risked implicating Moray's allies without incriminating the Queen. Their plan required most careful handling. Many of Bothwell's principal opponents were under oath to protect him after signing the Craigmillar bond. They could not openly oppose him and needed to deflect rumour of their own involvement. If he cited the bond in his defence, he would incriminate those who were trying to bring him down.

Moray needed more evidence than the innuendo in the placards to demonstrate Mary's involvement in her husband's murder. After receiving a safe conduct from Elizabeth, he left Edinburgh on 7 April,* five days before the trial. This left Bothwell overjoyed. Yet Moray was focused on implicating Mary and, to this end, Bothwell was being maliciously encouraged by Morton and Maitland into marrying her. This suited Moray and Cecil perfectly.

References

1. CSP Scottish, Moray to Cecil, 13 March 1567; cited in Weir, pp. 280, 321
2. Teulet, cited in Guy, p. 313 and Weir, pp. 284, 316
3. Guy, p. 313
4. Weir, p. 299
5. Acts of Parliament; T. F. Henderson, *The Casket Letters and Mary Queen of Scots*, Appendix D, p. 177, cited in Antonia Fraser, p. 407
6. Guy, p. 321
7. J. Robertson, p. 53; CSP, Foreign, VIII, p. 198; Gore-Browne, p. 374, cited in Antonia Fraser, p. 360
8. CSP Scottish, cited in Guy, p. 309, and Weir, p. 312
9. Register of the Privy Council of Scotland, I, p. 500; Anderson, cited in Antonia Fraser, p. 359, and Weir, p. 322
10. CSP Spanish, cited in Weir, p. 327
11. Keith, II, p. 532; CSP Foreign, VIII, p. 198, cited in Antonia Fraser, pp. 360–1, and Weir, p. 328
12. CSP Spanish, cited in Weir, p. 329
13. CSP Spanish, De Silva to Philip II, 21 April 1567; cited in Weir, p. 331

---

* While in London, Moray justified his departure to de Silva by saying that 'he did not intend to return until the Queen had punished the persons concerned in her husband's death, as he thought it was unworthy of his position to remain in a country where so strange and extraordinary a crime went unpunished. He believed that the truth might certainly be ascertained if due diligence were shown.'[13] This unctuous stance did not impress Archbishop Bethune, who warned de Alava that, despite his show of loyalty to Mary, he was in reality her deadly enemy. Before his departure, he appointed Mary as guardian of his infant daughter and would not have chosen her if he believed her guilty. He must have been confident that his supporters in Scotland would bring Mary and Bothwell down as soon as they married, and he could rely on Cecil.

30

Bothwell's Trial and its Aftermath

For those who argue that Mary was uninvolved in the conspiracy for the murder of her husband (and this account takes that view), the most difficult issue is to explain why Mary should have condoned a whitewash for Bothwell's trial with no evidence being presented. All the early commentators accepted the view of the propaganda that she had been involved with him in an amorous attachment and wanted to avoid a proper investigation. They thought she was completely in his thrall and was involved in a crime of passion. Yet there is no reliable evidence for this. It is argued that she was suffering a mental breakdown caused by her earlier illness and depression. Yet this was not in character and conflicts with her behaviour when Riccio was murdered, when in Glasgow in the previous month, and at Borthwick a month later.

We know from Mary's correspondence that she thought the King's murder was also aimed against her, and Moray was behind a conspiracy to bring her down. He was most suspiciously seeking to leave Scotland at a time when he had everything to gain if she was removed from the throne. The murder was much more likely to involve Moray or the returning exiles than Bothwell, who had been with her for most of the day beforehand. She was aware of the Reformers' long-standing objective of creating a Scottish republic. Their action to depose Mary's mother as Regent had begun a pattern of events, which continued with the Chaseabout Raid, the murder of Riccio and now the death of the King, all aimed at bringing down the Stuart dynasty. The nobility had another reason for acting against Mary. In December 1567, she would be twenty-five, the age when Scottish kings could revoke grants of land given during their earlier years. Most of the nobility had benefited, and she believed that they wanted her deposed to avoid their recall.

The only man Mary trusted for support was Bothwell, but she had been advised from several sources, including the placards in Edinburgh, that he had organised the murder. An enquiry might implicate the one man capable of protecting her throne, although, from what she knew, she would expect him to be exonerated. Instead of investigating further, she unwisely provided him with the church vestments taken from Strathbogie to make clothing, and reduced the forfeitures on a number of those who had been at Craigmillar. This implied that she was involved in a pay-off. Yet all her close advisers were discouraging her from holding a trial and, when Lennox forced her into it, the Privy Council so arranged it that his acquittal was a formality. The Council, with Bothwell present, met on Good Friday, 27 March, to assure this. Only Lennox, whom Mary despised and mistrusted, actively sought evidence against him, and, if she had pressed for it herself, she risked losing the one supporter who might protect her throne. On 24 March, at Lennox's insistence, Mary at last set 12 April as the date for Bothwell's trial. It was bound to be a whitewash. In his memoirs, Bothwell claimed to have called for it to silence the innuendo in the placards, and Mary seemed confident that he would be exonerated.

On 5 April, a Privy Council meeting was held at Seton, where it is alleged that Mary and Bothwell signed marriage contracts. There were two differing versions among the Casket Letters, one in French and one in Scots. Neither is dated, but it was claimed that each was completed on 5 April. As this predated Bothwell's trial, it implied that Mary had agreed to their marriage before he had been cleared and before his divorce from Jean Gordon, adding to the evidence of a crime of passion. The one in French has been thought to be an original document in Maitland's hand.* If so, it is the only original among the Casket Letters to have survived. The lords explained it by saying, 'Although some words therein seem to the contrary, they suppose [the contract] to have been made and written by her before the death of her husband.' Certainly the words are 'contrary' as they refer to her 'late husband Henry Stuart called Darnley', who had died on 10 February. [2] They also state that Bothwell was free to marry. This implies that it was written after his divorce from Jean Gordon on 3 May, which post-dated his trial on 12 April. Despite the claim that it was signed on 5 April, it includes extracts from the Ainslie's Tavern bond† not prepared until two weeks later. The one in Scots is only known through a transcript attached as an appendix to Buchanan's *Detectio*. Huntly is reputed to have witnessed it, implying that he approved of the marriage, although this would contradict Casket Letters VI and VII. If

---

* There is doubt about the authenticity of the French version as the Journal of the Commission records that this was written in a Roman hand in French, but the existing one is in an English hand. Although apparently signed by Mary, her signature is indisputably forged.[1]

† In addition to the extract from the Ainslie's Tavern bond, John Guy points out that it also refers to the gathering at Ainslie's Tavern because it says that Mary 'among the rest' had chosen Bothwell, which can only have been at that meeting held on 19 April.[3]

the contracts are not complete forgeries, both appear to have been written much later than 5 April. They thus lose relevance as incriminating evidence. Neither of them is the marriage contract which Mary and Bothwell indisputably signed, as would be usual, on 14 May, the day before their wedding.

Having pressed Mary to hold Bothwell's trial as soon as practicable, Lennox was left with insufficient time to gather evidence. Although treason trials required forty days' notice, Mary had wanted it resolved before Parliament met, and the Council agreed to fifteen days. Realising that there would be no prosecution unless he arranged it, Lennox wrote to Elizabeth on 4 April for help in seeking a delay. He was also concerned for his security after hearing that bonds were being signed by those he planned to prosecute. Yet he continued gathering evidence, and requested immunity from prosecution for Murray of Pardewis, so that he could be recalled from England. No doubt at Bothwell's persuasion, Mary refused this.

On 10 April, Lennox left Glasgow with 3,000 men. On reaching Linlithgow, he was advised that he would be limited by law to six supporters on arrival in Edinburgh. Yet he knew that Bothwell had 4,000 men there, and Mary was not insisting on them being reduced to the four permitted. Lennox again asked for time to obtain such evidence 'as the truth shall be known', without which 'you shall have not just trial'. When Mary would not agree, he returned to Glasgow.

Understanding Lennox's predicament, Elizabeth wrote to Mary seeking a postponement. She advised her to

> use such sincerity and prudence in this case, which touches you so closely, that all the world shall have reason to pronounce you innocent of a crime of such enormity, a thing which if you do it not, you would deserve to fall from the ranks of princesses.[4]

She wanted Bothwell brought to book to prevent Mary from marrying him, fearing that they would renew the Auld Alliance with France. Yet Elizabeth's ministers knew the game plan. They saw that Mary would be irretrievably damaged if she subsequently married Bothwell after a dubious acquittal. Elizabeth's letter arrived in Edinburgh at six o'clock on the morning of the trial, carried by John Selby, Provost Marshal of Berwick. Bothwell's kinsman, Thomas Hepburn, the Parson of Oldhamstocks, advised Selby to withdraw, as 'he saw no likelihood of any convenient time to serve his turn until after the assize'. Cockburn of Skirling then asked Selby if the letter was from Elizabeth or Cecil. Being told that Elizabeth had sent it, Cockburn told him, 'Then ye shall be soon discharged', and Hepburn escorted him from the premises. Selby continued waiting and, after ten o'clock Maitland and Bothwell appeared. They demanded the letter and took it indoors. When Maitland reappeared, Selby asked if the Queen had seen it, but he replied that, 'as yet, the Queen was sleeping, and therefore he had not delivered the letter, and that there would not be any meet time for it till after the assize.'[5] Yet he was caught out when Selby saw her at a window with Mary Fleming. This was a blatant breach of diplomatic etiquette to prevent the trial being delayed.

Bothwell set out for his trial riding ahead of his 4,000 men on the King's horse. The Queen gave him a friendly toss of the head, and there was a 'merry and lusty cheer' as he processed in state down the Canongate.[6] He was flanked by Morton and Maitland, his two traditional enemies, with 200 hackbutters. Argyll, the Justice-General, and Huntly presided as chief judges attended by four assessors, Lindsay, Robert Pitcairn, Commendator of Dumfermline, MacGill and a well-reputed Protestant lawyer, Henry Balnaves. With the judges assured of supporting an acquittal, the jury was drawn from all factions of the nobility. Their chancellor was the unsavoury Caithness, who had attended the meeting at Dunkeld aimed at bringing Bothwell down, although his son was by then betrothed to Bothwell's sister, Jean. The jury included two close Bothwell allies, Cockburn of Skirling and Mowbray of Barnbougle, and two Lennox supporters, Sempill and Ross. The remainder probably mistrusted him, but supported Mary. These were Cassillis, Rothes, Lord John Hamilton, recently returned from Italy, Boyd, Herries, Oliphant, John, Master of Forbes, Sir John Gordon of Lochinvar, Sir John Somerville of Cambusnethan and Ogilvy of Boyne. They were no doubt aware of what was expected of them. As the King's kinsman, Morton was excused from serving. In reality he wanted to avoid having to confirm Bothwell's innocence.

The trial started at noon and lasted seven hours. Lennox was represented by the capable Robert Cunningham, who immediately requested a forty-day adjournment to give more time to prepare his case. Bothwell's procurators countered this by tabling Lennox's request for 'a short and summary process'.[7] Cunningham then produced Lennox's letter to the Queen, naming those listed in the first two placards, but did not offer evidence. The jury retired and returned after a decent interval to acquit Bothwell of being 'art and part of the slaughter of the king'. Melville was later to state that they had acted 'some for fear, some for favour, and the greatest part in expectation of advantage'.[8] The hackbutters outside were no doubt intimidating. Yet, without evidence, the result was inevitable, and the Court Recorder wrote that 'Bothwell was made clean of the said slaughter, albeit that it was heavily murmured that he was guilty thereof'.[9]

The only concession to this travesty of justice was to give permission for a retrial, if evidence came forward in future. Bothwell immediately sent out a crier pronouncing his innocence and was prepared to fight anyone doubting it in single combat. A placard was posted by someone offering to prove that Bothwell was the 'chief author of the foul and horrible murder by law of arms', but no one appeared.[10] Yet the mud continued to fly, and Buchanan recorded that after 'this jolly acquittal ... suspicion was increased and retribution seemed only to be postponed.'[11] This made the other conspirators in the King's murder very nervous. Mary rejected Balfour's request for a similar trial, and his house remained protected by guards day and night. When he heard that one of his servants was planning to claim the reward by giving evidence against him, he arranged for him to be killed and secretly buried at night.

With the case settled, Mary implicated herself further by showering Bothwell with benefits. On 14 April, he carried the sceptre, while Argyll held the crown and Crawford the sword of state at the opening of Parliament. This was intended as an endorsement of his innocence and, at the Queen's request, he was granted Dunbar Castle to reward his 'great and manifold services'.[12] After having sold land to Home to resolve his financial commitments undertaken on the Crown's behalf, he also received the principal estates of the Earldom of March in recompense. In addition to the church vestments from Strathbogie provided to him before his trial, Mary now gave him genet fur from one of her mother's dresses to make a nightgown and, more naively, horses and rich clothing previously belonging to the King. The tailor making the alterations remarked that 'it was but right and according to the custom of the country for the clothes of the deceased to be given to the executioner'.[13]

Bothwell had to take control, and the remaining actions of Parliament have his stamp on them. Mary was provided with a guard of hackbutters in place of her traditional bailiffs. An Act concerning Religion gave Crown protection to the Kirk. In a step that she had previously avoided, Mary made Protestantism her official religion, despite still attending Catholic services in private. Bothwell's supporters replaced her more hostile advisers in key positions. Huntly was secretly promised the Lord Chancellorship in thanks for assuring Bothwell's acquittal at his trial. He replaced Morton, who was starting to be mistrusted. On 19 April, Huntly, Sutherland and their allies were officially confirmed back to their estates, although, in Huntly's case, this had been informally agreed two years earlier. To smooth the divorce from Jean Gordon, he received other parts of the March estates at Dunbar. Eleven forfeitures on dissident Protestants, including Morton and Argyll, were reduced. Argyll was granted estates previously belonging to the King. On 17 May, Boyd became a Privy Councillor and received other Lennox property. It all seemed like a pay-off. With his estates being usurped, Lennox realised his precarious position and left for England.

The restoration of the Sutherland estates resulted in tragedy. On 18 June, Sutherland went with his wife and fifteen-year-old son Alexander to hunt at Helmsdale Castle as guests of Isabel Sinclair, the widow of his great-uncle, Gilbert Gordon of Gartray. Her son, John, was next in line to the Sutherland earldom after Alexander. Isabel was a cousin of the reprehensible Caithness, who had persuaded her to arrange a dinner to poison Sutherland and his son so that her own son, John, would inherit the Sutherland earldom. This would enable the Sinclairs to take effective control of the Sutherland estates. At the dinner after the hunt, Isabel provided ale, which had been poisoned. Sutherland and his wife fell ill and, suspecting treachery, stopped Alexander, who returned later, from taking the meal being kept for him. Although they returned to Dunrobin, they died five days later. Isabel's son, John, was another victim, after inadvertently drinking the poisoned ale. In August, Isabel was sentenced to death after being found guilty of murder, but took her own life in Edinburgh Castle. Caithness still managed to become the young Sutherland's guardian and arranged for him to marry his 32-year-old daughter Barbara. This misalliance ended in divorce after five years, and she died a year later. Sutherland later remarried Jean Gordon, whose equally unhappy marriage to Bothwell had also been annulled.

Bothwell's dominance in government caused concern. As late as 13 March, Maitland, who was still trying to promote Mary's claim to the English throne, was advising her to marry a Protestant husband acceptable to the English, such as Leicester. Yet most Scots, particularly the Catholics, believed a fellow Scot would assure their independence. This played into Moray's hands. With a Catholic being unacceptable to the Reformers, he persuaded them that the Anglophobe Bothwell was the next best thing, but, when Mary accepted him, Moray quickly turned them against the couple.

On 19 April, at the end of the sitting of Parliament, Bothwell entertained twenty-eight members of the nobility to dinner at Ainslie's Tavern near Holyrood, ostensibly to celebrate his acquittal. With his guests well wined and dined, he produced a document intended as a bond. In addition to confirming his innocence, it suggested that the Queen was 'now destitute of a husband, in the which solitary state the commonwealth of this realm may not permit Her Highness to continue and endure'. It proposed that she should marry him, given his 'affectionate and hearty service . . . and his other good qualities', particularly as she might prefer 'one of her native-born subjects unto all foreign subjects'.[14] He will have needed tacit encouragement from Morton* (and probably even from Moray, who was still in Scotland despite his non-attendance) to make this proposal. By falling into their trap, he also helped to snare Mary. The bond called for signatories to back him for the sake of the realm. In return, they would be protected from prosecution for any past offences. It has been said that he kept his 200 hackbutters outside as an 'inducement', but, in all probability, he only sent the document round for signature on the following morning.[15] Cecil's copy indicates that all the lords signed, but this is not the case. It is known that the signatories included Morton, Huntly, Sutherland, Caithness, Rothes, Cassillis, Seton, Fleming, Sinclair, Boyd, Glamis, Sempill, Ross, Herries, Archbishop Hamilton and six bishops. It is also known that Argyll, deeply offended at Bothwell's presumption, and Eglinton refused to sign. Maitland, Atholl, Glencairn, Home, Lindsay of the Byres, Kirkcaldy and Sir James Melville neither attended the dinner nor signed it. Atholl will have been following Maitland's advice, but seemed to accept Moray's cynical assertion that Bothwell offered the best way of assuring Scottish independence. We know that Kirkcaldy always hated Bothwell. Despite his obsession with honour, he was an English spy, providing regular reports to Bedford, and had been at university with Randolph in Paris. Immediately after the dinner, he wrote to Bedford that the guests signed in

> fear of their lives and against honour and conscience and that if Mary will pursue revenge for the murder, she will win the hearts of all honest Scotsmen again.

He went on to say:

> She cares not to lose France, England and her own country for him, and will go with him to the world's end in a white petticoat before she leaves him ... Whatever is unhonest reigns presently in our court.[16]

Yet there is no contemporary record to suggest that she contemplated marrying him prior to seeing the Ainslie's Tavern bond. She told the Bishop of Dunblane that it was only when he started to play suit that he showed it to

---

* Although Morton signed the bond, his relationship with Bothwell was already strained, with the Chancellorship having been offered to Huntly. The fact that he signed has to be seen as further evidence of the crime of passion conspiracy. Yet it was he who insisted that Bothwell should not become King or wield royal powers on marriage.

her. Although there is a report that Bothwell took a marriage contract in Huntly's hand to Ainslie's Tavern to induce the guests to sign, those found in the casket could not have been prepared until later (and may have been outright forgeries).

While Mary relied on Bothwell, she did not always follow his advice and had ample opportunity to see his rougher side. When, on the day after the dinner, soldiers at Holyrood mutinied for lack of pay, Bothwell held their captain by the throat and swore profanely when they forced him to let go. Mary immediately produced 400 crowns from her purse to settle their arrears. Earlier while at Seton, an elderly former servant of the King had humbly asked Mary 'to give him some release' in his poverty. She was about to help him, when Bothwell struck him for his effrontery, shouting, 'Thou custrel, go thy ways! I shall so release you that you shall be sorry with yourself, churl!' The man was left with blood pouring from his mouth as he limped home, where he died two hours later.[17]

Armed with the Ainslie's Tavern bond and accompanied by Maitland and Patrick Bellenden, Bothwell went to see Mary, who had returned to Seton at the end of Parliament. He showed her the signatures supporting their marriage, but she turned down his suit, telling the Bishop of Dunblane that 'our answer was in no degree correspondent with his desire'.[18] She knew that their marriage would fatally prejudice relations with England and there were continuing rumours of his part in her husband's murder. Although he seemed to accept this with a good grace, the Council still offered him active support. Mary told Nau that she was

> circumvented on all sides by persuasions, requests, and importunities; both by general memorials signed by their hands, and presented to her in full council, and by private letters.[19]

Acting on instructions from the Privy Council, Maitland was sent, on 20 April, to speak to her privately to add his persuasion for the marriage, despite his hatred of Bothwell and his knowledge that it would destroy Mary's ambition to be recognised as Elizabeth's heir. It seems hardly credible that he should encourage her to marry the man who had kept him out of favour after Riccio's murder and had refused to hand back his estates after their release from attainder. Although he may have feared Bothwell revealing his part in the murder plan, the danger of this had disappeared with Bothwell's acquittal eight days earlier. Much has been made of Mary Fleming's influence on keeping Maitland loyal to Mary, but he knew that his role was to implicate the Queen in a crime of passion. Moray must have put pressure on him, and he felt sufficiently threatened that he also prepared the Casket Letters as the evidence. While his non-attendance at Ainslie's Tavern may seem surprising, he had always tried to avoid signing anything conspiratorial. When Maitland met Mary, he cited her recent lack of leadership, and advised that

> it had become absolutely necessary that some remedy should be provided for the disorder into which public affairs of the realm had fallen for want of a head.

He explained that it had been

> unanimously resolved to press her to take Bothwell for her husband. They knew he was a man of resolution, adapted to rule, the very character needed to give weight to the decisions and actions of the Council. All of them therefore pleaded in his favour.

When she expressed concern at continuing rumours of his part in the King's death, he responded

> that Lord Bothwell had been legally acquitted by the Council. They who made this request to her did so for the public good of the realm.

This was persuasive and she 'began to give ear to their overtures, without letting it be openly seen'.[20] Bothwell had been loyal and was a brave leader, a good administrator and powerful personality. Their marriage would strengthen the government, but, contrary to the propaganda, it was not an insatiable love match.

It is an irony that it was Maitland and Kirkcaldy, with their intense hatred of Bothwell, who linked up as Mary's most fervent supporters in captivity. Maitland tipped the balance in favour of her marrying him and Kirkcaldy considered her so 'far past all shame' by doing so.

References

1. Public Record Office, London, SP/52/2; Cecil Papers 252/1–4; Cotton MSS: Caligula, 1, folio 271; Goodall, Casket Letters, II, p. 54; Hosack, I, p. 549
2. Guy, p. 401, and Antonia Fraser, p. 467
3. Guy, p. 400

4. Weir, p. 333
5. Drury to Cecil, 15 April 1567, in Tytler; cited in Guy, pp. 323–4, and Weir, pp. 337–8
6. Drury to Cecil, 15 April 1567, in Tytler; cited in Guy, p. 324, and Weir, p. 338
7. Weir, p. 339
8. Melville, cited in Weir, p. 339
9. Diurnal of Occurrents, p. 108, cited in Antonia Fraser, p. 361, and Weir, p. 340
10. Antonia Fraser, p. 361, and Weir, p. 340
11. Buchanan, *Detectio*, cited in Weir, p. 340
12. Keith II, p. 558, cited in Weir, p. 341
13. Guy, p. 320, and Weir, p. 302
14. Keith, II, p. 562, Cotton MMS; CSP Scottish; Anderson, Collections, cited in Guy, p. 326, Antonia Fraser, p. 362, and Weir, p. 344
15. Weir, p. 345
16. Kirkcaldy to Bedford, 20 April 1567, State Papers in the Public Record Office, cited in Guy, p. 327, and Weir, pp. 343, 348
17. Guy, p. 322
18. Labanoff; cited in Weir, p. 346
19. Nau, p. 37; cited in Antonia Fraser, p. 363, and Weir, p. 347
20. Nau, cited in Antonia Fraser, p. 363, and Weir, pp. 346–7

31

Mary's Abduction and her Marriage to Bothwell

On 21 April 1567, Mary returned to Edinburgh to sign papers. Later that day, she set out secretly for Stirling to visit James, now aged ten months, for what would be their last meeting. Maitland, Huntly and Sir James Melville escorted her with thirty armed horsemen. While there, in the only letter she wrote in the month before her marriage, she told Mondovi, who was back in Turin:

> I beg of you to speak well of me to His Holiness, and not to let anyone persuade him to the contrary concerning the devotion I have to die in the Catholic faith and for the good of his church.[1]

This implies that it was written after she had decided to marry Bothwell. Mondovi had already said that she would need a husband for protection and had suggested Bothwell, 'who has ever been the Queen's most trusty and obedient adherent'.[2]

Bothwell did not go to Stirling, but remained in Edinburgh, where he raised a force on the pretext of going after Borderers, who had recently despoiled Biggar. Yet by 23 April, Lennox in Glasgow had 'heard from a well-informed source' that he was planning to kidnap the Queen.[3] On 29 April, Lennox left for England, not wanting to be in Scotland if they should marry. The kidnap plan was corroborated by Kirkcaldy; Bothwell may have leaked it to avoid causing a surprise. On 22 April, Kirkcaldy told Bedford:

> I doubt not but you have heard Bothwell had gathered many of his friends, some say to ride in Liddesdale, but I believe it not, for he is minded to meet the Queen this day, Thursday, and to take her by the way and bring her to Dunbar. Judge you if it be with her will or no.[4]

Buchanan claimed that Mary went to Stirling with a plan to move control of the Prince from Mar to Bothwell, who did not consider it to his own security to protect a boy who might one day become the avenger of his father's death; and he wanted no other to stand in the way of his own children in line of succession to the throne.[5]

Mar, who attended the Confederate meeting at Stirling four days later, thwarted this by retaining the Prince under his control at all times and, without Bothwell being there, Mary had no forcible means of abducting him. Drury even claimed that she had tried to poison the Prince with an apple, but he refused it, and a greyhound which ate it died. With her overriding determination to protect her precious son, this has to be another malicious falsehood.

After spending 22 April at Stirling, Mary left on the next morning without James, after pressing Mar 'to be vigilant and wary that he was not robbed of her son'.[6] She suffered a severe abdominal pain after leaving and rested at a cottage before reaching Linlithgow in the evening. Meanwhile, Bothwell had assembled 800 horse at Calder Castle, south-west of Edinburgh, from where he rode to Linlithgow to ask Huntly for help in abducting the Queen. Huntly's refusal to assist implies that Mary was unaware of Bothwell's plan. Yet Moray's allies spread rumours that she had colluded in her abduction; this would make the crime of passion story seem more plausible. Drury reported that, despite appearing to be taken by force, she had agreed to go with him.

Casket Letters VI, VII and VIII and the French love poem were produced as the evidence of Mary's collusion in her abduction. Casket Letter VI records Mary's mistrust for Huntly and is endorsed, 'From Stirling afore the ravissement – proves her mask [pretence] of ravishing.'[7] The letter exists in both a French transcript and an English translation. It has been seen as significant that the French version is written in an italic script unlike the English hand of the other letters, leading to speculation that it is the original missing document not returned by Moray to Morton in 1571. Italic script was generally used only by those brought up on the Continent, but it is not Mary's writing and is probably a transcript made by a secretary who happened to use italic calligraphy. It says:

Alas, my Lord, why is your trust put in a person so unworthy to mistrust that which is wholly yours? ... You had promised me ... that you would send me word every day what I should do. You have done nothing thereof. I advertise you well to take heed of your false brother-in-law. He came to me ... to say what he was to write on my behalf to explain...where and when you should come to me, ... and thereupon hath preached unto me that it was a foolish enterprise, and that with mine honour, I could never marry you, seeing that you being married, you did carry me away ... he is all contrary ... I told him ... that no persuasion nor death itself would make me fail of my promise. As touching the place ... Choose it yourself and send me word of it ... And seeing that your negligence doth put us both in danger of a false brother, if it succeed not well, I will never rise again ... I wish I were dead. For I see everything is going badly. You promised something very different in your prediction, but absence have power over you that have two strings to your bow.[8]

The letter is intended to imply that Bothwell has failed to tell Mary where he planned to kidnap her. She believes that, by sending Huntly, who disapproves of the marriage, he is risking it becoming known that she has colluded in her abduction. She fears that Bothwell is not getting on with it, as he still has 'two strings' (Mary and Jean Gordon).

Yet Huntly had already given approval for Bothwell to divorce his sister and did not criticise Mary until his argument with her at Dunbar. There is no record that he left her at either Stirling or Linlithgow to carry messages to Bothwell. It was Bothwell who came to him. Buchanan's *Detectio* also differs from Casket Letter VI as he claims that Mary had agreed with Bothwell where she would be abducted before going to Stirling. Casket Letter VI seems to be a transcript of a later genuine letter which Mary wrote to Bothwell from Dunbar, but predated to make it look as if it were from Stirling. By then Jean's divorce papers had been filed, and Huntly had quarrelled with Mary, as is confirmed in her correspondence with Robert Melville and the Bishop of Dunblane. Her letter shows her agitation that she is risking everything. Even Cecil's clerk realised that the English version had been predated as he corrected present to past tenses in a couple of places to show that it was written after her abduction, and headed it, 'Copie from Stirling after the ravissement'. Yet, if sent afterwards, it lost its point to provide evidence of a crime of passion. Even Cecil showed he was not above a little manipulation of his own, as he changed 'after' to 'afore'.[9]

No contemporary copy of Casket Letter VII survives, but the transcript shows that it was intended to be the second in a sequence of letters written by Mary from Stirling. It continues in a vein similar to Casket Letter VI, saying:

Of the place and time, I remit myself to your brother [Huntly] and to you. I will follow him and will fail in nothing on my part. He finds many difficulties. I think he does advertise you thereof and what he desires for the handling of himself. As for the handling of myself, I heard it once well devised. Methinks that your services, and the long amity, having the good will of the Lords, do well deserve a pardon, if above the duty of a subject you advance yourself, not to constrain me, but to assure yourself of such place near to me, that other admonitions or foreign persuasions may not let me from consenting to that that ye hope your service shall make me a day to attend. And to be short, to make yourself sure of the Lords and free to marry, and that you are constrained for your surety, and to be able to serve me faithfully, to use a humble request joined to an importune action. And to be short, excuse yourself, and persuade them the most you can, that you are constrained to make pursuit against your enemies. You shall say enough, if the matter or ground do like you, and many fair words to Lethington. If you like not the deed, send me word, and leave not the blame of all unto me.[10]

If genuine, the letter confirms that Mary knew of her abduction in advance and, by proposing that Bothwell deserves to be pardoned, it implicates her in the murder. Yet, if Casket Letter VI was written after the abduction, as seems certain, and this is intended to be before it, it can only be a complete forgery attempting to overcome the shortcomings of the earlier letter. It avoids mentioning any row with Huntly at this early stage, but demonstrates Mary's collusion in her abduction by telling Bothwell how to react. As a forgery, it shows remarkable insight. It is aware that there are 'other admonitions and foreign persuasions' disapproving of the marriage.[11] It knows that Bothwell has enemies, who need to be placated. As it singles out Lethington to receive 'many fair words', it must be concluded that Maitland wrote it. He hated Bothwell and wanted those seeing it to understand his behind the scenes efforts to oppose the marriage.

Casket Letter VIII was deemed to be the third in the same sequence of letters sent to Bothwell by Mary from Stirling, although she was not there for long enough for a third delivery. It refers to Huntly as 'your brother-in-law that was', who has come to her 'very sad' and in fear that he is acting treasonably.[12] Yet Bothwell had not by then divorced Jean Gordon. As it also mentions Sutherland being present, it fits as a genuine letter, written to Bothwell – by then her husband – at Melrose while she was at Borthwick. It will be discussed in that context.

It was also claimed that Mary wrote a long love poem to Bothwell from Stirling. Its twelve verses each take the form of a sonnet on a separate page.

They show her infatuation for a man to whom she has pledged her son, her honour, her life, her country and her subjects. Yet Mar had already prevented James being pledged to Bothwell. In line seventeen, it describes Scotland as 'my country', but Mary would always have referred to 'my Kingdom' or 'my Realm'.[13] Buchanan claimed that it was composed 'while her husband lived, but certainly before [Bothwell's] divorce from his wife', and he admired its 'tolerable elegance'.[14] Yet both Brantôme and Ronsard felt that its French was too unpolished to have been written by Mary, who was well trained in courtly phrasing and analogy, and its scansion is faulty. Buchanan probably wrote it himself and, despite its shortcomings, would have been one of the few in Scotland capable of it.

On 24 April, the royal party left Linlithgow, but when they approached the River Almond six miles from Edinburgh, Bothwell appeared from Calder, supported by 800 men with swords drawn. The royal party halted and Bothwell rode forward to take the Queen's bridle, as if she were captive. He told her that an insurrection was threatened in Edinburgh and he would take her to Dunbar for safety. Neither Mary nor her entourage seemed to believe this, but, when those around her prepared to defend her, she agreed to go with him 'rather than bloodshed and death should result'.[15] Huntly, Maitland and Melville went with her.

Mary's lack of resistance has added to the speculation of her collusion in her abduction. This was a critical argument for those who wanted to imply that she was involved in a crime of passion. Yet she sent James Borthwick into Edinburgh to warn the Provost and there is no plausible evidence to verify her collusion. There can be little doubt that she was abducted without forewarning. Yet Paris claimed that Black Ormiston spoke with Maitland at Linlithgow on the night before, implying that Maitland had been told, and Lennox and Kirkcaldy certainly knew in advance. Kirkcaldy told Bedford that 'the Queen was minded to cause Bothwell to ravish [seize] her', so that they could speed up their marriage, 'which she has promised before she caused murder her husband'. Given Kirkcaldy's later loyalty, he must have come to realise that this was a falsehood. It is only the falsified Casket Letters that suggest that Mary was also aware of his plan. If she had agreed to it in advance, Huntly would have assisted Bothwell, but he refused. Mary did not resist as she trusted Bothwell and wanted to avoid conflict. Although the Edinburgh town bell was rung to call the citizens 'to armour and weapons', there was little that could be done on foot against Bothwell's mounted force.[16] Despite being Bothwell's ally, Cockburn of Skirling trained the Castle guns on the royal party as they rode by safely out of range and they arrived at Dunbar, forty miles away, unchallenged well after midnight.

Those seeking to exonerate Mary claim she was raped by Bothwell at Dunbar and agreed to marriage only because of the resultant risk of being pregnant. She certainly wanted to give this impression. In two letters to France she claimed to have been taken by force. *The Diurnal of Occurrents* records that Bothwell 'ravished her and took her to his castle'.[17] Yet the word 'ravish' at this time meant 'seize'. She was certainly seized, but was she raped? With Dunbar full of people, she could have screamed for help. She was there for twelve days with her servants and advisers, and Bothwell was not always with her. On 26 April, he returned to Edinburgh with Mary's encouragement to assist in Jean Gordon's Protestant divorce petition. By then she had agreed to marry him – hardly likely if she had been raped.

Some have said that, despite having raped her, Bothwell was the first man to satisfy Mary sexually. The idea of rape providing sexual satisfaction is absurd and there will be evidence that his sexual methods did not appeal to her. Her relationship with King Henry, initially at least, was indisputably passionate, and Bothwell was the antithesis of the long-limbed androgynous man that seemed to attract her. After King Henry, Mary never allowed her heart to rule her head. There is no record of her succumbing to impropriety during her imprisonment, despite having admirers. She showed no lingering affection for Bothwell after they parted at Carberry Hill and never offered him sympathy in his later captivity.

A fortnight later, Mary sent an account of her abduction to the Bishop of Dunblane, explaining that Bothwell had

> asked pardon of the boldness he had taken to convey us to one of our own houses, whereunto he was driven by force, as well as constrained by love, the vehemence whereof had made him to set apart the reverence which naturally, as our subject, he bore us, as also for safety of his own life.[18]

If this suggests that she was flattered by his show of affection, she later expressed her indignation to Nau at what had happened, particularly as the pretext of an uprising in Edinburgh proved to be a fabrication. According to Nau, after arriving at Dunbar, she complained at her treatment to Bothwell, who retorted that

> she was in one of her own houses, that all her domestics were around her, that she could remain there in perfect liberty and freely exercise her lawful authority. Practically, however, all happened very differently,

for the greater part of her train was removed, nor had she full liberty until she had consented to the marriage, which had been proposed by the Lords of the Council.[19]

She later claimed to have 'sent secretly to the Governor of the town of Dunbar to sally out with his troops and rescue her', but no one came.[20] Bothwell saw her privately to explain that, although everyone claimed to be his friend, in reality they hated him without reason and he needed her protection. He wanted to marry her before his rumoured part in the King's murder became a public outcry. His intentions were entirely honourable and he would 'serve and obey' her for the rest of her life.[21] Yet she again refused him, even though he produced the Ainslie's Tavern bond, confirming the nobility's support.

Sir James Melville, who remained at Dunbar for the night, recorded that Bothwell planned to marry Mary, whether she would agree or not. He claimed that, despite being rebuffed, Bothwell dismissed her servants and raped her, laying her open to the loss of her reputation. Given the risk of pregnancy, she was left with no choice but to marry him. In her letter to the Bishop of Dunblane, she wrote:

Seeing ourselves in his power, sequestered from the company of our servants, and others of whom we might ask counsel ... already welded to his appetite, and so we left alone, as it were a prey to him ... [he] ever pressing us with continuous and importunate suit. In the end when we saw no hope to be rid of him, never man in Scotland making a move to secure our deliverance, we were compelled to mitigate our displeasure, and began to think upon that he propounded.[22]

She is saying that, although Bothwell put her under huge pressure, he won her round. With so many people in the castle, even though most of her servants had been dismissed, this has to be more likely than rape. Royal apartments provided adjacent rooms and Mary could have locked the access door or screamed for help.

If Bothwell did not rape Mary, he was indisputably insistent in his suit. He persuaded her that he offered the only chance for her of retaining power. They agreed to consummate their relationship, as there would be strong efforts by the rest of the nobility to separate them. Her pregnancy would then enable them to push through their marriage. Mary was taking a high-stake gamble. She did become pregnant, but could not have known this at their wedding three weeks after her abduction, and rape would have been a good defence if she had wanted to get out of it. Yet she did not bargain on the adverse effect of marriage on the esteem in which she had been held.

Mary now had to explain why she had accepted Bothwell, who was still seen as a principal in the King's murder. She wrote to Archbishop Bethune in Paris, but, with her strict sense of morality, did not admit to the French court that she had willingly entered into an adulterous relationship. Her letter was carefully worded. She needed a strong man

> to take pain upon his person in the execution of justice and suppressing their insolence that was rebel, the travails whereof we may no longer sustain in our own person, being already wearied and almost broken with the frequent uproars and rebellions raised against us since we came to Scotland. Bothwell had no equal in Scotland either for the reputation of his House, or for the worthiness of himself, as well in wisdom, valiance, as in all other good qualities. Albeit we found his doings rude, yet were his words and answers gentle. As by a bravado in the beginning he had won the first point, so ceased he never, till by persuasion and importunate suit, accompanied not the less with force, he had finally driven us to end the work begun, at such time and in such form as he thought best might serve his turn, wherein we cannot dissemble that he has tried us otherwise than we would have wished or yet deserved at his hand.[23]

She went on to say: 'The event is indeed strange and otherwise nor you would have looked for. But as it is succeeded, we must take the best of it.'[24] She was making clear that she had not submitted out of lust, but through his determined persuasion. Although he used force and 'tried her otherwise than she wished or yet deserved, yet were his words and answers gentle.'[25] She had little choice in the matter, but this was not rape. She also needed to show that their marriage would be lawful and to outline why the Nuncio had not come to Scotland, but her explanations are not convincing. She confirmed that his previous marriage had been properly dissolved, allowing him to remarry. She claimed to have encouraged the Nuncio's visit, but the King's murder had put him off. She was being economical with the truth.

Bothwell is known to have had a predilection for anal sex with both male and female partners. Mary's words that that she 'found his doings rude', and that his actions were 'in such form as he thought best might serve his turn', which 'tried us other than we would have wished or yet deserved', seem to

371

imply his 'unnatural' proclivities.*[26] Although it is difficult to judge, she provided later hints that her sexual experience with him was distasteful to her. While her infatuation for King Henry is in no doubt, Bothwell's rugged methods may not have appealed. For a man who relished his sexual pleasures with the lusty Bessie Crawford in a church tower, Mary may have seemed slightly tame. If true, she must have been a lot more submissive than she would have wanted the French court to know.

Buchanan later claimed that the Bishop of Ross encouraged Bothwell to abduct Mary by force and she had slept with him out of passion (having already done so on numerous occasions previously). Yet many of Buchanan's accusations were far-fetched attempts to blacken Mary's supporters. Ross always claimed that he tried to prevent the marriage, despite his friendship with Bothwell. Many believed that Mary was claiming to have been raped to cover a long-standing illicit affair, but all the contemporary evidence is that their first sexual encounter was at Dunbar. On 20 December 1567, the Confederates placed a Bill before Parliament recording that, in her weakened state of mind, 'she suspected no evil from any of her subjects, and least of all from him.'[27]

Both Maitland and Sir James Melville were soon doubting whether Bothwell's marriage plan would succeed and, with the guard at Holyrood becoming mutinous, the Queen seemed safer at Dunbar. Sir James told her that marriage to 'a man commonly adjudged her husband's murderer would leave a tash (slur) upon her name and give too much ground for jealousy'.[29] Even Huntly, still Bothwell's closest supporter, showed no enthusiasm for the marriage. Despite having argued the Privy Council's case in support of it, Maitland remained hostile to Bothwell and only wanted to escape from Dunbar, particularly after Bothwell threatened to murder him. He told Cecil that he survived only because the Queen intervened on his behalf.† Furious at Maitland's and Melville's sudden opposition, Bothwell jailed them both, although Melville left with Huntly the next day. Pragmatic as ever, Maitland probably acted on Moray's instruction by playing along with the marriage plan and he accompanied Mary and Bothwell to Edinburgh for their wedding.

Sitting in London, Elizabeth could not decide what to do. Unaware of

---

* A broadside ballad published in Edinburgh by Robert Sempill after Mary's abdication records:
   Such beastly buggery Sodom has not seen
   As ruled in him who ruled Realm and Queen.[28]

† Drury's record says that it was Huntly who attacked Maitland, but the Queen shielded him from his drawn sword with her body, threatening 'that she would cause him to forfeit lands and goods and lose his life unless he desisted'.[31] As Drury was not present, Melville's report that Bothwell was the assailant seems more likely.

events at Dunbar, she initially sent Lord Grey of Wilton to Scotland. She wanted Mary to bring the King's murderers to justice, and abhorred the favour being shown to 'such as have been by common fame most touched by the crime'. She also criticised 'the contempt or neglect in the burial of the King's body' and was determined that 'so monstrous an outrage [as Mary's marriage to Bothwell] must be prevented'.[30] Yet after he had left London, she recalled Grey, sending Bedford in his place to give Mary a warning and to enquire whether James could be brought up in England. It has been suggested that Elizabeth recalled Grey after realising that Mary's marriage would cause her to be implicated in the King's death. Although this reasoning may have caused Cecil to discourage the visit, Elizabeth would never have supported such a devious attitude.

At this stage Kirkcaldy unquestionably believed that Mary had committed a crime of passion with his enemy, Bothwell, and wanted Moray to be installed as Regent. On 26 April, two days after her abduction, he wrote to Bedford that

> many would revenge it but they fear your mistress [Elizabeth]. I am so suited for to enterprise the revenge that I must either take it in hand or leave the country, which I am determined to do, if I get licence: but Bothwell minds to cut me off ere I obtain it. I pray you let me know what your mistress will do, for if we seek France, we may find favour; but I would rather persuade to lean to England. No honest man is safe in Scotland under the rule of a murderer and a murderess.[32]

Yet he stayed on continuing to send increasingly vitriolic reports. On 8 May, he told Bedford that the Confederates would need Elizabeth's help to overthrow Bothwell and that du Croc had offered French assistance. Elizabeth refused to become involved, and when Kirkcaldy said that 'the barbarous tyrant' Bothwell was trying to poison James, she became incensed at the tone of his 'vile' letters. He sent correspondence via Bedford to be forwarded to Moray in France, advising him to wait in Normandy for the Confederates' call. Elizabeth looked on with wry interest.

Despite the rumblings of opposition, nothing would stop Bothwell from marrying Mary and he moved forward with all speed, believing that a Queen's consort could not be prosecuted for the King's murder. It took only three weeks from the abduction until their marriage. The biggest hurdle was the divorce from Jean Gordon, who willingly colluded in the civil proceedings put in motion within two days of the abduction. Adultery with Bessie Crawford provided acceptable grounds in the eyes of the Kirk, and the decree was confirmed on 3 May. Yet this would not allow a Catholic to remarry, and Bothwell asked Sir James Balfour to fix it for him. The only acceptable form of Catholic divorce was an annulment on grounds that they were within the fourth degree of consanguinity. Archbishop Hamilton, who had conducted their marriage, was approached and, on 7 May, signed the papers (notwithstanding that his consistorial powers had already been revoked), conveniently forgetting that he had granted a dispensation for consanguinity before their wedding in the previous year.* Mary knew the divorce was dubious, as she raised it with other bishops before the wedding. Yet the niceties were overlooked, and, with Bothwell so determined, she had little option. Hamilton was wise to sign; Bothwell's servants threatened the chief Commissioner for the divorce, John Manderstoun, canon of Dunbar collegiate church, that if it did not proceed promptly 'there shall not fail to be noses and lugges [ears] cut and far greater displeasures'.[33]

While Bothwell was in Edinburgh resolving the divorce, Huntly stayed in Dunbar, where he had a row with Mary over her planned marriage. This is mentioned in Casket Letter VI, which, as has been shown, was written by Mary from Dunbar and not prior to her abduction. Although Huntly had agreed to the divorce and was formally restored to his estates, he was becoming isolated in his support for the marriage, and later failed to provide his promised military support. This would become the nail in the coffin for Mary and Bothwell at Carberry Hill.

Like others of her traditional supporters, Bethune in Paris saw it as 'madness of folly' that Mary remained committed to the marriage. On 14 May, Clernault reported to him that she had not read his or any other advice sent from abroad. She was not prepared to explain that she might be pregnant out of wedlock, fearing that the scandal might cost her the throne. Bothwell kept her so closely shielded from growing opposition that many believed she was being held against her will. Yet attempting a rescue at

---

* Jean must have kept this dispensation hidden, as it was found at Dunrobin Castle in the nineteenth century by the historian John Stuart. She did not want the validity of her divorce from Bothwell questioned, and, if produced, it would have shown it to be improper, invalidating her later marriages. John Stuart wondered why she did not destroy it completely, but concluded that she required it to confirm her right to the jointure revenues from Crichton, which continued until her death. She wanted her part of the bargain and remained there to assure her proper recompense. On 2 May, Drury suggested that Archbishop Hamilton had signed the divorce papers to bring the Hamiltons a step closer to the throne. If Mary were deposed, only James stood between them and the Crown. Yet their later support for Mary, when in captivity, makes this hypothesis unlikely.

Dunbar was difficult and, with a general belief that she had played a part in the King's murder, it was not seriously attempted.*

Mary's ladies-in-waiting at Dunbar were picked by Bothwell to encourage the marriage. They included his sister Jean, widow of Lord John Stewart, and his former mistresses, Janet Bethune, the widow of Sir Walter Scott of Buccleuch, and her sister, Lady Forbes of Reres, the aunts of Mary Bethune. Jean was shortly to marry the Master of Caithness, whose father had presided over the jury at Bothwell's trial and staunchly supported Moray. Janet Bethune (see p. 25, footnote) was forty-eight, some sixteen years older than Bothwell, and had been widowed for the previous fifteen. Reres, who was now forty-one, had been recalled from supervising James's nursery. Yet none of them were as intimate with Mary as the Maries, who did not come to Dunbar and seem to have opposed the marriage, probably on Maitland's persuasion.

Bothwell's abduction of Mary and his scarcely credible divorce proceedings alienated the Catholic lords, and Mary was now in Moray's trap, having implicated herself in a crime of passion by agreeing to the marriage. Herries thought that Moray had arranged the Confederate alliance before leaving Scotland, and he probably had received encouragement from Cecil to organise its initial meeting at Dunkeld.

On 27 April, Morton met at Stirling with Argyll, Atholl and Mar, who all believed that Mary was being held against her will. Morton's presence shows that his alliance with Bothwell and his support for the marriage at Ainslie's tavern had only been skin-deep. It was the first time that he had let his opposition be seen publicly. As it was three days after Mary's abduction to Dunbar he was assured that they were now committed. He no longer needed to encourage a marriage, which would leave Moray out in the cold. He had not supported it in return for Bothwell helping in his rehabilitation, as is sometimes suggested. This had been formally confirmed on 7 March, but he flanked him with Maitland when he walked to his trial on 12 April and supported the marriage proposal at Ainslie's Tavern a week after that.

A gathering, which included all the rival factions, met at Stirling on 6 May with the common goal of bringing Bothwell down. In Moray's absence, Morton was given the task to 'manage all', and a letter was written to Moray seeking his return to Scotland.[34] The group also signed a bond as

---

* The lieges of Aberdeen sent Mary an offer of help, but there is no record that she received it or replied to them. On 3 May, Robert Melville complained to Cecil that Mary had received no support, despite requesting Elizabeth's help.

Confederate lords to 'pursue the Queen's liberty, preserve the Prince from his enemies in Mar's keeping, and purge the realm of the detestable murder of our king'.[35] They stopped short of accusing Mary of conspiring with him, despite a general belief that she had done so. Having been 'ravished and detained' against her will, they wanted her released from Bothwell's cruel 'tyranny and thralldom'.[36] According to Drury, the Confederates sent a message to her at Dunbar offering to put together a force to rescue her, but she replied that, although 'she had been evil and strangely handled', she was now treated 'so well that she had no cause to complain'. Yet Bothwell would have intercepted their communication, and she later complained of her nobles' 'profound silence'.[37] He still seemed to offer her the best hope of powerful leadership, and his control of the munitions at Dunbar and Edinburgh Castles seemed to prevent his opponents mounting a challenge. She found it hardly credible that support for him had evaporated, given the signatures on the Ainslie's Tavern bond.

The Confederates put on a drama at Stirling called *The Murder of Darnley and the Fate of Bothwell*. [38] Bothwell was beside himself with anger on hearing that they had hung the boy acting him so realistically that it took some time for him to be revived! The choice of Stirling, where Mar was Governor, shows that they now had his full support, and a future Regency would depend on him maintaining control of the Prince. The Confederates were now a force to be reckoned with. They included Argyll, militarily the most powerful of the Scottish magnates and traditionally a supporter of the Queen, Atholl, head of the Catholic party, and Glencairn, in the absence of Moray the most powerful of the Lords of the Congregation. Morton, Argyll and Glencairn were not natural allies of Atholl, who had been kept in the dark about the plot to murder the King. Yet, perhaps as a result of Maitland's influence, Atholl was just as determined to bring down Bothwell. It was he who had attracted the Catholic Tullibardine into the Confederate camp and Tullibardine had enlisted his brother-in-law, Mar. Other Catholics included Eglinton, Montrose and Innermeath, while among the Protestants were Caithness, Cassillis, newly converted by his wife Margaret Lyon, Boyd, Ochiltree, Ruthven, Drummond, Gray, Glamis, Lindsay of the Byres, Home, Herries and Kirkcaldy. Moray's half-brother, Sir William Douglas, also joined them, and offered Lochleven as a stronghold to imprison Mary when the time came. It had taken a major change of heart for Mar to turn against Mary, who held him in such respect that she accepted it as his absolute duty not to let the Prince out of his and his wife's control. Yet Bothwell had taken the governorship of Edinburgh Castle from him and he believed the tale that she had been a party to the King's murder. Melville saw him as:

a man of meik and humayne nature, inclinit to all kind of quietness and modestie. The fact that his abilities were not of the highest order rather fitted him than otherwise for the position [of neutrality].

The Catholics among the Confederates always remained loyal to the Queen, but took their lead from Atholl in believing that she was being held by Bothwell against her will. Eglinton, as a Catholic, and Herries and Cassillis, as Protestants, supported Atholl. Moray's mainly Protestant supporters had the broader objective of deposing Mary and appointing him as Regent. Those who had signed the Ainslie's Tavern bond* argued, somewhat cynically, that they had assumed that Bothwell had received the Queen's consent for marriage beforehand, but, as she had been abducted to Dunbar against her will, she must have agreed under duress. This was of course easier to explain than that they had encouraged the marriage to justify her downfall by implicating her in a crime of passion. Most importantly, the Confederates mustered 3,000 troops at short notice and, having overwhelming public support, were in a position to make a stand against Bothwell. On 5 May, Drury reported that, if the marriage took place, many of the signatories of the Ainslie's Tavern bond would support a regency for James.

Maitland failed to attend the meeting at Stirling, as he was still at Dunbar, and his non-appearance caused the Confederates to 'muse much'. He was probably not at this point being held strictly against his will, but chose pragmatically to sit on the fence. Commentators have suggested that his overriding consideration was salvaging the negotiations for peaceful union with England. Yet this could have been more easily achieved with a Protestant Regency for Prince James, who would become heir to the English throne. It is much more likely that he was still trying, with the help of Mary Fleming, to protect Mary's position by dissuading her from marrying Bothwell, but failed to do so. Yet he later seems to have concocted the Casket Letters, after being threatened by Moray that he would reveal his part in the murder plot if he failed to assist him. His schizophrenic stance left him mistrusted on all sides.

The Confederates believed that Huntly still supported Bothwell, but, with Châtelherault abroad, were uncertain of Hamilton affiliations. Balfour

---

* Some of those signing the Ainslie's Tavern bond began to be nervous that supporting the Queen, a reigning sovereign, to marry Bothwell, her subject, could be construed as treasonable. Before they consented to the marriage on 14 May, they obtained Mary's confirmation that neither she nor her heirs would ever 'impute a crime or offence to any of the subscribers thereof'.[39]

seemed to be in Bothwell's camp after being installed at Edinburgh Castle with equal rank to the Governor, Cockburn of Skirling. On 8 May, Bothwell appointed him sole Governor, an unlikely role for a lawyer, in an effort to assure his allegiance. Cockburn of Skirling was compensated with the lucrative post of Comptroller of Customs. Yet Balfour's loyalty remained in doubt, and, only six days later, Drury reported the governorship being offered to John Hepburn of Beanston. Melville later admitted having warned Balfour. He secretly asked him not to hand over the keys, but to hold the Castle for the Confederates in order to protect the Prince and the Queen 'who was so disdainfully handled'. With Balfour staying at his post, both the ordnance and royal treasure were retained for the Confederates. Yet he treacherously let Bothwell believe that he held the Castle on his behalf. This was to be a principal factor in Bothwell's undoing.

On 7 May, Robert Melville told Cecil in London that the Confederates were seeking support and had returned to their own localities to raise troops. Argyll had gone to the west, Atholl to the north and Morton to Fife, Angus and Kincardineshire. Although Mar remained at Stirling to protect the Prince, he was now exposed if Bothwell should try to gain control and he prepared for a siege. Randolph reported that Bothwell intended to send the Prince to France to prevent the Confederates from ruling in his name. Cecil provided the Confederates with all the help he could, without alerting Elizabeth to what he was doing, as she would not back a rebellion against her sister Queen, even though she was 'greatly scandalised' by events at Dunbar and would no longer accept Mary as her heir.[40] She promised to help Lennox avenge his son's murder, hoping that James would be brought to England into his grandmother's care.

Well aware of opposition building against him, Bothwell raised troops in the Borders, and with control of the munitions at Dunbar and, as he thought, at Edinburgh Castle, he seemed in an unassailable position. On 6 May, he set out with Mary from Dunbar, and, in the evening, with the Castle guns firing a salute 'most magnificently', they entered Edinburgh by the West Port, accompanied by Huntly and Maitland.[41] Bothwell was on foot, respectfully bareheaded, leading Mary's horse by its bridle through the sullen crowds. After they had taken up residence in the Castle, he positioned his 200 hackbutters outside Mary's rooms, hoping to limit communication with her, so that she did not realise the hostility they faced. Showing great personal loyalty, Herries came to explain to her the public concern at their intended marriage and, on his knees, begged her 'to remember her honour and dignity and the safety of the Prince'. She effected to wonder why reports of marriage were circulating, as 'there was no such thing in her mind'.[42]

Herries apologised and withdrew, but she was probably trying to avoid him having to confront Bothwell, who was in a volatile mood.

Sir James Melville also visited Mary in an attempt to stop the marriage, but this greatly endangered Maitland's position. He gave her a letter purportedly from a Scotsman, Thomas Bishop, living in England (although he seems to have been a fictional character). Bishop's letter declared that it was

> bruited that she was to marry the murderer of her husband, who at present had a wife of his own, a man full of vice; if she married him she would lose the favour of God, her own reputation and the hearts of England, Ireland and Scotland.

Mary gave it to Maitland, and when he asked what it said, she rounded on him that it was part of his design 'tending to the wreck of the Earl of Bothwell'. Maitland had clearly overplayed his hand. He took Melville on one side, asking what he was thinking about in producing such a letter, and warned him that 'so soon as Bothwell gets notice hereof, as I fear he will shortly, he will cause you to be killed'. When Melville argued that someone needed to tell her what people thought, as it was 'a sore matter to see that good princess run to utter wreck.' Maitland told him 'he had done more honestly than wisely; and therefore I pray you, retire diligently before Bothwell comes up from his dinner.' Mary protected Melville from Bothwell, but he admitted keeping out of sight 'till his fury was slaked; because I was advertised there was nothing but slaughter in case I had been gotten'.[43]

Drury reported that Bothwell's efforts to keep Mary away from her traditional advisers caused a quarrel between them lasting half a day. She wept when he would not allow her to look or be looked on by anybody, for he knew very well that she loved her pleasure and passed her time like any other devoted to the world.[44]

He concluded that they would not long agree after their marriage. Bothwell was ungovernably jealous of any favours she granted. 'He is offended for a horse which she gave to' Lord John Hamilton, claiming that he wanted it himself. She, in turn, 'much misliked' him writing to Jean Gordon, whom he visited at Crichton.[45] This led to speculation that they were continuing a relationship, even after his marriage to Mary. De Silva heard that he 'passes some days a week with the wife he has divorced'.[46] Maitland, who was still doing all he could to stop the marriage, advised Mary that her new husband 'had written to Jean more than once, to tell her that he still regarded her as his true wife, and Mary as a mere concubine'.[47] Du Croc confirmed to the French government that 'no one in this kingdom is in any doubt but that the Duke [Bothwell] loves his former wife a great deal more than he loves the Queen'.[48] Yet there is no evidence of a continuing affair with Jean, who probably always hated him. In the summer of 1567, when she eventually left Crichton* to return to Strathbogie, she told Lady Moray, who she visited, that 'she will never live with the Earl of Bothwell nor take him for her husband'.[49]

Bothwell deserves sympathy for being made the scapegoat for the King's murder and for assuming that he had the nobility's support to marry Mary. Yet he cannot be forgiven for taking the Queen captive to Dunbar, for separating her from her closest supporters and for pressurising her into sex with him. The Confederates had every reason to sign a bond to bring him down and had no choice but to take up arms after he had bullied those who warned Mary of his shortcomings, and members of the Church who were forced to confirm his divorce.

On 8 May, a proclamation was issued that Mary would marry Bothwell, with the banns to be read at both Holyrood and St Giles' on the next day. At St Giles', the minister John Craig, Knox's fearless assistant, refused to read them without having the Kirk's approval and until Mary provided a writ to confirm that she had not been ravished nor kept in captivity against her will. He was called before Bothwell and the Council to justify himself. Instead of apologising, he denounced the marriage, citing:

> the law of adultery, the ordinance of the Kirk, the law of ravishing, the suspicion of collusion between him [Bothwell] and his wife, the sudden divorce and proclaiming within the space of four days, and last the suspicion of the King's death, which his marriage would confirm.[50]

If, of course, Mary denied rape, then she had committed adultery. Amazingly, Bothwell kept his temper, but threatened to hang Craig if he failed to read the banns. The Council issued the writ, which was delivered by Justice-Clerk Bellenden on the same day, and the Kirk gave its assent. Craig had no choice, but had the temerity to preach that he took 'heaven and earth to

---

* At the start of their marriage, as has been seen, there is evidence that Jean resisted Bothwell's marital overtures, and she did not become pregnant in their year together. Yet when she remarried Alexander, 12th Earl of Sutherland, she produced seven children. Although her son did not consider his mother beautiful, he reported that she had a 'masculine intelligence'. If Bothwell was meeting her at Crichton, it is likely that he was seeking to extract himself from the financial stranglehold she held over him through her jointure on Crichton. He did not turn to her for assistance after Carberry Hill, and his request for Huntly's help was rejected.

witness that he abhorred and detested that marriage'. On 13 May, he was again brought before the Council and wrote that 'my Lords put me to silence and sent me away'.[51] He was lucky to survive.

On 12 May, Mary was escorted by the Lords of Session to the Tolbooth, accompanied by Rothes carrying the sword of state, Crawford the sceptre, and Huntly the crown. Bothwell wore a scarlet robe edged with ermine and was attended by Cockburn of Skirling carrying a blue banner emblazoned with his arms. To protect him from future prosecution, Mary publicly forgave his seizure of her person during her return from Stirling. Five of his men who had assisted him in it received pardons, and Black Ormiston was knighted. Bothwell was later created Duke of Orkney and Lord of Shetland (titles once borne by the 1st Earl of Bothwell), and Mary placed the ducal coronet on his head. In accordance with the Council's wishes, and on Morton's insistence, his future powers were curtailed. He was not made King and could not undertake public business or bestow gifts or privileges without Mary's consent. All official documents required her signature.

The Confederates made a last-ditch effort to make Mary pull back from marriage. On 13 May, they wrote that, unless she discharged her soldiers and paid heed to her nobility, they would not obey her commands. Yet the next day Mary and Bothwell signed the contract, which described her as a young widow, 'apt and able to procreate and bring forth more children' to maintain the Stuart dynasty, having been encouraged by the 'most part of her nobility' to marry. Its wording echoed the Ainslie's Tavern bond in declaring that she should 'so far humble herself' by choosing one of her subjects.[52] It was witnessed by Huntly, Maitland, Fleming, Lindsay, Bellenden and even Herries, whose loyalty to her outshone his hatred of the newly created Duke. In the evening, Melville took the risk of returning to court. In jovial mood, Orkney invited him to dine with his friends, but when 'he fell to discoursing of gentlewomen, speaking with such filthy language', Melville left to join the Queen.[53]

To appease the mainly Protestant lords that opposed him, Orkney insisted on the wedding taking place in the Great Hall at Holyrood in accordance with Reformist rites, and not in the Chapel Royal. This caused du Croc to organise a Catholic boycott. The marriage at ten o'clock in the morning on 15 May was conducted by Orkney's adherent (but no relation) Adam Bothwell, Bishop of Orkney, a recent Reformist convert, who preached to confirm the Duke's 'penitence' at having been an 'evil liver'.[54] They were then 'handfasted' as an exchange of rings was considered Popish. Yet Mary's approval of the Act concerning Religion and her participation in a Protestant ceremony later caused her great distress,* and lost her the last vestiges of papal support. Yet it demonstrates Orkney's dominance and the need for her to be seen to act for the good of her realm. She wore mourning clothes, but beneath these was a magnificent flowing black patterned velvet gown in the Italian style, richly embroidered with gold strapwork and gold and silver thread. Afterwards she changed into a shimmering yellow silk gown, which had been relined, and wore a refurbished black taffeta petticoat.

The service was not well attended, despite some of the Confederate lords feeling duty bound to be there. Huntly was a witness and Maitland, Crawford, Sutherland, Seton, Fleming, Boyd, Oliphant, Glamis, Livingston and Sir James Melville came, as did the four Maries, and the couple's servants. There were members of the Catholic clergy, including Archbishop Hamilton and the Bishops of Ross and Dunblane. 'There was neither pleasure nor pastime used as is wont to be used when princesses are married, no masques, no rich presents, no elaborate gowns, no balling, dancing and banqueting', no largesse, merely a wedding breakfast to which the public was invited, with the Queen sitting at the head of the table and Orkney at the foot eating in silence.[56] It was a pathetic little event compared to the glittering pageantry of her earlier marriage celebrations.

On the evening of the wedding a further placard appeared in Edinburgh quoting from Ovid, 'Mense malas maio nubere vulgus ait [As is commonly said, wantons marry in the month of May]'.[57] Cecil rubbed his hands in ill-disguised glee, writing that Scotland was 'in a quagmire; nobody seemeth to stand still; the most honest desire to go away; the worst tremble with the shaking of their conscience.'[58] Yet his own conscience seemed unaffected.

References

1. Guy, p. 327
2. Pollen, p. 386; Labanoff, cited in Antonia Fraser, p. 364, and Weir, p. 351
3. Weir, p. 352
4. State Papers in the Public Record Office; CSP Scottish, cited in Weir, p. 353
5. Buchanan, *Detectio*; cited in Weir, p. 350
6. Sir Arthur Salusbury MacNalty, *Mary Queen of Scots, The Daughter of Debate*, cited in Weir, p. 352

* 'On her return from that unlawful ceremony, the Queen could not help weeping', believing that she had put her immortal soul in peril. 'At once she sent for the Bishop of Ross, and with many tears unlocked the secret of her heart; she showed many clear signs of repentance and promised that she would never again do anything opposed to the rites of the Catholic Church.'[55]

7. Calendar of manuscripts at Hatfield House, I, p. 379, cited in Antonia Fraser, p. 463
8. Guy, pp. 425–7, and Antonia Fraser, p. 463
9. Guy, pp. 427–8
10. Henderson, *Casket Letters*, pp. 171, 172; Armstrong-Davison, p. 195; cited in Antonia Fraser, p. 464
11. Henderson, *Casket Letters*, pp. 171, 172; Armstrong-Davison, p. 195
12. Henderson, *Casket Letters*, pp. 171, 172; Armstrong-Davison, p. 195; cited in Antonia Fraser, p. 465
13. J. Hosack, *Mary Queen of Scots and Her Accusers*, Appendix F, p. 562
14. Buchanan, *Detectio*, cited in Weir, p. 361
15. De Silva to Philip II, May 1567; CSP Spanish, cited in Weir, p. 354
16. Robert Melville to Cecil, 7 May 1567, CSP Scottish, cited in Weir, p. 354
17. State Papers in the Public Record Office; CSP Scottish, cited in Guy, p. 329
18. Labanoff; CSP Scottish, cited in Weir, p. 354
19. Nau, cited in Weir, p. 354
20. CSP Spanish, cited in Weir, p. 355
21. Labanoff, cited in Weir, p. 355
22. Labanoff, cited in Guy, p. 361
23. Labanoff, II, p. 31; Teulet, cited in Guy, pp. 360–2, Antonia Fraser, p. 376, and Weir, pp. 355–6.
24. Fraser, p. 376, and Weir, p. 381
25. Labanoff, II, p. 31
26. Labanoff, II, p. 31
27. Acts of Parliament of Scotland, cited in Weir, pp. 359, 427
28. 'A Declaration of the Lords' Just Quarrel' in Satyrical Poems, by Robert Sempill; Phillips, p. 44, cited in Guy, p. 389 and Antonia Fraser, p. 368, footnote
29. Melville, cited in Weir, p. 362
30. Weir, p. 362
31. Drury to Cecil, 6 May 1567, CSP Foreign
32. State Papers on the Public Record Office; CSP Scottish, cited in Weir, p. 363
33. Calendar of Manuscripts at Hatfield House, XIII, p. 82, cited in Weir, p. 366
34. Keith, cited in Weir, p. 365
35. Guy, p. 331
36. Weir, p. 364
37. CSP Foreign; Buchanan, *Detectio*; cited in Weir, p. 365
38. De Silva to Philip II, 11 May, 1567, CSP Spanish; cited in Weir, p. 366
39. Cotton MMS; Caligula; Anderson; Buchanan, *Detectio*; cited in Weir, p. 373
40. CSP Spanish, cited in Weir, p. 365
41. Weir, p. 367
42. Melville, cited in Weir, p. 367
43. Melville, cited in Weir, p. 368
44. Keith, cited in Guy, p. 336, and Weir, p. 377
45. CSP Foreign, cited in Weir, p. 372
46. CSP Spanish, cited in Weir, p. 376
47. CSP Foreign, cited in Weir, p. 376

48. CSP, Foreign, VIII, p. 229; Teulet, II, p. 170, cited in Antonia Fraser, p. 374, and Weir, p. 376
49. Stuart, p. 48, cited in Marshall, p. 134
50. Knox; Hay Fleming, p. 454, cited in Guy, p. 332, Antonia Fraser, p. 371, and Weir, p. 369
51. Anderson, cited in Weir, p. 371; Keith, cited in Weir, p. 372
52. Guy, p. 333
53. Weir, p. 373
54. Drury to Cecil, 20 May 1567, CSP Foreign; cited in Weir, p. 374
55. Leslie; Keith; cited in Weir, p. 375
56. Diurnal of Occurrents, p. 111; cited in Weir, pp. 374–5; Calendar of Letters and State Papers in Rome
57. Ovid, 5th Book of the Fasti, cited in Antonia Fraser, p. 372, and Weir, p. 375
58. Alison Plowden, *Two Queens in One Isle*; cited in Guy, p. 335, and Weir, p. 352

32

The Confederate Alliance Challenges Mary and Orkney

After her wedding, Mary sent Robert Melville to Elizabeth to explain why she had married Orkney, and the Bishop of Dunblane was sent to the French court carrying letters from du Croc and to seek Catherine de Medici's and Charles IX's approval. Her letters confirmed that 'she had been very content to take him for our husband. From his first entering into his estate, he dedicated his whole service to his sovereign.'[1] She cited her personal exhaustion and her need for a consort to share the burden of government, noting his long-standing loyalty to both the Queen Regent and herself. She pointed out that he had been cleared by Parliament of all suspicion of murder and had the support of the other lords, although, with their factious nature, they were now trying to put him down. This lacked conviction when the other lords, speaking with one voice, were already seeking Elizabeth's help, but Mary wrote personally to Cecil for assistance in explaining her situation.

Mary was remarkably candid in instructions to the Bishop of Dunblane on how to explain the events leading to her marriage. He was to report that, following the King's death, as Orkney's 'pretences began to be higher, so his proceedings seemed somewhat more strange, but she was now so far committed to him that we must interpret all things to the best', despite his 'plain contempt of our person and use of force to have us in his power'.[2] Once again Mary was implying that she had been raped, but without quite saying so. He was also to say that 'destiny and necessity' had required a Protestant marriage service, as Orkney had been more concerned with placating the Protestants

> than regarding our contentation, or weighing what was convenient for us, that has been nourished in our own religion and never intends to leave the same for him or any man on Earth.[3]

Immediately after the wedding Mary seemed greatly distressed, and du Croc perceived a strange formality between her and her husband, which she begged me to excuse, saying that if I saw her sad, it was because she could not rejoice nor ever should again, for she did nothing but wish for death,

as she repeated on several occasions.[4] Arthur Erskine told Melville and du Croc that, while she was alone with Orkney in her cabinet, 'she cried aloud, then sought for a knife to stab herself, or else (said she) I will drown myself'. Du Croc 'counselled and comforted her as best I could these three times I have seen her'.[5] She called in the Bishop of Ross and, in floods of tears, told him of her regret at both her marriage and the Protestant service, and said she would never again offend the Catholic Church.

Mary's rapid disaffection with Orkney so soon after their wedding has caused great speculation. After being a virtual prisoner for three weeks at Dunbar, friction between them now became open hostility. While a continuing affair with Jean Gordon has been mentioned, there are other claims that his pleasure in anal sex distressed her. Sir James Melville reported that he 'mishandled' her in every way, and 'he was so beastly and suspicious'.[6] Yet this smacks of scurrilous tittle-tattle, and it is more likely that Orkney's frightening mood swings are to blame. Sometimes he was dour, distant and forbidding, sometimes embarrassingly over familiar and ribald. Although his display of Calvinistic demeanour seems out of character, he now forbade all frivolity, including music, cards, hunting, hawking and golf. Yet his foul language and overbearing manner in private reduced her to 'an abundance of salt tears'.[7] Drury reported that

the opinion of divers is that she is the most changed woman of face that in so little time, without extremity of sickness, they have ever seen. It is thought that the Queen has long had a spice of the falling sickness [epilepsy] and has of late been troubled therewith.[8]

Yet her fainting seems to have been caused by stress on her realisation that her marriage was extremely unpopular. Having been able to do no wrong since her return from France, public opinion was suddenly against her. She now recognised that the rumours of Orkney's part in murdering the King were likely to be true. She may have seen the Craigmillar bond, which he eventually gave to her at Carberry Hill, and was by then aware that most of the lords lining up against her were also implicated. Neither Moray nor Maitland, who might have been able to provide her with advice, was unscathed. She was being shunned by her Guise relations and severely criticised by both European heads of state and the Papacy. She had no shoulder to lean on.

As the Queen's consort, Orkney displayed 'great reverence' in public, doffing his cap in her presence, even though it was proper for a consort to wear it. This resulted in Mary showing that she 'would have otherwise, sometimes taking his cap and putting it on'.[9] To show that life continued as normal, they made a point of being seen with Mary in all her finery when they rode together. Drury reported that 'they now make outward show of great content'.[10] On 23 May, Orkney belatedly organised a celebration of their marriage with a masque, a water pageant on the shores of the Firth of Forth and a tournament in Edinburgh, at which he ran at the rings. Soldiers acted out a mock skirmish, but, despite this return to an air of fun, the court was sparsely attended.

Du Croc was not taken in by any illusion of marital harmony. On 18 May, he again wrote to Charles IX and Catherine de Medici, telling them to pay no attention to his letters sent with the Bishop of Dunblane, which were

merely delusive. You can suppose that I did not entrust to him what I write to you. Your majesties cannot do better than to make him very bad cheer, and find all amiss in the marriage, for it is very wretched and is already repented of.[11]

He reported that the Queen had summoned the Confederates, and had asked him to intercede on her behalf. He considered this futile and, as he did not expect them to appear, would withdraw from court.

Elizabeth was scandalised at Mary, and admonished her candidly:

To be plain with you, our grief has not been small threat: for how could a worse choice be made for your honour than in such haste to marry a subject who, besides other notorious lacks, public fame has charged with the murder of your late husband, besides touching yourself in some part, though we trust in that behalf, falsely. And with what peril you have married him, that hath another lawful wife, nor any children betwixt you legitimate. Thus you see our opinion plainly, and we are heartily sorry we can conceive no better. We are earnestly bent to do everything in our power to procure the punishment of that murder against any subject you have, how dear soever you should hold him, and next thereto to be careful how your son the Prince may be preserved to the comfort of you and the realm.[12]

The English had always disliked Bothwell and believed that he would colour Mary against them. Despite her hope that Robert Melville might win Elizabeth over, he had failed. Elizabeth was convinced that Orkney had murdered the King and posed a threat to James. Her main objective was to gain control of the Prince, placing him in Lady Margaret's care.

Realising that he was losing the propaganda battle, Orkney renewed his efforts to persuade the French court to accept the marriage. He wrote personally to Archbishop Bethune in Paris asking him 'to bestow your study, ingenuity and effectual labours in the ordering of this present message'. He explained:

> Her majesty might well have married with men of greater birth and estimation, but, we are well assured, never with one more affectionately inclined to do her honour and service.[13]

On 4 June, he made a last-ditch effort with both Elizabeth and Cecil, sending a letter to each of them with Robert Melville. Cecil must have been offended by his opening, which reads, 'Seeing God has called me to this place, I heartily desire to persevere in all good offices.'[14] Cecil knew only too well how the marriage had been arranged, and had no desire for him to 'persevere'. To placate Elizabeth, Orkney claimed that he did not deserve the evil reports she had heard of him. Although men of greater birth might have been preferred, none could be more eager for her friendship. He assured her that he would be 'careful to see Your two Majesties' amity continued by all good offices'.[15] His efforts did not achieve the desired effect.

It was Mary's remarriage, not the King's murder, which was now the focus of international scandal, and would prove her undoing. The broadsheets in Edinburgh had a field day, likening her to Delilah, Jezebel and Clytemnestra. In Catholic Europe, she was seen to have entered into a bigamous marriage with a heretic in an unlawful ceremony. Giovanni Correr, the Venetian ambassador in Paris, recognised that the Catholic cause in Scotland had been 'deprived of all hope of ever again raising its head'.[16] Catherine de Medici told Bethune that Mary 'had behaved so ill and made herself so hateful to her subjects' that France could no longer support her.[17] Her correspondence with her Guise relations evaporated. Having for so long been the focus for their counter-Reformation, the English Catholics could not believe that she:

> without fear of God, or respect for the world, has allowed herself to be induced by sensuality, or else by the persuasion of others to take one

who cannot be her husband and gives thereby a suspicion that she will go over by degrees to Protestantism.[18]

Her confessor, the Dominican friar Roche Mameret, resigned and returned to France.*

At some point shortly after the wedding, Mary must have realised that she was pregnant and there were already speculative rumours of this in England. Pregnancy was an insuperable barrier to her ending the marriage and she stood firmly behind her new husband. If he were found guilty of treason, their child's legitimacy would be questioned. The only matter of importance to her was providing a second heir to the throne. Despite James's robust health, life was fickle. Without her children, her death would result in anarchy in Scotland, with the Hamiltons and Lennox Stuarts, neither of whom offered decisive leadership, fighting it out. Yet the Confederates had no inkling of her pregnancy and could not understand her ignoring their advice for her to leave her husband.

On 17 May, Orkney presided over a Privy Council meeting and was now wielding sovereign power. He wrote: 'They placed the government of the country in my hands with the wish that I should bring some order into the country.'[19] He provided strong and intelligent leadership with 'a latent talent for diplomacy'.[20] There was to be a rota of Councillors, including Morton, in permanent attendance at court. He reintroduced an old regulation penalising those failing to attend. On 19 May, he banned counterfeit brass money, which was driving Scottish coinage out of circulation and prevented him paying his troops. To win over the Reformers, he blocked Catholic efforts to restore the Mass, annulling Mary's dispensation for Catholic nobles and her servants to worship with her in private. The Bishop of Ross prudently retired to join Balfour in Edinburgh Castle.† Orkney assured Craig, who had so recently opposed the marriage, that he would attend sermons at St Giles'. To ameliorate the nobility, he restored Morton to Tantallon and offered the Kers of Cessford a pardon for murdering the Abbot of Kelso. Fleming, who remained continuously loyal, was made Governor of the seemingly impregnable Dumbarton Castle and would continue to hold it for Mary until 1571. Yet Orkney lacked support and had no opportunity to demonstrate his qualities.

---

* While in London, Mameret was later to admit that, until Mary's marriage to Orkney, he had never seen a woman of greater virtue, courage and uprightness. He was certain that she had no knowledge of the King's murder, and that she was greatly grieved by it. He claimed that she had married Orkney as a means of settling religious differences in Scotland.

† When the castle was eventually handed over to Morton after Carberry Hill, the Bishop was permitted to escape by a postern gate.

On 6 June 1567, Huntly requested leave to visit his estates. Mary refused permission for him to depart from court and accused him 'with many bitter words' of plotting treason against her as his father had done.[21] On the same day, Maitland had a furious row with Orkney and, without taking leave of the Queen, left court* with Mary Fleming. Mary was distraught to lose her chief Marie. Before going to Stirling, he asked Atholl to affirm for him his loyalty to the Confederates, but they remained suspicious at him for staying with Mary for so long. They feared he was acting as her agent, and he later implied to Throckmorton and Melville that he had hoped to help her better after joining them. On 8 June, Atholl, Eglinton, Sempill and Tullibardine, all Catholic, accompanied him to meet with the Protestants led by Morton. These included Caithness, Boyd, Ochiltree, Ruthven, Drummond, Gray, Glamis, Lindsay of the Byres and Douglas of Lochleven, who all wanted Moray as Regent, while others, including Cassillis, Kirkcaldy of Grange, Herries and Argyll, supported Maitland in being loyal to the Queen, but would not tolerate Orkney. Despite the suspicions, Maitland's arrival proved a rallying point for the Confederates, who were also joined by Montrose and Innermeath, both Catholic. Even the Hamiltons and Home, hitherto Mary's supporters, became affiliated, but the Hamiltons were hoping to be recognised ahead of the Lennoxes as heirs to the throne after James.† Home brought Ker of Cessford and Kerr of Ferniehirst with him, but they were the only Border chiefs in support. Traditionally neutral Protestants in attendance included Mar and Ochiltree, who were so horrified at Mary's marriage that they too favoured her deposition. Finally there was Sir James Balfour, but, as he controlled Edinburgh Castle, this was kept secret. He made his backing conditional on receiving immunity from prosecution for the King's murder which he required 'by reason of his long familiarity with' Orkney.[22]

While the Confederates were united in their desire to bring Orkney down, the differences in their other objectives strained their loyalty for each other. They signed another bond confirming, as common ground, their intention

---

* Much has been written to try to explain Maitland's motives in leaving Mary at this time. She indisputably saw this as a betrayal, but *The Diurnal of Occurrents* states that he feared for his life after his row with Orkney. More likely, the pragmatic Maitland saw the balance of power swinging towards the Confederates and did not want to find himself isolated with Mary in a lost cause.

† There must be considerable doubt whether either Archbishop or Lord John Hamilton genuinely supported the Confederates at this stage, although the elderly Châtelherault, who was still in exile, may have done. All contemporary references suggest that they remained strong adherents of the Queen. Yet for a short period after Moray became Regent, he bought their loyalty in return for recognising their prior claim to the Lennoxes, but they soon mistrusted his own rival ambitions and rejoined Mary's supporters.

to liberate the Queen. Those, whose sole objective was to topple Orkney, expected her to desert him when she realised the extent of adverse public opinion facing her, but others saw the marriage as their pretext for removing her as their Catholic monarch. They did not want Orkney appointed as Governor and Protector of Scotland, and feared that, if he gained control of the Prince, he would proclaim himself King.

By 25 May, Orkney knew he faced a rebellion and told his supporters to prepare for action. He wanted to establish a standing army of 500 infantry and 200 cavalry, but Mary could not believe that such a defensive step was needed. With war inevitable, she had to raise 5,000 crowns and sent table silver and gold to be converted to coin at the Mint. Even Prince James's christening font was handed over, although it was so large that the furnace generated insufficient heat to melt it. The Privy Council summoned the Queen's lieges to attend her on 15 June at Melrose ostensibly to raid Liddesdale, but in fact to provide protection against the Confederates. Mary was shocked at the extent of opposition from hitherto loyal adherents. Sounding like Orkney, she poured scorn on them:

> For Argyll, I know well enough how to stop his mouth, and for Atholl, he is but feeble. I will deal well enough with him. And for Morton, his boots are but new pulled off him and not made clean. I will return him to exile.

She still trusted Mar, saying, 'He hath assured me to be mine and faithfully ever,' and James remained in his care.[23] Yet, by 1 June, it was strongly rumoured that Orkney was planning to kidnap the Prince at Stirling, and he was aware that Kirkcaldy had men ready to capture them on their return to Holyrood. He seems to have been informed by Argyll, who was in fear that, with his back to the wall, Orkney would reveal his signature on the Craigmillar bond. Although Orkney made repeated demands for the Prince to be handed over, Mary sent the Bishop of Ross to Stirling to forbid Mar from delivering James to anyone but herself, and Melville reported:

> But my Lord of Mar was a trew nobleman, and would not delyuer him out of his custody, alleging that he could not without consent of [Parliament].[24]

Although Mary wanted to visit Stirling, Orkney feared that he could not provide her with protection there. He was wise to forbid it.

As Holyrood was unfortified, Orkney hoped to move with Mary into

Edinburgh Castle. It is alleged that Balfour used masterly double bluff* to discourage this, while assuring them of his continuing loyalty. Without control of the Castle, they would lose the town. They now looked for a stronghold outside Edinburgh to await their levies being mustered at Melrose. On the day after Maitland's departure from court, Orkney took Mary to Borthwick Castle, twelve miles south-east of Edinburgh, and only two miles from Crichton, where Jean Gordon remained in residence. They arrived on 7 June, but, as a result of her hurried departure, Mary carried only her essentials, including a silver wash basin, a silver kettle, a small cabinet with lock and key for her papers, and pins to hold back her hair.

Borthwick Castle belonged to the Catholic William, 6th Lord Borthwick, Orkney's assured adherent. It was a fine fortress built in about 1425, surrounded by a curtain wall with twin towers 110 feet high at each corner, making it impregnable without cannon. At its centre was a three-storey keep with walls thirteen feet thick at the base, tapering to six feet at the battlements. It stood in a hollow surrounded by water with steeply rising ground on three sides. The only access was by a drawbridge, which made it difficult to provision in a lengthy siege. After installing Mary in the keep, Orkney left for Melrose (although this was a week before the lieges were due to meet). His plan was to link up with Home, not realising he had joined the Confederates. When his defection became clear, Orkney returned to Borthwick on 9 or 10 June. Mary now rearranged the muster of her levies to 12 June at Muirshead Abbey, but her 'proclamation was not so well obeyed, and so many as came had no heart to fight in that quarrel'.[25]

Casket Letter VIII was indisputably written by Mary from Borthwick on 8 June, while Orkney was at Melrose, notwithstanding that it is annotated as being from Stirling before her abduction.† Having asked to return to his estates three days earlier, Huntly feared that Mary would accuse him of treason, but he arrived from Edinburgh with 300 horse raised by Livingston and himself, aware that the Confederates planned to attack Borthwick on the following day (10 June). Mary's letter refers to him as 'your brother-in-law that was', and reports that he has promised his backing, supported by

---

* It is not clear how Balfour dissuaded them from moving into the Castle, but Orkney still trusted in his support, and later asked him to send troops to Borthwick. Even at Dunbar, he believed that he would have his support, if he returned to Edinburgh. This resulted in him playing into the Confederates' hands.

† The letter shows that Mary was well in control of herself at Borthwick, but there is no hint of passion to be expected from a wife most recently believing that she is pregnant. Being written from Borthwick, it could not have been found in the casket when originally opened in Edinburgh on 20 June. As Orkney never returned there afterwards, it must have been added later.

many folks here, and among others the Earl of Sutherland, who would rather die, considering the good they so lately received of me, than suffer me to be carried away, they conducting me, but wants advice on what to do after tomorrow.

Huntly's support is half-hearted and he

hath abashed me to see him so unresolved at the need. I assure myself he will play the part of the honest man; but I have thought good to advertise you of the fear he hath that he should be charged and accused of treason, to the end that, without mistrusting him, you may be the more circumspect.

By predating the letter, as if written from Stirling, the manipulator has used Mary's words of being 'carried away, they conducting me' to imply that she colluded in her abduction, although this makes no sense in the surrounding context.[26]

When Orkney returned to Borthwick he urgently requested support from Balfour, Lord John Hamilton and Huntly, who had returned to Edinburgh. On the evening of 10 June, Home joined Morton and Mar at Liberton Park, four miles south of Edinburgh, from where they advanced on Borthwick with between 700 and 800 mounted hackbutters. They were joined by Atholl, Glencairn, Lindsay, Sempill, Ruthven, Tullibardine, Kirkcaldy, and Ker of Cessford. Drury had tried to persuade Cecil to send English troops to support Home, but Elizabeth was still not openly prepared to oppose a fellow sovereign. Orkney was still trying to gather troops from levies and his allies; he could not risk becoming holed up at Borthwick with an inadequate force. Leaving Mary in command of a small garrison, he escaped by a postern gate with William Borthwick, younger of Crookston (a cadet branch of Lord Borthwick's family). Although William was captured, Orkney's horse outran his pursuers. He reached Haddington to seek reinforcements, trusting that the Confederates would not attack Borthwick with Mary there on her own. After intercepting two of her messengers sent to Huntly in Edinburgh, reiterating her urgent need for assistance, Morton sent them on their way to avoid being accused of treason.

Unaware of Orkney's escape, the Confederates lined out 2,000 men before Borthwick, taunting him with cries of, 'Traitor! Murderer! Butcher!' Late in the summer evening light, Mary shouted out from the battlements that he was not there. When they asked her to return to Edinburgh to assist in finding the King's murderers, she refused. This brought insults 'too evil and unseemly to be told, which the poor Princess did with her speech defend'.[27] Having no artillery for an attack, they withdrew to Dalkeith before returning to Edinburgh, claiming they had left after learning that the Queen was alone; their sole objective was to avenge the King's murder. On reaching Edinburgh, they found the gates had been barred by the Provost, but a small contingent scaled the walls to open the Cowgate Port. With Balfour offering no resistance from the Castle, the Provost surrendered and the Confederates were acclaimed by the townsfolk. On 12 June, a secret Council at the Tolbooth declared Orkney 'to be the principal author and murderer of the King's grace of good memory and ravishing of the Queen's Majesty'.[28] This had the effect of reversing his acquittal and gave legal substance to their call to arms. Morton's men ransacked the Abbey Kirk at Holyrood and plundered the gold collected at the Mint, including the still unmolten christening font. He now offered twenty shillings per month, a substantial rate, to anyone taking up arms to deliver the Queen from Orkney, and when Argyll at last arrived in Edinburgh with a substantial force, they boasted 3,000 men. As Orkney wrote much later, 'the city and castle of Edinburgh had abandoned us and gone over to them'.[29] Yet he still believed that Balfour was supporting him.

After receiving the Queen's messages, Huntly attempted, with Archbishop Hamilton's assistance, to generate support for her in Edinburgh. Yet they were forced to seek refuge in the Castle, still relying on Balfour's loyalty. To avoid his duplicity being revealed, they were permitted to leave the next day.* Huntly apparently hastened north to raise more troops, but his support for Mary and Orkney was evaporating. Hamilton headed south-west, but his family was also ambivalent about providing assistance.

At midnight on the following evening, Mary had the courage to escape from Borthwick Castle 'dressed in men's clothes, booted and spurred'. After being lowered by a rope from a window in the Great Hall, she left by the postern gate. After travelling a mile, she was met by Orkney's servants, who took her to join him at Black Castle on Cakemuir belonging to his allies, the Wauchopes. From here, they took a circuitous route to Dunbar, where Seton greeted their arrival at three o'clock in the morning with Hay of Yester, Borthwick and six local lairds.

Orkney's main objective was to regain control of Edinburgh, but he was still short of men and left Dunbar to raise troops in the Borders. Another

---

* Huntly's movements at this critical point are obscure. Suggestions that he remained under guard in Edinburgh Castle to prevent him from supporting Mary and Orkney are unlikely. If they had learned of this, Balfour would not have been able to induce them to return to Edinburgh.

message was sent to Huntly and Lord John Hamilton to bring men with all speed, but they no longer had the will to provide support against the substantial build-up of Confederate forces and arrived too late to assist. Both sides solicited wavering lieges, but Mary and Orkney lost the propaganda battle. By focusing only on executing justice on 'the murderer of the King and the ravisher of the Queen', the Confederates had outwitted them in their call to arms, and 'sundry libels were set out in both rhyme and prose, to move the hearts of the whole subjects to assist and take part in so good a cause'.[30] The Confederates soon had 4,000 men and the backing of the Reformist clergy. By 14 June, Orkney was back at Haddington with 1,600 men, but they were inferior troops provided by minor Border lairds, such as Ormiston, Langton, Wedderburn, Waughton and Bass. Drury had bribed the Elliots of Liddesdale to intercept and harry smaller contingents attempting to join him, so that much of his hoped-for support did not materialise. Although Mary wanted to look the part, her clothing had been left at Borthwick and she had to borrow garments from a countrywoman, 'a red petticoat' that barely covered her knees, 'sleeves tied with bows, a velvet hat and a muffler'.[31] Despite lacking the trappings of royalty, she left Dunbar to link with Orkney at Haddington, burning with defiance and supported by 200 hackbutters, sixty cavalry and three field guns. On arrival, she had 600 cavalry, and Seton had joined her, but she was dismayed at the small numbers coming to her banner. Unaware that they remained hopelessly outnumbered, she and Orkney marched on to Gladsmuir, where they made a proclamation that

> a number of conspirators, under pretext of preserving the Prince, were really trying to dethrone the Queen, that they might rule all things at their pleasure, [and that] very necessity compelled her to take up arms, and her hope was in the help of all faithful subjects, who would be rewarded with [the] lands and possessions of [the] rebels.[32]

Yet these brave words provided no appreciable increase in their support. The Confederates, with their numerical superiority, were anxious to confront her before rumours of her pregnancy started to attract sympathy.

Balfour now showed his true colours by enticing Orkney and Mary into a trap. On 13 June, he sent them a message

> to take the open field and to march direct to Edinburgh, so as to meet the insurgents on the road. He assured her that they would not keep their ground for a moment, especially when they knew that [as

The scene at Carberry Hill. Mary is shown twice, first on the right riding side-saddle among the soldiers at 'the Quince's Campe', and in the centre, riding to negotiate with the 'Lord of Grange' (Kirkcaldy), followed by Mary Seton on her pony. The NationalArchives/Photolibrary.com.

397

Governor of Edinburgh Castle] he had declared against them and would open fire upon their troops. If she did not do so, he would be compelled, he said, to come to terms with them.[33]

Even though they were still awaiting troops, Orkney and Mary set out immediately, unaware that they were outnumbered, billeting for the night at Prestonpans, from where they rode to Seton for what would be their last night together. The Confederates had taken no chances on Balfour's loyalty. Maitland interviewed him for three hours to gain assurance that Edinburgh Castle would be held for them and promised to back his retention as Governor. It is another irony that it was Balfour, Orkney's erstwhile colleague, encouraged by Maitland, so long Mary's champion, who caused their downfall.

Early on 15 June, bearing the lion rampant of Scotland and the St Andrew's Cross, Mary and Orkney moved forward to the slope of Carberry Hill overlooking the River Esk, seven miles east of Edinburgh. Their men were strategically placed inside an earthwork dug by Somerset prior to Pinkie Cleugh. Having left Edinburgh at two o'clock in the morning, the Confederates positioned themselves at the foot of a hill next to Cousland, two miles to the south-east. They carried banners between two spears, showing the infant James before his father's body praying, 'Judge and avenge my cause, O Lord.'[34] Morton and Home, with Ker of Cessford and Kerr of Ferniehirst, led the main body of cavalry, while Atholl, Mar, Glencairn, Lindsay, Sempill and Ruthven commanded the foot. Kirkcaldy controlled a smaller contingent of horse to block Mary from withdrawing to Dunbar.

Mary and Orkney played for time, vainly, as it turned out, having heard that Huntly and Archbishop Hamilton* were on their way with 800 men. The day was long and hot, and the Confederates had access to water from a stream. There was no inclination to fight on either side, and the time was spent in negotiation. Glencairn sent a message to the Queen that the Confederates had no quarrel with her and, if she handed over Orkney, the murderer of King Henry, they would 'restore her to her former authority as their natural sovereign'. She angrily refused, telling them to 'yield or take their chance in battle'.[35] Orkney seemed to offer her better prospects than the likes of Morton, Ruthven and Lindsay.

After three hours, du Croc appeared from Edinburgh offering to mediate through an interpreter. With instructions to improve French influence in

---

* Although troops led by Huntly and Lord John Hamilton set out to join them, they apparently received word that a compromise had been reached and did not continue. This may have been a convenient excuse.

Scotland not to bring down the monarchy, he tried to stop the Confederates from engaging their anointed Queen in battle. Morton explained that their complaint was against the King's murderers, not her. If Mary would not leave Orkney, one of the Confederates would face him in single combat. Du Croc crossed the open ground between the opposing armies to put this to Mary, who was sitting with Mary Seton. He apparently noticed that she was pregnant, even though she could not have been more than two months gone. After kissing her hand, he told her what the Confederates were proposing. She retorted in fury:

> It looks very ill of them to go against their own signed bond, after they themselves married me to him, having already acquitted him of the deed of which they would now accuse him.[36]

She told him to offer them a pardon for their offences, if they would submit. When Orkney arrived to ask what they proposed, du Croc greeted him, but would not take his hand. He loudly assured him of their loyalty to Mary, but told him quietly that they were his mortal enemies. Orkney complained:

> Is not the bond they gave to me well known to everyone? ... I have never meant to offend any of them, but rather to please them all, and they only speak of me as they do out of envy of my high estate.

In swashbuckling fashion, he affirmed:

> Fortune is free to those who may profit from it, and there is not a single one of them who would not gladly be in my place.[37]

The Confederates now sent a herald to Orkney with a written statement of their reasons for taking to the field. He later claimed:

> These were, firstly, to set the Queen free from the captivity, in which I was holding her, and also to avenge the death of the King, of which I had been accused.

He replied that he

> was not holding the Queen in any captivity, but that I loved and honoured her in all humanity as she deserved. There had not been any

question of my participating in, or consenting to, the murder of his Majesty,

having been cleared by Parliament. He was ready to defend his honour in the field against any comer, claiming, 'My cause is so just, I am quite sure that God is on my side.'[38] With typical bravado, he called on a Confederate to take up his challenge. James Murray of Pardewis immediately stepped forward, but the Queen vetoed him because of his inferior rank. Orkney then offered to fight Morton. As both of them had taken part in the murder plot, this was a macabre jest. Morton was now aged forty-seven, some fifteen years the elder, and was no longer considered proficient in armed combat, so Kirkcaldy offered to fight on his behalf. Wary of his awesome reputation, Orkney refused to fight with 'one who was only a baron', and suggested Moray's father-in-law, the reclusive Marischal. Despite his appropriate rank, Marischal was not fit, and Lindsay* claimed the right to fight, as a closer kinsman to King Henry than Morton, and took off his armour to limber up. He knelt to pray that God would preserve the innocent and punish the cruel and evil assassin who had shed his kinsman's blood. Having slain le Battu seven years earlier, Lindsay was no mean challenge. Morton provided him with Bell-the-Cat's two-handed sword to avenge Bell-the-Cat having been ousted from power by Orkney's great-grandfather. As the combatants prepared themselves, the Queen intervened in tears to prevent the fight. She knew she was pregnant, and feared her protector being killed. When du Croc backed her, Orkney likened him to the envoy who had tried in vain to arbitrate between Hannibal and Scipio before the Battle of Zama, only to witness the greatest spectacle he had ever seen. Du Croc returned to the Confederates with Mary's offer of clemency, but, when Glencairn retorted that they wanted revenge for the King's death, he could do no more and later rode back to Edinburgh 'with tears in my eyes'.

Time had elapsed, and, with the day hot, the Confederates had the advantage of shade in the valley in addition to water. Mary's troops on the hill became extremely thirsty in the full sun. When Orkney sent scouts in search of water, they were captured. Wine arrived in casks from Seton, but this only caused dehydration. As the day progressed, raw Border troops slipped away looking for refreshment causing morale to fall, so that others

---

* Neither Lindsay nor his wife was a closer kinsman to King Henry than Morton, but he had a better reputation in single combat. Morton's father, Sir George Douglas, was the brother of King Henry's grandfather, Angus, making him a first cousin once removed. Lindsay was a half second cousin, sharing the 1st Earl of Argyll as a great-grandfather. His wife, Euphemia Douglas, was a third cousin, sharing the 1st Earl and Countess of Lennox as great-great-grandparents.

disappeared or even deserted to the Confederates. According to Melville, they had heard rumours that Mary was negotiating terms, but would not make the first move to desert her husband. Although probably untrue, this proved devastating.

Despite Orkney facing unassailable numerical odds, du Croc had grudging respect for his management:

> I am obliged to say that I saw a great leader, speaking with great confidence and leading his forces boldly, gaily and skilfully. I admired him, for he saw his foes were resolute, he could not count on half his men, and yet was not dismayed. He had not on his side a single lord of note. Yet I rated his chances higher because he was in sole command.[39]

Mary would not surrender her throne lightly, but, with her army trickling away to no more than 400 men, the outcome of military action was no longer in doubt. She tried to leave the field, but found her way blocked by Kirkcaldy. When one of Orkney's men took aim at him, she immediately told the man not to shame her. Knowing that Kirkcaldy was an ally at heart, she sought terms. Maitland and Atholl were too embarrassed to negotiate, but Kirkcaldy assured her that, if she would go with them, Orkney could leave with a safe conduct until Parliament debated his guilt. Orkney begged her to retreat with him to Dunbar to raise another army: 'I told her they would take her prisoner and strip her of all authority.'[40] As so often when faced with a crucial decision, Mary took the wrong one and overrode her husband. She wanted him free to fight again, after lying low while she arranged for a proper review of the King's murder. Kirkcaldy heard her telling him that

> she owed a duty to the late King her husband, a duty which she would not neglect. Most willingly therefore would she authorise everyone to exercise the fullest liberty of inquiry into the circumstances of his death. She intended to do so herself, and to punish with all severity such as should be convicted thereof.[41]

She made clear that she would investigate both her enemies and her husband, which again implies that she was fully aware of the Craigmillar bond. She probably expected another whitewash. She told Orkney that, if found innocent,

> nothing would prevent her from rendering to him all that a true and lawful wife ought to do, but, if guilty, it would be to her an endless

source of regret that, by her marriage, she had ruined her good reputation, and from this she would endeavour to free herself by all possible means.[42]

By distancing herself from him, she hoped to demonstrate her own innocence.

Orkney left Mary in the hands of the Confederates. His safe conduct suited them, as they did not want his evidence revealed in an investigation. Mary wept as they embraced.* He gave her what seems to have been the Craigmillar bond, implicating many of their opponents, telling her to 'take good care of the paper'.[43] Seton and Fleming with between twelve and thirty horsemen went with him to Dunbar with a plan to raise reinforcements. He never saw her again.

Always chivalrous, Kirkcaldy assured Mary that

> he had been sent, at the unanimous consent of the rebels, for the sole purpose of offering to the Queen, as their rightful superior, their true allegiance, and to give her a guaranteed safe conduct to come amongst them. Furthermore, that each single one of them wanted no more than to accord her all honour and obedience in whatever way she wished to command them.[44]

Mary very quickly learned that this was not the general intention, and Kirkcaldy considered her subsequent treatment and imprisonment in Lochleven to have breached his honour. He led her on horseback to join the other Confederate lords. She was still in the clothes borrowed at Dunbar, begrimed from her day in the saddle. Yet she held her head high, and Mary Seton, who had remained with her on her pony, attended her. She was received with 'all due reverence' by Morton, Home and the other lords, who assured her that she was now in her rightful place among her own true and faithful subjects.[45] Yet their deference was short-lived. According to Drury, they produced the banner showing the dead King's body, which she later admitted 'she wished she had never seen'. Troops led by Atholl and Tullibardine roughly jostled her, shouting: 'Burn the whore! Burn the murderess of her husband!'[46] Kirkcaldy and other lords struck out with their swords at those taunting her, but to little effect. According to du Croc, she was in no

---

* The Confederates claimed that they kissed passionately in front of both armies, but this was no doubt for public consumption. Du Croc's eyewitness report says that they clasped hands. This seems more likely as they were both on horseback.

mood for conciliation, but 'talked of nothing but hanging and crucifying them all'.[47] She was furious, rounding on Morton:

> How is this, my Lord Morton? I am told that all this is done in order to get justice among the King's murderers. I am told that you are one of the chief of them.

He answered: 'Come, come, this is not the place to discuss such matters,' but was sufficiently disconcerted to move out of earshot.[48] She was escorted to Edinburgh under guard, with the banner showing the King's body ahead of her, and reached the gates after eight o'clock in the evening. When Lindsay gripped her by the wrist, she asserted: 'By the hand which is now in yours, I will have your head for this.'[49] Yet she was never able to do so, and Sir William Douglas of Hawick and Ker of Cessford took charge of her. The Confederates had packed the streets with people screaming: 'Burn the whore! Kill her! Drown her! She is not worthy to live!' 'All disfigured in dust and tears, she rode past amid execrations of the people from the windows and stairs.'[50]

Mary was not taken to Holyrood but, at Maitland's suggestion, to The Black Turnpike, a luxurious but fortified house on the High Street used by his brother-in-law, Sir Simon Preston, as Provost. On arrival at eleven o'clock at night, she was placed under guard in a sparsely furnished upper chamber. The banner depicting the dead King was positioned in the street opposite her window. The mob continued shouting abuse; 'the women be most furious and impudent against the Queen, and yet the men be mad enough'.[51] She was without servants and, with guards in her bedroom, could not undress even when she wanted to relieve herself. Although she was invited by her captors to join them for supper, she refused, perhaps in fear of poison. There was no chance to escape.

Sir James Melville heard a story, which he believed to be fabricated, that Mary wrote a letter to Orkney, 'her dear heart, whom she should never forget or abandon for absence', and gave it to a boy, who promptly handed it to her captors.[52] If true, it is surprising that it was not used in evidence against her. Buchanan's *Detectio* makes no mention of it, but claims that she tried to smuggle out a purse of gold for Orkney.

Mary had no one to turn to. If she were not already aware of its content, she had time to study the Craigmillar bond with so many of its signatories responsible for her detention. She realised that they would want her dead or removed from the throne. She was in fear of being suffocated, so that her captors could claim she had taken poison. She was too exhausted to sleep, but lay down fully dressed for the night with the clatter of guards outside her door. The next morning, in a desperate bid for help, she appeared in hysterics at her window with her tangled hair hanging loose. She opened her bodice to expose her breasts and, with 'piteous lamentations', appealed to those below. Although some continued to insult her, many were 'moved to compassion' until the guards pulled her out of view. Independent witnesses reported that the crowds were soon showing support for her, but when the lords promised to return her to Holyrood 'to do as she list, she was so pacified that the people willingly departed'.[53] Yet Home, with his cavalry, spent three hours in clearing the streets to prevent a rescue attempt.

References

1. Weir, p. 375
2. Guy, p. 359, and Weir, p. 375
3. Labanoff; Anderson; cited in Weir, p. 375
4. Du Croc to Catherine de Medici, 18 May 1567, Teulet; Anderson; Keith; cited in Guy, p. 337, and Weir, pp. 375–6
5. Melville, p. 154; Keith; cited in Guy, p. 337, and Weir, p. 376
6. Guy, p. 337
7. Melville, p. 68; cited in Guy, p. 337, and Weir, p. 377
8. Drury in CSP Foreign; cited in Guy, p. 336, and Weir, p. 378
9. Drury to Cecil, 27 May 1567, CSP Foreign, cited in Guy, p. 337–8, and Weir, p. 377
10. Weir, p. 377
11. Teulet; cited in Weir, p. 378
12. CSP Scottish; cited in Weir, p. 379
13. Tytler, New Edition, III, p. 3; Teulet, II, p. 156; Selections from Unpublished Manuscripts; cited in Antonia Fraser, p. 377, and Weir, p. 381
14. Guy, p. 339
15. Labanoff; CSP Scottish; cited in Weir, p. 383
16. CSP Venetian; cited in Weir, p. 382
17. Plowden, cited in Weir, p. 382
18. J. B. Black, *The Reign of Elizabeth*, in Weir, p. 382
19. Cockburn and Maitland, cited in Weir, p. 378
20. Weir, p. 378
21. CSP Foreign, cited in Weir, p. 384
22. Weir, p. 384
23. Guy, p. 338
24. Melville, cited in Weir, p. 380
25. Melville, cited in Weir, p. 385
26. Weir, pp. 361, 385–6
27. Nau; Drury to Cecil, CSP, Foreign, VIII, p. 246, cited in Guy, p. 341, Antonia Fraser, p. 379, and Weir, p. 387

28. Guy, pp. 341–2
29. Cockburn and Maitland, cited in Weir, p. 387
30. Melville, cited in Weir, p. 388
31. Drury to Cecil, 18 June 1567, CSP Foreign; Teulet; cited in Weir, p. 388
32. Cited in Gore-Browne and Weir, p. 389
33. Nau, cited in Weir, pp. 388–9
34. CSP Scottish; cited in Guy, p. 343, Antonia Fraser, p. 381 and Weir, p. 389
35. Cited by Sitwell and Weir, p. 390
36. Guy, p. 344
37. Guy, p. 345, and Weir, p. 390
38. Cockburn and Maitland; cited in Weir, p. 390
39. Cited in Antonia Fraser, p. 382, and Weir, pp. 390–1
40. Cockburn and Maitland, cited in Weir, p. 391
41. Nau, cited in Weir, p. 391
42. Nau, cited in Weir, p. 391
43. Cockburn and Maitland, cited in Weir, p. 392
44. Cockburn and Maitland, cited in Weir, p. 392
45. Melville, cited in Weir, p. 392
46. Melville, cited in Weir, p. 393
47. Du Croc to Catherine de Medici, 17 June 1567, Teulet; cited in Guy, p. 349, and Weir, p. 393
48. Nau, p. 48, cited in Antonia Fraser, pp. 383–4
49. Drury to Cecil, 18 June 1567, CSP Foreign; cited in Guy, pp. 349–50, and Weir, p. 393
50. Nau, cited in Antonia Fraser, p. 38
51. Cited by Neale, Wormald, *Mary, Queen of Scots*, p. 171, and Weir, p. 393
52. Melville, cited in Guy, p. 350, and Weir, p. 396
53. Melville, p. 156; Teulet; John Beaton in Sloane MMS; Hay Fleming, p. 165; cited in Weir, p. 394

33

Imprisonment in Lochleven and Mary's Deposition from the Throne

Mary had understood that her surrender at Carberry Hill would lead to a parliamentary investigation into King Henry's murder, but, as she came to realise, this was exactly what Morton, Maitland and Balfour were most anxious to avoid. It was unlikely to incriminate her, but would put at risk the signatories of the Craigmillar bond, which she now held.

The Confederates had to decide what to do with Mary. Some of them had achieved their objective of removing her from Orkney's control and would have restored her to the throne. Others wanted Moray as Regent and sought her immediate execution. John Spottiswood provided a letter, probably drafted by Knox, describing her as 'that wicked woman'. Morton, who needed to hold them together, gained a consensus to spare her life 'with provision of securitie of religion'.[1] There was general agreement that she should be held securely to stop Orkney attempting a rescue. They chose to imprison her at the island fortress of Lochleven, to keep her utterances, particularly about the Craigmillar bond, out of earshot. It is no surprise that this disappeared. It will have been removed from Mary and destroyed. They signed a new bond to confirm her imprisonment, despite the risk of it being treasonable. It was of critical importance to avoid her escaping and they would need immunity from prosecution, if she were ever to be freed.

Although Maitland's opposition to Mary evaporated as soon as she was separated from Orkney, he had become so implicated in the King's murder that he was blackmailed into continuing to assist Moray's allies. While still at The Black Turnpike, Mary saw him in the crowd below her window and, to his embarrassment, called out to him to come to her. Despite appearing to take no notice, Mary much later told Nau that he came privately.* He was

---

* In another version of this interview, Mary is said to have pleaded with Maitland to help her to escape, and to take her 'where fortune might conduct them', but he refused. Maitland may have put this about to explain their meeting, but Mary would hardly have chosen the effete Maitland as her swashbuckling saviour, and he was in no position to help her. Nau's version of events has a ring of truth to it and implies that Mary was innocent of playing any part in the murder plan, but had, by then, seen Morton, Balfour and Maitland's signatures on the Craigmillar bond.

apparently so mortified 'that he did not dare to raise his eyes and look her in the face'. He told her that she would be 'held in custody until everything had been done to authorise the investigation' of King Henry's death. It was suspected and feared that she meant to thwart the execution of justice. He told her that the Council would never permit her to return to Orkney, who, he said, ought to be hanged. Nau reported that he 'discoursed with something more than freedom on Orkney's habits, against whom he manifested an intensity of hatred'. She replied that she was fully aware of the false pretexts that the Lords were employing [in] charging her with wishing to hinder justice done for the murder, which they themselves had committed. She was ready to refute these accusations by joining with the lords in the inquiry (Mary was no doubt aware that it was the last thing they would want). She told Maitland that no one understood Orkney's involvement better than him. Morton, Balfour, and he, 'more than any others, hindered the inquiry into the murder, to which they were the consenting and guilty parties'. Orkney had told her that he had acted entirely by their persuasion and advice, and showed her their signatures ... They were all miserable wretches if they made her bear the punishment for their crimes.[2]

Mary told Maitland that if he continued to support the Confederates, she would reveal everything she had been told by Orkney of his involvement. He was furious and went so far as to say that, if she did so, she would drive him to greater lengths than he yet had gone in order to save his own life. On the other hand, if she let matters tone down little by little, the day would come when he might do her good service. He begged her not to ask to see him again, as this caused mistrust and put his life at risk. If she left him alone he might be able to protect her from being 'put out of the way'.[3] This seems a fairly accurate assessment of Maitland's dilemma.

As spokesman for the Confederates, Maitland provided du Croc with an official version of his conversation with Mary. By now the theme of a crime of passion, first hinted at in the placards, was being developed. He explained her passionate love for Orkney, claiming that she leaned out of the window at The Black Turnpike in tears to ask why she had been separated from the man, 'with whom she had hoped to live and die with the full approval of the world'.[4] Maitland claimed that he again warned her that he could show her a letter written by Orkney to Jean Gordon, in which she was treated as his true wife and Mary as his mistress. Yet Mary retorted that his letters to her contradicted this and, despite being miserable since marriage (which du Croc was well aware of), her desire to live and die with him was as violent as ever. She would willingly take ship with him to where the winds might take them, but, as this was impossible, she proposed that he should be exiled, a solution which Maitland apparently supported.

From his own interviews with Mary, du Croc must have had doubts about Maitland's assertion of Mary's passion for Orkney. Yet it was this passion, which provided the motive for her being involved in the murder and the justification for her arrest. As the Casket Letters also follow a theme of passion, this is further evidence that Maitland put them together. It was only much later that the idea was fed to Buchanan to enable him to prepare his *Detectio*. Maitland not only had the intellect to provide Classical metaphor and French poetry, but, as Secretary, had access to all Mary's correspondence (and could easily have obtained Orkney's). Despite being married to Mary Fleming, he failed his Queen to save his own skin by helping Moray. It was the falsified evidence in the Casket Letters at the Conference at Westminster that would justify Mary's continued detention. It was only when she was imprisoned in England that he belatedly demonstrated his support for her, but by then her cause was hopeless. Not without reason has history named Maitland as 'Meikle Wylie' [Much Wily].[5] This was a pun on Machiavelli, who believed that a prince could be devious to protect the State; Maitland was devious to protect himself.

Mary Fleming's loyalty has also been questioned, sometimes being seen as a major influence on her husband to support Mary and sometimes as the forger of Mary's handwriting in the Casket Letters. It is surprising, with her acknowledged hold over him, that she failed to curb his outrageous libels of the Queen. Yet there is only the flimsiest evidence that she was the forger of Mary's handwriting. Before the Conference at York, Mary was to suggest that her ladies might be able to counterfeit her writing, and 'principally such as are in company with' the Scottish Commissioners.[6] Mary Fleming certainly adopted similar calligraphy, learned during their schooling in France. Yet Mary's comment was intended to show that incriminating insertions could easily have been added to the Casket Letters (which she had not been able to examine). It is highly unlikely that Mary Fleming was ever disloyal. Her son born at this time was named James in honour of the Queen and the Prince, and all her family steadfastly backed Mary. Mary Bethune's writing bore an even closer similarity to Mary's and she was, at the time, being questioned by Mary on the whereabouts of some missing jewellery. Yet she and Ogilvy of Boyne were unfailingly faithful. Without original documents one can only speculate, but it is much more likely that Maitland made the manuscript insertions himself. He later admitted to Norfolk that from time to time he had forged Mary's handwriting. There were of course a number of able master forgers working for Walsingham in England at this time, even if

Maitland was not responsible. The masterstroke was to employ parts of Mary's own writing and idiom, so that branding the letters as forgeries would be so difficult.

Mary did nothing to contradict the innuendo of her passion for Orkney. Drury wrote:

> Though her body be restrained, yet her heart is not dismayed; she cannot be dissuaded from her affection to the Duke, but seems to offer sooner to receive harm herself than he should.[7]

Given the unhappiness of their short marriage witnessed by so many, her determination to stand behind him can only be explained by her being pregnant. Even though she knew that his signature was on the Craigmillar bond, she did not denounce him until after her miscarriage. His act of treason, if proved, would make their child illegitimate. Yet so long as she defended him, the Confederates would keep her imprisoned.

Maitland's first task on the Confederates' behalf was to arrange a deal with du Croc. They needed to gauge how the French would react to Mary being deposed. Du Croc advised that, if Mary were sent to France, where her guilt was now accepted, she would be shut up in a convent, but if she were sent to England, they would feel obliged to take her side. A secret pact was reached. Du Croc agreed that France would not interfere, so long as England did not assume control of Scottish government.

On 16 June, the day after Carberry Hill, the Confederates agreed to move Mary to Lochleven. With Orkney still at large and with an ugly mood in the Edinburgh streets, they feared a rescue being attempted by either Huntly or the Hamiltons. Yet arranging her imprisonment presented a dilemma for them, as any trial risked incriminating all the conspirators in the King's murder. Deposing her from the throne would require parliamentary approval, but parliament could only be called by Mary or a legally appointed regent. The solution was to imprison her for her safety away from Edinburgh and without trial. Although Kirkcaldy believed this was against his undertaking to her when she submitted to him, he was overruled.

The first step was to move Mary from The Black Turnpike to Holyrood. Morton left nothing to chance. He and Atholl escorted her with a guard of 200 hackbutters, still carrying the banner depicting the body of the King. They were followed by the other Confederates and a further 1,000 men. The crowd was again packed with people shouting, 'Burn her, burn her, she is not worthy to live, kill her, drown her.'[8] Mary shouted back to confirm her innocence, claiming that they had been deceived by false and cruel traitors.

On reaching Holyrood, she was reunited with Mary Seton and Mary Sempill (Livingston), but, while they ate, Morton stood behind her chair to stop any plotting for an escape. The Confederates arranged Mary's removal from Holyrood under cover of darkness, and during the meal Morton sent a message to establish if her horses were ready. When this was confirmed, she was abruptly told to leave. She had no time to pack, but set out with only the clothes she stood up in, a silk nightgown and a coarse brown cloak. She was permitted only two *femmes de chambre* to travel with her and believed that she would be taken to join her son at Stirling.

After mounting a waiting horse, Mary was taken to Leith, where she was handed over to Ruthven and Lindsay. They did not take her to Stirling, but boarded a ferry across the Forth to Kinross-shire. She seems to have received a message that the Hamiltons, with support from Hay of Yester, were planning a rescue. Although she tried to slow her captors, they whipped her in. She had no inkling of her destination while she was hurried north. They reached the shores of Loch Leven before daybreak, from where she was rowed out to one of the four islands with its austere five-storey keep with round turrets on each corner.

The choice of Lochleven had not been difficult and may have been taken by Moray before leaving Scotland. Being positioned on an island half a mile from the shore at its closest point,* it was extremely secure. Sir William Douglas was of undoubted loyalty; not only was he Morton's kinsman (he was later to become the 5th Earl of Morton), but a half-brother of Moray and nephew of Mar. Mary had debated there with Knox in 1563 and had visited with the King for hunting in Kinross-shire, but it must have seemed a forbidding setting early in the morning of 17 June 1567. The household included Sir William's brother, George ('pretty Geordie'), and their formidable mother, Margaret, née Erskine ('the old lady'), Mar's sister and Moray's mother. One of Sir William's sisters, Euphemia, was married to Lindsay, and both Lindsay and Ruthven remained there to guard her.

Mary was treated courteously, but despaired at the lack of appropriate furniture and was no doubt exhausted. For the next fortnight, she hardly ate, causing those around her to fear for her life. Although the Confederates' bond advocated her being restored to liberty once freed from Orkney, she was now incarcerated. An order of the Council for her indefinite detention

---

* Loch Leven was then twelve miles across, considerably larger and the islands smaller than today. In the nineteenth century, it was partially drained, making the castle seem less imposing.

was signed by Morton, Glencairn, Home, Mar, Atholl, Lindsay, Ruthven and others. Sir William insisted on a warrant confirming his authority to hold her. This was probably drafted by Maitland, as it explained that she had intended to 'fortify and maintain Orkney in his crimes, and was a woman of inordinate passion'.[9] Both Morton and Home had, of course, signed the Ainslie's Tavern bond in approval of the marriage.

The Confederates' show of solidarity did not crack, despite their treasonable actions. They were all determined to isolate Mary from communicating with Orkney. Moray's allies among them also planned her deposition from the throne. On 29 June, du Croc left Edinburgh with a letter from the Confederates to Charles IX setting out 'the justice of our cause'.[10] It is not known what was said, but in July Throckmorton told Elizabeth that 'du Croc carries with him matter little to the Queen's advantage'.[11] He may also have brought early versions of the Casket Letters. Broadsheets continued to emphasise her immorality, inciting public opinion against her, while from the pulpit Protestant ministers denounced her as a murderess. On 21 July, Knox returned to Edinburgh in triumph and thundered against 'the whore of Babylon and the scarlet adventuress'. Throckmorton said he threatened that 'God would send a great plague on the whole nation if Mary was spared from punishment'. Even the Pope withdrew his support. When, on 2 July, he became aware of her marriage to Orkney, he broke off diplomatic relations with her, unable to decide which of the two Queens of Britain was worse, and announced that it was not his intention to have any further communication with Mary, unless in times to come he shall see some better sign of her life and religion than he has witnessed in the past.[12]

Glencairn took possession of her silver and jewellery, which was eventually handed to Moray. Twenty-seven pieces of plate were sent to the Mint to be melted into silver coin. He infuriated the Catholic nobles by destroying the religious furnishings in the Chapel Royal at Holyrood with help from the Lords of the Congregation. All this brought her some sympathy, and Maitland believed that if she had been prepared to divorce Orkney, he could now have negotiated her freedom. Yet, with her pregnancy, this was not an option she would consider.

When appropriate quarters were at last refurbished at Lochleven, Mary was given two rooms of the third floor of the Round Tower. She could walk in the gardens, but the watchful Sir William Douglas gave her no opportunity for escape and insisted on 'the old lady' sleeping in her bedroom.[13] Mary was unaware that Morton had given instructions for her to be killed, if a rescue was attempted. Her humour improved, and Drury reported that she was 'better digesting' her captivity.[14] On 17 July, Bedford claimed that she was calmer and better quieted of late, and takes both rest and meat, and also some dancing and play at the cards, and much better than she was wont to do; and it is said that she is become fat.*[15]

Ruthven and Lindsay continued to guard her, but Ruthven became smitten and proposed a night-time tryst in a love letter to her. That night, Mary, now four months pregnant, hid her chamber women behind tapestries in her room as witnesses. At four o'clock in the morning, Ruthven burst in and, on his knees, begged her to marry him, notwithstanding that he was already married to Dorothea Stewart, Methven's daughter. He then offered to free her, if she would become his lover. Mary was indignant and Ruthven was removed.

Moray's allies would not have dared to hold Mary imprisoned without tacit approval from the English, and Cecil continued to pull the strings behind the scenes, always closely informed when new evidence against her came to light. On 23 June, Bedford reported to him that the Confederates did not want to keep her imprisoned longer than necessary, but would act as Elizabeth requested. This suggests that it was Cecil who had originally recommended Mary's imprisonment. At the end of June, he wrote to Moray in Paris sending packages thought to have contained transcripts of early versions of the Casket Letters. He also advised him to return at once to supervise inquiries into the King's murder.

Despite Cecil's efforts to assure England's security, he did not always harness Elizabeth to his views. She had watched the political changes in Scotland with trepidation, shocked at an anointed Queen being imprisoned by her subjects. She did not want other European heads of state to believe she supported Mary's deposition, for fear of them taking revenge on her. To placate them, she fulminated from afar, saying:

They have no warrant nor authority, by the law of God or man, to be as superiors, judges or vindicators over their prince and sovereign, for an example to all posterity. Though she were guilty of all they charge her with, I cannot assist them while their Queen is imprisoned.[16]

She threatened war, but Cecil dissuaded her, although she sent Throckmorton, Cecil's political opponent, to negotiate Mary's restoration and to offer to bring up James as her ward in England, proposing the sale of Orkney's attainted estates to pay for his education. Although Throckmorton

---

* Mary was eleven weeks pregnant with twins and, in all probability, this was beginning to show.

was instructed to visit Mary, he was secretly met by Home and Maitland at Fast Castle, where they refused him access to her probably on Cecil's advice, and Home escorted him back to Edinburgh with 400 horse. Throckmorton was now extremely concerned for Mary's safety and at her captors' brutality. Elizabeth faced a dilemma. She preferred to keep Mary on the throne as a powerless Catholic puppet, but she wanted Moray in power. Her attitude may have saved Mary's life, but failed to resolve Cecil's problem of providing a Protestant succession in England.

Everyone realised that control of Prince James would determine Scotland's destiny. Throckmorton heard that the French were offering Mary a 'peaceful reclusion' at the convent of St-Pierre-des-Dames in Reims with James to accompany her 'at the French devotion'. This would leave Scotland to be governed by a Council of Regency. Yet as no French ambassador was given access to her to make such a proposal, the story is unlikely and, with James in a secure family environment with Mar, he was in safe hands. Throckmorton recognised that James's future depended on whom Mar agreed to support. He asked Mar to protect Mary, but he replied, 'To save her life by endangering her son or his estate, or by betraying my marrows, I will never do it, my Lord Ambassador, for all the gowd in the world.' Mar believed the propaganda that Mary was morally indefensible and, with his absolute control of the Prince, his 'incorruptible integrity' sealed her and Orkney's fate. He had backed the Confederate cause to defeat them and signed the agreement committing her to Lochleven. He now favoured her being deposed to make way for Moray, his nephew, as Regent.

On his return to Edinburgh on 13 July, Throckmorton found no groundswell of sympathy for Mary, with 'the most part of Scotland incensed against the Queen'. Even Huntly and Herries supported Moray. Yet Elizabeth continued to fulminate that Mary's offences were nothing compared to the outrage committed 'by those that are by nature and law subject to her'.[17] Throckmorton again aired Elizabeth's concerns with Maitland, who, despite seeming wise and reasonable, would still not allow him to see the Queen. Maitland explained that she was being 'guarded very straitly because she had refused to lend herself to any plans to seek out the murderers of her husband'. This was untrue, but he continued to cite her passion for Orkney to justify her detention. He claimed that, given a choice between her Kingdom and her husband, she

avoweth constantly that she would rather live and die with him a simple damsel; she could never consent that he should fare worse or have more harm than herself.[18]

Throckmorton was politely told not to interfere, but he managed to send Mary messages carried in Robert Melville's scabbard, advising her of Elizabeth's desire to help, but also warning her to give up Orkney. Melville carried Mary's response that she was 'seven weeks gone with child' and, despite being in despair, divorce would make it a bastard and forfeit her honour. This was no protestation of undying love for Orkney as Maitland was claiming. Throckmorton feared that the Confederates would want to do away with her, as they were 'unsafe while she lives'.[19] He warned her that they were seeking her abdication, but, if she signed away her throne under duress, it would be illegal. When Maitland heard of Throckmorton's continuing interference, he sent him back to England carrying a letter from the Confederates to Elizabeth, confirming their need to keep Mary locked up, as she still reasserted the vehemence of her passion, and there was a need for breathing time and leisure to go forward in the prosecution of the murder. Yet the Casket Letters, said by Morton to have been found on 19 June, were not mentioned to Throckmorton, as they surely would have been, if they then existed.

On receiving Throckmorton's letter, Elizabeth defied Cecil and her Council by replying on 27 July that she would not negotiate while Mary remained imprisoned and was unimpressed with the Confederates' 'colourful defences' of their actions.[20] She told Cecil to threaten war if they deposed or executed Mary. He had already advised Moray in Paris to return to Scotland, knowing that she was to be deposed, but told Elizabeth that they were still undecided what to do.

After Cecil's initial contact with Moray, Sir James Melville arrived in Paris in early July bringing the Council's formal offer of the Regency. Moray set out immediately, arriving in London on 23 July to see Cecil. He then met Elizabeth to confirm his innocence. He made a show of sympathy for Mary by sending his secretary, Nicholas Elphinstone, on to Scotland to complain at her harsh treatment. He told Elizabeth that he

> could not fail to strive for her liberty because, besides being her brother, he was much beholden to her; but still, [Orkney's] business and the King's murder had much grieved him and had caused him to leave the country. He returned now to see what could be done in these troubles, although he feared they would be difficult to mend. Many of those concerned in the Queen's detention were his closest adherents ... He would therefore find some means by which she should remain Queen, but without sufficient liberty to do them any harm, whilst punishing at the same time the authors of the King's murder.[21]

Cecil will have carefully briefed him on what to say, but Moray had no intention of protecting her throne, although he was unaware that by then her abdication papers were already signed.

Moray will also have sought Cecil's guidance on how to handle the foreign ambassadors in London. He told de Silva what he had said to Elizabeth, but added that the discovery of the Casket Letters made Mary's abdication unavoidable. He claimed to have heard something of the content of one letter, which 'proved beyond doubt that she had been cognisant of the murder of her husband', but he had not felt able to discuss it with Elizabeth. He added that, in his opinion, Mary's worst crime was to 'pet and fondle' the King only hours before his murder. De Silva was not taken in by Moray's show of loyalty to his sister. He was 'more inclined to believe that he will do it for himself, if he has the chance'.[22]

Sometime between 20 and 24 July, Mary miscarried twins,* losing a great deal of blood. This no doubt was a result of stress at her imprisonment. Although well known in diplomatic circles, her miscarriage was not made public, in an effort to limit any upwelling of sympathy. The twins seem to have been conceived at Dunbar in April, shortly before her marriage, despite contemporary reports of conception prior to the King's murder.†

Now that she was separated from Orkney, Mary started to gain support. Rumblings of disquiet at her continued captivity began well before her abdication. Despite the Confederates' outward show of unity, they differed on how she should be treated. Seton, Livingston, Fleming and Eglinton had never wavered in their loyalty and met at Dumbarton during June to seek her freedom. They were joined by Atholl, Herries, Huntly, Crawford, Lord John and Archbishop Hamilton. Perhaps more surprisingly, Argyll, who had signed the Craigmillar bond, also appeared. Despite Knox's efforts to woo him back into Moray's camp, he had stood by Mary since her return from France. John Sempill (Mary Livingston's husband) also came to Dumbarton after failing in an attempt to rescue Mary from Lochleven. The Marians, as they would be called, signed a bond to seek her liberty, but when rescue

---

* There were unfounded rumours well into 1568 of a daughter having being born. In the seventeenth century, a footnote to Castelnau's edited memoirs claimed that she gave birth to a daughter at Lochleven, who was smuggled to France to be brought up in the convent of Soissons.

† Mary's pregnancy is not mentioned prior to May 1567, but in June de Silva in London received a report that she was 'five months gone with child'.[23] If this were true, it would have been noticed well beforehand, and she would have been unlikely to survive her miscarriage in July. The report should probably have indicated that she was five *weeks* pregnant. Nevertheless it implied that she had conceived in January, while the King was recovering from syphilis in Glasgow, which fitted with rumours of a long-running affair and a crime of passion.

seemed insuperable they could not agree what to do. On 29 June, the Bishop of Ross found them 'all being full of tumult', and withdrew to his see.

A rift opened between the Marians and Moray's supporters. On 27 July, Lord John Hamilton* went to the General Assembly to plead for her release, but was not permitted to attend. He then wrote to Throckmorton seeking Elizabeth's help to gain Mary's freedom and to pursue the King's murderers, while providing protection for James. Yet Throckmorton was suspicious of the mainly Catholic Marians, particularly Herries, who he saw as 'the cunning horse leech and wisest of the whole faction ...no one can be sure of him', and Elizabeth refused them assistance. Despite her continuing show of horror at Mary's imprisonment to placate her European counterparts, she never actively opposed the Confederates prior to Mary's deposition, drawn as they were from every faction. Cecil had persuaded her of the merits of Moray becoming Regent.

Moray's allies found the prospect of his Regency far more appealing than leaving Mary on the throne. Mary would be twenty-five in December, the age when she could recall grants of land made earlier in her reign. Many nobles stood to lose, and it was a further incentive for her removal from the throne. The Confederates sent Lindsay, in 'boasting humour', to obtain her signature on her abdication papers, while she lay recovering from her miscarriage. When she demanded the parliamentary enquiry as promised, Lindsay shocked Melville, who was with her, by threatening to cut her throat if she did not sign. She was forced to rely on Throckmorton's assurance that her signature given under duress would be invalid. There were three documents; the first said 'she was so vexed, broken and unquieted' that she could no longer continue as Queen; the second confirmed Moray as Regent; and the third appointed Châtelherault, Argyll, Morton, Glencairn and Mar to act as a Council of Regency until his return.[24] Although it was outrageous, she had no choice but to sign. Weakened by her miscarriage and under stress, she seems to have suffered a liver complaint. Her body swelled and her skin became jaundiced and covered with pustules. Yet she soon recovered after bleeding and a potion to strengthen her heart.

Maitland warned Throckmorton that, if he attempted to garner support for Mary, her life would be endangered. He claimed that 'the realm could never be worse governed than it was, for either the Queen was advised by the worse counsel or by no counsel'. Throckmorton tried to persuade the

---

* Lord John Hamilton's personal agenda was to persuade Mary to divorce Orkney. He hoped to gain the Crown for the Hamiltons by marrying her himself. Yet when she abdicated in favour of James, there was a short period when Hamilton support for her evaporated.

Lords to defer James's coronation, as it was not good to put the State in the hands of a child. Yet this took place on 29 July, when the documentation appointing Moray as Regent, which Mary had signed, was read out. Having instructions from Elizabeth not to attend, Throckmorton sought her consent to return to England, but was told to continue working for Mary's freedom. He was to report how much Elizabeth disliked *their* doing, but Cecil transformed Elizabeth's meaning by changing *their* to *her*. Elizabeth continued:

> We will take plain part against them, to revenge their sovereign, for example to all posterity ... You may assure them that we detest the murder of our cousin the king, and mislike the marriage of the queen with Bothwell as much as any of them. But think it not tolerable for them ... to call her ... to answer to their accusations by way of force; for we do not think it consonant in nature that the head should be subject to the foot.

This greatly comforted Mary and, on 29 July, Robert Melville replied on her behalf that 'she would rather herself and the prince were in your realm than elsewhere in Christendom'.[25] She was still relying on Elizabeth to support her when forced to flee Scotland.

Mary was not told of James's coronation in advance, but found that Sir William Douglas had prepared bonfires in the garden at Lochleven, with artillery being discharged. On demanding what was going on, Sir William asked her why she would not celebrate her son being crowned. Mary assured him that her son would avenge her and retired indoors weeping bitterly. From now on she signed herself as Marie R, whereas previously she was always Marie.

Sir James Melville hurried back from London to attend James's Coronation in a short-lived display of disapproval for Mary. Yet his brother, Robert, explained to him his concerns at her harsh treatment. Despite making an unsuccessful attempt to encourage the Hamiltons into the Confederate camp, Sir James later recalled that, with Maitland and Kirkcaldy, he now secretly supported the Queen. Yet his memory, as so often, must have been faulty. None of them were backing Mary following her escape from Lochleven. Kirkcaldy even led the decisive action against her at Langside, and Maitland was still concocting the Casket Letters.

On 5 August, Throckmorton reported to Elizabeth that he was more optimistic of Mary agreeing to divorce Orkney. Since her miscarriage, she was no longer bound to him, and any possibility of him rescuing her had become remote. He knew that Mary's restoration was a forlorn hope, but he focused on saving her life. By 7 August, Elizabeth knew that Mary had signed her abdication papers and considered recalling him. She contemplated sending English troops or funding the Hamiltons to raise an army on Mary's behalf. When Cecil warned her that this might cost Mary her life, she accused him of being lukewarm in her cause, but after seeing Throckmorton's report, she realised that he might be right. Having abandoned military plans, she instructed Throckmorton to support Moray in gaining the Regency, as Mary's best hope of protection. She threatened English vengeance, if Mary should be harmed before Moray's arrival. On 9 August, Maitland assured Throckmorton that Mary 'shall not die any violent death unless some new accident chance'.[26] Throckmorton believed that he had saved her life. On his eventual return to England, Elizabeth instructed him to refuse a gift of silver plate offered in King James's name, as she did not recognise Mary's abdication. He later told Leicester that this was 'the most dangerous legation of my life'.[27]

References

1. David Calderwood, *The True History of the Church of Scotland from the Beginning of the Reformation unto the End of the Reign of James VI*, ii p366
2. Nau, p. 52; cited in Weir, pp. 281, 394–5
3. Nau, cited in Weir, p. 395
4. Du Croc to Catherine de Medici, 17 June 1567, Teulet, cited in Weir, p. 396
5. Guy, p. 128
6. Antonia Fraser, p. 470
7. CSP Foreign, cited in Weir, p. 396
8. Nau, Memorials; Leslie, cited in Guy, p. 351
9. Guy, p. 352, and Weir, p. 397
10. Weir, p. 406
11. CSP Scottish, cited in Weir, p. 406
12. Pollen, cited in Wormald, *Mary, Queen of Scots*, p. 146, and Weir, p. 408
13. Antonia Fraser, p. 388
14. CSP, Foreign, VIII, p. 269, p. 287; cited in Antonia Fraser, p. 394
15. CSP Foreign; cited in Weir, p. 399
16. CSP Scottish; cited in Weir, p. 407
17. CSP Scottish; Keith; cited in Weir, p. 409
18. CSP Scottish; cited in Weir, p. 409
19. CSP, Scottish, II, p. 355; cited in Antonia Fraser, p. 396, and Weir, pp. 410, 413
20. CSP Scottish; Selections from Unpublished Manuscripts; Keith; cited in Weir, pp. 412, 415
21. Weir, p. 416

22. De Silva to Philip II, 2 August 1567, CSP Spanish; cited in Weir, pp. 417, 418
23. CSP Spanish; cited in Weir, pp. 403, 411
24. Register of the Privy Council; Diurnal of Occurrents; CSP Scottish, cited in Weir, p. 413
25. Keith, History, II, p. 702, cited in Marshall, p. 203
26. CSP Scottish; cited in Weir, p. 419
27. Guy, p. 364, and Weir, p. 407

34

The Discovery of the Silver Casket

On 19 June, four days after Carberry Hill, three of Orkney's supporters, George Dalgleish, his tailor, Thomas Hepburn, the parson of Oldmanstocks, and John Cockburn, brother of Cockburn of Skirling, came to Edinburgh from Dunbar, apparently to recover Orkney's clothes. After gaining access to the Castle, they were recognised by one of Balfour's men, and Buchanan much later reported that Dalgleish approached Balfour seeking to recover

> a small silver casket bearing inscriptions showing that it had once belonged to Francis, King of the French. In this there were letters nearly all of them written in the Queen's hand, in which the murder of the King and practically all that followed was clearly revealed.[1]

Not realising its significance, Balfour apparently handed it over, but reported their arrival to Morton, who was dining with Maitland in Edinburgh. Morton immediately sent Archibald and Robert Douglas, James Johnston of Westerrow and about thirteen of his own servants to arrest them, but they had by then already left the Castle. His men divided into three groups; Archibald Douglas searched for Hepburn, but could only find his horse; Johnston arrested Cockburn, who had nothing compromising found on him, and was later released; and Robert Douglas tracked down Dalgleish at a house in the Potterrow near Kirk o' Field, finding several of Orkney's papers in his possession. Morton later attested that the letters patent which created Orkney a Duke, were among them. Yet these were separately reported to have been found in the ballast of his ship in Denmark. Dalgleish was taken with the papers to Morton, but when he claimed that he held nothing else, they were suspicious and imprisoned him overnight. The next day he was placed in the Jayne (a cage too small to stand or lie down in) at the Tolbooth 'for furthering of the truth'. In terror and 'moved of conscience', he took Archibald and Robert Douglas back to the house, where he produced the locked casket from 'under the foot of a bed'.[2] This was taken to Morton, but, as it was eight o'clock in the evening, he did not open it and returned Dalgleish to his cell. Eighteen months later, Morton made a deposition for the Conference at Westminster recording how the casket was opened. On the next morning, 21 June, the lock was forced open before Morton, Maitland, Atholl, Glencairn, Home, Sempill, Tullibardine, Archibald Douglas and others. They examined the content, but left it with Morton for safekeeping. He confirmed:

> I have observed and kept the same box, and all letters, missives contracts, sonnets and other writings contained therein, surely without alteration, changing, eking [adding] or diminishing of anything found or received in the said box. This I testify and declare to be the undoubted truth.[3]

Despite its apparent significance, the casket's content was not initially made public. Although the Confederates presented accusations against Orkney in the Tolbooth three weeks after the discovery, the Queen was blamed only for failing to abandon him. If genuine, the correspondence would have justified her imprisonment and abdication. Given the treasonable nature of their actions, the Confederates would hardly have withheld it if it then existed. At the Westminster Conference, it became the principal evidence against her.

The story of the casket's discovery does not stand up to scrutiny. If Balfour was holding it, he would never have given it to Dalgleish unopened and allowed him to leave the Castle. Yet Morton was advised only after Dalgleish had already gone. Although Dalgleish was interviewed by the Council on 26 June, when he made a deposition that he had played no part in the murder, there was no mention of the casket's discovery. Either it was found later or its content was not thought to be incriminating. Dalgleish's name only became associated with its discovery at the Westminster Conference, by when he had been executed. Although, on 25 June, Drury reported:

> There is [information] here that the Queen has a box, wherein are the practices between her and France, wherein is little good meant to England,[4]

this does not seem to relate to the small silver casket or its purported content.

The silver casket which seems to have been found on 19 June probably contained a single innocuous letter, often conjectured to be the official report of Mary's discussion with the King written during her visit to Glasgow and forming the principal part of Casket Letter II. It would appear that this was progressively replaced by more incriminating documents, the creation of which started soon after the casket's discovery. It has already been shown that there were other seemingly more damaging letters which were not tabled at Westminster. Packages sent by Cecil to Moray in Paris at the end of June seem to have contained a transcript of one of them. This could have been the letter written on three sheets of paper, which Moray described to de Silva in London, before his return to Scotland to take up the Regency. Moray reported that Mary had written to Orkney

> not to delay putting into execution that which had been ordered because her husband [King Henry] used such fair words to deceive her and bring her to his will that she might be moved by them, if the other thing were not done quickly. She herself would go and fetch him [the King] and would stop at a house on the road, where she would try to give him a draught, but if this could not be done, she would put him in a house where the explosion was arranged for the night upon which one of her servants was to be married. [Orkney] was to try to get rid of his wife, either by putting her away or poisoning her, since she knew that [Mary] had risked all for him, her honour, her kingdom, her wealth which she had in France, and her God, contenting herself with his person alone.[5]

Incriminating though this is, it does not fit with the facts as known. It is implausibly indiscreet and unrealistically prescient of what was to happen. It bears no resemblance to any of the transcripts tabled at Westminster and predates them, as it was purportedly written before Mary went to Glasgow. Yet it seems to be an early attempt to provide evidence against Mary, later being replaced by something more subtle. It may be the letter which du Croc copied at about this time to Charles IX. Du Croc may have provided a second copy to de Silva, who arrived in London on 4 July, as eight days later de Silva reported that

> the Queen's adversaries assert positively that they know that she has been concerned in the murder of her husband, which was proved by letters under her own hand, copies of which were in his possession.[6]

His wording can be translated to mean 'letter' or 'letters'. It also seems similar to the one letter mentioned by Lennox in his Narrative, a fanciful record of events written by him for the Conferences at York and West-minster. Either de Silva or Moray could have told him of it.

It seems that the casket was chosen as the receptacle for incriminating letters from Mary to Bothwell to be used in evidence against her. Further falsified letters were added to a single apparently innocent letter, which it originally contained, and this in turn was manipulated. They were added progressively, with earlier less plausible attempts being removed. It can be conjectured that, when earlier documents failed to stand up to close scrutiny, they were destroyed. Yet from what is known, their content was far more incriminating than the often ambiguous wording for which transcripts remain.

On 28 November 1567, Drury reported that the lords met to discuss the casket's content, and this was 'kept to be shown' at the forthcoming December Parliament. The Act of Council* immediately beforehand claimed that on the evidence of

> divers her privy letters written and subscribed with her own hand and sent to James, Earl of Bothwell, chief executioner of the horrible murder, it is most certain that she was privy, art and part, and of the actual devise and deed of the murder of the King.[7]

This was signed by Morton, Maitland and Balfour, all signatories of the Craigmillar bond, and twenty-seven others. The Council debated whether to refer to the letters publicly, 'as the manifestation thereof may tend to the dishonour of the Queen', but they concluded that they must 'open and reveal the truth of the whole matter from the beginning, plainly and uprightly'.[8] Yet, on 12 September 1568, when Mary's adherents met at Dumbarton, they referred to what the Council had seen more than nine months earlier, saying:

> And if it be alleged that Her Majesty's writing should prove Her Grace culpable, it may be answered that there is no place mention[ed] in it by the which Her Highness may be convicted, albeit it were her own hand-writ, which it is not. And also, the same is devised by themselves [the Regency] in some principal and substantial clauses, which will be clearer nearer the light of day.[9]

---

* Although the Act of Council is known from a copy sent to Cecil, it is not mentioned in the official record of the Council's proceedings for 4 December.

They were saying that that the 'writing' contained incriminating additions, even if not a complete forgery. The Council must have tabled an original document, but perhaps only of one letter as they referred to the 'writing' as 'it', which could well have been the one described by Moray.

With changes to the letters being made progressively in an effort to provide more plausible evidence, Buchanan faced an issue in keeping his *Detectio*, first published in Latin in June 1568, consistent with them. Initially he refers to 'litterae' being found, and this can be translated to mean one letter or several, in which 'the whole wicked plot was exposed to view'. Yet in the English version of his *Detectio*, known as the *Book of Articles*, published shortly before Morton's declaration of their authenticity, he gives a much fuller description of

> such letters of the Queen's own handwriting direct to [Orkney] and other writings as clearly testified that, as he was the chief executor of the murder, so was she of the foreknowledge thereof, and that her ravishing [seizure] was nothing else but a coloured mask.[10]

Ultimately Morton claimed to have found twenty-two documents in the casket. Despite their shortcomings, they offer the only remotely plausible evidence on which to accuse Mary of involvement in her husband's murder. As Cecil undoubtedly realised, they would never withstand detailed scrutiny in a court of law, and Moray was always reluctant to provide the originals. Mary was never permitted to see them, although Moray quite improperly showed transcripts to the English Commissioners before the Conference at York to establish whether they seemed sufficiently incriminating to condemn her. Everyone became sceptical about tabling them at the Conferences.

Although each transcript is endorsed in an English hand to clarify its purpose, sometimes by Cecil himself, the meaning claimed in the endorsement is often obscure or applies to words taken out of context from the surrounding text. None of them is logical as a love letter. Yet taken together they contain a common thread, incriminating Bothwell in every step of a plan to marry the Queen. They imply that they were involved in a passionate relationship before the King's death, and this provided their motive for killing him. They show that Mary encouraged their marriage, even before Bothwell was cleared of the murder and before her abduction to Dunbar. They confirm that the plan to murder the King was premeditated. All this is too convenient. Murder conspiracies are not fully documented by the perpetrators in advance.

Du Croc later discussed the letters with Elizabeth. Having told her he understood that the Lords had letters proving Mary knew of the murder plan beforehand, Elizabeth replied that 'it was not true, although Lethington had acted badly in the matter', adding that if she saw him, 'she would say something that would not be at all to his taste'.[11] This implies that Elizabeth had become aware of Maitland's part in concocting them.

It is hardly surprising that the originals mysteriously disappeared in 1584. Yet, without them, their authenticity cannot be categorically disproved. After being handed to Moray by Cecil in January 1569, he took them back to Scotland and eventually, on 22 January 1571, returned them to Morton (twenty-one of the twenty-two were received by him and the whereabouts of the remaining one is unknown). Although further copies were made, these seem to have vanished immediately. After Morton's execution, one of his illegitimate sons passed them to the Earl of Gowrie (Ruthven). In 1584, Gowrie was also executed, and his estates forfeited, so the letters probably passed to James VI, but were never to be seen again. Although Gowrie may have destroyed them, it is much more likely to have been James. He was by then determined to restore his mother's reputation and had already arranged for Buchanan's *Detectio* and *Book of Articles* to be banned by Parliament. If the letters were seen to be falsified, it was Mary, not James, who was rightfully monarch. Destroying them removed this complication.

References

1. CSP, Scottish, II, p. 730; Buchanan, Book of Articles; cited in Weir, p. 400
2. CSP, Scottish, II, p. 730; cited in Weir, p. 401
3. Morton's Statement, CSP, Scottish, II, p. 73; cited in Weir, p. 402, p. 448
4. CSP Foreign; cited in Weir, p. 403
5. De Silva to Philip II, 2 August 1567, CSP Spanish; cited in Weir, p. 417
6. CSP Spanish; cited in Weir, p. 409, and Guy, p. 396
7. Acts of Parliament Scotland, III, 27, cited in Guy, p. 397, Wormald, *Mary, Queen of Scots*, p. 174 and Weir, p. 424
8. Goodall; Calendar of Manuscripts at Hatfield House; CSP Scottish; cited in Weir, p. 425
9. Goodall, cited in Guy, p. 397, Antonia Fraser, p. 439, and Weir, p. 447
10. Buchanan, *Detectio*; cited in Weir, p. 402
11. De Silva to Philip II, 21 July 1567, CSP Spanish; cited in Weir, pp. 411–2

35

Orkney's Escape to Denmark

After leaving Carberry Hill, Orkney fled with Seton to Dunbar, but was unable to raise troops in the Borders. Having sailed to Linlithgow, he travelled by land to Dumbarton. This proved a more successful rallying point, with fifty men of rank joining him, including Lord John and Archbishop Hamilton and Fleming, who still held Dumbarton Castle on Mary's behalf. They realised that an immediate attack on Lochleven would risk her life, but, while they dithered, support for Bothwell melted away. Still looking for assistance, he commandeered four men-of-war as Lord High Admiral and sailed with Seton and Fleming to Aberdeenshire. On arrival, he visited Strathbogie, but Huntly 'heartily wished both his sister and the Queen rid of so wicked a husband'[1] and would not raise the north to help him. Feeling suddenly isolated, Seton and Fleming refused him further assistance.

Although the Confederates had offered a reward of 1,000 crowns for Orkney's arrest, they made no serious effort to bring him to trial. Yet they called on Dunbar Castle to surrender, and gave him three weeks' notice, until 17 July, to come to the Tolbooth to answer for the King's murder. When, as expected, he failed to appear, his titles and estates were forfeited.* He had sailed north and by the end of July was with his kinsman the Bishop of Moray at Spynie.

Morton realised that he needed to be seen to bring Orkney to book, and, on 11 August, sent Kirkcaldy and Tullibardine after him. Kirkcaldy was not an experienced sailor and was probably chosen to neutralise his continuing opposition to Mary's imprisonment. He went to Dundee, where he fitted out four more men-of-war, considered the fastest in Scotland, and obtained five further ships before setting to sea on 19 August with cannon and 400 hackbutters. They had orders to seize Orkney and to execute him without trial.

---

* It was only now that Jean decided to leave Crichton Castle and to return to her mother in Aberdeenshire, wanting no more to do with her former husband. She may have realised that her mortgage was unlikely to be redeemed while the castle remained forfeited, but she continued to receive income from the estates.

Meanwhile, Orkney's arrival at Spynie had been betrayed by the Bishop's bastard sons, and he moved on with 200 men to Kirkwall in Orkney, planning to levy further ships to add to his existing four vessels. As Duke, he controlled Orkney Castle, but its bailiff, Gilbert Balfour, Sir James's brother, trained the castle guns on his ships to prevent them from landing, so he headed on for Shetland. Here at last his mother's kinsman, the pirate Olaf Sinclair, provided money and provisions. After acquiring two more ships, they sought booty by pirating English and Danish shipping in the vicinity.

On 25 August, Kirkcaldy and Tullibardine caught up with Orkney's ships anchored in Bressay Sound off Lerwick, while Orkney was on shore with most of his men. Despite facing immediate attack, Orkney managed to climb aboard his own vessel and cut the anchor. He scraped the bottom driving it over some rocks, but, when Kirkcaldy followed with his man-of-war, it was holed and sank. Orkney escaped to Unst, Shetland's main northern island, with three ships and 140 men, but his remaining three vessels were captured with all those on board, including his henchmen from Kirk o' Field, Cullen, Hay of Talla and Hepburn of Bolton. Kirkcaldy continued the chase with his three remaining men-of-war and, after again catching up with Orkney, fought out a battle for three hours, during which Orkney's mainmast was shot away. Although Kirkcaldy sent a boarding party, a violent storm came to Orkney's rescue. He transferred his remaining men, including Paris,* to his two remaining ships and sailed eastward before the wind to Norway, making the 250-mile crossing in record time. Although Kirkcaldy managed to follow for sixty miles, he was out-sailed and, by his own admission, was 'no good seaman'.[2]

Without Orkney in custody, the Confederates needed to be seen to bring his henchmen to book. They extracted depositions, often under torture, which were censored and manipulated to provide evidence against him and later to implicate Mary. Although these were designed to fit with the concocted tale of a crime of passion, they remained full of inconsistencies. Although, on 23 June, Powrie had explained the movement of the gunpowder to Kirk o' Field, on 3 July he made a second deposition, which contradicted much of the first. Yet, by 26 June, the Confederates claimed to have the evidence 'as well of witnesses as of writings' to prove Orkney's guilt.[3]

Cullen, Hay and Hepburn were brought back to Edinburgh, where they

---

* Paris was at last extradited from Denmark in June 1569 and, as has been seen, made two conflicting depositions after his return to Scotland. He was hung without trial, but from the scaffold shouted out, denying the content of what he had been forced to sign.

were imprisoned. Cullen had previously been arrested in June,* when he made a deposition, which apparently revealed 'the whole manner and circumstance' of the murder,[4] but this was conveniently suppressed. He was now interviewed again, but apparently said nothing useful and was released. Yet he knew a great deal. To silence his evidence† he was bribed by being appointed as an officer in the Edinburgh garrison. Hay initially told his captors that Orkney and Huntly had murdered the King. Yet, on 5 September, Bedford reported that he had revealed 'the whole device of the murder, declaring who were the executioners of the same, and went so far as to touch a great many not of the smallest'.[7]

On 3 January 1568, Moray, as Regent, arranged a public trial for Hay, Hepburn, Powrie and Dalgleish. They were not permitted to give evidence before being convicted. Hepburn, Powrie and Dalgleish were taken to the scaffold at the Mercat Cross in Edinburgh to be hanged and quartered, from where Drury reported that Hepburn named Huntly, Argyll, and Maitland, now in power, as being involved. There was nothing in either of the depositions of Powrie and Dalgleish to merit their execution, but their dismembered corpses were displayed on pikes above the gates of Glasgow, Hamilton, Dumbarton, Ayr and other towns in the west of Scotland, where the Queen had a stronger following. Drury informed Cecil that Hay was being spared until those he had accused in his depositions could be arrested. Yet they were never questioned. In the following May, he made a new deposition that accused Orkney alone, with his earlier depositions being suppressed. He too was taken to the scaffold, from where he shouted out that Orkney, Huntly, Argyll, Maitland and Balfour had subscribed to the Craigmillar bond, and 'diverse other nobles of the realm were [all] involved in the murder', and that 'Balfour and Maitland were notoriously known as the principal advisers and counsellors'.[8] Archbishop Bethune told the Cardinal of Lorraine that all the henchmen had

---

* According to Scrope, Cullen was already in custody by 11 June, four days before Carberry Hill. 'After some strict dealing [torture]', he 'uttered and revealed the murder, with the whole manner and circumstances thereof'.[5] Although it would have suited the Confederates to claim that they were gathering evidence at this early stage, it is more likely that he was arrested after Carberry Hill, as beforehand they were trying to trap Orkney and the Queen into marching on Edinburgh. Yet he must have been in custody by 20 June, as Drury reported that Cullen, Blackadder, Powrie and others had not been arraigned, because the authorities had been unable to track down as witnesses the tenants of the cottages in the gardens next to Kirk o' Field, where they were thought to have been hiding. Cullen was later freed (probably because he knew too much) in time to rejoin Orkney on his voyage north.

† After Cullen's second arrest, Moray referred to him as Orkney's 'chamberchild and one of the very executors, he may make us clear on the whole action as it proceeded'.[6] There has been great speculation what Moray meant. 'Chamberchild' could have homosexual connotations or may refer to him sharing a cabin with Orkney on board ship. If the 'action' relates to the murder rather than the naval chase, it is further evidence of him knowing a great deal more than was revealed.

confessed that they had amply deserved the punishment of death, yet declared the Queen's innocence, and accused ... especially Morton, Lethington and Balfour, and their own master, the Earl [of Bothwell].[9]

Moray's action in suppressing the evidence badly backfired. A fresh series of placards and broadsheets appeared in Edinburgh, one placed outside Moray's house, and another on the wall of the Council Chamber, asking 'why John Hepburn and John Hay were not compelled openly to declare the manner of the King's slaughter'. There was a clamour that the lords in power should also 'suffer for their demerits'.[10] There were uncomfortable rumours that servants were being made the scapegoats for their masters.

Cullen was not the only conspirator to escape trial. Black Ormiston and his uncle went into hiding in the Borders, from where Black Ormiston later took part in the Northern Rising, a rebellion started in the north of England to place Mary, as a Catholic, on the English throne. When Morton eventually tracked him down, he was taken to Edinburgh Castle, where, before his execution, he apparently confessed taking part in the King's murder to John Brand, Minister of the Canongate Kirk. The resultant deposition conflicted with that of Hay, Hepburn, Powrie, Dalgleish and Paris, despite obvious manipulation in an attempt to follow a consistent story. It claimed that he never discussed the murder with Mary, as he would have needed to do had she been involved. It blamed Maitland, who was already dead, and Balfour, who was by then disaffected with Morton.

The arrests seem to have assuaged public opinion, although several were blamed who played no part in the murder. Orkney's friend, William Blackadder, who had appeared in all innocence at Kirk o' Field immediately after the explosion, was captured off Leith while sailing with three others, John Blackadder, James Edmonstoun and Mynart Fraser, a Swedish sailor, to join Orkney at Dunbar. He was found guilty of being 'art and part' of the King's murder and was hanged and quartered at the Mercat Cross.[11] His dismembered limbs were posted on the gates of the principal burghs round Scotland. John Blackadder and Edmonstoun were executed in September, but Fraser was released back to his ship. Pagez and Francisco Busso were arrested after their mention in the placards, but were later freed, and Pagez served Mary during her captivity in England. John Spens, the Queen's advocate, also mentioned in the placards, was imprisoned, but freed after handing over coffers containing Orkney's money.

Meanwhile, Orkney arrived in Norway (then part of Denmark) and hove to at Karm Island, north of Stavanger, where he was arrested for suspected piracy. On 2 September, he was taken with his two ships and 140 men to the castle at Bergen, where the Governor, Eric Rosencrantz, uncertain whether he really was the Duke of Orkney, entertained him lavishly, while awaiting instructions. Yet Orkney's luck ran out. Anna Throndssen was now living in Bergen with her mother, and immediately sued him for breach of promise to marry her, sending some of her kinsmen to arrest him with creditors from his earlier visit to Denmark. To stop their action, Orkney promised to pay Anna an annuity in Scotland and handed over the smaller of his two ships. By now Rosencrantz had Frederick II's instructions to arrest Orkney for use as a bargaining counter for the return to Denmark of the disputed Orkney and Shetland Islands. A box of documents was found hidden in the ballast of his remaining ship. These apparently included the letters patent creating him a duke, proclamations published in Edinburgh showing that there was a price on his head, and a letter from Mary written after Carberry Hill complaining at the lack of support for them. None of these are extant.

After being brought before the Bergen magistrates, Orkney, on 23 September, was carried to Copenhagen on one of Frederick's ships for 'honourable confinement' in the castle.[12] There was little sympathy for him in Denmark, particularly as he had supported Sweden against them while in government in Scotland. Yet he was permitted to write to Charles IX seeking French assistance for Mary's release, for which he had her approval from Lochleven. Unfortunately for him, Moray had already arranged an *entente* with France, in which Orkney was branded as a pirate, murderer and traitor. Yet when Moray asked Charles IX to put pressure on Frederick to repatriate Orkney to Scotland, the French King does not appear to have done so, and Orkney was left as a potentially lucrative political hostage in Denmark. Although confined to his rooms, he was allowed visitors and books to read and initially was held in some comfort dressed in velvet clothes, even being escorted hunting.

On 5 January 1568, Orkney completed his memoirs, setting out a version of events aimed at procuring his release. He dictated them in French to a Danish secretary, later having them published as *Les Affaires du Conte Boduel*. He depicted himself as a chivalrous knight seeking to rescue Mary from the 'seditious lords', who 'did all they could to oppose her', especially Moray, who was attempting to usurp the throne. He blamed them for murdering both Riccio and the King. Having worked tirelessly to uncover the truth, his enemies had accused him to prevent him from solving the crime. Yet when they

> were convinced that there was no just cause of complaint against me ... I was, according to the laws and customs of the realm, by the

direction of the judges and with the consent of my accusers then present, declared innocent and found not guilty of all that which I had been accused ...

He had then been invited to marry the Queen 'as the man most suitable to be her husband' by those lords now demanding his extradition. Despite offering to settle their complaints by fighting Lindsay in single combat at Carberry Hill, Lindsay 'did not however turn up', and the Queen chose to negotiate to 'see if matters could be resolved peaceably'.[13] Having promised her safe passage 'without fear of treachery', she was immediately arrested.[14] He depicts himself as much more of a man of honour than his enemies were suggesting. He 'named the leaders and principal of all this trouble and sedition' as Moray, Atholl, Glencairn, Morton, Mar, Lindsay, Maitland, Bellenden, MacGill, Home, Ruthven, Balfour, Tullibardine, Sir Simon Preston and others, claiming:

I have been falsely accused, detained without justification, and prevented from going about the business I have in certain kingdoms with various princes and noblemen for the freeing of my princess.[15]

After making manuscript corrections, he arranged for a second copy to be sent to Frederick, but the Danish King remained unsympathetic and transferred him for greater security to Malmö Castle (now in Sweden) on the eastern side of the Sound into the Baltic. Yet he remained decently housed in a large vaulted chamber below the royal apartments.

Moray was determined to silence Orkney. Mary had been able to send him messages fairly freely from Lochleven, through his Danish page, Herman; Hepburn of Riccarton provided another communication conduit. On 13 January 1568, Mary had given Orkney authority to offer the Orkney and Shetland islands to Frederick II, if he would send Danish troops and ships to her assistance. Yet she was by then already deposed, and Moray, as Regent, would never have agreed. With Frederick hoping to recover the islands as a ransom for Orkney's release without having to risk a military invasion, Orkney remained in captivity.

When Mary escaped from Lochleven, Moray feared that Orkney might be freed by the Danes to give evidence at an enquiry into the King's death. Shortly before the Conference at York, he again pressed Frederick for his extradition to Scotland. He sent Captain John Clark, a Scottish mercenary serving in Denmark, to arrange for him to be extradited with Paris, but with instructions to take him 'dead or alive' or to allow Clark to execute him. On

30 October 1568, Clark gave their keeper, Peter Oxe, a receipt for Paris and William Murray, intending to bring them to Scotland for trial. Yet Frederick still saw Orkney as a bartering counter and again refused his extradition. Clark had come to Scotland in early 1567 with Danish money to raise mercenaries for Frederick's army, but Orkney warned Frederick that the money had been used to fund the Confederates at Carberry Hill. This led to Clark being court-martialled and imprisoned in Dragsholm Castle on the north-west Jutland coast.

As has been seen, there was no urgency to repatriate Paris and Murray. They did not reach Scotland until the Conferences in England had ended, after which Paris's two conflicting depositions were made under torture. Although Moray had assured Cecil that they would be found 'so authentic as the credit thereof shall not seem doubtful',[16] Cecil could see their obvious shortcomings and wrote to prevent Paris's execution. He called for Paris to be sent to London, but his letter (as perhaps he hoped) arrived too late. Moray had already arranged for him to be hung, drawn and quartered without trial.

In 1571, during Lennox's Regency, Thomas Buchanan renewed efforts for Orkney to be extradited back to Scotland. It had been discovered that Orkney was again discussing with Mary the transfer of the Orkney and Shetland Islands to Denmark in return for his freedom, which 'was prejudicial and hurtful to both our countries and to the discontentment of the Queen's Majesty of England'.[17] Yet again Frederick refused his release. It was not until 1573, after Elizabeth had at last recognised James as King of Scotland, that Frederick realised that he would never collect a ransom in return for freeing Orkney and moved him to join Clark at Dragsholm. Despite Morton making one further effort at extradition in June 1574, Frederick still refused.

Orkney was rumoured to have lived out his remaining days at Dragsholm in solitary confinement, chained to a post in a dungeon too small for him to stand. Yet the truth was less austere. Having resolved his differences with Clark, they drowned their sorrows in wine, resulting in Clark's death from alcoholic excess in July 1575. Although it was reported that Orkney had died four months later, he was 'but great swollen and not yet dead', but suffering from liver or kidney failure.[18]

Reports of Orkney's death brought rumours of a deathbed confession that exonerated Mary from any part in the King's murder. Her supporters scrambled for a copy, hoping that it might justify her release. On 1 June 1576, she asked Archbishop Bethune to investigate, and he paid 500 crowns for a courier to obtain a transcript, but the courier pocketed the money without visiting Denmark. At the end of July, Bethune admitted that it would prove too expensive to obtain. On 6 January 1577, Mary heard that Frederick II had sent a copy to Elizabeth and perhaps to Catherine de Medici, but neither of these survives. She was furious that Elizabeth would not show it to her. The partial transcripts that remain confirm that Mary 'never knew nor consented to the death of the King'. Orkney had been appointed to undertake the murder, 'divers Lords consenting, and subscribing thereunto, which were not there present at the deed doing'. It names Moray, Morton and, inexplicably, Lord Robert Stewart, Kirkcaldy, Boyd and 'John Hamilton, Bishop of St Andrews,* with divers others, whom he said he could not remember at that present'. It also claims that he bewitched the Queen, drugging her with *eau sucrée* to seduce her, and found means to put away his own wife to obtain the Queen. After the marriage was consummated, he sought all means how to destroy the infant Prince and the whole nobility that would not fall in with him.[19]

All this is of course implausible, suggesting that the confession was a forgery. It says that Orkney was writing 'sick unto death in the castle of Malmö'. Yet by then he was in Dragsholm and was not on his deathbed, but lived on for three more years in increasing insanity until 14 April 1578. He was buried there in the parish church, where it is claimed that his ghost still haunts the castle, now a hotel. Herries, who later visited Dragsholm, reported that Orkney had latterly become overgrown with hair and filth. Despite the shortcomings of his purported confession, it so impressed Lady Margaret Douglas that she at last saw Mary as a victim of a foul injustice. The young King James, who saw it much later, took it as a 'clear proof of her innocence'.[20]

References

1. Cited in Guy, p. 371, and Marshall, p. 135
2. CSP Scottish; cited in Weir, p. 419
3. Act of the Privy Council, cited in Weir, p. 405
4. CSP Scottish; cited in Weir, p. 423
5. CSP Scottish; cited in Weir, p. 400
6. CSP Scottish; cited in Weir, p. 422
7. State Papers in the Public Record Office; cited in Weir, p. 422

* Lord Robert Stewart and Archbishop Hamilton played no part in the murder, although they later attended Mary's wedding to Orkney, and Hamilton signed Orkney's divorce from Jean Gordon. Neither Sir James Balfour nor Archibald Douglas is mentioned, though Orkney would most certainly have known of their involvement.

8. Drury to Cecil, 4 January 1568; CSP Scottish; Diurnal of Occurrents; cited in Weir, pp. 282, 428
9. Archbishop Bethune to the Cardinal of Lorraine, 6 February 1568, Sloane MMS; cited in Weir, pp. 294, 428
10. Diurnal of Occurrents; cited in Weir, p. 428
11. Weir, p. 406
12. CSP Scottish, cited in Weir, p. 422
13. Cockburn and Maitland, cited in Guy, p. 374, 377, 378
14. Weir, p. 392
15. Weir, p. 429
16. Weir, p. 487
17. Guy, p. 380
18. State Papers in the Public Record Office, cited in Guy, p. 380, and Weir, p. 499
19. Guy, p. 381
20. Guy, p. 382

36

Moray's Acceptance of the Regency and the Aftermath for Mary

It was Morton who arranged for Moray to return to Scotland as Regent, although this was almost certainly planned prior to the King's murder. Only Moray had the necessary authority and skills to govern the factious nobility. Yet Morton did well to hold them together in his absence. Although Protestant Lords dominated the Council, they needed Moray's charisma and diplomatic skills to stop defections and to justify their treasonable action in holding Mary imprisoned.

On 31 July, Moray left London intending to wait in Berwick until everything was prepared for his return to Scotland. On 11 August, he arrived in Edinburgh to a rapturous welcome as Scotland's Reformist saviour, King in all but name, and took immediate control of the government. Four days later he went to Lochleven, riding one of Mary's horses and, to her amusement, fell off it into the loch. She noticed that he was addressed as 'your grace', despite his apparent reluctance to accept high office. She greeted him with 'great passion and weeping', but he remained 'cold and reserved', distressing her with a pious sermon on her wrongdoings.[1] He told her that Scotland was dissatisfied with her conduct and he threatened her with execution 'in such injurious language as was likely to break her heart'. Even though innocent before God, she should have had regard to her reputation in the eyes of the world, 'which judges by the outward appearance and not upon the inward sentiment'.[2] She was mortified, and Nau recorded: 'The injuries were such as they cut the thread of love betwixt him and the Queen for ever.' She objected to his appointment as Regent, insisting that she was 'innocent of all that could be laid to her charge', as God would 'manifest' in the end.[3] He swept out, leaving her 'with nothing but the hope of God's mercy', and Throckmorton was impressed with his sincerity, using his lofty sermonising to lead his people like the ancient prophets of Israel.[4]

With his calculated but cynical approach, Moray seems to have demonstrated to Mary that he was now in control and, on the following day, he returned to find her more conciliatory. He told her that he could not free her, but 'would assure her of her life and, as much as lay in him, the preservation of her honour' by preventing the publication of her letters. If she persisted in her affection for Orkney, her life would be in danger, and he would be unable to protect her. Yet if she were penitent and confirmed her abhorrence at the King's murder and did not seek revenge on the lords, 'so it might appear she detested her former life', she might 'one day be restored to the throne'.[5] Mary made a show of trusting him; she kissed him and begged him to accept the Regency. He told her he would do so only as a special act of kindness to her. Even on 30 August, he told Cecil that he had no real wish for it and privately shunned such grandeur and ambition, but he might be able to serve her as Regent, while others would ruin her. This show of modesty met with Elizabeth's approval, but she never formally recognised his appointment. In the broader arena of European politics, she could not be seen to accept Mary being deposed. According to Nau, Mary left Moray with a sting in the tail, warning, 'He, who does not keep faith where it is due, will hardly keep it where it is not due'.[6] If she, a born Queen, faced rebellion from her people, he, a bastard by birth and origin, would endure much more.

Moray had probably agreed with Cecil in London that Mary should be kept imprisoned without trial. Yet among the nobility there was a range of views on what to do with her. From the Lennox faction, Tullibardine urged her execution on grounds that, if freed, she might marry again and have more children, which would only cause difficulties.* This was countered by the Marians, including Argyll, Boyd and Livingston, who sought her release, and by Throckmorton, who claimed that if she were executed, the Hamiltons would seek the throne. Maitland had told Throckmorton that even Archbishop Hamilton wanted her executed, so that the nobility could meet without fear of the future. For once Maitland was probably telling the truth. For a temporary period after Mary's abdication, the Hamiltons undertook to support Moray as Regent, so long as their legitimacy was not questioned and they were acknowledged as heirs after James. They insisted on Charles Stuart, Lennox's second son, being debarred. If Mary were executed, only the life of an infant child stood between them and the Crown. Throckmorton was disgusted that they 'could have such double faces and such traitorous minds'.[7]

---

* It may seem surprising that Tullibardine, a Catholic, should continue to seek Mary's death, but, as the probable author of the broadsheets in Edinburgh, he undoubtedly believed that Mary had played a part in the murder of the King. His conviction will have persuaded his brother-in-law, Mar, to support Moray in keeping Mary imprisoned and in seeking her abdication. Tullibardine's views will also have rubbed off on Buchanan.

Mary's treatment by Moray was, of course, outrageous. She knew he was far more implicated in the King's murder than her. Yet she had only herself to blame. If she had listened to him initially, she would never have married the King. She did not realise that, with Cecil's support, he had duped her into marrying Orkney as the means of bringing her down. He somehow had to produce evidence of her complicity in the murder. The propaganda was well organised and proved sufficiently credible at the time, even if today it fails to stand up to examination. He held the whip hand. By keeping her imprisoned at Lochleven without trial, her Scottish supporters could not rescue her, and she no longer had the support of Catholics abroad.

*****

Whatever else may be concluded about Mary, she was politically naive. Her cosseted upbringing in France had left her ill-prepared to face the intransigence of either the Scottish nobility or the Kirk. Both were questioning the divine right of her rule. The threat to her authority was little different to that being faced by the monarchy in England and France, but she lacked the political astuteness of either Elizabeth or Catherine de Medici. Her naivety had led her to have unrealistic aspirations. She never understood that she had no realistic expectation of being accepted as the heir to the English throne by an English Parliament so long as she remained personally Catholic. Yet Mary would never subsume her faith to suit her political ambitions. This was unlike the Huguenot Henry of Navarre, when he became King Henry IV of France, who concluded that 'Paris is worth a mass'. She could not bring herself to be pragmatic when it came to her Catholicism. She had hoped that once she was accepted as Elizabeth's heir, she could rely on the English to protect her Scottish throne. Yet it was unrealistic to expect the English to protect her as a Catholic Queen on their northern border, particularly when she was a member of the belligerent and ultra-Catholic Guise family. The English were only interested in protecting their border with secure Protestant government.

Mary lost her throne, not because she may have had some knowledge of the conspiracy to murder King Henry, but because she organised Bothwell's trial so that it was seen to be a whitewash and then agreed to marry him, even though he was generally thought to have murdered her husband. It is really very difficult to show her in a good light. The claim that she married him because she was completely under his thrall, the result apparently of her dangerous illness and acute depression, is questionable. At considerable personal risk, she had stepped in to protect Maitland and Melville from his violent temper. She was in sufficient authority to quarrel with him immediately before their marriage. Her determination to go ahead with the marriage can be explained by her fear of being pregnant and her belief that the signatories of the Ainslie's Tavern bond supported him. Yet she knew from Elizabeth, Catherine de Medici and Lennox, and more recently from Herries, Melville and, almost certainly, Maitland, that she would be marrying her husband's murderer. She could hardly claim that she did not believe it, as she was aware of a bond being signed at Craigmillar. She also knew that marriage to Bothwell would preclude her from succeeding to the English throne and from any future Catholic support. Yet she was cajoled by him into believing that it provided them with mutual protection. If her first sexual encounter with him was in Dunbar on 24 April, she could not have known that she was pregnant by 9 May when the banns for her wedding to him were published. She had seen the way he bullied her traditional supporters and must have borne the brunt of much of his tantrums herself. She had only to claim that Bothwell had raped her, as everyone assumed, to explain her pregnancy. She always maintained that she married Bothwell for reasons of state. This was no love match and she made no effort to provide him with assistance after Carberry Hill. Yet, with muddle-headed logic, she spurned all rational advice and seemed to believe that marriage to the most powerful available Scotsman was the only way to protect her throne and, if she were pregnant, would legitimise another heir to secure her dynasty. She brought about her own downfall and it is hard to make a case that she deserves to have been treated better by history.

Yet the villain was Moray, who was encouraged by Cecil and had the support of Morton and Maitland (in his effort to save his own skin). Their conspiracy to persuade Mary and Bothwell to marry was underhand in the extreme. History has exonerated Cecil, perhaps because his loyalty was to Elizabeth, but he was the *eminence grise* behind Mary's undoing. The Protestant Lords needed his blessing to bring her down, and his meticulous records show the extent of his involvement. Yet they were almost caught out. When Mary escaped from Lochleven and was able to reach England, there had to be a trial and there had to be evidence to justify her detention. Would Moray be able to prove her involvement in a crime of passion when Mary had played no part in one? Would her supporters in Scotland gain sufficient strength to put her back on her throne? Many of these were Catholic, but despite her strong personal faith, she had previously let them down by failing to support their cause.

References

1. CSP Scottish; Keith; Nau; CSP Spanish; cited in Antonia Fraser, p. 401, and Weir, p. 420
2. CSP Scottish; Keith; Nau; CSP Spanish; cited in Antonia Fraser, p. 401, and Weir, p. 420
3. Nau, cited in Weir, p. 420
4. CSP Scottish; Keith; Nau, Memorials; CSP Spanish; cited in Weir, p. 420
5. CSP Scottish; cited in Weir, p. 420
6. Nau, p. 69; cited in Antonia Fraser, p. 402
7. CSP Scottish; cited in Weir, p. 419

Bibliography

Anderson, James, *Collections Relating to the History of Mary Queen of Scotland*, 1727

Armstrong-Davison, M. H., *The Casket Letters*, 1965

Balcomes Papers, *Foreign Correspondence with Marie of Lorraine Queen of Scotland*, Vol. I, 1537–48, Vol. II, 1548–57, Scot. Hist. Soc. Ed. Marguerite Wood

Bannatyne, R., *Bannatyne Manuscript*, ed. W. Tod Ritchie, Scottish Text Society, 1934

Bannatyne, R., *Memorials of Transactions in Scotland*, ed. R. Pitcairn, Bannatyne Club, Edinburgh, 1836

Bingham, Caroline, *James V, King of Scots*, William Collins Sons & Co Ltd, 1971.

Birrel, Robert, *Diary, 1532–1605, from Fragments of Scottish History*, ed. D. J. Dalyell

Black, J. B., *The Reign of Elizabeth*, 1959

Blackwood, Adam, *History of Mary, Queen of Scots: A Fragment*, Maitland Club, Edinburgh/Glasgow, 1834

Brantôme, Pierre, *Oeuvres Complètes*, Paris 1823

Brantôme, Pierre, *The Lives of Gallant Ladies*, trans. Alec Brown, London, 1961

Buchanan, George, *Detectio Mariae Reginae: Ane Detection of the Doings of Marie, Queen of Scots, touching the Murder of her Husband and her Conspiracy, Adultery and Pretensed Marriage with the Earl of Bothwell, and a Defence of the True Lords, Maintainers of the King's Majesty's Action and Authority*, Edinburgh, 1571, 1572

Buchanan, George, *The Tyrannous Reign of Mary Stewart*, ed. and trans. W. A. Gatherer, Edinburgh, 1958

Calderwood, David, *The True History of the Church of Scotland from the Beginning of the Reformation unto the End of the Reign of James VI*, ed. T. Thomson and D. Laing, Woodrow Society, Edinburgh, 1842–9

Castiglione, Baldassare, *The Book of the Courtier*, 1528, Aldine Press

Camden, William, *Annales Rerum Anglicarum et Hibernicarum Regnante Elizabetha*, Trans. R. Norton, 1635 and T. Hearne, 1717

Cockburn, H., and Maitland, T., (eds), *Les Affaires du Conte de Boduel*, Bannatyne Club, Edinburgh, 1829

Crawford of Jordanhill, Thomas, *Deposition*, Cambridge University Library, ed. CSP Scottish

de Beaugué, Jean, *Histoire de la Guerre en Ecosse*, Foreword by Comte de Montalembert, Maitland Club, 1862

de Castelnau, Michel, Seigneur de Mauvissière, *Memoirs*, ed. Le Laboureur, Paris, 1731

de Ruble, Alphonse, *La Première Jeunesse de Marie Stuart*, 1891

Donaldson, Gordon, *The Scottish Reformation*, 1960

Doran, Susan, *Mary Queen of Scots, An Illustrated Life*, The British Library, 2007.

Forneron, H., *Les Ducs de Guise et leur Epoque*, Paris, 1887

Fraser, Antonia, *Mary Queen of Scots*, Weidenfeld & Nicolson, 1969.

Fraser, Sir William, *The Lennox*, 1874

Frieda, Leonie, *Catherine de Medici*, Weidenfeld & Nicolson, 2003.

Goodall, W., *Examination of the (Casket) Letters said to be written by Mary Queen of Scots to James, Earl of Bothwell*, 1754

Gordon, Sir R., *Genealogical History of the Earldom of Sutherland*, Edinburgh, 1813

Gore-Browne, R., *Lord Bothwell*, 1935

Graham, Roderick, *An Accidental Tragedy, The Life of Mary Queen of Scots*, Birlinn Limited, 2008.

Guy, John, *My Heart is my Own*, Harper Perrenial, 2004.

Hay Fleming, D., *Mary Queen of Scots from her birth till her flight into England*, 1897

Henderson, T. F., *Mary Queen of Scots*, 1905

Henderson, T. F., *The Casket Letters and Mary, Queen of Scots*, Edinburgh and London, 1890

Herries, John Maxwell, *Historical Memoirs of the Reign of Mary Queen of Scots*, Abbotsford Club, ed. R. Pitcairn, Edinburgh, 1836

Holinshed, Raphael, *The Chronicles of England, Scotland and Ireland*, London, 1587, ed. Sir Henry Ellis, London, 1907–8

Hosack, J., *Mary Queen of Scots and her Accusers*, Edinburgh, 1969

Jebb, S., *De Vita et Rebus Gestis Sereuissima Principis Marie Scotorum Reginae*, Franciiae Dotariae, 1725

Keith, R., *History of the Affairs of Church and State in Scotland*

Knox, John, *History of the Reformation*, ed. and trans. W. Croft Dickinson

Knox, John, *Works of John Knox*, ed. D. Laing, Edinburgh, 1895

Labanoff, Prince (A. I. Lobanov-Rostovsky) *Lettres de Marie Stuart*, 1844

Leslie, John, Bishop of Ross, *The Historie of Scotland*, Ed. Fr. E. G. Gody and William Murison, Scottish Text Society

Lettres de Catherine de Medicis: ed. H. De la Ferrière-Percy, Paris, 1880

Levine, Mortimer, *Early Elizabethan Succession Question from Tudor Dynastic Problems*, California 1966

MacNalty, Sir Arthur Salusbury, *Mary Queen of Scots: The Daughter of Debate*, London, 1960

Mahon, R. H., *Mary Queen of Scots: a study of the Lennox Narrative*, 1924

Mahon, R. H., *The Tragedy of Kirk O'Field*, 1930

Marshall, Rosalind K, *Queen Mary's Women*, John Donald, 2006.

Melville, Sir James of Hallhill, *Memoirs of his own Life 1549–1593*, ed. Francis Steuart, 1929, ed. Gordon Donaldson, The Folio Society, 1969

Mumby, Frank Arthur, *The Fall of Mary Stuart: a Narrative in Contemporary Letters*, London, 1921

Nau, Claude, *Memorials of Mary Stewart*, ed. J. Stevenson, 1883

Neale, JE, *Queen Elizabeth I*, Jonathan Cape, 1934.

Neale, Sir J. E., *Elizabeth I and her Parliaments*, 1953

Noel Williams, Hugh, *Henry II: His Court and Times*, London, 1910

Oxford Dictionary of National Biography

Phillips, J. E., *Images of a Queen: Mary Stuart in 16th Century Literature*, California, 1964

Pitcairn, R., *Ancient Criminal Trials in Scotland*, Vol. I, Bannatyne Club, Edinburgh, 1833

Pitcairn, R., *Collections Relative to the Funereals of Mary Queen of Scots*, Edinburgh, 1822

Pitscottie, Robert Lindsay of, *History and Chronicles of Scotland*, Volumes I and II Scottish Text Society, ed. A. J. G. Mackay, 1899, 1911

Plowden, Alison, *Two Queens in One Isle: the Deadly Relationship of Elizabeth I and Mary, Queen of Scots*, Brighton, 1984

Pollen, J. H., *Papal Negotiations with Mary Queen of Scots*, Scottish History Society, 1st series, Edinburgh, 1901

Prebble, John, *The Lion of the North: One Thousand Years of Scotland's History*, London, 1971

Regnier de la Planche, Louis, *Estat de France sous François II*, ed. Henneschet, 1836

Robertson, J (ed), *Inventaires de la Royne d'Ecosse, Douairière de France*, Bannatyne Club, Edinburgh, 1883

Robertson, William, *The History of Scotland during the Reigns of Queen Mary and of King James VI til his Accession to the Crown of England*, London, 1759

Ruthven, Lord, *The Murder of Riccio, being Lord Ruthven's Own Account of the Transaction*, Holyrood Series, 1891

Sadler, Sir Ralph, *The State Papers and Letters of Sir Ralph Sadler*, ed. A. Clifford, Edinburgh, 1809

Sanderson, Margaret, *Mary Stewart's People*, Edinburgh, 1987

Schutte, Kim, *A Biography of Margaret Douglas, Countess of Lennox, 1515–1578; Niece of Henry VIII and Mother-in-law of Mary, Queen of Scots*, New York 2002

Selections from Unpublished Manuscripts in the College of Arms and the British Museum, illustrating the Reign of Mary, Queen of Scotland, 1543–68, ed. Joseph Stevenson, Maitland Club XLI, Glasgow, 1837

Sitwell, Edith, *The Queens and the Hive*, London, 1962

Sloane MSS: British Museum

Stoddart, Jane T., *The Girlhood of Mary Queen of Scots*, 1908

Strickland, Agnes, *The Lives of the Queens of Scotland*, 1854

Stuart, John, *A lost chapter in the history of Mary Queen of Scots recovered*, Edinburgh, 1874

Teulet, A, *Papiers d'État relatives à L'Histoire de l'Ecosse au 16e siècle*, Paris, 1862

Thomson, T. (ed), *Historie and Life of James Sext*, author unknown, Bannatyne Club, Edinburgh, 1860

Thomson, T., Diurnal of Occurrents, Bannatyne Club, Edinburgh, 1833

Tytler, P. F., *History of Scotland*, Edinburgh, 1841 and New Enlarged Edition, 1870

Weir, Alison, *Mary, Queen of Scots and the Murder Of Lord Darnley*, Jonathan Cape, 2003.

Wood, Marguerite (ed), 'Foreign Correspondence with Marie de Lorraine Queen of Scotland from the originals in the Balcarres papers', Scottish History Society, 3rd Series, IV, Edinburgh, 1923 and 1925

Wormald, Jenny, *Court, Kirk and Community, Scotland, 1470–1625, (The New History of Scotland series)*, Edward Arnold (Publishers) Ltd, 1981.

Wormald, Jenny, *Mary, Queen of Scots, Politics, Passion and a Kingdom Lost*, Tauris Parke Paperbacks, 2001.

Papers

Calendar of manuscripts at Hatfield House: Calendar of the Manuscripts of the Marquess of Salisbury at Hatfield House, Historic Manuscripts Commission, 1883

Cecil Papers, Hatfield House

Chronicles of the Families of Atholl and Tullibardine, ed. 7th Duke of Atholl, Edinburgh, 1908

Cotton MSS: British Museum

CSP Foreign: Calendar of State Papers, Foreign Series, *Edward VI*, ed. W. Turnbull, 1861

CSP Foreign: Calendar of State Papers, Foreign Series, *Elizabeth*, ed. J. Stevenson, 1863

CSP Roman: Calendar of State Papers relating to English affairs (Rome), ed. JM Rigg, 1916

CSP Scottish: Calendar of State Papers relating to Scottish affairs, ed. J. Bain, 1898

CSP Spanish: Calendar of State Papers, Spanish, *Elizabeth*, ed. M. A. S. Home, London, 1892

CSP Venetian: Calendar of State Papers Venetian, ed. R. Brown and G. C. Bentinck, 1890

Hamilton Papers: ed. J. Bain, Edinburgh, 1890

Index